P9-CKC-782

• The Complete Guide •

Rocky Mountain Camping

by Tom Stienstra and Robyn Schlueter

51495
9 780935 701531

Copyright 1989, 1991, 1993
by Thomas F. Stienstra
ROCKY MOUNTAIN CAMPING: 1993-94 Edition

All rights reserved. This book may not be reproduced in full or in part without the written permission of the publisher, except for use by a reviewer in the context of a review. Inquiries and excerpt requests should be addressed to:

Foghorn Press
555 DeHaro Street, Suite 220
San Francisco, CA 94107
(415) 241-9550

To order books, please phone (800)842-7477.

Senior Research Editor — Robyn Schlueter
Managing Editor — Ann Marie Brown
Copy Editing and Indexing — Samantha Trautman, Howard Rabinowitz
Maps and Book Design — Luke Thrasher, David Ergo
Research Editors, Previous Editions — Julie Lancelle, Nancy Christensen
Cover Photo — Ben Davidson

Library of Congress Cataloging-in-Publication Data
Stienstra, Tom.
Rocky Mountain camping: the complete guide to Montana, Wyoming & Colorado's recreation areas/ Tom Stienstra — 1991-92 ed.
p. cm.
Includes index.
ISBN 0-935701-53-2 (softcover): $14.95
1.Campsites, facilities, etc. — Rocky Mountains Region — Directories.
2.Camping — Rocky Mountains Region — Guidebooks.
3.Rocky Mountains Region — Description and travel — Guidebooks.
I. Title.
GV191.42.R63S75 1993
647.9478'09 — dc20 91-15665

• The Complete Guide •

Rocky Mountain Camping

by Tom Stienstra and Robyn Schlueter

Dear Camper,

To update this year's 1993-1994 edition of Rocky Mountain Camping, every campground was reviewed for accuracy and updated with longer trip notes, better directions, and the latest campground facts. Every effort has been made to make this book as accurate and up-to-date as possible. We recommend that you use the phone numbers provided for each campground to make last-minute checks on campground availability, weather and road conditions, plus the short-term effects of drought, fire or flood.

We welcome your comments, questions and suggestions. Please write to us at Foghorn Press, 555 DeHaro Street, Suite 220, San Francisco, CA 94107.

—Tom Stienstra and Robyn Schlueter

As a publisher of outdoor and recreation guidebooks,
Foghorn Press is committed to protecting the environment.
This book is printed on the California standard for recycled paper,
which is 50% recycled paper and 10% post-consumer waste.

Contents

Introduction	**i**
Food and Cooking Gear	**1**
Clothing and Weather Protection	**9**
Hiking and Foot Care	**13**
Sleeping Gear	**18**
First Aid and Insect Protection	**24**
Fishing and Camp Fun	**35**
Camping Options: Boat-In and Desert	**47**
Ethics	**50**
Resource Guide	**52**
Camping Gear Checklist	**56**
Colorado Campgrounds	**59**
Montanta Campgrounds	**283**
Wyoming Campgrounds	**437**
Index	**555**
About the Author	**583**

Contents

Introduction i
Food and Cooking Gear 1
Clothing and Weather Protection 9
Hiking and Foot Care 13
Sleeping Gear 18
First Aid and Insect Protection 24
Fishing and Camp Fun 35
Camping Options: Boat-In and Desert 47
Ethics 50
Resource Guide 52
Camping Gear Checklist 56

Colorado Campgrounds 59
Montanta Campgrounds 283
Wyoming Campgrounds 437

Index 555
About the Author 583

Introduction

Going on a camping trip can be like trying to put hiking boots on an octopus. You've tried it too, eh? Instead of the relaxing, exciting sojourn that was intended, a camping trip can turn into a scenario called You Against The World. You want something easy? Try fighting an earthquake.

But it doesn't have to be that way and that's what this book is all about. If you give it a chance, it can put the mystery, excitement and fun back into your camping vacations—and remove the fear of snarls, confusion and occasional temper explosions of volcanic proportions that keep people at home, locked away from the action.

Mystery? There are hundreds of hidden, rarely used campgrounds listed and mapped in this book that you have never dreamed of. Excitement? At many of them you'll find the sizzle with the steak, the hike to a great lookout, the big fish at the end of the line. Fun? The how-to section of this book can help you take the futility out of your trips and put the fun back in. Add it up, put it in your cash register and you can turn camping into the satisfying adventure it is meant to be, whether it's just an overnight quicky or a month-long expedition.

It has been documented that 95 percent of American vacationers use only five percent of the available recreation areas. With this book, you can leave the herd to wander and be free, and join the inner circle, the five percenters who know the great, hidden areas used by so few people. To join the Five Percent Club, you should take a hard look at the maps for the areas you wish to visit and the corresponding listings of campgrounds. As you study the camps, you will start to feel a sense of excitement building, a feeling that you are about to unlock a door and venture into a world that is rarely viewed. When you feel that excitement, act on it. Parlay that energy into a great trip.

The campground maps and guide lists can serve in two ways: 1—If you're on the road late in the day and you are stuck for a spot for the night, you can likely find one nearby; or 2—If you are planning in advance, you can tailor a vacation to fit exactly into your plans, rather than heading off, and hoping—maybe praying—it turns out all right.

For the latter, you may wish to obtain additional maps, particularly if you are venturing into areas governed by the U.S. Forest Service or Bureau of Land Management. Both are federal agencies and have low-cost maps available that detail all hiking trails, lakes, streams and backcountry camps reached via logging roads. How to obtain these and other maps is described in the Resource Guide on pages 53 to 56.

Backcountry camps listed in this book are often in primitive and rugged settings, but provide the sense of isolation that you may want for a trip. They also provide good jump-off points for backpacking trips, if that is your calling. These camps are also often free, and we have listed hundreds of them.

At the other end of the spectrum are the developed parks for motor homes, parks that offer a home away from home with everything from full hookups to a grocery store and laundromat. These spots are just as important as the remote camps with no facilities. Instead of isolation, an RV park provides a place to shower, get outfitted for food and clean clothes, and for motor home cruisers, is a place to stay in high style while touring the area. RV parks range in price from $8 to $20 per night, depending on location, and an advance deposit may be necessary in summer months.

Somewhere between the two extremes — the remote, unimproved camps and the lavish motor home parks — are hundreds and hundreds of campgrounds that provide a compromise: beautiful settings and some facilities, with a small overnight fee. Piped water, vault toilets and picnic tables tend to come with the territory, along with a fee that usually ranges from $7 to $15, with the higher-priced sites located near population centers. Because they offer a bit of both worlds, they are in high demand. Reservations are usually advised, and at state parks, particularly during the summer season, you can expect company. This does not mean you need to abandon them in hopes of a less confined environment. For one thing, most state parks have set up quotas so that you don't feel like you've been squeezed in with a shoehorn, and for another, the same parks are often uncrowded during the off-season or on weekdays.

Prior to your trip, you will want to get organized, and that's where you must start putting socks on that giant octopus. The key to organization for any task is breaking it down to its key components, then solving each element independent of the others. Remember the octopus. Grab a moving leg, jam on a boot, and make sure it's on tight before reaching for another leg. Do one thing at a time, in order, and all will get done quick and right.

In the stories that follow, we have isolated the different elements of camping, and you should do the same when planning for your trip. There are separate stories on each of the primary ingredients for a successful trip: 1 — Food and cooking gear; 2 — Clothes and weather protection; 3 — Foot and leg care and how to choose the right boots and socks; 4 — Sleeping gear; 5 — Combatting bugs and some common sense first-aid; 6 — Recreation gear and catching fish. We've also included sections on boat-in and desert camping and ethics in the outdoors, as well as a camping gear checklist.

Now you can become completely organized for your trip in just one week, spending just a little time each evening. Getting organized is an unnatural act for many. By splitting up the tasks, you take the pressure out and put the fun back in.

As a full-time outdoors writer, the question I get asked more than any other is, "Where are you going this week?" For the Rocky Mountain area, all of the answers are in this book.

Food and Cooking Gear

It was a warm, crystal clear day, the kind of day when if you had ever wanted to go skydiving, you would go skydiving. That was exactly the case for my old pal Foonsky, who had never before tried the sport. But a funny thing happened after he jumped out of the plane and pulled on the rip cord for the first time: his parachute didn't open.

In total free-fall, Foonsky watched the earth below getting closer and closer. Not one to panic, he calmly pulled the rip cord on the emergency parachute. But nothing happened then either. No parachute, no nothing.

The ground was getting closer and closer, and as he tried to search for a soft place to land, Foonsky detected a small object shooting up toward him, getting larger as it approached. It looked like a camper.

Foonsky figured this could be his last chance, so as they passed in mid-flight, he shouted, "Hey, do you know anything about parachutes?"

The other fellow just shouted back as he headed off into space, "Do you know anything about lighting camping stoves?"

Well, Foonsky got lucky and his parachute opened. As for the other fellow, well, he's probably in orbit like a NASA weather satellite. If you've ever had a mishap lighting a camping stove, you know exactly what I'm talking about.

When it comes to camping, all things are not created equal. Nothing is more important than lighting your stove easily and having it reach full heat without feeling like you're playing with a short fuse to a miniature bomb. If your stove does not work right, your trip can turn into a disaster, regardless of how well you have planned the other elements. In addition, a bad stove will add an underlying sense of foreboding to your day. You will constantly have the inner suspicion that your darn stove is going to foul up again.

Camping Stoves

If you are buying a camping stove, remember this one critical rule: Do not leave the store with a new stove unless you have been shown exactly how to use it.

Know what you are getting. Many stores that specialize in outdoor recreation equipment now provide experienced campers/employees who will demonstrate the use of every stove they sell, and while they're at it, describe their respective strengths and weaknesses.

Never buy a stove that uses kerosene for fuel. Kerosene is smelly and messy, provides low heat, needs priming, and in America, is virtually obsolete as a camp fuel. As a test, I tried using a kerosene stove once. I could scarcely boil a pot of water. In addition, some kerosene leaked out when the stove was packed, and it ruined everything it touched. The smell of kerosene never did go away. Kerosene remains popular in Europe only because the campers haven't heard much of white gas yet, and when they do, they will demand it.

That leaves white gas or butane as the best fuels, and either one can be right for you, depending on your special preferences.

White gas is the most popular, because it can be purchased at most outdoor recreation stores, at many supermarkets, and is inexpensive and effective. It burns hot, has virtually no smell, and evaporates quickly if it should spill. If you get caught in wet, miserable weather and can't get a fire going, you can use it as an emergency fire starter, although its use as such should be sparing and never on an open flame.

White gas is a popular fuel both for car campers who use the large, two-burner stoves equipped with a fuel tank and a pump, and for hikers who use a lightweight backpacking stove. On the latter, lighting can require priming with a gel called priming paste, which some people dislike. Another problem with white gas is that it can be extremely explosive.

As an example, I once almost burned off my beard completely in a mini-explosion while lighting one of the larger stoves designed for car camping. I was in the middle of cooking dinner when the flame suddenly shut down. Sure enough, the fuel tank was empty, and after refilling it, I pumped the tank 50 or 60 times to regain pressure. When I lit a match, the sucker ignited from three feet away. The resulting explosion was like a stick of dynamite going off, and immediately the smell of burning beard was in the air. In the quick flash of an erred moment, my once thick, dark beard had been reduced to a mass of little, yellow, burned curly-Qs.

My error? After filling the tank, I forgot to shut the fuel cock off while pumping up the pressure in the tank. As a result, when I pumped the tank, the stove burners were slowly producing the gas/air mixture, filling the air space above the stove. The strike of a match even from a few feet away and ka-boom!

That problem can be solved by using stoves that use bottled butane fuel. Butane requires no pouring, pumping or priming, and stoves that use butane are the easiest to light of all camping stoves. Just turn a knob and light, that's it. On the minus side, because it comes in bottles, you never know precisely how much fuel you have left, and when a bottle is empty, you have a potential piece of litter. Never litter. Ever.

The other problem with butane as a fuel is that it just plain does not work well in cold weather, or when there is little fuel left in the cartridge. Since you cannot predict mountain weather in spring or fall, you can use more fuel than originally projected. That can be frustrating, particularly if your stove starts wheezing with several days left in your trip. In addition, with most butane cartridges, if there is any chance of the temperature falling below freezing, you often have to sleep with the cartridge to keep it warm, or otherwise forget using it come morning.

Personally, I prefer using a small, lightweight stove that uses white gas so I can closely gauge fuel consumption. My pal Foonsky uses one with a butane bottle because it lights so easily. We have contests to see who can boil a pot of water faster and the difference is usually negligible. Thus, other factors are important when choosing a stove.

Of the other elements, ease of cleaning the burner is the most important. If you camp much, especially with the smaller stoves, the burner holes will eventually become clogged. Some stoves have a built-in cleaning needle; a quick twist of a knob and you're in business. On the other hand, others require disassembling and a protracted session using special cleaning tools. If a stove is difficult to clean, you will tend to put off doing it, and your stove will sputter and pant while you get humiliated watching the cold pot of water sitting on it.

Before making a purchase, have the salesman show you how to clean the burner head. Except in the case of the large, multi-burner family camping stoves, which rarely require cleaning, this test can do more to determine the long-term value of a stove than any other factor.

Building Fires

One summer expedition took me to the Canadian wilderness in British Columbia for a 75-mile canoe trip on the Bowron Lake Circuit, a chain of 13 lakes, six rivers and seven portages. It is one of the true great canoe trips of the world, a loop trip that ends just a few hundred feet from the start. But at the first camp at Kibbee Lake, my camp stove developed a fuel leak at the base of the burner and the nuclear-like blast that followed just about turned Canada into a giant crater.

As a result, the final 70 miles of the trip had to be completed without a stove, cooking on open fires each night. The problem was compounded by the weather. It rained eight of the ten days. Rain? In Canada, raindrops the size of silver dollars fall so hard they actually bounce on the lake surface. We had to stop paddling a few times in order to empty the rain water out of the canoe. At the end of the day, we'd make camp, and then came the test. Either make a fire or go to bed cold and hungry.

With an ax, at least we had a chance for success. As soaked as all the downed wood was, I was able to make my own fire-starting tinder from the chips of splitting logs; no matter how hard it rains, the inside of a log is always dry.

In miserable weather, matches don't stay lit long enough to get the tinder started. Instead, we used either a candle or the little, wax-like, fire-starter cubes that stay lit for several minutes. From those, we could get the tinder going. Then we added small, slender strips of wood that had been axed from the interior of the logs. When the flame reached a foot high, we added the logs, with the dry interior of them facing in. By the time the inside of the logs had caught fire, the outside would be drying from the heat. It wasn't long before a royal blaze was brightening the rainy night.

That's a worst case scenario and perhaps you will never face anything like it. Nevertheless, being able to build a good fire and cook on it can be one of the more satisfying elements of a camping trip. At times, just looking into the flames can provide a special satisfaction at the end of a good day.

However, never expect to build a fire for every meal, or in some cases, even to build one at all. Many state and federal campgrounds have been picked clean of downed wood, or forest fire danger forces rangers to prohibit fires altogether during the fire season. In either case, you either use your camp stove or you go hungry.

But when you can build a fire, and the resources are available to do so, it will add to the quality of your camping trip. Of the campgrounds listed in this book, the sites that allow for fires will usually already have fire rings available. In primitive areas where you can make your own, you should dig a ring eight inches deep, line the edges with rock, and clear all the needles and twigs in a five-foot radius. The next day, when the fire is dead, you can discard the rocks, fill over the black charcoal with dirt, then scatter pine needles and twigs over it. Nobody will even know you camped there. That's the best way I know to keep a secret spot a real secret.

When you start to build a campfire, the first thing you will notice is that no matter how good your intentions, your fellow campers will not be able to resist moving the wood around. Watch. You'll just be getting ready to add a key piece of wood at just the right spot, and your companion will stick his mitts in, confidently believing he has a better idea. He'll shift the fire around and undermine your best thought-out plans.

So I make a rule on camping trips. One person makes the fire and everybody else stands clear, or is involved with other camp tasks, like gathering wood, getting water, putting up tents or planning dinner. Once the fire is going strong, then it's fair game; anyone adds logs at their discretion. But in the early, delicate stages of the campfire, it's best to leave it to one person.

Before a match is struck, a complete pile of firewood should be gathered. Then start small, with the tiniest twigs you can find, and slowly add in larger twigs as you go, criss-crossing them like a miniature tepee. Eventually, you will get to the big chunks that will produce high heat. The key is to get one piece of wood burning into another, which then burns to another, setting off what I call the "chain of flame." Conversely, single pieces of wood, set apart from each other, will not burn.

On a dry, summer evening, at a campsite where plenty of wood is available, about the only way you can blow the deal is to get impatient and try to add the big pieces too quickly. Do that and you'll just get smoke, not flames, and it won't be long before every one of your fellow campers is poking at your fire. It will drive you crazy, but they just won't be able to help it.

Cooking Gear

I like traveling light, and I've found all I need for cooking is a pot, small frying pan, metal pot grabber, fork, knife, cup and matches. If you want to keep the price of food low and also cook customized dinners each night, a small pressure cooker can be just the ticket (see "Keeping the Price Down.") I keep all my gear in one small bag, which fits into my pack. If I'm camping out of my four-wheel drive rig, the little bag of cooking gear is easy to keep track of. Going simple, not complicated, is the key to keeping a camping trip on the right track.

You can get more elaborate by purchasing complete cook kits with plates, a coffee pot, large pots, and other cookware, but what really counts is having one single pot you're happy with. It needs to be just the right size, not too big or small, and stable enough so it won't tip over, even if it is at a slight angle on a fire, full of water at a full boil. Mine is just six inches wide and four-and-a-half inches deep, holds better than a quart of water, and has served well for several hundred camp dinners.

The rest of your cook kit is easy to complete. The frying pan should be small, light-gauge aluminum, teflon-coated, with a fold-in handle so it's no hassle to store. A pot grabber is a great addition. It's a little aluminum gadget that will clamp to the edge of pots and allow you to lift them and pour water with total control, without burning your fingers. For cleanup, take a small bottle filled with dish cleaner and a plastic scrubber, and you're in business.

A Sierra Cup, which is a wide aluminum cup with a wire handle, is an ideal cup to carry because you can eat out of it as well as use it for drinking. This means no plates to clean after dinner, so cleanup is quick and easy. In addition, if you go for a hike, you can clip it to your belt with its wire handle.

If you want a more formal setup, complete with plates, glasses, silverware and the like, you can end up spending more time preparing and cleaning up from meals than you do enjoying the country you are exploring. In addition, the more equipment you bring, the more loose ends you will have to deal with, and loose ends can cause plenty of frustration. If you have a choice, choose simple.

And remember what Thoreau said: "A man is rich in proportion to what he can do without."

Food and Cooking Tricks

On a trip to the Bob Marshall Wilderness in western Montana, I woke up one morning, yawned, and said, "What've we got for breakfast?"

The silence was ominous. "Well," finally came the response, "we don't have any food left."

"What!?"

"Well, I figured we'd catch trout for meals every other night."

On the return trip, we ended up eating wild berries, buds, and yes, even roots (not too tasty). When we finally landed the next day at a Kalispell pizza parlor, we nearly ate the wooden tables.

Running out of food on a camping trip can do more to turn reasonable people into violent grumps than any other event. There's no excuse for it, not when a system for figuring meals can be outlined with precision and little effort. You should not go out and buy a bunch of food, throw it in your rig, and head off for yonder. That leaves too much to chance. And if you've ever been in the woods and real hungry, you'll know to take a little effort to make sure a day or two of starvation will not occur. A three-step process offers a solution:

1 — Make a general meal-by-meal plan and make sure your companions like what is on it.

2 — Tell your companions to buy any specialty items (like a special brand of coffee) on their own and not to expect you to take care of everything.

3 — Put all the food on your living room floor and literally figure every day of your trip meal-by-meal, bagging the food in plastic bags as you go. You will know exact food quotas and will not go hungry.

Fish for meals? There's a guaranteed rule for that: If you expect to catch fish for meals, you will most certainly get skunked. If you don't expect to catch fish for meals, you will probably catch so many they'll be coming out of your ears. I've seen it a hundred times.

Keeping the Price Down

"There must be some mistake," I said with a laugh. "Who ever paid $750 for some camp food?"

But the amount was as clear as the digital numbers on the cash register: $753.27.

"How is this possible?" I asked the clerk at the register.

"Just add it up," she responded, irritated.

Then I started figuring. The freeze-dried backpack dinners cost $6 apiece. A small pack of beef jerky went for $2, the beef sticks for 75 cents, granola bars for 50 cents apiece. Then multiply it by four hungry men, including Foonsky, for 21 days. This food was for a major expedition—four guys hiking 250 miles over three weeks from Mount Whitney to Yosemite Valley.

The dinners alone cost close to $500. Add in the usual goodies—the jerky, granola bars, soups, dried fruit, oatmeal, Tang, candy and coffee—and I was handed a bill that felt like an earthquake.

A lot of campers have received similar shocks. In preparation for their trips, campers shop with enthusiasm. Then after hearing the price, they pay the bill in horror.

Well, there are solutions, lots of them. You can eat gourmet style in the outback without having your wallet cleaned out. But it means do-it-yourself cooking, more planning, and careful shopping. It also means transcending the push-button "I-want-it-now" philosophy that so many people try to take with them to the mountains.

The secret is to bring along a small pressure cooker. A reader, Mike Bettinger of San Francisco, passed this tip on to me. Little pressure cookers weigh about two pounds, and for backpackers and backcountry campers, that may sound like a lot. But when three or four people are on a trip, it actually saves weight.

The key is that it allows campers to bring items that are difficult to cook at high altitudes, such as brown and white rice, red, black, pinto and lima beans, and lentils. You pick one or more for a basic staple and then add a variety of freeze-dried ingredients to make a complete dish. Available are packets of meat, vegetables, onions, shallots and garlic. Sun-dried tomatoes, for instance, reconstitute wonderfully in a pressure cooker. Add herbs, spices, and maybe a few rainbow trout and you will be eating better out of a backpack than most people eat in their homes.

"In the morning, I have used the pressure cooker to turn dried apricots into apricot sauce to put on the pancakes we made with sourdough starter," Bettinger said. "The pressure cooker is also big enough for washing out cups and utensils. The days when backpacking meant eating terrible freeze-dried food are over. It doesn't take a gourmet cook to prepare these meals, only some thought beforehand."

Now when Foonsky, Mr. Furnai, Rambob and me sit down to eat such a meal, we don't call it "eating." We call it "hodgepacking," or "time to pack your hodge." After a particularly long day on the trail, you can do some serious hodgepacking.

If your trip is a shorter one, like for a weekend, that means you can bring more fresh food to add some sizzle to the hodge. You can design a hot soup/stew mix that is good enough to make and eat at home.

You start by bringing a pot of water to a full boil, then adding pasta, ramen noodles or macaroni. While it simmers, cut in a potato, carrot, onion and garlic clove, and let it cook for about 10 minutes. When the vegetables have softened, add in a soup mix or two, maybe some cheese, and you are just about in business. But you can still ruin it and turn your hodge into slodge. Make sure you read the directions on the soup mix to determine cooking time. It can vary widely. In addition, make sure you stir the whole thing up, otherwise you will get these hidden dry clumps of soup mix that can taste like garlic sawdust.

How do I know? Well, it was up near Kearsage Pass, where, feeling half-starved, I will never forget the first bite of that night's hodge. I damn near gagged to death. Foonsky laughed at me, until he took his first bite (a nice big one), then turned green.

Another way to trim food costs is to make your own beef jerky, the trademark staple of campers for more than 200 years. But hey, a tiny, little packet of beef jerky costs $2. On that 250-mile expedition, I spent $150 on jerky alone. Never again. Now we make our own and get big strips of jerky that taste better than anything you can buy.

Foonsky settled on the following recipe, starting with a couple pieces of meat, lean top round, sirloin or tri-tip. At home, cut it in 3/16-inch strips across the grain, trimming out the membrane, gristle and fat. Marinate the strips for 24 hours, placing them in a glass dish. The fun begins in picking a marinade. Try two-thirds teriyaki sauce, one-third Worcestershire. You can customize the recipe by adding pepper, ground mustard, bay leaf, red wine vinegar, garlic, and for the brave, Tabasco sauce. After a day or so, squeeze out each strip of meat with a rolling pin, lay them in rows on a cooling rack over a cookie sheet, place them in an oven and dry them at 125 degrees for 12 hours. Thicker pieces can take as long as 18 to 24 hours.

That's it. The hardest part is cleaning the cookie sheet when you are done. The easiest part is eating your own homemade jerky while sitting at a lookout on a mountain ridge. The do-it-yourself method for jerky may take a day or so, but it is cheaper and can taste better than anything you can buy pre-made.

If all this still doesn't sound like your idea of a gourmet but low-cost camping meal, well, you are forgetting the main course: rainbow trout. The law of the wild is that if you expect to catch trout for meals, you will starve to death. However, if you plan to catch none, you will have plenty to top off each night's hodgepacking.

Some campers go to great difficulties to cook their trout, bringing along frying pans, butter, grills, tin foil, and more, but all you really need is some seasoned salt and a campfire.

Rinse the trout off, and while it's still wet, sprinkle a good dose of seasoned salt on it, both inside and out. Clear any burning logs to the side of the campfire, then lay the trout right on the coals, turning it once so both sides are cooked. Sound ridiculous? Sound like you are throwing the fish away?

Sound like the fish will burn up? Sound like you will have to eat the campfire ash? Wrong on all counts. The fish cooks perfectly, the ash doesn't stick, and after cooking trout this way, you may never fry a trout again.

But if you can't convince your buddies, who may insist the trout should be fried, then make sure you have butter to fry them in, not oil. And also make sure you cook them all the way through, so the meat strips off the back bone in two nice, clean fillets. The fish should end up looking like Sylvester the Cat just dipped it in his mouth, leaving only the head, tail and a perfect skeleton.

You can supplement your eats with sweets, nuts, freeze-dried fruits and drink mixes. In any case, make sure you keep the dinner menu varied. If you and your buddies look into your dinner cups and groan, "Ugh, not this again," you will soon start dreaming of cheeseburgers and french fries on your trip instead of hiking, fishing and finding beautiful campsites.

If you are car camping and have a big ice chest, you can bring virtually anything to eat and drink. If you are on the trail, and don't mind paying the price, the new era of pre-made freeze-dried dinners provide another option.

Some of the biggest advances in the outdoors industry have come in freeze-dried dinners now available for campers. Some of them are almost good enough to serve in restaurants. Sweet-and-sour pork over rice, tostadas, burgundy chicken . . . it sure beats the poopy goop we used to eat, like the old, soupy chili mac dinners that tasted bad and looked so unlike "food" that consumption was near impossible, even for my dog, Rebel. Foonsky managed to get it down, however, but just barely.

To provide an idea of how to plan a menu, consider what my companions and I ate while hiking 250 miles on California's John Muir Trail:

Breakfast — Instant soup, oatmeal (never get plain), one beef or jerky stick, coffee or hot chocolate.

Lunch — One beef stick, two jerky sticks, one granola bar, dried fruit, half cup of pistachio nuts, Tang, small bag of M&Ms.

Dinner — Instant soup, freeze-dried dinner, milk bar, rainbow trout.

What was that last item? Rainbow trout? Right! Lest you plan on it, you can catch them every night.

Clothing and Weather Protection

What started as an innocent pursuit of a perfect campground evolved into one heck of a predicament for Foonsky and me.

We had parked at the end of a logging road and then bushwhacked our way down a canyon to a pristine trout stream. On my first cast, a little flip into the plunge pool of a waterfall, I caught a 16-inch rainbow trout, a real beauty that jumped three times. Magic stuff.

Then just across stream, we saw it. The Perfect Camping Spot. On a sandbar on the edge of the forest, there lay a flat, high and dry spot above the river. Nearby was plenty of downed wood collected by past winter storms that we could use for firewood. And, of course, this beautiful trout stream was bubbling along just 40 yards from the site.

But nothing is perfect, right? To reach it, we had to wade across the river, although it didn't appear to be too difficult. The cold water tingled a bit, and the river came up surprisingly high, just above the belt. But it would be worth it to camp at The Perfect Spot.

Once across the river, we put on some dry clothes, set up camp, explored the woods, and fished the stream, catching several nice trout for dinner. But late that afternoon, it started raining. What? Rain in the summertime? Nature makes its own rules. By the next morning, it was still raining, pouring like a Yosemite waterfall from a solid gray sky.

That's when we noticed The Perfect Spot wasn't so perfect. The rain had raised the river level too high for us to wade back across. We were marooned, wet and hungry.

"Now we're in a heck of a predicament," said Foonsky, the water streaming off him.

Getting cold and wet on a camping trip with no way to get warm is not only unnecessary and uncomfortable, but it can be a fast ticket to hypothermia, the Number One killer of campers in the woods. By definition, hypothermia is a condition where body temperature is lowered to the point where it causes illness. It is particularly dangerous because the afflicted are usually unaware it is setting in. The first sign is a sense of apathy, then a state of confusion, which can lead eventually to collapse (or what appears to be sleep), then death.

You must always have a way to get warm and dry in short order, regardless of any conditions you may face. If you have no way of getting dry, then you must take emergency steps to prevent hypothermia. Those steps are detailed in the following pages on first-aid.

But you should never reach that point. For starters, always have different sets of clothes tucked away, so no matter how cold and wet you might get, you always have something dry. On hiking trips, I always carry a second set of clothes, sealed to stay dry, in a plastic garbage bag. I keep a third set waiting back at the truck.

If you are car camping, your vehicle can cause an illusionary sense of security. But with an extra set of dry clothes stashed safely away, there is no illusion. The security is real. And remember, no matter how hot the weather is when you start on your trip, always be prepared for the worst. Foonsky and I learned the hard way.

So both of us were soaking wet on that sandbar, and with no other choice, we tried holing up in the tent for the night. A sleeping bag with Quallofil, or another polyester fiber fill, can retain warmth even when wet, because the fill is hollow and retains its loft. So as miserable as it was, we made it through the night.

The rain finally stopped the next day, and the river dropped a bit, but it was still rolling big and angry. Using a stick as a wading staff, Foonsky crossed about 80 percent of the stream before he was dumped, but he made a jump for it and managed to scramble to the river bank. He waved for me to follow. "No problem," I thought.

It took me 20 minutes to reach nearly the same spot where Foonsky had been dumped. The heavy river current was above my belt and pushing hard. Then, in the flash of an instant, my wading staff slipped on a rock. I teetered in the river current, and was knocked over like a bowling pin. I became completely submerged. I went tumbling down the river, heading right toward the waterfall. While underwater, I looked up at the river surface and can remember how close it appeared, yet how out of control I was. Right then, this giant hand appeared, and I grabbed it. It was Foonsky. If it wasn't for that hand, I would have sailed right over the nearby waterfall.

My momentum drew Foonsky right into the river, and we scrambled in the current, but I suddenly sensed the river bottom under my knees. On all fours, the two of us clambered ashore. We were safe.

"Thanks ol' buddy," I said.

"Man, we're wet," he responded. "Let's get to the rig and get some dry clothes on."

Dressing in Layers

After falling in the river, Foonsky and I looked like a couple of cold swamp rats. When we eventually reached the truck and finally started getting into warm clothes, a strange phenomenon hit both of us. Now that we were warming up, we started shivering and shaking like old engines trying to start. That's the body's built-in heater. Shivering is how the body tries to warm itself, producing as much heat as if you were jogging.

To retain that heat, you should dress in "layers." The interior layer, what you wear closest to your skin, and the exterior layer, what you wear to repel the weather, are the most important.

In the good ol' days, campers wore long underwear made out of wool, which was scratchy, heavy, and sometimes sweaty. Well, times have changed. You can now wear long underwear made of polypropylene, a synthetic material that is warm, light, and wicks dampness away from your skin. It's ideal to wear in a sleeping bag on cold nights, during cool evenings after the sun goes down, or for winter snow sports. Poly shirts come in three weights: light, medium and heavy. The medium weight is ideal for campers. The light weight clings too much to your body. We call it Indian Underwear, because it keeps creeping up on you. And the heavy weight is too warm and bulky. For most folks, the medium is just right.

The next layer of clothes should be a light cotton shirt or a long-sleeve cotton/wool shirt, or both, depending on the coolness of the day. For pants, many just wear blue jeans when camping, but blue jeans can be hot, tight, and once wet, they tend to stay that way. Putting on wet blue jeans on a cold morning is a torturous way to start the day. I can tell you that from experience since I have suffered that fate a number of times. A better choice are pants made from a cotton/canvas mix, which are available at outdoors stores. They are light, have a lot of give, and dry quickly. If the weather is quite warm, shorts that have some room to them can be the best choice.

Vests and Parkas

In cold weather, you should take the layer system one step further with a warm vest and a parka jacket. Vests are especially useful because they provide warmth without the bulkiness of a parka. The warmest vests and parkas are either filled with down, Quallofil, or are made with a cotton/wool mix. Each has its respective merits and problems. Downfill provides the most warmth for the amount of weight, but becomes useless when wet, taking on a close resemblance to a wet dish rag. Quallofil keeps much of its heat-retaining qualities even when wet, but is expensive. Vests made of cotton/wool mixes are the most attractive and also are quite warm, but can be as heavy as a ship's anchor when wet.

Sometimes the answer is combining the two. One of my best camping companions wears a good-looking, cotton-wool vest, and a parka filled with Quallofil. The vest never gets wet, so weight is not a factor.

Rain Gear

One of the most miserable nights I ever spent in my life was on a camping trip where I didn't bring my rain gear or a tent. Hey, it was early August, the temperature had been in the 90s for weeks, and if anybody told me it was going to rain, I would have told them to consult a brain doctor. But rain it did. And as I got more and more wet, I kept saying to myself, "Hey, it's summer, it's not supposed to rain." Then I remembered one of the Ten Commandments of camping: forget your rain gear and you can guarantee it will rain.

To stay dry, you need some form of water-repellent shell. It can be as simple as a $5 poncho made out of plastic or as elaborate as a Gore-Tex rain jacket and pants set that costs $300. What counts is not how much you spend, but how dry you stay.

Some can do just fine with a cheap poncho, and note that ponchos can serve other uses in addition to a rain coat. Ponchos can be used as a ground tarp, as a rain cover for supplies or a backpack, or in a pinch, can be roped up to trees to provide a quick storm ceiling if you don't have a tent. The problem with ponchos is that in a hard rain, you just don't stay dry. First your legs get wet, then they get soaked. Then your arms follow the same pattern. If you're wearing cotton, you'll find that once part of the garment gets wet, the water will spread until, alas, you are dripping wet, poncho and all. Before long you start to feel like a walking refrigerator.

One high-cost option is buying a Gore-Tex rain jacket and pants. Gore-Tex is actually not a fabric, as is commonly believed, but a laminated film that coats a breathable fabric. The result is a lightweight, water repellent, breathable jacket and pants. They are perfect for campers, but they cost a fortune.

Some hiking buddies of mine have complained that the older Gore-Tex rain gear loses some water-repellent qualities over time. However, manufacturers insist that this is the result of water seeping through seams, not leaks in the jacket. At each seam, tiny needles will have pierced through the fabric, and as tiny as the holes are, water will find a way through. An application of Seam Lock, especially at major seams around the shoulders of a jacket, can usually end the problem.

If you don't want to spend the big bucks for Gore-Tex rain gear, but want more rain protection than a poncho affords, a coated nylon jacket is the compromise that many choose. They are inexpensive, have the highest water repellent qualities of any rain gear, and are warm, providing a good outer shell for your layers of clothing. But they are not without fault. These jackets don't breathe at all, and if you zip them up tight, you can sweat like an Eskimo.

My brother, Rambob, gave me a $20 nylon jacket prior to a mountain climbing expedition. I wore that $20 special all the way to the top with no complaints; it's warm and 100 percent waterproof. The one problem with nylon is when the temperatures drop below freezing. It gets so stiff that it feels like you are wearing a straight jacket. But at $20, it seems like a treasure, especially compared to the $180 Gore-Tex jackets. And its value increases every time it rains.

Other Gear, And a Few Tips

What are the three items most commonly forgotten on a camping trip? A hat, sunglasses and chapstick. A hot day is unforgiving without them.

A hat is crucial, especially when you are visiting high elevations. Without one you are constantly exposed to everything nature can give you. The sun will dehydrate you, sap your energy, sunburn your head, and in worst cases, cause sunstroke. Start with a comfortable hat. Then finish with sunglasses, chapstick and sunscreen for additional protection. They will help protect you from extreme heat.

To guard against extreme cold, it's a good idea to keep a pair of thin ski gloves stashed away with your emergency clothes, along with a wool ski cap. The gloves should be thick enough to keep your fingers from stiffening up, but pliable enough to allow full movement, so you don't have to take them off to complete simple tasks, like lighting a stove. An alternative to gloves are glovelets, which look like gloves with no fingers. In any case, just because the weather turns cold doesn't mean that your hands have to.

And if you fall into a river like Foonsky and I did, well, I hope you have a set of dry clothes waiting back at your rig. Oh, and a hand reaching out to you.

Hiking and Foot Care

We had set up a nice little camp in the woods, and my buddy, Foonsky, was strapping on his hiking boots, sitting against a big Douglas fir.

"New boots," he said with a grin. "But they seem pretty stiff."

We decided to hoof it down the trail for a few hours, exploring the mountain wildlands that are said to hide Bigfoot and other strange creatures. After just a short while on the trail, a sense of peace and calm seemed to settle in. The forest provides you the chance to be purified with clean air and the smell of trees, freeing you from all troubles.

But it wasn't long before the look of trouble was on Foonsky's face. And no, it wasn't from seeing Bigfoot.

"Got a hot spot on a toe," he said.

Immediately we stopped. He pulled off his right boot, then socks, and inspected the left side of his big toe. Sure enough, a blister had bubbled up, filled with fluid, but not popped. From his medical kit, Foonsky cut a small piece of moleskin to fit over the blister, then taped it to hold it in place. A few minutes later, we were back on the trail.

A half hour later, there was still no sign of Bigfoot. But Foonsky stopped again and pulled off his other boot. "Another hot spot." Another small blister had started on the little toe of his left foot, over which he taped a Band-Aid to keep it from further chafing against the inside of his new boot.

In just a few days, ol' Foonsky, a strong, 6-foot-5, 200-plus pound guy, was walking around like a sore-hoofed horse that had been loaded with a month of supplies and then ridden over sharp rocks. Well, it wasn't the distance that had done Foonsky in; it was those blisters. He had them on eight of his ten toes and was going through Band-Aids, moleskin, and tape like he was a walking emergency ward. If he used any more tape, he would've looked like a mummy from an Egyptian tomb.

If you've ever been in a similar predicament, then you know the frustration of wanting to have a good time, wanting to hike and explore the area at which you have set up a secluded camp, only to be turned gimp-legged by several blisters. No one is immune, neither big, strong guys nor small, innocent-looking women. All are created equal before the blister god. You can be forced to bow to it unless you get your act together.

That means wearing the right style boots for what you have in mind and then protecting your feet with a careful selection of socks. And then, if you are still so unfortunate as to get a blister or two, it means knowing how to treat them fast so they don't turn your walk into a sore-footed endurance test.

What causes blisters? In almost all cases, it is the simple rubbing of your foot against the rugged interior of your boot. That can be worsened by several factors:

1 —A very stiff boot, or one in which your foot moves inside the boot as you walk, instead of the boot flexing as if it was another layer of skin.

2 —Thin, ragged or dirty socks. This is the fastest route to blisters. Thin socks will allow your feet to move inside of your boots, ragged socks will allow

your skin to chafe directly against the boot's interior, and dirty socks will wrinkle and fold, also rubbing against your feet instead of cushioning them.

3 — Soft feet. By themselves, soft feet will not cause blisters, but in combination with a stiff boot or thin socks, they can cause terrible problems. The best way to toughen up your feet is to go barefoot. In fact, some of the biggest, toughest-looking guys you'll ever see from Hells Angels to pro football players have feet that are as soft as a baby's butt. Why? Because they never go barefoot and don't hike much.

Selecting the Right Books

One summer I hiked 400 miles, including 250 miles in three weeks, along the crest of California's Sierra Nevada, and another 150 miles over several months in an earlier general training program. In that span, I got just one blister, suffered on the fourth day of the 250-miler. I treated it immediately, and suffered no more. One key is wearing the right boot, and for me, that means a boot that acts as a thick layer of skin that is flexible and pliable to my foot. I want my feet to fit snugly in them, with no interior movement.

There are three kinds of boots: mountaineering boots, hiking boots and canvas walking shoes. Either select the right one for you or pay the consequences.

The stiffest of the lot is the mountaineering boot. These boots are often identified by mid-range tops, laces that extend almost as far as the toe area, and ankle areas that are as stiff as a board. The lack of "give" in them is what endears them to mountaineers. Their stiffness is preferred when rock climbing, walking off-trail on craggy surfaces, or hiking down the edge of stream beds where walking across small rocks can cause you to turn your ankle. Because these boots don't give on rugged, craggy terrain, they reduce ankle injuries and provide better traction.

The drawback to stiff boots is that if careful selection of socks is not made and your foot starts slipping around in them, you will get a set of blisters that would raise even Foonsky's eyebrows. But if you just want to go for a walk, or a good tromp with a backpack, then hiking shoes or backpacking boots are better designed for those uses.

Canvas walking shoes are the lightest of all boots, designed for day walks or short backpacking trips. Some of the newer models are like rugged tennis shoes, designed with a canvas top for lightness and a lug sole for traction. These are perfect for people who like to walk but rarely carry a backpack. Because they are flexible, they are easy to break in, and with fresh socks, rarely cause blister problems. And because they are light, general hiking fatigue is greatly reduced.

On the negative side, because canvas shoes have shallow lug soles, traction can be far from good on slippery surfaces. In addition, they provide less than ideal ankle support, which can be a problem in rocky areas, such as along a stream where you might want to go trout fishing. Turn your ankle and your trip can be ruined.

My preference is for a premium backpacking boot, the perfect medium between the stiff mountaineering boots and the soft canvas hiking shoes. The deep lug bottom provides traction, the high ankle coverage provides support, yet the soft, waterproof leather body gives each foot a snug fit. Add it up and that means no blisters. On the negative side, they can be quite hot, weigh a ton, and, if they get wet, take days to dry.

There are a zillion styles, brands and price ranges of boots to choose from. If you wander about, looking at them equally, you will get as confused as a kid in a toy store. Instead, go into the store with your mind clear with what you want, then find it and buy it. If you want the best, expect to spend $60 to $80 for canvas walking shoes, from $100 to $140 and sometimes more for hiking or mountaineering boots. This is one area you don't want to scrimp on, so try not to yelp about the high cost. Instead, walk out of the store believing you deserve the best, and that's exactly what you just paid for.

If you plan on using the advice of a shoe salesman for your purchase, first look at what kind of boots he is wearing. If he isn't even wearing boots, then any advice he might tender may not be worth a plug nickel. Most people I know who own quality boots, including salesmen, will wear them almost daily if their job allows, since boots are the best footwear available. However, even these well-meaning folks can offer sketchy advice. Every hiker I've ever met will tell you he wears the world's greatest boot.

Instead, enter the store with a precise use and style in mind. Rather than fish for suggestions, tell the salesman exactly what you want, try two or three different brands of the same style, and always try on the matching pair of boots simultaneously so you know exactly how they'll feel. If possible, walk up and down stairs with them. Are they too stiff? Are your feet snug yet comfortable, or do they slip? Do they have that "right" kind of feel when you walk?

If you get the right answers to those questions, then you're on your way to blister-free, pleasure-filled days of walking.

Socks

The poor gent was scratching his feet like ants were crawling over them. I looked closer. Huge yellow calluses had covered the bottom of his feet, and at the ball and heel, the calluses were about a quarter of an inch thick, cracking and sore.

"I don't understand it," he said. "I'm on my feet a lot, so I bought a real good pair of hiking boots. But look what they've done to my feet. My feet itch so much I'm going crazy."

People can spend so much energy selecting the right kind of boot that they virtually overlook wearing the right kind of socks. One goes with the other.

Your socks should be thick enough to provide a cushion for your foot, as well as a good, snug fit. Without good socks, you might try to get the boot laces too tight and that's like putting a tourniquet on your feet. You should have plenty of clean socks on hand, or plan on washing what you have on your trip. As socks are worn, they become compressed, dirty and damp. Any one of those factors can cause problems.

My camping companions believe I go overboard when it comes to socks, that I bring too many, wear too many. But it works, so that's where the complaints stop. So how many do I wear? Well, would you believe three socks on each foot? It may sound like overkill, but each has its purpose, and like I said, it works.

The interior sock is thin, lightweight, and made out of polypropylene or silk synthetic materials designed to transport moisture away from your skin. With a poly interior sock, your foot stays dry when it sweats. Without a poly sock, your foot can get damp and mix with dirt, which can cause a "hot spot" to start on your foot. Eventually you get blisters, lots of them.

The second sock is for comfort, and can be cotton, but a thin wool-based composite is ideal. Some made of the latter can wick moisture away from the skin, much like the qualities of polypropylene. If wool itches your feet, a thick cotton sock can be suitable, though cotton collects moisture and compacts more quickly than other socks. If you're on a short hike though, cotton will do just fine.

The exterior sock should be made of high quality, thick wool—at least 80 percent wool. It will cushion your feet, provide that "just right" snug fit in your boot, and in cold weather, give you some additional warmth and insulation. It is critical to keep the wool sock clean. If you wear a dirty wool sock over and over again, it will compact and lose its cushion, start wrinkling while you hike, and your feet will catch on fire from the blisters that start popping up.

A Few Tips

If you are like most folks, that is, the bottom of your feet are rarely exposed and quite soft, you can take additional steps in their care. The best tip is keeping a fresh foot pad in your boot made of sponge rubber. Another cure for soft feet is to get out and walk or jog on a regular basis prior to your camping trip.

If you plan to use a foot pad and wear three socks, you will need to use these items when sizing boots. It is an unforgiving error to wear thin cotton socks when buying boots, then later trying to squeeze all this stuff, plus your feet, into your boots. There just won't be enough room.

The key to treating blisters is fast work at the first sign of a hot spot. But before you remove your socks, first check to see if the sock has a wrinkle in it, a likely cause of the problem. If so, either change socks or pull them tight, removing the tiny folds, after taking care of the blister. Cut a piece of moleskin to cover the offending toe, securing the moleskin with white medical tape. If moleskin is not available, small Band-Aids can do the job, but these have to be replaced daily, and sometimes with even more frequency. At night, clean your feet and sleep without socks.

Two other items that can help your walking is an Ace bandage and a pair of gaiters.

For sprained ankles and twisted knees, an Ace bandage can be like an insurance policy to get you back on the trail and out of trouble. Over the years, I have had serious ankle problems and have relied on a good wrap with a four-inch bandage to get me home. The newer bandages come with the clips permanently attached, so you don't have to worry about losing them.

Gaiters are leggings made of plastic, nylon or Gore-Tex which fit from just below your knees, over your calves, and attach under your boots. They are of particular help when walking in damp areas, or in places where rain is common. As your legs brush against ferns or low-lying plants, gaiters will deflect the moisture. Without them, your pants will be soaking wet in short order.

Should your boots become wet, a good tip is never to try to force dry them. Some well-meaning folks will try to speed-dry them at the edge of a campfire or actually put the boots in an oven. While this may dry the boots, it can also loosen the glue that holds them together, ultimately weakening them until one day they fall apart in a heap.

A better bet is to treat the leather so the boots become water repellent. Silicone-based liquids are the easiest to use and least greasy of the treatments available.

A final tip is to have another pair of lightweight shoes or moccasins that you can wear around camp, and in the process, give your feet the rest they deserve.

Sleeping Gear

One mountain night in the pines on an eve long ago, my dad, brother and I had rolled out our sleeping bags and were bedded down for the night. After the pre-trip excitement, a long drive, an evening of trout fishing and a barbecue, we were like three tired doggies who had played too much.

But as I looked up at the stars, I was suddenly wide awake. The kid was still wired. A half hour later? No change—wide awake.

And as little kids can do, I had to wake up ol' dad to tell him about it. "Hey, Dad, I can't sleep."

"This is what you do," he said. "Watch the sky for a shooting star and tell yourself that you cannot go to sleep until you see at least one. As you wait and watch, you will start getting tired, and it will be difficult to keep your eyes open. But tell yourself you must keep watching. Then you'll start to really feel tired. When you finally see a shooting star, you'll go to sleep so fast you won't know what hit you."

Well, I tried it that night and I don't even remember seeing a shooting star, I went to sleep so fast.

It's a good trick, and along with having a good sleeping bag, ground insulation, maybe a tent or a few tricks for bedding down in a pickup truck or motor home, you can get a good sleep on every camping trip.

Some 20 years after that camping episode with my dad and brother, we made a trip to the Planetarium at the Academy of Sciences in San Francisco to see a show on Halley's Comet. The lights dimmed, and the ceiling turned into a night sky, filled with stars and a setting moon. A scientist began explaining phenomenons of the heavens.

After a few minutes, I began to feel drowsy. Just then, a shooting star zipped across the Planetarium ceiling. I went into a deep sleep so fast it was like I was in a coma. I didn't wake up until the show was over, the lights were turned back on, and the people were leaving.

Feeling drowsy, I turned to see if ol' Dad had liked the show. Oh yeah? Not only had he gone to sleep too, but he apparently had no intention of waking up, no matter what. Just like a camping trip.

Sleeping Bags

What could be worse than trying to sleep in a cold, wet sleeping bag on a rainy night without a tent in the mountains?

Answer: Trying to sleep in a cold, wet sleeping bag on a rainy night without a tent in the mountains, when your sleeping bag is filled with down.

Water will turn a down-filled sleeping bag into a mushy heap. Many campers do not like a high-tech approach, but the state-of-the-art polyfiber sleeping bags can keep you warm even when wet. That factor, along with temperature rating and weight, is key when selecting a sleeping bag.

A sleeping bag is a shell filled with a heat-retaining insulation. By itself, it is not warm. Your body provides the heat, and the sleeping bag's ability to retain that heat is what makes it warm or cold.

The old-styled canvas bags are heavy, bulky, cold, and, when wet, useless. With other options available, their use is limited. Anybody who sleeps outdoors or backpacks should choose otherwise. Instead, buy and use a sleeping bag filled with down or one of the quality poly-fills. Down is light, warm, and aesthetically pleasing to those who don't think camping and technology mix. If you like down bags, be sure to keep it double wrapped in plastic garbage bags on your trips in order to keep it dry. Once wet, you'll spend your nights howling at the moon.

The polyfiber-filled bags are not necessarily better than those filled with down, but they can be. Their one key advantage is that even when wet, some poly-fills can retain up to 80 to 85 percent of your body heat. This allows you to sleep and get valuable rest even in miserable conditions. And my camping experience is that no matter how lucky you may be, there comes a time when you will get caught in an unexpected, violent storm and everything you've got will get wet, including your sleeping bag. That's when a poly-fill bag becomes priceless. You either have one and can sleep, or you don't have one and suffer. It is that simple. Of the synthetic fills, Quallofil made by Dupont is the leader of the industry.

But as mentioned, just because a sleeping bag uses a high-tech poly-fill doesn't necessarily make it a better bag. There are other factors.

The most important are a bag's temperature rating and weight. The temperature rating of a sleeping bag refers to how cold it can get before you start actually feeling cold. Many campers make the mistake of thinking, "I only camp in the summer, so a bag rated at a 30 or 40 degrees should be fine." Later, they find out it isn't so fine, and all it takes is one cold night to convince them of that. When selecting the right temperature rating, visualize the coldest weather you might ever confront, and then get a bag rated for even colder weather.

For instance, if you are a summer camper, you may rarely experience a night in the low 30s or high 20s. A sleeping bag rated at 20 degrees would be appropriate, keeping you snug, warm and asleep. For most campers, I advise bags rated at zero or ten degrees.

If you buy a poly-filled sleeping bag, never leave it squished in your stuff sack between camping trips. Instead, keep it on a hanger in a closet or use it as a blanket. One thing that can reduce a polyfilled bag's heat-retaining qualities is if you lose the loft out of the tiny hollow fibers that make up the fill. You can avoid this with proper storage.

The weight of a sleeping bag can also be a key factor, especially for backpackers. When you have to carry your gear on your back, every ounce becomes important. To keep your weight to a minimum, sleeping bags that weigh just three pounds are available, although expensive. But if you hike much, it's worth the price. For an overnighter, you can get away with a four or four-and-a-half-pound bag without much stress. However, bags weighing five pounds and up should be left back at the car.

I have two sleeping bags: a seven-pounder that feels like I'm in a giant sponge, and a little three-pounder. The heavy duty model is for pickup truck camping in cold weather and doubles as a blanket at home. The lightweight bag is for hikes. Between the two, I'm set.

Insulation Pads

Even with the warmest sleeping bag in the world, if you just lay it down on the ground and try to sleep, you will likely get as cold as a winter cucumber. That is because the cold ground will suck the warmth right out of your body. The solution is to have a layer of insulation between you and the ground. For this, you can use a thin Insulite pad, a lightweight Therm-a-Rest inflatable pad, or an air mattress. Here is a capsule summary of them:

Insulite pads — They are light, inexpensive, roll up quick for trans- port, and can double as a seat pad at your camp. The negative side is that in one night, they will compress, making you feel like you are sleeping on granite.

Therm-a-Rest pads — They are a real luxury, because they do every- thing an Insulite pad does, but also provide a cushion. The negative side to them is that they are expensive by comparison, and if they get a hole in them, they become worthless unless you have a patch kit.

Air mattress — OK for car campers, but their bulk, weight and the amount of effort necessary to blow them up make them a nuisance.

A Few Tricks

When surveying a camp area, the most important consideration should be to select a good spot to sleep. Everything else is secondary. Ideally, you want a flat spot that is wind-sheltered, on ground soft enough to drive stakes into. Yeah, and I want to win the lottery, too.

Sometimes that ground will have a slight slope to it. In that case, always sleep with your head on the uphill side. If you sleep parallel to the slope, every time you roll over in your sleep, you'll find yourself rolling down the hill. If you sleep with your head on the downhill side, you'll get a headache that feels like an ax is embedded in your brain.

When you've found a good spot, clear it of all branches, twigs, and rocks, of course. A good tip is to dig a slight indentation in the ground where your hip will fit. Since your body is not flat, but has curves and edges, it will not feel comfortable on flat ground. Some people even get severely bruised on the sides of their hips when sleeping on flat, hard ground. For that reason alone, they learn to hate camping. Instead, bring a spade, dig a little depression in the ground for your hip, and sleep well.

After the ground is prepared, throw a ground cloth over the spot, which will keep much of the morning dew off you. In some areas, particularly where fog is a problem, morning dew can be quite heavy and get the outside of your sleeping bag quite wet. In that case, you need overhead protection, such as a tent or some kind of roof, like that of a poncho or tarp, with its ends tied to trees.

Tents and Weather Protection

All it takes is to get caught in the rain once without a tent and you will never go anywhere without one again. A tent provides protection from rain, wind and mosquito attacks. In exchange, you can lose a starry night's view, though some tents now even provide moon roofs.

A tent can be as complex as a four-season, tubular-jointed dome with a rain fly, or nothing more complicated than two ponchos snapped together and roped up to a tree. They can be as cheap as a $10 tube tent, which is nothing more than a hollow piece of plastic, or as expensive as a $500 five-person deluxe expedition dome model. They vary greatly in size, price and put-up time. If you plan on getting a good one, then plan on doing plenty of shopping and asking lots of questions. The key ones are: Will it keep me dry? How hard is it to put up? Is it roomy enough? How much does it weigh?

With a little bit of homework, you can get the right answers to these questions.

Will it keep me dry? On many one and two-person tents, the rain fly does not extend far enough to keep water off the bottom sidewalls of the tent. In a driving rain, water can also drip from the rain fly and to the bottom sidewalls of the tent. Eventually the water can leak through to the inside, particularly through the seams where the tent has been sewed together.

You must be able to stake out your rain fly so it completely covers all of the tent. If you are tent shopping and this does not appear possible, then don't buy the tent. To prevent potential leaks, use a seam water proofer like Seam Lock, a glue-like substance, to close potential leak areas on tent seams. On the large umbrella tents, keep a patch kit handy.

Another way to keep water out of your tent is to store all wet garments outside the tent, under a poncho. Moisture from wet clothes stashed in the tent will condense on the interior tent walls. If you bring enough wet clothes in the tent, by the next morning you can feel like you're camping in a duck blind.

How hard is it to put up? If a tent is difficult to erect in full sunlight, you can just about forget it at night. Some tents can go up in just a few minutes, without requiring help from another camper. This might be the kind of tent you want.

The way to compare put-up time of tents when shopping is to count the number of connecting points from the tent poles to the tent, and also the number of stakes required. The fewer, the better. Think simple. My tent has seven connecting points and, minus the rain fly, requires no stakes. It goes up in a few minutes. If you need a lot of stakes, it is a sure tip-off to a long put-up time. Try it at night or in the rain, and you'll be ready to cash your chips and go for broke.

Another factor is the tent poles themselves. Some small tents have poles that are broken into small sections that are connected by bungee cords. It takes only an instant to convert them to a complete pole.

Some outdoor shops have tents on display on their showroom floor. Before buying the tent, have the salesman take the tent down and put it back up. If it takes him more than five minutes, or he says he "doesn't have time," then keep looking.

Is it roomy enough? Don't judge the size of a tent on floor space alone. Some tents small on floor space can give the illusion of roominess with a high ceiling. You can be quite comfortable in them and snug.

But remember that a one-person or two-person tent is just that. A two-person tent has room for two people plus gear. That's it. Don't buy a tent expecting it to hold more than it is intended to.

How much does it weigh? If you're a hiker, this becomes the preeminent question. If it's much more than six or seven pounds, forget it. A 12-pound tent is bad enough, but get it wet and it's like carrying a piano on your back. On the other hand, weight is scarcely a factor if you camp only where you can take your car. My dad, for instance, used to have this giant canvas umbrella tent that folded down to this neat little pack that weighed about 500 pounds.

An Option

If you like going solo and choose not to own a tent at all, a bivvy bag, short for bivouac bag, can provide the weather protection you require. A bivvy bag is a water repellent shell in which your sleeping bag fits. They are light and tough, and for some, are a perfect alternative to a heavy tent. On the down side, however, there is a strange sensation when you try to ride out a rainy night in one. You can hear the rain hitting you, and sometimes even feel the pounding of the drops through the bivvy bag. It can be unsettling to try and sleep under such circumstances.

Pickup Truck Campers

If you own a pickup truck with a camper shell, you can turn it into a self-contained campground with a little work. This can be an ideal way to go: it's fast, portable, and you are guaranteed a dry environment.

But that does not necessarily mean it is a warm environment. In fact, without insulation from the metal truck bed, it can be like trying to sleep on an iceberg. That is because the metal truck bed will get as cold as the air temperature, which is often much colder than the ground temperature. Without insulation, it can be much colder in your camper shell than it would be on the open ground.

When I camp in my rig, I use a large piece of foam for a mattress and insulation. The foam measures four inches thick, is 48 inches wide and 76 inches long. It makes for a bed as comfortable as anything one might ask for. In fact, during the winter, if I don't go camping for a few weeks because of writing obligations, I sometimes will throw the foam on the living room floor, lay down the old sleeping bag, light a fire, and camp right in my living room. It's in my blood, I tell you.

If you camp in cold areas in your pickup truck camper shell, a Coleman catalytic heater can keep you toasty. When using a catalytic heater, it is a good idea to keep ventilation windows partially open to keep the air fresh. Don't worry about how cold it is — the heater will take the snap out of the air.

Motor Homes

The problems motor home owners encounter come from two primary sources: lack of privacy and light intrusion.

The lack of privacy stems from the natural restrictions of where a "land yacht" can go. Without careful use of the guide portion of this book, motor home owners can find themselves in parking lot settings, jammed in with plenty of neighbors. Because motor homes often have large picture windows, you lose your privacy, causing some late nights, and come daybreak, light intrusion forces an early wake-up. The result is you get shorted on your sleep.

The answer is always to carry inserts to fit over the inside of your windows. This closes off the outside and retains your privacy. And if you don't want to wake up with the sun at daybreak, you don't have to. It will still be dark.

First Aid and Insect Protection

The mountain night could not have been more perfect, I thought as I lay in my sleeping bag.

The sky looked like a mass of jewels and the air tasted sweet and smelled of pines. A shooting star fireballed across the sky, and I remember thinking, "It just doesn't get any better."

Just then, as I was drifting into sleep, this mysterious buzz appeared from nowhere and deposited itself inside my left ear. Suddenly awake, I whacked my ear with the palm of my hand, hard enough to cause a minor concussion. The buzz disappeared. I pulled out my flashlight and shined it on my palm, and there, lit in the blackness of night, lay the squished intruder. A mosquito, dead amid a stain of blood.

Satisfied, I turned off the light, closed my eyes, and thought of the fishing trip planned for the next day. Then I heard them. It was a squadron of mosquitos, flying landing patterns around my head. I tried to grab them with an open hand, but they dodged the assault and flew off. Just 30 seconds later another landed in my left ear. I promptly dispatched the invader with a rip of the palm.

Now I was completely awake, so I got out of my sleeping bag to retrieve some mosquito repellent. But while en route, several of the buggers swarmed and nailed me in the back and arms. Later, after applying the repellent and settling snugly again in my sleeping bag, the mosquitos would buzz a few inches from my ear. After getting a whiff of the poison, they would fly off. It was like sleeping in a sawmill.

The next day, drowsy from little sleep, I set out to fish. I'd walked but 15 minutes when I brushed against a bush and felt this stinging sensation on the inside of my arm, just above the wrist. I looked down: a tick had his clamps in me. I ripped it out before he could embed his head into my skin.

After catching a few fish, I sat down against a tree to eat lunch, and just watch the water go by. My dog, Rebel, sat down next to me and stared at the beef jerky I was munching as if it was a T-bone steak. I finished eating, gave him a small piece, patted him on the head, and said, "Good dog." Right then, I noticed an itch on my arm where a mosquito had drilled me. I unconsciously scratched it. Two days later, in that exact spot, some nasty red splotches started popping up. Poison oak. By petting my dog and then scratching my arm, I had transferred the oil residue of the poison oak leaves from Rebel's fur to my arm.

On returning back home, Foonsky asked me about the trip.

"Great," I said. "Mosquitos, ticks, poison oak. Can hardly wait to go back."

"Sorry I missed out," he answered.

Mosquitos, No-See-Ums, Gnats and Horseflies

On a trip to Canada, Foonsky and I were fishing a small lake from the shore when suddenly a black horde of mosquitos could be seen moving across the lake toward us. It was like when the French Army looked across the Rhine and saw the Wehrmacht coming. There was a literal buzz in the air. We fought them off for a few minutes, then made a fast retreat to the truck and jumped in, content the buggers had been fooled. But somehow, still unknown to us, the mosquitos gained entry to the truck. In 10 minutes, we squished 15 of them while they attempted to plant their oil derricks in our skin. Just outside the truck, the black horde waited for us to make a tactical error, like roll down a window. It finally took a miraculous hailstorm to wipe out the attack.

When it comes to mosquitos, no-see-ums, gnats and horseflies, there are times when there is nothing you can do. However, in most situations you can muster a defense to repel the attack.

The first key with mosquitos is to wear clothing too heavy for them to drill through. Expose a minimum of skin, wear a hat, and, around your neck, tie a bandanna, one that has preferably been sprayed with repellent. If you try to get by with just a cotton T-shirt, you will be declared a federal mosquito sanctuary.

So first your skin must be well covered, exposing only your hands and face. Second, you should have your companion spray your clothes with repellent. Third, you should dab liquid repellent directly on your skin.

Taking Vitamin B1 and eating garlic are reputed to act as natural insect repellents, but I've met a lot of mosquitos that are not convinced. A better bet is to examine the contents of the repellent in question. The key is the percentage of the ingredient called "non-diethyl-metatoluamide." That is the poison, and the percentage of it in the container must be listed and will indicate that brand's effectiveness. Inert ingredients are just excess fluids used to fill the bottles.

At night, the easiest way to get a good sleep without mosquitos buzzing in your ear is to sleep in a bug-proof tent. If the nights are warm and you want to see the stars, new tent models are available that have a skylight covered with mosquito netting. If you don't like tents on summer evenings, mosquito netting rigged with an air space at your head can solve the problem. Otherwise prepare to get bit, even with the use of mosquito repellent.

If your problems are with no-see-ums or biting horseflies, then you need a slightly different approach.

No-see-ums are tiny, black insects that look like nothing more than a sliver of dirt on your skin. Then you notice something stinging, and when you rub the area, you scratch up a little no-see-um. The results are similar to mosquito bites, making your skin itch, splotch, and, when you get them bad, puffy. In addition to using the techniques described to repel mosquitos, you should go one step further.

The problem is, no-see-ums are tricky little devils. Somehow they can actually get under your socks and around your ankles where they will bite to their heart's content all night long while you sleep, itch, sleep, and itch some more. The best solution is to apply a liquid repellent to your ankles, then wear clean socks.

Horseflies are another story. They are rarely a problem, but when they get their dander up, they can cause problems you'll never forget.

One such episode occurred when Foonsky and I were paddling a canoe along the shoreline of a large lake. This giant horsefly, about the size of a fingertip, started dive-bombing the canoe. After 20 minutes, it landed on his thigh. Foonsky immediately slammed it with an open hand, then let out a blood-curdling "yeeeee-ow" that practically sent ripples across the lake. When Foonsky whacked it, the horsefly had somehow turned around and bit him in the hand, leaving a huge, red welt.

In the next 10 minutes, that big fly strafed the canoe on more dive-bomb runs. I finally got my canoe paddle, swung it as if it was a baseball bat, and nailed that horsefly like I'd hit a home run. It landed about 15 feet from the boat, still alive and buzzing in the water. While I was trying to figure what it would take to kill this bugger, a large rainbow trout surfaced and snatched it out of the water, finally avenging the assault.

If you have horsefly or yellowjacket problems, you'd best just leave the area. One, two or a few can be dealt with. More than that and your fun camping trip will be about as fun as being roped to a tree and stung by an electric shock rod.

On most trips, you will spend time doing everything possible to keep from getting bit by mosquitos or no-see-ums. When that fails, you must know what to do next, and fast, if you are among those ill-fated campers who get big, red lumps from a bite inflicted from even a microscopic-sized mosquito.

A fluid called "After Bite," or a dab of ammonia, should be applied immediately to the bite. To start the healing process, apply a first-aid gel, not a liquid, such as Campho-Phenique.

Ticks

Ticks are nasty little vermin that will wait in ambush, jump on unsuspecting prey, and then crawl to a prime location before filling their bodies with their victim's blood.

I call them Dracula Bugs, but by any name they can be a terrible camp pest. Ticks rest on grass and low plants and attach themselves to those who brush against the vegetation (dogs are particularly vulnerable). Typically, they are no more than 18 inches above ground, and if you stay on the trails, you can usually avoid them.

There are two common species of ticks. The common coastal tick is larger, brownish in color, and prefers to crawl around prior to putting its clamps on you. The latter habit can give you the creeps, but when you feel it crawling, you can just pick it off and dispatch it. The coastal tick's preferred destination is usually the back of your neck, just where the hairline starts. The other species, a wood tick, is small and black, and when he puts his clamps in, it's immediately painful. When a wood tick gets into a dog for a few days, it can cause a large, red welt. In either case, ticks should be removed as soon as possible.

If you have hiked in areas infested with ticks, it is advisable to shower as soon as possible, washing your clothes immediately. If you just leave your clothes in a heap, a tick can crawl from your clothes and invade your home. They like warmth, and one way or another, they can end up in your bed. Waking up in the middle of the night with a tick crawling across you chest can really give you the creeps.

Once a tick has its clampers on you, you must decide how long it has been there. If it has been a short time, the most painless and effective method for removal is to take a pair of sharp tweezers and grasp the little devil, making certain to isolate the mouth area, then pull him out. Reader Johvin Perry sent in the suggestion to coat the tick with Vaseline, which will cut off its oxygen supply, after which it may voluntarily give up the hunt.

If the tick has been in longer, you may wish to have a doctor extract it. Some people will burn a tick with a cigarette, or poison it with lighter fluid, but this is not advisable. No matter how you do it, you must take care to remove all of it, especially its claw-like mouth.

The wound, however small, should then be cleansed and dressed. This is done by applying liquid peroxide, which cleans and sterilizes, and then applying a dressing coated with a first-aid gel such as First-Aid Cream, Campho-Phenique, or Neosporin.

Lyme disease, which can be transmitted by the bite of the deer tick, is rare but common enough to warrant some attention. To prevent tick bites, some people tuck their pant legs into their hiking socks and spray tick repellent, called Permamone, on their pants.

The first symptom of Lyme disease is that the bite area will develop a bright red, splotchy rash. Other early symptoms sometimes include headache, nausaea, fever and/or a stiff neck. If this happens, or if you have any doubts, you should see your doctor immediately. If you do get Lyme disease, don't panic. Doctors say it is easily treated in the early stages with simple antibiotics. If you are nervous about getting Lyme disease, carry a small plastic bag with you when you hike. If a tick manages to get his clampers into you, put it in the plastic bag after you pull it out. Then give it to your doctor for analysis, to see if the tick is a carrier of the disease.

Poison Oak

After a nice afternoon hike, about a five-miler, I was concerned about possible exposure to poison oak, so I immediately showered and put on clean clothes. Then I settled into a chair with my favorite foamy elixir to watch the end of a baseball game. The game went 18 innings and meanwhile, my dog, tired from the hike, went to sleep on my bare ankles.

A few days later I had a case of poison oak. My feet looked like they had been on fire and put out with an ice pick. The lesson? Don't always trust your dog, give him a bath as well, and beware of extra-inning ball games.

You can get poison oak only from direct contact with the oil residue from the leaves. It can be passed in a variety of ways, as direct as skin to leaf contact or as indirect as leaf to dog, dog to sofa, sofa to skin. Once you have it, there is little you can do but itch yourself to death. Applying Caladryl lotion or its equivalent can help because it contains antihistamines, which attack and dry the itch.

A tip that may sound crazy but seems to work is advised by my pal Furniss. You should expose the afflicted area to the hottest water you can stand, then suddenly immerse it in cold water. The hot water opens the skin pores and gets the "itch" out, and the cold water then quickly seals the pores.

In any case, you're a lot better off if you don't get poison oak to begin with. Remember the old Boy Scout saying: "Leaves of three, let them be." Also remember that poison oak can disguise itself. In the spring, it is green, then it gradually turns reddish in the summer. By fall, it becomes a bloody, ugly-looking red. In the winter, it loses its leaves altogether and appears to be nothing more than barren, brown sticks of small plant. However, at any time and in any form, skin contact can cause quick infection.

Some people are more easily afflicted than others, but if you are one of the lucky few who aren't, don't cheer too loudly. While some people can be exposed to the oil residue of poison oak with little or no effect, the body's resistance can gradually be worn down with repeated exposures. At one time, I could practically play in the stuff and the only symptom would be a few little bumps on the inside of my wrist. Now, some 15 years later, my resistance has broken down. If I merely rub against poison oak now, in a few days the exposed area can look like it was used for a track meet.

So regardless if you consider yourself vulnerable or not, you should take heed to reduce your exposure. That can be done by staying on trails when you hike and making sure your dog does the same. Remember, the worst stands of poison oak are usually brush-infested areas just off the trail. Protect yourself also by dressing so your skin is completely covered, wearing long-sleeve shirts, long pants and boots. If you suspect you've been exposed, immediately wash your clothes, then wash yourself with aloe vera, rinsing with a cool shower.

And don't forget to give your dog a bath as well.

Sunburn

The most common injury suffered on camping trips is sunburn, yet some people wear it as a badge of honor, believing that it somehow enhances their virility. Well, it doesn't. Neither do suntans. And too much sun can lead to serious burns or sunstroke.

It is easy enough to avoid. Use a high-level sunscreen on your skin, chapstick on your lips, and wear sunglasses and a hat. If any area gets burned, apply First-Aid Cream, which will soothe and provide moisture for your parched, burned skin.

The best advice is not to get even a suntan. Those who do are involved in a practice that can be eventually ruinous to their skins.

A Word About Giardia

You have just hiked in to your secret backwoods fishing or hunting spot, you're thirsty and a bit tired, but you smile as you consider the prospects. Everything seems perfect—you have a campsite along a stream that tumbles into a nearby lake, there's not a stranger in sight, and you have nothing to do for a week but fish or hunt with your pals.

You toss down your gear, grab your cup and dip it into the stream, and take a long drink of that ice cold mountain water. It seems crystal pure and sweeter than anything you've ever tasted. It's not till later that you find out that it can be just like drinking a cup of poison.

By drinking what appears to be pure mountain water without treating it, you can ingest a microscopic protozoan called Giardia lamblia. The pain of the ensuing abdominal cramps can make you feel like your stomach and intestinal tract are in a knot, ready to explode. With that comes long-term diarrhea that is worse than even a bear could imagine.

Doctors call the disease giardiasis, or Giardia for short, but it is difficult to diagnose. One friend of mine who contracted Giardia was told he might have stomach cancer before the proper diagnosis was made.

Drinking directly from a stream or lake does not mean you will get Giardia, but you are taking a giant chance. There is no reason to take such a risk, potentially ruining your trip and enduring weeks of misery.

A lot of fishermen and hunters are taking that risk. I made a personal survey of backpackers in the Yosemite National Park Wilderness last year, and found that roughly only one in 20 were equipped with some kind of water purification system. The result, according to the Public Health Service, is that an average of four percent of all backpackers and campers suffer giardiasis. According to the Parasitic Diseases Division of the Center for Infectious Diseases, the rates range from 1 percent to 20 percent across the country.

But if you get Giardia, you are not going to care about the statistics. "When I got Giardia, I just about wanted to die," said Henry McCarthy, a California camper. "For about ten days, it was the most terrible thing I have ever experienced. And through the whole thing, I kept thinking, 'I shouldn't have drunk that water, but it seemed all right at the time.'"

That is the mistake most campers make. The stream might be running free, gurgling over boulders in the high country, tumbling into deep, oxygenated pools. It looks pure. Then the next day, the problems suddenly start. Drinking untreated water from mountain streams is a lot like Russian roulette. Sooner or later, the gun goes off.

If you camp, fish and hunt in primitive settings, there are some clear-cut answers to the water purification problem. I have tested them all. Here are my findings:

Katadyn Water Filter: This is the best system for screening out Giardia, as well as other microscopic bacteria more commonly found in stream and lake water that can also cause stomach problems.

This filter works by placing the nozzle in the water, then pumping the water directly from a spout at the top of the pump into a canteen. The pumping can be fairly rigorous, especially as the filter becomes plugged. On the average, it takes a few minutes to fill a canteen.

The best advantages are that the device has a highly advanced screening system (a ceramic element), and it can be cleaned repeatedly with a small brush.

The drawbacks are that the filter is expensive, it can easily break when dropped because its body is made of porcelain, and if you pack very light, its weight (about two pounds) may be a factor. But those are good trade-offs when you can drink ice cold stream water without risk.

First-Need Water Purifier: This is the most cost-effective water purification system for a variety of reasons.

The unit is far less expensive than the Katadyn, yet provides much better protection than anything cheaper. It is small and lightweight, so it doesn't add much to the weight of your pack. And if you use some care to pump water from sediment-free sources, the purifier will easily last a week, the length of most outdoor trips.

These devices consist of a plastic pump and a hose that connects to a separate filter canister. They pump faster and with less effort than the Katadyn, but one of the reasons for that is because the filter is not as fine-screened.

The big drawback is that if you pump water from a mucky lake, the filter can clog in a few days. Therein lies the weakness. Once plugged up, it is useless and you have to replace it or take your chances.

One trick to extend the filter life is to fill your cook pot with water, let the sediment settle, then pump from there. It is also advisable always to have a spare filter canister as an insurance policy.

Boiling Water: Except for water filtration, this is the only treatment that you can use with complete confidence. According to the federal Center for Disease Control, it takes a few minutes at a rolling boil to be certain to kill Giardia lamblia. At high elevations, the advice is to boil for three to five minutes. A side benefit is that you'll also kill other dangerous bacteria that live undetected in natural waters.

But to be honest, boiling water is a thorn for most people on backcountry fishing and hunting trips. For one thing, if you boil water on an open fire, what should taste like crystal-pure mountain water tastes instead like a mouthful of warm ashes. If you don't have a campfire, it wastes stove fuel. And if you are thirsty now, forget it. The water takes hours to cool.

The one time boiling always makes sense, however, is when you are preparing dinner. The ash taste will disappear in whatever freeze-dried dinner, soup or hot drink you have planned.

Water purification pills are the preference for most anglers and hunters and it can get them in trouble. The pills come cheap at just $3 to $8 per bottle, which can figure to just a few cents per canteen. In addition, they kill most of the bacteria, regardless of whether you use iodine crystals or potable aqua iodine tablets.

They just don't always kill Giardia lamblia, and that is the one critter worth worrying about on your trip. That makes water treatment pills unreliable and dangerous.

Another key element is the time factor. Depending on the water's temperature, organic content and pH level, these pills can take a long time to do the job. A minimum wait of 20 minutes is prescribed. Most people don't like waiting that long, especially when hot and thirsty after a long hike, "and what the heck, the water looks fine."

And then there is the taste. On one trip, my water filter clogged and we had to use the iodine pills instead. It doesn't take long to get tired of the iodine-tinged taste of the water. Mountain water should be one of the greatest tasting beverages of the world, but the iodine kills that.

No treatment: This is your last resort and, using extreme care, can be executed with success. One of my best hiking buddies, Michael Furniss, is a hydrologist for the Forest Service, and on wilderness fishing trips he has showed me the difference between "safe" and "dangerous" water sources.

Long ago, people believed that just finding water running over a rock used to be a guarantee of its purity. Imagine that. What we've learned is that the safe water sources are almost always small creeks or springs located in high, craggy mountain areas. The key is making sure no one has been upstream from where you drink.

Furniss mentioned that another problem you can have if you bypass water treatment is that even in settings free of Giardia, you can still ingest other bacteria that can cause stomach problems.

The only sure way to beat the problem is to filter or boil your water before drinking, eating or brushing your teeth. And the best way to prevent the spread of Giardia is to bury your waste products at least eight inches deep and 100 feet away from natural waters.

Hypothermia

No matter how well planned your trip might be, a sudden change in weather can turn it into a puzzle for which there are few answers. Bad weather or an accident can set in motion a dangerous chain of events.

Such a chain of episodes occurred for my brother, Rambob, and me on a fishing trip one fall day just below the snow line. The weather had suddenly turned very cold and ice was forming along the shore of the lake. Suddenly, the canoe became terribly imbalanced and just that quick, it flipped. The little life vest seat cushions were useless, and using the canoe as a paddle board, we tried to kick our way back to shore where my dad was going crazy at the thought of his two sons drowning before his eyes.

It took 17 minutes in that 38-degree water, but we finally made it to the shore. When they pulled me out of the water, my legs were dead, not strong enough even to hold up my weight. In fact, I didn't feel so much cold as tired, and I just wanted to lay down and go to sleep.

I closed my eyes, and my brother-in-law, Lloyd Angal, slapped me in the face several times, then got me on my feet and pushed and pulled me about.

In the celebration over making it to shore, only Lloyd had realized that hypothermia was setting in, in which the temperature of the body is lowered to the point that it causes poor reasoning, apathy and collapse. It can look like the afflicted person is just tired and needs to sleep, but that sleep can be the next step to a coma.

Ultimately, my brother and I shared what little dry clothing remained. Then we began hiking around to get muscle movement, creating internal warmth. We ate whatever munchies were available because the body produces heat by digestion. But most important, we got our heads as dry as possible. More body heat is lost through wet hair than any other single factor.

A few hours later, we were in a pizza parlor replaying the incident, talking about how only a life vest can do the job of a life vest. We decided never again to rely on those little flotation seat cushions that disappear when the boat flips.

Almost by instinct we had done everything right to prevent hypothermia: Don't go to sleep, start a physical activity, induce shivering, put dry clothes on, dry your head, and eat something. That's how you fight hypothermia. In a dangerous situation, whether you fall in a lake or a stream or get caught unprepared in a storm, that's how you can stay alive.

After being in that ice-bordered lake for almost 20 minutes, and then finally pulling ourselves to the shoreline, a strange, eerie phenomena occurred. My canoe was flipped right-side up, and almost all of its contents were lost: tackle box, floatation cushions and cooler. But remaining was one paddle and one fishing rod, the trout rod my grandfather had given me for my 12th birthday.

Lloyd gave me a smile. "This means that you are meant to paddle and fish again," he said with a laugh.

Getting Unlost

You could not have been more lost. But there I was, a guy who is supposed to know about these things, transfixed by confusion, snow and hoof prints from a big deer.

I discovered it is actually quite easy to get lost. If you don't get your bearings, getting found is the difficult part. This occurred on a wilderness trip where I'd hiked in to a remote lake and then set up a base camp for a deer hunt.

"There are some giant bucks up on that rim," confided Mr. Furnai, who lives near the area. "But it takes a mountain man to even get close to them."

That was a challenge I answered. After four-wheeling it to the trailhead, I tromped off with pack and rifle, gut-thumped it up 100 switchbacks over the rim, then followed a creek drainage up to a small but beautiful lake. The area was stark and nearly treeless, with bald granite broken only by large boulders. To keep from getting lost, I marked my route with piles of small rocks to act as directional signs for the return trip.

But at daybreak the next day, I stuck my head out of my tent and found eight inches of snow on the ground. I looked up into a gray sky filled by huge, cascading snowflakes. Visibility was about 50 yards, with fog on the mountain rim. "I better get out of here and get back to my truck," I said to myself. "If my truck gets buried at the trailhead, I'll never get out."

After packing quickly, I started down the mountain. But after 20 minutes, I began to get disoriented. You see, all the little piles of rocks I'd stacked to mark the way were now buried in snow, and I had only a smooth white blanket of snow to guide me. Everything looked the same, and it was snowing even harder now.

Five minutes later I started chewing on some jerky to keep warm, then suddenly stopped. Where was I? Where was the creek drainage? Isn't this where I was supposed to cross over a creek and start the switchbacks down the mountain?

Right then I looked down and saw the tracks of a huge deer, the kind Mr. Furnai had talked about. What a predicament: I was lost and snowed in, and seeing big hoof prints in the snow. Part of me wanted to abandon all safety and go after that deer, but a little voice in the back of my head won out. "Treat this as an emergency," it said.

The first step in any predicament is to secure your present situation, that is, to make sure it does not get any worse. I unloaded my rifle (too easy to slip, fall and have a misfire), took stock of my food (three days worth), camp fuel (plenty), and clothes (rain gear keeping me dry). Then I wondered, "Where the hell am I?"

I took out my map, compass and altimeter, then opened the map and laid it on the snow. It immediately began collecting snowflakes. I set the compass atop the map, and oriented it to north. Because of the fog, there was no way to spot landmarks, such as prominent mountain tops, to verify my position. Then I checked the altimeter, which read 4,900 feet. Well, the elevation at my lake was 5,320 feet. That was critical information.

I scanned the elevation lines on the map and was able trace the approximate area of my position, somewhere downstream from the lake, yet close to 4,900 feet elevation. "Right here," I said, point to a spot on the map with a finger. "I should pick up the switchback trail down the mountain somewhere off to the left, maybe just 40 or 50 yards away."

Slowly and deliberately, I pushed through the light, powdered snow. In five minutes, I suddenly stopped. To the left, across a 10-foot depression in the snow, appeared a flat spot that veered off to the right. "That's it! That's the crossing."

In minutes, I was working down the switchbacks, on my way, no longer lost. I thought of the hoof prints I had seen, and now that I knew my position, I wanted to head back and spend the day hunting. Then I looked up at the sky, saw it filled with falling snowflakes, and envisioned my truck buried deep in snow. Alas, this time logic won out over dreams.

In a few hours, now trudging through more than a foot of snow, I was at my truck at a spot called Doe Flat, and next to it was a giant, all-terrain Forest Service vehicle and two rangers.

"Need any help?" I asked them.

They just laughed. "We're here to help you," one answered. "It is a good thing you filed a trip plan with our district office in Gasquet. We wouldn't have known you were out here."

"Winter has arrived," said the other. "If we don't get your truck out now, it will be stuck here until next spring. If we hadn't found you, you might have been here until the end of time."

They connected a chain from the rear axle of their giant rig to the front axle of my truck and started towing me out, back to civilization. On the way to pavement, I figured I had gotten some of the more important lessons of my life. Always file a trip plan, have plenty of food, fuel and a camp stove you can rely on. Make sure your clothes, weather gear, sleeping bag and tent will keep you dry and warm. Always carry a compass, altimeter and map with elevation lines, and know how to use them, practicing in good weather to get the feel of it.

And if you get lost and see the hoofprints of a giant deer, well, there are times when it is best to pass them by.

Fishing and Camp Fun

Feet tired and hot, stomachs hungry, we stopped our hike for lunch beside a beautiful little river pool that was catching the flows from a long but gentle waterfall. My brother, Rambob, passed me a piece of jerky. I took my boots off, then slowly dunked my feet into the cool, foaming water.

I was gazing at a towering peak across a canyon, when suddenly, Wham! There was a quick jolt at the heel of my right foot. I pulled my foot out of the water and incredibly, a trout had bitten it.

My brother looked at me like I had antlers growing out of my head. "Wow!" he exclaimed, "That trout almost caught himself an outdoors writer!"

It's true that in remote areas trout sometimes bite on almost anything, even feet. On one high-country trip, I have caught limits of trout using nothing but a bare hook. The only problem is that the fish will often hit the splitshot sinker instead of the hook. Of course, fishing isn't usually that easy. But it gives you an idea of what is possible.

America's wildlands are home for a remarkable abundance of fish and wildlife. Deer browse with little fear of man, bears keep an eye out for your food, and little critters like squirrels and chipmunks are daily companions. Add in the fishing and you've got yourself a camping trip.

Your camping trips will evolve into premium outdoor experiences if you can work in a few good fishing trips, avoid bear problems, and occasionally add a little offbeat fun with some camp games.

Trout and Bass

He creeps up on the stream as quiet as an Indian scout, keeping his shadow off the water. With his little spinning rod, he'll zip his lure within an inch or two of its desired mark, probing along rocks, the edges of riffles, pocket water, or wherever he can find a change in river habitat. It's my brother, Rambob, trout fishing, and he's a master at it.

In most cases, he'll catch a trout on his first or second cast. After that it's time to move up the river, giving no spot much more than five minutes due. Stick and move, stick and move, stalking the stream like a bobcat zeroing in on a unsuspecting rabbit. He might keep a few trout for dinner, but mostly he releases what he catches. Rambob doesn't necessarily fish for food. It's the feeling that comes with it.

Fishing can give you a sense of exhilaration, like taking a hot shower after being coated with dust. On your walk back to camp, the steps come easy. You suddenly understand what John Muir meant when he talked of developing a oneness with nature, because you have it. That's what fishing can provide.

You don't need a million dollars worth of fancy gear to catch fish. What you need is the right outlook, and that can be learned. That goes regardless of whether you are fishing for trout or bass, the two most popular fisheries in America. Your fishing tackle selection should be as simple and as clutter-free as possible.

At home, I've got every piece of fishing tackle you might imagine, more than 30 rods and many tackle boxes, racks and cabinets filled with all kinds of stuff. I've got one lure that looks like a chipmunk and another that resembles a miniature can of beer with hooks. If I hear of something new, I want to try it, and usually do. It's a result of my lifelong fascination with the sport.

But if you just want to catch fish, there's an easier way to go. And when I go fishing, I take that path. I don't try to bring everything. It would be impossible. Instead, I bring a relatively small amount of gear. At home I will scan my tackle boxes for equipment and lures, make my selections, and bring just the essentials. Rod, reel and tackle will fit into a side pocket of my backpack or a small carrying bag.

So what kind of rod should be used on an outdoor trip? For most camper/anglers, I suggest the use of a light, multi-piece spinning rod that will break down to a small size. One of the best deals on the fishing market is the six-piece Daiwa 6.5-foot pack rod, No. 6752. It retails for as low as $30, yet is made of a graphite/glass composite that gives it the quality of a much more expensive model. And it comes in a hard plastic carrying tube for protection. Other major rod manufacturers, such as Fenwick, offer similar premium rods. It's tough to miss with any of them.

The use of graphite-glass composites in fishing rods has made them lighter and more sensitive, yet stronger. The only downside to graphite as a rod material is that it can be brittle. If you rap your rod against something, it can crack or cause a weak spot. That weak spot can eventually snap when under even light pressure, like setting a hook or casting. Of course, a bit of care will prevent that from ever occurring.

If you haven't bought a fishing reel in some time, you will be surprised at the quality and price of micro spinning reels on the market. The reels come tiny and strong, with rear-control drag systems. Sigma, Shimano, Cardinal, Abu and others all make premium reels. They're worth it. With your purchase, you've just bought a reel that will last for years and years.

The one downside to spinning reels is that after long-term use, the bail spring will weaken. The result is that after casting and beginning to reel, the bail will sometimes not flip over and allow the reel to retrieve the line. Then you have to do it by hand. This can be incredibly frustrating, particularly when stream fishing, where instant line pickup is essential. The solution is to have a new bail spring installed every few years. This is a cheap, quick operation for a tackle expert.

You might own a giant tackle box filled with lures, but on your fishing trip you are better off to fit just the essentials into a small container. One of the best ways to do that is to use the Plano Micro-Magnum 3414, a tiny two-sided tackle box for trout fishermen that fits into a shirt pocket. In mine, I can fit 20 lures in one side of the box and 20 flies, splitshot and snap swivels in the other. For bass lures, which are larger, you need a slightly larger box, but the same principle applies.

There are more fishing lures on the market than you can imagine, but a few special ones can do the job. I make sure these are in my box on every trip. For trout I carry: a small black Panther Martin spinner with yellow spots, a small gold Kastmaster, a yellow Roostertail, a gold Z-Ray with red spots, a Super Duper, and a Mepps Lightning spinner.

You can take it a step further using insider's wisdom. My old pal Ed the Dunk showed me his trick of taking a tiny Dardevle spoon, then spray painting it flat black and dabbing five tiny red dots on it. It's a real killer, particularly in tiny streams where the trout are spooky.

The best trout catcher I've ever used on rivers is a small metal lure called a Met-L Fly. On days when nothing else works, it can be like going to a shooting gallery. The problem is that the lure is near impossible to find. Rambob and I consider the few we have remaining so valuable that if the lure is snagged on a rock, a cold swim is deemed mandatory for its retrieval. These lures are as hard to find in tackle shops as trout can be to catch without one.

For bass, you can also fit all you need into a small plastic tackle box. I have fished with many bass pros and all of them actually use just a few lures: a white spinner bait, a small jig called a Gits-It, a surface plug called a Zara Spook, and plastic worms. At times, like when the bass move into shoreline areas during the spring, shad minnow imitations like those made by Rebel or Rapala can be dynamite. My favorite is the one-inch blue-silver Rapala. Every spring, as the lakes begin to warm and the fish snap out of their winter doldrums, I like to float and paddle around in my small raft. I'll cast that little Rapala along the shoreline and catch and release hundreds of bass, bluegill and sunfish. The fish are usually sitting close to the shoreline, awaiting my offering.

A Few Tricks

There's an old angler's joke about how you need to "think like a fish." But if you're the one getting zilched, you may not think it's so funny.

The irony is that it is your mental approach, what you see and what you miss, that often determines your fishing luck. Some people will spend a lot of money on tackle, lures and fishing clothes, and that done, just saunter up to a stream or lake, cast out and wonder why they are not catching fish. The answer is their mental outlook. They are not attuning themselves to their surroundings.

You must live on nature's level, not your own. Try this and you will start to feel things you never believed even existed. Soon you will see things that will allow you to catch fish. You can get a head start by reading about fishing, but to get your degree in fishing, you must attend the University of Nature.

On every fishing trip, regardless what you fish for, try to follow three hard-and-fast rules:

1—Always approach the fishing spot so you will be undetected.

2—Present your lure, fly or bait in a manner so it appears completely natural, as if no line was attached.

3—Stick and move, hitting one spot, working it the best you can, then move to the next.

Here's a more detailed explanation.

1—Approach: No one can just walk up to a stream or lake, cast out, and start catching fish as if someone had waved a magic wand. Instead, give the fish credit for being smart. After all, they live there.

Your approach must be completely undetected by the fish. Fish can sense your presence through sight and sound, though this is misinterpreted by most people. By sight, this rarely means the fish actually see you, but more likely, they will see your shadow on the water, or the movement of your arm or rod while casting. By sound, it doesn't mean they hear you talking, but that they will detect the vibrations of your footsteps along the shore, kicking a rock, or the unnatural plunking sound of a heavy cast hitting the water. Any of these elements can spook them off the bite. In order to fish undetected, you must walk softly, keep your shadow off the water, and keep your casting motion low. All of these keys become easier at sunrise or sunset, when shadows are on the water. At midday, a high sun causes a high level of light penetration in the water, which can make the fish skittish to any foreign presence.

Like hunting, you must stalk the spots. When my brother Rambob sneaks up on a fishing spot, he is like a burglar sneaking through an unlocked window.

2 — Presentation: Your lure, fly or bait must appear in the water as if no line was attached, so it appears as natural as possible. My pal Mo Furniss has skin-dived in rivers to watch what the fish see when somebody is fishing.

"You wouldn't believe it," he said. "When the lure hits the water, every trout within 40 feet, like 15, 20 trout, will do a little zigzag. They all see the lure and are aware something is going on. Meanwhile, onshore the guy casting doesn't get a bite and thinks there aren't any fish in the river."

If your offering is aimed at fooling a fish into striking, it must appear as part of its natural habitat, as if it is an insect just hatched or a small fish looking for a spot to hide. That's where you come in.

After you have snuck up on a fishing spot, you should zip your cast upstream, then start your retrieve as soon as it hits the water. If you let the lure sink to the bottom, then start the retrieve, you have no chance. A minnow, for instance, does not sink to the bottom then start swimming. On rivers, the retrieve should be more of a drift, as if the "minnow" was in trouble and the current was sweeping it downstream.

When fishing on trout streams, always hike and cast up river, then retrieve as the offering drifts downstream in the current. This is effective because trout will sit almost motionless, pointed upstream, finning against the current. This way they can see anything coming their direction, and if a potential food morsel arrives, all they need to do is move over a few inches, open their mouths, and they've got an easy lunch. Thus you must cast upstream.

Conversely, if you cast downstream, your retrieve will bring the lure from behind the fish, where he cannot see it approaching. And I've never seen a trout that had eyes in its tail. In addition, when retrieving a downstream lure, the river current will tend to sweep your lure inshore to the rocks.

3 — Finding spots: A lot of fishermen don't catch fish and a lot of hikers never see any wildlife. The key is where they are looking.

The rule of the wild is that fish and wildlife will congregate wherever there is a distinct change in the habitat. This is where you should begin your search.

To find deer, for instance, forget probing a thick forest, but look for when it breaks into a meadow, or a clear-cut has splayed a stand of trees. That's where the deer will be.

In a river, it can be where a riffle pours into a small pool, a rapid that plunges into a deep hole and flattens, a big boulder in the middle of a long riffle, a shoreline point, a rock pile, a submerged tree. Look for the changes. Conversely, long straight stretches of shoreline will not hold fish — the habitat is lousy.

On rivers, the most productive areas are often where short riffles tumble into small oxygenated pools. After sneaking up from the downstream side and staying low, you should zip your cast so the lure plops gently in the white water just above the pool. Starting your retrieve instantly, the lure will drift downstream and plunk into the pool. Bang! That's where the trout will hit. Take a few more casts, then head upstream to the next spot.

With a careful approach and lure presentation, and by fishing in the right spots, you have the ticket to many exciting days on the water.

Of Bears and Food

The first time you come nose-to-nose with a bear, it can make your skin quiver.

Even mild-mannered black bears, the most common bear in America, can send shock waves through your body. They range from 250 to 400 pounds and have large claws and teeth that are made to scare campers. When they bound, the muscles on their shoulders seem to roll like ocean breakers.

Bears in camping areas are accustomed to sharing the mountains with hikers and campers. They have become specialists in the food-raiding business. As a result, you must be able to make a bear-proof food hang, or be able to scare the fellow off. Many campgrounds provide bear and raccoon-proof food lockers. You can also stash your food in your vehicle, but that puts a limit on your trip.

If you are in a particularly remote area, there will be no food lockers available. Your car will not be there either. The answer is making a bear-proof food hang, suspending all of your food wrapped in a plastic garbage bag from a rope in mid-air, ten feet from the trunk of a tree and 20 feet off the ground. (Counter-balancing two bags with a rope thrown over a tree limb is very effective, but an extensive search must often be made to find an appropriate limb.)

This is accomplished by tying a rock to a rope, then throwing it over a high but sturdy tree limb. Next, tie your food bag to the rope, and hoist it up in the air. When you are satisfied with the position of the food bag, tie off the end of the rope to another tree. In a bear-troubled area, a good food bag is a necessity — nothing else will do.

I've been there. On one trip, Foonsky and Rambob had left to fish, and I was stoking up an evening campfire when I felt the eyes of an intruder on my back. I turned around and this big bear was heading straight for our camp. In the next half hour, I scared the bear off twice, but then he got a whiff of something sweet in my brother's pack.

In most situations you can spook a black bear by banging on a pot and shouting like a lunatic. But some bears are on to the old banging-the-pot trick. If so, and he gets a whiff of your Tang, banging on a pot and shouting can be like trying to stop a tank with a roadblock.

In this case, the bear rolled into camp like a semi truck, grabbed my brother's pack, ripped it open and plucked out the Tang and the Swiss Miss. The bear, a 350-pounder, then sat astride a nearby log and lapped at the goodies like a thirsty dog finding water.

I took two steps toward the pack and that bear jumped off the log and galloped across the camp right at me. Scientists say a man can't outrun a bear, but they've never seen how fast I can go up a granite block with a bear on my tail. Once a bear gets his mitts on your gear, he considers it his.

Shortly thereafter, Foonsky returned while I was still perched on top of the rock, and demanded to know how I could let a bear get our Tang. But it took all three of us, Foonsky, Rambob, and myself, all charging at once and shouting like madmen, to clear the bear out of the camp and send him off over the ridge. It was a lesson never to let food sit unattended again—a lesson learned the hard way.

The Grizzly

When it comes to grizzlies, well, my friends, you need what we call an "attitude adjustment." Or that big ol' bear may just decide to adjust your attitude for you and make your stay at the park a short one.

Grizzlies are nothing like black bears. They are bigger, stronger, have little fear, and take what they want. Some people believe there are many different species of this critter, like Alaskan brown, silvertip, cinnamon and Kodiak, but the truth is they are all grizzlies. Any difference in appearance has to do with diet, habitat, and life habits, not speciation. By any name, they all come big.

The first thing you must do is determine if there are grizzlies in the area where you are camping. That can usually be done by asking rangers in the area. If you are heading into Yellowstone or Glacier National Park, or the Bob Marshall Wilderness of Montana, well, you don't have to ask. They're out there, and they're the biggest and potentially most dangerous critters you could run into.

One general way to figure the size of a bear is from his footprint. Take the width of the footprint in inches, add one to it—and you'll have an estimated length of the bear in feet. For instance, a nine-inch footprint equals a 10-foot bear. Any bear that big is a grizzly, my friends. In fact, most grizzly footprints average about nine to ten inches across, and black bears (though they may be brown in color) tend to have footprints only four-and-a-half to six inches across.

If you are hiking in a wilderness area that may have grizzlies, then it becomes a necessity to wear bells on your pack. That way, the bear will hear you coming and likely get out of your way. Keep talking, singing, or maybe even debate the country's foreign policy, but whatever, do not fall into a silent hiking vigil. And if a breeze is blowing in your face, you must make even more noise (now a good excuse to rant and rave about the government's domestic affairs). Noise is important, because your smell will not be carried in the direction you are hiking. As a result, the bear will not smell you coming.

If a bear can hear you and smell you, it will tend to get out of the way and let you pass without your knowing it was even close by. The exception is if you are carrying fish, lots of sweets in your pack, or are wearing heavy, sweet deodorants or makeup. All three are bear attractants.

Most encounters with grizzlies occur when hikers fall into a silent march in the wilderness with the wind in their faces, and they walk around a corner and right into a big, unsuspecting grizzly. If you do this, and see a big hump just behind its neck, well, gulp, don't think twice, it's a grizzly.

And then what should you do? Get up a tree, that's what. Grizzlies are so big that their claws cannot support their immense weight, and thus they cannot climb trees. And although their young can climb, they rarely want to get their mitts on you.

If you do get grabbed, every instinct in your body will tell you to fight back. Don't believe it. Play dead. Go limp. Let the bear throw you around a little, because after awhile you become unexciting play material, and the bear will get bored. My grandmother was grabbed by a grizzly in Glacier National Park and after a few tosses and hugs, was finally left alone to escape.

Some say it's a good idea to tuck your head under his chin, since therefore, the bear will be unable to bite your head. I'll take a pass on that one. If you are taking action, any action, it's a signal that you are a force to be reckoned with, and he'll likely respond with more aggression. And bears don't lose many wrestling matches.

What grizzlies really like to do, believe it or not, is to pile a lot of sticks and leaves on you. Just let them, and keep perfectly still. Don't fight them; don't run. And when you have a 100-percent chance (not 98 or 99) to dash up a nearby tree, that's when you let fly. Once safely in a tree, then you can hurl down insults and let your aggression out.

In a wilderness camp, there are special precautions you should take. Always hang your food at least 100 yards downwind of your camp and get it high, 30 feet is reasonable. In addition, circle your camp with rope, and hang the bells from your pack on it. Thus, if a bear walks into your camp, he'll run into your rope, the bells will ring, and everybody will have a chance to get up a tree before ol' griz figures out what's going on. Often, the unexpected ringing of bells is enough to send him off in search of a quieter environment.

You see, more often than not, grizzlies tend to clear the way for campers and hikers. So, be smart, don't act like bear bait, and always have a plan if you are confronted by one.

My pal Foonsky had such a plan during a wilderness expedition in Montana's northern Rockies. On our second day of hiking, we started seeing scratch marks on the trees, 13 to 14 feet off the ground.

"Mr. Griz made those," Foonsky said. "With spring here, the grizzlies are coming out of hibernation and using the trees like a cat uses a scratch board to stretch the muscles."

The next day, I noticed Foonsky had a pair of track shoes tied to the back of his pack. I just laughed.

"You're not going to outrun a griz," I said. "In fact, there's hardly any animals out here in the wilderness that man can outrun."

Foonsky just smiled.

"I don't have to outrun a griz," he said. "I just have to outrun you!"

Fun and Games

"Now what are we supposed to do?" the young boy asked his dad.

"Yeah, Dad, think of something," asked another son.

Well, Dad thought hard. This was one of the first camping trips he'd taken with his sons and one of the first lessons he received was that kids don't want the philosophic release of mountain quiet. They want action, and lots of it. With a glint in his eye, Dad searched around the camp and picked up 15 twigs, breaking them so each was four inches long. He laid them in three separate rows, three twigs in one row, five twigs in another, and seven in the other.

"OK, this game is called 3-5-7," said dad. "You each take turns picking up sticks. You are allowed to remove all or as few as one twig from a row, but here's the catch: You can only pick from one row per turn. Whoever picks up the last stick left is the loser."

I remember this episode well because those two little boys were my brother Bobby, as in Rambobby, and me. And to this day, we still play 3-5-7 on campouts, with the winner getting to watch the loser clean the dishes. What I have learned in the span of time since that original episode is that it does not matter what your age is: campers need options for camp fun.

Some evenings, after a long hike or ride, you are likely to feel too worn-out to take on a serious romp downstream to fish, or a climb up to a ridge for a view. That is especially true if you have been in the outback for a week or more. At that point a lot of campers will spend their time resting and gazing at a map of the area, dreaming of the next day's adventure, or just take a seat against a rock, watching the colors of the sky and mountain panorama change minute-by-minute. But kids in the push-button video era, and a lot of adults too, want more. After all, "I'm on vacation; I want some fun."

There are several options, like the 3-5-7 twig game, and they should be just as much a part of your pre-trip planning as arranging your gear.

For kids, plan on games, the more physically challenging the competition, the better. One of the best games is to throw a chunk of wood into a lake, then challenge the kids to hit it by throwing rocks. It wreaks havoc on the fishing, but it can keep kids totally absorbed for some time. Target practice with a wrist-rocket slingshot is also all-consuming for kids, firing rocks away at small targets like pine cones set on a log.

You can also set kids off on little missions near camp, like looking for the footprints of wildlife, searching out good places to have a "snipe hunt," picking up twigs to get the evening fire started, or having them take the water purifier to a stream to pump some drinking water into a canteen. The latter is an easy, fun, yet important task that will allow kids to feel a sense of equality they often don't get at home.

For adults, the appeal should be more to the intellect. A good example is star and planet identification, and while you are staring into space, you're bound to spot a few asteroids, or shooting stars. A star chart can make it easy to locate and identify many distinctive stars and constellations, such as Pleiades (the Seven Sisters), Orion, and several from the zodiac, depending on the time of year. With a little research, this can add a unique perspective to your trip. You could point to Polaris, one of the most easily identified of all stars, and note that navigators in the 1400s used it to find their way. Polaris, of course, is the "North Star," and is at the end of the handle of the Little Dipper. Pinpointing Polaris is quite easy. First find the Big Dipper, then locate the outside stars of the ladle of the Big Dipper. They are called the "Pointer Stars" because they point right at Polaris.

A tree identification book can teach you a few things about your surroundings. It is also a good idea for one member of the party to research the history of the area you have chosen and another to research the geology. With shared knowledge, you end up with a deeper love of wild places.

Another way to add some recreation into your trip is to bring a board game, a number of which have been miniaturized for campers. The most popular are chess, checkers and cribbage. The latter comes with an equally miniature set of playing cards. And if you bring those little cards, that opens a vast set of other possibilities. With kids along, for instance, just take the Queen of Clubs out of the deck and you can instantly play Old Maid.

But there are more serious card games and they come with high stakes. Such occurred on one high country trip where Foonsky, Rambob and myself sat down for a late afternoon game of poker. In a game of seven-card stud, I caught a straight on the sixth card and felt like a dog licking on a T-bone. Already, I had bet several Skittles and peanut M&Ms on this promising hand.

Then I examined the cards Foonsky had face up. He was showing three sevens, and acting as happy as a grizzly with a pork chop, like he had a full house. He matched my bet of two peanut M&Ms, then raised me three SweetTarts, one Starburst and one sour apple Jolly Rancher. Rambob folded, but I matched Foonsky's bet and hoped for the best as the seventh and final card was dealt.

Just after Foonsky glanced at that last card, I saw him sneak a look at my grape stick and beef jerky stash.

"I raise you a grape stick," he said.

Rambob and I both gasped. It was the highest bet ever made, equivalent to a million dollars laid down in Las Vegas. Cannons were going off in my chest. I looked hard at my cards. They looked good, but were they good enough?

Even with a great hand like I had, a grape stick was too much to gamble, my last one with 10 days of trail ahead of us. I shook my head and folded my cards. Foonsky smiled at his victory.

But I still had my grape stick.

Old Tricks Don't Always Work

Most people are born honest, but after a few camping trips, they usually get over it.

I remember some advice I got from Rambob, normally an honest soul, on one camping trip. A giant mosquito had landed on my arm and he alerted me to some expert advice.

"Flex your arm muscles," he commanded, watching the mosquito fill with my blood. "He'll get stuck in your arm, then he'll explode."

For some unknown reason, I believed him. We both proceeded to watch the mosquito drill countless holes in my arm.

Alas, the unknowing face sabotage from their most trusted companions on camping trips. It can arise at any time, usually in the form of advice from a friendly, honest-looking face, as if to say, "What? How can you doubt me?" After that mosquito episode, I was a little more skeptical of my dear, old brother. Then, the next day, when another mosquito was nailing me in the back of the neck, out came this gem:

"Hold your breath," he commanded. I instinctively obeyed. "That will freeze the mosquito," he said, "then you can squish him."

But in the time I wasted holding my breath, the little bugger was able to fly off without my having the satisfaction of squishing him. When he got home, he probably told his family, "What a dummy I got to drill today!"

Over the years, I have been duped numerous times with dubious advice:

On a grizzly bear attack: "If he grabs you, tuck your head under the grizzly's chin, then he won't be able to bite you in the head." This made sense to me until the first time I looked face to face with a nine-foot grizzly, 40 yards away. In seconds, I was at the top of a tree, which suddenly seemed to make the most sense.

On coping with animal bites: "If a bear bites you in the arm, don't try to jerk it away. That will just rip up your arm. Instead force your arm deeper into his mouth. He'll lose his grip and will have to open it to get a firmer hold, and right then you can get away." I was told this in the Boy Scouts, and when I was 14, I had a chance to try it out when a friend's dog bit me when I tried to pet it. What happened? When I shoved my arm deeper into his mouth, he bit me about three extra times.

On cooking breakfast: "The bacon will curl up every time in a camp frying pan. So make sure you have a bacon stretcher to keep it flat." As a 12-year-old Tenderfoot, I spent two hours looking for the bacon stretcher until I figured out the camp leader had forgotten it. It wasn't for several years until I learned that there is no such thing.

On preventing sore muscles: "If you haven't hiked for a long time and you are facing a rough climb, you can keep from getting sore muscles in your legs, back and shoulders by practicing the `Dead Man's Walk.' Simply let your entire body go slack, and then take slow, wobbling steps. This will clear your muscles of lactic acid, which cause them to be so sore after a rough hike." Foonsky pulled this one on me. Rambob and I both bought it, then tried it while we were hiking up Mount Whitney, which requires a 6,000-foot elevation gain in six miles. In one 45-minute period, about 30 other hikers passed us and looked at us as if we were suffering from some rare form of mental aberration.

Fish won't bite? No problem: "If the fish are not feeding or will not bite, persistent anglers can still catch dinner with little problem. Keep casting across the current, and eventually, as they hover in the stream, the line will feed across their open mouths. Keep reeling and you will hook the fish right in the side of the mouth. This technique is called `lining.' Never worry if the fish will not bite, because you can always line 'em." Of course, heh, heh, heh, that explains why so many fish get hooked in the side of the mouth.

How to keep bears away: "To keep bears away, urinate around the borders of your campground. If there are a lot of bears in the area, it is advisable to go right on your sleeping bag." Yeah, surrrrre.

What to do with trash: "Don't worry about packing out trash. Just bury it. It will regenerate into the earth and add valuable minerals." Bears, raccoons, skunks and other critters will dig up your trash as soon as you depart, leaving one huge mess for the next camper. Always pack out everything.

Often the advice comes without warning. That was the case after a fishing trip with a female companion, when she outcaught me two-to-one, the third such trip in a row. I explained this to a shopkeeper, and he nodded, then explained why.

"The male fish are able to detect the female scent on the lure, and thus become aroused into striking."

Of course! That explains everything!

Getting Revenge

I was just a lad when Foonsky pulled the old snipe-hunt trick on me. It's taken 30 years to get revenge.

You probably know about snipe hunting. That is where the victim is led out at night in the woods by a group, then is left holding a bag.

"Stay perfectly still and quiet," Foonsky explained. "You don't want to scare the snipe. The rest of us will go back to camp and let the woods settle down. Then when the snipe are least expecting it, we'll form a line and charge through the forest with sticks, beating bushes and trees, and we'll flush the snipe out right to you. Be ready with the bag. When we flush the snipe out, bag it. But until we start our charge, make sure you don't move or make a sound or you will spook the snipe and ruin everything."

I sat out there in the woods with my bag for hours, waiting for the charge. I waited, waited and waited. Nothing happened. No charge, no snipe. It wasn't until well past midnight that I figured something was wrong. When I finally returned to camp, everybody was sleeping.

Well, I tell ya, don't get mad at your pals for the tricks they pull on you. Get revenge. Some 25 years later, on the last day of a camping trip, the time finally came.

"Let's break camp early," Foonsky suggested to Mr. Furnai and me. "Get up before dawn, eat breakfast, pack up, then be on the ridge to watch the sun come up. It will be a fantastic way to end the trip."

"Sounds great to me," I replied. But when Foonsky wasn't looking, I turned his alarm clock ahead three hours. So when the alarm sounded at the appointed 4:30 a.m. wakeup time, Mr. Furnai and I knew it was actually only 1:30 a.m.

Foonsky clambered out of his sleeping bag and whistled with a grin. "Time to break camp."

"You go ahead," I answered. "I'll skip breakfast so I can get a little more sleep. At the first sign of dawn, wake me up, and I'll break camp."

"Me too," said Mr. Furnai.

Foonsky then proceeded to make coffee, cook a breakfast and eat it, sitting on a log in the black darkness of the forest, waiting for the sun to come up. An hour later, with still no sign of dawn, he checked his clock. It now read 5:30 a.m. "Any minute now we should start seeing some light," he said.

He made another cup of coffee, packed his gear and sat there in the middle of the night, looking up at the stars, waiting for dawn. "Anytime now," he said. He ended up sitting there all night long.

Revenge is sweet. Prior to a fishing trip at a lake, I took Foonsky aside and explained that the third member of the party, Jimbobo, was hard of hearing and very sensitive about it. "Don't mention it to him," I advised. "Just talk real loud."

Meanwhile, I had already told Jimbobo the same thing. "Foonsky just can't hear very good."

We had fished less than 20 minutes when Foonsky got a nibble.

"GET A BITE?" shouted Jimbobo.

"YEAH!" yelled back Foonsky, smiling. "BUT I DIDN'T HOOK HIM!"

"MAYBE NEXT TIME!" shouted Jimbobo with a friendly grin.

Well, they spent the entire day yelling at each other from the distance of a few feet. They never did figure it out. Heh, heh, heh.

That is, I thought so, until we made a trip salmon fishing. I got a strike that almost knocked my fishing rod out of the boat. When I grabbed the rod, it felt like Moby Dick was on the other end. "At least a 25-pounder," I said. "Maybe bigger."

The fish dove, ripped off line and then bulldogged. "It's acting like a 40-pounder," I announced, "Huge, just huge. It's going deep. That's how the big ones fight."

Some 15 minutes later, I finally got the "salmon" to the surface. It turned out to be a coffee can that Foonsky had clipped on the line with a snap swivel. By maneuvering the boat, he made the coffee can fight like a big fish.

This all started with a little old snipe hunt years ago. You never know what your pals will try next. Don't get mad. Get revenge!

Camping Options

Boat-in Seclusion

Most campers would never think of trading in their car, pickup truck or motor home for a boat, but people who go by boat on a camping trip have a virtual guarantee of seclusion and top-quality outdoor experiences.

Camping with a boat is a do-it-yourself experiment in living in primitive circumstances. Yet at the same time you can bring any luxury item you wish, from giant coolers, stoves and lanterns to portable gasoline generators. Weight is almost never an issue.

In the West, many outstanding boat-in campgrounds are available in many beautiful areas. The best are on the shores of lakes accessible by canoe or skiff, and at offshore islands reached by saltwater cruisers. Several boat-in camps are detailed in this book. Some of the best are in the Northern Rockies in Montana on the Kootenai River near the Canadian border, and also on the Missouri River near Virgelle.

If you want to take the adventure a step further and create your own boat-in camp, perhaps near a special fishing spot, this is a go-for-it deal that provides the best way possible to establish your own secret campsite. But most people who set out without planning forget three critical items for boat-in camping: a shovel, a sunshade and an ax. Here is why these three items can make a key difference in your trip:

1—A shovel: Many lakes and virtually all reservoirs have steep, sloping banks. At reservoirs subject to drawdowns, what was lake bottom in the spring can be a prospective campsite in late summer. If you want a flat area for a tent site, the only answer is to dig one out yourself. A shovel gives you that option.

2—A sunshade: The flattest spots to camp along lakes often have a tendency to support only sparse tree growth. As a result, a natural shield from sun and rain is rarely available. What? Rain in the summer? Oh yeah, don't get me started. A light tarp, set up with poles and staked ropes, solves the problem.

3—An ax: Unless you bring your own firewood, necessary at some sparsely wooded reservoirs, there is no substitute for a good, sharp ax. With an ax, you can almost always find dry firewood, since the interior of an otherwise wet log will be dry. When the weather turns bad is precisely when you will most want a fire. You may need an ax to get one going.

In the search to create your own personal boat-in campsite, you will find that the flattest areas are usually the tips of peninsulas and points, while the protected back ends of coves are often steeply sloped. At reservoirs, the flattest areas are usually near the mouths of the feeder streams, and the points are quite steep. On rivers, there are usually sand bars on the inside of tight bends that make for ideal campsites.

At boat-in campsites developed by government agencies, virtually all are free of charge, but you are on your own. Only in extremely rare cases is piped water available.

Any way you go, by canoe, skiff or power cruiser, you end up with a one-in-a-million campsite you can call your own.

Desert Outings

It was a cold, snowy day in Missouri when 10-year-old Rusty Ballinger started dreaming about the vast deserts of the West.

"My dad was reading aloud from a Zane Grey book called Riders of the Purple Sage," Ballinger said. "He would get animated when he got to the passages about the desert. It wasn't long before I started to have the same feelings."

That was in 1947. Ballinger, now in his 50s, has spent a good part of his life exploring the West, camping along the way. "The deserts are the best part," he says. "There's something about the uniqueness of each little area you see," Ballinger said. "You're constantly surprised. Just the time of day and the way the sun casts a different color. It's like the lady you care about. One time she smiles, the next time she's pensive. The desert is like that. If you love nature, you can love the desert."

A desert adventure is not just an antidote for a case of cabin fever in the winter. Whether you go by motor home, pickup truck, car, or on foot, it provides its own special qualities.

Mountain Desert—Monument Valley on the Navajo Indian Reservation in southern Utah is a classic mountain desert; no sand or soil, just solid rock. "You look at the rock formations and imagine the massive forces that eroded the earth away and formed these huge spires and cathedral rocks," Ballinger said. "The sun strikes them in certain ways and the top of them turns bright gold, then red. On a cloudy day, sun will pour through an opening and hit a cathedral and you will feel like you are witnessing a miracle in the making."

Inland Desert Valleys—Death Valley, the lowest point in America, located east of Mount Whitney, and nearby Panamint Valley, are classic examples of this kind of desert. "Death Valley has different areas with totally different looks and formations of nature's work," Ballinger said. "On the valley floor, there is an area called the Devil's Golf Course where soupy, acidic underground water has come to the surface and evaporated. It takes the salt with it and forms stalagmites right out in the open. At Death Valley's lowest point, it is totally ugly. It is so ugly that you appreciate the uniqueness of it, like a really ugly dog you love. It is foreboding, dangerous, and you can feel it. Then there are beautiful areas, the furnace wells, and areas that look like an artist's pallette."

Sonoran Desert—This is a forbidding-looking area in southern Arizona, New Mexico and northern Mexico. "When you first look at it, you'd swear there's nothing there but sand, rock, scrub and a few cactus," Ballinger said. "When you look close, it is so alive you can't believe it—all kinds of rodents, birds, snakes, and in March and April, tiny blooming flowers."

Great Basin Desert—The Great Basin is the vast Nevada wasteland that spans south to the rim of the Grand Canyon. "West of the Ruby Mountains, the Great Basin looks like miles of desolate country, devoid of life," explained

Ballinger. "Then the Humboldt River gives it a little bit of green and it looks like the Garden of Eden."

Painted Desert—This is reddish, stark Arizona land that spans from Winslow to Page, and west to Flagstaff on the Navajo Indian Reservation. "This is very close to what you envision as Hell," Ballinger said. "It is totally desolate. It gets its name because the rock cones, gullies and washes are so many different colors that it is like an artist's palette that is totally screwed up, from coal black to native pinks and yellows, all mixed together."

High Plains Deserts—This is the high, flat country set in eastern Wyoming and Colorado. "You get absolute solitude here," Ballinger explained. "You get out in parts of Wyoming, and it will be totally flat and there will not be one thing taller than a blade of grass for miles. Because of that, you get incredible sunsets. Sometimes, close to the earth's surface, there will be a turquoise look, and above that a pinkish tinge."

On one of my trips cruising south from Jackson Hole along the Green River in Wyoming, I spent the night watching thunderstorms moving across the plains, with dramatic lightning strikes that could be seen for a hundred miles.

If you go camping in the desert, your approach has to be as unique as the setting. For starters, don't plan on any campfires, but bring a camp stove instead. And unlike in the mountains, do not camp near a water hole. The reason is that an animal, such as a badger, coyote or desert bighorn, might be desperate for water, and if you set up camp in the animal's way, you may be forcing a confrontation.

In some areas, there is a danger of flash floods. An intense rain can fall in one area, collect in a pool, then suddenly burst through a narrow canyon. If you are in its path, you could be injured or drowned. The lesson? Never camp in a gully.

"Some people might wonder, 'What good is this place?'" Ballinger said. "The answer is that it is good for looking at. It is one of the world's unique places."

Ethics

The perfect place to set up a base camp for a camping trip turned out to be not so perfect. In fact, according to Doug Williams of California, "it did not even exist."

Williams and his son, James, had driven deep into National Forest land, prepared to set up camp and then explore the surrounding area on foot. But when they reached their destination, no campground existed.

"I wanted a primitive camp in a national forest where I could teach my son some basics," said the senior Williams. "But when we got there, there wasn't much left of the camp and it had been closed. It was obvious that the area had been vandalized."

It turned out not to be an isolated incident. A lack of outdoor ethics practiced by a few people using the non-supervised campgrounds available on national forest land has caused the U.S. Forest Service to close a few of them, and make extensive repairs to others.

"There have been sites closed, especially in Angeles and San Bernardino National Forests in Southern California," said David Flohr, regional campground coordinator for the Forest Service. "It's an urban type of thing, affecting forests near urban areas, and not just Los Angeles. They get a lot of urban users and they bring with them a lot of the same ethics they have in the city. They get drinking and they're not afraid to do things. They vandalize and run. Of course, it is a public facility, so they think nobody is getting hurt."

But somebody is getting hurt, starting with the next person who wants to use the campground. And if the ranger district budget doesn't have enough money to pay for repairs, the campground is then closed for the next arrivals. Just ask Doug and James Williams.

In an era of considerable fiscal restraint for the Forest Service, vandalized campgrounds could face closures instead of repair in the next few years. The Williams had a taste of it, but Flohr, as camping coordinator, gets a steady diet.

"It starts with behavior," Flohr said. "General rowdiness, drinking, partying and then vandalism. They burn up tables, burn barriers. They'll burn up signs for firewood, even the shingles right off the roofs of the bathrooms."

The National Park Service had a similar problem 10 years ago, especially with rampant littering. Park Director Bill Mott responded by creating an interpretive program that attempts to teach visitors how to use natural areas, and to have all park workers set examples by picking up litter and reminding others to do the same.

The Forest Service has responded with a similar program, with brochures available that detail the wise use of national forests. The four most popular brochures are titled: "Rules for Visitors to the National Forest," "Recreation in the National Forests," "Is the Water Safe?" and "Backcountry Safety Tips." These include details on campfires, drinking water from lakes or streams, hypothermia, safety and outdoor ethics. They are available for free by writing Public Affairs, Rocky Mountain Region, Forest Service, 11177 West Eighth Avenue, P.O. Box 25127, Lakewood, CO 80225 or phoning (303)236-9660. In Montana, write Public Affairs, Forest Service, Federal Building, P.O. Box 7669, Missoula, MT 59807 or phone (406)329-3511.

Flohr said even experienced campers sometimes cross over the ethics line unintentionally. The most common example, he said, is when campers toss garbage into the outhouse toilet, rather than packing it out in a plastic garbage bag.

"They throw it in the vault toilet bowls, and that just fills them up," Flohr said. "That creates an extremely high cost to pump it. You know why? Because that stuff has to be picked out piece-by-piece by some poor guy. It can't be pumped."

At most backcountry sites, the Forest Service has implemented a program called, "Pack it in, pack it out," even posting signs that remind all visitors to do so. But unfortunately, a lot of people don't do it.

On a trip to a secluded lake near Carson Pass in the Sierra Nevada, I arrived at a small, little-known camp where the picnic table had been spray painted and garbage had been strewn about. A pristine place, the true temple of God, had been defiled.

Then I remembered back 30 years, and advice my dad gave me. "There are two dogs inside of you," he said, "a good one, and a bad one. The one you feed is the one that will grow. Always try to feed the good dog."

Resource Guide

Now you're ready to join the Five Percent Club, that is, the five percent of campers who know the secret spots where they can camp, fish and hike, and have the time of their lives doing it.

To aid in that pursuit, there are a number of contacts, map sources and reservation systems available for your use. These include contacts for national forests, state parks, national parks, and the Bureau of Land Management offices for each state. The state and federal agencies listed can provide detailed maps at low costs and any additional information you might require.

National Forests

The Forest Service provides many secluded camps and permits camping anywhere except where it is specifically prohibited. If you ever want to clear the cobwebs and get away from it all, this is the way to go.

Many Forest Service campgrounds are quite remote and have no developed water. You don't need to check in, you don't need reservations and there is no fee. At many Forest Service campgrounds that provide piped water, the camp fee is often only a few dollars, with payment made on the honor system. Because most of these camps are in mountain areas, they are subject to closure from snow or mud during the winter.

Dogs are permitted in national forests with no extra charge and no hassle. Conversely, in state and national parks, dogs are not allowed on trails.

Maps for national forests are among the best you can get. They detail all backcountry streams, lakes, hiking trails and logging roads for access. They cost $2. For maps of national forests in Colorado and Wyoming, write Rocky Mountain Region, Forest Service, 11177 West Eighth Avenue, P.O. Box 25127, Lakewood, CO 80225 or phone (303)236-9660 or (303)236-9431. For maps of forests in Montana, write Forest Service, Federal Building, P.O. Box 7669, Missoula, MT 59807 or phone (406)329-3511.

I've found the Forest Service personnel to be the most helpful of the government agencies when obtaining camping or hiking trail information. Unless you are buying a map, it is advisable to phone, not write, to get the best service. For specific information on a national forest, write or phone the following:

Montana National Forests

Beaverhead National Forest, 610 North Montana, Dillon MT 59725; phone (406)683-3900.

Bitterroot National Forest, 316 North Third Street, Hamilton, MT 59840; phone (406)363-3131.

Custer National Forest, 2602 First Avenue North, P.O. Box 2556, Billings MT 59103; phone (406)657-6361.

Deerlodge National Forest, Box 400, Butte, MT 59703; phone (406)496-3400.

Flathead National Forest, 1935 Third Avenue East, Kalispell, MT 59901; phone (406)755-5401.

Gallatin National Forest, Box 130, Bozeman, MT 59715; phone (406)587-6700.

Helena National Forest, Federal Building, Drawer 10014, Helena, MT 59626; phone (406)449-5201.

Lewis & Clark National Forest, 1101 15th Street North, Box 871, Great Falls, MT 59403; phone (406)791-7700.

Kootenai National Forest, 506 U.S. Highway 2, Libby, MT 59923; phone (406)293-6211.

Lolo National Forest, Building 24, Ft. Missoula, Missoula, MT 59801; phone (406)329-3750.

Shoshone National Forest, P.O. Box 2140, Cody, WY 82414; phone (307)587-6241.

Wyoming National Forests

Bridger-Teton National Forest, 340 North Cache Street, P.O. Box 1888, Jackson, WY 83001; phone (307)733-2752.

Black Hills National Forest, Forest Service, P.O. Box 680, Sundance, WY 82729; phone (307)283-1361.

Bighorn National Forest, 1969 S. Sheridan Avenue, Sheridan, WY 82801; phone (307)672-0751.

Medicine Bow National Forest, 605 Skyline Drive, Laramie, WY 82070; phone (307)745-8971.

Shoshone National Forest, 225 W. Yellowstone, P.O. Box 2140, Cody, WY 82414; phone (307)527-6241.

Colorado National Forests

Arapaho and Roosevelt National Forests, 240 West Prospect Road, Fort Collins, CO 80526-2098; phone (303)498-1277.

Grand Mesa-Uncompahgre and Gunnison National Forests, 2250 Highway 50, Delta, CO 81416-8723; phone at (303)874-7691.

Pike and San Isabel National Forests, 1920 Valley Drive, Pueblo, CO 81008; phone (719)545-8737.

Rio Grande National Forest, 1803 West Highway 160, Monte Vista, CO 81144; phone (719)852-5941.

Routt National Forest, 29587 West U.S. 40, Suite 20, Steamboat Springs, CO 80487; phone (303)879-1722.

San Juan National Forest, 701 Camino del Rio, Room 301, Durango, CO 81301; phone (303)247-4874.

White River National Forest, 9th and Grand, P.O. Box 948, Glenwood Springs, CO 81602; phone (303)945-2521.

State Parks

State parks provide many popular camping spots. They range widely in style, from developed, numbered sites available in Colorado to primitive and little-known areas in Montana. Some state parks are well-known, but there are still many rarely-visited gems where campers can get seclusion even in summer months, especially in Montana.

For maps or information, write or phone the following:

Montana Department of Fish, Wildlife & Parks, 1420 East 6th Avenue, Helena, MT 59620; phone (406)444-2535.

Wyoming State Parks and Historic Sites, Wyoming Recreation Commission, Cheyenne, WY 82002; phone (307)777-7695.

Colorado Division of Parks and Recreation, 1313 Sherman Street, No. 618, Denver, CO 80203; phone (303)866-3437.

National Parks

The national parks of the Rocky Mountains are natural wonders, ranging from the spectacular and world-reknowned Yellowstone and Glacier Parks to the stark Devils Tower in northeastern Wyoming. For more information, write or phone the following:

Montana National Parks

Bighorn Canyon National Recreation Area, P.O. Box 458, Fort Smith, MT 59035; phone (406)666-2412.

Glacier (International Peace) National Park, P.O. Box 128, West Glacier, MT 59936; phone (406)888-5441.

Wyoming National Parks

Devils Tower National Monument, Devils Tower, WY 82714; phone (307)467-5370.

Grand Teton National Park, P.O. Drawer 170, Moose, WY 83012; phone (307)733-2880.

Yellowstone National Park, P.O. Box 168, Yellowstone National Park, WY 82190; phone (307)344-7381.

Colorado National Parks

Black Canyon of the Gunnison National Monument, Box 1648, Montrose, CO 81402; phone (303)249-7036.

Colorado National Monument, Fruita, CO 81521; phone (303) 242-7906.

Curecanti National Recreation Area, P.O. Box 1040, Gunnison, CO 81230; phone (303)641-2505.

Dinosaur National Monument, Box 210, Dinosaur, CO 81610; phone (303)374-2216.

Great Sand Dune National Monument, Mosca, CO 81146; phone (719)378-2312.

Mesa Verde National Park, Mesa Verde, CO 81330; phone (303)529-4474 or (303)529-4421.

Rocky Mountain National Park, Estes Park, CO 80517; phone (303)586-2371.

Bureau of Land Management

The Bureau of Land Management offers unique opportunities on wild lands that are often overlooked, or lost in the much larger shadow of the national parks and national forests. The numbers are:

Montana — Bureau of Land Management, P.O. Box 36800, Billings, MT 59107; phone (406)255-2913.

Wyoming — Bureau of Land Management, Box 1828, Cheyenne, WY 82001; phone (307)772-2334.

Colorado — Bureau of Land Management, 1037 20th Street, Denver, CO 80202; phone (303)236-2100.

Camping Gear Checklist

Cooking Gear

Matches bagged in zip-lock bags
Fire-starter cubes or candle
Camp stove
Camp fuel
Pot, pan, cup
Pot grabber
Knife, fork
Dish soap and scrubber
Salt, pepper, spices
Itemized food
Plastic spade

OPTIONAL
Ax or hatchet
Wood or charcoal for barbecue
Ice chest
Spatula
Grill
Tinfoil
Dust pan
Tablecloth
Whisk broom
Clothespins

Camping Clothes

Polypropylene underwear
Cotton shirt
Long sleeve cotton/wool shirt
Cotton/canvas pants
Vest
Parka
Rain jacket, pants or poncho
Hat
Sunglasses
Chapstick

OPTIONAL
Seam Lock
Shorts
Swimming suit
Gloves
Ski cap

Hiking and Foot Care

Quality hiking boots
Backup lightweight shoes
Polypropylene socks
Thick cotton socks
80 percent wool socks
Strong boot laces
Innersole or foot cushion
Moleskin and medical tape
Gaiters
Water repellent boot treatment

Sleeping

Sleeping bag
Insulite or Therm-a-Rest pad
Ground tarp
Tent

OPTIONAL
Air pillow
Mosquito netting
Foam pad for truck bed
Windshield light screen for RV
Catalytic heater

First Aid

Band-Aids
Sterile gauze pads
Roller gauze
Athletic tape
Moleskin
Thermometer
Aspirin
Ace bandage
Mosquito repellent
After Bite or ammonia
Campho-Phenique gel
First-Aid cream
Sunscreen
Neosporin
Caladryl
Biodegradable soap
Towelette

OPTIONAL
Water purification system
Coins for emergency phoning
Extra set of matches
Tweezers
Mirror for signaling

Fishing/Recreational Gear

Fishing rod
Fishing reel with fresh line
Small tackle box with lures, splitshot and snap swivels
Pliers
Knife

OPTIONAL
Stargazing chart
Tree identification handbook
Deck of cards
Backpacking cribbage board
Knapsack for each person

Miscellaneous

Maps
Flashlight
Nylon rope for food hang
Handkerchief
Camera and film
Plastic garbage bags
Toilet paper
Compass
Watch

OPTIONAL
Binoculars
Notebook and pen
Towel
altimeter

COLORADO

Colorado Map C1
50 listings
Pages 60-83

North—Wyoming
East (C2)—see page 84
South (C5)—see page 184
West—Utah

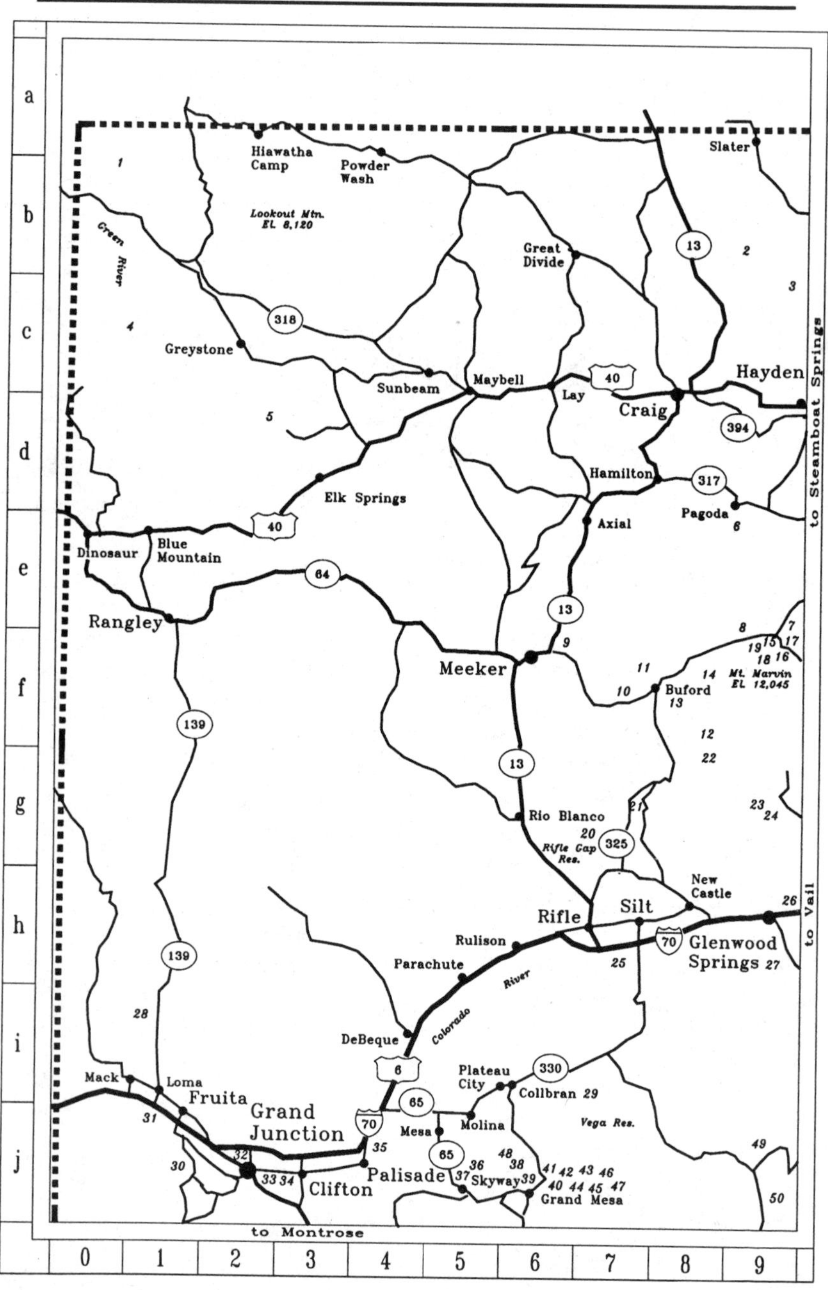

Featuring: Beaver Creek, Brown's Park National Wildlife Refuge, Elkhead Mountains, Routt National Forest, Freeman Reservoir, Green River, Dinosaur National Monument, Yampa River, North Fork of White River, White River National Forest, White River, Lake Avery, South Fork of White River, Marvine Creek, Trappers Lake, Rifle Gap Reservoir, East Rifle Creek, Deep Lake, Heart Lake, Colorado River, Roaring Fork River, Vega Reservoir, Colorado National Monument, Mesa Lakes, Grand Mesa National Forest, Island Lake, Eggleston Lake, Larger Leon Lake, Bull Basin, Lee Creek, Gunnison National Forest

---

1) COLD SPRINGS

Reference: near Beaver Creek, Brown's Park National Wildlife Refuge; map C1, grid b0.

Campsites, facilities: Tents, trailers and campfires are permitted in designated areas only, otherwise there are no facilities available. There is **no piped water.**

Reservations, fee: No reservations necessary; no fee. Open May to October.

Who to contact: Phone Colorado Division of Wildlife at (303) 248-7175 or write to 711 Independent Avenue, Grand Junction, CO 81505.

Location: From Maybell, travel northwest on Highway 318 to County Road 10 and north on County Road 10 to County Road 72. Turn west on County Road 72 to Cold Springs Unit or drive further west to the Wiggins Unit (about 70 miles from Maybell).

Trip note: Set in sagebrush country, these two wildlife management units are part of Brown's Park National Wildlife Refuge. They are extremely primitive, so be sure to bring all your own provisions, including water. Another unit at nearby Beaver Creek Canyon is open for day-use and offers fishing for native Colorado cutthroat trout. See the trip note for Gates of Lodore camp for information on nearby wildlife refuge.

---

2) SAWMILL CREEK

Reference: in Elkhead Mountains, Routt National Forest; map C1, grid b9.

Campsites, facilities: There are five sites for tents, trailers or motor homes up to 21 feet long. Picnic tables and grills are provided. Vault toilets are also available. There is **no piped water.** Pets are permitted on leashes.

Reservations, fee: No reservations necessary; no fee. Open mid-June to mid-November.

Who to contact: Phone Routt National Forest at (303) 824-9438 or write to Bears Ears Ranger District, 356 Ranney Street, Craig, CO 81625.

Location: From Craig, travel 13 miles northeast on Highway 13 and then 12.5 miles northeast on Forest Service Road 110.

Trip note: This campground is set at 9,000 feet, near Sawmill Creek in the Elkhead Mountains. A trailhead near camp runs to the east, providing access to numerous beaver ponds. It's a good base camp for hiking trips. There are also four-wheel-drive roads in the area that make good mountain biking trails. See a Forest Service map.

---

3) FREEMAN

Reference: on Freeman Reservoir, Routt National Forest; map C1, grid b9.

Campsites, facilities: There are 17 sites for tents, trailers or motor homes up to 22 feet long. Picnic tables and grills are provided. Piped water and vault toilets are also available. Some facilities are **wheelchair accessible.** Pets are permitted on leashes.

Reservations, fee: No reservations necessary; $5 fee per night. Open mid-June to mid-November.

Who to contact: Phone Routt National Forest at (303) 824-9438 or write to Bears Ears Ranger District, 356 Ranney Street, Craig, CO 81625.

Location: From Craig, travel 13 miles northeast on Highway 13 and nine miles northeast on Forest Service Road 112.

Trip note: This campground is set at 8,800 feet, near the shore of Freeman Reservoir, a popular fishing spot. There is a trailhead about two miles west of camp that is routed to the north, leading to the North Fork of Fortification Creek and continuing into the surrounding national forest. There is another slightly easier trail you can access directly out of camp; it heads south for one mile.

---

4) GATES OF LODORE

Reference: on Green River, Dinosaur National Monument; map C1, grid c1.

Campsites, facilities: There are 17 sites for tents, trailers or motor homes up to 30 feet long. Picnic tables and grills are provided. Vault toilets and piped water are available. Pets are permitted on leashes. Raft launching facilities are nearby.

Reservations, fee: No reservations necessary; no fee. Open mid-May to mid-October.

Who to contact: Phone Dinosaur National Monument at (303) 374-2216 or write to P.O. Box 210, Dinosaur, CO 81610.

Location: From Maybell, travel 41 miles northwest on Highway 318 and four miles southwest on unpaved roads to the campground.

Trip note: This primitive campground is set along the banks of the Green River in Dinosaur National Monument. Whitewater rafting trips are available through outfitters; call the Park Service for details. The dinosaur discovery site is accessible from the south entrance to the park. Nearby is Brown's Park National Wildlife Refuge, a good sidetrip during the fall and spring waterfowl migrations; the gravel entrance road is to the left on Highway 318 northwest of camp.

5) ECHO PARK

Reference: on Yampa and Green Rivers, Dinosaur National Monument; map C1, grid d2.

Campsites, facilities: There are 14 primitive tent sites. No trailers or motor homes. Picnic tables and grills are provided. Piped water is also available. Pets are permitted on leashes.

Reservations, fee: No reservations necessary; no fee. Open mid-May to mid-October.

Who to contact: Phone Dinosaur National Monument at (303) 374-2216 or write to P.O. Box 210, Dinosaur, CO 81610.

Location: Travel two miles east of Dinosaur on US 40, 25 miles north on Harpers Corner Road, and 13 miles northeast on an unpaved road (Echo Park Road) to the campground. The road is graded but suitable only for cars and four-wheel-drive vehicles. Any rain will make the road impassable.

Trip note: This primitive campground is set at a spectacular location at the confluence of the Yampa and Green Rivers in Dinosaur National Monument. Many good hiking trails are in the area. Day river trips are available through outfitters in town. Contact the Park Service at (303) 866-3437 for details.

6) INDIAN RUN STATE WILDLIFE REFUGE

Reference: near Pagoda; map C1, grid d9.

Campsites, facilities: Camping is permitted in designated areas, but there are no developed campsites. Pit toilets and a corral are available, but there is **no piped water.**

Reservations, fee: No reservations necessary; no fee. Open all year.

Who to contact: Phone Colorado Division of Wildlife at (303) 878-4493 or write to P.O. Box 1181, Meeker, CO 81641.

Location: Travel 14 miles south of Craig on Highway 13 to Hamilton and 12 miles east on Highway 317 to Pagoda. Turn south on County Road 67, and drive six miles to the entrance.

Trip note: This area covers 2,000 acres and offers fishing for native trout along four miles of creeks. Some frontage along the South Fork of the Williams Fork River is in private ownership, so be sure you're on public property before fishing. Hunting, hiking and photography are some other options.

7) VAUGHN LAKE

Reference: in Routt National Forest; map C1, grid e9.

Campsites, facilities: There are seven sites for tents, trailers or motor homes up to 22 feet long. Picnic tables and grills are provided. Vault toilets are also available. There is **no piped water,** and no firewood available. Pets are permitted on leashes. Primitive boat docks and launching facilities are nearby.

Reservations, fee: No reservations necessary; no fee. Open mid-June through October.

Who to contact: Phone Routt National Forest at (303) 638-4516 or write to Yampa Ranger District, P.O. Box 7, Yampa, CO 80483.

Location: Travel 25 miles southwest of the town of Steamboat Springs to Phippsburg. From Phippsburg, drive 300 yards south on Highway 131 and 28 miles west on Forest Service Road 16 to the campground.

Trip note: This campground is set at 9,500 feet and is along the shore of Vaughn Lake. Fishing is popular here, but note that no gasoline motors are permitted on the lake. An excellent hiking trail is available by driving four miles north on Forest Service Road 16. The trailhead is located adjacent to the Pyramid Guard Station. This area is known for its abundant wildlife and beautiful scenery, so photographers, take your cameras.

---

8) NORTH FORK

Reference: on the North Fork of White River, White River National Forest; map C1, grid e9.

Campsites, facilities: There are 39 sites for tents, trailers or motor homes up to 60 feet long. Group camping facilities are available for up to 50 people. Picnic tables and grills are provided. Piped water, vault toilets and firewood are also available. Pets are permitted on leashes.

Reservations, fee: No reservations necessary; $5 fee per night. Open mid-May to mid-November.

Who to contact: Phone White River National Forest at (303) 878-4039 or write to Blanco Ranger District, 317 East Market Street, Meeker, CO 81641.

Location: From Meeker, drive two miles east on Highway 13 and 31 miles east on County Road 8.

Trip note: This campground is set at 7,800 feet and is along the banks of the North Fork of the White River. The Flat Tops Trail Scenic Byway (County Road 8) is adjacent to the camp, and makes a good sidetrip. There are no hiking trails leading directly from the camp, but there are two trails, Long Park and Lost Park, about 1.5 miles to the west. Motorcycle and bicycle trails are available close by; see a Forest Service map for details. There is excellent fishing in the White River just across the road from camp.

---

9) MEEKER PASTURE

Reference: on White River; map C1, grid f6.

Campsites, facilities: There are several primitive, undesignated sites for trailer or tent camping. There are no toilets and **no piped water**. Pets are permitted on leashes.

Reservations, fee: No reservations necessary; no fee. Open year-round.

Who to contact: Phone Colorado Division of Wildlife at (303) 878-4493 or write P.O. Box 1181, Meeker, CO 81641.

Location: Go four miles east of Meeker on Highway 132.

Trip note: This spot is out there in what we call "booger country"—remote, primitive, and beautiful. It's simple and undeveloped, but perfect for those looking to get away from the city. It's set along the White River, and few know or use it. There are a total of 40 acres. Great spot for fishing and small game hunting.

---

10) OAK RIDGE STATE WILDLIFE AREA

Reference: on Lake Avery; map C1, grid f7.

Campsites, facilities: There are campsites for tents or small trailers in three designated areas. Pit toilets, corrals and horse loading ramps are provided. Piped water is available at the east entrance at the turn-off from County Road 8. A boat ramp is located on Lake Avery.

Reservations, fee: No reservations necessary; no fee. Open mid-July to late October.

Who to contact: Phone Colorado Division of Wildlife at (303) 878-4493 or write P.O. Box 1181, Meeker, CO 81641.

Location: From Meeker, travel 1.5 miles north on Highway 13 and nine miles east on County Road 8 to the first entrance. There are several entrances.

Trip note: Though primitive, this camp is perfect for a short hunting or fishing trip. The 8,000-acre wildlife area offers fishing for native trout and whitefish on Lake Avery during spring and summer and hunting in fall. Boats with motors are permitted on Lake Avery, but the speed limit is 20 miles per hour. No waterskiing is permitted on the lake.

---

11) HILL CREEK

Reference: east of Meeker, White River National Forest; map C1, grid f7.

Campsites, facilities: There are ten tent sites. No trailers are permitted. Picnic tables, pit toilets and non-potable water are provided. Pets are permitted on leashes.

Reservations, fee: No reservations; $5 fee per night. Open late May through mid-November.

Who to contact: Phone White River National Forest at (303) 878-4039 or write to Blanco Ranger District, 317 East Market Street, Meeker, CO 81641.

Location: From Meeker, drive one mile east on Highway 13. Turn right and travel 18 miles on County Road 8, then turn right on County Road 10 (South Fork Road) and continue for 10 miles. Turn left on Hill Creek Road and continue for one mile to the campground.

Trip note: The road into this camp is steep and rough, which keeps out trailers and campers with BMWs. This is a trailhead camp for Hill Creek Trail, used primarily by campers heading off on pack-trip expeditions. There are loading docks and hitch racks for horses.

---

12) SOUTH FORK

Reference: on the South Fork of White River, White River National Forest; map C1, grid f8.

Campsites, facilities: There are 18 sites for tents, trailers or motor homes up to 20 feet long. Picnic tables and grills are provided. Hand-pumped well water, vault toilets and firewood are also available. Some facilities are **wheelchair accessible.** Pets are permitted on leashes.

Reservations, fee: No reservations necessary; $5 fee per night. Open mid-May to mid-November.

Who to contact: Phone White River National Forest at (303) 878-4039 or write to Blanco Ranger District, 317 East Market Street, Meeker, CO 81641.

Location: From Meeker, travel two miles east on Highway 13, 20 miles east on County Road 8, and 9.5 miles south on County Road 10.

Trip note: This campground is set at 8,000 feet and is along the South Fork of the White River. It is a beautiful camp, surrounded by huge evergreens and providing superb fishing access. Trails from camp provide access to numerous lakes and streams in Flat Tops Wilderness including one trail that follows the South Fork of the White River through South Fork Canyon. For spelunkers, the Cliff Lake Trail also accesses Spring Cave. Be sure to bring a light. There is a **wheelchair accessible** bridge for anglers.

---

13) BEL AIRE UNIT

Reference: on the South Fork of White River; map C1, grid f8.

Campsites, facilities: There are several campsites for tents or small trailers. Picnic tables are provided. Piped water and pit toilets are also available.

Reservations, fee: No reservations necessary; no fee. Open mid-July to late October.

Who to contact: Phone Colorado Division of Wildlife at (303) 878-4493 or write P.O. Box 1181, Meeker, CO 81641.

Location: From Meeker, travel 1.5 miles north on Highway 13, and 20.5 miles east on County Road 8 to County Road 17 (Buford/Newcastle Road). Turn south and drive one mile. Turn west on the dirt road before the second bridge and drive to the campground.

Trip note: This camp is remote, fairly primitive, and gets little use from anyone but locals. The primary attraction here is fishing. The wildlife area offers a fishing pond near the entrance and fishing for native trout and whitefish along the South Fork of the White River.

14) MARVINE

Reference: on Marvine Creek, White River National Forest; map C1, grid f8.

Campsites, facilities: There are 25 sites for tents, trailers or motor homes up to 30 feet long. Picnic tables and grills are provided. Hand-pumped water, vault toilets and firewood are also available. Pets are permitted on leashes.

Reservations, fee: No reservations necessary; $5 fee per night. Open late May to mid-November.

Who to contact: Phone White River National Forest at (303) 878-4039 or write to Blanco Ranger District, 317 East Market Street, Meeker, CO 81641.

Location: Travel two miles east of Meeker on Highway 13, 23 miles east on County Road 8, and six miles southeast on County Road 12.

Trip note: This campground is set at 8,100 feet and is along the banks of Marvine Creek. It's a unique, pretty camp, with open sites encircled by evergreens and aspen. A trailhead provides access to the Marvine Lakes and other lakes in the Flat Tops Wilderness. Fishing is good in the three branches of Marvine Creek.

15) BUCKS

Reference: near Trappers Lake, White River National Forest; map C1, grid f9.

Campsites, facilities: There are 10 sites for tents, trailers or motor homes up to 36 feet long. Picnic tables and grills are provided. Piped water, vault toilets and firewood are also available. Pets are permitted on leashes. Boat and horse rentals are nearby.

Reservations, fee: No reservations necessary; $7 fee per night. Open mid-June to mid-September.

Who to contact: Phone White River National Forest at (303) 878-4039 or write to Blanco Ranger District, 317 East Market Street, Meeker, CO 81641.

Location: From Meeker, travel two miles east on Highway 13 and 41 miles east on County Road 8. Continue 10 miles southeast on Forest Service Road 205.

Trip note: This campground is set at 9,800 feet and is near the shore of Trappers Lake, the largest lake in the area. Nearby trails provide access to numerous smaller backcountry lakes in the Flat Tops Wilderness Area. A good sidetrip is the Ripple Creek Overlook, located on County Road 8 four miles beyond the Trappers Lake turnoff. A bicycle trail is available north of the campground in a new wilderness area.

16) TRAPLINE

Reference: on Trappers Lake, White River National Forest; map C1, grid f9.

Campsites, facilities: There are 12 sites for tents, trailers or motor homes up to 36 feet long. Picnic tables and grills are provided. Piped water, vault toilets and firewood are also available. Pets are permitted on leashes. Boat and horse rentals are nearby.

Reservations, fee: No reservations necessary; $7 fee per night. Open mid-June to mid-September.

Who to contact: Phone White River National Forest at (303) 878-4039 or write to Blanco Ranger District, 317 East Market Street, Meeker, CO 81641.

Location: From Meeker, drive two miles east on Highway 13, 41 miles east on County Road 8, and 10 miles southeast on Forest Service Road 205.

Trip note: This campground is set at 9,800 feet and is on the western shore of Trappers Lake, on the border of the Flat Tops Wilderness. This is a popular camp, so get here early; during the week if you can. Trappers Lodge, located at the north end of the lake, offers cabins, horse rentals and boat rentals. No motors are allowed on the lake, providing a serene, quiet environment. The silver-gray vegetation that covers the ground you see facing the Flat Top Wilderness is actually the remains of thousands of Engelmann spruce trees, killed in the 1940s by a spruce beetle epidemic.

---

17) CUTTHROAT

Reference: near Trappers Lake, White River National Forest; map C1, grid f9.

Campsites, facilities: There are 14 sites for tents, trailers or motor homes up to 36 feet long. Picnic tables and grills are provided. Piped water, vault toilets and firewood are also available. Pets are permitted on leashes. Boat and horse rentals are nearby.

Reservations, fee: No reservations necessary; $7 fee per night. Open mid-June to late September.

Who to contact: Phone White River National Forest at (303) 878-4039 or write to Blanco Ranger District, 317 East Market Street, Meeker, CO 81641.

Location: Drive two miles east of Meeker on Highway 13, 41 miles east on County Road 8, and 10 miles southeast on Forest Service Road 205.

Trip note: This is an option to Bucks Camp, also being set north of Trappers Lake. Nearby trails provide access to many backcountry lakes in the Flat Tops Wilderness. See previous trip note for details on Trappers Lake.

---

18) SHEPHERD'S RIM

Reference: near Trappers Lake, White River National Forest; map C1, grid f9.

Campsites, facilities: There are 20 sites for tents, trailers or motor homes up to 36 feet long. Picnic tables and grills are provided. Piped water, vault toilets and firewood are also available. Pets are permitted on leashes. Boat and horse rentals are nearby.

Reservations, fee: No reservations necessary; $7 fee per night. Open mid-June to mid-November.

Who to contact: Phone White River National Forest at (303) 878-4039 or write to Meeker, CO 81641.

Location: Travel two miles east of Meeker on Highway 13, 41 miles east on County Road 8, and 10 miles southeast on Forest Service Road 205.

Trip note: This campground is the northernmost of several in this area, set on the border of the Flat Tops Wilderness. A good base camp for hikers or anglers. See trip notes for Trapline Camp for details on the area.

---

19) HIMES PEAK

Reference: on the North Fork of White River, White River National Forest; map C1, grid f9.

Campsites, facilities: There are 11 sites for tents, trailers or motor homes up to 36 feet long. Picnic tables and grills are provided. Piped water, vault toilets and firewood are also available. Pets are permitted on leashes. Boat and horse rentals are nearby.

Reservations, fee: No reservations necessary; $5 fee per night. Open late May to mid-November.

Who to contact: Phone White River National Forest at (303) 878-4039 or write to Blanco Ranger District, 317 East Market Street, Meeker, CO 81641.

Location: Drive two miles east of Meeker on Highway 13, 41 miles east on County Road 8, and five miles southeast on Forest Service Road 205.

Trip note: This campground is set at 8,800 feet and is along the North Fork of the White River, approximately four miles north of Trappers Lake. A trailhead at camp provides access to Boulder Lake, Big Fish Lake and numerous backcountry lakes in the Flat Tops Wilderness.

---

20) RIFLE GAP STATE RECREATION AREA

Reference: on Rifle Gap Reservoir; map C1, grid g7.

Campsites, facilities: There are 46 drive-through sites for tents, trailers or motor homes of any length. Picnic tables and grills are provided. Piped water, vault toilets and sanitary disposal services are also available. Pets are permitted on leashes. Boat docks and launching facilities are nearby.

Reservations, fee: Reserve sites by calling (800) 678-CAMP ($6.75 reservation fee); $6-$10 fee per night plus $3 entrance fee. Open all year with limited winter facilities.

Who to contact: Phone (303) 625-1607 or write to 0050 County

Road 219, Rifle, CO 81650.

Location: Drive three miles north on Highway 13 from Rifle and five miles northeast on Highway 325.

Trip note: This campground is set along the shore of Rifle Gap Reservoir and has an elevation of 6,000 feet. It offers access to the lake and a myriad of activities to choose from. Waterskiing, horseback riding, hunting (in the fall) and ice fishing (in winter) are some of your options.

---

21) RIFLE FALLS STATE RECREATION AREA

Reference: on East Rifle Creek; map C1, grid g7.

Campsites, facilities: There are seven tent sites and 11 drive-through sites for trailers or motor homes up to 18 feet long. Picnic tables and grills are provided. Piped water and vault toilets are also available. Pets are permitted on leashes.

Reservations, fee: Reserve sites by calling (800) 678-CAMP ($6.75 reservation fee); $6-$10 fee per night plus $3 entrance fee. Open all year with limited winter facilities.

Who to contact: Phone (303) 625-1607 or write to 0050 County Road 219, Rifle, CO 81650.

Location: From Rifle, drive three miles north on Highway 13 and 10 miles northeast on Highway 325.

Trip note: Set at 6,600 feet and along East Rifle Creek, this state park offers hiking trails, a beautiful waterfall, and limestone caves. This is a popular campground, so it's advisable to get your reservation in early.

---

22) MEADOW LAKE

Reference: in White River National Forest; map C1, grid g8.

Campsites, facilities: There are 10 sites for tents, trailers or motor homes up to 16 feet long. Picnic tables and grills are provided. Piped water, vault toilets and firewood are also available. Pets are permitted on leashes. Boat docks are nearby.

Reservations, fee: No reservations necessary; $5 fee per night. Open mid-June to mid-November.

Who to contact: Phone White River National Forest at (303) 625-2371 or write to Rifle Ranger District, P.O. Box 289, Rifle, CO 81650.

Location: From the town of Glenwood Springs, drive west 10 miles to New Castle. Travel nine miles northwest of New Castle on County Road 245, 20.5 miles north on Forest Service Road 244, and 3.5 miles east on Forest Service Road 601.

Trip note: This campground is set at 9,600 feet and is along the shore of Meadow Lake. Nearby dirt roads provide backcountry access for four-wheel-drive vehicles or mountain bikes. See a National Forest map for trail access into the nearby Flat Tops Wilderness.

23) DEEP LAKE

Reference: on Deep Lake, White River National Forest; map C1, grid g9.

Campsites, facilities: There are 45 sites for tents, trailers or motor homes up to 36 feet long. Picnic tables and grills are provided. Vault toilets and firewood are also available. There is **no piped water.** Pets are permitted on leashes. Boat docks are nearby.

Reservations, fee: No reservations necessary; no fee. Open July to late October.

Who to contact: Phone White River National Forest at (303) 328-6388 or write to Eagle Ranger District, P.O. Box 720, Eagle, CO 81631.

Location: Travel 17 miles east of Glenwood Springs on Interstate 70; two miles north on County Road 301, and 26.5 miles northwest on Forest Service Road 600.

Trip note: This popular campground is set at 10,500 feet and is along the shore of Deep Lake, one of several lakes in the area. It is currently quite primitive, but scheduled to be renovated within one year. Be sure to phone before you plan a trip to make sure it's open.

24) SUPPLY BASIN

Reference: near Heart Lake, White River National Forest; map C1, grid g9.

Campsites, facilities: There are eight sites for tents, trailers or motor homes up to 22 feet long. Picnic tables and grills are provided. Pit toilets and firewood are also available. There is **no piped water.** Pets are permitted on leashes.

Reservations, fee: No reservations necessary; no fee. Open July to late October.

Who to contact: Phone White River National Forest at (303) 328-6388 or write to Eagle Ranger District, P.O. Box 720, Eagle, CO 81631.

Location: From Glenwood Springs, drive 17 miles east on Interstate 70; two miles north on County Road 301, and 25.5 miles northwest on Forest Service Road 600.

Trip note: This campground is set at 10,800 feet and is near the shore of Heart Lake, the largest of several lakes in the area. It is primitive, but considering the fee, you can't complain. Nearby dirt roads provide access to backcountry lakes for four-wheel-drive vehicles. A Forest Service map details all secluded lakes, trails, and roads.

25) VIKING RV PARK

Reference: on Colorado River; map C1, grid h7.

Campsites, facilities: There are 30 tent sites and 52 sites for trailers or motor homes of any length. Electricity, piped water, sewer hookups and picnic tables are provided. Flush toilets, sanitary disposal services, showers, firewood, a store, cafe, bottled gas, ice and a playground are also available. Pets and motorbikes are permitted. Pets must be on leash.

Reservations, fee: Reservations accepted; $9-$14 fee per night; American Express, MasterCard and Visa accepted. Open year-round.

Who to contact: Phone (303) 876-2443 or write to P.O. Box 190, Silt, CO 81652.

Location: From Glenwood Springs, travel 19 miles west on Interstate 70 to Silt. Take exit 97. Go south to the frontage road, and continue a half mile west to the park.

Trip note: This campground is set along the banks of the Colorado River, with a choice of pretty open or shaded sites. There is good fishing on the Colorado River. Nearby recreation options include a riding stable and tennis courts.

---

26) ROCK GARDENS

Reference: on Colorado River; map C1, grid h9.

Campsites, facilities: There are 25 tent sites and 50 sites for trailers or motor homes of any length. Electricity, piped water and picnic tables are provided. Flush toilets, showers, a sanitary disposal station, firewood, a store and ice are also available. Pets are permitted on leashes.

Reservations, fee: Reservations accepted; $13-$17 fee per night; MasterCard and Visa accepted. Open mid-April to November.

Who to contact: Phone (303) 945-6737 or write to 1308 County Road 129, Glenwood Springs, CO 81601.

Location: From Glenwood Springs, travel two miles east on Interstate 70. Take exit 119 (the exit has no name) to the campground.

Trip note: This campground is set along the Colorado River, with sites on the river bank or up above on higher ground. A bike path goes up the canyon or west into Glenwood Springs to the hot springs pool. Other nearby recreation options include golf courses, hiking trails and tennis courts. Fishing and river rafting are available right out of the campground.

---

27) THE HIDEOUT CABINS

Reference: near Roaring Fork River; map C1, grid h9.

Campsites, facilities: There are 13 tent sites and 47 drive-through sites for trailers or motor homes of any length. Electricity, piped water, sewer hookups and picnic tables are provided. Flush toilets, sanitary disposal services, showers, firewood, a recreation hall, store, ice and a playground are also available. Bottled gas and cafe are located within one mile. Pets and motorbikes are permitted. There are also 12 cabins available for rental.

Reservations, fee: Reservations accepted; $13-$17 fee per night; cabins are $38-$120 per night; MasterCard and Visa accepted. Open all year.

Who to contact: Phone (303) 945-5621 or write to 1293 Road 117, Glenwood Springs, CO 81601.

Location: From the town of Glenwood Springs, go two miles south on Sunlight Ski Road.

Trip note: This campground is set near the Roaring Fork River. It has shady sites on the river banks. Nearby recreation options include hot springs pools, golf courses, bike paths, a riding stable and tennis courts. Twelve miles west of Glenwood Springs near New Castle is the Garfield Creek State Wildlife Area, a 13,000-acre tract that provides year-round range and protection for elk and many other animals.

---

28) HIGHLINE STATE RECREATION AREA

Reference: northwest of Grand Junction; map C1, grid i1.

Campsites, facilities: There are 12 tent sites and 13 sites for trailers or motor homes of any length. Piped water, grills and picnic tables are provided. Sanitary disposal services and a playground are available. Some facilities are **wheelchair accessible.** Pets are permitted on leashes. Boat docks and launching facilities are available nearby.

Reservations, fee: Reserve sites by calling (800) 678-CAMP ($6.75 reservation fee); $6-$7 fee per night plus $3 entrance fee. Open all year with limited winter facilities.

Who to contact: Phone (303) 858-7208 or write to 1800 11.8 Road, Loma, CO 81524.

Location: From Grand Junction, drive west on Interstate 70 to the Loma exit (County Road 139). Drive north for six miles to Q Road, west 1.2 miles to 11.8 Road, and north one mile to the park entrance.

Trip note: At an elevation of 4,700 feet, this state park offers grassy areas, shade trees, and two lakes. There are many recreation options: in the summer, you can fish, waterski, swim, sail or windsurf; in the fall and winter, choose from , ice fishing and ice skating. This camp fills up quickly during the summer months; get your reservation in early.

---

29) VEGA STATE RECREATION AREA

Reference: on Vega Reservoir; map C1, grid i7.

Campsites, facilities: There are 64 sites for tents, trailers or motor homes of any length. Picnic tables, piped water, pit toilets and a sanitary disposal station are provided. A store and a playground are available nearby. A coffee shop and laundromat are located within one mile. Pets are permitted on leashes. There are boat launching facilities at Vega Reservoir.

Reservations, fee: Reserve sites by calling (800) 678-CAMP ($6.75 reservation fee); $6 fee per night plus $3 entrance fee. Open all year with limited winter facilities.

Who to contact: Phone (303) 487-3407 or write to P.O. Box 186, Collbran, CO 81624.

Location: Travel east of Grand Junction on Interstate 70 for about 12 miles to the Highway 65 exit. Continue east on Highway 65 for 10 miles, then drive 11 miles east on Highway 330 to Collbran. From Collbran continue on County Road 330E east for six miles to the Silt/Vega exit. Go to the right and continue for six miles into the park.

Trip note: This camp is set in the 898-acre Vega State Park, near Vega Reservoir, a 900-acre lake—not huge, but still the biggest body of water for many miles. Recreation options include waterskiing, fishing and hiking in the summer, and snowmobiling, cross-country skiing and ice fishing in the winter. No other camps are located within 25 miles, so it is advisable to call ahead for weather conditions prior to hitting the road.

30) FRUITA JUNCTION

Reference: near Colorado River; map C1, grid j1.

Campsites, facilities: There are 28 tent sites and 121 sites for trailers or motor homes of any length. Electricity, piped water, sewer hookups and picnic tables are provided. Flush toilets, bottled gas, sanitary disposal station, showers, laundromat, small store, ice and a playground are available. A coffee shop is available within one mile. Pets and motorbikes are permitted.

Reservations, fee: Reservations accepted; $12-$14 fee per night; Open all year.

Who to contact: Phone (303) 858-3155 or write to 607 Highway 340, Fruita, CO 81521.

Location: From Interstate 70, a few miles west of Grand Junction, take the Fruita exit 19 and drive a quarter mile on Highway 340 to the park.

Trip note: This developed campground provides a layover spot for Interstate 70 cruisers. It's one of six campgrounds in the immediate vicinity set near the Colorado River. This one has both shaded and open sites, all pull-through. Good sidetrips include visiting the Colorado National Monument, the Colorado River or Dinosaur Valley, a museum located at Fourth and Main Streets in Grand Junction, which features fossil finds from the Grand Junction area. Nearby recreation options include a golf course, hiking trails and bike paths.

31) SADDLE HORN

Reference: near Fruita, Colorado National Monument; map C1, grid j1.

Campsites, facilities: There are 81 tent sites and 50 sites for trailers or motor homes up to 32 feet long. Picnic tables are provided. Piped water and both flush and pit toilets are available. Pets are permitted on leashes.

Reservations, fee: No reservations; $8 fee per night. Open all year, but facilities limited in the winter.

Who to contact: Phone Colorado National Monument at (303) 858-3617 or write to Fruita, CO 81521.

Location: From Fruita on Interstate 70, take the Highway 340 exit and drive south for 2 miles to the campground entrance.

Trip note: The best spot in the area for tent campers, quite popular for out-of-town cruisers looking for a layover. Hiking and bicycle trails are available in the park, with maps, exhibits and a 10-minute slide show available at the visitor center at the park entrance. A recreation program is provided in the summer, and in the winter, this is a popular spot for cross-country skiing.

---

32) JUNCTION WEST RV PARK

Reference: near Grand Junction; map C1, grid j2.

Campsites, facilities: There are 12 tent sites and 30 drive-through sites for trailers or motor homes of any length. Piped water and picnic tables are provided. Flush toilets, sanitary disposal station, showers, a store, propane, laundromat, ice and a playground are available. A coffee shop is located within one mile. Motorbikes are permitted.

Reservations, fee: Reservations accepted; $12-$15 fee per night; MasterCard and Visa accepted. Open all year.

Who to contact: Phone (303) 245-8531 or write to 793-22 RD, Grand Junction, CO 81505.

Location: From Interstate 70 in Grand Junction, take exit 26 and drive a half mile west on US 6/50. Turn north on County Road 22 and drive a half mile to the park.

Trip note: This 14-acre motor home park is an option to Highline State Recreation Area, which is in a more rural setting. This one offers open, pull-through sites. A good sidetrip is to visit the Colorado National Monument, to the south. Nearby recreation options include a golf course and hiking trails.

---

33) BIG J CAMPER COURT

Reference: near Grand Junction; map C1, grid j3.

Campsites, facilities: There are 25 tent sites and 110 drive-through sites for trailers or motor homes of any length. Picnic tables are provided. Flush toilets, bottled gas, sanitary disposal station, showers, recreation hall, a store, laundromat, ice, playground and a swimming pool are available. A coffee shop is located within one mile. Pets and motorbikes are permitted.

Reservations, fee: Reservations accepted; $13-$16 fee per night; MasterCard and Visa accepted. Open all year.

Who to contact: Phone (303) 242-2527 or write to 2819 Highway 50, Grand Junction, CO 81503.

Location: From Interstate 70 in Grand Junction, take the US 50 exit and drive 2.5 miles south on US 50 to the campground.

Trip note: The biggest of the seven campgrounds in the area, with more accommodations for tent campers than the preceding listed camps. It's in a fairly rural setting, but close to town. It has open sites. See trip note for Highline State Recreation Area for sidetrip options.

---

34) ROSE PARK MOBILE VILLAGE

Reference: in Grand Junction; map C1, grid j3.

Campsites, facilities: There are 26 sites for trailers or motor homes of any length. Electricity, piped water and sewer hookups are provided. Flush toilets, sanitary disposal station, showers and laundromat are available. Bottled gas, a store, coffee shop and ice are available within one mile. Pets are permitted on leashes.

Reservations, fee: Reservations accepted; $10 fee per night. Open all year.

Who to contact: Phone (303) 243-1292 or write to 2910 North Avenue, Grand Junction, CO 81504.

Location: From Interstate 70 in Grand Junction, take the US 50/6 exit. Take the Highway 6 split (North Avenue) and drive about three miles to the park on the left.

Trip note: This is a privately-run park designed expressly for motor home users. It's located on the highway right on the border of the city limits. The park is in an urban setting, paved and graveled with very little vegetation. Nearby attractions include an amusement park and a golf course. Restaurants and shopping are a short distance away.

---

35) ISLAND ACRES STATE PARK

Reference: on Colorado River; map C1, grid j4.

Campsites, facilities: There are 32 sites for tents or motor homes of any length. Picnic tables, piped water and pit toilets are provided. A sanitary disposal station is available. A store and a coffee shop are available within one mile. Pets are permitted on leashes.

Reservations, fee: Reserve sites by calling (800) 678-CAMP ($6.75 reservation fee); $6 fee per night plus $3 entrance fee. Open all year.

Who to contact: Phone (303) 464-0548 or write to P.O. Box B, Palisade, CO 81526.

Location: From Interstate 70 east of Grand Junction, take exit 47 and drive to the park six miles east of Palisade.

Trip note: This camp is set in the Island Acres State Park, which used to be an actual island in the middle of the Colorado River until a dike was built in the 1950s. There are four lakes within the park, which offer campers opportunities to boat (no motors), fish (except in Lake #2), swim and windsurf. In the winter, the park is open for ice skating and ice fishing. There is a short nature trail that follows the river, but serious hikers should explore trails at nearby Colorado National Monument.

36) JUMBO

Reference: near Mesa Lakes, Grand Mesa National Forest; map C1, grid j5.

Campsites, facilities: There are 26 sites for tents, trailers or motor homes up to 22 feet long. Picnic tables are provided. Piped water and vault toilets are available. A store, coffee shop and ice are located within one mile. A boat ramp and rentals are nearby.

Reservations, fee: No reservations necessary; $7 fee per night. Open late June to mid-September.

Who to contact: Phone Grand Mesa National Forest at (303) 487-3534 or write to Collbran Ranger District, P.O. Box 330, Collbran, CO 81624.

Location: From Interstate 70 east of Grand Junction, take Highway 65 drive 26 miles east then south on Highway 65. Continue south on Forest Service Road 252 to the campground.

Trip note: This campsite is just enough off the beaten path to get missed by virtually all out-of-towners. The elevation is 9,800 feet. The Mesa Lakes and some nice trails are in the vicinity, including the scenic West Bench Trail. See a Forest Service map for details.

37) SPRUCE GROVE

Reference: near Mesa, Grand Mesa National Forest; map C1, grid j5.

Campsites, facilities: There are 16 sites for trailers or motor homes up to 32 feet long. Picnic tables are provided. Piped water and pit toilets are available. A store, coffee shop and ice are located within one mile. Boat docks and rentals are nearby.

Reservations, fee: No reservations necessary; $5 fee per night. Open late June to mid-October.

Who to contact: Phone Grand Mesa National Forest at (303) 487-3534 or write to Collbran Ranger District, P.O. Box 330, Collbran, CO 81624.

Location: From Interstate 70 east of Grand Junction, take Highway 65 and drive 20 miles south on Highway 65 to the campground.

Trip note: A good layover for self-contained campers, this campsite is far enough from Interstate 70, 20 miles, to provide a feeling of separation from the freeway burners. It is just 12 miles from Mesa, where you can re-supply. A number of hiking trails and lakes are located just south in the Mesa Lakes area. There is also a four-wheel-drive road to the east that leads to several pretty alpine lakes.

38) ISLAND LAKE

Reference: north of Cedaredge, Grand Mesa National Forest; map C1, grid j6.

Campsites, facilities: There are 41 tent sites and 41 sites for trailers or motor homes up to 22 feet long. Picnic tables are provided. Piped water, flush and vault toilets are available. A store and coffee shop are available within one mile. Boat docks and rentals are nearby.

Reservations, fee: Reserve through MISTIX at (800) 283-CAMP ($6 MISTIX fee); $6 fee per night. Open late June to mid-October.

Who to contact: Phone Grand Mesa National Forest at (303) 242-8211 or write to Grand Junction Ranger District, 764 Horizon Drive, Grand Junction, CO 81502.

Location: From Delta, travel east on Highway 92 for about four miles, then north on Highway 65 to Cedaredge. Continue north on Highway 65 for 16 miles and one mile west on Forest Service Road 116.

Trip note: This is an option to Little Bear and is one of two camps that sits on pretty Island Lake. There is a trail at the northeast end of the lake that leads into the high country and several little lakes. Or, you can head to the southwest end and take the dirt four-wheel-drive road up to Granby Reservoirs and Big Battlement Lake.

---

39) LITTLE BEAR

Reference: on Island Lake, Grand Mesa National Forest; map C1, grid j6.

Campsites, facilities: There are 36 sites for tents, trailers or motor homes up to 22 feet long. Picnic tables are provided. Piped water, flush and vault toilets are available. A store and coffee shop are located within one mile. Boat docks and rentals are nearby.

Reservations, fee: Reserve through MISTIX at (800) 283-CAMP ($6 MISTIX fee); $7 fee per night. Open late June to mid-October.

Who to contact: Phone Grand Mesa National Forest at (303) 242-8211 or write to Grand Junction Ranger District, 764 Horizon Drive, Grand Junction, CO 81502.

Location: From Delta, travel east on Highway 92 for about four miles, then north on Highway 65 to Cedaredge. Continue north on Highway 65 for 16 miles and a half mile west on Forest Service Road 116.

Trip note: This is one of the more developed campgrounds in the area. It is set on Island Lake at 10,200 feet. There's good boating and fishing in summer months. There are many hiking options, too; see the trip note for Island Lake Camp.

---

40) CARP LAKE

Reference: north of Cedaredge, Grand Mesa National Forest; map C1, grid j6.

Campsites, facilities: There are 20 sites for tents, trailers or motor homes up to 22 feet long. Piped water and picnic tables are provided. Vault toilets are available. A store and coffee shop are located within one mile. Boat docks and rentals are nearby.

Reservations, fee: Reserve through MISTIX at (800) 283-CAMP ($6 MISTIX fee); $6 fee per night. Open late June to mid-October.

Who to contact: Phone Grand Mesa National Forest at (303) 242-8211 or write to Grand Junction Ranger District, 764 Horizon Drive, Grand Junction, CO 81502.

Location: From Delta travel east on Highway 92 for about four miles, then north on Highway 65 to Cedaredge. Continue north on Highway 65 for 16 miles to the campground.

Trip note: One of nine on this mesa, this campground is set at an elevation of 10,300 feet. There are numerous hiking and fishing opportunities in the area; see a Forest Service map for details. By the way, we didn't catch any carp.

---

41) WARD LAKE

Reference: north of Cedaredge, Grand Mesa National Forest; map C1, grid j6.

Campsites, facilities: There are 27 sites for tents, trailers or motor homes up to 22 feet long. Piped water and picnic tables are provided. Vault toilets are available. A store and coffee shop are located within one mile. Boat docks and launching facilities are nearby.

Reservations, fee: Reserve through MISTIX at (800) 283-CAMP ($6 MISTIX fee); $7 fee per night. Open late June to mid-October.

Who to contact: Phone Grand Mesa National Forest at (303) 242-8211 or write to Grand Junction Ranger District, 764 Horizon Drive, Grand Junction, CO 81502.

Location: From Delta travel east on Highway 92 for about four miles, then north on Highway 65 to Cedaredge. Continue north on Highway 65 for 16 miles and 0.1 mile east on Forest Service Road 121.

Trip note: This is one of the more developed campgrounds on this mesa. The camp has an elevation of 10,200 feet and is set along the banks of Ward Lake, one of the dozen small lakes in the immediate area. There are no hiking trails in the immediate area, but several good ones are located to the north, leading up to many lakes and streams.

---

42) TRICKLE PEAK

Reference: on Eggleston Lake, Grand Mesa National Forest; map C1, grid j6.

Campsites, facilities: There are five sites for tents, trailers or motor homes up to 22 feet long. Picnic tables are provided. Pit toilets are available. There is **no piped water.** Boat docks are nearby.

Reservations, fee: No reservations necessary; no fee. Open late June to late September.

Who to contact: Phone Grand Mesa National Forest at (303) 242-8211 or write to Grand Junction Ranger District, 764 Horizon Drive,

Grand Junction, CO 81502.

Location: From Delta travel east on Highway 92 for about four miles, then north on Highway 65 to Cedaredge. Continue north on Highway 65 for 16 miles, then 0.8 mile east on Forest Service Road 121.

Trip note: There are a dozen other lakes in the area, but Eggleston is by far the largest. It is a nice camp, with large sites, encircled by forest to the south. A Forest Service map will detail recreation options.

---

43) KISER CREEK

Reference: near Eggleston Lake, Grand Mesa National Forest; map C1, grid j6.

Campsites, facilities: There are 12 sites for tents, trailers or motor homes up to 16 feet long. Picnic tables are provided. Pit toilets are available, and there is hand-pumped water. A store and coffee shop are located within one mile. Boat docks and rentals are nearby.

Reservations, fee: No reservations necessary; no fee. Open late June to late September.

Who to contact: Phone Grand Mesa National Forest at (303) 242-8211 or write to Grand Junction Ranger District, 764 Horizon Drive, Grand Junction, CO 81502.

Location: From Delta, travel east on Highway 92 for about four miles, then north on Highway 65 to Cedaredge. Continue north on Highway 65 for 16 miles, then east three miles on Forest Service Road 121, then 0.1 mile south on Forest Service Road 123.

Trip note: This is the least known of the nine campgrounds in the area, and is unique, being free but still offering drinking water and the basic amenities. It is set on Kiser Creek near Eggleston Lake at 10,100 feet. A Forest Service map is advisable.

---

44) CRAG CREST

Reference: on Eggleston Lake, Grand Mesa National Forest; map C1, grid j6.

Campsites, facilities: There are nine tent sites and eight sites for trailers or motor homes up to 22 feet long. Picnic tables are provided. Piped water and vault toilets are available. A store and coffee shop are located within one mile.

Reservations, fee: No reservations necessary; $6 fee per night. Open late June to mid-October.

Who to contact: Phone Grand Mesa National Forest at (303) 242-8211 or write to Grand Junction Ranger District, 764 Horizon Drive, Grand Junction, CO 81502.

Location: From Delta, travel east on Highway 92 for about four miles, then north on Highway 65 to Cedaredge. Continue north on Highway 65 for 16 miles, then east for 3.5 miles on Forest Service Road 121.

Trip note: This is one of three campgrounds on Eggleston Lake and one of nine campgrounds in the area. The area is called by some the "Land of Lakes." This is another take-your-pick situation in the Rocky Mountain high country.

---

45) EGGLESTON LAKE

Reference: northeast of Delta, Grand Mesa National Forest; map C1, grid j6.

Campsites, facilities: There are six sites for tents, trailers or motor homes up to 16 feet long. Picnic tables are provided. Pit toilets and well water are available. A store and coffee shop are located within one mile. Boat docks and rentals are nearby.

Reservations, fee: No reservations necessary; $5 fee per night. Open late June to mid-October.

Who to contact: Phone Grand Mesa National Forest at (303) 242-8211 or write to 764 Horizon Drive, Grand Junction, CO 81502.

Location: From Delta, travel east on Highway 92 for about four miles, then north on Highway 65 to Cedaredge. Continue north on Highway 65 for 16 miles, then east for four miles on Forest Service Road 121.

Trip note: A lesser used, primitive option to the other more developed camps on Eggleston Lake. It can be just what you're looking for if you desire peace, quiet and solitude.

---

46) TWIN LAKE

Reference: north of Cedaredge, Grand Mesa National Forest; map C1, grid j6.

Campsites, facilities: There are 13 sites for tents, trailers or motor homes up to 22 feet long. Picnic tables are provided. Pit toilets are available, but there is **no piped water.**

Reservations, fee: No reservations necessary; no fee. Open late June to late September.

Who to contact: Phone Grand Mesa National Forest at (303) 242-8211 or write to Grand Junction Ranger District, 764 Horizon Drive, Grand Junction, CO 81502.

Location: From Delta, travel east on Highway 92 for about four miles, then north on Highway 65 to Cedaredge. Continue north on Highway 65 for 16 miles, then east for 10 miles on Forest Service Road 121. Turn and drive two miles east on Forest Service Road 126.

Trip note: This camp is adjacent to Twin Lakes and close to numerous other small lakes. It is small, primitive and little known. It doesn't offer many luxuries, but you get what you pay for.

47) WEIR & JOHNSON

Reference: near Larger Leon Lake, Grand Mesa National Forest; map C1, grid j6.

Campsites, facilities: There are 12 sites for tents, trailers or motor homes up to 22 feet long. Picnic tables are provided. Pit toilets and well water are available.

Reservations, fee: No reservations necessary; no fee. Open late June to mid-October.

Who to contact: Phone Grand Mesa National Forest at (303) 242-8211 or write to Grand Junction Ranger District, 764 Horizon Drive, Grand Junction, CO 81502.

Location: From Delta, travel east on Highway 92 for about four miles, then north on Highway 65 to Cedaredge. Continue north on Highway 65 for 16 miles, then east for 10 miles on Forest Service Road 121. Turn and drive three miles east on Forest Service Road 126.

Trip note: Bet you didn't know about this one—and it's worth knowing about. The camp is set at the end of the Forest Service road at a small lake. There is a one-mile trail from camp routed to Larger Leon Lake. Camp elevation is at 10,500 feet. It offers basic conveniences, and you sure can't beat the price.

48) COTTONWOOD LAKE

Reference: near Bull Basin, Grand Mesa National Forest; map C1, grid j6.

Campsites, facilities: There are 42 sites for tents, trailers or motor homes up to 22 feet long. Picnic tables are provided. Pit toilets are available, but there is **no piped water.** A boat ramp is nearby.

Reservations, fee: No reservations necessary; $5 fee per night. Open late June to late September.

Who to contact: Phone Grand Mesa National Forest at (303) 487-3534 or write to Collbran Ranger District, P.O. Box 338, Collbran, CO 81624.

Location: From Interstate 70 east of Grand Junction, take Highway 65 and drive 10 miles east. Continue 11 miles northeast on Highway 330 to Collbran, 12 miles south on Forest Service Road 121, and four miles west on Forest Service Road 257.

Trip note: This camp is set at the largest of five lakes in the area known as the Cottonwood Lakes. This is a good base camp for a fishing trip, if you don't mind the lack of piped water. A trail leads west to the Bull Basin Reservoirs. A hiking trail, starting at the end of the road at Lake No. 1, leads west to a number of high-country lakes. See a Forest Service map.

49) McCLURE

Reference: on Lee Creek, Gunnison National Forest; map C1, grid j9.

Campsites, facilities: There are four tent sites and 15 sites for trailers or motor homes up to 30 feet long. Picnic tables are provided. Well water and pit toilets are available. Pets are permitted on leashes.

Reservations, fee: No reservations necessary; $7 fee per night. Open June to mid-November.

Who to contact: Phone Gunnison National Forest at (303) 527-4131 or write to Paonia Ranger District, P.O. Box AG, Paonia, CO 81428.

Location: From the town of Glenwood Springs, take the Highway 82 exit from Interstate 70 and drive south for 11 miles. Continue south on Highway 133 for about 29 miles to the campground.

Trip note: This is the most accessible of three camps in the immediate vicinity. It is set along Lee Creek, fairly close to McClure Pass (9,018 feet). A trailhead at McClure Pass leads south, skirting the Raggeds Wilderness and running across several small lakes.

50) PAONIA RESERVOIR STATE RECREATION AREA

Reference: northeast of Delta; map C1, grid j9.

Campsites, facilities: There are 31 sites for tents, trailers or motor homes of any length. Picnic tables are provided. Vault toilets are available, but there is **no piped water.** Pets are permitted on leashes. Boat launching facilities are nearby.

Reservations, fee: Reserve sites by calling (800) 678-CAMP ($6.75 reservation fee); $6 fee per night plus $3 entrance fee. Open all year with limited winter facilities.

Who to contact: Phone (303) 874-4258 or write to P.O. Box 147, Crawford, CO 81415.

Location: From Delta on US 50 drive east on Highway 92 for 20 miles, then northeast on Highway 133 for 19 miles to the reservoir entrance.

Trip note: This camp is set on a long, narrow reservoir which provides a spot for fishing and waterskiing in summer, and ice fishing and ice skating in winter. The sides are steep, which makes the area also good for snow tubing and cross-country skiing in winter.

Colorado Map C2
140 listings
Pages 84-147

North—Wyoming
East (C3)—see page 148
South (C6)—see page 216
West (C1)—see page 60

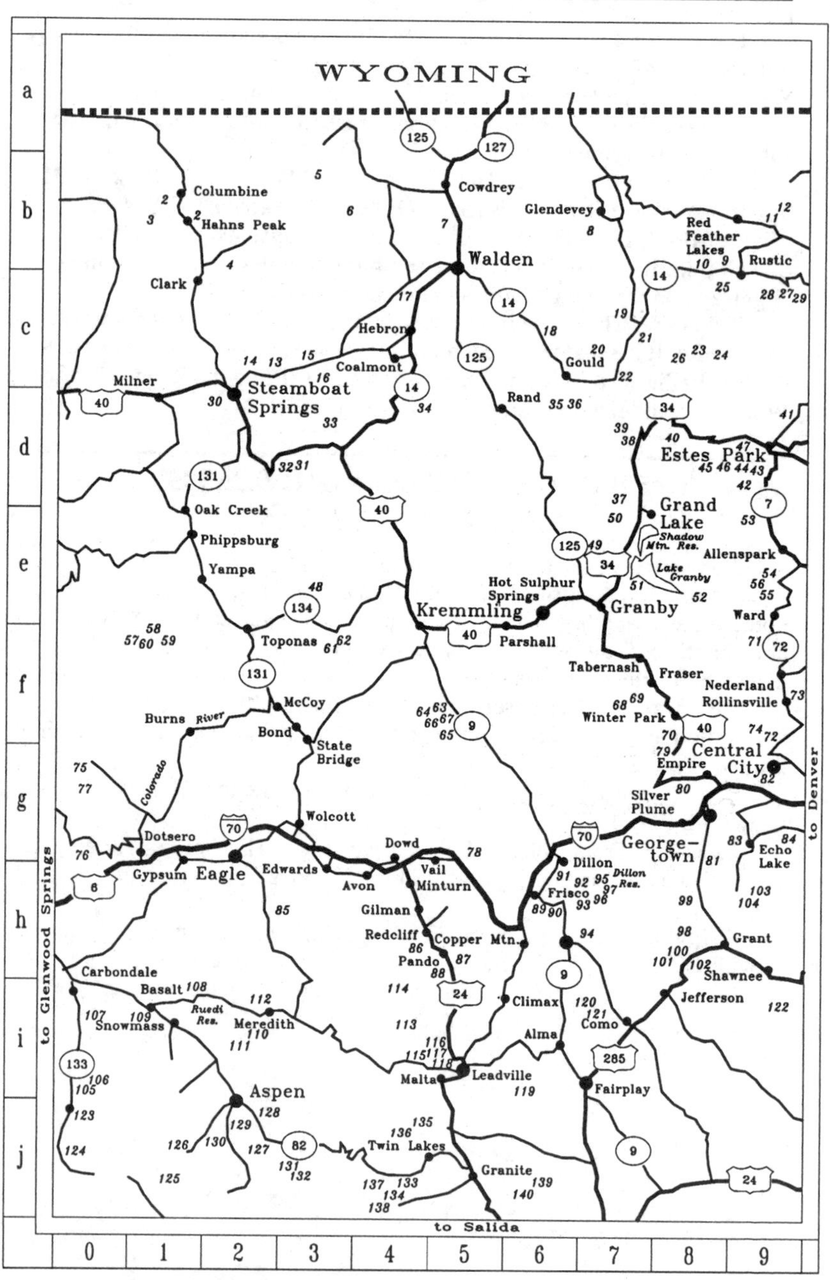

Featuring: Routt National Forest, Pearl Lake, Hahns Peak, Elk River, Jinks Creek, North Fork of Cache La Poudre River, Roosevelt National Forest, Laramis Mountains, Cache La Poudre River, South Shore of Dowdy Lake, Mount Zirkel Wilderness, Buffalo Pass, Park Mountain Range, Colorado State Forest, Rawah Wilderness, Laramie River, Michigan River, Joe Wrights Creek, Long Draw Reservoir, Comanche Peak Wilderness, Dumont Lake, South Fork of Michigan River, Rocky Mountain National Park, Grand Lake, Arapaho National Forest, Big Thompson River, Mary's Lake, Glacier Creek, Fall River, Willow Creek, Shadow Mountain Reservoir, Lake Granby, Willow Creek Reservoir, Middle St. Vrain Creek, Stillwater Reservoir, Yampa Reservoir, Gore Mountain Range, Green Mountain Reservoir, White River National Forest, Fraser Experimental Forest, Vasquez Mountains, Fraser River, Indian Peaks Wilderness,. Silver Creek, Glacier Rim, Flat Tops Wilderness, Mount Evans Wilderness, Lake Edith, Holy Cross Wilderness, Eagle River, East Fork of Eagle River, Dillon Reservoir, Swan River, Jefferson Lake, Pike National Forest, Jefferson Cree, Mount Evans Wilderness, Bear Creek, Geneva Creek, Kenosha Pass, Elk Creek, Avalanche Creek, Crystal River, Elk Mountains, Ruedi Reservoir, Roaring Fork River, North Fork of Frying Pan River, Frying Pan Lake, Turquoise Lake, San Isabel National Forest, Holy Cross Wilderness, Mount Sherman, Tarryall Creek, Lost Creek, East River, Gunnison National Forest, Maroon Creek, Roaring Fork River, Lincoln Creek, Maroon Bells Snowmass Wilderness, Grizzly Reservoir, Lost Man Creek, Twin Lakes, Mount Elbert, Twin Lakes Reservoir, Mount Massive Wilderness, Elbert Creek, South Fork of South Platte River

---

1) HAHNS PEAK LAKE

Reference: north of Steamboat Springs, Routt National Forest; map C2, grid b1.

Campsites, facilities: There are 26 sites for tents, trailers or motor homes up to 40 feet long. Picnic tables and grills are provided. Piped water and vault toilets are also available. A store, cafe and ice are located within five miles. Pets are permitted on leashes. Boat launching facilities are nearby.

Reservations, fee: Reserve through MISTIX at (800) 283-CAMP ($6 MISTIX fee); $7 fee per night. Open Memorial Day to mid-October.

Who to contact: Phone Routt National Forest at (303) 879-1870 or write to Hahns Peak Ranger District, P.O. Box 771212, Steamboat Springs, CO 80477.

Location: From the town of Steamboat Springs, drive north for 18 miles on County Road 129 to Clark. Continue 10.5 miles north of Clark on County Road 129 and 2.5 miles west on Forest Service Road 486.

Trip note: This campground is set at 8,500 feet and is along the shore of Hahns Peak Lake in a pretty, wilderness-like setting. There's good fishing in the spring for trout, but note that no gasoline motors are permitted on the lake. Steamboat Lake State Park is two miles south of camp. A nearby trail accesses some backcountry streams. It is all detailed on a Forest Service map.

---

2) PEARL LAKE STATE PARK

Reference: on Pearl Lake; map C2, grid b1.

Campsites, facilities: There are 41 sites for tents, trailers or motor homes of any length. Picnic tables and grills are provided. Piped water, vault toilets and sanitary disposal services are also available. Pets are permitted on leashes. Boat launching facilities are nearby.

Reservations, fee: Reserve sites by calling (800) 678-CAMP ($6.75 reservation fee); $6 fee per night plus $3 entrance fee. Open all year with limited winter facilities.

Who to contact: Phone (303) 879-3922 or write to P.O. Box 750, Clark, CO 80428.

Location: Travel 23 miles north of the town of Steamboat Springs on County Road 129 and east two miles on Pearl Lake Road.

Trip note: This cozy spot is set at 8,065 feet and is along the shore of little Pearl Lake. This is a very popular campground, often crowded to capacity during the summer months. Boating is permitted, but only low-speed. If you make a wake, you're out of luck. Other recreation options include fishing, hunting, and, in the winter, cross-country skiing, snowmobiling and ice fishing.

---

3) STEAMBOAT LAKE STATE PARK

Reference: near Hahns Peak; map C2, grid b1.

Campsites, facilities: There are 182 sites for tents, trailers or motor homes of any length. Picnic tables and grills are provided. Piped water, vault toilets, sanitary disposal services and firewood are also available. Pets are permitted on leashes. Boat docks, rentals and launching facilities are nearby.

Reservations, fee: Reserve sites by calling (800) 678-CAMP ($6.75 reservation fee); $6 fee per night plus $3 entrance fee. Open all year.

Who to contact: Phone (303) 879-3922 or write to P.O. Box 750, Clark, CO 80428.

Location: Travel 25 miles north of the town of Steamboat Springs on County Road 129.

Trip note: This lake covers over 1000 acres and is set at the base of Hahns Peak (elevation 10,800 feet). It's a beautiful park with something for everybody. Adventures include fishing, hiking, waterskiing, sailboarding, and in the winter, snowmobiling, cross-country skiing, ice fishing and snow tubing. With so much to do, you certainly won't be alone; campers pack in here like sardines in the high season. Reserve a spot early.

4) HINMAN

Reference: on Elk River, Routt National Forest; map C2, grid b2.

Campsites, facilities: There are 13 sites for tents, trailers or motor homes up to 22 feet long. Picnic tables and grills are provided. Piped well water and pit toilets are also available. Pets are permitted on leashes.

Reservations, fee: No reservations necessary; $5 fee per night. Open Memorial Day to Labor Day.

Who to contact: Phone Routt National Forest at (303) 879-1870 or write to Hahns Peak Ranger District, P.O. Box 771212, Steamboat Springs, CO 80477.

Location: From the town of Steamboat Springs, drive 18 miles north on Highway 129 to Clark. Continue one mile further north on County Road 129, four miles northeast on Forest Service Road 400 and a half mile southwest on Forest Service Road 440.

Trip note: This campground is set along the banks of the Elk River. Two nearby trails provide good sidetrips. One reaches Hinman Lake, about two miles north, and the other heads southeast into the Mount Zirkel Wilderness. A Forest Service map details the possibilities.

5) BIG CREEK LAKE

Reference: in Routt National Forest; map C2, grid b3.

Campsites, facilities: There are 37 tent sites and 17 sites for trailers or motor homes up to 22 feet long. Picnic tables and grills are provided. Piped water and vault toilets are also available. Pets are permitted on leashes. Boat docks and launching facilities are nearby.

Reservations, fee: Reserve through MISTIX at (800) 283-CAMP ($6 MISTIX fee); $7 fee per night. Open mid-June to early September.

Who to contact: Phone Routt National Forest at (303) 879-1722, or write to North Park Ranger District, 29587 West US 40, Suite 20, Steamboat Springs, CO 80487.

Location: From Walden, travel 13 miles north on Highway 127 to Cowdrey, 18 miles northwest on County Road 6, and 5.5 miles southwest on Forest Service Road 600.

Trip note: This campground is set at 9,000 feet and is located along the shore of Big Creek Lake. A nearby trail accesses numerous backcountry lakes and streams as it winds its way westward (through Mount Zirkel Wilderness) across the Continental Divide to Columbine.

6) LAKE JOHN

Reference: north of Walden; map C2, grid b3.

Campsites, facilities: There are several primitive undesignated sites for tents, trailers or motor homes up to 18 feet long. Vault toilets are available, but there is **no piped water.** Pets are permitted on leashes. Boat launching facilities are nearby.

Reservations, fee: No reservations necessary; no fee. Open all year with limited winter facilities.

Who to contact: Phone Colorado Division of Wildlife at (303) 297-1192 or write to 6060 Broadway, Denver, CO 80216.

Location: From Walden, travel a half mile west on Highway 14, then 7.8 miles northwest on County Road 12, and seven miles north on County Road 7.

Trip note: The 563-acre lake offers fishing for big rainbow, cutthroat, and brown trout. The browns can get quite big here, but are quite elusive. This camp is primarily used by fishermen and hunters, with little use by tourists. It can be a good spot for peace, quiet and privacy.

---

7) COWDREY LAKE

Reference: north of Walden; map C2, grid b5.

Campsites, facilities: There are several, undesignated primitive sites for tents, trailers or motor homes up to 18 feet long. Vault toilets are available, but there is **no piped water.** Pets are permitted on leashes. Boat launching facilities are nearby.

Reservations, fee: No reservations necessary; no fee. Open all year with limited winter facilities.

Who to contact: Phone Colorado Division of Wildlife at (303) 297-1192 or write to 6060 Broadway, Denver, CO 80216.

Location: From Walden, travel 7.5 miles north on Highway 125.

Trip note: Small and primitive, this sparse area isn't known to many. Local anglers are the main dwellers here. It is a good base camp for a trout fishing trip. Cowdrey Lake, covering 80 acres, offers decent fishing for rainbow trout. Another option is three miles away at the North Platte River (nine miles of which is managed by the Division of Wildlife). To get there, take Big Creek Lake Road west from Cowdrey. The Michigan River provides another 9.5 miles of river and is located just north of Walden.

---

8) BROWNS PARK

Reference: on Jinks Creek; map C2, grid b7.

Campsites, facilities: There are 28 sites for tents, trailers or motor homes up to 30 feet long. Picnic tables and grills are provided. Vault toilets are also available, but there is **no piped water.** Pets are permitted on leashes.

Reservations, fee: No reservations necessary; no fee. Open June through November.

Who to contact: Phone Roosevelt National Forest at (303) 498-1375 or write to Red Feather Ranger District, University Square Office Building, 1311 South College Avenue, Fort Collins, CO 80524.

Location: From Fort Collins, drive 21 miles north on Highway 287, then turn left on Red Feather Lakes Road and travel 44 miles west. Turn south on Forest Service Road 190 and continue for eight miles to the campground.

Trip note: Here's an ideal spot for a base camp or jump-off spot for a backcountry hiking trip. This campground is set at 8,440 feet and is along Jinks Creek. Adjacent is the Link McIntyre trailhead which accesses many alpine lakes and streams in the Rawah Wilderness up in the Medicine Bow Mountains.

---

9) NORTH FORK POUDRE

Reference: on the North Fork of Cache La Poudre River, Roosevelt National Forest; map C2, grid b8.

Campsites, facilities: There are nine sites for tents, trailers or motor homes up to 30 feet long. Picnic tables and grills are provided. Vault toilets are also available, but there is **no piped water.** Pets are permitted on leashes.

Reservations, fee: No reservations necessary; no fee. Open June through November.

Who to contact: Phone Roosevelt National Forest at (303) 498-1375 or write to Red Feather Ranger District, University Square Office Building, 1311 South College Avenue, Fort Collins, CO 80524.

Location: From Red Feather, drive one mile south on County Road 4 and seven miles west on Forest Service Road 162.

Trip note: This campground is set at 9,150 feet and is along the North Fork of the Cache La Poudre River. A nearby trail follows Killpecker Creek south for about five miles to Middle Bald Mountain. This camp gets heavy use during hunting season.

---

10) BIG BEND

Reference: on Cache La Poudre River, Roosevelt National Forest; map C2, grid b8.

Campsites, facilities: There are nine sites for tents, trailers or motor homes up to 30 feet long. Picnic tables and grills are provided. Water and vault toilets are also available. A sanitary disposal station is located within five miles. Pets are permitted on leashes.

Reservations, fee: No reservations necessary; $7 fee per night. Open year-round.

Who to contact: Phone Roosevelt National Forest at (303) 482-3822 or write to Estes-Poudre Ranger District, 148 Remington Street, Fort Collins, CO 80524.

Location: From Laporte, drive four miles north on US 287 and 41 miles west on Highway 14.

Trip note: This campground is set along the banks of the Cache La Poudre River near the Roaring Creek trailhead which follows Roaring Creek for five miles into the Laramie Mountains. This is one of several camps along the banks of the Cache la Poudre. The Roaring Creek trailhead is located about a half mile west on Highway 14; it follows Roaring Creek north for about five miles.

11) DOWDY LAKE

Reference: on south shore of Dowdy Lake, Roosevelt National Forest; map C2, grid b9.

Campsites, facilities: There are 55 single sites for tents, trailers or motor homes up to 45 feet long, and seven double-occupancy sites. Picnic tables and grills are provided. Piped water and vault toilets are also available. Pets are permitted on leashes.

Reservations, fee: Reserve through MISTIX at (800) 283-CAMP ($6 MISTIX fee); $7 fee per night for singles sites; $14 per night for double sites. Open May through September.

Who to contact: Phone Roosevelt National Forest at (303) 498-1375 or write to Red Feather Ranger District, University Square Office Building, 1311 South College Avenue, Fort Collins, CO 80524.

Location: From Fort Collins, drive 21 miles north on Highway 287, then 22 miles west on Red Feather Lakes Road. Turn north (right) on the Red Feather Lakes access road and drive a short distance, then turn right on Forest Service Road 218 and continue east to the campground.

Trip note: This campground is set at 8,140 feet and is along the south shore of Dowdy Lake. Forest Service Road 216, which leads around the lake, winds north and ends up near the base of Mount Margaret (7,957 feet). This is one of several campgrounds in the immediate area, so pick and choose for the least-used spot.

12) WEST LAKE

Reference: near Red Feather, Roosevelt National Forest; map C2, grid b9.

Campsites, facilities: There are 29 sites for tents, trailers or motor homes up to 45 feet long. Picnic tables and grills are provided. Piped water and vault toilets are also available. Pets are permitted on leashes.

Reservations, fee: Reserve through MISTIX at (800) 283-CAMP ($6 MISTIX fee); $7 fee per night. Open May to mid-November.

Who to contact: Phone Roosevelt National Forest at (303) 498-1375 or write to Red Feather Ranger District, University Square Office Building, 1311 South College Avenue, Fort Collins, CO 80524.

Location: From Fort Collins, drive 21 miles north on Highway 287, then 22 miles west on Red Feather Lakes Road. Turn north (right) on the Red Feather Lakes access road and continue to the campground.

Trip note: This campground is set along the shore of one of the smaller of the Red Feather Lakes. It's not far from Dowdy Lake South Shore Camp. See that trip note for details.

13) SUMMIT LAKE

Reference: near Mount Zirkel Wilderness, Routt National Forest; map C2, grid c2.

Campsites, facilities: There are 16 sites for tents, trailers or motor homes up to 16 feet long. Picnic tables and grills are provided. Vault toilets are available. There is **no piped water.** Pets are permitted on leashes.

Reservations, fee: No reservations necessary; no fee. Open mid-July to early September.

Who to contact: Phone Routt National Forest at (303) 879-1870 or write to Hahns Peak Ranger District, P.O. Box 771212, Steamboat Springs, CO 80477.

Location: Travel two miles on Strawberry Park Road, then two miles on County Road 36, and then 11.5 miles east on Forest Service Road 60.

Trip note: This is an idyllic spot located next to small Summit Lake near Buffalo Pass (elevation 10,300 feet). It is a good jump-off spot for a wilderness adventure. The camp is adjacent to the boundary of Mount Zirkel Wilderness, and a trail from camp accesses numerous backcountry lakes. Fishing prospects are good at Summit Lake. RVers should note that the access road in is quite rough.

14) DRY LAKE

Reference: near Buffalo Pass, Routt National Forest; map C2, grid c2.

Campsites, facilities: There are eight sites for tents, trailers or motor homes up to 16 feet long. Picnic tables and grills are provided. Vault toilets are also available. There is no water available. Pets are permitted on leashes.

Reservations, fee: No reservations necessary; no fee. Open Memorial Day to mid-October.

Who to contact: Phone Routt National Forest at (303) 879-1870 or write to Hahns Peak Ranger District, P.O. Box 771212, Steamboat Springs, CO 80477.

Location: Travel two miles on Strawberry Park Road, then two miles north on County Road 36 and two miles east on Forest Service Road 60.

Trip note: Little-known and intimate, you can count on finding the "quiet America" here. This campground is set at 8,000 feet and is at the bottom of Buffalo Pass. The name? Well, we can tell you that the shoe fits.

15) GRIZZLY CREEK

Reference: near Mount Zirkel Wilderness, Routt National Forest;

map C2, grid c3.

Campsites, facilities: There are 12 sites for tents, trailers or motor homes up to 22 feet long. Picnic tables and grills are provided. Piped water and vault toilets are also available. Pets are permitted on leashes.

Reservations, fee: No reservations necessary; $5 fee per night. Open mid-June to early September.

Who to contact: Phone Routt National Forest at (303) 879-1722, or write to North Park Ranger District, 29587 West US 40, Suite 20, Steamboat Springs, CO 80487.

Location: Travel 13 miles southwest of Walden on Highway 14, 10.5 miles west on County Road 24, and a half mile west on Forest Service Road 60.

Trip note: This small, quiet camp is missed by all the out-of-towners, which is great for those in-the-know (like you). It is set at 8,500 feet beside Grizzly Creek. A trail to the north provides access to the Mount Zirkel Wilderness.

16) HIDDEN LAKES

Reference: in Park Mountain Range, Routt National Forest; map C2, grid c3.

Campsites, facilities: There are nine sites for tents, trailers or motor homes up to 22 feet long. Picnic tables and grills are provided. Piped water and vault toilets are also available. Pets are permitted on leashes.

Reservations, fee: No reservations; $7 fee per night. Open mid-June to early September.

Who to contact: Phone Routt National Forest at (303) 879-1722, or write to North Park Ranger District, 29587 West US 40, Suite 20, Steamboat Springs, CO 80487.

Location: Travel 13 miles southwest of Walden on Highway 14, 10.5 miles west on County Road 24, and two miles west on Forest Service Road 60. Continue four miles south on Forest Service Road 20 to the camp.

Trip note: This is an ideal camp for a multi-day backpacking adventure. It is set at 8,900 feet and near several small lakes. A trail to the south provides access to the other lakes in the Park Mountain Range before arriving in the town of Steamboat Springs. See a Forest Service map for directions.

17) DELAYNEY BUTTE LAKES

Reference: west of Walden; map C2, grid c4.

Campsites, facilities: There are 150 primitive sites for tents, trailers or motor homes up to 18 feet long. Vault toilets are available, but there is **no piped water.** Pets are permitted on leashes. Boat launching facilities are nearby.

Reservations, fee: No reservations necessary; no fee. Open all year with limited winter facilities.

Who to contact: Phone Colorado Division of Wildlife at (303) 297-1192 or write to 6060 Broadway, Denver, CO 80216.

Location: From Walden, travel a half mile west on Highway 14, then 4.5 miles west on County Road 18, and one mile north on County Road 5.

Trip note: This large, primitive campground is set among three small lakes, a perfect site for a fishing trip. Rainbow and brook trout can be found in the East and South Lakes, and big brown trout inhabit the North Lake. Fishing for wild trout is available in the nearby Division of Wildlife stream easements along the North Fork and Roaring Fork of the North Platte River.

---

18) KOA NORTH PARK

Reference: near Colorado State Forest; map C2, grid c6.

Campsites, facilities: There are six tent sites and 20 sites for trailers or motor homes of any length. Camping cabins are also available. Electricity, piped water, sewer hookups and picnic tables are provided. Flush toilets, bottled gas, sanitary disposal services, showers, firewood, a recreation hall, store, laundromat, ice and a playground are also available. Pets and motorbikes are permitted.

Reservations, fee: Reservations accepted; $13-$16 fee per night; camping cabins are $22 per night. MasterCard and Visa accepted. Open late May to mid-November.

Who to contact: Phone (303) 723-4310 or write to State Route Box 90A, Walden, CO 80480.

Location: From Gould, go two miles north on Highway 14.

Trip note: This campground is near the North Fork entrance into Colorado State Forest. It's missed by out-of-towners cruising the interstate. It's quite beautiful, in a forested setting with large, shaded sites. Nearby recreation options include hunting, fishing and hiking. This camp gets especially heavy use by hunters in the fall.

---

19) TUNNEL

Reference: on Laramie River, Roosevelt National Forest; map C2, grid c7.

Campsites, facilities: There are 49 sites for tents, trailers or motor homes up to 30 feet long. Picnic tables and grills are provided. Water and vault toilets are also available. Pets are permitted on leashes.

Reservations, fee: No reservations necessary; $7 fee per night. Open May to September.

Who to contact: Phone Roosevelt National Forest at (303) 498-1375 or write to Red Feather Ranger District, University Square Office Building, 1311 South College Avenue, Fort Collins, CO 80524.

Location: From Fort Collins, drive 11 miles north on Highway 287, then turn west on Highway 14 and travel 16.5 miles. Turn north on County Road 103 and continue for six miles to the camp.

Trip note: This campground is set at 8,600 feet and is along the banks of the Laramie River. The West Branch trailhead is just north of camp and offers access to the Rawah Wilderness, skirting several alpine lakes and intersecting with several other major trails, including the Rawah Trail and the Blue Lake Trail. If it sounds good, that's because it is good.

---

20) COLORADO STATE FOREST

Reference: near Michigan River; map C2, grid c7.

Campsites, facilities: There are 104 sites for tents, trailers or motor homes of any length, and some backcountry sites. Picnic tables and grills are provided. Piped water, vault toilets, firewood and sanitary disposal services are also available. Pets are permitted on leashes. Boat launching facilities are located at Michigan Creek Reservoir.

Reservations, fee: Reserve sites by calling (800) 678-CAMP ($6.75 reservation fee); $6 fee per night plus $3 entrance fee. Open all year with limited winter facilities.

Who to contact: Phone (303) 723-8366 or write to Star Route Box 91, Walden, CO 80480.

Location: From Walden, go 21 miles southeast on Highway 14 to park headquarters.

Trip note: Here's a great state park set 150 miles from Denver. It covers 70,000 acres along the western slopes of the Medicine Bow Mountain Range. It offers 50 miles of hiking trails and 100 miles of horseback riding trails. Fishing can be quite good along the banks of the Michigan River and on the numerous backcountry streams and lakes. Other options include bicycling in the summer and snowmobiling and ice fishing in the winter.

---

21) SLEEPING ELEPHANT

Reference: on Cache La Poudre River, Roosevelt National Forest; map C2, grid c7.

Campsites, facilities: There are 15 sites for tents, trailers or motor homes up to 22 feet long. Picnic tables and grills are provided. Water and vault toilets are also available. A sanitary disposal station is located within five miles. Pets are permitted on leashes.

Reservations, fee: No reservations necessary; $7 fee per night. Open May to late November.

Who to contact: Phone Roosevelt National Forest at (303) 482-3822 or write to Estes-Poudre Ranger District, 148 Remington Street, Fort Collins, CO 80524.

Location: From Fort Collins, drive 11 miles north on Highway 287 and 46 miles west on Highway 14.

Trip note: This campground is set at 7,850 feet and is along the banks of the Cache La Poudre River near Sleeping Elephant Mountain. Someone reportedly decided that the profile of the mountain looked like a snoozing elephant, but as one forest ranger remarked, "You need a lot of imagination to see it."

22) ASPEN GLEN

Reference: on Joe Wrights Creek, Roosevelt National Forest; map C2, grid c7.

Campsites, facilities: There are eight sites for tents, trailers or motor homes up to 30 feet long. Picnic tables and grills are provided. Pit toilets and water are available. Pets are permitted on leashes. Boat launching facilities are nearby at Chambers Lake.

Reservations, fee: No reservations necessary; $7 fee per night. Open mid-May to mid-November.

Who to contact: Phone Roosevelt National Forest at (303) 498-1375 or write to Red Feather Ranger District, University Square Office Building, 1311 South College Avenue, Fort Collins, CO 80524.

Location: From Fort Collins, drive 11 miles north on Highway 287 and 51 miles west on Highway 14.

Trip note: This campground is set at 8,660 feet and is along the banks of Joe Wrights Creek which is two miles from Chambers Lake, Lost Lake and Barnes Meadow Reservoir. Trails from that area access numerous smaller lakes in the Comanche Peak Wilderness. See a Forest Service map for options. Also note other campgrounds listed in the area.

23) GRAND VIEW

Reference: on Long Draw Reservoir, Roosevelt National Forest; map C2, grid c8.

Campsites, facilities: There are eight tent sites. Picnic tables and grills are provided. Pit toilets are also available, but there is **no piped water.** Pets are permitted on leashes.

Reservations, fee: No reservations necessary; no fee. Open mid-June to mid-November.

Who to contact: Phone Roosevelt National Forest at (303) 498-1375 or write to Red Feather Ranger District, University Square Office Building, 1311 South College Avenue, Fort Collins, CO 80524.

Location: From Fort Collins drive 11 miles north on Highway 287 and 24 miles west on Highway 14. Turn south on Forest Service Road 156 and drive 10 miles to the camp.

Trip note: This remote campground is set at the west end of Long Draw Reservoir on the northern boundary of Rocky Mountain National Park. The nearby Neota trailhead, 1.5 miles to the west, follows Neota Creek north for several miles into the Neota Wilderness.

24) LONG DRAW

Reference: on Long Draw Reservoir, Roosevelt National Forest; map C2, grid c8.

Campsites, facilities: There are 31 sites for tents, trailers or motor homes up to 45 feet long. Picnic tables and grills are provided. Vault toilets are also available, but there is **no piped water.** Pets are permitted on leashes. Boat docks are nearby at Long Draw Reservoir.

Reservations, fee: No reservations necessary; no fee. Open mid-June to late September.

Who to contact: Phone Roosevelt National Forest at (303) 498-1375 or write to Red Feather Ranger District, University Square Office Building, 1311 South College Avenue, Fort Collins, CO 80524.

Location: From Fort Collins, drive 11 miles north on Highway 287 and 24 miles west on Highway 14. Turn south on Forest Service Road 156 and drive seven miles.

Trip note: This campground is set near the east end of Long Draw Reservoir on the northern boundary of Rocky Mountain National Park. The nearby Corral Creek trailhead follows the Cache la Poudre River into Rocky Mountain National Park and branches out in several directions from there. Options? You got a bundle of 'em.

25) GLEN ECHO RESORT

Reference: on Cache La Poudre River; map C2, grid c8.

Campsites, facilities: There are 75 sites for trailers or motor homes up to 30 feet long. Cabins are also available for rent. Electricity, piped water, sewer hookups and picnic tables are provided. Flush toilets, bottled gas, showers, store, coffee shop, laundromat, ice and a playground are also available. Sanitary disposal services are located within one mile. Pets are permitted on leashes.

Reservations, fee: Reservations accepted; $15-$20 fee per night; MasterCard and Visa accepted. Open May to November.

Who to contact: Phone (303) 881-2208 or write to 31503 Poudre Canyon Drive, Bellevue, CO 80512.

Location: From Fort Collins, travel 10 miles northwest on US 287 and 31 miles west on Highway 14.

Trip note: This privately-owned campground is set in the canyon of the Cache La Poudre River in the Roosevelt National Forest. This is the country of high peaks, steep canyon walls, sparse spruce and lodgepole pines. There are some good hiking trails on adjacent national forest land.

26) TOM BENNETT

Reference: near Comanche Peak Wilderness, Roosevelt National Forest; map C2, grid c8.

Campsites, facilities: There are eight sites for tents, trailers or motor homes up to 16 feet long. Picnic tables and grills are provided. Vault toilets are also available, but there is **no piped water.** Pets are permitted on leashes.

Reservations, fee: No reservations necessary; no fee. Open mid-May to late October.

Who to contact: Phone Roosevelt National Forest at (303) 482-3822 or write to 148 Remington Street, Fort Collins, CO 80524.

Location: From Laporte, go four miles north on US 287, then 27 miles west on Highway 14, and 11 miles south on County Road 131.

Trip note: This campground is set at 9,000 feet and is near Cache la Poudre River. It's a good starting point for a wilderness adventure. Adjacent to the camp is the Beaver Creek trailhead which provides access to several lakes and streams within the Comanche Peak Wilderness. Also nearby is the Stormy Peaks trailhead which heads south into Rocky Mountain National Park.

---

27) MOUNTAIN PARK

Reference: on Cache La Poudre River, Roosevelt National Park; map C2, grid c9.

Campsites, facilities: There are 45 sites for tents, trailers or motor homes up to 45 feet long. Picnic tables and grills are provided. Piped water and vault toilets are also available. Showers, a sanitary disposal station, a store, coffee shop, laundromat and ice are located within five miles. Pets are permitted on leashes.

Reservations, fee: Reserve through MISTIX at (800) 283-CAMP ($6 MISTIX fee); $7 fee per night. Open mid-May to late September.

Who to contact: Phone Roosevelt National Forest at (303) 482-3822 or write to Estes-Poudre Ranger District, 148 Remington Street, Fort Collins, CO 80524.

Location: From Laporte, drive four miles north on US 287 and 25 miles west on Highway 14.

Trip note: This campground is set along the banks of the Cache La Poudre River, near the Cache La Poudre Wilderness. It's a good base camp for a hiking trip. The Mount McConnell Trail is located nearby.

---

28) KELLY FLATS

Reference: on Cache La Poudre River, Roosevelt National Forest; map C2, grid c9.

Campsites, facilities: There are 23 sites for tents, trailers or motor homes up to 45 feet long. Picnic tables and grills are provided. Piped water and vault toilets are also available. A sanitary disposal station is located within five miles. Pets are permitted on leashes.

Reservations, fee: No reservations necessary; $7 fee per night. Open mid-May to mid-November.

Who to contact: Phone Roosevelt National Forest at (303) 482-3822 or write to Estes-Poudre Ranger District, 148 Remington Street, Fort Collins, CO 80524.

Location: From Laporte, drive four miles north on US 287 and 26 miles west on Highway 14.

Trip note: This campground is set at 6,750 feet and is along the banks of the Cache La Poudre River, right on the border of the Cache La Poudre Wilderness. You can hop onto the Mount McConnell trailhead here. With piped water, it's a more attractive alternative than several other camps in this area.

---

29) STOVE PRAIRIE LANDING

Reference: on Cache La Poudre River, Roosevelt National Forest; map C2, grid c9.

Campsites, facilities: There are nine sites for tents, trailers or motor homes up to 30 feet long. Picnic tables and grills are provided. Vault toilets are also available, but there is **no piped water.** A sanitary disposal station is located within five miles. Pets are permitted on leashes.

Reservations, fee: No reservations necessary; no fee. Open all year.

Who to contact: Phone Roosevelt National Forest at (303) 482-3822 or write to Estes-Poudre Ranger District, 148 Remington Street, Fort Collins, CO 80524.

Location: Travel four miles north of Laporte on US 287 and 17 miles west on Highway 14.

Trip note: This campground is one of several campgrounds set along the banks of the Cache La Poudre River. It's primitive with little camper traffic. The Cache La Poudre Wilderness lies just across the highway. An excellent hike is the trail to Mount McConnell; see previous two camps for details.

---

30) SKI TOWN

Reference: near Steamboat Springs; map C2, grid d2.

Campsites, facilities: There are 37 tent sites and 73 sites for trailers or motor homes of any length. Electricity, piped water, sewer hookups and picnic tables are provided. Flush toilets, bottled gas, sanitary disposal services, showers, firewood, recreation hall, a store, laundromat, ice, heated pool, hot tub and a playground are also available. Pets are permitted on leashes.

Reservations, fee: Reservations accepted; $14.50-$18.75 fee per night; MasterCard and Visa accepted. Open all year.

Who to contact: Phone (303) 879-0273 or write to 29135 West US 40, Steamboat Springs, CO 80487.

Location: From the town of Steamboat Springs, go two miles west on US 40.

Trip note: A good year-around spot, particularly for motor home cruisers. The camp is set along the Yampa River, with grassy, shaded sites. Fishing can be excellent in the Yampa River. For those without a pole, there is a miniature golf course at the park, and bike rentals are available. Other nearby recreation options include an 18-hole golf course, a riding stable and tennis courts.

31) WALTON CREEK

Reference: southeast of Steamboat Springs, Routt National Forest; map C2, grid d3.

Campsites, facilities: There are 14 sites for tents, trailers or motor homes up to 22 feet long. Picnic tables are provided along with well water. There are vault toilets. Pets are permitted on leashes.

Reservations, fee: Reservations accepted; $6 fee per night. Open July to October.

Who to contact: Phone Routt National Forest at (303) 879-1870 or write to Hahns Peak Ranger District, Steamboat Springs, CO 80487.

Location: From the town of Steamboat Springs, drive 17 miles southeast on US 40.

Trip note: This is a nice spot set along Walton Creek, with good fishing prospects. It's in a small, cozy area right off the highway. Excellent hiking opportunities can be found in the nearby Rabbit Ears Pass Area. You can also hike or mountain bike to Walton Peak via Forest Service Roads 302 and 251.

32) MEADOWS

Reference: near Dumont Lake, Routt National Forest; map C2, grid d3.

Campsites, facilities: There are 30 sites for tents, trailers or motor homes up to 22 feet long. Picnic tables are provided along with piped water. There are vault toilets. Pets are permitted on leashes.

Reservations, fee: Reserve through MISTIX at (800) 283-CAMP ($6 MISTIX fee); $6 fee per night. Open July to late October.

Who to contact: Phone Routt National Forest at (303) 879-1870 or write to Hahns Peak Ranger District, Steamboat Springs, CO 80487.

Location: From the town of Steamboat Springs, drive 15 miles southeast on US 40.

Trip note: A nice spot for folks cruising US 40. It's close to the highway, yet in a serene location, surrounded by tall evergreens. Some good trout streams are nearby. Fishing can be good for brook trout during the evening bite in early summer. A sidelight is that the area is loaded with elk, and nearby Dumont Lake can provide a sidetrip.

33) DUMONT LAKE

Reference: southeast of Steamboat Springs, Routt National Forest; map C2, grid d3.

Campsites, facilities: There are 22 sites for tents, trailers or motor homes up to 22 feet long. Picnic tables and grills are provided. Well water and pit toilets are also available. Some of the facilities, including three campsites, are **wheelchair accessible**. Pets are permitted on leashes.

Reservations, fee: Reserve through MISTIX at (800) 283-CAMP ($6 MISTIX fee); $7 fee per night. Open July to late October.

Who to contact: Phone Routt National Forest at (303) 879-1870 or write to Hahns Peak Ranger District, Steamboat Springs, CO 80487.

Location: From the town of Steamboat Springs, drive 22 miles southeast on US 40 and 1.5 miles northeast on Forest Service Road 312.

Trip note: This campground is located about 500 yards from the shoreline of Dumont Lake, bordering on the Continental Divide on top of the Park Range. Sensational mountain views can be had from the camp. Picnic facilities are located along the lake and are **wheelchair accessible.** Hiking, boating (electric motors only), fishing, mountain biking and birdwatching are among the recreation options here. Spectacular wildflower displays can be found nearby in the spring.

---

34) SEYMOUR LAKE

Reference: southwest of Walden; map C2, grid d4.

Campsites, facilities: There are several, undesignated primitive primitive sites for tents, trailers or motor homes up to 18 feet long. Vault toilets are available, but there is **no piped water.** Pets are permitted on leashes. Boat launching facilities are nearby.

Reservations, fee: No reservations necessary; no fee. Open all year with limited winter facilities.

Who to contact: Phone Colorado Division of Wildlife at (303) 297-1192 or write to 6060 Broadway, Denver, CO 80216.

Location: From Walden, travel 14 miles southwest on Highway 14, one mile on County Road 28, three miles on County Road 11. Then take County Road 28B and follow for a half mile to the campground.

Trip note: This is a tiny, primitive camp that doesn't offer much in the way of amenities, but it is private and quiet. It gets heavy use from anglers who know about the sometimes excellent fishing on this 11-acre lake. Rainbow trout are the standard fare. A Routt National Forest map details backcountry roads and other smaller lakes in the area.

---

35) PINES

Reference: on the South Fork of Michigan River, Routt National Forest; map C2, grid d6.

Campsites, facilities: There are 11 sites for tents, trailers or motor homes up to 22 feet long. Picnic tables and grills are provided. Piped water and vault toilets are also available. Pets are permitted on leashes.

Reservations, fee: No reservations necessary; $6 fee per night. Open mid-June to early September.

Who to contact: Phone Routt National Forest at (303) 879-1722, or write to North Park Ranger District, 29587 West US 40, Suite 20, Steamboat Springs, CO 80487.

Location: Travel 21 miles southeast of Walden on Highway 14 to Gould. From Gould, drive four miles southeast on Forest Service Road 740.

Trip note: Rustic and private, this campground is set at 9,200 feet and is along the South Fork of the Michigan River. A dirt road travels east to a pair of tiny alpine lakes, providing a possible excursion, and Forest Service Roads 780 and 781 to the south (both four-wheel-drive roads) lead to the trio of Ranger Lakes in the Colorado State Forest. See a Forest Service map for specifics.

---

36) ASPEN

Reference: on the South Fork of Michigan River, Routt National Forest; map C2, grid d6.

Campsites, facilities: There are seven sites for tents, trailers or motor homes up to 22 feet long. Picnic tables and grills are provided. Piped water and vault toilets are also available. Pets are permitted on leashes.

Reservations, fee: No reservations necessary; $6 fee per night. Open mid-June to early September.

Who to contact: Phone Routt National Forest at (303) 879-1722, or write to North Park Ranger District, 29587 West US 40, Suite 20, Steamboat Springs, CO 80487.

Location: Travel 21 miles southeast of Walden on Highway 14 to Gould. From Gould drive one mile southwest on Forest Service Road 740 and 100 yards west on Forest Service Road 741.

Trip note: This spot is just enough off the beaten path to get missed by just about everybody. The camp has an altitude of 8,900 feet and is along the South Fork of the Michigan River. It's just a few miles from the entrance to the Colorado State Forest. See trip note for Pines Camp for recreation possibilities.

---

37) WINDING RIVER

Reference: near Rocky Mountain National Park; map C2, grid d7.

Campsites, facilities: There are 80 tent sites and 77 sites for trailers or motor homes of any length. Electricity, piped water, sewer hookups and picnic tables are provided. Flush toilets, sanitary disposal services, showers, firewood, a store, ice and a playground are also available. Pets are permitted on leashes.

Reservations, fee: Reservations accepted; $14-$18 fee per night; MasterCard and Visa accepted. Open year-round.

Who to contact: Phone (303) 627-3215 or write to P.O. Box 629, Grand Lake, CO 80447.

Location: Drive one mile north of the town of Grand Lake on US 34 and 1.5 miles west on County Road 491 West (a paved and gravel road).

Trip note: This camp is set just outside the southwest edge of Rocky Mountain National Park. It's in a pretty setting, with grassy sites shaded by lodgepole pines. Shadow Mountain Reservoir is set to the south, and several other lakes are in the vicinity.

---

38) TIMBER CREEK

Reference: north of Grand Lake, Rocky Mountain National Park; map C2, grid d7.

Campsites, facilities: There are 50 tent sites and 50 sites for trailers or motor homes up to 30 feet long. Picnic tables are provided. Flush toilets, sanitary disposal services, firewood and ice are also available. Pets are permitted on leashes.

Reservations, fee: No reservations; $7 fee per night. Open all year with limited winter facilities.

Who to contact: Phone Rocky Mountain National Park at (303) 586-2371 or write to Estes Park, CO 80517.

Location: From the town of Grand Lake, go 10 miles north on US 34.

Trip note: This is one of six campgrounds in Rocky Mountain National Park. This fantastic parkland attracts visitors from across America. It offers the full spectrum of camping possibilities from rocky, glacier-created landscapes of the high country, to alpine meadows, to valleys with a sea of conifers. An option is backcountry camping where five primitive walk-in camps are available. Check with park headquarters for permit information. The country is loaded with wildlife including elk, bighorn sheep, deer and marmots.

---

39) DENVER CREEK

Reference: northwest of Granby, Arapaho National Forest; map C2, grid d7.

Campsites, facilities: There are 25 sites for tents, trailers or motor homes up to 30 feet long. Picnic tables are provided. There is water available. Pets are permitted on leashes.

Reservations, fee: No reservations necessary; $7 fee per night. Open early June to early October.

Who to contact: Phone Arapaho National Forest at (303) 887-3301 or write to Sulphur Ranger District, 62429 Highway 40, P.O. Box 10, Granby, CO 80446.

Location: From Granby, go three miles northwest on US 40 and 12 miles northwest on Highway 125.

Trip note: This primitive camp is set at the confluence of Denver and Willow Creeks and has an altitude of 8,600 feet. It's a decent base camp for a hiking trip. A nearby two-mile trail cuts into Arapaho National

Forest. It's all detailed on the Forest Service map. If you're looking for a quiet camp, note that this one is located just two miles east of an airstrip. Sawmill Gulch Camp provides a more secluded option.

40) NATIONAL PARK RESORT

Reference: near Estes Park, Rocky Mountain National Park; map C2, grid d8.

Campsites, facilities: There are 82 tent sites and 20 sites for trailers or motor homes of any length. Electricity, piped water, sewer hookups and picnic tables are provided. Flush toilets, Sanitary disposal services, showers, firewood and ice are also available. A store, coffee shop and laundromat are located within one mile. Pets are permitted on leashes.

Reservations, fee: Reservations accepted; $16.50-$18.50 fee per night. Open May to late September.

Who to contact: Phone (303) 586-4563 or write to Moraine Route, Estes Park, CO 80517.

Location: From Estes Park, go west about five miles on US 34 to the Fall River entrance of Rocky Mountain National Park.

Trip note: This is a good jump-off point for an adventure into Rocky Mountain National Park. A park map details the options. Nearby recreation options include a golf course, hiking trails and a riding stable.

41) KOA ESTES PARK

Reference: near Rocky Mountain National Park; map C2, grid d9.

Campsites, facilities: There are 20 tent sites and 65 sites for trailers or motor homes of any length. Camping cabins are also available. Electricity, piped water, sewer hookups and picnic tables are provided. Flush toilets, sanitary disposal services, showers, firewood, recreation hall, a store, laundromat, ice, miniature golf course and a playground are also available. A coffee shop is located within one mile. Pets and motorbikes are permitted.

Reservations, fee: Reservations accepted; $13-$16 fee per night. Camping cabins are $22 per night. MasterCard and Visa accepted. Open April through October.

Who to contact: Phone (303) 586-2888 or write to Devils Gulch, Estes Park, CO 80517.

Location: From Estes Park, go 1.5 miles east on US 34.

Trip note: This is a privately developed campground set just outside the boundaries of Rocky Mountain National Park. Though not quite as scenic as the National Park camps, it does have incredible mountain views and it offers a less-crowded alternative and close proximity to the amenities in town. Estes Park is a quaint little town, with lots of antique stores and rock shops for tourists. It is also the home of the huge Stanley Hotel, made famous by the movie *The Shining*.

42) PARADISE TRAVEL PARK

Reference: near Big Thompson River; map C2, grid d9.

Campsites, facilities: There are three tent sites and 30 sites for trailers or motor homes up to 35 Feet. Electricity, piped water, sewer hookups and picnic tables are provided. Flush toilets, sanitary disposal services, showers, laundromat and ice are also available. Bottled gas and a coffee shop are located within one mile. Pets are not permitted.

Reservations, fee: Reservations recommended; $15-$18 fee per night. Open May to mid-October.

Who to contact: Phone (303) 586-5513 or write to Moraine Route, Estes Park, CO 80517.

Location: From Estes Park, go two miles southwest on US 36 and a half mile west on Highway 66.

Trip note: This is a small, private park for motor homes. It's set near the Big Thompson River and the entrance to Rocky Mountain National Park. It has shaded sites, some on the river banks. This park is classified as "adult oriented," meaning it's probably best to leave the little ones behinds. Nearby recreation options include a golf course, hiking trails and bike paths. See trip note for Estes Park KOA for area information.

43) MARY'S LAKE

Reference: near Rocky Mountain National Park; map C2, grid d9.

Campsites, facilities: There are 40 tent sites and 110 sites for trailers or motor homes of any length. Electricity, piped water, sewer hookups and picnic tables are provided. Flush toilets, bottled gas, sanitary disposal services, showers, firewood, recreation hall, a store, laundromat, ice, playground and a swimming pool are also available. Pets are permitted on leashes.

Reservations, fee: Reservations accepted; $15.50-$19.50 fee per night; MasterCard and Visa accepted. Open mid-May to late September.

Who to contact: Phone (303) 586-4411 or write to P.O. Box 2514, Estes Park, CO 80517.

Location: From Estes Park, go 2.5 miles south on Highway 7 and 1.5 miles west on Peakview Drive.

Trip note: This is one of several private campgrounds just outside the eastern border of Rocky Mountain National Park. It offers large, comfortable campsites with mountain views. Nearby recreation options include an 18-hole golf course and hiking trails. See trip note for Estes Park KOA for other details.

44) SPRUCE LAKE RV PARK

Reference: near Mary's Lake; map C2, grid d9.

Campsites, facilities: There are 110 sites for trailers or motor homes of any length. Electricity, piped water, sewer hookups and picnic tables are provided. Flush toilets, sanitary disposal services, showers, recreation hall, cable TV, a store, bottled gas, laundromat, ice, playground, miniature golf course, trout pond and a swimming pool are also available. A coffee shop is located within one mile. Pets are permitted on leashes.

Reservations, fee: Reservations accepted; $18-$21 fee per night; MasterCard and Visa accepted. Open all year.

Who to contact: Phone (303) 586-2889 or write to P.O. Box 2497, Estes Park, CO 80517.

Location: Drive 1.3 miles west of Estes Park on US 36, then 300 yards south on Mary's Lake Road.

Trip note: This is a big motor home park, no tent camping allowed. The sites are large, airy and clean, some on the river banks. It is just far enough out of town to provide a feeling of separation, yet it's close to all facilities. Fishing is available out of camp. Nearby recreation options include an 18-hole golf course, hiking trails, bike paths, and a riding stable. Mary's Lake is nearby.

---

45) GLACIER BASIN

Reference: near Glacier Creek, Rocky Mountain National Park; map C2, grid d8.

Campsites, facilities: There are 150 sites for tents, trailers or motor homes up to 30 feet long. There is also a group area that will accommodate up to 50 people. Picnic tables and grills are provided. Flush toilets, sanitary disposal services, firewood and ice are also available. Pets are permitted on leashes.

Reservations, fee: Reserve through MISTIX by calling (800) 283-CAMP; $10 fee per night for single sites, $20-$50 per night for group area. Open early June to early September.

Who to contact: Phone Rocky Mountain National Park at (303) 586-2371 or write to Estes Park, CO 80517.

Location: Drive nine miles southwest of Estes Park on Bear Lake Road.

Trip note: This campground is set at 8,600 feet and located near Glacier Creek in spectacular Rocky Mountain National Park. It's also excellent for large group trips, since it is the only camp with group facilities. Nearby trails access numerous lakes and streams. See the trip notes for Timber Creek and Aspenglen Camps for backcountry camping information and park details.

---

46) MORAINE PARK

Reference: near Big Thompson River, Rocky Mountain National Park; map C2, grid d8.

Campsites, facilities: There are 247 sites for tents, trailers or motor homes up to 30 feet long. Picnic tables and grills are provided. Flush toilets, piped water, sanitary disposal services, firewood and ice are also available. Pets are permitted on leashes.

Reservations, fee: Reserve through MISTIX at (800) 283-CAMP; $10 fee per night. Open all year.

Who to contact: Phone Rocky Mountain National Park at (303) 586-2371 or write to Estes Park, CO 80517.

Location: From Estes Park, travel seven miles west on Highway 36.

Trip note: This is one of the biggest campgrounds of the national parks in the Rockies. It is set near Big Thompson River not far from the visitor center. Hiking, horseback riding and fishing are some of the options here. See trip note for Timber Creek Camp for park details.

---

47) ASPENGLEN

Reference: near Fall River, Rocky Mountain National Park; map C2, grid d9.

Campsites, facilities: There are 54 sites for tents, trailers or motor homes up to 30 feet. Picnic tables and grills are provided. Flush toilets, piped water, firewood and ice are also available. Pets are permitted on leashes.

Reservations, fee: No reservations necessary; $7 fee per night. Open late May to mid-September.

Who to contact: Phone Rocky Mountain National Park at (303) 586-2371 or write to Estes Park, CO 80517.

Location: From Estes Park, drive five miles west on US 34.

Trip note: This is a beautiful campground in Rocky Mountain National Park and is set beside the Fall River near the Bighorn Ranger Station. Hiking trails access many lakes and backcountry streams. Primitive backcountry campsites are available. For permit information, contact the backcountry office at Rocky Mountain National Park at the phone number and address listed above.

---

48) LYNX PASS

Reference: near Toponas, Routt National Forest; map C2, grid e3.

Campsites, facilities: There are 11 sites for tents, trailers or motor homes up to 22 feet long. Picnic tables, piped water and vault toilets are provided. Pets are permitted on leashes.

Reservations, fee: No reservations necessary; $6 fee per night. Open mid-June to mid-November.

Who to contact: Phone Routt National Forest at (303) 638-4516 or write to Yampa Ranger District, P.O. Box 7, Yampa, CO 80483.

Location: From Toponas, drive a half mile south on Highway 131. Turn east on Highway 134 and drive eight miles, then turn north on Forest Service Road 270 and continue for 2.5 miles to the campground.

Trip note: This is a popular, pretty campground set at 8,900 feet elevation. It is relatively primitive, but drinking water is supplied, and there are numerous recreation options in the immediate vicinity. La Gunita Lake is nearby, with good fishing prospects, and there are miles of hiking trails in the area. You can access Morrison Divide Trail directly from the campground. See a Forest Service map for details.

---

49) SAWMILL GULCH

Reference: on Willow Creek, Arapaho National Forest; map C2, grid e7.

Campsites, facilities: There are five sites for tents, trailers or motor homes up to 30 feet long. Picnic tables are provided. Water is available. Pets are permitted on leashes.

Reservations, fee: No reservations necessary; $7 fee per night. Open early June to early October.

Who to contact: Phone Arapaho National Forest at (303) 887-3301 or write to Sulphur Ranger District, 62429 Highway 40, P.O. Box 10, Granby, CO 80446.

Location: Drive three miles northwest of Granby on US 40 and 10 miles northwest on Highway 125.

Trip note: This is small, quiet camp set just off the road, yet it's along pretty Willow Creek. It's primarily a layover spot, but hiking trails are available in the surrounding Arapaho National Forest. The camp is at 8,500 feet. Arapaho National Recreation Area is located to the southeast, providing fishing, boating and swimming options.

---

50) STILLWATER

Reference: on Lake Granby, Arapaho National Forest; map C2, grid e7.

Campsites, facilities: There are 148 sites for tents, trailers or motor homes up to 45 feet long. Picnic tables are provided. Piped water and flush toilets are also available. Pets are permitted on leashes. A boat ramp is nearby.

Reservations, fee: Reserve through MISTIX at (800) 283-CAMP ($6 MISTIX fee); $9 fee per night. Open late May to early September.

Who to contact: Phone Arapaho National Forest at (303) 887-3301 or write to Sulphur Ranger District, 62429 Highway 40, P.O. Box 10, Grand Lake, CO 80447.

Location: From the town of Grand Lake, go 6.5 miles southwest on US 34.

Trip note: This is one of the largest national forest campgrounds in Colorado, and it's a beautiful spot set on the east shore of Lake Granby. You can choose from a multitude of activities here, ranging from waterskiing to fishing to just lying in the sun. Trailheads on the southeast end of the lake lead into the adjacent Indian Peaks Wilderness.

---

51) WILLOW CREEK

Reference: on Willow Creek Reservoir, Arapaho National Forest;

map C2, grid e7.

Campsites, facilities: There are 35 sites for tents, trailers or motor homes up to 20 feet long. Picnic tables are provided. Pets are permitted on leashes. Boat launching facilities are nearby.

Reservations, fee: No reservations necessary; $7 fee per night. Open late May to early September.

Who to contact: Phone Arapaho National Forest at (303) 887-3331 or write to Sulphur Ranger District, 62429 Highway 40, P.O. Box 10, Granby, CO 80447.

Location: From Granby, drive approximately six miles northeast on US 34 and then 3.5 miles west on County Road 40.

Trip note: This is beautiful spot on Willow Creek Reservoir, set in the surrounding Arapaho National Forest. It is set a few miles west of huge Lake Granby, which affords several recreation alternatives.

---

52) ARAPAHO BAY

Reference: on Lake Granby, Arapaho National Forest; map C2, grid e8.

Campsites, facilities: There are 84 sites for tents, trailers or motor homes up to 35 feet long. Picnic tables are provided. Water is also available. Pets are permitted on leashes. Boat launching facilities are nearby.

Reservations, fee: Reserve through MISTIX at (800) 283-CAMP ($6 MISTIX fee); $9 fee per night. Open late May to early September.

Who to contact: Phone Arapaho National Forest at (303) 887-3301 or write to Sulphur Ranger District, 62429 Highway 40, P.O. Box 10, Granby, CO 80447.

Location: Drive 6.5 miles northeast of Granby on US 34 and nine miles east on County Road 6.

Trip note: This camp is set on the east end of Lake Granby. It can be used as a base camp for a fishing trip on the lake or used as "home" for a multi-day backpack adventure into the nearby wildlands. It is located right on the border of the Indian Peaks Wilderness, with a trail routed out of camp along Roaring Fork Creek. This is a large camp, second in popularity only to Stillwater Camp, so get your reservation in as early as possible, and expect crowds.

---

53) LONGS PEAK

Reference: south of Estes Park, Rocky Mountain National Park; map C2, grid e9.

Campsites, facilities: There are 26 tent sites. Picnic tables are provided. Piped water, flush toilets, firewood and ice are available. Pets are permitted on leashes.

Reservations, fee: No reservations; $7 fee per night. Open all year.

Who to contact: Phone Rocky Mountain National Park at (303) 586-

2371 or write to Estes Park, CO 80517.

Location: From Estes Park, go 11 miles south on Highway 7, then one mile west.

Trip note: This camp is right on the border of Rocky Mountain National Park. It is used heavily by rock climbers and mountaineers attempting to climb Longs Peak (14,255 feet), one of the famed Colorado "fourteeners." If you want to attempt it yourself, plan for a full day of rigorous hiking, and check the weather. It is a beautiful area, with several other hiking trails in the vicinity.

---

54) OLIVE RIDGE

Reference: near Rocky Mountain National Park, Roosevelt National Forest; map C2, grid e9.

Campsites, facilities: There are 56 sites for tents, trailers or motor homes up to 40 feet long. Picnic tables and vault toilets are provided. Piped water is available. Some facilities are **wheelchair accessible.** Pets are permitted on leashes.

Reservations, fee: Reserve through MISTIX at (800) 283-CAMP ($6 MISTIX fee); $8 fee per night. Open May to late October.

Who to contact: Phone Roosevelt National Forest at (303) 444-6600 or write to Boulder Ranger District, 2995 Baseline Road, Room 110, Boulder, CO 80303.

Location: From Estes Park, go 15 miles south on Highway 7. Turn right and follow the signs to the campground.

Trip note: This park is set outside the boundary of Rocky Mountain National Park. It is a good base camp for backpackers, with nearby hiking trails that lead into Rocky Mountain National Park and many small, hidden lakes. This is a popular camp, often fill to capacity on weekends and holidays, so get your reservation in early.

---

55) PEACEFUL VALLEY

Reference: near Middle St. Vrain Creek, Roosevelt National Forest; map C2, grid e9.

Campsites, facilities: There are 15 sites for tents, trailers or motor homes up to 30 feet long. Picnic tables and vault toilets are provided. Piped water is available. Pets are permitted on leashes.

Reservations, fee: No reservations; $7 fee per night. Open mid-May to late October.

Who to contact: Phone Roosevelt National Forest at (303) 444-6600 or write to Boulder Ranger District, 2995 Baseline Road, Room 110, Boulder, CO 80303.

Location: From Lyons, go 11 miles west on Highway 7, then four miles south on Highway 72. Turn right and proceed a quarter mile to the campground.

Trip note: This camp is set at 8,500 feet elevation, adjacent to

Middle St. Vrain Creek. Hiking and fishing are popular recreation activities here. Since no reservations are accepted here, it's advisable to get here as early as possible to insure that you get a site. On the drive in, look to the west for prime views of one of Colorado's famed "fourteeners," Longs Peak (14,251 feet). If this camp is full, try Camp Dick one mile to the west.

---

56) CAMP DICK

Reference: near Middle St. Vrain Creek, Roosevelt National Forest; map C2, grid e9.

Campsites, facilities: There are 34 sites for tents, trailers or motor homes up to 40 feet long. Picnic tables are provided. Water is available. Pets are permitted on leashes.

Reservations, fee: No reservations; $7 fee per night. Open mid-May to late October.

Who to contact: Phone Roosevelt National Forest at (303) 444-6600 or write to Boulder Ranger District, 2995 Baseline Road, Room 110, Boulder, CO 80303.

Location: Drive 11 miles west of Lyons on Highway 7, then four miles south on Highway 72. Turn right and drive one mile west to the campground.

Trip note: This camp is set adjacent to Middle St. Vrain Creek, in a glaciated valley. It's an ideal spot for four-wheel-drive vehicles. Via a rugged dirt road, you can reach Beaver Reservoir and Stapp Lake for sidetrips. Hikers can take the Middle St. Vrain trail to venture into the Indian Peaks Wilderness. The camp is set at 8,650 feet elevation.

---

57) HORSESHOE

Reference: near Stillwater Reservoir, Routt National Forest; map C2, grid f1.

Campsites, facilities: There are seven sites for tents, trailers or motor homes up to 30 feet long. Hand-pumped water, picnic tables and grills are provided. Vault toilets and trash collection are available. Pets are permitted on leashes on leash.

Reservations, fee: No reservations necessary; $7 fee per night. Open mid-June through October.

Who to contact: Phone Routt National Forest at (303) 638-4516 or write to Yampa Ranger District, P.O. Box 7, Yampa, CO 80483.

Location: Drive 31 miles south of the town of Steamboat Springs on Highway 131 to Yampa. Travel seven miles southwest of Yampa on County Route 7 and 8.1 miles southwest on Forest Service Road 900.

Trip note: This campground is set next to Cold Springs Camp. It is at 10,000 feet elevation near the Flat Tops Wilderness. There are several trail accesses here: East Fork Trail, Bear River Trail and North Derby Trail. No motors are permitted on Stillwater Reservoir, making fishing from a canoe, raft or pram ideal. This is a beautiful area, known for its exceptional scenery and wildlife.

58) BEAR LAKE

Reference: near Yampa Reservoir, Routt National Forest; map C2, grid f1.

Campsites, facilities: There are 29 sites for tents, trailers or motor homes up to 30 feet long. Picnic tables and grills are provided. Piped water and vault toilets are also available. Pets are permitted on leashes on leash. Some sites are **wheelchair accessible,** as are restrooms and fishing area.

Reservations, fee: No reservations necessary; $7 fee per night. Open mid-June to mid-October.

Who to contact: Phone Routt National Forest at (303) 638-4516 or write to Yampa Ranger District, P.O. Box 7, Yampa, CO 80483.

Location: Drive 31 miles south of the town of Steamboat Springs on Highway 131 to Yampa. Travel seven miles southwest of Yampa on County Route 7 and 5.9 miles southwest on Forest Service Road 900.

Trip note: This campground is set at 9,600 feet and is near the shore of Yampa Reservoir and the banks of Bear River. A nearby trail (Mandall Trail) provides access to backcountry lakes. Boating (row boats, canoes, rafts) is available.

59) STILLWATER

Reference: near Stillwater Reservoir, Routt National Forest; map C2, grid f1.

Campsites, facilities: There are 29 sites for tents, trailers or motor homes of any length. Picnic tables, piped water, and vault toilets are provided. Some facilities are **wheelchair accessible.** Pets are permitted on leashes. Boat launching facilities are available nearby at Stillwater Reservoir.

Reservations, fee: No reservations necessary; $7 fee per night. Open mid-June through October.

Who to contact: Phone Routt National Forest at (303) 638-4516 or write to Yampa Ranger District, P.O. Box 7, Yampa, CO 80483.

Location: From Steamboat Springs, drive 31 miles south on Highway 131 to Yampa. Turn southwest on County Road 7 and drive seven miles, then continue southwest on Forest Service Road 900 for 5.9 miles.

Trip note: This is a prime camp, set in the high country at 9,500 feet elevation, with access to a multitude of recreation opportunities. There are several lakes and streams with good fishing prospects, including Stillwater Reservoir, Yamcolo Reservoir, Bear River and Mandall Creek. Non-motorized boating is available at Bear Lake as well. In addition, Mandall Trail is nearby, leading into the Flat Tops Wilderness. This is an exceptionally beautiful area with spectacular scenery, so bring along your camera.

60) COLD SPRINGS

Reference: on Stillwater Reservoir, Routt National Forest; map C2, grid f1.

Campsites, facilities: There are five sites for tents, trailers or motor homes up to 22 feet long. Picnic tables and grills are provided. Piped water and vault toilets are also available. Pets are permitted on leashes. There is trash collection at this site. There is no firewood available.

Reservations, fee: No reservations necessary; $7 fee per night. Open mid-June to mid-November.

Who to contact: Phone Routt National Forest at (303) 638-4516 or write to Yampa Ranger District, P.O. Box 7, Yampa, CO 80483.

Location: Drive 31 miles south of the town of Steamboat Springs on Highway 131 to Yampa. Travel seven miles southwest of Yampa on County Route 7 and 8.5 miles southwest on Forest Service Road 900 to the campground.

Trip note: This campground is set at 10,500 feet and is along the shore of Stillwater Reservoir. Fishing can be good here, and anglers should explore Smith Lake and Bear River as well. Several nearby trails provide access to the numerous backcountry lakes in the Flat Tops Wilderness (bring your own oxygen). This camp gets heavy use on weekends, holidays and during big game season, so claim your spot early.

61) BLACKTAIL CREEK

Reference: in Gore Mountain Range, Routt National Forest; map C2, grid f3.

Campsites, facilities: There are two sites for tents, and six sites for trailers or motor homes up to 22 feet long. Picnic tables, fireplaces and vault toilets are provided. Piped water is also available. Pets are permitted on leashes. There is no firewood.

Reservations, fee: No reservations necessary; $6 fee per night. Open late May to mid-November.

Who to contact: Phone Routt National Forest at (303) 638-4516 or write to Yampa Ranger District, P.O. Box 7, Yampa, CO 80483.

Location: From Toponas, drive a half mile south on Highway 131 and 13 miles east on Highway 134.

Trip note: This is a small, pristine camp, set at 9,100 feet elevation in the Gore Mountain Range. Anglers can fish in nearby Rock Creek, and history enthusiasts can check out the historic Wells Fargo Stage Stop that exists on Forest Service Road 206 (adjacent to Rock Creek). If you're planning on camping during big game season, plan on having some company. This is a popular base camp for hunters.

62) GORE PASS

Reference: east of Toponas, Routt National Forest; map C2, grid f3.

Campsites, facilities: There are 12 sites for tents, trailers or motor homes up to 22 feet long. Picnic tables, fireplaces and vault toilets are provided. Piped water is also available. Pets are permitted on leashes. There is no firewood.

Reservations, fee: No reservations necessary; $6 fee per night. Open June to mid-November.

Who to contact: Phone Routt National Forest at (303) 638-4516 or write to Yampa Ranger District, P.O. Box 7, Yampa, CO 80483.

Location: From Toponas, drive a half mile south on Highway 131 and 15.5 miles east on Highway 134.

Trip note: This camp is set at 9,500 feet, the high spot in the area. If you're looking for privacy, this is the place to find it. This camp is little-used, which is surprising considering the amenities (piped water, large sites) it offers. Gore Pass Historic Monument is located at the campground entrance.

63) WILLOWS

Reference: on Green Mountain Reservoir, White River National Forest; map C2, grid f5.

Campsites, facilities: There are 35 primitive sites for tents, trailers or motor homes up to 32 feet long. Picnic tables are provided. Vault toilets are also available. There is **no piped water.** Pets are permitted on leashes. Boat docks are nearby.

Reservations, fee: No reservations necessary; no fee. Open late May to late September.

Who to contact: Phone White River National Forest at (303) 468-5400 or write to Dillon Ranger District, P.O. Box 620, Silverthorne, CO 80498.

Location: From Dillon, drive northwest on Highway 9 for 30.2 miles and one mile southwest on County Road 30 to the campground.

Trip note: This is one of two primitive camps set at the northwest end of Green Mountain Reservoir. Of the two, this one is by far the most primitive and gets less use than nearby Elliot Creek Camp. Cow Creek Swimming Beach is located just across the lake.

64) ELLIOT CREEK

Reference: on Green Mountain Reservoir, White River National Forest; map C2, grid f5.

Campsites, facilities: There are 64 primitive sites for tents, trailers or motor homes up to 22 feet long. Picnic tables are provided. There is **no piped water.** Vault toilets and firewood are available. A store, a coffee shop and ice are located within two miles. Pets are permitted on leashes.

Boat docks, launching facilities and rentals are nearby.

Reservations, fee: No reservations necessary; no fee. Open late May to late September.

Who to contact: Phone White River National Forest at (303) 468-5400 or write to Dillon Ranger District, P.O. Box 620, Silverthorne, CO 80498.

Location: From Dillon, drive northwest on Highway 9 for 30.2 miles and three miles southwest on County Road 30 to the campground.

Trip note: This is a nearby option Willows Camp. It's set on the northwest shore of Green Mountain Reservoir. The Eagles Nest Wilderness is located to the south; access is available from Cataract Lake to the south.

---

65) PRAIRIE POINT

Reference: on Green Mountain Reservoir, White River National Forest; map C2, grid f5.

Campsites, facilities: There are 33 sites for tents, trailers or motor homes up to 22 feet long. Picnic tables are provided. Hand-pumped water, vault toilets and firewood are also available. Pets are permitted on leashes. Boat docks are nearby.

Reservations, fee: No reservations necessary; $6 fee per night. Open late May to late September.

Who to contact: Phone White River National Forest at (303) 468-5400 or write to Dillon Ranger District, P.O. Box 620, Silverthorne, CO 80498.

Location: From Dillon, drive northwest on Highway 9 for 22.1 miles.

Trip note: This one of five campgrounds on Green Mountain Reservoir. This one, along with Davis Springs Camp and McDonald Flats Camp, are located on the southwest shore of the lake. Willows Camp and Elliot Creek Camp, set on the north end of the lake, provide other alternatives. Eagles Nest Wilderness, located south of the lake, offers a myriad of hiking trails and lakes.

---

66) McDONALD FLATS

Reference: on Green Mountain Reservoir, White River National Forest; map C2, grid f5.

Campsites, facilities: There are 13 sites for tents, trailers or motor homes up to 21 feet long. Picnic tables are provided. Piped water, vault toilets and a boat ramp are also available. A store, a coffee shop and ice are located within five miles. Pets are permitted on leashes. Boat docks and rentals are nearby.

Reservations, fee: No reservations necessary; $6 fee per night. Open late May to late September.

Who to contact: Phone White River National Forest at (303) 468-

5400 or write to Dillon Ranger District, P.O. Box 620, Silverthorne, CO 80498.

Location: From Dillon, drive northwest on Highway 9 for 19.2 miles and five miles northwest on County Road 30 to the campground.

Trip note: This is one of five campgrounds on Green Mountain Reservoir. Because it has drinking water available, this is a preferred option to Davis Springs. Fishing, swimming and boating are recreation options here, or you can strap on your boots and head south for a backpacking trip into the Eagles Nest Wilderness.

---

67) DAVIS SPRINGS

Reference: on Green Mountain Reservoir, White River National Forest; map C2, grid f5.

Campsites, facilities: There are seven sites for tents, trailers or motor homes up to 15 feet long. Vault toilets are available, but there is **no piped water.** A store, a coffee shop and ice are available within five miles. Pets are permitted on leashes. Boat docks, launching facilities and rentals are nearby.

Reservations, fee: No reservations necessary; no fee. Open late May to late September.

Who to contact: Phone White River National Forest at (303) 468-5400 or write to Dillon Ranger District, P.O. Box 260, Silverthorne, CO 80498.

Location: From Dillon, drive northwest on Highway 9 for 19.2 miles, then three miles northwest on County Road 30 to the campground.

Trip note: This is a primitive camp set on Green Mountain Reservoir. For some, it's a nice option to the more heavily used Dillon Reservoir to the south. See previous trip note for possible sidetrips.

---

68) BYERS CREEK

Reference: near Fraser Experimental Forest, Arapaho National Forest; map C2, grid f7.

Campsites, facilities: There are six sites for tents, trailers or motor homes up to 22 feet long. Picnic tables are provided. Water and vault toilets are also available. Pets are permitted on leashes.

Reservations, fee: No reservations necessary; $7 fee per night. Open late June to early September.

Who to contact: Phone Arapaho National Forest at (303887-3301 or write to Sulphur Ranger District, 62429 Highway 40, P.O. Box 10, Granby, CO 80446.

Location: From Granby, drive south on US 40 to Fraser. Travel 6.5 miles southwest on Forest Service Road 160 to the campground.

Trip note: This is a little-known campground that is located at confluence of St. Louis Creek and Byers Creek in the Fraser Experimental Forest. Some hiking trails are in the area. It's a quiet little spot.

69) ST. LOUIS CREEK

Reference: near Vasquez Mountains, Arapaho National Forest; map C2, grid f7.

Campsites, facilities: There are 18 sites for tents, trailers or motor homes up to 30 feet long. Picnic tables are provided. Vault toilets are available. There is water. Pets are permitted on leashes.

Reservations, fee: No reservations necessary; $7 fee. Open late June to early September.

Who to contact: Phone Arapaho National Forest at (303) 887-3301 or write to Sulphur Ranger District, 62429 Highway 40, P.O. Box 10, Granby, CO 80446.

Location: From Granby, drive south on US 40 to Fraser. Travel three miles southwest on Forest Service Road 160 to the campground.

Trip note: This is the most primitive of three camps in the immediate area, although it is the closest to developed services. It is set along St. Louis Creek on the border of the Fraser Experimental Forest, and is a good base camp for a backpacking trip. A trailhead 1.5 miles away routes into the Vasquez Mountain wildlands.

70) IDLEWILD

Reference: on Fraser River, Arapaho National Forest; map C2, grid f8.

Campsites, facilities: There are 26 sites for tents, trailers or motor homes up to 30 feet long. Picnic tables are provided. Piped water and vault toilets are also available. A laundromat and store are nearby. Pets are permitted on leashes.

Reservations, fee: No reservations; $7 fee per night. Open mid-July to early September.

Who to contact: Phone Arapaho National Forest at (303) 887-3301 or write to Sulphur Ranger District, 62429 Highway 40, P.O. Box 10, Granby, CO 80446.

Location: From Granby, travel south on US 40 to the town of Winter Park. Continue one mile south on US 40 to the campground.

Trip note: This camp is set along the Fraser River at the foot of the Continental Divide. It‘s the most developed of three campgrounds in the vicinity. In the winter, there are some ski resorts in the area. This is a pretty camp with easy highway access, so expect company.

71) PAWNEE

Reference: west of Ward, Roosevelt National Forest; map C2, grid f9.

Campsites, facilities: There are 55 sites for tents, trailers or motor homes up to 45 feet long. Picnic tables and vault toilets are provided. Piped water is available. Pets are permitted on leashes.

Reservations, fee: Reserve through MISTIX at (800) 283-CAMP ($6 MISTIX fee); $9 fee per night. Open July through October.

Who to contact: Phone Roosevelt National Forest at (303) 444-6600 or write to Boulder Ranger District, 2995 Baseline Road, Room 110, Boulder, CO 80303.

Location: From Ward, go six miles west on Forest Service Road 112.

Trip note: Situated within the Brainard Lake Recreation Area at the foot of the Continental Divide, this is an ideal starting point for backpackers. It is set in the high country at 10,350 elevation, with many small lakes set in the nearby Indian Peaks Wilderness. This is a popular camp; reserve early to insure getting a site.

---

72) COLD SPRINGS

Reference: near Blackhawk, Arapaho National Forest; map C2, grid f9.

Campsites, facilities: There are 36 sites for tents, trailers or motor homes up to 45 feet long. Picnic tables are provided. Piped water and vault toilets are also available. Showers, a store, a coffee shop, laundromat and ice are located within five miles. Pets are permitted on leashes.

Reservations, fee: No reservations necessary; $7 fee per night. Open late May to mid-October.

Who to contact: Phone Arapaho National Forest at (303) 567-2901 or write to Clear Creek Ranger District, P.O. Box 3307, Idaho Springs, CO 80524.

Location: From Blackhawk, travel 4.5 miles north on Highway 119 to the campground.

Trip note: This is a good base camp for explorers with four-wheel-drive vehicles. There are lots of rugged Forest Service roads in the area. Idle campers can always head up to Central City or Blackhawk and try their luck at the craps tables or slot machines.

---

73) KELLY DAHL

Reference: near Indian Peaks Wilderness, Roosevelt National Forest; map C2, grid f9.

Campsites, facilities: There are 46 sites for tents, trailers or motor homes up to 40 feet long. Picnic tables are provided. Piped water and vault toilets are also available. Pets are permitted on leashes.

Reservations, fee: Reserve through MISTIX at (800) 283-CAMP ($6 MISTIX fee); $7 fee per night. Open mid-May to late October.

Who to contact: Phone Roosevelt National Forest at (303) 444-6600 or write to Boulder Ranger District, 2995 Baseline Road, Room 110, Boulder, CO 80303.

Location: From Boulder, drive west on Highway 119 to Nederland and three miles south on Highway 119 to the campground.

Trip note: This is a pretty camp, nestled at 8,600 feet adjacent to the Peak-to-Peak National Scenic Byway. The head of the Hessie Trail, a trail leading to many backcountry lakes and the Indian Peaks Wilderness is located 10 miles away. Spectacular views of the Continental Divide are available from the campground.

---

74) PICKLE GULCH GROUP CAMP

Reference: on Silver Creek, Arapaho National Forest; map C2, grid f9.

Campsites, facilities: There is one group area with 30 tent sites. Picnic tables are provided, with a large group picnic area available by reservation as well. Vault toilets are also available. There is piped water. A store, a coffee shop, laundromat and ice are located within four miles. Pets are permitted on leashes.

Reservations, fee: Reserve through MISTIX at (800) 283-CAMP ($6 MISTIX fee); phone ahead for fee. Open late May to mid-October.

Who to contact: Phone Arapaho National Forest at (303) 893-1474 or write to Clear Creek Ranger District, P.O. Box 3307, Idaho Springs, CO 80524.

Location: From Blackhawk, travel three miles north on Highway 119 and one mile west on a gravel road to the campground.

Trip note: This secluded, primitive camp is set near Silver Creek. A trail west of camp is routed along the creek, providing a pretty nature hike. This is an ideal camp for large family trips or club gatherings, with fairly easy access and intimate campsites.

---

75) RAINBOW LAKES

Reference: near Glacier Rim, Roosevelt National Forest; map C2, grid g0.

Campsites, facilities: There are 16 sites for tents, trailers or motor homes up to 20 feet long. Picnic tables and vault toilets are provided. There is **no piped water**. Pets are permitted on leashes.

Reservations, fee: No reservations; no fee. Open late June to mid-October.

Who to contact: Phone Roosevelt National Forest at (303) 444-6600 or write to Boulder Ranger District, 2995 Baseline Road, Room 110, Boulder, CO 80303.

Location: From Nederland, go 6.5 miles north on Highway 72. Turn left and proceed five miles west on County Road 116 to the campground.

Trip note: This is a primitive camp set in a pretty, forested setting. Though the road in is only five miles long, plan on about a 40-minute drive, as it's very rough and rocky. Good sidetrips for hikers include tromping out to Glacier Rim and the Indian Peaks Wilderness. A Forest Service map is essential.

76) COFFEE POT SPRINGS

Reference: in White River National Forest; map C2, grid g0.

Campsites, facilities: There are ten primitive sites for tents, trailers or motor homes up to 21 feet long. Picnic tables and grills are provided. Pit toilets are also available. There is **no piped water.** Pets are permitted on leashes.

Reservations, fee: No reservations necessary; no fee. Open mid-June to mid-November.

Who to contact: Phone White River National Forest at (303) 328-6388 or write to Eagle Ranger District, P.O. Box 720, Eagle, CO 81631.

Location: From Glenwood Springs, drive 18 miles east on Interstate 70; two miles north on County Road 301, and 21 miles northwest on Forest Service Road 600.

Trip note: This secluded campground is set at 10,100 feet and is at Coffee Pot Springs. A good spot for four-wheel-drive cowboys. Forest Service roads provide access to backcountry streams.

77) SWEETWATER LAKE

Reference: near Flat Tops Wilderness, White River National Forest; map C2, grid g0.

Campsites, facilities: There are 10 sites for tents, trailers or motor homes up to 20 feet long. Picnic tables and grills are provided. Vault toilets and firewood are also available. There is **no piped water** in the camp itself, but there is one faucet available outside the campground. Pets are permitted on leashes. Boat docks, launching facilities and rentals are nearby.

Reservations, fee: No reservations necessary; $7 fee per night. Open May to mid-November.

Who to contact: Phone White River National Forest at (303) 328-6388 or write to Eagle Ranger District, P.O. Box 720, Eagle, CO 81631.

Location: From Glenwood Springs, travel 18 miles east on Interstate 70 to Dotsero. Turn north and go 7 miles on County Road 37 and 10 miles northwest on County Road 17. The camp is 600 yards south on Forest Service Road 607.

Trip note: This campground is set at 7,700 feet and is along the shore of Sweetwater Lake. Trails from camp and at the end of the nearby Forest Service Road provide access to backcountry areas in all directions including the Flat Tops Wilderness Area.

78) GORE CREEK

Reference: near Gore Mountain Range, White River National Forest; map C2, grid g5.

Campsites, facilities: There are 17 sites for tents, trailers or motor homes up to 60 feet long. Picnic tables are provided. Piped water and

vault toilets are also available. Pets are permitted on leashes.

Reservations, fee: No reservations necessary; $7 fee per night. Open June to early September.

Who to contact: Phone White River National Forest at (303) 827-5715 or write to Holy Cross Ranger District, P.O. Box 190, Minturn, CO 81645.

Location: From Vail, drive four miles east on Interstate 70. Turn south and drive 2.5 miles on the Forest Service (frontage) road to the campground.

Trip note: This is a prime spot either for hikers looking for a jump-off point or for Interstate 70 cruisers looking for a quiet overnight layover. The camp is set on Gore Creek on the edge of the Eagles Nest Wilderness, with nearby trails routed up various creeks into the backcountry. A Forest Service map details the options.

---

79) ROBBERS ROOST

Reference: in Arapaho National Forest; map C2, grid g8.

Campsites, facilities: There are 11 sites for tents, trailers or motor homes up to 16 feet long. Picnic tables are provided. Vault toilets and piped water are also available. A store, a coffee shop, laundromat, ice and a playground are located within five miles. Pets are permitted on leashes.

Reservations, fee: No reservations necessary; $7 fee per night. Open late June to early September.

Who to contact: Phone Arapaho National Forest at (303) 887-3301 or write to Sulphur Ranger District, 62429 Highway 40, P.O. Box 10, Granby, CO 80446.

Location: From the town of Winter Park, travel five miles south on US 40 to the site.

Trip note: This is a pretty site, set at the confluence of Eva Creek and the Fraser River. It's right off the highway and close to the quaint town of Winter Park, where sightseeing options abound. There is excellent skiing nearby in the winter months. Stream fishing and hiking nearby trails are two possibilities for the outdoor enthusiast.

---

80) MIZPAH

Reference: west of Idaho Springs, Arapaho National Forest; map C2, grid g8.

Campsites, facilities: There are 10 sites for tents, trailers or motor homes up to 20 feet long. Picnic tables are provided. Water and vault toilets are also available. Pets are permitted on leashes.

Reservations, fee: No reservations necessary; $7 fee per night. Open late May to mid-October.

Who to contact: Phone Arapaho National Forest at (303) 567-2901 or write to Clear Creek Ranger District, P.O. Box 3307, Idaho Springs, CO 80524.

Location: From Idaho Springs, drive seven miles west on Interstate 70, then seven miles west on US 40 to the campground.

Trip note: This camp is set right off of the highway near the West Fork of Clear Creek. It's small, quiet, provides easy access, all facilities nearby, and the area is loaded with little creeks. You get beautiful views of the Rockies on the drive in. Possible sidetrips include visiting some of the nearby ski areas; many offer summer tours.

---

81) CLEAR LAKE

Reference: near Mount Evans Wilderness, Arapaho National Forest; map C2, grid g8.

Campsites, facilities: There are eight tent sites and two sites for trailers or motor homes up to 30 feet long. Picnic tables are provided. Piped water and pit toilets are also available. Showers, a store, a coffee shop, laundromat and ice are located within four miles. Pets are permitted on leashes.

Reservations, fee: No reservations necessary; $7 fee per night. Open late May to mid-November.

Who to contact: Phone Arapaho National Forest at (303) 567-2901 or write to Clear Creek Ranger District, P.O. Box 3307, Idaho Springs, CO 80524.

Location: From Georgetown, drive four miles south on County Road 118.

Trip note: This is a small, intimate camp located along South Clear Creek on the border of the Mount Evans Wilderness. Lower Cabin Creek Reservoir is located just to the north. Travel south a bit and you get a great view of Mount Evans, which, at 14,264 feet, is one of Colorado's famed "fourteeners." Excellent hiking trails are located within the wilderness.

---

82) COLUMBINE

Reference: near Central City, Arapaho National Forest; map C2, grid g9.

Campsites, facilities: There are 47 sites for tents, trailers or motor homes up to 35 feet long. Picnic tables are provided. Piped water and vault toilets are also available. Showers, a store, a coffee shop, laundromat and ice are located within three miles. Pets are permitted on leashes.

Reservations, fee: No reservations necessary; $7 fee per night. Open late May to mid-October.

Who to contact: Phone Arapaho National Forest at (303) 567-2901 or write to Clear Creek Ranger District, P.O. Box 3307, Idaho Springs, CO 80524.

Location: From Central City, travel 2.1 miles northwest on County Road 279 to the campground.

Trip note: All you four-wheel-drive cowboys, here's a trail camp with your name on it. There are several roads routed out of camp. There are some good hiking in the area, too. If ghost stories around the campfire get a little slow, the gambling saloons and historic sites in Central City can provide a diversion.

---

83) ECHO LAKE

Reference: in Arapaho National Forest; map C2, grid g9.

Campsites, facilities: There are 18 sites for tents, trailers or motor homes up to 30 feet long. Picnic tables are provided. Water and vault toilets are also available. A coffee shop is located within one mile. Pets are permitted on leashes.

Reservations, fee: Reserve through MISTIX at (800) 283-CAMP ($6 MISTIX fee); $7 fee per night. Open late May to mid-November.

Who to contact: Phone Arapaho National Forest at (303) 567-2901 or write to Clear Creek Ranger District, P.O. Box 3307, Idaho Springs, CO 80524.

Location: From Idaho Springs, drive 14 miles southwest on Highway 103.

Trip note: This is another idyllic spot set near little Echo Lake. A trail from camp follows Beaverdam Creek into the adjacent Mount Evans Wilderness. There are several other lung-pounding hikes in the wilderness; see a Forest Service map for details.

---

84) WEST CHICAGO CREEK

Reference: near Idaho Springs, Arapaho National Forest; map C2, grid g9.

Campsites, facilities: There are 11 sites for tents, trailers or motor homes up to 30 feet long. Picnic tables are provided. Water and vault toilets are also available. Pets are permitted on leashes.

Reservations, fee: Reserve through MISTIX at (800) 283-CAMP ($6 MISTIX fee); $7 fee per night. Open late May to mid-November.

Who to contact: Phone Arapaho National Forest at (303) 567-2901 or write to Clear Creek Ranger District, P.O. Box 3307, Idaho Springs, CO 80524.

Location: From Idaho Springs, drive six miles southwest on Highway 103 and four miles southwest on Forest Service Road 188 to the campground.

Trip note: This is a beautiful, private, secluded spot set near little Lake Edith (a privately owned lake). For a sidetrip, hike the trail out of camp that follows West Chicago Creek into the Mount Evans Wilderness for four miles.

85) FULFORD CAVE

Reference: near Holy Cross Wilderness, White River National Forest; map C2, grid h3.

Campsites, facilities: There are six sites for tents, trailers or motor homes up to 32 feet long. Picnic tables are provided. Piped water and vault toilets are also available.

Reservations, fee: No reservations necessary; $6 fee per night. Open mid-June to late October.

Who to contact: Phone White River National Forest at (303) 328-6388 or write to Eagle Ranger District, P.O. Box 720, Eagle, CO 81633.

Location: From Eagle, drive south for 12.1 miles on County Road 307 and six miles east on Forest Service Road 15415.

Trip note: This campground is at the end of the road at a trailhead that provides access to lakes in the Holy Cross Wilderness. See a Forest Service map for details.

86) HORNSILVER

Reference: on Eagle River, White River National Forest; map C2, grid h4.

Campsites, facilities: There are 12 sites for tents, trailers or motor homes up to 30 feet long. Picnic tables are provided. Piped water and vault toilets are also available. A store and a coffee shop are located within two miles. Pets are permitted on leashes.

Reservations, fee: No reservations necessary; $6 fee per night. Open June to early September.

Who to contact: Phone White River National Forest at (303) 827-5715 or write to Holy Cross Ranger District, P.O. Box 190, Minturn, CO 81645.

Location: From Redcliff, travel 2.5 miles south on US 24 to the campground.

Trip note: This is a pretty little spot set alongside the Eagle River. It's a good jump-off point for a backpacking trip because it's located on the border of the Holy Cross Wilderness. See a Forest Service map for trailhead locations. A sidetrip option is visiting nearby Homestake Reservoir, which provides, fishing, swimming, hiking and boating opportunities.

87) CAMP HALE MEMORIAL

Reference: on the East Fork of Eagle River, White River National Forest; map C2, grid h5.

Campsites, facilities: There are 21 sites for tents, trailers or motor homes up to 60 feet long. Picnic tables are provided. Vault toilets and piped water are also available. Pets are permitted on leashes.

Reservations, fee: Reserve through MISTIX at (800) 283-CAMP

($6 MISTIX fee); $6 fee per night. Open June to early September.

Who to contact: Phone White River National Forest at (303) 827-5715 or write to Holy Cross Ranger District, P.O. Box 190, Minturn, CO 81645.

Location: From Leadville, travel 17 miles north on US 24, a quarter mile east on Forest Service Road 729, and one mile south on Forest Service Road 716 to the campground.

Trip note: This idyllic, little-known spot is set along the East Fork of the Eagle River in the Camp Hale Recreation Area. You can choose from fishing in the river, mountain biking on Forest Service roads or hiking into the wilderness areas to the west. If this camp is crowded, try Blodgett Camp, a few miles north.

---

88) BLODGETT

Reference: on Eagle River; map C2, grid h5.

Campsites, facilities: There are six sites for tents, trailers or motor homes up to 30 feet long. Picnic tables are provided. Piped water and vault toilets are also available. A store and a coffee shop are located within four miles. Pets are permitted on leashes.

Reservations, fee: No reservations necessary; $6 fee per night. Open June to early September.

Who to contact: Phone White River National Forest at (303) 827-5715 or write to Holy Cross Ranger District, P.O. Box 190, Minturn, CO 81645.

Location: From Redcliff, travel three miles south on US 24 and a half mile southwest on Forest Service Road 703 to the campground.

Trip note: This is a preferred alternative to nearby Hornsilver Camp. It is smaller and has piped water. Situated at the confluence of Homestake Creek and the Eagle River, the camp is also pretty. It borders the Holy Cross Wilderness and is just a few miles north of Homestake Reservoir.

---

89) PINE COVE

Reference: on Dillon Reservoir, White River National Forest; map C2, grid h6.

Campsites, facilities: There are 55 sites for trailers or motor homes up to 30 feet long. Piped water is provided. Vault toilets and a boat ramp are also available. A store, a coffee shop, laundromat and ice are located within one mile. Pets are permitted on leashes. Boat docks are nearby.

Reservations, fee: No reservations necessary; $7 fee per night. Open late May to early September.

Who to contact: Phone White River National Forest at (303) 468-5400 or write to Dillon Ranger District, P.O. Box 620, Silverthorne, CO 80498.

Location: From Frisco, drive one mile east on County Road 9 to the site.

Trip note: This is one of several campgrounds located on Dillon Reservoir. It's a perfect vacation destination, offering full facilities nearby as well as a myriad of recreation options—fishing, boating, swimming and hiking—but plan on plenty of company.

---

90) PEAK ONE

Reference: on Dillon Reservoir, White River National Forest; map C2, grid h6.

Campsites, facilities: There are 79 sites for trailers or motor homes up to 50 feet long. Picnic tables are provided. Piped water, flush toilets and firewood are also available. A store, a coffee shop, laundromat and ice are located within one mile. Pets are permitted on leashes. Boat docks, launching facilities and rentals are nearby.

Reservations, fee: Reserve through MISTIX at (800) 283-CAMP ($6 MISTIX fee); $8 fee per night. Open late May to late September.

Who to contact: Phone White River National Forest at (303) 468-5400 or write to Dillon Ranger District, P.O. Box 260, Silverthorne, CO 80498.

Location: From Frisco, drive 2.3 miles on County Road 9 to the campground.

Trip note: This camp is set on the shore of Dillon Reservoir and is one of the larger Forest Service camps in the region. It's also one of the more popular, being one of the rare camps that offers luxuries like flush toilets. Alternative camps include Prospector, Heaton Bay, Windy Point and Pine Cove. For recreation options, see the trip note for Pine Cove camp.

---

91) PROSPECTOR

Reference: on Dillon Reservoir, White River National Forest; map C2, grid h6.

Campsites, facilities: There are 107 sites for tents, trailers or motor homes up to 32 feet long. Picnic tables are provided. Piped water and vault toilets are also available. A store, a coffee shop and ice are located within five miles. Pets are permitted on leashes. Boat docks and launching facilities are nearby.

Reservations, fee: Reserve through MISTIX at (800) 283-CAMP ($6 MISTIX fee); $7 fee per night. Open late May to early September.

Who to contact: Phone White River National Forest at (303) 468-5400 or write to Dillon Ranger District, P.O. Box 260, Silverthorne, CO 80498.

Location: From Dillon, drive 3.5 miles southeast on US 6 and three miles west on County Road CH001 to the campground.

Trip note: This is one of the bigger camps set on Dillon Reservoir. It's a take-your-pick deal, with several camps available at the lake. See trip notes for two previous camps.

92) HEATON BAY

Reference: on Dillon Reservoir, White River National Forest; map C2, grid h6.

Campsites, facilities: There are 72 sites for tents, trailers or motor homes up to 100 feet long. Picnic tables are provided. Vault toilets and piped water are also available. A store, a coffee shop, laundromat and ice are located within one mile. Pets are permitted on leashes. Boat docks, launching facilities and rentals are nearby.

Reservations, fee: Reserve through MISTIX at (800) 283-CAMP ($6 MISTIX fee); $8 fee per night. Open late May to late September.

Who to contact: Phone White River National Forest at (303) 468-5400 or write to Dillon Ranger District, P.O. Box 620, Silverthorne, CO 80498.

Location: From Frisco, drive two miles north on US 6, then five miles northeast on County Road CH007 to the campground.

Trip note: This is probably the best of the campgrounds at Dillon Reservoir. It's a big lake and ideal for boating and fishing. It also borders on Eagles Nest Wilderness. Hiking trails near the camp provide access. A paved bike path is routed through the campground entrance.

93) WINDY POINT GROUP CAMP

Reference: on Dillon Reservoir, White River National Forest; map C2, grid h7.

Campsites, facilities: There are 72 sites for up to 200 people in trailers or motor homes up to 32 feet long. Picnic tables are provided. Vault toilets are also available. A store, a coffee shop and ice are located within one mile. Pets are permitted on leashes. Boat docks and launching facilities are nearby.

Reservations, fee: Reserve through MISTIX at (800) 283-CAMP ($6 MISTIX fee); call for fee. Open late May to early September.

Who to contact: Phone White River National Forest at (303) 468-5400 or write to Dillon Ranger District, P.O. Box 620, Silverthorne, CO 80498.

Location: From Dillon, drive six miles east on US 6 and 2.5 miles southwest on County Road CH001. Continue one mile northwest on Forest Service Road FH210 to the camp area.

Trip note: Calling all motor homes—this is for you. This is the one camp at Dillon Reservoir made expressly for RVs. It's perfect for large, club-type excursions, with large, airy sites and easy lake access.

94) TIGER RUN RESORT

Reference: on Swan River; map C2, grid h7.

Campsites, facilities: There are 250 sites for trailers or motor homes up to 55 feet. Electricity, piped water, sewer hookups and picnic tables are provided. Flush toilets, showers, recreation hall, a store, laundromat, tennis courts, volleyball, horseshoes and a swimming pool are also available. Bottled gas can be found within six miles. No pets allowed. Boat docks and launching facilities are nearby.

Reservations, fee: Reservations accepted; $25-$30 fee per night; MasterCard and Visa accepted. Open all year.

Who to contact: Phone (303) 453-9690 or write to P.O. Box 815, Breckenridge, CO 80424.

Location: From Frisco, drive south on Highway 9 for about six miles to the resort.

Trip note: This large, privately developed motor home park is located at the confluence the Swan River and the Blue River, about three miles from Dillon Reservoir. Most of the sites are open and grassy, some on the riverside. The park is surrounded on all sites by mountains, providing excellent views. Nearby recreation options include an 18-hole golf course, bicycle paths, a riding stable and tennis courts.

---

95) JEFFERSON CREEK

Reference: near Jefferson Lake, Pike National Forest; map C2, grid h7.

Campsites, facilities: There are 17 sites for tents, trailers or motor homes up to 22 feet long. Picnic tables are provided. Well water and pit toilets are also available. Pets are permitted on leashes. Boat launching facilities are nearby on Jefferson Lake.

Reservations, fee: No reservations necessary; $7 fee per night. Open late May to early September.

Who to contact: Phone Pike National Forest at (303) 236-7386 or write to South Park Ranger District, P.O. Box 219, Fairplay, CO 80440.

Location: From Jefferson, drive two miles northwest on County Road 35, one mile north on County Road 37, and 2.9 miles northwest on Forest Service Road 401 to the campground.

Trip note: This is a nice spot set along side Jefferson Creek and is less than a mile from Jefferson Lake. A trail at Beaver Ponds Picnic Ground to the south leads into the surrounding national forest. This is the closest campground to Jefferson Lake, and the most popular of the three in the immediate area. The other two, Lodgepole and Aspen, provide more private alternatives.

---

96) LODGEPOLE

Reference: near Jefferson, Pike National Forest; map C2, grid h7.

Campsites, facilities: There are 35 sites for tents, trailers or motor homes up to 22 feet long. Picnic tables are provided. Well water and pit toilets are also available. A store and ice are located within five miles. Pets are permitted on leashes. Boat launching facilities are available two miles north on Jefferson Lake.

Reservations, fee: No reservations necessary; $7 fee per night. Open late May to early September.

Who to contact: Phone Pike National Forest at (303) 236-7386 or write to South Park Ranger District, P.O. Box 219, Fairplay, CO 80440.

Location: From Jefferson, drive two miles northwest on County Road 35, one mile north on County Road 37, and 1.4 miles northwest on Forest Service Road 401 to the campground.

Trip note: This is the first of three campgrounds you'll come across on this road. It is the largest and most developed, with fishing access to Jefferson Creek, nearby hiking trails, and all the amenities. Aspen Camp provides an alternative.

---

97) ASPEN

Reference: on Jefferson Creek, Pike National Forest; map C2, grid h7.

Campsites, facilities: There are 12 sites for tents, trailers or motor homes up to 22 feet long. Picnic tables are provided. Well water and pit toilets are also available. A store and ice can be found within five miles. Pets are permitted on leashes. Boat launching facilities are nearby.

Reservations, fee: No reservations necessary; $7 fee per night. Open mid-May to late September.

Who to contact: Phone Pike National Forest at (303) 236-7386 or write to South Park Ranger District, P.O. Box 219, Fairplay, CO 80440.

Location: From Jefferson, drive two miles northwest on County Road 5, one mile north on County Road 37, and 1.8 miles northwest on Forest Service Road 401 to the campground.

Trip note: There's a little bit of both worlds here. The camp is set on Jefferson Creek, yet just two miles south of Jefferson Lake. Plus, a hiking trail (Colorado Trail) runs right through camp. And it's pretty, too, with shaded sites set amidst towering pine trees. What more could you want?

---

98) BURNING BEAR

Reference: on Bear Creek, Pike National Forest; map C2, grid h8.

Campsites, facilities: There are 13 sites for tents, trailers or motor homes up to 16 feet long. Picnic tables are provided. Well water and pit toilets are also available. Pets are permitted on leashes.

Reservations, fee: No reservations necessary; no fee. Open May to mid-October.

Who to contact: Phone Pike National Forest at (303) 236-7386 or write to South Platte Ranger District, P.O. Box 25127, Lakewood, CO 80225.

Location: From Grant, drive northwest on Forest Service Road 118 for 5.2 miles to the campground.

Trip note: Of the backcountry Forest Service camps in this region, this is one of the easier ones to reach and has many excellent qualities. It is located near the confluence of Bear Creek and Scott Gomer Creek, and trails leading from camp follow both. Backpackers should consider the route along South Gomer, which eventually leads into the Mount Evans Wilderness. The reward is the fantastic view of majestic Mount Evans (14,258 feet), one of the state's renowned "fourteeners." The really ambitious can even try to climb it.

---

99) GENEVA PARK

Reference: on Geneva Creek, Pike National Forest; map C2, grid h8.

Campsites, facilities: There are 26 sites for tents, trailers or motor homes up to 16 feet long. Picnic tables are provided. Well water and pit toilet are also available. Pets are permitted on leashes.

Reservations, fee: No reservations necessary; no fee. Open May to mid-October.

Who to contact: Phone Pike National Forest at (303) 236-7386 or write to South Platte Ranger District, P.O. Box 25127, Lakewood, CO 80225.

Location: From Grant, drive northwest on Forest Service Road 118 for seven miles and northwest for a quarter mile on Forest Service Road 119 to the campground.

Trip note: This is a quiet camp set on Geneva Creek that is flat out missed by out-of-towners. There are hiking trails in the area, although none that lead directly out of the camp. There are trailheads at nearby Burning Bear Camp and north of camp on Road 119. In the winter, there is skiing at Geneva Basin, located a few miles to the north.

---

100) HALL VALLEY

Reference: near Kenosha Pass, Pike National Forest; map C2, grid h8.

Campsites, facilities: There are nine sites for tents, trailers or motor homes up to 16 feet long. Picnic tables are provided. Well water and pit toilets are also available. Pets are permitted on leashes.

Reservations, fee: No reservations necessary; no fee. Open May to mid-October.

Who to contact: Phone Pike National Forest at (303) 236-7386 or write to South Platte Ranger District, P.O. Box 25127, Lakewood, CO 80225.

Location: From Grant, drive west on US 285 for 3.1 miles and northwest on Forest Service Road 120 for 4.7 miles to the campground.

Trip note: Set on the beautiful North Fork of the South Platte River, this camp, along with adjacent Handcart Camp, provides solitude, quiet, and a chance to "get back to nature." With all the larger, more developed camps in the area, this one is often overlooked, and can provide just the right amount of seclusion. There is fishing in the South Platte River, and hiking trails are routed right out of camp.

101) HANDCART

Reference: on the North Fork of South Platte River, Pike National Forest; map C2, grid h8.

Campsites, facilities: There are 10 sites for tents, trailers or motor homes up to 16 feet long. Picnic tables are provided. Well water and pit toilets are also available. Pets are permitted on leashes.

Reservations, fee: No reservations necessary; no fee. Open May to mid-October.

Who to contact: Phone Pike National Forest at (303) 236-7386 or write to South Platte Ranger District, P.O. Box 25127, Lakewood, CO 80225.

Location: From Grant, drive west on US 285 for 3.1 miles and northwest on Forest Service Road 120 for 4.9 miles to the campground.

Trip note: This is an idyllic little spot set near the headwaters of the North Fork of the South Platte River. Got that? Well, it's worth a look, even if it sounds confusing. An option for well-conditioned backpackers is taking a trail from camp that travels many miles (a lot of it up) to Guanella Pass. See trip note for Hall Valley Camp for further information.

102) KENOSHA

Reference: near Jefferson, Pike National Forest; map C2, grid h8.

Campsites, facilities: There are 25 sites for tents, trailers or motor homes up to 16 feet long. Picnic tables are provided. Well water and pit toilets are also available. A store and ice are located within four miles. Pets are permitted on leashes.

Reservations, fee: No reservations necessary; $6 fee per night. Open May to mid-October.

Who to contact: Phone Pike National Forest at (303) 236-7386 or write to South Platte Ranger District, P.O. Box 25127, Lakewood, CO 80225.

Location: From Jefferson, drive 4.2 miles northeast on US 285 to the campground.

Trip note: This is the high country. The campground is perched at the 10,000-foot Kenosha Pass. A backpacker's trail (Colorado Trail) passes right through camp and provides a sidetrip option. Due to its close proximity to the highway, this is a quite popular camp. Hall Valley and Handcart are two more private, though primitive, options.

103) DEER CREEK

Reference: near Mount Evans Wilderness, Pike National Forest; map C2, grid h9.

Campsites, facilities: There are 13 sites for tents, trailers or motor homes up to 16 feet long. Picnic tables are provided. Well water and pit toilets are also available. Pets are permitted on leashes.

Reservations, fee: No reservations necessary; $6 fee per night. Open April to mid-November.

Who to contact: Phone Pike National Forest at (303) 236-7386 or write to South Platte Ranger District, P.O. Box 25127, Lakewood, CO 80225.

Location: From Bailey, drive 2.4 miles north on US 285 and eight miles northwest on Forest Service Road 100 to the campground.

Trip note: This is another prime spot for hikers and is an option to Meridian Camp. This small camp is set along Deer Creek, with a major trailhead at the edge of camp that provides access into the Mount Evans Wilderness. This is used primarily as a base camp for backpackers. It's great for overnighters, too, with developed services within a few miles.

---

104) MERIDIAN

Reference: on Elk Creek, Pike National Forest; map C2, grid h9.

Campsites, facilities: There are 18 sites for tents, trailers or motor homes up to 16 feet long. Picnic tables are provided. Well water and pit toilets are also available. Pets are permitted on leashes.

Reservations, fee: No reservations necessary; no fee. Open May to mid-October.

Who to contact: Phone Pike National Forest at (303) 236-7386 or write to South Platte Ranger District, P.O. Box 25127, Lakewood, CO 80225.

Location: From Bailey, drive 2.4 miles north on US 285, then 6.6 miles northwest on Forest Service Road 100, and 1.1 miles north on Forest Service Road 102 to the campground.

Trip note: This is a good base camp for backpackers. It has a trail from camp routing into the Mount Evans Wilderness and is set along Elk Creek. It has easy access, and is an alternative to Deer Creek Camp.

---

105) JANEWAY

Reference: on Avalanche Creek and Crystal River, White River National Forest; map C2, grid i0.

Campsites, facilities: There are nine sites for tents, trailers or motor homes up to 35 feet long. Picnic tables are provided. Vault toilets only. A coffee shop is located within one mile. There is **no piped water** available. Pets are permitted on leashes.

Reservations, fee: No reservations necessary; no fee. Open late May to early November.

Who to contact: Phone White River National Forest at (303) 963-2266 or write to Sopris Ranger District, P.O. Box 248, Carbondale, CO 81623.

Location: From the town of Glenwood Springs, take the Highway 82 exit. Drive south for 12 miles. Continue south for 10.4 miles and east on Forest Service Road 310 for 0.6 mile to the campground.

Trip note: This primitive spot is located in steep and rugged country at the confluence of Avalanche Creek and Crystal River. The camp elevation is 6,800 feet, yet just three miles away is Mount Sopris at 12,953 feet. A four-wheel-drive road nearby leads to a mining area on the border of the Maroon Bells Snowmass Wilderness. A trail at nearby Avalanche Camp leads to many backcountry lakes and streams in the wilderness. Avalanche Camp may provide a less crowded option.

---

106) AVALANCHE

Reference: near Elk Mountains, White River National Forest; map C2, grid i0.

Campsites, facilities: There are 13 sites for tents, trailers or motor homes up to 25 feet long. Picnic tables are provided. Vault toilets only. There is piped water available. Pets are permitted on leashes.

Reservations, fee: No reservations necessary; $6 fee per night. Open late May to early November.

Who to contact: Phone White River National Forest at (303) 963-2266 or write to Sopris Ranger District, P.O. Box 248, Carbondale, CO 81623.

Location: From the town of Glenwood Springs, take Highway 82, and drive south for 12 miles. Continue south for 10.4 miles and east on Forest Service Road 310 for 2.6 miles to the campground.

Trip note: This primitive Forest Service camp is situated along side Avalanche Creek. Some good hiking trails are nearby, including routes that venture into the Maroon Bells Snowmass Wilderness in the Elk Mountains. There are many small, hidden lakes in the backcountry. Janeway Camp, which you pass on the way in, is an alternative.

---

107) BRB RESORT

Reference: on Crystal River; map C2, grid i0.

Campsites, facilities: There are 32 sites for tents, and 15 sites for trailers or motor homes of any length. Electricity, piped water and picnic tables are provided. Flush toilets, showers, firewood, ice and a playground are available. Pets and motorbikes are permitted. There are also 13 cabins available for use and one teepee for rent.

Reservations, fee: Reservations accepted; $12.50-$18.50 fee per night; Cabins range from $55-$90 per night; Teepee is $27 per night; MasterCard and Visa accepted. Open May through October.

Who to contact: Phone (303) 963-2341 or write to 7202 Highway 133, Carbondale, CO 81623.

Location: From the town of Glenwood Springs, travel eight miles south to Carbondale. Continue six miles south on Highway 133 to the campground.

Trip note: This campground is situate on the banks of Crystal River, set amidst cottonwood and pine trees. Recreation options abound here; you have a choice of volleyball, basketball, tetherball, badminton or horseshoes in the campground itself and fishing and hiking nearby.

---

108) RUEDI

Reference: on Ruedi Reservoir, White River National Forest; map C2, grid i1.

Campsites, facilities: There are 68 sites for tents, trailers or motor homes up to 40 feet long. Piped water and picnic tables are provided. Flush toilets and sanitary disposal station are available. A store and ice are located within five miles. Pets are permitted on leashes. Boat docks and launching facilities are available nearby.

Reservations, fee: No reservations necessary; $6-$9 fee per night. Open late May to mid-September.

Who to contact: Phone White River National Forest at (303) 963-2266 or write to Sopris Ranger District, P.O. Box 248, Carbondale, CO 81623.

Location: From the town of Glenwood Springs, drive 24 miles southeast on Highway 82 to Basalt and east on County Road FH 105 for 15.5 miles to the campground.

Trip note: This is the largest of two camps on Ruedi Reservoir and comes with a full-service marina nearby. Fishing, waterskiing and boating are all popular during the summer months. The camp elevation is 7,800 feet. This camp is known primarily as an RV overflow camp, so tenters, beware.

---

109) KOA ASPEN BASALT

Reference: on Roaring Fork River; map C2, grid i1.

Campsites, facilities: There are 37 tent sites and 79 sites for trailers or motor homes of any length. Electricity, piped water, sewer hookups and picnic tables are provided. Flush toilets, bottled gas, sanitary disposal services, showers, firewood, a recreation hall, a store, coffee shop, laundromat, ice, playground, hot tub and a heated swimming pool are available. Pets and motorbikes are permitted.

Reservations, fee: Reservations accepted; $15-$19 fee per night; MasterCard and Visa accepted. Open all year.

Who to contact: Phone (303) 927-3532 or write to P.O. Box 880, Basalt, CO 81621.

Location: The campground is located two miles west of the town of Basalt, right off of Highway 82.

Trip note: This campground is set along the banks of the Roaring Fork River, not far from Aspen, where the recreation options are legendary. The campground has large, grassy sites near the river. The park is very clean and well-maintained, but often filled to capacity due to its proximity to Aspen. Reserve a spot early.

110) ELK WALLOW

Reference: on the North Fork of Frying Pan River, White River National Forest; map C2, grid i2.

Campsites, facilities: There are seven sites for tents, trailers or motor homes up to 30 feet long. Picnic tables are provided. Vault toilets are available. A store, a coffee shop and ice are located within five miles. There is **no piped water.** Pets are permitted on leashes.

Reservations, fee: No reservations necessary; no fee. Open late May to early November.

Who to contact: Phone White River National Forest at (303) 963-2266 or write to Sopris Ranger District, P.O. Box 248, Carbondale, CO 81623.

Location: From the town of Glenwood Springs, drive 24 miles southeast on Highway 82 to Basalt, east on County Road 15105 for 23 miles, and 3.3 miles east on Forest Service Road 15501.

Trip note: The camp is nestled along the North Fork of the Frying Pan River, a primitive, little-known camp. It is advisable to obtain a Forest Service map of the area, which details access roads and trails into the adjacent Holy Cross Wilderness. The camp elevation is 8,800 feet, and about eight miles from Ruedi Reservoir.

111) DEARHAMMER

Reference: on Ruedi Reservoir, White River National Forest; map C2, grid i2.

Campsites, facilities: There are 13 sites for tents, trailers or motor homes up to 35 feet long. Piped water and picnic tables are provided. Vault toilets, firewood, a store and ice are available. Pets are permitted on leashes. Boat docks and launching facilities are available nearby.

Reservations, fee: No reservations necessary; $7 fee per night. Open late May to early November.

Who to contact: Phone White River National Forest at (303) 963-2266 or write to Sopris Ranger District, P.O. Box 248, Carbondale, CO 81623.

Location: From the town of Glenwood Springs, drive 24 miles southeast on Highway 82 to Basalt and east on County Road 15105 for 20.5 miles to the campground.

Trip note: This is a pretty spot set at the east end of Ruedi Reservoir. This is the smaller of two camps on the lake, and one of four camps in the immediate area. The camp elevation is 7,800 feet. There are numerous four-wheel-drive roads near camp that are excellent for mountain biking; many also lead to the network of trails that are routed south into the Hunter-Frying Pan Wilderness.

112) CHAPMAN

Reference: on Frying Pan Lake, White River National Forest; map C2, grid i2.

Campsites, facilities: There are 83 sites for tents, trailers or motor homes up to 50 feet long. Piped water and picnic tables are provided. Vault toilets, a store, a coffee shop and ice are available within five miles. Some facilities are **wheelchair accessible.** Pets are permitted on leashes.

Reservations, fee: Reserve through MISTIX at (800) 283-CAMP ($6 MISTIX fee); $7 fee per night. Open late May to late September.

Who to contact: Phone White River National Forest at (303) 963-2266 or write to Sopris Ranger District, P.O. Box 248, Carbondale, CO 81623.

Location: From the town of Glenwood Springs, drive 24 miles southeast on Highway 82 to Basalt and east on County Road 15105 for 24.5 miles to the campground.

Trip note: A pretty little spot with an elevation of 8,800 feet, this camp sits beside the Frying Pan River. It is one of four camps in the immediate area. There are many options for sidetrips, including hiking trails in White River National Forest, where several small lakes are hidden in the Hunter-Frying Pan Wilderness. Ruedi Reservoir, located six miles to the west, provides another sidetrip.

113) MAY QUEEN

Reference: on Turquoise Lake, San Isabel National Forest; map C2, grid i4.

Campsites, facilities: There are 34 sites for tents, trailers or motor homes up to 31 feet long. Picnic tables are provided. Pit toilets and well water are also available. A sanitary disposal station is located within six miles. Pets are permitted on leashes. Boat docks and launching facilities are nearby.

Reservations, fee: No reservations necessary; $9 fee per night. Open late May to late September.

Who to contact: Phone San Isabel National Forest at (719) 486-0752 or write to Leadville Ranger District, 2015 North Poplar, Leadville, CO 80461.

Location: From Leadville, travel 8.5 miles northwest on County Road 105 to the campground.

Trip note: One of several campgrounds set along Turquoise Lake, this camp is on the west shore. Nearby trails provide access to other smaller lakes in the adjacent Holy Cross Wilderness. Nearby Leadville is a charming little historic mining town, and worth a sidetrip.

114) GOLD PARK

Reference: near Holy Cross Wilderness, White River National Forest; map C2, grid i4.

Campsites, facilities: There are 11 sites for tents, trailers or motor homes up to 40 feet long. Picnic tables are provided. Piped water and pit toilets are also available. Pets are permitted on leashes.

Reservations, fee: No reservations necessary; $6 fee per night. Open June to early September.

Who to contact: Phone White River National Forest at (303) 827-5715 or write to Holy Cross Ranger District, P.O. Box 190, Minturn, CO 81645.

Location: From Redcliff, travel three miles south on US 24, then nine miles southwest on Forest Service Road 703 to the campground.

Trip note: This camp provides an ideal jump-off point for a multi-day backpack trip. Nearby trails follow creeks to lakes in the Holy Cross Wilderness. If you don't want to hike, the camp is a pretty enough spot just to stay put. Located at the confluence of several small creeks, just watching the water go by is enough for some folks. A sidetrip option is to visit Homestake Reservoir, located four miles south of camp at the end of the road.

---

115) FATHER DYER

Reference: on Turquoise Lake, San Isabel National Forest; map C2, grid i5.

Campsites, facilities: There are 26 sites for tents, trailers or motor homes up to 30 feet long. Picnic tables are provided. Piped water and flush toilets are also available. Showers, a store, a coffee shop, laundromat and ice are located within five miles. Pets are permitted on leashes. A boat launch is nearby.

Reservations, fee: Reservations accepted; $10 fee per night. Open late May to late September.

Who to contact: Phone San Isabel National Forest at (719) 486-0752 or write to Leadville Ranger District, 2015 North Poplar, Leadville, CO 80461.

Location: From Leadville, drive 4.2 miles west on Forest Service Road 105 and 1.9 miles northeast on Forest Service Road 104 to the campground.

Trip note: This spot is set along the east shore of Turquoise Lake and is one of several camps. Leadville is just a few miles away, with full facilities. The lake is near two wilderness areas, Holy Cross Wilderness and Mount Massive Wilderness. Both provide superb hiking trails and spectacular views. See a National Forest map for trails.

---

116) MOLLY BROWN

Reference: on Turquoise Lake, San Isabel National Forest; map C2, grid i5.

Campsites, facilities: There are 49 sites for tents, trailers or motor homes up to 30 feet long. Picnic tables are provided. Piped water and

flush toilets are also available. Showers, a store, a coffee shop, laundromat and ice are located within five miles. Pets are permitted on leashes. A boat launch is nearby.

Reservations, fee: Reservations accepted; $10 fee per night. Open late May to early September.

Who to contact: Phone San Isabel National Forest at (719) 486-0752 or write to Leadville Ranger District, 2015 North Poplar, Leadville, CO 80461.

Location: From Leadville, drive 4.2 miles west on Forest Service Road 105, 1.5 miles northeast on Forest Service Road 104, then a half mile northwest on Forest Service Road 129 to the campground.

Trip note: One of several campgrounds set at Turquoise Lake, this one is located on the northeast shore. It's one of the larger, more developed camps on the lake, and quite popular, so get there early. This camp is used primarily by families for extended summer trips, but it along with the other camps in the immediate area can make suitable base camps for backpackers heading into the adjacent wilderness areas.

---

117) BELLE OF COLORADO

Reference: on Turquoise Lake, San Isabel National Forest; map C2, grid i5.

Campsites, facilities: There are 19 tent sites. Picnic tables are provided. Piped water and flush toilets are also available. Showers, a store, a coffee shop, laundromat and ice are located within three miles. Pets are permitted on leashes. A boat launch is nearby.

Reservations, fee: No reservations necessary; $9 fee per night. Open late May to early September.

Who to contact: Phone San Isabel National Forest at (719) 486-0752 or write to Leadville Ranger District, 2015 North Poplar, Leadville, CO 80461.

Location: From Leadville, drive 4.2 miles southwest on Forest Service Road 105 and a half mile northeast on Forest Service Road 104 to the campground.

Trip note: This camp is set on the east shore of Turquoise Lake. It is one of several camps on the lake. See trip notes for Father Dyer and Molly Brown Camps.

---

118) BABY DOE

Reference: on Turquoise Lake, San Isabel National Forest; map C2, grid i5.

Campsites, facilities: There are 50 sites for tents, trailers or motor homes up to 31 feet long. Picnic tables are provided. Piped water and flush toilets are also available. A sanitary disposal station is located within one mile. A store, a coffee shop and ice are located within five miles. Pets are permitted on leashes. Boat launching facilities are nearby.

Reservations, fee: Reservations accepted; $10 fee per night. Open late May to early September.

Who to contact: Phone San Isabel National Forest at (719) 486-0752 or write to Leadville Ranger District, 2015 North Poplar, Leadville, CO 80461.

Location: From Leadville, drive 1.9 miles west on County Road 37 and 2.4 miles west on County Road 4. Continue 2.2 miles north on County Road 9C to the campground.

Trip note: This is the largest of the campgrounds at Turquoise Lake. It is located on the east shore. If you want a smaller camp, scan the others available at this lake. See trip notes for Father Dyer and Molly Brown camps for recreation possibilities.

---

119) FOURMILE

Reference: near Mount Sherman, Pike National Forest; map C2, grid i6.

Campsites, facilities: There are 14 sites for tents, trailers or motor homes up to 22 feet long. Picnic tables are provided. Well water and pit toilets are also available. Pets are permitted on leashes.

Reservations, fee: No reservations necessary; $6 fee per night. Open mid-May to mid-October.

Who to contact: Phone Pike National Forest at (719) 836-2031 or write to South Park Ranger District, P.O. Box 219, Fairplay, CO 80440.

Location: From Fairplay, drive 1.4 miles south on US 285, then eight miles west on County Road 18 to the campground.

Trip note: This quiet spot is set along Fourmile Creek and is not far from Mount Sherman to the west. It offers a unique point-of-interest; a grove of 1,000-year old trees is just a short hike away.

---

120) MICHIGAN CREEK

Reference: northwest of Jefferson, Pike National Forest; map C2, grid i7.

Campsites, facilities: There are 13 sites for tents, trailers or motor homes up to 22 feet long. Picnic tables are provided. Well water and pit toilets are also available. Pets are permitted on leashes.

Reservations, fee: No reservations necessary; $6 fee per night. Open mid-May to late October.

Who to contact: Phone Pike National Forest at (719) 836-2081 or write to South Park Ranger District, P.O. Box 219, Fairplay, CO 80440.

Location: From Jefferson, drive three miles northwest on County Road 35, 2.1 miles northwest on County Road 54, and continue northwest one mile on Forest Service Road 34.

Trip note: This camp is just enough off the beaten path that cruisers on US 285 (without this kind of inside info) will always miss it. And in this area, that's a big plus if you're looking for solitude. It's a quiet little spot set beside Michigan Creek.

121) SELKIRK

Reference: near Tarryall Creek, Pike National Forest; map C2, grid i7.

Campsites, facilities: There are 15 sites for tents, trailers or motor homes up to 22 feet long. Picnic tables are provided. Pit toilets are also available. There is **no piped water**. A coffee shop is located within five miles. Pets are permitted on leashes.

Reservations, fee: No reservations necessary; no fee. Open early June to mid-October.

Who to contact: Phone Pike National Forest at (719) 836-2031 or write to South Park Ranger District, Box 219, Fairplay, CO 80440.

Location: From Como, drive 3.5 miles northwest on County Road 33, three-quarters of a mile northwest on County Road 50, and 1.8 miles northwest on Forest Service Road 801 to the campground.

Trip note: A secluded, little-known spot set near Tarryall Creek, this camp promises quiet and solitude. If that's what you want, go for it. If you brought your fishing pole, you can follow the road north along Tarryall Creek and plunk it in.

122) LOST PARK

Reference: on Lost Creek, Pike National Forest; map C2, grid i9.

Campsites, facilities: There are 10 sites for tents, trailers or motor homes up to 16 feet long. Picnic tables are provided. Well water and pit toilets are also available. Pets are permitted on leashes.

Reservations, fee: No reservations necessary; no fee. Open late May to mid-October.

Who to contact: Phone Pike National Forest at (719) 836-2031 or write to South Park Ranger District, P.O. Box 219, Fairplay, CO 80440.

Location: From Jefferson, drive 1.2 miles northeast on US 285, then 19.7 miles east on Forest Service Road 56.

Trip note: This one is way out there in "booger country." The camp is set along side Lost Creek, near the trailhead for hiking routes into the Lost Creek Wilderness. If you want to get lost, this is the best place to do it.

123) REDSTONE

Reference: on Crystal River, White River National Forest; map C2, grid j0.

Campsites, facilities: There are 24 sites for tents, trailers or motor homes up to 22 feet long. Picnic tables are provided. Piped water and vault toilets are available. A store and ice are located within one mile. Pets are permitted on leashes.

Reservations, fee: No reservations necessary; $6 fee per night. Open late May to late September.

Who to contact: Phone White River National Forest at (303) 963-2266 or write to Sopris Ranger District, P.O. Box 248, Carbondale, CO 81623.

Location: From the town of Glenwood Springs, take the Highway 82 exit south to Carbondale. Continue south on Highway 133 for 13 miles and east for one mile on County Road 15308.

Trip note: This is one of three camps set on the Crystal River in the immediate area. A major trailhead is located just east of the town of Redstone, following East Creek into the Maroon Bells Snowmass Wilderness. Bogan Flats or Janeway Camps are two alternatives, all within a few miles of each other.

---

124) BOGAN FLATS

Reference: on Crystal River, White River National Forest; map C2, grid j0.

Campsites, facilities: There are 37 sites for tents, trailers or motor homes up to 30 feet long. Picnic tables are provided. Vault toilets and piped water are available. Pets are permitted on leashes.

Reservations, fee: Reserve through MISTIX at (800) 283-CAMP ($6 MISTIX fee); $7 fee per night. Open late May to late September.

Who to contact: Phone White River National Forest at (303) 963-2266 or write to Sopris Ranger District, P.O. Box 248, Carbondale, CO 81623.

Location: From the town of Glenwood Springs, take the Highway 82 exit south to Carbondale. Continue south on Highway 133 for 20.5 miles and 1.5 miles south on County Road 314.

Trip note: This pretty camp is set beside the Crystal River. It is one of three camps in the immediate area. There are many options in the area. Some small ponds are nearby, but hikers should consider multi-day trips into the Maroon Bells Snowmass Wilderness (a trailhead is located nearby at Lily Lake Ranger Station), or into the Raggeds Wilderness, which is loaded with wildlife. See a National Forest map for access points.

---

125) AVERY PEAK

Reference: near East River, Gunnison National Forest; map C2, grid j1.

Campsites, facilities: There are 10 sites for tents, trailers or motor homes up to 16 feet long. Picnic tables are provided. Vault toilets are available. There is **no piped water.** Pets are permitted on leashes.

Reservations, fee: No reservations necessary; no fee. Open early June to late October.

Who to contact: Phone Gunnison National Forest at (303) 641-0471 or write to Taylor River Ranger District, 216 North Colorado, Gunnison, CO 81230.

Location: From US 50 in Gunnison, take Highway 135 and drive north for 28 miles to Crested Butte. Continue north for 7.3 miles on County Road 3 and 1.5 miles north on Forest Service Road 317.

Trip note: This camp is set at 9,600 feet, at the foot of Avery Peak (12,653 feet). The East River is located nearby, and trails are available that route into Gunnison National Forest. A Forest Service map details the options. There is fishing in the East River.

---

126) SILVER QUEEN

Reference: on Maroon Creek, White River National Forest; map C2, grid j1.

Campsites, facilities: There are six sites for tents, trailers or motor homes up to 16 feet long. Picnic tables are provided. Vault toilets, piped water and firewood are available. Pets are permitted on leashes.

Reservations, fee: Reserve through MISTIX at (800) 283-CAMP ($6 MISTIX fee); $8 fee per night. Open mid-June to late September.

Who to contact: Phone White River National Forest at (303) 925-3445 or write to Aspen Ranger District, 806 West Hallam Street, Aspen, CO 81611.

Location: From Aspen, drive 1.4 miles west on Highway 82 and southwest for 5.9 miles on Forest Service Road 125 to the campground.

Trip note: This camp is set along Maroon Creek at an elevation of 9,100 feet. It is adjacent to the Maroon Bells Snowmass Wilderness, with a trail starting here that provides access for backpackers. This is a spectacularly beautiful area, but due to its close proximity to Aspen, a major vacation destination, you will most likely have lots of company.

---

127) WELLER

Reference: on Roaring Fork River, White River National Forest; map C2, grid j2.

Campsites, facilities: There are 11 sites for tents, trailers or motor homes up to 16 feet long. Picnic tables are provided. Vault toilets, piped water and firewood are available. Pets are permitted on leashes.

Reservations, fee: No reservations necessary; $5 fee per night. Open mid-June to late September.

Who to contact: Phone White River National Forest at (303) 925-3445 or write to Aspen Ranger District, 806 West Hallam Street, Aspen, CO 81611.

Location: From Aspen, drive 11.4 miles southeast on Highway 82 and south for 100 yards on Forest Service Road 104 to the campground.

Trip note: A primitive and spectacular setting on the Roaring Fork River. The camp elevation is at 9,200 feet with the Collegiate Peaks towering nearby, all over 12,000 feet. Weller Lake is located just over the wilderness border to the south. For access points into the adjacent Collegiate Peaks Wilderness, obtain a Forest Service map. Alternative camps are Lincoln Gulch and Difficult.

128) DIFFICULT

Reference: on Roaring Fork River, White River National Forest; map C2, grid j2.

Campsites, facilities: There are 47 sites for tents, trailers or motor homes up to 47 feet long, and one large group site. Picnic tables are provided. Piped water, vault toilets and firewood are available. A store, a coffee shop, a laundromat and ice are located within one mile. Pets are permitted on leashes.

Reservations, fee: No reservations for single sites; reserve group site through MISTIX at (800) 283-CAMP ($6 MISTIX fee). $8 fee per night for single sites; call for group rates. Open late May to late September.

Who to contact: Phone White River National Forest at (303) 925-3445 or write to Aspen Ranger District, 806 West Hallam Street, Aspen, CO 81611.

Location: From Aspen, drive 4.3 miles southeast on Highway 82 and 0.6 miles southeast on Forest Service Road 108 to the campground.

Trip note: This is one in a series of four camps located just east of Aspen. The camp elevation is at 8,000 feet and located at the confluence of Roaring Fork River and Difficult Creek. It is adjacent to the Collegiate Peaks Wilderness, with a trail routed south directly from the campground. This is the most popular of the three camps in the area; Lincoln Gulch and Weller Camps may offer quieter alternatives.

129) LINCOLN GULCH

Reference: on Lincoln Creek, White River National Forest; map C2, grid j2.

Campsites, facilities: There are six sites for tents, trailers or motor homes up to 16 feet long. Picnic tables are provided. Vault toilets and piped water are available. Pets are permitted on leashes.

Reservations, fee: No reservations necessary; $5 fee per night. Open July to mid-September.

Who to contact: Phone White River National Forest at (303) 925-3445 or write to Aspen Ranger District, 806 West Hallam Street, Aspen, CO 81611.

Location: From Aspen, drive 10.4 miles southeast on Highway 82, a half mile southwest on Forest Service Road 106, and 0.2 mile west on Forest Service Road 106 to the campground.

Trip note: One of three camps in the immediate area, this is a primitive spot set at the confluence of Lincoln Creek and the Roaring Fork River. It gets little use, and is one of the best camps for relative privacy, if not guaranteed solitude. You are just outside of Aspen, after all. It is adjacent to Collegiate Peaks Wilderness.

130) MAROON LAKE

Reference: near Maroon Bells Snowmass Wilderness, White River National Forest; map C2, grid j2.

Campsites, facilities: There are 44 sites for tents, trailers or motor homes up to 22 feet long. Picnic tables are provided. Piped water and vault toilets are available. Pets are permitted on leashes.

Reservations, fee: No reservations necessary; $10 fee per night. Open mid-June to mid-October.

Who to contact: Phone White River National Forest at (303) 925-3445 or write to Aspen Ranger District, 806 West Hallam Street, Aspen, CO 81611.

Location: From Aspen, drive 1.4 miles west on Highway 82 and southwest for 8.9 miles on Forest Service Road 125 to the campground.

Trip note: This is a nice spot set along Maroon Lake, sandwiched between the borders of the Maroon Bells Snowmass Wilderness. The elevation is 9,600 feet. This is an ideal base camp for backpackers, with a trail from camp providing access to numerous small lakes in the wilderness.

131) PORTAL

Reference: on Grizzly Reservoir, White River National Forest; map C2, grid j3.

Campsites, facilities: There are seven sites for tents, trailers or motor homes up to 16 feet long. Picnic tables are provided. Vault toilets and firewood are available. There is **no piped water.** Pets are permitted on leashes. Boat docks are nearby.

Reservations, fee: No reservations necessary; no fee. Open mid-July to late September.

Who to contact: Phone White River National Forest at (303) 925-3445 or write to Aspen Ranger District, 806 West Hallam Street, Aspen, CO 81611.

Location: From Aspen, drive 10.4 miles southeast on Highway 82 and southeast for 6.6 miles on Forest Service Road 15106, a four-wheel drive road, to the campground.

Trip note: This is a beautiful spot set in the high country along Grizzly Reservoir and is accessible to four-wheel-drive vehicles. The camp elevation is 10,700 feet, and it is located adjacent to the Collegiate Peaks Wilderness. There are trails nearby to several other smaller lakes. A Forest Service map provides details.

132) LOST MAN

Reference: on Lost Man Creek, White River National Forest; map C2, grid j3.

Campsites, facilities: There are nine sites for tents, trailers or motor homes up to 22 feet long. Picnic tables are provided. Vault toilets, piped water and firewood are available. Pets are permitted on leashes.

Reservations, fee: No reservations necessary; $5 fee per night. Open July to late September.

Who to contact: Phone White River National Forest at (303) 925-3445 or write to Aspen Ranger District, 806 West Hallam Street, Aspen, CO 81611.

Location: From Aspen, drive 14.2 miles southeast on Highway 82 to the campground.

Trip note: This is a spectacular spot, surrounded by high mountain peaks and set at the confluence of Lost Man Creek and the Roaring Fork River. The camp elevation is 10,700 feet, with four-wheel-drive roads and trails nearby that route into the Hunter-Frying Pan Wilderness.

---

133) PARRY PEAK

Reference: near Twin Lakes, San Isabel National Forest; map C2, grid j4.

Campsites, facilities: There are 26 sites for tents, trailers or motor homes up to 16 feet long. Picnic tables are provided. Piped water and pit toilets are also available. Sanitary disposal station, a store, cafe and ice are located within five miles. Pets are permitted on leashes. Boat launching facilities are nearby on Twin Lakes Reservoir.

Reservations, fee: No reservations necessary; $7 fee per night. Open late May to early September.

Who to contact: Phone San Isabel National Forest at (719) 486-0752 or write to Leadville Ranger District, 2015 North Poplar, Leadville, CO 80461.

Location: From the town of Lakes, drive 2.7 miles southwest on Highway 82 to the campground.

Trip note: This campground is more developed than nearby Lakeview and is also closer to Twin Lakes. You can reach the southern shore of Twin Lakes on a trail that starts at camp. Fishing for big mackinaw trout can be good, although they are often pretty deep in the lake. It's a scenic place, with mountain peaks rising above the lakes.

---

134) TWIN PEAKS

Reference: near Mount Elbert, San Isabel National Forest; map C2, grid j4.

Campsites, facilities: There are 37 sites for tents, trailers or motor homes up to 22 feet long. Picnic tables are provided. Piped water and pit toilets are also available. A store, cafe and ice are located within five miles. Pets are permitted on leashes. A boat launch is nearby.

Reservations, fee: No reservations necessary; $7 fee per night. Open late May to early September.

Who to contact: Phone San Isabel National Forest at (719) 486-0752 or write to Leadville Ranger District, 2015 North Poplar, Leadville, CO 80461.

Location: From the town of Twin Lakes, travel three miles west on Highway 82 to the campground.

Trip note: This is an uncrowded campground that has good hiking trails. It is set along Lake Creek adjacent to the La Plata Basin section of the Collegiate Peaks Wilderness. Nearby trails lead north to Mount Elbert. The trails can be hiked by anyone in decent physical condition—just give yourself a full day for the round trip.

---

135) WHITE STAR

Reference: near Twin Lakes, San Isabel National Forest; map C2, grid j4.

Campsites, facilities: There are 64 sites for tents, trailers or motor homes up to 22 feet long. Picnic tables are provided. Piped water and pit toilets are also available. A store, cafe and ice are located within one mile. Pets are permitted on leashes. Boat launching facilities are nearby.

Reservations, fee: No reservations necessary; $8 fee per night. Open mid-May to late September.

Who to contact: Phone San Isabel National Forest at (719) 486-0752 or write to Leadville Ranger District, 2015 North Poplar, Leadville, CO 80461.

Location: From the town of Twin Lakes, travel one mile northeast on Highway 82 and then drive 200 yards southeast on Forest Service Road 172.

Trip note: For visitors to the Twin Lakes area, this camp provides an option to Lakeview and Parry Peak camps. See trip note for Parry Peak.

---

136) LAKEVIEW

Reference: near Twin Lakes Reservoir, San Isabel National Forest; map C2, grid j4.

Campsites, facilities: There are 59 sites for tents, trailers or motor homes up to 32 feet long. Picnic tables are provided. Piped water and pit toilets are also available. A store, cafe and ice are located within five miles. Pets are permitted on leashes. Boat launching facilities are nearby.

Reservations, fee: No reservations necessary; $7 fee per night. Open mid-May to early September.

Who to contact: Phone San Isabel National Forest at (719) 486-0752 or write to Leadville Ranger District, 2015 North Poplar, Leadville, CO 80461.

Location: From the town of Twin Lakes, drive 2.6 miles northeast on Highway 82, and then 1.2 miles northwest on County Road 24 to the campground.

Trip note: No matter which way you look, this is a scenic camp. The campground is across the highway and overlooks Twin Lakes Reservoir. To the north is Mount Elbert. At an elevation of 14,433 feet, it is the highest mountain in Colorado. In the lower 48 states, it is second in height only to Mount Whitney in California. For backpackers, there's a good trail out of camp leading north to the Colorado Trail which accesses the Mount Massive Wilderness.

---

137) ELBERT CREEK

Reference: near Mount Massive Wilderness, San Isabel National Forest; map C2, grid j4.

Campsites, facilities: There are 17 sites for tents, trailers or motor homes up to 16 feet. Picnic tables are provided. Well water and pit toilets are also available. Pets are permitted on leashes.

Reservations, fee: No reservations necessary; $6 fee per night. Open late May to late September.

Who to contact: Phone San Isabel National Forest at (719) 486-0752 or write to Leadville Ranger District, 2015 North Poplar, Leadville, CO 80461.

Location: From Leadville, drive six miles southwest on Forest Service Road 110 to the campground.

Trip note: This is a great little spot set at the foot of the highest mountain in Colorado, Mount Elbert (elevation 14,433 feet). The camp is located at the confluence of Elbert Creek and Half Moon Creek. You can use the camp as a jump-off point because the Colorado Trail passes right through camp. It provides access to the Mount Massive Wilderness to the north and Mount Elbert to the south.

---

138) HALFMOON

Reference: near Elbert Creek, San Isabel National Forest; map C2, grid j4.

Campsites, facilities: There are 24 sites for tents, trailers or motor homes up to 16 feet long. Picnic tables are provided. Well water and pit toilets are also available. Pets are permitted on leashes.

Reservations, fee: No reservations necessary; $6 fee per night. Open late May to late September.

Who to contact: Phone San Isabel National Forest at (719) 486-0752 or write to Leadville Ranger District, 2015 North Poplar, Leadville, CO 80461.

Location: From Leadville, drive 3.7 miles west on US 24, three-quarters of a mile west on Highway 300, and 5.6 miles southwest on Forest Service Road 110 to the campground.

Trip note: This site is a nearby option to the adjacent Elbert Creek campground, about a mile down the road. See trip note for that camp for information.

139) WESTON PASS

Reference: on the South Fork of South Platte River, Pike National Forest; map C2, grid j6.

Campsites, facilities: There are 14 sites for tents, trailers or motor homes up to 16 feet long. Picnic tables are provided. Well water and pit toilets are also available. Pets are permitted on leashes.

Reservations, fee: No reservations necessary; no fee. Open late May to mid-October.

Who to contact: Phone Pike National Forest at (719) 836-2031 or write to South Park Ranger District, P.O. Box 219, Fairplay, CO 80440.

Location: From Fairplay, travel south on US 285 for 4.5 miles; southwest on County Road 5 for seven miles, and then southwest on County Road 22 for four miles to the campground.

Trip note: This is a good base camp for a hiking trip. It is set on the South Fork of the South Platte River. It is the trailhead for the Rich Creek-Buffalo Meadows Trail and Rich Creek-Tumble Creek Trail. They form a 12-mile loop and trace the creeks en route. For the ambitious, it's five miles to the 11,921-foot Weston Pass.

140) BUFFALO SPRINGS

Reference: north of Antero Junction, Pike National Forest; map C2, grid j6.

Campsites, facilities: There are 17 sites for tents, trailers or motor homes up to 32 feet long. Picnic tables are provided. Well water and pit toilets are also available. Pets are permitted on leashes.

Reservations, fee: No reservations necessary; no fee. Open late May to early November.

Who to contact: Phone Pike National Forest at (719) 836-2031 or write to South Park Ranger District, P.O. Box 219, Fairplay, CO 80440.

Location: From Antero Junction, travel north on US 285 for 6.5 miles; turn west on Forest Service Road 431 and drive a half of a mile to the campground.

Trip note: This camp offers both convenience and seclusion: convenience because it is just one mile off the main road and seclusion because out-of-town visitors don't know about it. There's not a whole lot to do out here, but sometimes that's just what you need.

Colorado Map C3
67 listings
Pages 148-179

North—Wyoming
East (C4)—see page 180
South (C7)—see page 262
West (C2)—see page 84

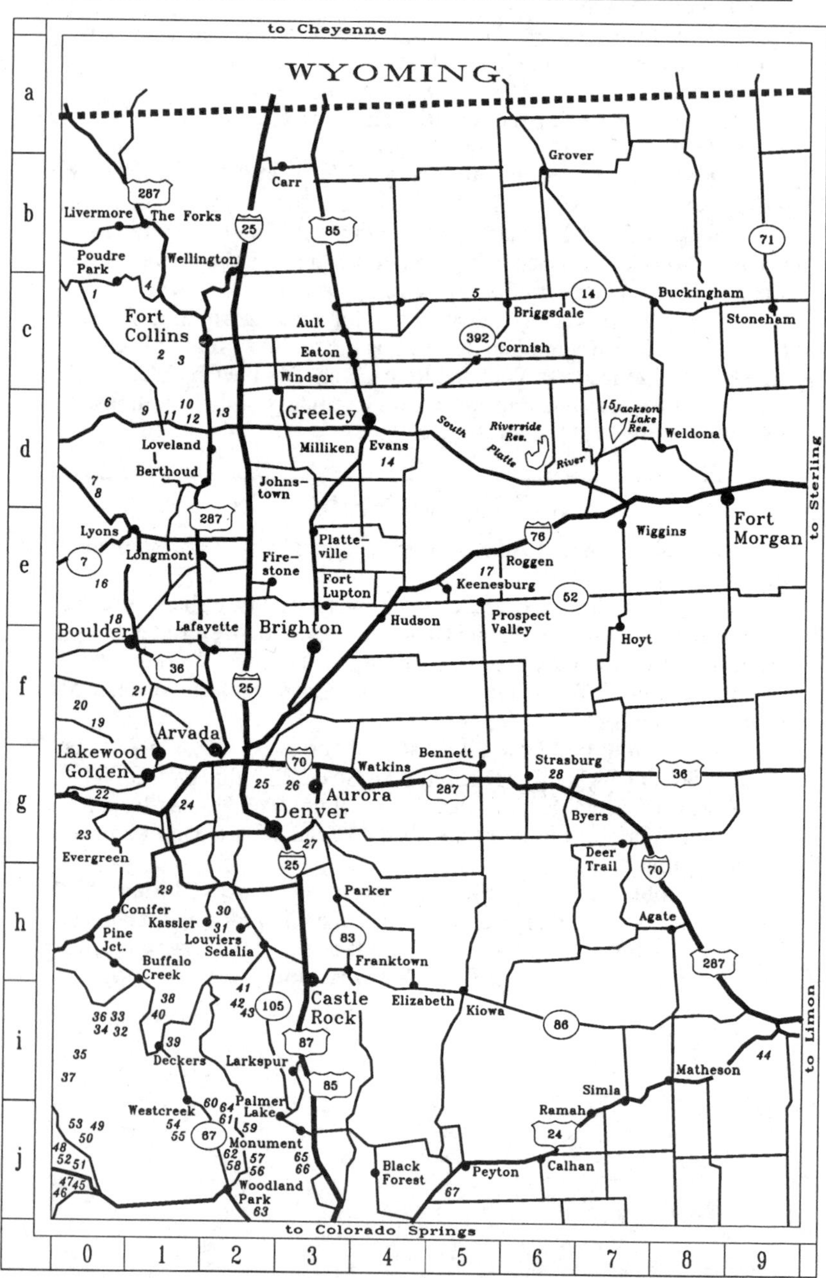

Featuring: Cache La Poudre River, Roosevelt National Forest, Horsetooth Reservoir, Pawnee National Grasslands, Big Thompson River, Rocky Mountain National Park, Little Thompson River, Carter Lake, South Platte River, Jackson Lake, Golden Gate Canyon State Park, Platte River, Cherry Creek Lake, Redskin Creek, Baldy Peak, Sixmile Creek, Buffalo Creek, Wellington Lake, Devil's Head, Trail Creek, Eleven Mile Reservoir, Lake George, Lost Creek Wilderness, Turkey Creek, Pike's Peak, Manitou Forest, Ryan Gulch, Trout Creek, Rampart Reservoir

1) ANSEL WATROUS

Reference: on Cache La Poudre River, Roosevelt National Forest; map C3, grid c0.

Campsites, facilities: There are 19 sites for tents, trailers or motor homes up to 45 feet long. Picnic tables and grills are provided. Piped water and vault toilets are also available. Pets are permitted on leashes.

Reservations, fee: No reservations necessary; $7 fee per night. Open all year.

Who to contact: Phone Roosevelt National Forest at (303) 482-3822 or write to Estes-Poudre Ranger District, 148 Remington Street, Fort Collins, CO 80524.

Location: Travel four miles north of Laporte on US 287 and 14.5 miles west on Highway 14.

Trip note: This site is set at 5,800 feet and is in the canyon of the Cache La Poudre River, which is in the Cache La Poudre Wild and Scenic river corridor. Typical rocky mountain environment: high peaks, low-density ponderosa pine and juniper, narrow canyon. Mule deer and bighorn sheep roam the country, so bring a camera and telephoto lens.

2) HORSETOOTH RESERVOIR

Reference: near Fort Collins; map C3, grid c1.

Campsites, facilities: There are 100 tent sites and 115 sites for trailers or motor homes of any length. Picnic tables are provided. Sanitary disposal services, firewood, a store, coffee shop and ice are available. Pets are permitted on leashes. Boat docks, launching facilities and rentals are nearby.

Reservations, fee: No reservations necessary; $4 fee per night. Open all year.

Who to contact: Phone (303) 226-4517, or write 4200 West County Road 38E, Fort Collins, CO 80526.

Location: From Fort Collins, drive three miles west on County Road 38E, off of Taft Hill Road, to park.

Trip note: This county-operated campground is set along the southwest shore of Horsetooth Reservoir and is just west of Fort Collins. The sites are somewhat grassy, overlooking the reservoir. There is a marina for boaters and trails for hikers (recommended is a trail that is routed to Lory State Park). When we stayed here, we were kept up all night by the roar of cars on the road that runs next to the camp as well as the racket of teenagers partying nearby, but if it's late and you're hard up for a campsite, it will do.

---

3) LORY STATE PARK

Reference: on Horsetooth Reservoir; map C3, grid c1.

Campsites, facilities: There are seven tent sites. Picnic tables and grills are provided. Piped water and vault toilets are also available. Pets are permitted on leashes.

Reservations, fee: Reserve sites by calling (800) 678-CAMP ($6.75 reservation fee); $6 fee per night plus $3 entrance fee. Open all year.

Who to contact: Phone (303) 493-1623, or write 708 Lodge Pole Drive, Bellevue, CO 80512.

Location: From Fort Collins, travel north on Highway 287 through Laporte. Turn left at the Bellevue exit, and drive one mile; turn left on County road 23 and drive 1.4 miles. Then continue right on County Road 25-G for 1.6 miles.

Trip note: This state park is set along the shore of Horsetooth Reservoir and offers hiking, fishing, horseback riding and picnicking. Also available at the reservoir is boating, sailboarding and waterskiing.

---

4) FORT COLLINS MILE HIGH KOA

Reference: near Cache La Poudre River; map C3, grid c1.

Campsites, facilities: There are 20 tent sites and 40 sites for trailers or motor homes of any length. Electricity, piped water, sewer hookups and picnic tables are provided. Flush toilets, sanitary disposal services, showers, recreation hall, a store, coffee shop, laundromat, ice, playground and a swimming pool are also available. Pets and motorbikes are permitted.

Reservations, fee: Reservations accepted; $14-$19 fee per night; MasterCard and Visa accepted. Open mid-April through October.

Who to contact: Phone (303) 493-9758 or write to P.O. Box 600, La Porte, CO 80535.

Location: Travel 10 miles northwest of Fort Collins on US 287/Highway 14 to the north junction of US 287/Highway 14.

Trip note: This campground is set near the Cache La Poudre River. The sites are set on a hill and shaded. It's a good overnighter for highway cruisers taking the Highway 287 shortcut between Fort Collins and Laramie. The Cache La Poudre River is especially pretty in the spring and fall; photographers should bring along lots of film.

5) CROW VALLEY

Reference: in Pawnee National Grasslands; map C3, grid c5.

Campsites, facilities: There are five sites for tents, trailers or motor homes up to 32 feet long. Picnic tables are provided. Piped water and pit toilets are also available. A store, coffee shop and ice are located within one mile. Pets are permitted on leashes.

Reservations, fee: No reservations necessary; $6 fee per night. Open mid-April to December.

Who to contact: Phone Roosevelt National Forest at (303) 353-5004, or write 660 O Street, Suite A, Greeley, CO 80631.

Location: From the town of Briggsdale, drive a half mile west on Highway 14, and then another half mile north on County Route 77 to the campground.

Trip note: Bet you didn't know about this one; it just might come to the rescue. It's a tiny little camp set in the Pawnee National Grasslands. No other camp choices are in the area. The closest option is Greeley RV Park, 30 miles away in Greeley.

6) RIVER BEND

Reference: near Big Thompson River; map C3, grid d0.

Campsites, facilities: There are 10 tent sites and 30 sites for trailers or motor homes up to 23 feet long. Electricity, piped water and picnic tables are provided. Flush toilets, showers, firewood, barbecue pits, a store, coffee shop and ice are also available. Pets and motorbikes are permitted.

Reservations, fee: No reservations; $6-$11 fee per night. Open May to late September.

Who to contact: Phone (303) 667-3641 or write to 1520 Big Thompson, Loveland, CO 80537.

Location: Drive 16 miles west of Loveland on US 34.

Trip note: This campground is set along the banks of the Big Thompson River, shaded by the mountains set behind it. Some sites are on the river, and there is a large grassy area for tents. There is also a gazebo for barbecues or parties. Hiking trails are nearby.

7) PARK PLACE RESORT

Reference: near Rocky Mountain National Park; map C3, grid d0.

Campsites, facilities: There are 45 tent sites and 50 sites for trailers or motor homes of any length. Cabins are also available for rental. Electricity, piped water, sewer hookups and picnic tables are provided. Flush toilets, sanitary disposal services, showers, firewood, a recreation hall, store, laundromat, ice, playground and a swimming pool are also available. Pets are permitted on leashes.

Reservations, fee: Reservations accepted; $12-$17 fee per night; cabins are $24-$60 per night. MasterCard and Visa accepted. Open May through September.

Who to contact: Phone (303) 586-4230 or write to P.O. Box 4608, Estes Park, CO 80517.

Location: From Estes Park, go 5.5 miles east on US 36.

Trip note: This 35-acre private campground is set at 8,500 feet and is less than 10 miles from the entrance into Rocky Mountain National Park. It offers scenic mountain views and shaded hillside sites. Other nearby recreation options include a golf course, hiking trails, and a riding stable.

---

8) STONE MOUNTAIN LODGE

Reference: near Little Thompson River; map C3, grid d0.

Campsites, facilities: There are three tent sites and 10 sites for trailers or motor homes of any length. Electricity, piped water and picnic tables are provided. Flush toilets, showers and a swimming pool are also available. No pets allowed. Motorbikes are permitted.

Reservations, fee: Reservations accepted; $7.50-$12 fee per night; MasterCard and Visa accepted. Open all year.

Who to contact: Phone (303) 823-6091 or write to 18055 North St. Vrain Drive, Lyons, CO 80540.

Location: Drive two miles northwest of Lyons on US 36.

Trip note: This small motor home park is set near the Little Thompson River in the tiny town of Lyons. It's right off the highway and is not particularly scenic, but Rocky Mountain National Park is just a short drive away. Nearby recreation options include a riding stable. There are some good hiking trails in the nearby National Forest; see a Forest Service map for details.

---

9) LOVELAND RV VILLAGE

Reference: east of Loveland; map C3, grid d1.

Campsites, facilities: There are 200 sites for trailers or motor homes of any length. Piped water, picnic tables, showers, flush toilets and a sanitary disposal station are provided. A heated pool, laundromat, store, propane and a playground are available. Pets are permitted.

Reservations, fee: Reservations accepted; $13-$21 per night. Open year-round.

Who to contact: Phone (303) 667-1204 or write 4421 US 34 East, Loveland, CO 80537.

Location: From Interstate 25 just east of Loveland, take exit 257B and drive one mile west on US 34 to the campground.

Trip note: This is a good layover spot for motor home cruisers heading south to Denver or southern Colorado. It has large, grassy, shaded sites. There's not much to do around Loveland, but the park tries to make up for that by offering delightful activities like hay rides and miniature golf. They even have a recreation program in the summertime. Nice folks here, too.

---

10) RIVERVIEW

Reference: on Big Thompson River; map C3, grid d1.

Campsites, facilities: There are 35 tent sites and 140 for trailers or motor homes of any length. Electricity, piped water, sewer hookups and picnic tables are provided. Flush toilets, bottled gas, sanitary disposal services, showers, firewood, a recreation hall, store, coffee shop, laundromat, ice and a playground are also available. Pets and motorbikes are permitted.

Reservations, fee: Reservations accepted; $10.50-$16 fee per night. Open all year.

Who to contact: Phone (303) 667-9910 or write to 7806 West US 34, Loveland, CO 80537.

Location: From Loveland, drive six miles west on US 34.

Trip note: This campground is set along the banks of the Big Thompson River, and it's ideal for overnighters. The pretty, riverside sites are shaded, and offer direct fishing access. Nearby recreation options include a golf course, hiking trails, bike paths and a riding stable.

---

11) CARTER VALLEY

Reference: near Carter Lake; map C3, grid d1.

Campsites, facilities: There are 10 tent sites and 50 sites for trailers or motor homes of any length. Electricity, piped water, sewer hookups and picnic tables are provided. Flush toilets, sanitary disposal services, showers, firewood, a recreation hall, store, coffee shop, laundromat, ice and a playground are also available. Pets and motorbikes are permitted.

Reservations, fee: Reservations accepted; $12-$15 fee per night; MasterCard and Visa accepted. Open all year.

Who to contact: Phone (303) 663-3131 or write to 1326 North Carter Lake Road, Loveland, CO 80537.

Location: Drive seven miles west of Loveland on US 34 and one-half mile south on North Carter Lake Road.

Trip note: This is a private, developed campground set within ten miles of the Thompson River and many other lakes. Sites are grassy, set on a hillside with beautiful views of Carter Valley. Carter Lake, about four miles away, offers fishing access. A riding stable is nearby.

---

12) FIRESIDE MOTEL

Reference: near Big Thompson River; map C3, grid d1.

Campsites, facilities: There are 12 tent sites and 28 sites for trailers or motor homes of any length. Electricity, piped water, sewer hookups

and picnic tables are provided. Flush toilets, showers, a store, laundromat, ice and a playground are also available. Pets are permitted on leashes.

Reservations, fee: Reservations accepted; $12-$13 fee per night; American Express, MasterCard and Visa accepted. Open all year.

Who to contact: Phone (303) 667-2903 or write to 6850 West US 34, Loveland, CO 80537.

Location: From Loveland, drive five miles west on US 34.

Trip note: This campground is set adjacent to a motel, about 200 yards from the Big Thompson River. There is fishing in the river, but it's anyone's guess what you'll catch. The sites are graveled and shaded with cement pads. There are some good hiking trails in the area.

---

13) BOYD LAKE STATE RECREATION AREA

Reference: near Loveland; map C3, grid d2.

Campsites, facilities: There are a total of 148 sites for tents, trailers or motor homes of any length. Picnic tables are provided. Flush toilets, piped water, sanitary disposal services, showers, firewood, a store, coffee shop and ice are also available. Some facilities are **wheelchair accessible.** Pets are permitted on leashes. Boat docks, launching facilities and rentals are nearby. A large picnic area is also available.

Reservations, fee: Reserve sites by calling (800) 678-CAMP ($6.75 reservation fee); $7 fee per night plus $3 entrance fee. Open April through October.

Who to contact: Phone (303) 669-1739, or write 3720 North County Road 11C, Loveland, CO 80538.

Location: Take the Highway 34 exit off Interstate 25 twelve miles south of Fort Collins, and turn north on Madison Avenue one mile east of Loveland. Travel three miles to the park (well-signed).

Trip note: This is a good base camp for a fishing trip. Boyd Lake provides good walleye fishing in the spring. Other recreation options are boating, hiking, windsurfing and hunting. There is also a swim beach with showers. In the winter, this is a good spot for cross-country skiing.

---

14) GREELEY RV PARK

Reference: near South Platte River; map C3, grid d4.

Campsites, facilities: There are 18 tent sites and 80 drive-through sites for trailers or motor homes of any length. Electricity, piped water, sewer hookups and picnic tables are provided. Flush toilets, bottled gas, sanitary services, showers, recreation hall, a store, laundromat, ice and a playground are also available. A coffee shop is located within one mile. Pets are permitted on leashes.

Reservations, fee: Reservations accepted; $10.50 to $15.50 fee per night; MasterCard and Visa/BankAmericard accepted. Open all year.

Who to contact: Phone (303) 353-6476, or write 501 East 27th Street, Greeley, CO 80631.

Location: From the town of Greeley, drive a quarter mile east on the US 34 Bypass from the junction with US 85 to the campground.

Trip note: This privately developed camp is set near the South Platte River and is a good layover for cruisers looking for a break from Highway 34. The sites are level and shaded. Greeley has one of the largest outdoor rodeos in the nation every July 4th.

---

15) JACKSON LAKE STATE RECREATION AREA

Reference: on Jackson Lake; map C3, grid d7.

Campsites, facilities: There are 185 sites for tents, trailers or motor homes of any length. Picnic tables are provided. Piped water, flush toilets, sanitary disposal station and showers are also available. Pets are permitted on leashes. Boat docks, launching facilities and rentals are available.

Reservations, fee: Reserve sites by calling (800) 678-CAMP ($6.75 reservation fee); $7 fee per night plus $3 entrance fee. Open all year with limited winter facilities.

Who to contact: Phone (303) 645-2551, or write 26363 County Road 3, Orchard, CO 80649.

Location: From the town of Fort Morgan, drive 22 miles northwest on Highway 144 to the park entrance.

Trip note: This big camp is set along Jackson Lake, one of the prime lakes in the area for boating, fishing, windsurfing, swimming and waterskiing. In the winter you can choose from cross-country skiing, ice fishing, or ice skating. Although there are several lakes in the area, this is the only one with a campground. It is 80 miles from Denver and midway between Greeley RV Park and Brush Memorial Camp which are each about a half hour drive away.

---

16) BARBOUR PONDS STATE PARK

Reference: near Longmont; map C3, grid e0.

Campsites, facilities: There are 48 sites for tents, trailers or motor homes. Picnic tables are provided. Sanitary disposal services are also available. Bottled gas is located within one mile. Pets are permitted on leashes.

Reservations, fee: Reserve sites by calling (800) 678-CAMP ($6.75 reservation fee); $9 fee per night plus $3 entrance fee. Open all year.

Who to contact: Phone (303) 669-1739 or write to 3720N County Road 11-C, Loveland, CO 80538.

Location: Drive west from Longmont on Highway 119 to County Road 7. Turn north and follow for one mile to park.

Trip note: This camp provides a little of both worlds—city and country. It is located close to town where all the amenities are available, yet is close to a small lake where you can boat and fish. It is set back from the highway in a sparse, grassy setting. A unique sidetrip is a quarter-mile nature trail with a floating boardwalk. This is the only camp around for several miles, so take advantage.

17) DENVER NORTHEAST / PEPPER POD KOA

Reference: near Hudson; map C3, grid e5.

Campsites, facilities: There are 15 tent sites and 60 sites for trailers or motor homes up to 35 feet long. Picnic tables are provided. Flush toilets, bottled gas, sanitary disposal station, showers, recreation hall, a store, laundromat, ice, playground, swimming pool and a wading pool are also available. A coffee shop is located within one mile. Pets and motorbikes are permitted.

Reservations, fee: Reservations accepted; $15 to $21 fee per night; MasterCard and Visa/BankAmericard accepted. Open all year with limited winter facilities.

Who to contact: Phone (303) 536-4763, or write P.O. Box 445, Hudson, CO 80642.

Location: In the town of Hudson on Interstate 76, take exit 31 and drive two blocks to the campground.

Trip note: This one is just enough off the beaten path that it gets missed by most Interstate 76 cruisers. A 15-minute drive gets you here. You'll find a quiet, nine-acre spot in a rural setting. It's a good layover for visitors with motor homes. The sites are open and level. The country is rather barren, but if you're just looking for a place to lay down your head, it will do.

18) BOULDER MOUNTAIN LODGE

Reference: on Boulder Creek; map C3, grid f0.

Campsites, facilities: There are 25 sites for tents, trailers or motor homes. Picnic tables, showers, flush toilets, and piped water are provided. Electricity, a hot tub and a heated pool are available. Pets are permitted.

Reservations, fee: Reservations accepted; $14-$15 fee per night. Open year-round.

Who to contact: Phone (303) 444-0882 or write to 91 Four Mile Canyon Road, Boulder, CO 80302.

Location: From Highway 36 in Boulder, turn west on Highway 119 (Canyon Boulevard) and drive four miles up the canyon. Turn right on Four Mile Canyon Road and proceed one mile to the campground.

Trip note: This is the only camp within miles of Boulder. It's a nice option for those who want to be near the town, but don't want to pay the exorbitant hotel fees there. The campground is small, set in a pretty, wooded area, with some sites on the creek. Sidetrips include the drive west up Boulder Canyon to Nederland or nearby Flagstaff Mountain. Rocky Mountain National Park is a 45-minute drive north. This is an extremely popular area for rock climbing.

19) GOLDEN GATE CANYON STATE PARK

Reference: west of Golden; map C3, grid f0.

Campsites, facilities: There are 70 tent sites and 70 sites for trailers or motor homes of any length. Picnic tables are provided. Flush toilets, piped water, sanitary disposal station, showers, firewood and a laundromat are also available. Pets are permitted on leashes.

Reservations, fee: Reserve sites by calling (800) 678-CAMP ($6.75 reservation fee); $7 fee per night plus $3 entrance fee. Open all year with limited winter facilities.

Who to contact: Phone (303) 592-1502 or write to 3873 Highway 46, Golden, CO 80403.

Location: From Golden, travel west on US 6 to Highway 119 and drive through Black Hawk. At second park entrance go right and follow signs for 1.6 miles to campground.

Trip note: This is a popular year-round camp. In the fall, the deciduous trees brighten the hillsides in yellows and oranges, and it's especially beautiful. In spring and summer, there is good fishing in the streams, along with hiking and horseback riding. In winter, ice skating and snowmobiling are popular. A possible sidetrip is a tour of the Coors Brewery in Golden.

---

20) CENTRAL CITY / BLACK HAWK KOA

Reference: near Golden Gate Canyon State Park; map C3, grid f0.

Campsites, facilities: There are six tent sites and 17 sites for trailers or motor homes of any length. Electricity, piped water, sewer hookups and picnic tables are provided. Flush toilets, bottled gas, sanitary disposal station, showers, firewood, cable TV, recreation hall, a store, laundromat, ice, playground and a swimming pool are also available. Pets and motorbikes are permitted.

Reservations, fee: Reservations accepted; $18-$22 fee per night; MasterCard and Visa accepted. Open all year.

Who to contact: Phone (303) 582-9979 or write to 661 Highway 46, Golden, CO 80403.

Location: From Interstate 70 east of Idaho Springs, travel north on Highway 119 to Black Hawk, continue for six miles north to Highway 46, then drive east for a half mile to the campground.

Trip note: This is a small, developed campground for folks who want full facilities and adventure at the same time. It has shaded, open sites and is close to both the town of Golden and the western entrance to Golden Gate Canyon State Park. This offers a less-crowded alternative to the state park, but is not quite as scenic. Black Hawk and Central City, which offer limited stakes gambling, are a short drive away.

---

21) DENVER NORTH KOA

Reference: in Broomfield; map C3, grid f1.

Campsites, facilities: There are 22 tent sites and 157 sites for trailers or motor homes of any length. Electricity, piped water, sewer hookups

and picnic tables are provided. Flush toilets, bottled gas, sanitary disposal station, showers, recreation hall, a store, laundromat, ice, playground and a swimming pool are also available. Pets and motorbikes are permitted.

Reservations, fee: Reservations accepted; $14-$19 fee per night; MasterCard and Visa accepted. Open all year.

Who to contact: Phone (303) 452-4120 or write to 16700 North Washington, Broomfield, CO 80020.

Location: From Denver, travel 15 miles north on Interstate 25. Take exit 229 and go about 300 feet east on Highway 7.

Trip note: If you're visiting Denver, but in no way do you want to stay there, this campground is a viable option, located about 20 minutes by car outside of the city. Broomfield, however, is not exactly the wilderness either; it's basically a suburb of Boulder with wall-to-wall housing developments. Driving over to the Platte River to the east on Highway 7, or exploring the mountains to the west of Boulder are good sidetrips.

---

22) CHIEF HOSA

Reference: west of Denver; map C3, grid g0.

Campsites, facilities: There are 150 sites for tents, trailers or motor homes of any length. Picnic tables are provided. Flush toilets, sanitary disposal station, showers, recreation hall, a store, laundromat, ice, playground, wading pool and a swimming pool are also available. Electricity, piped water and firewood are available at an additional charge. A coffee shop is located within one mile. No pets are allowed.

Reservations, fee: Reservations accepted; $13-$16 fee per night; MasterCard and Visa accepted. Open mid-May to October.

Who to contact: Phone (303) 526-0364 or write to 27661 Genesee Drive, Golden, CO 80401.

Location: From Denver, travel 20 miles west on Interstate 70 and take exit 253 to the campground.

Trip note: This one is far enough out of Denver to provide the feeling of separation from the masses that most motor home cruisers desire. It's a beautiful park, set in a wooded mountain area that offers gorgeous scenic views. Hiking trails are available from the campground. Nearby recreation options include a golf course and tennis courts.

---

23) MOUNT EVANS STATE WILDLIFE AREA

Reference: west of Evergreen; map C3, grid g0.

Campsites, facilities: There are 15 primitive tent sites. Pit toilets are available. Pets are permitted on leashes. There is **no piped water.**

Reservations, fee: No reservations necessary; no fee. Open mid-June through December.

Who to contact: Phone Colorado Division of Wildlife at (303) 297-1192 or write to 6060 Broadway, Denver, CO 80216.

Location: From Evergreen, travel 10 miles west on Highway 74 to Upper Bear Creek Road and the campground.

Trip note: This is an ideal spot for anglers and hunters, especially those in Denver looking for a primitive spot without having to drive too far. The Mount Evans Wildlife Area covers 4,800 acres and includes small streams for fishing. In the fall, it is a good area for hunting. Call for information.

---

24) EAST TIN CUP VILLAGE

Reference: in Golden; map C3, grid g1.

Campsites, facilities: There are 13 tent sites and 90 sites for trailers or motor homes of any length. Electricity, piped water, sewer hookups and picnic tables are provided. Flush toilets, bottled gas, sanitary disposal station, showers and a laundromat are also available. A store and a coffee shop are located within one mile. Pets and motorbikes are permitted.

Reservations, fee: Reservations accepted; $12-$16 fee per night; MasterCard and Visa accepted. Open all year.

Who to contact: Phone (303) 279-6279 or write to 17921 West Colfax, Golden, CO 80401.

Location: In Golden, take exit 262 off Interstate 70, and drive two miles west on US 40 to the campground.

Trip note: This campground is set just outside the major Denver area. The tent sites are set in grass, with graveled RV sites. Nearby recreational options including a golf course, hiking trails and bicycle paths. A good sidetrip is visiting the spectacular Red Rocks Ampitheater, a natural rock phenomenon located a short drive away.

---

25) DELUX RV PARK

Reference: in Denver; map C3, grid g2.

Campsites, facilities: There are two tent sites and 29 sites for trailers or motor homes of any length. Electricity, piped water, sewer hookups and picnic tables are provided. Flush toilets, sanitary disposal station, showers, laundromat and ice are also available. Bottled gas, a store and a coffee shop are located within two miles. Pets and motorbikes are permitted.

Reservations, fee: Reservations accepted; $10-$17 fee per night. Open all year.

Who to contact: Phone (303) 433-0452 or write to 5520 North Federal, Denver, CO 80221.

Location: In Denver, go north on Federal Boulevard off Interstate 70 to the campground (on the east side of Federal Boulevard).

Trip note: This is an option to camping in the Denver area, a decent overnighter. It's located about ten minutes from downtown, but still offers trees and grass. If you're looking for a more rural option, head west to Golden.

26) CHERRY CREEK STATE RECREATION AREA

Reference: on Cherry Creek Lake; map C3, grid g3.

Campsites, facilities: There are 102 drive-through sites for tents, trailers or motor homes of any length. Piped water is provided. Flush toilets, picnic tables, sanitary disposal station, showers, a coffee shop, laundromat, ice and a playground are also available. Firewood costs extra. Bottled gas, a store and a swimming pool are located within one mile. Some facilities are **wheelchair accessible.** Pets are permitted on leashes. Boat docks, launching facilities and rentals are nearby.

Reservations, fee: Reserve sites by calling (800) 678-CAMP ($6.75 reservation fee); $7-$10 fee per night plus $3 entrance fee. Open April through October.

Who to contact: Phone (303) 699-3860 or write to 4201 South Parker, Aurora, CO 80014.

Location: From the junction of Interstate 225 and Parker Road in Aurora, travel three-quarters of a mile south on Parker Road to the campground.

Trip note: This is a popular camp set at Cherry Creek Lake. It can get crowded on summer weekends. Recreational options include horseback riding, bicycle paths, hiking trails, fishing, windsurfing, boating and a golf course. There are cross-country ski trails for winter campers.

27) DENVER MEADOWS

Reference: in Denver; map C3, grid g3.

Campsites, facilities: There are 50 tent sites and 278 sites for trailers or motor homes of any length. Electricity, piped water, sewer hookups and picnic tables are provided. Flush toilets, sanitary disposal station, showers, recreation hall, laundromat, ice, playground and a swimming pool are also available. A store and a coffee shop are located within one mile. No pets or motorbikes are permitted.

Reservations, fee: Reservations accepted; $16 fee per night; MasterCard and Visa accepted. Open all year.

Who to contact: Phone (303) 364-9483 or write to 2075 Potomac, Aurora, CO 80011.

Location: From the junction of Interstate 225 and US 40/287 in Aurora, travel one block west on Colfax and six blocks north on Potomac to the campground.

Trip note: This is a big urban camp for folks visiting the Denver area. Nearby recreation options include a golf course. There are many tourist attractions in Denver and the surrounding area. It's not the ideal camping destination, but it's cheaper than a hotel.

28) DENVER EAST STRASBURG KOA

Reference: east of Denver; map C3, grid g6.

Campsites, facilities: There are 30 tent sites and 84 sites for trailers or motor homes of any length. Picnic tables are provided. Flush toilets, bottled gas, sanitary disposal station, showers, firewood, recreation hall, a store, a laundromat, ice, a playground and a swimming pool are also available. Pets and motorbikes are permitted.

Reservations, fee: Reservations accepted; $13.50 to $17 fee per night; MasterCard and Visa/BankAmericard accepted. Open all year.

Who to contact: Phone (303) 622-9274, or write P.O. Box 597, Strasburg, CO 80136.

Location: From the town of Denver, drive 36 miles east on Interstate 70. Take exit 310 and drive north, and then east on the frontage road to the campground.

Trip note: This is a major layover spot for motor home cruisers on Interstate 70 who are looking to avoid the Denver crush. Situated 20 miles east of Denver, this privately developed park covers 14 acres in a rural, high prairie setting. The sites are level and shaded. The park offers a "social program" in the summer.

---

29) STAGE STOP

Reference: east of Conifer; map C3, grid h1.

Campsites, facilities: There are 20 sites for tents, trailers or motor homes up to 32 feet long. Picnic tables are provided. Piped water, flush toilets, sanitary disposal station, firewood, ice and playground are also available. Showers are available at an additional charge. Bottled gas, a store and a coffee shop are located within three miles. Pets are permitted on leashes.

Reservations, fee: Reservations accepted; $12 fee per night. Open May to October.

Who to contact: Phone (303) 697-4901 or write to 8884 South US 285, Morrison, CO 80465.

Location: From Conifer, travel five miles east on US 285 to the campground.

Trip note: This is a good layover spot for cruisers on US 285. It's a pretty spot, set near forest wildlands. Morrison is a quaint little town, with lots of antique shops for tourists.

---

30) CHATFIELD STATE RECREATION AREA

Reference: southwest of Denver; map C3, grid h2.

Campsites, facilities: There are 76 tent sites and 77 drive-through sites for trailers or motor homes of any length. Picnic tables are provided. Piped water, flush toilets, sanitary disposal station, showers, firewood and a playground are also available. Electricity costs extra. A store and a coffee shop are located within one mile. Pets are permitted on leashes. Boat docks, launching facilities and rentals are nearby.

Reservations, fee: Reserve sites by calling (800) 678-CAMP ($6.75 reservation fee); $7-$10 fee per night plus $3 entrance fee. Open April through mid-October

Who to contact: Phone (303) 791-7275 or write to 11500 North Roxborough, Littleton, CO 80125.

Location: From Denver, go south on Wadsworth to Highway 121. Continue south until you see the Deer Creek Entrance. Head east and into park.

Trip note: This is a popular and easy-to-reach park just eight miles from Denver. The park covers 5,600 acres and the adjacent lake covers 1,150 acres. All water sports allowed. Bike paths, hiking trails and horse rentals provide sidetrip options. In the winter, it's a good spot for ice skating, cross-country skiing and ice fishing.

---

31) INDIAN CREEK

Reference: west of Sedalia, Pike National Forest; map C3, grid h2.

Campsites, facilities: There are 10 sites for tents, trailers or motor homes up to 16 feet long. Picnic tables are provided. Piped water and pit toilets are also available. A store and a coffee shop are located within one mile. Pets are permitted on leashes.

Reservations, fee: No reservations necessary; $6 fee per night. Open April to mid-November.

Who to contact: Phone Pike National Forest at (303) 236-7386 or write to South Platte Ranger District, P.O. Box 25127, Lakewood, CO 80225.

Location: From Sedalia, drive 10 miles west on Highway 67 and a quarter mile west on County Road 67 to the campground.

Trip note: Set on Indian Creek, few people, with the exception of locals, know about this nice little spot. It's located just beyond the Indian Creek Ranger Station, which can provide maps and local information. There is a primitive road leading north out of camp that is perfect for mountain biking. A National Forest map will detail routes of the various hiking trails in the area.

---

32) MEADOWS GROUP CAMP

Reference: on Redskin Creek, Pike National Forest; map C3, grid i0.

Campsites, facilities: There are 40 sites for tents, trailers or motor homes up to 16 feet long. This site can accommodate up to 300 people. Picnic tables are provided. Piped water and pit toilets are also available. Pets are permitted on leashes.

Reservations, fee: Reserve through MISTIX at (800) 283-CAMP ($6 MISTIX fee); $25-$300 fee per night. Open April to mid-November.

Who to contact: Phone Pike National Forest at (303) 236-7386 or write to South Platte Ranger District, P.O. Box 25127, Lakewood, CO 80225.

Location: From the town of Buffalo Creek, drive a half mile southeast on County Road 126, 5.7 miles southwest on Forest Service Road 543 and a half mile east on Forest Service Road 550 to the campground.

Trip note: This camp is set along Redskin Creek. It's a good spot for hikers because a trail (Colorado Trail) passes through camp that leads to Lost Creek Wilderness. It's a five-mile hike to the west. It's a pretty, wide-open campground, perfect for large gatherings.

---

33) BALDY

Reference: near Baldy Peak, Pike National Forest; map C3, grid i0.

Campsites, facilities: There are eight sites for tents, trailers or motor homes. Picnic tables are provided. Piped water and pit toilets are also available. A store is located within one mile. Pets are permitted on leashes.

Reservations, fee: No reservations necessary; no fee. Open May to mid-October.

Who to contact: Phone Pike National Forest at (303) 236-7386 or write to South Platte Ranger District, P.O. Box 25127, Lakewood, CO 80225.

Location: From the town of Buffalo Creek, drive a half mile southeast on County Road 126 and 4.8 miles southwest on Forest Service Road 543 to the campground.

Trip note: This camp gets its name from nearby Baldy Peak, (7,872 feet). A visit to nearby Buffalo Creek is a good sidetrip. It's tiny, private and secluded, a quieter and more primitive option to Buffalo Camp. Buffalo Picnic Ground is located nearby.

---

34) BUFFALO

Reference: on Buffalo Creek, Pike National Forest; map C3, grid i0.

Campsites, facilities: There are 41 sites for tents, trailers or motor homes up to 16 feet long. Picnic tables are provided. Piped water and pit toilets are also available. Pets are permitted on leashes.

Reservations, fee: Reserve through MISTIX at (800) 283-CAMP ($6 MISTIX fee); $6 fee per night. Open April to mid-November.

Who to contact: Phone Pike National Forest at (303) 236-7386 or write to South Platte Ranger District, P.O. Box 25127, Lakewood, CO 80225.

Location: From the town of Buffalo Creek, drive a half mile southeast on County Road 126, 5.7 miles southwest on Forest Service Road 543 and a quarter mile east on Forest Service Road 550 to the campground.

Trip note: This camp is difficult to reach, but still very popular. It is set near Buffalo Creek, which can provide good fishing. A major trail is available just south of camp, and is routed west for several miles into the

Lost Creek Wilderness. The trail also runs east into the adjacent National Forest lands. See a National Forest map for detailed information.

35) KELSEY

Reference: on Sixmile Creek, Pike National Forest; map C3, grid i0.

Campsites, facilities: There are 17 sites for tents, trailers or motor homes up to 16 feet long. Picnic tables are provided. Piped water and pit toilets are located. Pets are permitted on leashes.

Reservations, fee: No reservations necessary; $7 fee per night. Open May to mid-October.

Who to contact: Phone Pike National Forest at (303) 236-7386 or write to South Platte Ranger District, P.O. Box 25127, Lakewood, CO 80225.

Location: From the town of Buffalo Creek drive 7.9 miles south on County Road 126 to the campground.

Trip note: This is a quiet spot on Sixmile Creek. There isn't much around here except water and trees, but sometimes that's all you need, or want. There are no hiking trails in the immediate area, but a major trail crosses the road about 3.5 miles to the north.

36) TRAMWAY

Reference: on Buffalo Creek, Pike National Forest; map C3, grid i0.

Campsites, facilities: There are six sites for tents, trailers or motor homes. Picnic tables are provided. Piped water and pit toilets are also available. Pets are permitted on leashes.

Reservations, fee: No reservations necessary; no fee. Open May to mid-October.

Who to contact: Phone Pike National Forest at (303) 236-7386 or write to South Platte Ranger District, P.O. Box 25127, Lakewood, CO 80225.

Location: From the town of Buffalo Creek, drive four-tenths of a mile southeast on County Road 126 and 5.2 miles southwest on Forest Service Road 543 to the campground.

Trip note: Little known and little used, this camp provides quiet and a place to watch the water roll by. Set along Buffalo Creek, Hoosier Pass and the Continental Divide are not far to the north. This is a primitive option to Buffalo Camp.

37) GREEN MOUNTAIN

Reference: near Wellington Lake, Pike National Forest; map C3, grid i0.

Campsites, facilities: There are six sites for tents, trailers or motor homes. Picnic tables are provided. Piped water and pit toilets are also available. Pets are permitted on leashes.

Reservations, fee: No reservations necessary; no fee. Open May to mid-October.

Who to contact: Phone Pike National Forest at (303) 236-7386 or write to South Platte Ranger District, P.O. Box 25127, Lakewood, CO 80225.

Location: From the town of Buffalo Creek, drive a half mile southeast on County Road 126 and 7.7 miles southwest on Forest Service Road 543 to the campground.

Trip note: This can be a perfect little spot. It is less than a mile from Wellington Lake, is also close to Buffalo Creek, and a trailhead on the other side of Wellington Lake provides access to the Lost Creek Wilderness. And, with just six campsites, you know there won't be scarcely a soul around.

---

38) TOP OF THE WORLD

Reference: in Pike National Forest; map C3, grid i1.

Campsites, facilities: There are seven sites for tents, trailers or motor homes up to 16 feet long. Picnic tables are provided. Pit toilets are also available. A store is located within one mile. There is **no piped water.** Pets are permitted on leashes.

Reservations, fee: No reservations necessary; no fee. Open April to mid-November.

Who to contact: Phone Pike National Forest at (303) 236-7386 or write to South Platte Ranger District, P.O. Box 25127, Lakewood, CO 80225.

Location: From the town of Buffalo Creek, drive 2.7 miles southeast on County Road 126 and a quarter mile southeast on Forest Service Road 537 to the campground.

Trip note: Height is always relative. The Top of the World campground is set at 7,500 feet, low compared to the high Rockies. But when compared to the surrounding country, you feel much higher. A trail passes near camp, but no creeks are in the immediate area; be sure to bring your own water. Buffalo Creek Ranger Station is nearby on Road 126, and can provide maps and information.

---

39) HORSE CREEK

Reference: near Sedalia; map C3, grid i1.

Campsites, facilities: There are 13 tent sites and 19 sites for trailers or motor homes of any length. Sewer hookups and picnic tables are provided. Flush toilets, bottled gas, sanitary disposal station, showers, a coffee shop, ice and a playground are also available. Firewood costs extra. Pets on leashes and motorbikes are permitted.

Reservations, fee: Reservations accepted; $10-$13 fee per night. Open Memorial Day to Labor Day.

Who to contact: Phone (303) 647-2329 or write to Route 2, P.O. Box 104, Sedalia, CO 80135.

Location: From Colorado Springs, drive 20 miles west on US 24 and 20 miles north on Highway 67 to the campground.

Trip note: This is a privately developed park located beside Horse Creek. It's a pretty area, surrounded by national forest. The nearby recreation options include hiking trails and bicycle paths.

---

40) LONE ROCK

Reference: on South Platte River, Pike National Forest; map C3, grid i1.

Campsites, facilities: There are 19 sites for tents, trailers or motor homes up to 16 feet long. Picnic tables are provided. Piped water and pit toilets are also available. A store, a coffee shop and ice are located within one mile. Pets are permitted on leashes.

Reservations, fee: Reserve through MISTIX at (800) 283-CAMP ($6 MISTIX fee); $8 fee per night. Open April to November.

Who to contact: Phone Pike National Forest at (303) 236-7386 or write to South Platte Ranger District, P.O. Box 25127, Lakewood, CO 80225.

Location: From the town of Buffalo Creek, drive 16.7 miles southeast on County Road 126 to the campground.

Trip note: You get a little of both worlds here: rustic beauty, yet nearby facilities. This camp is set on the South Platte River, but supplies are available just a mile away. So when you figure out what you forgot, you can still get it. This is one of the few camps in the area that takes reservations, which shows you how many people are trying to get in. Expect plenty of company in the summer months.

---

41) FLAT ROCKS

Reference: southwest of Sedalia, Pike National Forest; map C3, grid i2.

Campsites, facilities: There are 20 sites for tents, trailers or motor homes up to 16 feet long. Picnic tables are provided. Piped water and pit toilets are also available. Pets are permitted on leashes.

Reservations, fee: No reservations necessary; $6 fee per night. Open May to mid-October.

Who to contact: Phone Pike National Forest at (303) 236-7386 or write to South Platte Ranger District, P.O. Box 25127, Lakewood, CO 80225.

Location: From Sedalia, drive 10 miles west on Highway 67 and 4.8 miles south on Forest Service Road 300.

Trip note: There's not much out here except trees and squirrels, but you'll probably have the place to yourself. Not many people know about this place. It is pretty, though, and is perfect if you're looking for peace and quiet. If you like Flat Rocks Camp, then you'll love Devil's Head Camp and Jackson Creek Camp. Just drive south on Road 300.

---

42) DEVIL'S HEAD

Reference: southwest of Sedalia, Pike National Forest; map C3, grid i2.

Campsites, facilities: There are 22 sites for tents, trailers or motor homes up to 16 feet long. Picnic tables are provided. Piped water and pit toilets are also available. Pets are permitted on leashes.

Reservations, fee: No reservations necessary; $6 fee per night. Open May to mid-October.

Who to contact: Phone Pike National Forest at (303) 236-7386 or write to South Platte Ranger District, P.O. Box 25127, Lakewood, CO 80225.

Location: From Sedelia, drive 10 miles west on Highway 67, 9.1 miles south on Forest Service Road 300, and four-tenths of a mile southeast on Forest Service Road 30008C.

Trip note: This camp is set near the legendary Devil's Head, a big rock at 9,748 feet and just a short hike away. Some say it is a place of power and mystery. Devil's Head Fire Lookout is the only manned lookout station in Colorado; visitors are welcome. A trail is also available.

---

43) JACKSON CREEK

Reference: near Devil's Head, Pike National Forest; map C3, grid i2.

Campsites, facilities: There are nine sites for tents, trailers or motor homes up to 16 feet long. Picnic tables are provided. Piped water and pit toilets are also available. Pets are permitted on leashes.

Reservations, fee: No reservations necessary; $6 fee per night. Open May to mid-October.

Who to contact: Phone Pike National Forest at (303) 236-7386 or write to South Platte Ranger District, P.O. Box 25127, Lakewood, CO 80225.

Location: From Sedalia, drive 10 miles west on Highway 67, 13.9 miles south on Forest Service Road 300, and 1.5 miles northeast on Forest Service Road 502 to the campground.

Trip note: This is a quiet spot on Jackson Creek. You get a view of the back of Devil's Head (see trip note for Devil's Head Camp). This camp is harder to reach and definitely more remote than nearby Devil's Head Camp, but it's nice, situated by a rippling stream, and no people for miles.

44) KOKO'S CAMPGROUND

Reference: in Limon; map C3, grid i9.

Campsites, facilities: There are 22 sites for trailers or motor homes of any length. Electricity, piped water and picnic tables are provided. Flush toilets, bottled gas, sanitary disposal station, ice and a playground are also available. A store, a coffee shop and laundromat are located within one mile. Pets are permitted on leashes.

Reservations, fee: Reservations accepted; $6-$8 fee per night; MasterCard and Visa/BankAmericard accepted. Open all year with limited winter facilities.

Who to contact: Phone (719) 775-9797, or write 378 Main Street, P.O. Box 367, Limon, CO 80828.

Location: In the town of Limon, take exit 362 off Highway 71 where it meets US 24 and drive five blocks west to the campground.

Trip note: This is a small (one acre) urban motor home park. It's set in the middle of town, adjacent to a service station. You get the picture. Nearby recreation options include a golf course and tennis courts. Some local attractions are the historic railroad, which offers tours, and the Genoa Tower, from the top of which, they say, you can see seven states on a clear day.

45) RIVERSIDE

Reference: on South Platte River, Pike National Forest; map C3, grid j0.

Campsites, facilities: There are 19 sites for tents, trailers or motor homes up to 21 feet long. Picnic tables are provided. Well water and pit toilets are also available. Sanitary disposal station, a store, a coffee shop and ice are located within five miles. Pets are permitted on leashes.

Reservations, fee: No reservations necessary; $7 fee per night. Open mid-May to early November.

Who to contact: Phone Pike National Forest at (719) 836-2031 or write to South Park Ranger District, P.O. Box 219, Fairplay, CO 80440.

Location: From the town of Lake George, drive one mile southwest on County Road 61, then one mile on Forest Service Road 96 to the campground.

Trip note: This is a nearby option to Blue Mountain Camp. It's take-your-pick deal, with trout fishing available, and also visits to Elevenmile Reservoir or Florissant Fossil Beds National Monument. A nearby option is Blue Mountain Camp.

46) BLUE MOUNTAIN

Reference: near South Platte River, Pike National Forest; map C3, grid j0.

Campsites, facilities: There are 21 sites for tents, trailers or motor homes up to 22 feet long. Picnic tables are provided. Well water and pit toilets are also available. A store, a coffee shop and ice are located within one mile. Pets are permitted on leashes.

Reservations, fee: Reserve through MISTIX at (800) 283-CAMP ($6 MISTIX fee); $6 fee per night. Open mid-May to late October.

Who to contact: Phone Pike National Forest at (719) 836-2031 or write to South Park Ranger District, P.O. Box 219, Fairplay, CO 80440.

Location: From the town of Lake George, drive 1.6 miles southwest on County Road 61 to the campground.

Trip note: This is an option to nearby Riverside Campground. The sites here are more shaded. A 1.5-mile nature trail is located at the camp, offering access to the beautiful South Platte River. For details on the sidetrip to Florissant Fossil Beds National Monument, see the trip note for Homestead Camp.

---

47) SPRINGER GULCH

Reference: on South Platte River, Pike National Forest; map C3, grid j0.

Campsites, facilities: There are 15 sites for tents, trailers or motor homes up to 22 feet long. Picnic tables are provided. Piped water and pit toilets are also available. Pets are permitted on leashes.

Reservations, fee: No reservations necessary; $7 fee per night. Open mid-May to late September.

Who to contact: Phone Pike National Forest at (719) 836-2031 or write to South Park Ranger District, P.O. Box 219, Fairplay, CO 80440.

Location: From the town of Lake George, travel southwest one mile on County Road 61, then southwest on Forest Service Road 96 for 5.6 miles to the campground.

Trip note: This is one in a series of Forest Service campgrounds in the immediate vicinity. See trip notes for Riverside and Elevenmile State Park for sidetrip possibilities.

---

48) WILDHORN

Reference: near Trail Creek, Pike National Forest; map C3, grid j0.

Campsites, facilities: There are nine sites for tents, trailers or motor homes up to 16 feet long. Picnic tables are provided. Hand-pumped water and pit toilets are also available. Pets are permitted on leashes.

Reservations, fee: No reservations necessary; no fee. Open late May to October.

Who to contact: Phone Pike National Forest at (719) 636-1602 or write to Pike's Peak Ranger District, 601 South Weber, Colorado Springs, CO 80903.

Location: From Florissant, drive 12.2 miles north on Forest Service Road 200 and then three-quarters of a mile west on Forest Service Road 361 to the campground.

Trip note: This is a hidden little camp set near Trail Creek. It's a good spot for hikers. One trail from camp leads eight miles west to South Platte River. Pick up a Forest Service map for details on trails and access roads.

49) HAPPY MEADOWS

Reference: on South Platte River, Pike National Forest; map C3, grid j0.

Campsites, facilities: There are seven sites for tents, trailers or motor homes up to 22 feet long. Picnic tables are provided. Well water and pit toilets are also available. Sanitary disposal station, a store, a coffee shop and ice are located within five miles. Pets are permitted on leashes.

Reservations, fee: No reservations necessary; $7 fee per night. Open mid-May to mid-November.

Who to contact: Phone Pike National Forest at (719) 836-2031 or write to South Park Ranger District, P.O. Box 219, Fairplay, CO 80440.

Location: From the town of Lake George, travel northwest for 1.2 miles on US 24; north for 1.2 miles on County Road 77 and then northeast on County Road 112 for three-quarters of a mile to the campground.

Trip note: This is a secluded spot set along the South Platte River. It is a good option if you want to avoid the people crunch you are likely to get at nearby Elevenmile Canyon. By heading north up the road a ways, you can hop on trails that follow Vermillion and Crystal Creeks.

50) ROUND MOUNTAIN

Reference: near Elevenmile Reservoir, Pike National Forest; map C3, grid j0.

Campsites, facilities: There are 16 sites for tents, trailers or motor homes up to 32 feet long. Picnic tables are provided. Well water and pit toilets are also available. A store and ice are located within five miles. Pets are permitted on leashes.

Reservations, fee: No reservations necessary; $6 fee per night. Open mid-May to early November.

Who to contact: Phone Pike National Forest at (719) 836-2031 or write to South Park Ranger District, P.O. Box 219, Fairplay, CO 80440.

Location: From the town of Lake George, travel 5.4 miles northwest on US 24 to the campground.

Trip note: This is a good Forest Service camp for Highway 24 cruisers looking for an easy-access layover spot. The campground is located right off the highway. Sidetrip options include trips to Elevenmile Reservoir and Florissant Fossil Beds National Monument.

51) HOMESTEAD

Reference: near Lake George; map C3, grid j0.

Campsites, facilities: There are 10 tent sites and 16 sites for trailers or motor homes. Electricity, piped water, sewer hookups and picnic tables are provided. Flush toilets, sanitary disposal station, showers, firewood, ice and a playground are also available. Bottled gas, a store and coffee shop are located within one mile. Pets and motorbikes are permitted.

Reservations, fee: Reservations accepted; $6-$12 fee per night; Open all year.

Who to contact: Phone (719) 748-3822 or write to Star Route 2, P.O. Box 8966, Lake George, CO 80827.

Location: Drive one mile northwest of the town of Lake George on US 24 to the campground.

Trip note: This camp is a layover spot for visitors heading to nearby Lake George and Elevenmile Canyon. Florissant Fossil Beds National Monument provides a sidetrip. It is a 6,000-acre park with unique geology and hiking possibilities. The fossils include petrified sequoia stumps. For information, phone (719) 748-3253.

52) WAGON TONGUE

Reference: near South Platte River, Pike National Forest; map C3, grid j0.

Campsites, facilities: There are seven sites for tents, trailers or motor homes up to 16 feet long. Picnic tables and pit toilets are provided. There is **no piped water**. Pets are permitted on leashes.

Reservations, fee: No reservations necessary; no fee. Open mid-May to late October.

Who to contact: Phone Pike National Forest at (719) 836-2031 or write to South Park Ranger District, P.O. Box 219, Fairplay, CO 80440.

Location: From the town of Lake George, travel one mile southwest on County Road 61, then southwest on Forest Service Road 96 for seven miles to the campground.

Trip note: A take-your-pick deal with the three preceding camps providing close options. This is the smallest and most primitive of the lot, and is also located slightly off the highway, which provides a bit more seclusion than the others.

53) SPRUCE GROVE

Reference: near Lost Creek Wilderness, Pike National Forest; map C3, grid j0.

Campsites, facilities: There are 28 sites for tents, trailers or motor homes up to 32 feet long. Picnic tables are provided. Well water and pit toilets are also available. Pets are permitted on leashes.

Reservations, fee: No reservations necessary; $6 fee per night. Open mid-May to early November.

Who to contact: Phone Pike National Forest at (719) 836-2031 or write to South Park Ranger District, P.O. Box 219, Fairplay, CO 80440.

Location: From the town of Lake George, travel 1.2 miles northwest on US 24 and 12.2 miles northwest on County Road 77 to the campground.

Trip note: This pretty camp is set alongside Tarryall Creek. It's a good base camp for backpackers who arrive late. The Lizard Rock trailhead leads directly from camp into the Lost Creek Wilderness, as does the Twin Eagles Trail, located one mile northwest.

---

54) TRAIL CREEK

Reference: in Pike National Forest; map C3, grid j1.

Campsites, facilities: There are seven sites for tents, trailers or motor homes up to 16 feet long. Picnic tables are provided. Hand-pimped water and pit toilets are also available. Pets are permitted on leashes.

Reservations, fee: No reservations necessary; no fee. Open late May to October.

Who to contact: Phone Pike National Forest at (719) 636-1602 or write to Pike's Peak Ranger District, 601 South Weber Street, Colorado Springs, CO 80903.

Location: From the town of Woodland Park, drive 13.5 miles northwest on Highway 67 (to Westport); 1.5 miles south on Forest Service Road 340/200 and then 1.5 miles southwest on Forest Service Road 200 to the campground.

Trip note: A hidden spot along Trail Creek, this is an ideal base camp for hikers. The ambitious can take a network of forest service roads to the west and jump on to a trail that follows the Platte River. A Forest Service map detailing both access roads and the numerous trails in the area is advised. A nearby option is Big Turkey Camp to the west.

---

55) BIG TURKEY

Reference: on Turkey Creek, Pike National Forest; map C3, grid j1.

Campsites, facilities: There are 10 sites for tents, trailers or motor homes up to 16 feet long. Picnic tables are provided. Hand-pumped water and pit toilets are also available. Pets are permitted on leashes.

Reservations, fee: No reservations necessary; no fee. Open May to mid-October.

Who to contact: Phone Pike National Forest at (719) 236-7386 or write to South Platte Ranger District, P.O. Box 25127, Lakewood, CO 80225.

Location: From the town of Woodland Park, drive 13.5 miles northwest on Highway 67 (to Westport); three-quarters of a mile southwest on Forest Service Road 200 and then 3.9 miles southwest on Forest Service Road 360 to the campground.

Trip note: This is a intimate, secluded camp set alongside Turkey Creek near Turkey Rock. It's small, primitive and quiet. There is a hiking trail about a mile south of camp, routed west into the surrounding national forest.

---

56) COACH LIGHT

Reference: in Woodland Park; map C3, grid j2.

Campsites, facilities: There are 10 tent sites and 25 sites for trailers or motor homes of any length. Electricity, piped water, sewer hookups and picnic tables are provided. Flush toilets, sanitary disposal station, showers, recreation hall, laundromat, ice and a playground are also available. Firewood costs extra. Bottled gas and a coffee shop are located within one mile. Pets and motorbikes are permitted.

Reservations, fee: Reservations accepted; $12-$16 fee per night. Open all year.

Who to contact: Phone (719) 687-2645 or write to 19253 Highway 24, Woodland Park, CO 80863.

Location: Located in Woodland Park on US 24 (east of town).

Trip note: This is one of several privately developed campgrounds in the immediate area. It covers 12 acres and offers pretty, grassy and shaded sites. Nearby recreation options include hiking trails and a riding stable. A sidetrip is the drive up Pike's Peak (14,110 feet).

---

57) BIG PINES

Reference: near Woodland Park; map C3, grid j2.

Campsites, facilities: There are 24 drive-through sites for trailers or motor homes of any length. Picnic tables are provided. Flush toilets, sanitary disposal station and a playground are also available. Bottled gas, a store, coffee shop and laundromat are located within one mile. Pets are permitted on leashes.

Reservations, fee: Reservations accepted; $10-$12 fee per night. Open all year.

Who to contact: Phone (719) 687-9160 or write to P.O. Box 915, Woodland Park, CO 80863.

Location: From the town of Woodland Park, drive two miles east on US 24.

Trip note: This is one of three parks in the immediate area. The sites are graveled and shaded with pine trees. The park is set at the foot of Pike's Peak, a granite hulk of a mountain that looms high at 14,110 feet. If your car is up to it, you can drive right up near the peak (but don't turn your engine off, it may not start again). Nearby recreation options include hiking trails, bike paths and a riding stable.

58) TOWN & COUNTRY

Reference: in Woodland Park; map C3, grid j2.

Campsites, facilities: There are four tent sites and 53 sites for trailers or motor homes of any length. Electricity, piped water, sewer hookups and picnic tables are provided. Flush toilets, sanitary disposal station, showers, recreation hall, a store, coffee shop, laundromat and ice are also available. Bottled gas is located within one mile. Pets and motorbikes are permitted.

Reservations, fee: Reservations accepted; $14-$17 fee per night; MasterCard and Visa accepted. Open May through September.

Who to contact: Phone (719) 687-9518 or write to P.O. Box 368, Woodland Park, CO 80866.

Location: From the junction of US 24 and Highway 67 in Woodland Park, drive four blocks north on Highway 67 to the park.

Trip note: One of many motor home parks in the area, this one covers four acres. It has large, shaded sites and is very well kept. Nearby recreation options include a golf course, a riding stable, tennis courts, and of course, the drive up Pike's Peak.

59) SOUTH MEADOWS

Reference: near Manitou Experimental Forest, Pike National Forest; map C3, grid j2.

Campsites, facilities: There are 64 sites for tents, trailers or motor homes up to 32 feet long. Picnic tables are provided. Piped water, pit toilets and a sanitary disposal station are also available. Showers, a laundromat and ice are located within five miles. Some facilities are **wheelchair accessible.** Pets are permitted on leashes.

Reservations, fee: No reservations necessary; $7 fee per night. Open May to mid-October.

Who to contact: Phone Pike National Forest at (719) 636-1602 or write to Pike's Peak Ranger District, 601 South Weber Street, Colorado Springs, CO 80903.

Location: From the town of Woodland Park, drive 5.8 miles north on Highway 67 to the campground.

Trip note: This is one of three Forest Service campgrounds in the immediate area. All are adjacent to the Manitou Experimental Forest. There are good hiking trails and small creeks in the area. Since Pike National Forest is close to the Denver-Colorado Springs corridor, this area gets heavy use by visitors.

60) PAINTED ROCKS

Reference: near Ryan Gulch, Pike National Forest; map C3, grid j2.

Campsites, facilities: There are 18 sites for tents, trailers or motor homes up to 22 feet long. Picnic tables are provided. Piped water and pit toilets are also available. Showers, a laundromat and ice are located within five miles. Pets are permitted on leashes.

Reservations, fee: No reservations necessary; $6 fee per night. Open late May to early September.

Who to contact: Phone Pike National Forest at (719) 636-1602 or write to 601 South Weber Street, Colorado Springs, CO 80903.

Location: From the town of Woodland Park, drive eight miles north on Highway 67 and then a half mile west on Forest Service Road 341 to the campground.

Trip note: This is a nearby option to Colorado Camp. Possible sidetrips include visiting Manitou Picnic Ground at the tiny lake north of camp, or taking the primitive road that runs west, through Manitou Experimental Forest, near the base of Mount Deception. There is a also trail south of camp that follows Ryan Gulch.

---

61) COLORADO

Reference: near Trout Creek, Pike National Forest; map C3, grid j2.

Campsites, facilities: There are 81 sites for tents, trailers or motor homes up to 32 feet long. Picnic tables are provided. Piped water, pit toilets and a sanitary disposal station are also available. Showers, a laundromat and ice are located within five miles. Some facilities are **wheelchair accessible.** Pets are permitted on leashes.

Reservations, fee: No reservations necessary; $7 fee per night. Open late May to early September.

Who to contact: Phone Pike National Forest at (719) 636-1602 or write to 601 South Weber Street, Colorado Springs, CO 80903.

Location: From the town of Woodland Park, drive 6.9 miles north on Highway 67 to the campground.

Trip note: This camp is set near a small reservoir on nearby Trout Creek and adjacent to Manitou Experimental Forest. A few hiking trails, but mostly logging roads, are nearby and provide access to Pike National Forest. See trip note for Painted Rocks Camp for sidetrip details.

---

62) DIAMOND

Reference: in Woodland Park; map C3, grid j2.

Campsites, facilities: There are 10 tent sites and 150 drive-through sites for trailers or motor homes of any length. Electricity, piped water, sewer hookups and picnic tables are provided. Flush toilets, sanitary disposal station, showers, recreation hall, laundromat, ice and a playground are also available. Firewood costs extra. Bottled gas, a store and coffee shop are located within one mile. Pets and motorbikes are permitted.

Reservations, fee: Reservations accepted; $15 fee per night; MasterCard and Visa accepted. Open May to October.

Who to contact: Phone (719) 687-9684 or write to 900 North Highway 67, Woodland Park, CO 80863.

Location: From the town of Woodland Park, drive a quarter mile north on Highway 67 to the campground.

Trip note: This is a 20-acre, privately developed park, set up primarily for motor homes. The sites are heavily treed. The park is situated adjacent to Pike National Forest, which offers a myriad of recreation options including hiking trails, fishing in backcountry lakes and hunting. A nearby riding stable provides a sidetrip possibility.

---

63) HI-VU

Reference: near Pike National Forest; map C3, grid j2.

Campsites, facilities: There are 24 tent sites and 54 sites for trailers or motor homes of any length. Picnic tables are provided. Flush toilets, sanitary disposal station, showers, recreation hall, laundromat, ice, playground and a swimming pool are also available. Firewood are available at an additional charge. Bottled gas, a store and a coffee shop are located within one mile. Pets and motorbikes are permitted.

Reservations, fee: Reservations accepted; $9-$13 fee per night; MasterCard and Visa accepted. Open May to October.

Who to contact: Phone (719) 684-9044 or write to P.O. Box 215, Green Mountain Falls, CO 80819.

Location: Take exit 141 off Interstate 25 in Colorado Springs and drive 15 miles northwest on US 24 to milepost 290 and the campground entrance.

Trip note: Pike's Peak overlooks this privately developed camp set near the Pike National Forest. It's a pretty park, with campsites set on a hill and spectacular mountain views. Nearby recreation options include hiking trails and a riding stable.

---

64) RAINBOW FALLS

Reference: near Trout Creek; map C3, grid j2.

Campsites, facilities: There are 200 tent sites and 40 sites for trailers or motor homes of any length. Picnic tables are provided. Flush toilets, sanitary disposal station, showers, firewood, a store, coffee shop, ice and a playground are also available. Pets and motorbikes are permitted.

Reservations, fee: Reservations accepted; $10-$14 fee per night; MasterCard and Visa accepted. Open all year.

Who to contact: Phone (719) 687-9074 or write to P.O. Box 9062, Woodland Park, CO 80866.

Location: From the town of Woodland Park, drive north on Highway 67 for 10 miles. Turn east at the sign for Rainbow Falls park and drive two miles northeast to the campground.

Trip note: This is a large but relatively secluded park that covers 61 acres. It gets its name from small waterfalls at the nearby Trout Creek.

Some hiking trails are available close by in Pike National Forest. There are eight lakes within the park that are great for fishing. Horseback riding, hay rides and chuckwagon dinners are some of the extra attractions.

65) THUNDER RIDGE

Reference: near Rampart Reservoir, Pike National Forest; map C3, grid j3.

Campsites, facilities: There are 21 sites for tents, trailers or motor homes up to 22 feet long. Picnic tables are provided. Piped water and pit toilets are also available. Pets are permitted on leashes. Boat launching facilities are nearby.

Reservations, fee: Reserve through MISTIX at (800) 283-CAMP ($6 MISTIX fee); $9 fee per night. Open late May to early September.

Who to contact: Phone Pike National Forest at (719) 636-1602 or write to Pike's Peak Ranger District, 601 South Weber Street, Colorado Springs, CO 80903.

Location: From the town of Woodland Park, drive 4.5 miles northeast on Forest Service Road 393, four miles southeast on Forest Service Road 300 and then 1.4 miles northeast on Forest Service Road 306 to the campground.

Trip note: This is a popular camp, set near the west shore of Rampart Reservoir in the Rampart Reservoir Recreation Area. Your options include fishing, swimming, boating, hiking or just lying in the sun. Get your reservation in early—this is a favored camp for local Colorado families, and you may find yourself wrestling for a site if you show up on Fourth of July weekend. An alternative camp is Meadow Ridge.

66) MEADOW RIDGE

Reference: on Rampart Reservoir, Pike National Forest; map C3, grid j3.

Campsites, facilities: There are 19 sites for tents, trailers or motor homes up to 22 feet long. Picnic tables are provided. Piped water and pit toilets are also available. Pets are permitted on leashes. Boat launching facilities are nearby.

Reservations, fee: Reserve through MISTIX at (800) 283-CAMP ($6 MISTIX fee); $9 fee per night. Open May to mid-October.

Who to contact: Phone Pike National Forest at (719) 636-1602 or write to Pikes Peak Ranger District, 601 South Weber Street, Colorado Springs, CO 80903.

Location: From the town of Woodland Park, drive 4.5 miles northeast on Forest Service Road 393, four miles southeast on Forest Service Road 300 and then 1.4 miles northeast on Forest Service Road 306 to the campground.

Trip note: This is one of two popular camps set aside Rampart Reservoir. A puffer of a sidetrip is the 13-mile hike around the lake. See trip note for Thunder Ridge Camp for other options.

---

67) FALCON MEADOW

Reference: east of Colorado Springs; map C3, grid j5.

Campsites, facilities: There are 10 tent sites and 20 sites for trailers or motor homes of any length. Picnic tables are provided. Flush toilets, bottled gas, sanitary disposal station, showers, recreation hall, a store, laundromat, ice and a playground are also available. A coffee shop is located within one mile. Pets are permitted on leashes.

Reservations, fee: Reservations accepted; $9-$10.50 fee per night; MasterCard and Visa/BankAmericard accepted. Open all year.

Who to contact: Phone (719) 495-2694, or write 11150 East Highway 24, Falcon, CO 80831.

Location: From Interstate 25 in the town of Colorado Springs, drive 15 miles east on US 24 to the campground.

Trip note: This a relatively unknown, privately developed camp that provides a layover spot for Highway 24 cruisers who want to avoid the city and are en route to Colorado Springs. It's a rural park covering seven acres. It is a prairie-type setting with grassy sites. There are no attractions to speak of in the immediate area; continue to Colorado Springs for many recreation options.

Colorado

Colorado Map C4
6 listings
Pages 180-183

North—Wyoming
East —Nebraska/Kansas
South (C8)—see page 280
West (C3)—see page 148

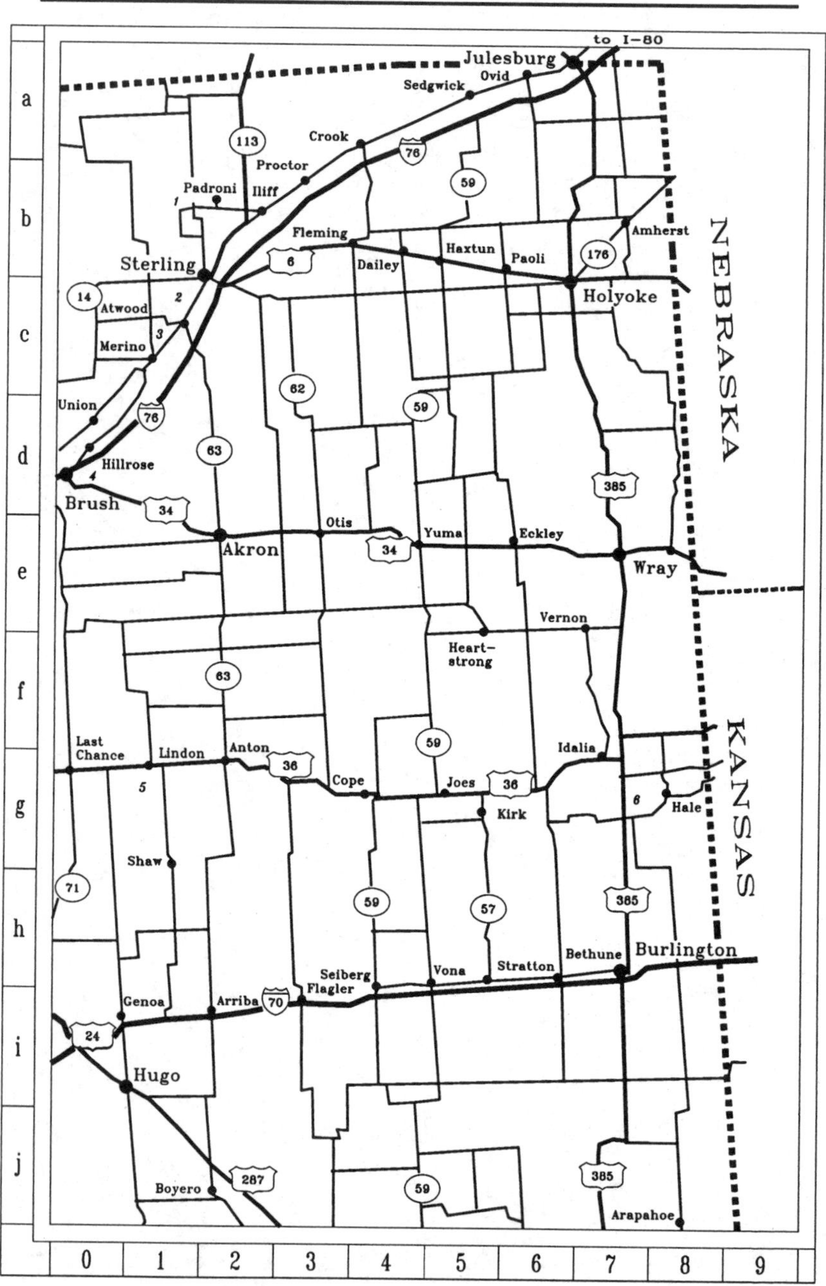

Featuring: North Sterling Reservoir, Prewitt Reservoir, Bonny Dam Reservoir

---

1) NORTH STERLING RESERVOIR CAMPGROUND

Reference: on North Sterling Reservoir; map C4, grid b1.

Campsites, facilities: There are several undesignated, primitive sites. Picnic tables are provided. Pit toilets and sanitary dump station are also available. There is **no piped water.** Pets are permitted on leashes. A boat ramp is available nearby.

Reservations, fee: No reservations necessary; no fee. Open all year.

Who to contact: Phone (303) 824-5234, or write Colorado Division of Wildlife, 6060 Broadway, Denver, CO 80216.

Location: From the town of Sterling, drive eight miles north on Seventh Avenue. Turn left on County Road 46 and drive two miles west, then one mile north on County Road 33 to the campground.

Trip note: This campground is set on North Sterling Reservoir and provides an option to Prewitt Reservoir Campground. North Sterling covers 3000 acres and has good fishing in early summer and waterfowl hunting in the fall. The camp is used primarily by hunters and fishermen in the fall, and is often close to empty in the early summer.

---

2) BUFFALO HILLS CAMPER PARK

Reference: near Sterling; map C4, grid c1.

Campsites, facilities: There are 16 tent sites and 84 sites for trailers or motor homes of any length. Picnic tables are provided. Flush toilets, bottled gas, sanitary disposal station, showers, recreation hall, a store, laundromat, ice, playground, swimming pool, wading pool and a miniature golf course are also available. A coffee shop is located within one mile. Pets are permitted on leashes.

Reservations, fee: Reservations accepted; $13.50-$16.50 fee per night; MasterCard and Visa/BankAmericard accepted. Open all year with limited winter facilities.

Who to contact: Phone (303) 522-2233, or write 22018 Highway 6, Sterling, CO 80751.

Location: From the junction of Interstate 76 and US 6 in the town of Sterling, drive a quarter of a mile east on US 6 and take exit 125A to the campground.

Trip note: If you're heading north on Interstate 76 and looking for a spot, you'd best stop here. It's the last call until you hit Nebraska. The terrain is high prairie, used now for agricultural land. The sites are grassy and shaded. An added bonus for motor home cruisers—the park sells a full stock of RV supplies and parts. A tennis court is available nearby in Sterling.

3) PREWITT RESERVOIR CAMPGROUND

Reference: on Prewitt Reservoir; map C4, grid c1.

Campsites, facilities: There are several undesignated, primitive sites. Picnic tables are provided. Pit toilets are also available. There is **no piped water.** Pets are permitted on leashes. A boat ramp is available nearby.

Reservations, fee: No reservations necessary; $3-$5 fee per night. Open all year.

Who to contact: Phone (303) 824-5234, or write Colorado Division of Wildlife, 6060 Broadway, Denver, CO 80216.

Location: From the town of Brush, drive 15 miles northeast on US 6, and then one mile east on the Wildlife Management Area access road.

Trip note: This is a primitive camp on Prewitt Reservoir, ideal for fishermen in the early summer and hunters in the fall. The lake covers 2400 acres and is seven miles from the 1500-acre Elliot State Wildlife Area. Between the two, you've got hunting for upland game, waterfowl, small game as well as fishing.

4) BRUSH MEMORIAL CAMPGROUND

Reference: near Brush; map C4, grid d0.

Campsites, facilities: There are 10 tent sites and 24 sites for trailers or motor homes of any length. Electricity, piped water and picnic tables are provided. Flush toilets, sanitary disposal station, showers, playground, swimming pool and a wading pool are also available. Bottled gas, a store, cafe, laundromat and ice are located within one mile. Pets are permitted on leashes.

Reservations, fee: No reservations necessary; first night free, thereafter $10 fee per night. Open May to late-October.

Who to contact: Phone (303) 842-5001, or write P.O. Box 363, Brush, CO 80723.

Location: From the town of Brush, drive two miles south on Highway 34 to Clayton Street, and then four blocks south to the park.

Trip note: This city park is located on the outskirts of city limits. It's in a nice, grassy area with all the amenities of town close by. Nearby recreation options include a golf course and tennis courts. An option is Prewitt Reservoir Campground, a primitive camp that's 20 minutes northeast.

5) MEADOWLARK MOTEL AND CAMPGROUND

Reference: in Lindon; map C4, grid g1.

Campsites, facilities: There are undesignated tent sites and 12 sites for trailers or motor homes of any length. Electricity, piped water, sewer hookups and picnic tables are provided. Flush toilets, sanitary disposal station, showers, a store, cafe, laundromat, ice and a playground are also available. Pets are permitted on leashes.

Reservations, fee: No reservations necessary; $5-$15 fee per night; MasterCard and Visa/BankAmericard accepted. Open late May to late October.

Who to contact: Phone (303) 383-2298, or write P.O. Box 8, Lindon, CO 80740.

Location: From Interstate 70 west of Denver, take the Highway 36 exit at Byers. Drive 73 miles east to Lindon. The campground is located in town, one block north of Highway 36.

Trip note: If you're stuck on Highway 36, this five-acre park will give you a quick spot to relax for awhile. It's in a high-prairie setting, with large grassy sites bordered by lilacs. The nearest camp is an hour's drive west to Denver East Strasburg KOA. There's nothing to the east until you approach Bonny Lake State Park and Kansas.

---

6) BONNY LAKE STATE PARK

Reference: on Bonny Dam Reservoir; map C4, grid g7.

Campsites, facilities: There are 200 sites for tents, trailers or motor homes of any length. Picnic tables are provided. Piped water, flush toilets, sanitary disposal station, showers, a store, snack bar, laundromat, ice and a playground are also available. Pets are permitted on leashes. Boat docks, launching facilities and rentals are nearby.

Reservations, fee: Reserve sites by calling (800) 678-CAMP ($6.75 reservation fee); $7 fee per night plus $3 entrance fee. Open all year with limited winter facilities.

Who to contact: Phone (303) 354-7306, or write 3010 County Road 3, Idalia, CO 80735.

Location: From the town of Burlington, drive 25 miles north on US 385, and then two miles east on a dirt road (County Road 3) to the park.

Trip note: This camp is the class act of the region. Set on Bonny Dam Reservoir with a 1900-acre lake, the camp has an adjoining 5000-acre wildlife and recreation area. It's a warm water lake and popular for boating, fishing and waterskiing. This is the only camp for miles around; a few more miles east and you're in the fields of Kansas.

Colorado Map C5
66 listings
Pages 184-215

North (C1)—see page 60
East (C6)—see page 216
South—New Mexico
West—Utah

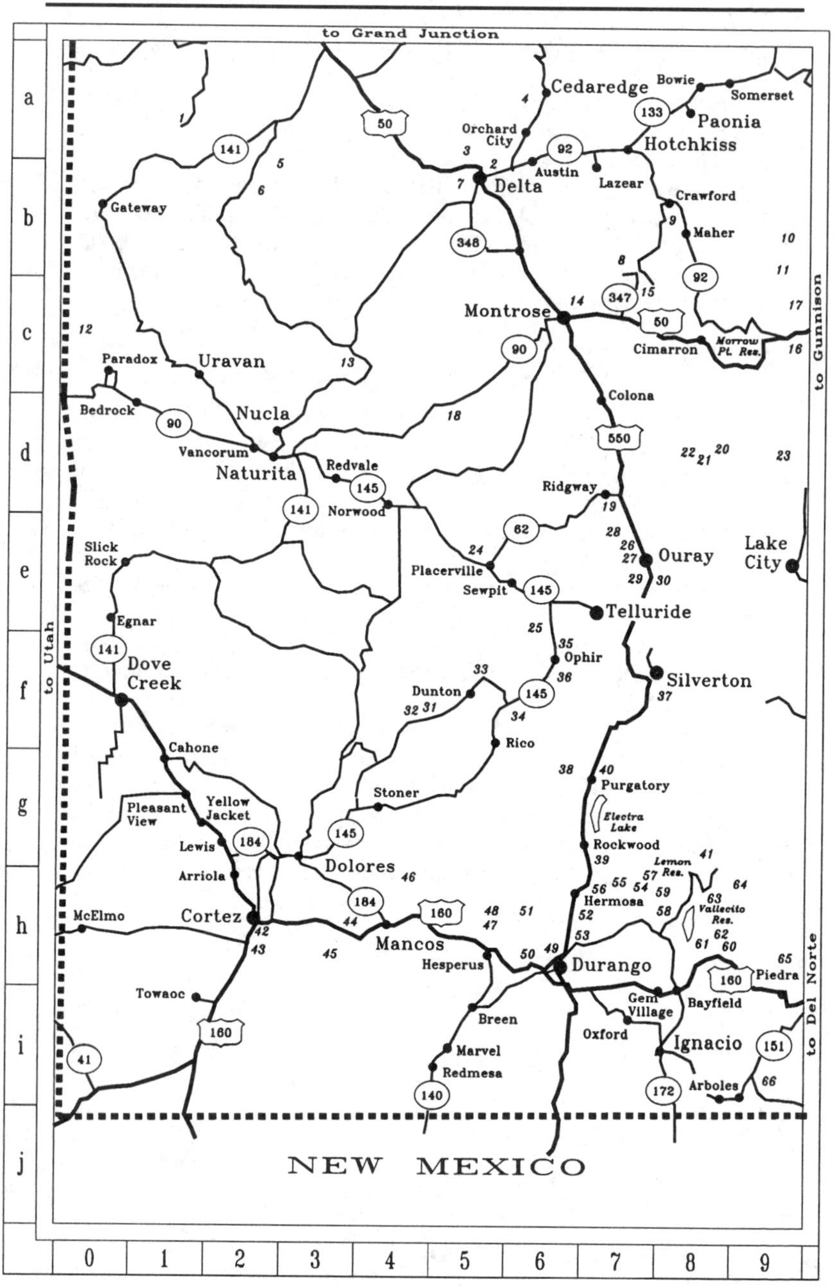

Featuring: Little Fruita Reservoir, Grand Mesa National Forest, Big Dominquez Creek, Uncompahgre National Forest, Black Canyon, Gunnison National Monument, Crawford Lake, Soap Creek, West Elk Wilderness, Buckeye Reservoir, Manti Lasal National Forest, Uncompahgre Plateau, Blue Mesa Reservoir, Curecanti National Recreation Area, Blue Mesa Lake, Curecanti National Recreational Area, Uncompahgre River, Silver Jack Reservoir, Cimarron River, Big Blue Creek, Cushman Lake, Uncompahgre Primitive Area, West Dolores River, San Juan National Forest, Barlow Creek, Dolores River, South Fork Of Mineral Creek, South Fork Of San Miguel River, Animas River, East Fork Of Hermosa Creek, Weminuche Wilderness, Vallecito Creek, Mesa Verde National Park, Mancos River, La Plata River, Lightner Creek, Timber Creek, Los Pinos River, Lemon Reservoir, Vallecito Reservoir, Piedra River, Navajo Lake

---

1) HAYPRESS

Reference: on Little Fruita Reservoir, Grand Mesa National Forest; map C5, grid a1.

Campsites, facilities: There are 11 sites for tents, trailers or motor homes up to 16 feet long. Picnic tables are provided. Pit toilets are available, but there is **no piped water.**

Reservations, fee: No reservations necessary; no fee. Open late May to November.

Who to contact: Phone Grand Mesa National Forest at (303) 242-8211 or write to Grand Mesa Ranger District, 764 Horizon Drive, Grand Junction, CO 81502.

Location: From Grand Junction, drive 10 miles southwest on Highway 340 and 20 miles south on County Road 400 to the campground.

Trip note: This little camp is nestled along little Fruita Reservoir No. 3 on Hay Press Creek. Fruita Picnic Area is located about two miles to the east, with a road/trail leading to Fruita Reservoir No. 1. The nearest campgrounds are the developed parks in Grand Junction.

---

2) DELTA-GRAND MESA KOA

Reference: in Delta; map C5, grid a5.

Campsites, facilities: There are 20 tent sites and 42 sites for trailers or motor homes of any length. Picnic tables are provided. Flush toilets, bottled gas, sanitary disposal station, showers, firewood, recreation hall, a store, laundromat, ice, playground, whirlpool and a swimming pool are available. Electricity, piped water, sewer hookups and air conditioning or heater hookups are available for an extra fee. A coffee shop is located within one mile. Pets and motorbikes are permitted. Boat rentals are nearby.

Reservations, fee: Reservations accepted; $13-$18.50 fee per night; MasterCard and Visa accepted. Open mid-April to mid-October.

Who to contact: Phone (303) 874-3918 or write to 1675 Highway 92, Delta, CO 81416.

Location: Drive one mile east of the junction of US 50 and Highway 92 in Delta on Highway 92 to the campground.

Trip note: With a rural setting in Delta, this is one of three camps in the immediate area. The sites are level and partially shaded. An 18-hole golf course is nearby.

---

3) RIVERWOOD INN

Reference: on Gunnison River; map C5, grid a5.

Campsites, facilities: There are 10 tent sites and 29 sites for trailers or motor homes of any length. Electricity, piped water, sewer hookups and picnic tables are provided. Flush toilets, showers, a coffee shop, laundromat, ice and a playground are available. Bottled gas, sanitary disposal station and a store are located within one mile. Pets and motorbikes are also permitted.

Reservations, fee: Reservations accepted; $11-$15 fee per night; MasterCard and Visa accepted. Open all year.

Who to contact: Phone (303) 874-5787 or write to 677 Highway 50 North, Delta, CO 81416.

Location: From the junction of US 50 and Highway 92 in Delta, drive a half mile north on US 50.

Trip note: This is one of three campgrounds in Delta and is strategically located near the intersection of Highways 50 and 92. It is set along the Gunnison River with several sites available on the riverside. It's a pretty, wooded area with lots of grass and trees. Fishing on the Gunnison River can be excellent. Nearby recreation options include an 18-hole golf course and tennis courts.

---

4) ASPEN TRAILS

Reference: near Cedaredge; map C5, grid a6.

Campsites, facilities: There are six tent sites and 20 drive-through sites for trailers or motor homes of any length. Electricity, piped water, sewer hookups and picnic tables are provided. Flush toilets, bottled gas, sanitary disposal station, showers, firewood, a store, ice, playground and a swimming pool are available. Pets are permitted on leashes.

Reservations, fee: Reservations accepted; $7.50-$14.50 fee per night; MasterCard and Visa accepted. Open mid-March to mid-November.

Who to contact: Phone (303) 856-6321 or write to 1997 Highway 65, Cedaredge, CO 81413.

Location: From Delta on US 50 drive east on Highway 92 four miles to Highway 65. Turn north and drive about 11 miles to the campground on the left.

Trip note: This is a good layover spot for cross-country cruisers looking for a spot near Cedaredge. It's not as heavily wooded as the camps in the national forest land to the north, but its proximity to Highway 65 and Highway 92 makes it strategically located. There are several other options north of this camp in Grand Mesa.

5) BIG DOMINGUEZ

Reference: on Big Dominguez Creek; map C5, grid b2.

Campsites, facilities: There are five sites for tents, trailers or motor homes up to 16 feet long. Pit toilets are available, and there is piped water.

Reservations, fee: No reservations necessary; no fee. Open late May to November.

Who to contact: Phone Bureau of Land Management at (303) 239-3600 or write to 1037 20th Street, Denver, CO 80202.

Location: From Grand Junction, travel south on US 50 to Whitewater, then southwest on Highway 141 for 14 miles. Turn left at the Uncompahgre National Forest border (signed) and follow the signs to the campground.

Trip note: This hidden spot is located beside Big Dominguez Creek at 8,400 feet. It's quite primitive, but it does offer water, and you're likely to be the only one here. No one knows about this spot but the locals. A Forest Service map is advised which details access roads and adjacent hiking trails that route into the surrounding wildlands.

6) DIVIDE FORK

Reference: in Uncompahgre National Forest; map C5, grid b2.

Campsites, facilities: There are nine sites for tents, trailers or motor homes up to 16 feet long. Picnic tables are provided. Piped water and pit toilets are available.

Reservations, fee: No reservations necessary; no fee. Open late May to November.

Who to contact: Phone Uncompahgre National Forest at (303) 242-8211 or write to Grand Junction Ranger District, 764 Horizon Drive, Grand Junction, CO 81502.

Location: From Grand Junction, travel south on US 50 to Whitewater and southwest on Highway 141 for 13 miles. Continue southwest on Forest Service Road 402 for 15 miles to the campground.

Trip note: This is an alternative to Big Dominguez Camp, but set deeper into the Forest Service country at 9,200 feet. Forest Service maps detail hiking trails in the area. This is good headquarters for four-wheel-drive cowboys, and folks with off-highway vehicles.

7) FLYING A CAMPGROUND

Reference: in Delta; map C5, grid b5.

Campsites, facilities: There are five tent sites and 19 sites for trailers or motor homes of any length. Electricity, piped water, sewer hookups and picnic tables are provided. Flush toilets, bottled gas, sanitary disposal station, showers, laundromat, cable TV, ice and a playground are available. A store and a coffee shop are located within one mile. Pets and motorbikes are permitted. Boat launching facilities are nearby.

Reservations, fee: Reservations accepted; $9-$13 fee per night; MasterCard and Visa accepted. Open all year.

Who to contact: Phone (303) 874-9659 or write to 676 Highway 50 North, Delta, CO 81416.

Location: From Delta, drive north on Highway 50 across the Gunnison River Bridge. The campground is on the left.

Trip note: This is a nice spot near the Gunnison River where you can recharge your batteries. It is very well-maintained, with shaded and open sites near the river banks. Fishing access is available in the campground. Nearby recreation options include an 18-hole golf course and tennis courts. This is one of three developed campgrounds in Delta.

8) NORTH RIM

Reference: near Black Canyon, Gunnison National Monument; map C5, grid b7.

Campsites, facilities: There are 13 sites for tents, small trailers and motor homes up to 24 feet long. Picnic tables are provided. Vault toilets are available. There is **limited water** so bring your own. Pets are permitted on leashes.

Reservations, fee: No reservations; $6 fee per night. Open mid-May to mid-November.

Who to contact: Phone Black Canyon of Gunnison National Monument at (303) 249-7036 or write to P.O. Box 1648, Montrose, CO 81402.

Location: From Delta, drive east on Highway 92 to Hotchkiss and veer right. Drive 10 miles to Crawford. Continue two miles on Highway 92 and head southeast for 12 miles on a gravel road.

Trip note: Of the options at Black Canyon in Gunnison National Monument, North Rim is by far the more primitive of the two camps. A dirt road can make access difficult for motor homes. See trip note for South Rim for details of the area.

9) CRAWFORD STATE RECREATION AREA

Reference: on Crawford Lake; map C5, grid b8.

Campsites, facilities: There are 55 sites for tents, trailers or motor homes of any length. Piped water and picnic tables are provided. Flush toilets and a sanitary disposal station are available. Firewood is an additional fee. A store is located within one mile. Pets are permitted on leashes. Boat launching facilities are nearby.

Reservations, fee: Reserve sites by calling (800) 678-CAMP ($6.75 reservation fee); $6 fee per night plus $3 entrance fee. Open all year with limited winter facilities.

Who to contact: Phone (303) 921-5721 or write to P.O. Box 147, Crawford, CO 81415.

Location: From Delta, drive east on Highway 92 to Hotchkiss and veer right. Drive 10 miles to Crawford. The park is one mile south.

Trip note: This is a developed state park camp set beside Crawford Lake. It's a big lake that's popular for boating, fishing and waterskiing. Ask park rangers for a map of the area which details hiking trails.

10) COMMISSARY

Reference: on Soap Creek, Gunnison National Forest; map C5, grid b9.

Campsites, facilities: There are seven sites for tents and trailers up to 16 feet long. Picnic tables are provided. Vault toilets are available, but there is **no piped water.** Pets are permitted on leashes.

Reservations, fee: No reservations necessary; no fee. Open early June to early September.

Who to contact: Phone Gunnison National Forest at (303) 641-0471 or write to Taylor River Ranger District, 216 North Colorado, Gunnison, CO 81230.

Location: From Gunnison, drive 26.1 miles west on US 50. Turn northwest on Highway 92 and drive six-tenths of a mile, then 9.2 miles north on Forest Service Road 721 to the campground.

Trip note: This primitive, little known spot is nestled along Soap Creek. The West Elk Wilderness is nearby; there are no trails from this camp, but trailheads are available from Soap Creek Camp and Ponderosa Camp, both to the south. There is fishing in Soap Creek, so be sure to bring along your pole and frying pan. Camp elevation is 7,900 feet.

11) SOAP CREEK

Reference: near West Elk Wilderness, Gunnison National Forest; map C5, grid b9.

Campsites, facilities: There are 13 sites for tents, trailers or motor homes up to 22 feet long. Picnic tables are provided. Pit toilets and piped water are available. Pets are permitted on leashes.

Reservations, fee: No reservations necessary; no fee. Open early June to early September.

Who to contact: Phone Gunnison National Forest at (303) 641-0471 or write to Taylor River Ranger District, 216 North Colorado, Gunnison, CO 81230.

Location: From Gunnison, drive 26.1 miles west on US 50. Turn northwest on Highway 92 and drive six-tenths of a mile, then 7.2 miles north on Forest Service Road 721. Continue for six-tenths of a mile northeast on Forest Service Road 824 to the campground.

Trip note: This is good jump-off point for a multi-day backpack trip into the adjacent West Elk Wilderness. A trailhead adjacent to camp is the starting point for the trip. It is advisable to obtain a Forest Service map for access roads and backcountry trails. The elevation is 7,700 feet.

---

12) BUCKEYE

Reference: on Buckeye Reservoir, Manti Lasal National Forest; map C5, grid c0.

Campsites, facilities: There are several undesignated primitive sites for tents, trailers or motor homes up to 22 feet long. Picnic tables and grills are provided. Firewood and vault toilets are available. There is **no piped water.** Pets are permitted on leashes.

Reservations, fee: No reservations necessary; no fee. Open June to early September.

Who to contact: Phone Manti Lasal National Forest at (801) 259-7155 or write to Moab Ranger District, 125 West 200 South, Moab, UT 84532.

Location: From Highway 90 at Paradox, take Forest Service Road 371 and travel 11.5 miles northwest to the campground.

Trip note: This campground is set at 7,200 feet on the west side of Buckeye Reservoir. Small boats are permitted with good trolling in early summer. Hiking is available along old logging roads. This is a nice little spot.

---

13) COLUMBINE

Reference: on Uncompahgre Plateau, Uncompahgre National Forest; map C5, grid c3.

Campsites, facilities: There are six tent sites. Picnic tables are provided. Vault toilets are available, but there is **no piped water.**

Reservations, fee: No reservations necessary; no fee. Open early June to late September.

Who to contact: Phone Uncompahgre National Forest at (303) 249-3711 or write to Ouray Ranger District, 2505 South Townsend, Montrose, CO 81401.

Location: From Delta, travel 30 miles southwest on County Road 214 to the campground.

Trip note: This one is really out there in No Man's Land. It's located near Columbine Pass on the Uncompahgre Plateau at 8,700 feet. You get guaranteed solitude but not a whole lot else.

14) MONTROSE KOA

Reference: near Montrose; map C5, grid c6.

Campsites, facilities: There are 43 sites for tents, trailers or motor homes of any length. Piped water and picnic tables are provided. Flush toilets, sanitary disposal station, showers, recreation hall, a store, laundromat, ice, playground and a swimming pool are available. Bottled gas and a coffee shop are located within one mile. Pets and motorbikes are permitted.

Reservations, fee: Reservations accepted; $13.50-$18.50 fee per night; MasterCard and Visa accepted. Open April to November.

Who to contact: Phone (303) 249-9177 or write to 200 North Cedar, Montrose, CO 81401.

Location: From Montrose at the junction of US 550 and US 50, travel 1.3 miles east on US 50 to the campground.

Trip note: This is a good layover spot for folks burning up the highway on vacation. It's a well-maintained park, located in town. Nearby recreation options include a golf course, bike paths, a riding stable and tennis courts. In summer months, a recreational program is offered.

15) SOUTH RIM

Reference: near Black Canyon, Gunnison National Monument; map C5, grid c7.

Campsites, facilities: There are 102 drive-through sites for tents, trailers or motor homes up to 24 feet long. Picnic tables are provided. Piped water, pit toilets, a store and a coffee shop are available. Pets are permitted on leashes.

Reservations, fee: No reservations; $3 fee per night. Open May to mid-November.

Who to contact: Phone Black Canyon of Gunnison National Monument at (303) 249-7036 or write to P.O. Box 1648, Montrose, CO 81402.

Location: From Montrose, travel six miles east on US 50 and five miles north on Highway 347 to the campground.

Trip note: This is one of two camps at the Gunnison National Monument. It is set at 8,200 feet near the rim of Black Canyon, an awesome gorge that plunges 1,800 feet, carved by the Gunnison River. It's one of Colorado's most spectacular sights. Note: Motor home campers should plan to stay here. Access to the North Rim Camp is poor because of a dirt road.

16) LAKE FORK

Reference: on Blue Mesa Reservoir, Curecanti National Recreation Area; map C5, grid c9.

Campsites, facilities: There are five walk-in tent sites and 82 sites for trailers or motor homes up to 30 feet long. Flush toilets, piped water and sanitary disposal station are available. Bottled gas, a store and ice are located within one mile. Some facilities are **wheelchair accessible.** Pets are permitted on leashes. Boat docks, launching facilities and rentals are at a marina nearby.

Reservations, fee: No reservations; $8 fee per night. Open Memorial Day to Labor Day with limited winter facilities.

Who to contact: Phone Curecanti National Recreation Area at (303) 641-2337 or write to 102 Elk Creek, Gunnison, CO 81230.

Location: From Gunnison drive 27 miles west on US 50 and a half mile west on Highway 92 to the campground.

Trip note: One of nine camps on Blue Mesa Reservoir. There is a marina and boat ramp nearby, and a visitor center and nature program are available to campers. Recreation options include fishing and waterskiing. See trip note for Ponderosa Camp for specific fishing details.

---

17) PONDEROSA

Reference: near Blue Mesa Lake, Curecanti National Recreational Area; map C5, grid c9.

Campsites, facilities: There are five walk-in sites and 16 drive-in sites for tents, trailers or motor homes. Picnic tables are provided. Piped water and pit toilets are available. Pets and motorbikes are permitted. Horse corral and boat launching facilities are nearby.

Reservations, fee: No reservations necessary; $7 fee per night. Open mid-May to mid-September.

Who to contact: Phone Curecanti National Recreation Area at (303) 641-2337 or write to 102 Elk Creek, Gunnison, CO 81230.

Location: From Gunnison, drive 27 miles west on US 50 and six miles north on Soap Creek Road to the campground. Note: The first seven miles of Soap Creek Road can be very hazardous during rainy months for recreational vehicles.

Trip note: This is a premium area for anglers. There is excellent trout and salmon fishing at Blue Mesa Reservoir, the largest of the lakes in the area. There are two other man-made lakes on the Gunnison River here than can provide sidetrips. There are nine campgrounds in the area under the management of the Curecanti National Recreation Area, so be sure to obtain a map and guide at the entrance station.

---

18) IRON SPRING

Reference: southwest of Montrose, Uncompahgre National Forest; map C5, grid d5.

Campsites, facilities: There are 10 sites for trailers or motor homes up to 22 feet long. Picnic tables and grills are provided. Vault toilets are available, but there is **no piped water.** Pets are permitted on leashes.

Reservations, fee: No reservations necessary; no fee. Open early June to late September.

Who to contact: Phone Uncompahgre National Forest at (303) 249-3711 or write to Ouray Ranger District, 2505 South Townsend, Montrose, CO 81401.

Location: From Montrose, drive 24 miles southwest on Highway 90.

Trip note: This campground is set at 9,500 feet at Iron Spring. It has no water, but it's small, free and private. Sometimes that's all you need.

---

19) WEBER'S CAMP

Reference: on Uncompahgre River; map C5, grid d7.

Campsites, facilities: There are 40 sites for tents, trailers or motor homes of any length. Electricity, piped water, sewer hookups and picnic tables are provided. Flush toilets, sanitary disposal services, showers, firewood, a laundromat, ice and a playground are also available. Pets are permitted on leashes.

Reservations, fee: Reservations accepted; $9-$13 fee per night. Open May to November.

Who to contact: Phone (303) 626-5383 or write to 20725 US Highway 550, Ridgway, CO 81432.

Location: From Montrose, drive 27 miles south on US 550 to Ridgway. At the filling station in Ridgway go south and travel for 2.5 miles (on US 550) to campground on the right.

Trip note: A good layover for vacationers cruising US 550, this campground is set at 7,200 feet and offers terraced sites along the Uncompahgre River. Fishing access is available. It is one of six camps in the vicinity.

---

20) SILVER JACK

Reference: near Silver Jack Reservoir, Uncompahgre National Forest; map C5, grid d8.

Campsites, facilities: There are 60 sites for tents, trailers or motor homes up to 31 feet long. Picnic tables and grills are provided. Piped water, vault toilets, a store and ice are available. Pets are permitted on leashes. This campground is **wheelchair accessible.**

Reservations, fee: Reserve through MISTIX at (800) 283-CAMP ($6 MISTIX fee); $6 fee per night. Open early June to mid-September.

Who to contact: Phone Uncompahgre National Forest at (303) 249-3711 or write to Ouray Ranger District, 2505 South Townsend, Montrose, CO 81401.

Location: From Montrose, travel 20 miles east on US 50 and 22 miles south on County Road 69.

Trip note: This campground is near the shore of Silver Jack Reservoir. It's an ideal destination for canoe campers since no motorized boats are allowed on the lake. It is the most modern campground in the area, a perfect spot for RV campers or families. Swimming, fishing and hiking are among the recreation options available. This is a popular hunter's camp during deer season.

---

21) BEAVER LAKE

Reference: southeast of Montrose, Uncompahgre National Forest; map C5, grid d8.

Campsites, facilities: There are 11 sites for tents, trailers or motor homes up to 22 feet long. Picnic tables and grills are provided. Piped water, vault toilets, a store and ice are available. Pets are permitted on leashes. Boat docks are nearby.

Reservations, fee: No reservations necessary; $7 fee per night. Open early June to late September.

Who to contact: Phone Uncompahgre National Forest at (303) 249-3711 or write to Ouray Ranger District, 2505 South Townsend, Montrose, CO 81401.

Location: From Montrose, travel 20 miles east on US 50 and 20 miles south on County Road 69.

Trip note: This campground is set at 8,800 feet along the shore of Beaver Lake. Only non-motorized boats are permitted. This is a good spot for a canoe camping and fishing adventure. Special note: a **wheelchair accessible** trail circles the lake, offering pretty views and fishing access.

---

22) BIG CIMARRON

Reference: on Cimarron River, Uncompahgre National Forest; map C5, grid d8.

Campsites, facilities: There are 18 sites for tents, trailers or motor homes up to 22 feet long. Picnic tables and grills are provided, but there is **no piped water.** Pit toilets, a store and ice are available. Pets are permitted on leashes.

Reservations, fee: No reservations necessary; no fee. Open early June to late September.

Who to contact: Phone Uncompahgre National Forest at (303) 249-3711 or write to Ouray Ranger District, 2505 South Townsend, Montrose, CO 81401.

Location: From Montrose, travel 20 miles east on US 50 and 20 miles south on County Road 69.

Trip note: Here's a good spot that gets missed by a lot of folks, yet is good for a weekender. The camp is set along the banks of the Cimarron River with several small lakes nearby. A National Forest map details all trails, lakes and streams in the area. Note: Call the ranger before you head out to this one to check for possible closure.

23) BIG BLUE

Reference: on Big Blue Creek, Uncompahgre National Forest; map C5, grid d9.

Campsites, facilities: There are 11 sites for tents, trailers or motor homes up to 16 feet long. Picnic tables and grills are provided. Pit toilets are available, but there is **no piped water.** Pets are permitted on leashes.

Reservations, fee: No reservations necessary; no fee. Open mid-June to late October.

Who to contact: Phone Uncompahgre National Forest at (303) 327-4261 or write to Norwood Ranger District, P.O. Box 388, Norwood, CO 81423.

Location: From Gunnison, travel 10 miles west on Highway 50. Turn south on Highway 149 and drive 36 miles, then nine miles northwest on Forest Service Road 868.

Trip note: This remote campground is set at 9,800 feet at a trailhead that provides access to Big Blue Creek to the north and south as well as other nearby creeks. A good spot for hikers, this camp is primitive with relatively little use. There is access to the Big Blue Wilderness.

24) MIRAMONTE RESERVOIR

Reference: south of Norwood; map C5, grid e5.

Campsites, facilities: There are 50 sites for trailers or motor homes of any length. Picnic tables are provided. Firewood is also available. Pets are permitted on leashes. Boat launching facilities are nearby.

Reservations, fee: No reservations necessary; no fee. Open all year.

Who to contact: Phone (303) 626-5822 or write to Ridgway State Recreation Office at 28555 Highway 550, Ridgway, CO 81432.

Location: From Norwood, go two miles south on Highway 145 and take the Miramonte Road turn-off. Follow the road for about 18 miles to reservoir (first 10 miles are paved, last eight are dirt and gravel).

Trip note: This is more of a parking lot than anything else, but what the heck, it does provide a layover spot for those visiting Miramonte Reservoir. And it's free, to boot. Miramonte Reservoir is a great place for fishing, boating and swimming.

25) SUNSHINE

Reference: near Cushman Lake, Uncompahgre National Forest; map C5, grid e6.

Campsites, facilities: There are 15 sites for tents, trailers or motor homes up to 16 feet long. Picnic tables and grills are provided. Piped water and vault toilets are also available. A store, cafe, laundromat and ice are located within five miles. Pets are permitted on leashes. Boat docks are nearby.

Reservations, fee: No reservations necessary; $7 fee per night. Open late May to late September.

Who to contact: Phone Uncompahgre National Forest at (303) 327-4261 or write to Norwood Ranger District, P.O. Box 388, Norwood, CO 81423.

Location: From Telluride, drive eight miles southwest on Highway 145.

Trip note: This is a rustic, alpine camp set at 9,500 feet. It's located near Cushman Lake, and it's a pretty nice spot, so you can usually expect company. If you prefer a stream setting, there are several nearby along the Dolores River to the south. If you're around in the summer, check out the nationally-acclaimed Telluride Blues Festival (but get tickets early—they won't even let you in town without one). In the winter, Telluride is an extremely popular skiing destination.

---

26) TIMBER RIDGE

Reference: near Uncompahgre River; map C5, grid e7.

Campsites, facilities: There are 30 tent sites and 67 sites for trailers or motor homes of any length. Electricity, piped water, sewer hookups and picnic tables are provided. Flush toilets, bottled gas, showers, firewood, a recreation hall, laundromat, ice and a playground are also available. A store and cafe are located within one mile. Pets and motorbikes are permitted.

Reservations, fee: Reservations accepted; $10-$15 fee per night; American Express, MasterCard and Visa accepted. Open May to November.

Who to contact: Phone (303) 325-4523 or write to P.O. Box 606, Ouray, CO 81427.

Location: From US 550 in Ouray, drive to the north end of town.

Trip note: This campground is set near the Uncompahgre River. Nearby recreation options include hiking trails, a riding stable and tennis courts. Ouray is a popular spot for rock climbing and in the winter, ice climbing. This is one of six camps in the area.

---

27) FOUR J TRAILER PARK

Reference: on Uncompahgre River; map C5, grid e7.

Campsites, facilities: There are 80 sites for tents, trailers or motor homes of any length. Electricity, piped water, sewer hookups and picnic tables are provided. Flush toilets, sanitary disposal services, showers, firewood, laundromat, ice and playground are also available. Bottled gas, a store and cafe are located within one mile. Pets and motorbikes are permitted.

Reservations, fee: Reservations accepted; $14-$16 fee per night. Open May to November.

Who to contact: Phone (303) 325-4418 or write to P.O. Box 79, Ouray, CO 81427.

Location: This campground is on Seventh Avenue in Ouray, right off US 550.

Trip note: This campground is set at 7,900 feet and is along the banks of the Uncompahgre River. Nearby recreation options include hiking trails and a riding stable. This campground has been family owned and operated since the 1950s, and it's very well maintained, with pretty, grassy sites surrounded by mountains. Riverside sites are available.

---

28) KOA OURAY

Reference: on Uncompahgre River; map C5, grid e7.

Campsites, facilities: There are 110 sites for tents, trailers or motor homes of any length. Picnic tables are provided. Flush toilets, sanitary disposal services, showers, hot tub, firewood, recreation hall, a store, cafe, laundromat, ice and a playground are also available. Pets and motorbikes are permitted. There are also six cabins available for use.

Reservations, fee: Reservations accepted; $16-$20 fee per night; Cabins are $25 per night; MasterCard and Visa accepted. Open mid-May through September.

Who to contact: Phone (303) 325-4736 or write to P.O. Box J, Ouray, CO 81427.

Location: From Ouray, travel four miles north on US 550 and a quarter mile west on Highway 23.

Trip note: This campground is set along the banks of the Uncompahgre River. You get a choice of wooded or riverside sites and scenic mountain views. There is fishing access from the camp, and hiking trails are nearby. The campground also offers pancake breakfasts and on-site barbecue dinners for those who forgot their stoves or just plain don't want to cook.

---

29) POLLY'S JEEP RENTAL CAMP AND MOTEL

Reference: in Ouray; map C5, grid e7.

Campsites, facilities: There are 14 sites for trailers or motor homes of any length. Electricity, piped water, sewer hookups and picnic tables are provided. Flush toilets, sanitary disposal services, showers, store, laundromat and ice are also available. Pets and motorbikes are permitted.

Reservations, fee: Reservations accepted; $14 fee per night; MasterCard and Visa accepted. Open May through October.

Who to contact: Phone (303) 325-4061 or write to P.O. Box 342, Ouray, CO 81427.

Location: This camp is located in Ouray at the north end of town.

Trip note: Nearby recreation options include hiking trails, bike paths and a riding stable. The campsites are on the river, with a view of Mount Abrams. Ouray is a beautiful, quaint little town with many scenic qualities. This is one of six camps in the immediate area.

30) AMPITHEATRE

Reference: near Uncompahgre Primitive Area, Uncompahgre National Forest; map C5, grid e8.

Campsites, facilities: There are 15 tent sites and 12 sites for trailers or motor homes up to 16 feet long. Picnic tables and grills are provided. Pit toilets and firewood are also available. There is piped water. A store, cafe, laundromat and ice are within one mile. Pets are permitted on leashes.

Reservations, fee: No reservations necessary; $10 fee per night. Open late May to early September.

Who to contact: Phone Uncompahgre National Forest at (303) 249-3711 or write to Ouray Ranger District, 2505 South Townsend, Montrose, CO 81401.

Location: From Ouray, travel a half mile south on US 550 and a half mile east on Forest Service Road 885.

Trip note: You get a little of both worlds here. This campground is spartan, in a rugged setting close to the backcountry, yet it is located just a mile southeast of Ouray, so full facilities are nearby. It is advisable to obtain a National Forest map, which will detail hiking options.

31) WEST DOLORES

Reference: on West Dolores River, San Juan National Forest; map C5, grid f4.

Campsites, facilities: There are 13 sites for tents, trailers or motor homes up to 35 feet long. Picnic tables and grills are provided. Piped water, a sanitary dump station and vault toilets are also available. Pets are permitted on leashes.

Reservations, fee: No reservations necessary; $6 fee per night. Open mid-May to mid-November.

Who to contact: Phone San Juan National Forest at (303) 882-7296 or write to Dolores Ranger District, P.O. Box 210, Dolores, CO 81323.

Location: From Dolores, travel 13 miles northeast on Highway 145 and 7.5 miles northeast on County Road 535.

Trip note: This is one of a series of camps set along the banks of the West Dolores River. It has shady, level sites. A good sidetrip is visiting the thermal hot springs 15 miles past the campground. The drive there is beautiful, following a lush river valley. There are several roads leading into the backcountry, but be aware of signs indicating private land.

32) MAVREESO

Reference: on West Dolores River, San Juan National Forest; map C5, grid f4.

Campsites, facilities: There are 14 sites for tents, trailers or motor homes up to 35 feet long. Picnic tables and grills are provided. Piped water, a sanitary dump station and vault toilets are also available. Pets are permitted on leashes. One site is **wheelchair accessible.**

Reservations, fee: Reserve through MISTIX at (800) 283-CAMP ($6 MISTIX fee); $6 fee per night. Open mid-May to mid-November.

Who to contact: Phone San Juan National Forest at (303) 882-7296 or write to Dolores Ranger District, P.O. Box 210, Dolores, CO 81323.

Location: From Dolores, drive 13 miles northeast on Highway 145 and six miles northeast on County Road 535.

Trip note: This campground is set at 7,600 feet and is one of several in the area located along the banks of the West Dolores River. Most of the sites are set close to the river, shaded by pine and fir trees. This is a good spot for fishing, with parking area for day use at the campground entrance.

---

33) BURRO BRIDGE

Reference: on West Dolores River, San Juan National Forest; map C5, grid f5.

Campsites, facilities: There are 15 sites for tents, trailers or motor homes up to 35 feet long. Picnic tables and grills are provided. Piped water and vault toilets are also available. Pets are permitted on leashes.

Reservations, fee: No reservations necessary; $5 fee per night. Open mid-May to mid-November.

Who to contact: Phone San Juan National Forest at (303) 882-7296 or write to Dolores Ranger District, P.O. Box 210, Dolores, CO 81323.

Location: From Dolores, drive 12.5 miles northeast on Highway 145 and 23 miles northeast on County Road 535.

Trip note: This campground is set at 9,000 feet and is near the headwaters of the West Dolores River. The sites rest on a hillside above the river, with some shady areas. This camp gets less use than others on this river, making it ideal for a peace-and-quiet trip. There are some excellent trails in the area. The Navajo Lake Trailhead is located about a mile beyond camp; follow the signs. It heads into the Navajo Basin, which is circled by several of Colorado's "fourteener" peaks—El Diente, Wilson Peak and Mount Wilson. About four miles north of the campground is the Calico National Recreation Trail, which heads south for many miles.

---

34) CAYTON

Reference: on Barlow Creek and Dolores River, San Juan National Forest; map C5, grid f6.

Campsites, facilities: There are 27 sites for tents, trailers or motor homes up to 35 feet long. Picnic tables and grills are provided. Piped water and vault toilets are also available. Pets are permitted on leashes.

Reservations, fee: Reserve through MISTIX at (800) 283-CAMP ($6 MISTIX fee); $7 fee per night. Open mid-May to mid-November.

Who to contact: Phone San Juan National Forest at (303) 882-7296 or write to Dolores Ranger District, P.O. Box 210, Dolores, CO 81323.

Location: From Rico, drive six miles northeast on Highway 145 and a half mile east on County Road 578.

Trip note: This campground is set at 9,400 feet and is near the confluence of Barlow Creek and the Dolores River. The camp is a popular one, especially with anglers, and is usually crowded in the summer. The camp offers a choice of sunny or shaded sites, with many recreation options. Continue on Road 578 past the campground and you will see the signs for the Colorado Trail, which follows the ridge along Bolam Pass. Views are particularly spectacular from this point. Nearby Rico is a point of historical interest, with mining and rail remains.

---

35) SOUTH MINERAL

Reference: on the South Fork of Mineral Creek, San Juan National Forest; map C5, grid f6.

Campsites, facilities: There are 26 sites for tents, trailers or motor homes up to 45 feet long. Picnic tables and grills are provided. Piped water, vault toilets and firewood are also available. Pets are permitted on leashes.

Reservations, fee: No reservations necessary; $7 fee per night. Open late May to mid-October.

Who to contact: Phone San Juan National Forest at (303) 385-1283 or write to Animas Ranger District, 701 Camino Del Rio, Durango, CO 81301.

Location: From Silverton, travel four miles northwest on US 550 and five miles southwest on Forest Service Road 2585.

Trip note: This campground is set along the South Fork of Mineral Creek. There is a trailhead that provides access to little Ice Lake, two miles from the campground. The sites are well-spaced and private, some shaded by spruce and fir, others sunny and open. Be sure to check out the waterfall on the creek just upstream from camp.

---

36) MATTERHORN

Reference: on the South Fork of San Miguel River, Uncompahgre National Forest; map C5, grid f6.

Campsites, facilities: There are 23 sites for tents, trailers or motor homes up to 16 feet long. Picnic tables and grills are provided. Piped water and vault toilets are also available. A store, cafe, laundromat and ice are located within five miles. Pets are permitted on leashes.

Reservations, fee: Reserve through MISTIX at (800) 283-CAMP ($6 MISTIX fee); $7 fee per night. Open late May to late September.

Who to contact: Phone Uncompahgre National Forest at (303) 327-4261 or write to Norwood Ranger District, P.O. Box 388, Norwood, CO 81423.

Location: From Telluride, travel 12 miles southwest on Highway 145 to the campground.

Trip note: This alpine camp is set at 9,500 feet and sits along the South Fork of the San Miguel River. The camp is situated across the road from the Wilson Mountains Primitive Area, a particularly beautiful piece of wilderness. There is no trail access from this camp, but a trailhead can be found off the road about four miles south. The nearby Matterhorn Ranger Station provides maps and information. Fishing is good in the San Miguel River.

---

37) RED MOUNTAIN LODGE

Reference: near Animas River; map C5, grid f8.

Campsites, facilities: There are 12 sites for trailers or motor homes. Electricity, piped water, sewer hookups and picnic tables are provided. Flush toilets, sanitary disposal services, showers, cable TV, laundromat and ice are also available. Bottled gas, a store and cafe are located within one mile. Pets and motorbikes are permitted.

Reservations, fee: No reservations necessary; $15 fee per night; MasterCard and Visa accepted. Open mid-May to mid-October.

Who to contact: Phone (303) 387-5512 or write to 664 Green, P.O. Box 346, Silverton, CO 81433.

Location: Drive one block off US 550 in Silverton, and you'll find the campground on Main Street.

Trip note: This is a good layover for motor home cruisers. Silverton is an enjoyable town set along the Animas River. The Western Narrow Gauge Railroad line starts in this town and runs south to Durango—a great trip. Nearby recreational options include hiking trails, bike paths, a riding stable and tennis courts.

---

38) SIG CREEK

Reference: near the East Fork of Hermosa Creek, San Juan National Forest; map C5, grid g6.

Campsites, facilities: There are nine sites for tents, trailers or motor homes up to 35 feet long. Picnic tables and grills are provided. Piped water, vault toilets and firewood are also available. Pets are permitted on leashes.

Reservations, fee: No reservations necessary; $6 fee per night. Open mid-May to November.

Who to contact: Phone San Juan National Forest at (303) 385-1283 or write to Animas Ranger District, 701 Camino Del Rio, Durango, CO 81306.

Location: From Silverton, travel 21 miles southwest on US 550 and six miles west on Forest Service Road 578 (Hermosa Park Road).

Trip note: This campground is set at 9,400 feet and is set about a quarter mile from the East Fork of Hermosa Creek. If you want to hike in the nearby backcountry, there is a trail about two miles west of camp at the end of the developed Forest Service road that runs along Hermosa Creek. Note for history buffs: A good part of the campground access road (Forest Service Road 578) follows the path that was once the Pinkerton Trail and Scotch Creek Toll Road, which provided access from Rico to the Animas Valley back in the 1800s. The route was abandoned in 1891 when the Rio Grande Southern Railroad came to Rico.

39) HAVILAND LAKE

Reference: north of Durango, San Juan National Forest; map C5, grid g7.

Campsites, facilities: There are 47 sites for tents, trailers or motor homes up to 30 feet long. Picnic tables and grills are provided. Piped water, vault toilets and firewood are also available. Boat docks are nearby.

Reservations, fee: Reserve through MISTIX at (800) 283-CAMP ($6 MISTIX fee); $8 fee per night. Open mid-May to November.

Who to contact: Phone San Juan National Forest at (303) 385-1283 or write to Animas Ranger District, 701 Camino Del Rio, Durango, CO 81301.

Location: From Durango, travel 16.5 miles north on US 550 and one mile east on Forest Service Road 671.

Trip note: This is a good spot for vacationers cruising US 550 that want a nice spot at a lake. Haviland Lake is right here, offering spectacular views of Hermosa Cliffs and excellent fishing. If you're camping in fall, bring your camera; this is a superb spot to catch the autumn colors.

40) PURGATORY

Reference: near Weminuche Wilderness, San Juan National Forest; map C5, grid g7.

Campsites, facilities: There are 14 sites for tents, trailers or motor homes up to 35 feet long. Picnic tables and grills are provided. Piped water, vault toilets and firewood are also available. Pets are permitted on leashes.

Reservations, fee: No reservations necessary; $6 fee per night. Open mid-May to mid-November.

Who to contact: Phone San Juan National Forest at (303) 385-1283 or write to Animas Ranger District, 701 Camino Del Rio, Durango, CO 81301.

Location: From Silverton, travel 22 miles southwest on US 550.

Trip note: This is an easy-access camp that provides an ideal spot for a hike into the wilderness. The campground is set at 8,800 feet, across from Purgatory Ski Area. Purgatory Trail follows Cascade Creek for four miles to the Animas River. From there, several trails are routed into the Weminuche Wilderness.

41) VALLECITO

Reference: at Vallecito Creek; map C5, grid g6.

Campsites, facilities: There are 80 sites for tents, trailers or motor homes up to 35 feet long. Picnic tables and grills are provided. Piped water and vault toilets are also available. Pets are permitted on leashes. Boat docks, launching facilities and rentals are nearby.

Reservations, fee: Reservations accepted; $8 fee per night. Open May to November.

Who to contact: Phone San Juan National Forest at (303) 884-2512 or write to Pine Ranger District, P.O. Box 439, Bayfield, CO 81122.

Location: From Bayfield, drive 18 miles north on County Road 501 and 2.5 miles north on County Road 600.

Trip note: This campground is one of the most heavily-used in the area, a large, conifer-ringed area located at the popular Vallecito Trailhead, a major access route into the Weminuche Wilderness. The Endlich Mesa Trail, a common path for equestrians, is located at the north end of Vallecito Reservoir. See a Forest Service map for backcountry options. The Weminuche is a spectacular wilderness with fishing, lookouts and pristine camps.

42) LAZY G RV PARK

Reference: near Mesa Verde National Park; map C5, grid h2.

Campsites, facilities: There are 25 tent sites and 53 sites for tents, trailers or motor homes of any length. Electricity, piped water, sewer hookups and picnic tables are provided. Flush toilets, sanitary disposal services, showers, cable TV, cafe, laundromat, sauna, whirlpool, wading pool and a heated pool are also available. Pets are permitted on leashes.

Reservations, fee: Reservations accepted; $14.50-$18.50 fee per night; American Express, MasterCard and Visa accepted. Open all year.

Who to contact: Phone (303) 565-8577 or write to P.O. Box 1048, Cortez, CO 81321.

Location: From Cortez, travel 1.5 miles east on US 160 to the intersection of Highway 145.

Trip note: This campground is adjacent to a motel, located near the junction of Highways 160 and 666 and is complete with all the amenities. It's close to a large shopping center and restaurants. Mesa Verde National Park is a good sidetrip and is located to the immediate southeast. Other nearby recreation options include a golf course and a riding stable.

43) MESA OASIS

Reference: south of Cortez; map C5, grid h2.

Campsites, facilities: There are 60 tent sites and 58 sites for trailers or motor homes of any length. Electricity, piped water, sewer hookups and picnic tables are provided. Flush toilets, sanitary disposal services, showers, firewood, a recreation hall, store, cafe, laundromat, ice and a playground are also available. Bottled gas is located within one mile. Pets are permitted on leashes.

Reservations, fee: Reservations accepted; $13-$17.50 fee per night; MasterCard and Visa accepted. Open all year.

Who to contact: Phone (303) 565-8716 or write to 5608 Highway 160, Cortez, CO 81321.

Location: From Cortez, travel four miles south on US 160.

Trip note: This is a nice, clean camp, with grassy sites and a few trees along with excellent views of Ute Mountain and Mesa Verde National Park. One of the largest attractions in the area is the Ute Mountain Casino, which offers high-stakes bingo and limited-stakes gambling.

---

44) MESA VERDE POINT KAMPARK

Reference: near Mesa Verde National Park; map C5, grid h3.

Campsites, facilities: There are 12 tent sites and 33 sites for trailers or motor homes of any length. Electricity, piped water, sewer hookups and picnic tables are provided. Flush toilets, bottled gas, sanitary disposal services, showers, firewood, a recreation hall, store, laundromat, ice and a playground are also available. Pets are permitted on leashes.

Reservations, fee: Reservations accepted; $13-$18.50 fee per night; MasterCard and Visa accepted. Open April to November.

Who to contact: Phone (303) 533-7421 or write to 35303 Highway 160, Mancos, CO 81328.

Location: From Mancos, drive seven miles west on US 160.

Trip note: This campground is less than a mile from the entrance to Mesa Verde National Park. It has large, open sites. It is not quite as luxurious as nearby Morefield Campground, but it may be easier to find a site here. The two camps are usually packed to the brim in the summer. Other options are Target Tree and Transfer, both National Forest camps. A riding stable is nearby.

---

45) MOREFIELD

Reference: in Mesa Verde National Park; map C5, grid h3.

Campsites, facilities: There are 477 sites for tents, trailers or motor homes up to 30 feet long. Picnic tables and grills are provided. Flush toilets, bottled gas, sanitary disposal services, showers, firewood, a store, restaurant, laundromat and ice are also available. Pets are permitted on leashes.

Reservations, fee: No reservations necessary; $8-$15.50 fee per night. Open May to mid-October.

Who to contact: Phone Mesa Verde National Park at (303) 529-4465 or write to Mancos, CO 81330.

Location: Travel 10 miles east of Cortez on US 160 to the park entrance. Continue five miles south.

Trip note: This huge campground, named Morefield Camp, is the only camp in Mesa Verde National Park. This park contains the site of Native American cliff dwellings. Evening campfire programs are offered by the rangers. The sites are large and private. A nature program, hiking trails and a riding stable offer other recreational options.

---

46) TRANSFER

Reference: on Mancos River, San Juan National Forest; map C5, grid h4.

Campsites, facilities: There are 13 sites for tents, trailers or motor homes up to 45 feet long. Picnic tables and grills are provided. Piped water, firewood and vault toilets are also available. Pets are permitted on leashes.

Reservations, fee: Reserve through MISTIX at (800) 283-CAMP ($6 MISTIX fee); $5 fee per night. Open mid-June to mid-November.

Who to contact: Phone San Juan National Forest at (303) 533-7716 or write to Mancos Ranger District, P.O. Box 330, Mancos, CO 81328.

Location: From Mancos, travel a quarter mile north on Highway 184 and 12 miles northeast on Forest Service Road 561.

Trip note: Remote and pristine, this camp is just enough off the beaten path to be missed by most folks. This campground is set at 8,500 feet, surrounded by aspens near the Mancos River. The Transfer Trail provides excellent fishing access to the river. Chicken Creek Trail, located about a quarter mile north of the campground, is eight miles long and follows Chicken Creek south to Jackson Gulch Reservoir. Several other excellent trails exist nearby; see a Forest Service map.

---

47) TARGET TREE

Reference: near Mesa Verde National Park, San Juan National Forest; map C5, grid h5.

Campsites, facilities: There are 51 sites for tents, trailers or motor homes up to 45 feet long. Picnic tables and grills are provided. Piped water, firewood and pit toilets are also available. Pets are permitted on leashes.

Reservations, fee: Reserve through MISTIX at (800) 283-CAMP ($6 MISTIX fee); $5 fee per night. Open mid-May to early November.

Who to contact: Phone San Juan National Forest at (303) 533-7716 or write to Mancos Ranger District, P.O. Box 330, Mancos, CO 81328.

Location: From Mancos, travel seven miles east on US 160.

Trip note: This campground is set alongside US 160. It is the easiest to reach and largest of the Forest Service camps in the vicinity. It's a pretty camp, overlooking the Cherry Creek Valley. The area is known for its diverse population of birds; informational signs are posted throughout the camp. The camp got its name from the Ute Indians, who used the trees in the area for target practice with rifles, bows and arrows. A trail leads out of camp to one of the remaining scarred trees.

48) KROEGER

Reference: near La Plata River, San Juan National Forest; map C5, grid h5.

Campsites, facilities: There are 10 sites for tents, trailers or motor homes up to 35 feet long. Picnic tables and grills are provided. Piped water, firewood and vault toilets are also available. Pets are permitted on leashes.

Reservations, fee: No reservations necessary; $6 fee per night. Open mid-June to mid-October.

Who to contact: Phone San Juan National Forest at (303) 533-7716 or write to P.O. Box 330, Mancos, CO 81328.

Location: Travel 11 miles west of Durango to Hesperus. From Hesperus, drive 200 yards northwest on US 160 and seven miles north on Forest Service Road 571.

Trip note: This campground is set at 9,000 feet and is in the La Plata River Canyon. This is a hot spot for fishing, so expect company if you bring your pole. It's a pretty camp, shielded by a mixture of spruce, fir, aspen and cottonwood trees. Many hiking trails are available in the surrounding area; a National Forest map details the options.

49) COTTONWOOD CAMPER PARK

Reference: in Durango; map C5, grid h6.

Campsites, facilities: There are five tent sites and 69 drive-through sites for trailers or motor homes of any length. Electricity, piped water, sewer hookups and picnic tables are provided. Flush toilets, sanitary disposal services, showers and ice are also available. Bottled gas, a store, cafe and laundromat are located within one mile. Pets and motorbikes are permitted.

Reservations, fee: Reservations accepted; $14-$16 fee per night. Open May through October.

Who to contact: Phone (303) 247-1977 or write to 21636 US 160, Durango, CO 81301.

Location: This camp is located at the west end of Durango on US 160.

Trip note: This is an alternative to Alpen Rose Camp and United Campground of Durango. This camp is located within walking distance of town. Lightner Creek runs through it, with sites available on the creekside and fishing access available. Other points of interest include the Narrow Gauge Railroad, the Animas River and old historic buildings downtown.

50) LIGHTNER CREEK

Reference: on Lightner Creek; map C5, grid h6.

Campsites, facilities: There are 30 tent sites and 66 sites for trailers or motor homes of any length. Electricity, piped water, sewer hookups

fire rings and picnic tables are provided. Flush toilets, bottled gas, sanitary disposal services, showers, firewood, a recreation hall, store, laundromat, ice, playground and a swimming pool are also available. Pets are permitted on leashes.

Reservations, fee: Reservations accepted; $17-$21 fee per night; MasterCard and Visa accepted. Open May through September.

Who to contact: Phone (303) 247-5406 or write to 1567 County Road 207, Durango, CO 81301.

Location: From Durango, drive three miles west on US 160 and 1.5 miles north on Lightner Creek Road.

Trip note: This campground is set along the banks of Lightner Creek. Most sites are directly on the edge of the creek, and many are private and wooded. Nature trails and fishing are two options within the campground; if you want to travel a bit, the Narrow Gauge Railroad is a short drive away. Nearby dirt roads provide access to some backcountry areas for four-wheel-drive cowboys.

---

51) JUNCTION CREEK

Reference: near Durango, San Juan National Forest; map C5, grid h6.

Campsites, facilities: There are 34 sites for tents, trailers or motor homes up to 50 feet long. Picnic tables and grills are provided. Piped water, vault toilets, showers and firewood are also available. Sanitary disposal services, a store, laundromat and ice are located within five miles. Some facilities are **wheelchair accessible.** Pets are permitted on leashes.

Reservations, fee: No reservations necessary; $7 fee per night. Open May to mid-November.

Who to contact: Phone San Juan National Forest at (303) 385-1283 or write to Animas Ranger District, 701 Camino Del Rio, Durango, CO 81301.

Location: From Durango, drive one mile north on US 550. Turn northwest on County Road 204 and drive 3.5 miles, then 1.5 miles northwest on Forest Service Road 2574.

Trip note: This campground is set along the banks of Junction Creek about five miles from Durango. It's just far enough out of the city to provide the separation from the masses that many vacationers desire. Fishing can be good in Junction Creek, with prospects best upstream from camp. The southern end of the famous Colorado Trail is located 1.5 miles east of camp, back at the forest boundary where the pavement ends. A good sidetrip is to continue north up Forest Service Road 543 to the Animas Overlook, where you can take an easy hike along an interpretive trail (it's also **wheelchair accessible**) and enjoy spectacular views of the Animas Valley and surrounding high peaks.

52) ALPEN ROSE RV PARK

Reference: on Animas River; map C5, grid h7.

Campsites, facilities: There are eight tent sites and 90 drive-through sites for trailers or motor homes of any length. Electricity, piped water, sewer hookups and picnic tables are provided. Flush toilets, bottled gas, showers, a recreation hall, swimming pool, video arcade, store, laundromat and ice are also available. Pets and motorbikes are permitted.

Reservations, fee: Reservations accepted; $15.50-$18.50 fee per night. Open May to mid-October.

Who to contact: Phone (303) 247-5540 or write to 3518 County Road 203, Durango, CO 81301.

Location: From Durango, travel 1.5 miles north on US 550.

Trip note: This campground is set along the banks of the Animas River. It has a choice of open or shady sites and a recreation program in the summer. There is a fishing pond available for campers' use. Durango offers many activities including the Western Narrow Gauge Railroad that travels through the backcountry between Durango and Silverton. Other recreational options include a golf course, hiking trails, a riding stable and tennis courts.

53) UNITED CAMPGROUND OF DURANGO

Reference: near Animas River; map C5, grid h7.

Campsites, facilities: There are 99 tent sites and 103 sites for trailers or motor homes of any length. Electricity, piped water, sewer hookups and picnic tables are provided. Flush toilets, bottled gas, sanitary disposal services, showers, a recreation hall, store, laundromat, ice and a swimming pool are also available. A cafe is located within one mile. Pets and motorbikes are permitted.

Reservations, fee: Reservations accepted; $13-$25 fee per night; MasterCard and Visa accepted. Open April to late October.

Who to contact: Phone (303) 247-3853 or write to 1322 Animas View Drive, Durango, CO 81301.

Location: From Durango, travel one mile north on US 550. The park is on the right.

Trip note: This is one of several camps to choose from in Durango. It is located in the Animas Valley on a hillside. The Animas River runs through the park, as does the Narrow Gauge Train. The park is heavily wooded, with clean, pretty sites. See trip note for Alpen Rose Camp for other recreation possibilities.

54) TRANSFER PARK

Reference: on Timber Creek, San Juan National Forest; map C5, grid h7.

Campsites, facilities: There are 25 sites for tents, trailers or motor homes up to 35 feet long. Picnic tables and grills are provided. Piped water and vault toilets are also available. Pets are permitted on leashes.

Reservations, fee: Reserve through MISTIX at (800) 283-CAMP ($6 MISTIX fee); $7 fee per night. Open May to November.

Who to contact: Phone San Juan National Forest at (303) 884-2512 or write to Pine Ranger District, P.O. Box 439, Bayfield, CO 81122.

Location: From Bayfield, drive 11 miles northwest on County Road 501. Continue for three miles northwest on County Road 240, then five miles north on County Road 243.

Trip note: In many ways, this is an ideal place. It is just far enough off the main road to get little attention from out-of-towners, yet it is located at the foot of the Weminuche Wilderness and not far from Lemon Reservoir. It is set at 8,600 feet and is right along Timber Creek. Burnt Timber Trail runs out of the camp into the wilderness. How did this camp get its name, you ask? It was once used for transferring ore and supplies between pack mules and wagons during the mining era.

---

55) HERMOSA MEADOWS

Reference: on Animas River; map C5, grid h7.

Campsites, facilities: There are 73 tent sites and 67 sites for trailers or motor homes of any length. Electricity, piped water, sewer hookups and picnic tables are provided. Flush toilets, bottled gas, sanitary disposal services, showers, firewood, a recreation hall, store, laundromat, ice and a playground are also available. Pets and motorbikes are permitted.

Reservations, fee: Reservations accepted; $11-$17 fee per night; MasterCard and Visa accepted. Open all year with limited winter facilities.

Who to contact: Phone (303) 247-3055 or write to 31420 US 550, Durango, CO 81301.

Location: From Durango, travel eight miles north on US 550 and a half mile east (on a well-signed road) to the campground.

Trip note: This spacious, family-run park is set along the banks of the Animas River where tubing and rafting are big sports. Hay wagon rides operate daily to the Western Narrow Gauge Railroad which runs through the backcountry from Durango to Silverton. Other recreational options include a golf course, hiking trails, bike paths and a riding stable.

---

56) PONDEROSA KOA

Reference: on Animas River; map C5, grid h7.

Campsites, facilities: There are 30 tent sites and 120 sites for trailers or motor homes of any length. Electricity, piped water, sewer hookups and picnic tables are provided. Flush toilets, sanitary disposal services, showers, firewood, a recreation hall, store, cafe, laundromat, ice, playground and a swimming pool are also available. Pets are permitted on leashes.

Reservations, fee: Reservations accepted; $12.50-$20.50 fee per night; MasterCard and Visa accepted. Open May to mid-October.

Who to contact: Phone (303) 247-4499 or write to 13391 CR 250, Durango, CO 81301.

Location: From Durango, drive 12 miles north on US 550.

Trip note: This campground is set along the banks of the Animas River. It has sheltered sites on the river's edge. A bus is available to ferry campers back and forth from Narrow Gauge Train tours. Horseback rentals are also available. See the trip note for Alpen Rose Camp for details about the area.

---

57) FLORIDA

Reference: near Weminuche Wilderness, San Juan National Forest; map C5, grid h7.

Campsites, facilities: There are 20 single sites for tents, trailers or motor homes up to 22 feet long, and one adjoining group site that can accommodate up to 65 people. Picnic tables and grills are provided. Piped water and vault toilets are also available. Pets are permitted on leashes.

Reservations, fee: Reserve through MISTIX at (800) 283-CAMP ($6 MISTIX fee); $7 fee per night for single sites. Phone ahead for group rates. Open May to November.

Who to contact: Phone San Juan National Forest at (303) 884-2512 or write to Pine Ranger District, P.O. Box 439, Bayfield, CO 81122.

Location: From Bayfield, drive 11 miles northwest on County Road 501. Continue for three miles northwest on County Road 240, then four miles north on County Road 243.

Trip note: This campground is several miles north of Lemon Reservoir at a trailhead that leads into the Weminuche Wilderness. It's a pretty camp, surrounded by Colorado blue spruce, Douglas fir and aspen trees. It's a good spot to set up your first night's camp in preparation for a wilderness expedition.

---

58) FIVE BRANCHES

Reference: on Los Pinos River; map C5, grid h8.

Campsites, facilities: There are 10 tent sites and 102 sites for trailers or motor homes of any length. Electricity, piped water, sewer hookups and picnic tables are provided. Flush toilets, bottled gas, sanitary disposal services, showers, firewood, a recreation hall, store, laundromat, ice and a playground are also available. Pets are permitted on leashes. Boat docks, launching facilities and rentals are nearby.

Reservations, fee: Reservations accepted; $10-$20 fee per night; MasterCard and Visa accepted. Open early May to October.

Who to contact: Phone (303) 884-2582 or write to 4677 County Road 501A, Bayfield, CO 81122.

Location: From Durango, drive approximately 15 miles northeast on County Road 240 and then 10 miles on County Road 501 to the park.

Trip note: This campground is set along the banks of the Los Pinos River not far from Vallecito Reservoir. Nearby recreation options include hiking trails and a riding stable. It is an ideal spot for motor home cruisers.

---

59) MILLER CREEK

Reference: on Lemon Reservoir, San Juan National Forest; map C5, grid h8.

Campsites, facilities: There are 11 sites for tents, trailers or motor homes up to 35 feet long. Picnic tables and grills are provided. Piped water and vault toilets are also available. Pets are permitted on leashes. Launching facilities are nearby.

Reservations, fee: No reservations necessary; $7 fee per night. Open May to November.

Who to contact: Phone San Juan National Forest at (303) 884-2512 or write to Pine Ranger District, P.O. Box 439, Bayfield, CO 81122.

Location: From Bayfield, drive 11 miles northwest on County Road 501. Continue for three miles northwest on County Road 240, then two miles north on County Road 243.

Trip note: This campground is located where Miller Creek runs into Lemon Reservoir. It is the only campground along the shore of the reservoir. A trailhead for the Weminuche Wilderness can be found five miles north at the Transfer Park campground. Fishing access is available 1.5 miles north of camp at the Upper Lemon Day Use Area. Florida Camp provides an alternative just north of the lake.

---

60) PINE POINT

Reference: on Vallecito Reservoir, San Juan National Forest; map C5, grid h8.

Campsites, facilities: There are 30 sites for tents, trailers or motor homes up to 35 feet long. Picnic tables and grills are provided. Piped water and vault toilets are also available. Pets are permitted on leashes. Boat docks, launching facilities and rentals are nearby.

Reservations, fee: No reservations necessary; $7 fee per night. Open May to November.

Who to contact: Phone San Juan National Forest at (303) 884-2512 or write to Pine Ranger District, P.O. Box 439, Bayfield, CO 81122.

Location: From Bayfield, drive 14 miles north on County Road 501 and four miles northeast on County Road 501A.

Trip note: This is one of several campgrounds set along Vallecito Reservoir. See the trip note for Graham Creek Camp.

---

61) GRAHAM CREEK

Reference: on Vallecito Reservoir, San Juan National Forest; map C5, grid h8.

Campsites, facilities: There are 25 sites for tents, trailers or motor homes up to 22 feet long. Picnic tables and grills are provided. Piped water and vault toilets are also available. Pets are permitted on leashes. Boat docks, launching facilities and rentals are nearby.

Reservations, fee: Reservations accepted; $8 fee per night. Open May to November.

Who to contact: Phone San Juan National Forest at (303) 884-2512 or write to Pine Ranger District, P.O. Box 439, Bayfield, CO 81122.

Location: From Bayfield, drive 14 miles north on County Road 501 and three miles northeast on County Road 501A.

Trip note: This is one of several campgrounds set along the eastern shore of Vallecito Reservoir (elevation 7,900 feet). There are numerous trails in the area, some of which lead north to creeks and lakes in the Weminuche Wilderness including Emerald Lake, a large natural lake with a native population of rainbow trout.

---

62) NORTH CANYON

Reference: on Vallecito Reservoir, San Juan National Forest; map C5, grid h8.

Campsites, facilities: There are 21 sites for tents, trailers or motor homes up to 35 feet long. Picnic tables and grills are provided. Piped water and vault toilets are also available. Pets are permitted on leashes. Boat docks, launching facilities and rentals are nearby.

Reservations, fee: No reservations necessary; $7 fee per night. Open May to November.

Who to contact: Phone San Juan National Forest at (303) 884-2512 or write to Pine Ranger District, P.O. Box 439, Bayfield, CO 81122.

Location: From Bayfield, drive 14 miles north on County Road 501 and 3.5 miles northeast on County Road 501A.

Trip note: This is one of several camps in the immediate vicinity along Vallecito Reservoir. See the trip note for Graham Creek Camp.

---

63) MIDDLE MOUNTAIN

Reference: on Vallecito Reservoir, San Juan National Forest; map C5, grid h8.

Campsites, facilities: There are 24 sites for tents, trailers or motor homes up to 35 feet long. Picnic tables and grills are provided. Piped water and vault toilets are also available. Pets are permitted on leashes. Boat docks, launching facilities and rentals are nearby.

Reservations, fee: Reservations accepted; $8 fee per night. Open May to November.

Who to contact: Phone San Juan National Forest at (303) 884-2512 or write to Pine Ranger District, P.O. Box 439, Bayfield, CO 81122.

Location: From Bayfield, drive 21 miles northeast on County Road 501.

Trip note: One of several campgrounds in the immediate area, this campground is set on the eastern shore of Vallecito Reservoir. Take your pick.

---

64) PINE RIVER

Reference: near Weminuche Wilderness, San Juan National Forest; map C5, grid h9.

Campsites, facilities: There are six sites for tents, trailers or motor homes up to 35 feet long. Picnic tables and grills are provided. Piped water and vault toilets are also available. Pets are permitted on leashes.

Reservations, fee: No reservations necessary; no fee. Open May to November.

Who to contact: Phone San Juan National Forest at (303) 884-2512 or write to Pine Ranger District, P.O. Box 439, Bayfield, CO 81122.

Location: From Bayfield, drive 25 miles northeast on County Road 501.

Trip note: This campground is set at the trailhead for the Weminuche Wilderness and a good spot to start a wilderness expedition. A Forest Service map details all trails, backcountry lakes and streams. See the trip note for Graham Creek Camp for options at nearby Vallecito Reservoir.

---

65) LOWER PIEDRA

Reference: on Piedra River, San Juan National Forest; map C5, grid h9.

Campsites, facilities: There are 17 sites for tents, trailers or motor homes up to 35 feet long. Picnic tables are provided. Piped water, vault toilets and firewood are also available. Pets are permitted on leashes.

Reservations, fee: No reservations necessary; no fee. Open May to November.

Who to contact: Phone San Juan National Forest at (303) 884-2512 or write to Pine Ranger District, P.O. Box 439, Bayfield, CO 81122.

Location: From the town of Pagosa Springs, travel west on US 160 for about 20 miles to Piedra and one mile north on Forest Service Road 621.

Trip note: This camp isn't that far from pavement, yet it gets missed by almost everybody. It's a good one set along the banks of the Piedra River. All that privacy and it's free to boot. See a Forest Service map for hiking possibilities.

---

66) NAVAJO STATE RECREATION AREA

Reference: on Navajo Lake; map C5, grid i9.

Campsites, facilities: There are 19 sites for tents only, and 52 sites for tents, trailers or motor homes of any length. Picnic tables and grills are provided. Some electrical hookups, flush toilets, sanitary disposal services, a store, cafe, ice and a playground are also available. Pets are permitted on leashes. Boat docks, launching facilities and rentals are nearby.

Reservations, fee: Reserve sites by calling (800) 678-CAMP ($6.75 reservation fee); $6-$10 fee per night plus $3 entrance fee. Open all year with limited winter facilities.

Who to contact: Phone (303) 883-2208 or write to P.O. Box 1697, Arboles, CO 81121.

Location: From the town of Pagosa Springs, travel 17 miles west on US 160. Turn left and drive 18 miles southwest on Highway 151 to Arboles. From Arboles, drive two miles south on County Road 982.

Trip note: This campground is set along the north shore of Navajo Lake. Boating, fishing, windsurfing, waterskiing, hiking and hunting are among your options here. Fishing licenses from both Colorado and New Mexico are required—the typical government gouge job.

Colorado Map C6
98 listings
Pages 216-261

North (C2)—see page 84
East (C7)—see page 262
South—New Mexico
West (C5)—see page 184

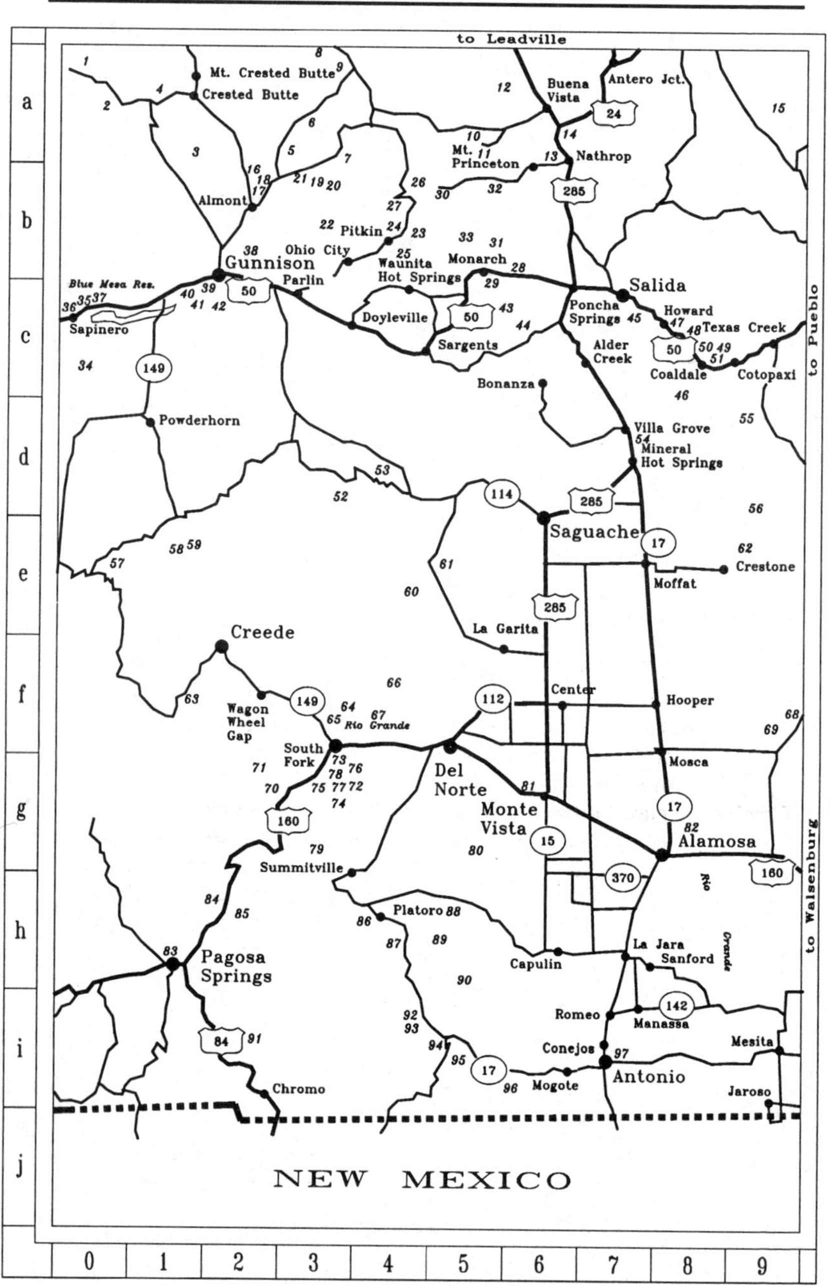

Featuring: Anthracite Creek, Gunnison National Forest, West Elk Wilderness, Ruby Mountain Range, Spring Creek Reservoir, Taylor River, Taylor Park Reservoir, Collegiate Peaks Wilderness, Cottonwood Creek, San Isabel National Forest, Elevenmile Reservoir, Middle Quartz Creek, Quartz Creek, Canyon Creek, Chalk Creek, North Quartz Creek, South Arkansas River, Poncha Springs, Lake Fork Gunnison River, Curecanti National Recreation Area, Poncha Creek, Rainbow Trail, Hayden Creek, South Fork of Carnero Creek, Rio Grande National Forest, Middle Fork of Carnero Creek, Sangre De Cristo Range, Mill Creek, La Garita Wilderness, Cebolla Creek, Cochetopa Pass, Continental Divide, San Juan Mountains, Rio Grande River, Cathedral Creek, San Dunes National Monument, West Fork of San Juan River, Big Meadows Reservoir, Beaver Creek Reservoir, Pass Creek, Alamosa River, South Fork of Rock Creek, Platoro Reservoir, Conejos River, Rio Blanco River, Trujillo Meadows Reservoir

---

1) ERIKSON SPRINGS

Reference: on Anthracite Creek, Gunnison National Forest; map C6, grid a0.

Campsites, facilities: There are 18 sites for tents, trailers or motor homes up to 32 feet long. Picnic tables are provided. Vault toilets are available. Hand-pumped water is available.

Reservations, fee: No reservations necessary; $7 fee per night. Open mid-May to mid-November.

Who to contact: Phone Gunnison National Forest at (303) 527-4131 or write to Paonia Ranger District, P.O. Box AG, Paonia, CO 81428.

Location: From Delta on US 50, drive east on Highway 92 for 20 miles. Turn left and continue northeast on Highway 133 for 23.6 miles, then seven miles east on County Road 12 to the campground.

Trip note: This is a little-known, tiny spot located along Anthracite Creek at an elevation of 6,800 feet. There are many sidetrip options. The best is a trail that is routed up Dark Canyon along Anthracite Creek which leads into the Raggeds Wilderness. Another alternative is visiting Paonia Reservoir and the Paonia State Recreation Area which is located just six miles away. Anthracite Ranger Station is located just north of the camp.

---

2) LOST LAKE

Reference: near West Elk Wilderness, Gunnison National Forest; map C6, grid a0.

Campsites, facilities: There are 11 sites for tents. Motor homes and trailers are not recommended due to the rough access road. Picnic tables are provided. Pit toilets are available. There is **no piped water.**

Reservations, fee: No reservations necessary; no fee. Open mid-June to mid-November.

Who to contact: Phone Gunnison National Forest at (303) 527-4131 or write to Paonia Ranger District, P.O. Box AG, Paonia, CO 81428.

Location: From Gunnison, drive 20.5 miles north on Highway 135 to Crested Butte. Travel west on County Road 12 for 15 miles, then south on Forest Service Road 706 for three miles to the campground.

Trip note: You'll feel like you're a bit lost here, and that's just what you might want. The small, quiet, pretty camp is beside Lost Lake Slough at 9,600 feet. Two smaller lakes, Dollar Lake and Lost Lake, are nearby, and there are trails that access a network of trails and tiny alpine lakes in the West Elk Wilderness.

---

3) CEMENT CREEK

Reference: in Gunnison National Forest; map C6, grid a1.

Campsites, facilities: There are 13 sites for tents, trailers or motor homes up to 32 feet long. Picnic tables are provided. Piped water and vault toilets are available. A coffee shop is located within one mile.

Reservations, fee: No reservations necessary; $7 fee per night. Open mid-May to late October.

Who to contact: Phone Gunnison National Forest at (303) 641-0471 or write to Taylor River Ranger District, 216 North Colorado, Gunnison, CO 81230.

Location: From Gunnison, drive 20.5 miles north on Highway 135. Turn northeast on Forest Service Road 740 and drive four miles to the campground.

Trip note: This can be an idyllic spot for those willing to take advantage of it. The campground is at 9,000 feet and is set along the banks of Cement Creek. The fishing can be quite good here. The bonus is that there are two hot springs just two miles away. A Forest Service map details the hiking trails. The campground is surrounded by aspen trees.

---

4) LAKE IRWIN

Reference: near Ruby Mountain Range, Gunnison National Forest; map C6, grid a1.

Campsites, facilities: There are 32 sites for tents, trailers or motor homes up to 32 feet long. Picnic tables are provided. Pit toilets only. There is hand-pumped water only. A boat ramp is nearby.

Reservations, fee: Reserve through MISTIX at (800) 283-CAMP ($6 MISTIX fee); $7 fee per night. Open early June to late October.

Who to contact: Phone Gunnison National Forest at (303) 641-0471 or write to Taylor River Ranger District, 216 North Colorado, Gunnison, CO 81230.

Location: From Gunnison, drive 20.5 miles north on Highway 135 to Crested Butte. Travel west on County Road 12 for 7.2 miles, then north on Forest Service Road 826 for 2.6 miles to the campground.

Trip note: This is a prime spot on the shore of Lake Irwin at an elevation of 10,200 feet. It's a great jump-off point for hikers and is set at the foot of the Ruby Mountain Range with numerous trails to alpine lakes. Several small waterfalls are within a half mile. There is also access to the spectacular Raggeds Wilderness.

5) MOSCA

Reference: on Spring Creek Reservoir, Gunnison National Forest; map C6, grid a3.

Campsites, facilities: There are 16 sites for tents, trailers or motor homes up to 22 feet long. Picnic tables are provided. Vault toilets and piped water are available. Boat docks and launching facilities are nearby.

Reservations, fee: No reservations necessary; $7 fee per night. Open early June to mid-October.

Who to contact: Phone Gunnison National Forest at (303) 641-0471 or write to Taylor River Ranger District, 216 North Colorado, Gunnison, CO 81230.

Location: From Gunnison, drive 11 miles north on Highway 135 to Almont. Continue northeast on Forest Service Road 742 for 7.2 miles, then north on Forest Service Road 744 for 12.1 miles to the campground.

Trip note: This pretty little spot is located along Spring Creek Reservoir at an elevation of 10,000 feet. There is good fishing in the reservoir, and anglers will appreciate the boat ramp near the campground. A trailhead a few miles from camp leads east to Taylor Park Reservoir. See a Forest Service map for details.

6) RIVER'S END

Reference: on Taylor River, Gunnison National Forest; map C6, grid a3.

Campsites, facilities: There are 15 sites for tents, trailers or motor homes up to 32 feet long. Picnic tables are provided. Hand-pumped water and vault toilets are available. A store and coffee shop are located within three miles. Boat docks, launching facilities and rentals are nearby.

Reservations, fee: No reservations necessary; $7 fee per night. Open late May to late October.

Who to contact: Phone Gunnison National Forest at (303) 641-0471 or write to Taylor River Ranger District, 216 North Colorado, Gunnison, CO 81230.

Location: From Gunnison, drive 11 miles north on Highway 135 to Almont. Continue northeast on Forest Service Road 742 for 28.3 miles to the campground.

Trip note: This is a nice spot where the Taylor River empties into the north end of Taylor Park Reservoir. This is one of two camps on the reservoir and one of four camps in the immediate area on the Taylor River. There are several hiking trails around the reservoir; see a National Forest map for trailhead locations.

7) LAKEVIEW

Reference: on Taylor Park Reservoir, Gunnison National Forest; map C6, grid a3.

Campsites, facilities: There are 40 sites for tents, trailers or motor homes up to 22 feet long. Picnic tables are provided. Piped water and vault toilets are available. A store and a coffee shop are located within one mile. Boat docks, launching facilities and rentals are nearby. Some facilities are **wheelchair accessible.**

Reservations, fee: Reserve through MISTIX at (800) 283-CAMP ($6 MISTIX fee); $7 fee per night. Open late May to late October.

Who to contact: Phone Gunnison National Forest at (303) 641-0471 or write to Taylor River Ranger District, 216 North Colorado, Gunnison, CO 81230.

Location: From Gunnison, drive 11 miles north on Highway 135 to Almont. Continue northeast on Forest Service Road 742 for 23.2 miles.

Trip note: This camp is located along the south shore of Taylor Park Reservoir. Good boating and fishing, the latter especially in early summer. A trail is routed south from camp to Park Cone; it's a relatively short hike and a pleasant sidetrip. This is the more popular of the two camps, so get your reservation in early or plan on staying at River's End Camp.

8) DORCHESTER

Reference: near Collegiate Peaks Wilderness, Gunnison National Forest; map C6, grid a3.

Campsites, facilities: There are 10 sites for tents, trailers or motor homes up to 32 feet long. Piped water and picnic tables are provided. Vault toilets only.

Reservations, fee: No reservations necessary; $7 fee per night. Open early June to mid-October.

Who to contact: Phone Gunnison National Forest at (303) 641-0471 or write to Taylor River Ranger District, 216 North Colorado, Gunnison, CO 81230.

Location: From Gunnison, drive 11 miles north on Highway 135 to Almont. Continue northeast on Forest Service Road 742 for 39.5 miles.

Trip note: This is a good starting point for a hiking trip, with a trail leading from camp that routes to several small lakes within five to seven miles. The camp has an elevation of 9,800 feet and is located at the base of the Collegiate Peaks Wilderness, near the Continental Divide. Dorchester Ranger Station is located adjacent to the camp; they can provide maps and answer any questions.

9) DINNER STATION

Reference: on Taylor River, Gunnison National Forest; map C6, grid a3.

Campsites, facilities: There are 22 sites for tents, trailers or motor homes up to 32 feet long. Picnic tables are provided. Piped water and vault toilets are available.

Reservations, fee: Reserve through MISTIX at (800) 283-CAMP ($6 MISTIX fee); $7 fee per night. Open late May to late October.

Who to contact: Phone Gunnison National Forest at (303) 641-0471 or write to Taylor River Ranger District, 216 North Colorado, Gunnison, CO 81230.

Location: From Gunnison, drive 11 miles north on Highway 135 to Almont. Continue northeast on Forest Service Road 742 for 32.5 miles to the campground.

Trip note: This camp is located on the Taylor River, a few miles above Taylor Park Reservoir. Fishing on the Taylor River can be excellent in early fall. An alternate camp is River's End, about four miles south.

---

10) COTTONWOOD LAKE

Reference: southwest of Buena Vista, San Isabel National Forest; map C6, grid a5.

Campsites, facilities: There are 28 sites for trailers or motor homes up to 22 feet long. No tents are allowed. Picnic tables are provided. Piped water and pit toilets are also available. Pets are permitted on leashes.

Reservations, fee: Reservations accepted; $7 fee per night. Open late May to late October.

Who to contact: Phone San Isabel National Forest at (719) 539-3591 or write to Salida Ranger District, 325 West Rainbow Boulevard, Salida, CO 81201.

Location: From Buena Vista, travel seven miles southwest on County Road 306 and drive 3.5 miles southwest on County Road 344 to the campground.

Trip note: Set on little Cottonwood Lake in the Cottonwood Lake Recreation Area, this is a rustic site for a motor home park (tenters need not apply). Some hiking trails which trace small creeks are nearby. Mount Princeton, a Colorado "Fourteener" at 14,197 feet, can be seen to the southeast.

---

11) COLLEGIATE PEAKS

Reference: on Cottonwood Creek, San Isabel National Forest; map C6, grid a5.

Campsites, facilities: There are 56 sites for trailers or motor homes up to 22 feet long. Picnic tables are provided. Pit toilets are also available. Pets are permitted on leashes.

Reservations, fee: Reserve through MISTIX at (800) 283-CAMP ($6 MISTIX fee); $7 fee per night. Open late May to late October.

Who to contact: Phone San Isabel National Forest at (719) 539-3591 or write to Salida Ranger District, 325 West Rainbow Boulevard, Salida, CO 81201.

Location: From Buena Vista, travel 10.6 miles west on County Road 306 to the campground.

Trip note: This camp is set on Cottonwood Creek adjacent to Collegiate Peaks Wilderness. Although there are no trails that lead directly from the camp, trails located nearby can be hiked to gain access to the wilderness area. A Forest Service map details all trails and the surrounding wildlands. The camp is easy to get to, and full services are just a few miles away in Buena Vista.

---

12) CRAZY HORSE

Reference: north of Buena Vista; map C6, grid a5.

Campsites, facilities: There are 11 tent sites and 89 sites for trailers or motor homes of any length. Picnic tables are provided. Flush toilets, bottled gas, sanitary disposal station, showers, recreation hall, a store, cafe, laundromat, ice, miniature golf course, horse corral, playground and a swimming pool are also available. Pets are permitted on leashes.

Reservations, fee: Reservations accepted; $12.50-$16.50 fee per night; MasterCard and Visa accepted. Open April to mid-November.

Who to contact: Phone (719) 395-2323 or write to 33975 Highway 24, Buena Vista, CO 81211.

Location: From Buena Vista, travel five miles north on US 24 to the resort.

Trip note: One of the more scenic areas for motor home parks you might find, this camp has the Collegiate Peaks providing a panoramic backdrop for pretty, open sites. Rafting on the Arkansas River is a good summer sidetrip and can be arranged through outfitters in Buena Vista. Other nearby recreation options include a golf course, hiking trails and bike paths.

---

13) BROWN'S

Reference: south of Buena Vista; map C6, grid a6.

Campsites, facilities: There are 12 tent sites and 45 sites for trailers or motor homes of any length. Picnic tables are provided. Flush toilets, sanitary disposal station, showers, laundromat, ice and playground are also available. Firewood costs extra. Bottled gas and a store are located within one mile. Pets on leashes and motorbikes are permitted.

Reservations, fee: Reservations accepted; $8-$12 fee per night; MasterCard and Visa accepted. Open May to mid-September.

Who to contact: Phone (719) 395-8301 or write to P.O. Box 39, Nathrop, CO 81236.

Location: From Buena Vista, drive eight miles south on US 285.

Trip note: This is a rural campground in a beautiful area. It has two levels, with the upper sites open and sunny, and the lower sites set in the trees along Chalk Creek. Nearby attractions include hot springs, horseback riding, hiking, fishing, river rafting and kayaking.

14) BUENA VISTA FAMILY RESORT

Reference: near Buena Vista; map C6, grid a6.

Campsites, facilities: There are 43 tent sites and 57 drive-through sites for trailers or motor homes of any length. Picnic tables are provided. Flush toilets, bottled gas, sanitary disposal station, showers, recreation hall, a store, a coffee shop, laundromat, ice and a playground are also available. Electricity, piped water, sewer hookups and firewood are available at an additional charge. Pets and motorbikes are permitted.

Reservations, fee: Reservations accepted; $12-$16.50 fee per night; MasterCard and Visa accepted. Open all year.

Who to contact: Phone (719) 395-8318 or write to 27700 County Road 303, Buena Vista, CO 81211.

Location: From Buena Vista, travel 2.5 miles south, then 1.5 miles east on US 24 to the campground.

Trip note: This is a super-deluxe campground, complete with mountain views and all the amenities. This resort has it all, including hay rides, river rafting, van tours, four-wheel-drive and motorcycle trails and horseback riding. In the winter, there are trails for snowmobiling and cross-country skiing. It's a large, homey campground, the kind you might not want to leave. Crazy Horse Camp provides an option if this one is full.

15) ELEVENMILE STATE PARK

Reference: on Elevenmile Reservoir; map C6, grid a9.

Campsites, facilities: There are 274 sites for tents, trailers or motor homes of any length. Some backcountry sites are also available. Picnic tables are provided. Piped water, pit toilets, a sanitary disposal station and a playground are also available. Firewood costs extra. A store, coffee shop and ice are located within one mile. Pets are permitted on leashes. Boat docks, launching facilities and rentals are nearby.

Reservations, fee: Reserve sites by calling (800) 678-CAMP ($6.75 reservation fee); $6 fee per night plus $3 entrance fee. Open all year with limited winter facilities.

Who to contact: Phone (719) 748-3401 or write to Star Route 2, P.O. Box 4229, Lake George, CO 80827.

Location: From the town of Lake George, drive a half mile west on Highway 24 and then 10 miles south on County Road 92 to the park.

Trip note: This is a 4,000-acre park set alongside the long Eleven Mile Reservoir. It's a good reservoir for small boats and fishing. No waterskiing is permitted. Windsurfing, however, is allowed, and is quite popular here. This reservoir can provide some of Colorado's best fishing for trout and northern pike. On winter weekends, it's a popular spot for ice skating, ice fishing, snow tubing and cross-country skiing.

16) ONE MILE

Reference: on Taylor River, Gunnison National Forest; map C6, grid b2.

Campsites, facilities: There are 27 sites for tents, trailers or motor homes up to 32 feet long. Picnic tables are provided. Piped water and pit toilets are available. A store and a coffee shop are located within one mile.

Reservations, fee: No reservations necessary; $7 fee per night. Open late May to late October.

Who to contact: Phone Gunnison National Forest at (303) 641-0471 or write to Taylor River Ranger District, 216 North Colorado, Gunnison, CO 81230.

Location: From Gunnison, drive 11 miles north on Highway 135 to Almont. Continue northeast on Forest Service Road 742 for 7.9 miles to the campground.

Trip note: This is a pretty spot on the bottom of Taylor Canyon. The camp is set right along the Taylor River. A trailhead is located at adjacent Taylor Canyon Picnic Area, and is routed south along Beaver Creek. There are several other trails available in the area as well; see a Forest Service map. This section of river is ideal for guided river float trips.

17) NORTH BANK

Reference: on Taylor River, Gunnison National Forest; map C6, grid b2.

Campsites, facilities: There are 17 sites for tents, trailers or motor homes up to 22 feet long. Picnic tables are provided. Piped water and vault toilets are available. A store and a coffee shop are located within one mile.

Reservations, fee: No reservations necessary; $7 fee per night. Open late May to mid-October.

Who to contact: Phone Gunnison National Forest at (303) 641-0471 or write to Taylor River Ranger District, 216 North Colorado, Gunnison, CO 81230.

Location: From Gunnison, drive 11 miles north on Highway 135 to Almont. Continue northeast on Forest Service Road 742 for 7.8 miles to the campground on the left.

Trip note: This is a nearby option to One Mile Camp, located less than one mile distant on the other side of the Taylor River. The camp is at 8,600 feet and has several hiking trails available. One is routed north directly from camp, traveling along Browns Gulch for about two miles.

18) SPRING CREEK

Reference: in Gunnison National Forest; map C6, grid b2.

Campsites, facilities: There are 12 sites for tents, trailers or motor homes up to 32 feet long. Picnic tables are provided. Piped water and

vault toilets are available. A store and a coffee shop are located within one mile.

Reservations, fee: No reservations necessary; $7 fee per night. Open early June to mid-October.

Who to contact: Phone Gunnison National Forest at (303) 641-0471 or write to Taylor River Ranger District, 216 North Colorado, Gunnison, CO 81230.

Location: From Gunnison, drive 11 miles north on Highway 135 to Almont. Continue northeast on Forest Service Road 742 for 7.2 miles, then two miles north on Forest Service Road 744 to the campground.

Trip note: This is a favorite for folks who want a bit of both worlds. It is a rustic, little-known camp set along the banks of Spring Creek, but if you need facilities and supplies, a store is just a two-minute drive away. This is an alternative to North Bank, One Mile or Rosy Lane Camps.

---

19) LODGEPOLE

Reference: on Taylor River, Gunnison National Forest; map C6, grid b3.

Campsites, facilities: There are 16 sites for tents, trailers or motor homes up to 32 feet long. Picnic tables are provided. Pit toilets and piped water are available.

Reservations, fee: Reserve through MISTIX at (800) 283-CAMP ($6 MISTIX fee); $7 fee per night. Open late May to late October.

Who to contact: Phone Gunnison National Forest at (303) 641-0471 or write to Taylor River Ranger District, 216 North Colorado, Gunnison, CO 81230.

Location: From Gunnison, drive 11 miles north on Highway 135 to Almont. Continue northeast on Forest Service Road 742 for 14.7 miles to the campground.

Trip note: This is an ideal spot for backpackers looking for a jump-off point for a hiking a trip into the Fossil Ridge Area. It is set at 8,800 feet along the Taylor River, with a major trailhead just south of the camp that provides access to the surrounding wildlands. Due to its close proximity to this popular trailhead, this camp is often full to capacity in the summer; reserve your spot early.

---

20) LOTTIS CREEK

Reference: on Taylor River, Gunnison National Forest; map C6, grid b3.

Campsites, facilities: There are 27 sites for tents, trailers or motor homes up to 32 feet long. Picnic tables are provided. Piped water and vault toilets are available. Two sites are **wheelchair accessible.**

Reservations, fee: No reservations necessary; $7 fee per night. Open late May to late October.

Who to contact: Phone Gunnison National Forest at (303) 641-0471 or write to Taylor River Ranger District, 216 North Colorado, Gunnison, CO 81230.

Location: From Gunnison, drive 11 miles north on Highway 135 to Almont. Continue northeast on Forest Service Road 742 for 17.4 miles to the campground.

Trip note: One of several camps situated along the Taylor River, this one is on Lottis Creek at an elevation of 9,000 feet. A good sidetrip for hikers is the trail that parallels Lottis Creek. Another possible sidetrip is a day at Taylor Park Reservoir, only five miles north of camp, with fishing, boating and swimming among your options.

---

21) COLD SPRING

Reference: on Taylor River, Gunnison National Forest; map C6, grid b3.

Campsites, facilities: There are six sites for tents, trailers or motor homes up to 16 feet long. Picnic tables are provided. Vault toilets are available. There is **no piped water.**

Reservations, fee: No reservations necessary; no fee. Open late May to late October.

Who to contact: Phone Gunnison National Forest at (303) 641-0471 or write to Taylor River Ranger District, 216 North Colorado, Gunnison, CO 81230.

Location: From Gunnison, drive 11 miles north on Highway 135 to Almont. Continue northeast on Forest Service Road 742 for 16.1 miles to the campground.

Trip note: This is the most primitive and smallest of the camps in the area. It is nestled at the bottom of Taylor Canyon at 9,000 feet. The Taylor River runs right past the campsites. It's quite pretty, and a great, inexpensive option to the more developed camps nearby. Just bring your own drinking water, and get there plenty early to insure getting a site.

---

22) GOLD CREEK

Reference: north of Ohio, Gunnison National Forest; map C6, grid b3.

Campsites, facilities: There are six tent sites. Picnic tables are provided. Vault toilets are also available. Pets are permitted on leashes.

Reservations, fee: No reservations necessary; no fee. Open June to September.

Who to contact: Phone Gunnison National Forest at (303) 641-0471 or write to Cebolla Ranger District, 216 North Colorado, Gunnison, CO 81230.

Location: From Ohio City, drive north on Forest Service Road 771 for about eight miles (the last five are dirt) to the campground.

Trip note: A small, primitive and little-used camp way out there in what we call "booger country." Set at 10,000 feet elevation along Gold

Creek, with trails from camp branching out in several directions to numerous high-country lakes. The main trail starts at camp and zigzags its way west, shooting up north to pretty little Boulder Lake, then back west, tracing Fossil Ridge.

---

23) MIDDLE QUARTZ

Reference: on Middle Quartz Creek, Gunnison National Forest; map C6, grid b4.

Campsites, facilities: There are seven tent sites. Picnic tables are provided. Vault toilets are also available. There is **no piped water.** Pets are permitted on leashes.

Reservations, fee: No reservations necessary; no fee. Open late June to late October.

Who to contact: Phone Gunnison National Forest at (303) 641-0471 or write to Cebolla Ranger District, 216 North Colorado, Gunnison, CO 81230.

Location: From Salida, travel 56 miles west on US 50 to Parlin and then head northeast on BLM Route 3101 for about 18 miles to Pitkin. From Pitkin, drive 1.5 miles northeast on Forest Service Road 765 and 5.5 miles east on Forest Service Road 767.

Trip note: This is a primitive, virtually unknown and hard-to-reach camp. But if you want to get away from it all, it's worth it. It's set at 10,200 feet on Middle Quartz Creek. You are strongly advised to obtain a Forest Service map detailing the backroads. There are fish in Quartz Creek, so bring your pole, along with a big frying pan.

---

24) PITKIN

Reference: on Quartz Creek, Gunnison National Forest; map C6, grid b4.

Campsites, facilities: There are 22 tent sites and nine sites for trailers or motor homes up to 16 feet long. Picnic tables are provided. Piped water and vault toilets are also available. Showers, a store, a coffee shop, laundromat and ice are located within one mile. Pets are permitted on leashes.

Reservations, fee: Reservations accepted; $7 fee per night. Open late May to September.

Who to contact: Phone Gunnison National Forest at (303) 641-0471 or write to Cebolla Ranger District, 216 North Colorado, Gunnison, CO 81230.

Location: From Salida, travel 56 miles west on US 50 to Parlin and then head northeast on BLM Route 3101 for about 18 miles to Pitkin. Continue one mile east on Forest Service Road 765 to the campground.

Trip note: This camp is located just east of Pitkin where you can get supplies. Yet, set at 9,300 feet on Quartz Creek, it has a nice out-of-the-way feel to it. There is a ranger station in Pitkin that can answer any questions you may have. Several four-wheel-drive roads in the vicinity make great trails for mountain bikers.

---

25) SNOWBLIND

Reference: on Canyon Creek, Gunnison National Forest; map C6, grid b4.

Campsites, facilities: There are 23 sites for tents, trailers or motor homes up to 22 feet long. Picnic tables and vault toilets are provided, but there is **no piped water** at this site. Pets are permitted on leashes.

Reservations, fee: No reservations necessary; no fee. Open June to late October.

Who to contact: Phone Gunnison National Forest at (303) 641-0471 or write to Cebolla Ranger District, 216 North Colorado, Gunnison, CO 81230.

Location: From Sargents, drive 1.1 mile northeast on US 50 and then 6.9 miles north on Forest Service Road 888 to the campground.

Trip note: A good Forest Service camp, located on Canyon Creek, with many sidetrips available. And it's quite large for a primitive, free camp, which means that you're almost guaranteed a site. One nearby trail loops 15 miles along Horseshoe and Canyon Creeks to the northwest of camp. To the northeast are some primitive roads that can be explored by four-wheel-drive cowboys or mountain bikers.

---

26) IRON CITY

Reference: on Chalk Creek, San Isabel National Forest; map C6, grid b4.

Campsites, facilities: There are 17 sites for tents, trailers or motor homes up to 16 feet long. Picnic tables are provided. Piped water and pit toilets are also available. Pets are permitted on leashes.

Reservations, fee: No reservations necessary; $6 fee per night. Open early June to late September.

Who to contact: Phone San Isabel National Forest at (719) 539-3591 or write to Salida Ranger District, 325 West Rainbow Boulevard, Salida, CO 81201.

Location: From Nathrop, drive a half mile south on US 285. Turn right and drive 15 miles west on County Road 162, then a half mile north on Forest Service Road 292 to the campground.

Trip note: This is a pretty spot set along Chalk Creek. There are numerous trails in the area, most which run alongside streams and creeks. A worthwhile sidetrip is visiting St. Elmo, an historic mining town that looks virtually unchanged from its original era. Another is the trip to Mount Princeton Hot Springs, where you can soak up some minerals and rinse off some of that camping grime.

27) QUARTZ

Reference: on North Quartz Creek, Gunnison National Forest; map C6, grid b4.

Campsites, facilities: There are 10 sites for tents, trailers or motor homes up to 16 feet long. Picnic tables are provided. Piped water and vault toilets are also available. Showers, a store, a coffee shop, laundromat and ice are located within five miles. Pets are permitted on leashes.

Reservations, fee: No reservations necessary; $7 fee per night. Open late May to late October.

Who to contact: Phone Gunnison National Forest at (303) 641-0471 or write to Cebolla Ranger District, 216 North Colorado, Gunnison, CO 81230.

Location: From Salida, travel 56 miles west on US 50 to Parlin and then head northeast on BLM Route 3101 for about 18 miles to Pitkin. Continue four miles northeast on Forest Service Road 765 to the campground.

Trip note: This secluded little camp is of geologic interest. It is located on the west side of the Continental Divide at 9,800 feet. North Quartz Creek runs adjacent to the camp. It's hidden, with shaded, private sites and few people. If you dig around long enough, you may even find a few quartz crystals buried in the earth.

28) HEART OF THE ROCKIES

Reference: west of Salida; map C6, grid b5.

Campsites, facilities: There are 20 tent sites and 54 sites for trailers or motor homes of any length. Picnic tables are provided. Flush toilets, sanitary disposal station, showers, recreation hall, a store, laundromat, ice, playground and a swimming pool are also available. Firewood costs extra. Pets and motorbikes are permitted.

Reservations, fee: Reservations accepted; $5-$17 fee per night; MasterCard and Visa accepted. Open mid-May to mid-October and some off-season weekends.

Who to contact: Phone (719) 539-2025 or write to 16105 Highway 50, Salida, CO 81201.

Location: From Salida, drive 11 miles west on US 50 (check road conditions in the winter).

Trip note: This camp is on the flank of Mount Shavano and close to the Arkansas River. It has gorgeous mountain views. In the spring and fall, the weather is milder here in comparison to other areas of Colorado. The Salida area provides many possible sidetrips. They include river rafting, visiting hot springs or a fish hatchery, and touring a ghost town. Other recreation options include a golf course, hiking trails and bike paths.

29) GARFIELD

Reference: on South Arkansas River, San Isabel National Forest; map C6, grid b5.

Campsites, facilities: There are 11 sites for tents, trailers or motor homes up to 16 feet long. Picnic tables are provided. Piped water and pit toilets are also available. Showers, a store, a coffee shop and ice are located within one mile. Pets are permitted on leashes.

Reservations, fee: No reservations necessary; $7 fee per night. Open June to early October.

Who to contact: Phone San Isabel National Forest at (719) 539-3591 or write to Salida Ranger District, 325 West Rainbow Boulevard, Salida, CO 81201.

Location: From Salida, drive 18 miles west on US 50 to the campground.

Trip note: This is a nice spot with easy access. It's set along the South Arkansas River. For a good sidetrip, take the trail out of camp that leads to two nearby small lakes. Note: it can get a little noisy here at times; the Denver-Rio Grande Western Railroad runs right next to the campground.

30) CASCADE

Reference: on Chalk Creek, San Isabel National Forest; map C6, grid b5.

Campsites, facilities: There are 23 sites for tents, trailers or motor homes up to 22 feet long. Picnic tables are provided. Piped water and pit toilets are also available. A coffee shop is located within five miles. Pets are permitted on leashes.

Reservations, fee: Reserve through MISTIX at (800) 283-CAMP ($6 MISTIX fee); $6 fee per night. Open late May to mid-September.

Who to contact: Phone San Isabel National Forest at (719) 539-3591 or write to Salida Ranger District, 325 West Rainbow Boulevard, Salida, CO 81201.

Location: From Nathrop, drive a half mile south on US 285, then 8.5 miles west on County Road 162 to the campground.

Trip note: This is a relatively secluded spot. Chalk Creek runs alongside the camp and Mount Princeton, to the north, can be spotted on clear days. See trip note for Iron City Camp for some fascinating sidetrips.

31) NORTH FORK RESERVOIR

Reference: northwest of Poncha Springs, San Isabel National Forest; map C6, grid b5.

Campsites, facilities: There are eight sites for tents, trailers or motor homes up to 16 feet long. Picnic tables are provided. Pets are permitted on leashes. Boat docks are also available.

Reservations, fee: No reservations necessary; no fee. Open late June to late September.

Who to contact: Phone San Isabel National Forest at (719) 539-3591 or write to Salida Ranger District, 325 West Rainbow Boulevard, Salida, CO 81201.

Location: From the town of Poncha Springs, drive six miles west on US 50 and then 10.2 miles north on County Road 240.

Trip note: This is the Rocky Mountain high country with an elevation of 11,000 feet. This camp is set along North Fork Lake. There are smaller lakes in the area, some which can be reached by trail. Though it's primitive, it's quite pretty, and being one of the only free campgrounds in the San Isabel National Forest, it's a pretty good deal.

---

32) CHALK LAKE

Reference: on Chalk Creek, San Isabel National Forest; map C6, grid b5.

Campsites, facilities: There are 21 sites for tents, trailers or motor homes up to 22 feet long. Picnic tables are provided. Piped water and pit toilets are also available. A coffee shop is also located within five miles. Pets are permitted on leashes.

Reservations, fee: Reserve through MISTIX at (800) 283-CAMP ($6 MISTIX fee); $8 fee per night. Open late May to mid-October.

Who to contact: Phone San Isabel National Forest at (719) 539-3591 or write to Salida Ranger District, 325 West Rainbow Boulevard, Salida, CO 81201.

Location: From Nathrop, drive a half mile south on US 285 and then 7.5 miles west on County Road 162 to the campground.

Trip note: This campground is one of three camps set along Chalk Creek. For other options, check out nearby Iron City Camp and Cascade Camp. Be sure to see the trip note for Iron City Camp for fun side excursions.

---

33) ANGEL OF SHAVANO GROUP CAMP

Reference: on the North Fork of South Arkansas River, San Isabel National Forest; map C6, grid b5.

Campsites, facilities: There is one group site that can accommodate tents, trailers or motor homes up to 16 feet long. Picnic tables are provided. Piped water and pit toilets are also available. A coffee shop is located within five miles. Pets are permitted on leashes.

Reservations, fee: Call ranger for reservation and fee information. Open early May to early October.

Who to contact: Phone San Isabel National Forest at (719) 539-3591 or write to Salida Ranger District, 325 West Rainbow Boulevard, Salida, CO 81201.

Location: From Salida, drive 10 miles west on US 50 and then five miles north on County Road 240 to the campground.

Trip note: This camp is set alongside the North Fork of South Arkansas River in the shadow of Mount Shavano (14,229 feet). The Colorado Trail can be accessed nearby and connects to the trail leading to Mount Shavano. North Fork Reservoir Camp provides a nearby alternative.

34) GATEVIEW

Reference: on Lake Fork of the Gunnison River, Curecanti National Recreation Area; map C6, grid c0.

Campsites, facilities: There are seven tent sites. Picnic tables are provided. Piped water and pit toilets are available. Pets and motorbikes are permitted.

Reservations, fee: No reservations necessary; no fee. Open all year.

Who to contact: Phone Curecanti National Recreation Area at (303) 641-2337 or write to 102 Elk Creek, Gunnison, CO 81230.

Location: From Gunnison, drive 10 miles west on US 50. Turn left and drive 20 miles south on Highway 149, then six miles north on a gravel road to the campground.

Trip note: This is a small, very private setting where Lake Fork of the Gunnison River empties into a long narrow inlet of Blue Mesa Reservoir. It is primitive, little used, and the only free campground in the park. Most campers in the area use the more-developed campgrounds at the north shore of the reservoir. If you're into "roughing" it, you might have the place to yourself.

35) RED CREEK

Reference: on Blue Mesa Reservoir, Curecanti National Recreation Area; map C6, grid c0.

Campsites, facilities: There are seven sites for tents, trailers or motor homes of any length. Picnic tables are provided. Piped water and pit toilets are available. Pets and motorbikes are permitted. Boat docks and launching facilities are nearby.

Reservations, fee: No reservations necessary; $7 fee per night. Open mid-May to mid-September.

Who to contact: Phone Curecanti National Recreation Area at (303) 641-2337 or write to 102 Elk Creek, Gunnison, CO 81230.

Location: From Gunnison, drive west on US 50 for 19 miles to the campground.

Trip note: The smallest of the nine campgrounds at Curecanti National Recreation Area, this site is set where Red Creek enters Blue Mesa Reservoir. See trip note for Ponderosa Camp for recreation options.

36) DRY GULCH

Reference: on Blue Mesa Reservoir, Curecanti National Recreation Area; map C6, grid c0.

Campsites, facilities: There are 10 sites for tents, trailers or motor homes of any length. Picnic tables are provided. Piped water and pit toilets are available. Pets and motorbikes are permitted.

Reservations, fee: No reservations necessary; $7 fee per night. Open mid-May to mid-September.

Who to contact: Phone Curecanti National Recreation Area at (303) 641-2337 or write to 102 Elk Creek, Gunnison, CO 81230.

Location: From Gunnison, drive west on US 50 for 17 miles to the campground.

Trip note: This is one of the smaller, more intimate campgrounds in the beautiful Curecanti National Recreation Area at Blue Mesa Reservoir. See trip note for Ponderosa Camp.

37) ELK CREEK

Reference: on Blue Mesa Reservoir, Curecanti National Recreation Area; map C6, grid c0.

Campsites, facilities: There are 179 sites for tents, trailers or motor homes up to 30 feet long. Piped water and picnic tables are provided. Flush toilets and a sanitary disposal station are available. Showers cost an extra fee. Some facilities are **wheelchair accessible.** A store, a coffee shop and ice are located within one mile. Pets are permitted on leashes. Boat docks, launching facilities and rentals are nearby.

Reservations, fee: No reservations necessary; $8 fee per night. Open Memorial Day to Labor Day with limited winter facilities.

Who to contact: Phone Curecanti National Recreation Area at (303) 641-2337 or write to 102 Elk Creek, Gunnison, CO 81230.

Location: From Gunnison, drive west on US 50 for 16 miles to the campground.

Trip note: This is by far the largest, most developed campground at Curecanti National Recreation Area at Blue Mesa Reservoir. It is set where Elk Creek pours into the lake. There is a boat ramp and marina for anglers, a nature program and a visitor center. Other options at the lake include windsurfing and waterskiing. In the winter, cross-country skiing is popular here.

38) THREE RIVERS RESORT

Reference: north of Gunnison; map C6, grid b2.

Campsites, facilities: There are 24 tent sites and 41 sites for trailers or motor homes of any length. Electricity, piped water, sewer hookups and picnic tables are provided. Flush toilets, showers, recreation hall, a store, laundromat, ice and a playground are available. Firewood costs extra. Pets and motorbikes are permitted. Boat launching facilities and rentals are nearby.

Reservations, fee: Reservations accepted; $12-$14 fee per night. Open all year.

Who to contact: Phone (303) 641-1303 or write to P.O. Box 339, Almont, CO 81210.

Location: From Gunnison, drive 10 miles north on Highway 135 and a half mile on County Road 742 to the campground.

Trip note: This is good camp if you want rural beauty but all the comforts, too. The camp is set at the base of Taylor Canyon, in a unique spot where the Taylor River and the East River join together to form the headwaters of the Gunnison River. The campground is divided into two parts, one with densely wooded sites along the Taylor River, and one on a hillside overlooking the Taylor Canyon. Bighorn sheep, elk and deer roam the area year-round. Taylor Reservoir is 17 miles to the east, and Mesa Reservoir is 17 miles to the west. Nearby recreation options include hiking, fishing, biking and horseback riding.

---

39) GUNNISON KOA

Reference: near Gunnison River; map C6, grid c1.

Campsites, facilities: There are 32 tent sites and 92 sites for trailers or motor homes of any length. Picnic tables are provided. Flush toilets, sanitary disposal station, showers, recreation hall, a store, laundromat, ice and a playground are available. Electricity, piped water and sewer hookups are available at an additional charge. Bottled gas and a coffee shop are located within one mile. Pets and motorbikes are permitted.

Reservations, fee: Reservations accepted; $13.50-$19.50 fee per night; MasterCard and Visa accepted. Open mid-May to mid-November.

Who to contact: Phone (303) 641-1358 or write to P.O. Box 1144, Gunnison, CO 81230.

Location: From Gunnison, drive one mile west on US 50 and a half mile south and follow the signs to the campground.

Trip note: This is a good layover spot for highway burners looking for a rest from the grind on US 50. You get large, open sites and some fun activities to choose from, including fishing, bike riding (they have rentals) and splashing around in paddle boats. The Gunnison River or a nearby golf course can provide another respite.

---

40) STEVENS CREEK

Reference: on Blue Mesa Reservoir, Curecanti National Recreation Area; map C6, grid c1.

Campsites, facilities: There are 54 sites for tents, trailers or motor homes up to 30 feet long. Picnic tables are provided. Piped water and vault toilets are available. A store and ice are located within one mile. Pets are permitted on leashes. Boat docks and launching facilities are nearby. Some facilities are **wheelchair accessible**.

Reservations, fee: No reservations; $7 fee per night. Open Memorial Day to Labor Day.

Who to contact: Phone Curecanti National Recreation Area at (303) 641-2337 or write to 102 Elk Creek, Gunnison, CO 81230.

Location: From Gunnison, drive west on US 50 for 12 miles to the campground.

Trip note: This may be what you're looking for in Curecanti National Recreation Area: not too big, not too primitive, a balance between the two. A hiking trail that starts at the camp provides a sidetrip option, and there is an informative nature program available. Fishing is good around this camp.

---

41) SUNNYSIDE

Reference: on Blue Mesa Reservoir; map C6, grid c1.

Campsites, facilities: There are 20 tent sites and 93 sites for trailers or motor homes of any length. Picnic tables are provided. Flush toilets, piped water, showers, recreation hall, a store, laundromat and ice are available. Firewood costs extra. Pets and motorbikes are permitted. Boat docks, launching facilities and rentals are nearby.

Reservations, fee: Reservations accepted; $10-$14 fee per night; MasterCard and Visa accepted. Open April through November.

Who to contact: Phone (303) 641-0477 or write to 28357 West Highway 50, Gunnison, CO 81230.

Location: From Gunnison, drive west on US 50 for 12 miles to the campground on the Blue Mesa Reservoir.

Trip note: This developed park is set just across the road from Blue Mesa Reservoir. It's an option to the more rustic campgrounds offered by the National Park Service. Sites are open and spacious, with scattered trees around the park. It gets packed here in the summertime, with many families returning year after year for the entire summer, so be sure to reserve a spot early. Fishing for trout and salmon can be excellent at the reservoir.

---

42) MESA

Reference: near Gunnison; map C6, grid c2.

Campsites, facilities: There are 15 tent sites and 135 sites for trailers or motor homes of any length. Electricity, piped water, sewer hookups and picnic tables are provided. Flush toilets, bottled gas, sanitary disposal station, showers, recreation hall, a store, laundromat, ice and a playground are available. A coffee shop is located within one mile. Pets are permitted on leashes.

Reservations, fee: Reservations preferred; $11-$15 fee per night; MasterCard and Visa accepted. Open May to mid-November.

Who to contact: Phone (303) 641-3186 or write to 36128 West Highway 50, Gunnison, CO 81230.

Location: From Gunnison, travel two miles west on US 50 to the campground.

Trip note: This is an option to Gunnison KOA, although it is a developed park designed primarily for motor homes. It has grassy sites with some trees. A golf course and riding stable are available nearby.

---

43) MONARCH PARK

Reference: on South Arkansas River, San Isabel National Forest; map C6, grid c5.

Campsites, facilities: There are 38 sites for tents, trailers or motor homes up to 22 feet long. Picnic tables are provided. Piped water and pit toilets are also available. A store, a coffee shop and ice are located within five miles. Pets are permitted on leashes.

Reservations, fee: Reservations accepted; $6 fee per night. Open June to mid-September.

Who to contact: Phone San Isabel National Forest at (719) 539-3591 or write to Salida Ranger District, 325 West Rainbow Boulevard, Salida, CO 81201.

Location: From Salida, drive 19.5 miles west on US 50 and then drive south just under a mile on Forest Service Road 231 to the campground.

Trip note: This is the high country. The camp is set at 10,500 feet on the South Arkansas River, just a few miles north of Monarch Pass (11,386-foot elevation). A nearby trail is routed to Waterdog Lakes and makes a good sidetrip. Monarch Ski Area is a popular ski resort in the winter months.

---

44) O'HAVER LAKE

Reference: near Poncha Creek, San Isabel National Forest; map C6, grid c6.

Campsites, facilities: There are 29 sites for tents, trailers or motor homes up to 16 feet long. Picnic tables are provided. Piped water and pit toilets are also available. A store is located within five miles. Pets are permitted on leashes.

Reservations, fee: Reserve through MISTIX at (800) 283-CAMP ($6 MISTIX fee); $8 fee per night. Open early May to mid-October.

Who to contact: Phone San Isabel National Forest at (719) 539-3591 or write to Salida Ranger District, 325 West Rainbow Boulevard, Salida, CO 81201.

Location: From the town of Poncha Springs, drive 4.5 miles south on US 285. Turn right and drive 4.6 miles southwest on County Road 200, then a half mile west on County Road 202 to the campground.

Trip note: O'Haver Lake isn't gigantic. It's an intimate little lake that provides a good site for camping. It is popular though, probably due to the fact that it's the only developed campground for miles. A trail accessible to both hikers and pack animals is nearby along Poncha Creek and Starvation Creek. It leads to Marshall Pass, an historic point of interest.

45) FOUR SEASONS RV PARK

Reference: near Salida; map C6, grid c7.

Campsites, facilities: There are 60 sites for tents, trailers or motor homes of any length. Piped water, sewer hookups and picnic tables are provided. Flush toilets, showers, firewood, laundromat and ice are also available. Pets are permitted on leashes.

Reservations, fee: Reservations accepted; $10-$20 fee per night. Open all year.

Who to contact: Phone (719) 539-3084 or write to 4305 Highway 50, Salida, CO 81201.

Location: From Salida, drive 1.5 miles east on US 50 to milepost 223 and the campground.

Trip note: This is a developed motor home park located near the Arkansas River. It's an exceptionally clean, well-maintained park with friendly folks running it. The Salida area provides many recreation options including a fish hatchery, river rafting, visiting the hot springs and touring a ghost town. The spring and fall are often milder here than in other areas of Colorado.

46) HAYDEN CREEK

Reference: near Rainbow Trail, San Isabel National Forest; map C6, grid c8.

Campsites, facilities: There are eleven sites for tents, trailers or motor homes up to 16 feet long. Picnic tables are provided. Piped water and pit toilets are also available. Showers, a store and ice are located within five miles. Pets are permitted on leashes.

Reservations, fee: No reservations necessary; no fee. Open late May to mid-October.

Who to contact: Phone San Isabel National Forest at (719) 539-3591 or write to Salida Ranger District, 325 West Rainbow Boulevard, Salida, CO 81201.

Location: From Coaldale, drive 5.1 miles southwest on County Road 6 to the campground.

Trip note: This camp is set near one of the trailheads for the Rainbow Trail. The trail branches off several times, leading to some beautiful high-country lakes that offer gorgeous scenery and good fishing. Coaldale Camp is a nearby option.

47) SUGARBUSH

Reference: east of Salida; map C6, grid c8.

Campsites, facilities: There are seven tent sites and 32 sites for trailers or motor homes of any length. Piped water and picnic tables are provided. Flush toilets, sanitary disposal station, showers, a full-service grocery store, gift shop, laundromat, ice and a playground are also available. Electricity, sewer hookups and firewood are available at an additional charge. Bottled gas and a coffee shop are located within one mile. Pets are permitted on leashes. There are also four cabins available for use.

Reservations, fee: Reservations accepted; $10-$15 fee per night; cabins are $24-$50 per night. Open all year.

Who to contact: Phone (719) 942-3363 or write to 9229 Highway 50, Howard, CO 81233.

Location: From Salida, drive 12 miles east on US 50 to the campground.

Trip note: This is a perfect base camp for Colorado tourists. It's heavily wooded, with quiet, spacious sites near the Arkansas River. There is a trail from camp leading down to the river, where campers can enjoy excellent fishing or watch for local wildlife, including bald eagles and some extraordinarily tame deer. Attractions in Salida and the surrounding area include rafting, hot springs, a fish hatchery, several old ghost towns, hiking trails and antique hunting.

---

48) PLEASANT VALLEY

Reference: in Howard; map C6, grid c8.

Campsites, facilities: There are 10 tent sites and 52 sites for trailers or motor homes of any length. Electricity, piped water, sewer hookups and picnic tables are provided. Showers, toilets, bottled gas, sanitary disposal station, firewood, recreation hall, laundromat, ice and a playground are also available. Showers are available at an additional charge. A store and a coffee shop are located within one mile. Pets and motorbikes are permitted.

Reservations, fee: Reservations accepted; $5-$17 fee per night. Open all year.

Who to contact: Phone (719) 942-3484 or write to P.O. Box 0018, County Road 47, Howard, CO 81233.

Location: From Salida, drive 13 miles east on US 50 to Howard and the campground.

Trip note: This camp provides a good layover spot for tourists or highway cruisers. The sites are graveled and well-spaced, with lots of trees and grass around. See the trip note for Sugarbush Camp for area details.

---

49) HIDDEN VALLEY LAKE

Reference: near Arkansas River; map C6, grid c8.

Campsites, facilities: There are 100 tent sites and 25 sites for trailers or motor homes of any length. Picnic tables are provided. Flush toilets, sanitary disposal station, showers, firewood, recreation hall, a store, laundromat, ice and a playground are also available. Pets and motorbikes are permitted.

Reservations, fee: Reservations accepted; $9-$13.50 fee per night; MasterCard and Visa accepted. Open mid-April to mid-November.

Who to contact: Phone (719) 942-4171 or write to P.O. Box 220, Coaldale, CO 81222.

Location: From Canon City, drive 37 miles west on Highway 50. Exit between mileposts 242 and 243 to the campground.

Trip note: Set near the Arkansas River, this is one of the few privately-developed campgrounds that isn't designed expressly for motor homes. Cottonwood Creek, which offers good fishing, runs through the camp. The sites are shaded, grassy and fairly spacious. Nearby recreation options include hiking trails up Hayden Creek and a riding stable.

---

50) COALDALE

Reference: on Hayden Creek, San Isabel National Forest; map C6, grid c8.

Campsites, facilities: There are 11 tent sites. Picnic tables are provided. Piped water and pit toilets are also available. Showers are located within one mile and a store within five miles. Pets are permitted on leashes.

Reservations, fee: No reservations necessary; no fee. Open late May to mid-October.

Who to contact: Phone San Isabel National Forest at (719) 539-3591 or write to Salida Ranger District, 325 West Rainbow Boulevard, Salida, CO 81201.

Location: From Coaldale, drive 4.1 miles southwest on County Road 6 to the campground.

Trip note: This is a secluded camp along Hayden Creek that provides some hiking possibilities on the Rainbow Trail. It's advisable to obtain a Forest Service map. The road ends one mile further at Hayden Creek Camp which provides one of the most direct access points to the Rainbow Trail.

---

51) LAZY J RESORT AND RAFT COMPANY

Reference: in Coaldale; map C6, grid c8.

Campsites, facilities: There are 25 tent sites and 25 sites for trailers or motor homes of any length. Picnic tables are provided. Flush toilets, sanitary disposal station, showers, a store, a coffee shop, laundromat, ice, playground and a swimming pool are also available. Electricity, piped water, sewer hookups and firewood are available at an additional charge. Pets are permitted on leashes.

Reservations, fee: Reservations accepted; $10-$13.50 fee per night; American Express, MasterCard and Visa accepted. Open early April to November.

Who to contact: Phone (719) 942-4274 or write to P.O. Box 109, Coaldale, CO 81222.

Location: From Salida, drive 20 miles east on US 50 to the campground in Coaldale.

Trip note: This privately-developed camp is good for people in need of a break from driving US 50. The sites are graveled, with trees by each one. The resort offers river rafting trips right out of camp. Other options include mountain climbing, hiking, bike paths and a riding stable. It's set near the Arkansas River.

---

52) POSO

Reference: on the South Fork of Carnero Creek, Rio Grande National Forest; map C6, grid d3.

Campsites, facilities: There are 11 sites for tents, trailers or motor homes up to 16 feet long. Picnic tables are provided. Piped water, vault toilets and firewood are also available. Pets are permitted on leashes.

Reservations, fee: No reservations necessary; no fee. Open late May to late September.

Who to contact: Phone Rio Grande National Forest at (719) 655-2547 or write to Sagauche Ranger District, P.O. Box 67, Sagauche, CO 81149.

Location: From La Garita, drive 10 miles northwest on County Road 690 and 1.5 miles west on Forest Service Road 675 to the campground.

Trip note: This is a nearby option to Storm King Camp. This secluded little spot is set along the South Fork of Carnero Creek. A Forest Service map is advisable for campers heading into the area. It will show the four-wheel-drive roads that lead away from camp as well as show access to some trails about four miles south of camp.

---

53) STORM KING

Reference: on the Middle Fork of Carnero Creek, Rio Grande National Forest; map C6, grid d4.

Campsites, facilities: There are 11 sites for trailers or motor homes up to 16 feet long. Picnic tables are provided. Piped water, vault toilets and firewood are also available. Pets are permitted on leashes.

Reservations, fee: No reservations necessary; no fee. Open late May to late September.

Who to contact: Phone Rio Grande National Forest at (719) 655-2547 or write to Sagauche Ranger District, P.O. Box 67, Sagauche, CO 81149.

Location: From La Garita, drive 14 miles northwest on County Road 690 to the campground.

Trip note: This remote camp is set on the Middle Fork of Carnero Creek. Its elevation is 9,200 feet and it's situated at the base of Storm King Mountain (10,849 feet). There are no trails to the top. To reach the peak, you'd have to go cross country. However, there are some roads leading away from the mountain that are accessible for four-wheel-drive vehicles. They are good for mountain bikes as well.

54) SAN LUIS VALLEY

Reference: near Villa Grove; map C6, grid d7.

Campsites, facilities: There are 10 tent sites and 10 sites for trailers or motor homes of any length. Sewer hookups and picnic tables are provided. Flush toilets, sanitary disposal station, showers, ice and firewood are also available. Bottled gas, a store, a coffee shop and a laundromat are located within one mile. Pets and motorbikes are permitted.

Reservations, fee: Reservations accepted; $6-$8 fee per night. Open mid-May to mid-November.

Who to contact: Phone (719) 655-2220 or write to P.O. Box 145, Villa Grove, CO 81155.

Location: From Villa Grove, drive two miles south on US 285.

Trip note: This privately-developed camp provides a good layover spot for cruisers looking for a break from US 285. The sites are pretty, with trees and grass surrounded by mountains. A point of interest is the ghost town of Bonanza, just a short distance away. Some hiking trails and bike paths are nearby.

55) LAKE CREEK

Reference: near Rainbow Trail, San Isabel National Forest; map C6, grid d9.

Campsites, facilities: There are 11 sites for tents, trailers or motor homes up to 16 feet long. Picnic tables are provided. Hand-pumped water and pit toilets are also available. A store and a coffee shop are located within five miles. Pets are permitted on leashes.

Reservations, fee: No reservations necessary; $6-$8 fee per night. Open mid-May to late October.

Who to contact: Phone San Isabel National Forest at (719) 275-4119 or write to San Carlos Ranger District, 326 Dozier Street, Canon City, CO 81212.

Location: From Canon City, drive 26 miles west on US 50 to the town of Texas Creek and then drive south for 11 miles on Highway 69 to Hillside. Continue for three miles west on Forest Service Road 300 to the campground.

Trip note: This hidden camp is set on Lake Creek close to the trailhead for the Rainbow Trail. A four-wheel-drive road is also nearby. This is the only campground around for miles, and with easy access and close proximity to hiking trails, you won't be the only one looking for a spot. Get there early.

56) ALVARADO

Reference: near Sangre de Cristo Range, San Isabel National Forest; map C6, grid d9.

Campsites, facilities: There are 47 sites for tents, trailers or motor homes up to 16 feet long. Picnic tables are provided. Piped water and pit toilets are also available. A coffee shop is located within one mile. Pets are permitted on leashes.

Reservations, fee: No reservations necessary; $6-$8 fee per night. Open late May to late October.

Who to contact: Phone San Isabel National Forest at (719) 275-4119 or write to San Carlos Ranger District, 326 Dozier Street, Canon City, CO 81212.

Location: From Westcliffe, drive 3.5 miles south on Highway 69. Turn right and drive 5.2 miles west on County Road 302, then 1.3 miles southwest on Forest Service Road 302 to the campground.

Trip note: This camp isn't far from town, yet is in a remote setting just the same. It is an ideal base camp for hikers and anglers. The Rainbow Trail runs out from camp and along the base of Sangre de Cristo Range. Many other trails bisect the Rainbow Trail and lead along streams to many mountain lakes. Horn Peak at 13,499 feet towers above it all. There are no other campgrounds within many, many miles.

57) SLUMGULLION

Reference: near Mill Creek, Gunnison National Forest; map C6, grid e0.

Campsites, facilities: There are 21 sites for tents, trailers or motor homes up to 22 feet long. Picnic tables are provided. Piped water and pit toilets are also available. Pets are permitted on leashes.

Reservations, fee: No reservations necessary; $6 fee per night. Open mid-June to late October.

Who to contact: Phone Gunnison National Forest at (303) 641-0471 or write to Cebolla Ranger District, 216 North Colorado, Gunnison, CO 81230.

Location: From Lake City, drive nine miles southeast on Highway 149 and 200 yards northeast on Forest Service Road 788.

Trip note: This little camp is in the Rocky Mountain high country (11,361 feet) and located near Slumgullion Pass. Nearby Mill Creek provides a sidetrip option. A scenic point of interest is the nearby Windy Point Overlook, just west of camp. There are several trails in the vicinity; see a Forest Service map for trailhead locations. Where this camp got its title is anyone's guess; rest assured it's prettier than its name.

58) SPRUCE

Reference: on Cebolla Creek, Gunnison National Forest; map C6, grid e1.

Campsites, facilities: There are nine sites for tents, trailers or motor homes up to 22 feet long. Picnic tables are provided. Piped water and pit toilets are also available. Pets are permitted on leashes.

Reservations, fee: No reservations necessary; $6 fee per night. Open mid-June to late October.

Who to contact: Phone Gunnison National Forest at (303) 641-0471 or write to Cebolla Ranger District, 216 North Colorado, Gunnison, CO 81230.

Location: From Lake City, drive nine miles southeast on Highway 149 and eight miles northeast on Forest Service Road 788.

Trip note: This is one of four very secluded camps in the area. It is set along Cebolla Creek on the border of La Garita Wilderness. Thus, it is an ideal base camp for a multi-day backpack trip. Nearby trails follow the creek into the wilderness. To the north is the Powderhorn Primitive Area.

59) CEBOLLA

Reference: on Cebolla Creek, Gunnison National Forest; map C6, grid e1.

Campsites, facilities: There are five sites for tents, trailers or motor homes up to 16 feet long. Picnic tables are provided. Piped water and pit toilets are also available. Pets are permitted on leashes.

Reservations, fee: No reservations necessary; $6 fee per night. Open mid-June to late October.

Who to contact: Phone Gunnison National Forest at (303) 641-0471 or write to Cebolla Ranger District, 216 North Colorado, Gunnison, CO 81230.

Location: From Lake City, drive nine miles southeast on Highway 149 and 8.8 miles northeast on Forest Service Road 788.

Trip note: This camp provides a nearby alternative to Spruce Camp. The difference is that this camp is much smaller, lesser used, and known by very few people. Except you. There is fishing in Cebolla Creek.

60) LUDERS CREEK

Reference: near Cochetopa Pass, Rio Grande National Forest; map C6, grid e4.

Campsites, facilities: There are six sites for tents, trailers or motor homes up to 16 feet long. Picnic tables are provided. Piped water, vault toilets and firewood are also available. Pets are permitted on leashes.

Reservations, fee: No reservations necessary; no fee. Open late May to late September.

Who to contact: Phone Rio Grande National Forest at (719) 655-2547 or write to Sagauche Ranger District, P.O. Box 67, Sagauche, CO 81149.

Location: From Sagauche, drive 22 miles northwest on Highway 114 and 11 miles northwest on Forest Service Road 750 to the campground.

Trip note: This is a tiny, primitive, little-known area set just below Cochetopa Pass at 10,032 feet and located near the Continental Divide. The camp is set along Luders Creek. No maintained hiking trails are in the area, but some obscure animal routes can be traced—for the rough and rowdy. This camp is located just west of the Gunnison National Forest border.

---

61) BUFFALO PASS

Reference: near the Continental Divide, Rio Grande National Forest; map C6, grid e5.

Campsites, facilities: There are 30 sites for tents, trailers or motor homes up to 22 feet long. Picnic tables are provided. Piped water, vault toilets and firewood are also available. Pets are permitted on leashes.

Reservations, fee: No reservations necessary; no fee. Open late May to late September.

Who to contact: Phone Rio Grande National Forest at (719) 655-2547 or write to Sagauche Ranger District, P.O. Box 67, Sagauche, CO 81149.

Location: From Sagauche, drive 27.6 miles northwest on Highway 114 and 1.7 miles west on Forest Service Road 775 to the campground.

Trip note: This remote spot set just below the Continental Divide and situated four miles from North Pass at 10,149 feet. There are some Forest Service roads in the area that are good for mountain biking. Some trails are routed to the north; see a National Forest map for details.

---

62) NORTH CRESTONE CREEK

Reference: in Rio Grande National Forest; map C6, grid e9.

Campsites, facilities: There are 14 sites for tents, trailers or motor homes up to 16 feet long. Picnic tables are provided. Piped water, vault toilets and firewood are also available. Showers, a store, coffee shop, laundromat and ice are located within one mile. Pets are permitted on leashes.

Reservations, fee: No reservations necessary; $7 fee per night. Open late May to late September.

Who to contact: Phone Rio Grande National Forest at (719) 655-2547 or write to Sagauche Ranger District, P.O. Box 67, Sagauche, CO 81149.

Location: From Crestone, drive 1.2 miles north on Forest Service Road 950 to the campground.

Trip note: This Forest Service camp gets moderate use and provides access to some nearby backcountry hiking trails. It has nice, shaded sites and gets relatively little use.

---

63) BROADACRES TRAVELIN' TEEPEE

Reference: near San Juan Mountains; map C6, grid f1.

Campsites, facilities: There are 20 tent sites and 20 sites for trailers or motor homes up to 38 feet long. Electricity, piped water, sewer hookups and picnic tables are provided. Flush toilets, sanitary disposal services, showers and a playground are also available. Pets are permitted on leashes.

Reservations, fee: Reservations accepted; $12-$15 fee per night. Open June through September.

Who to contact: Phone (719) 658-2291 or write to P.O. Box 39, Creede, CO 81130.

Location: From Creede, drive four miles southwest on Highway 149 to Broadacres Ranch and the campground.

Trip note: This is a 20-acre, privately developed park set up for both motor homes and tenters. The folks here are friendly, and the camp offers a mountain atmosphere, with wooded and grassy sites. Be sure to make time to explore Creede's unique underground railroad and museum. The closest campground is quite a ways to the southeast near the town of South Fork. This one is set near the San Juan Mountains.

---

64) UTE BLUFF

Reference: near Rio Grande River; map C6, grid f3.

Campsites, facilities: There are 45 sites for trailers or motor homes of any length. Electricity, piped water, sewer hookups and picnic tables are provided. Flush toilets, sanitary disposal station, showers, firewood, coffee shop, laundromat, three hot tubs, a game room, ice and a playground are also available. Bottled gas and a store are located within one mile. Pets and motorbikes are permitted.

Reservations, fee: Reservations accepted; $12-$14 fee per night; MasterCard and Visa accepted. Open all year.

Who to contact: Phone (719) 873-5595 or write to P.O. Box 119, South Fork, CO 81154.

Location: From South Fork, drive 1.5 miles east on US 160 to the campground.

Trip note: This is large motor home park that covers 20 acres near South Fork, which is set on the Rio Grande River. The back side of the camp is against a bluff, with grassy sites and some trees. Nearby attractions include Wolf Creek Pass, where mountain bikers can catch a ride up and plummet down, and the nearby town of Creede, which boasts a unique underground fire station and museum. A fun sidetrip is to take a horse-and-buggy ride up to a lake located at the top of a nearby mountain, where guest are treated to scenic views and a barbecue dinner.

Snowmobiling is popular in the winter. Other recreation options include hiking trails, bike paths and a riding stable.

---

65) CHINOOK

Reference: near Rio Grande River; map C6, grid f3.

Campsites, facilities: There are five tent sites and eight sites for trailers or motor homes up to 28 feet long. Electricity, piped water, sewer hookups and picnic tables are provided. Flush toilets, bottled gas, showers, a store, coffee shop and ice are also available. A laundromat is located within one mile. Pets and motorbikes are permitted.

Reservations, fee: Reservations preferred; $10 fee per night; American Express, MasterCard and Visa accepted. Open May to October.

Who to contact: Phone (719) 873-9993 or write to P.O. Box 530, South Fork, CO 81154.

Location: This campground is at the east end of South Fork on US 160.

Trip note: One of three small camps in the South Fork area. South Fork is a small town set on the Rio Grande River. See trip note for Ute Bluff Camp for sidetrip details.

---

66) CATHEDRAL

Reference: near Cathedral Creek, Rio Grande National Forest; map C6, grid f4.

Campsites, facilities: There are 33 sites for tents, trailers or motor homes up to 22 feet long. Picnic tables are provided. Piped water, vault toilets and firewood are also available. Pets are permitted on leashes.

Reservations, fee: No reservations necessary; no fee. Open mid-June to mid-September.

Who to contact: Phone Rio Grande National Forest at (719) 657-3321 or write to Del Norte Ranger District, P.O. Box 40, Del Norte, CO 81132.

Location: From Del Norte, drive 8.8 miles west on US 160. Turn right and continue 1.5 miles north on County Road 18, then 3.1 miles north on Forest Service Road 650. Turn left and drive seven miles northwest on Forest Service Road 640 (a dirt road).

Trip note: This one is way out there in "booger country." Don't go without a Forest Service map which details access roads and a number of good sidetrips. Among the best of the sidetrips are fishing along Cathedral and Embargo Creeks and hiking out to the La Garita Mountain backcountry. You can try your hand at fishing in Cathedral Creek, but to be honest, it's better known for its beauty than catch rates.

---

67) SPRUCE LODGE

Reference: near Rio Grande River; map C6, grid f4.

Campsites, facilities: There are 13 sites for trailers or motor homes up to 28 feet long. Electricity, piped water, sewer hookups and picnic tables are provided. Flush toilets, sanitary disposal station, showers, a store, coffee shop, ice and a playground are also available. Bottled gas can be found within one mile. Pets and motorbikes are permitted.

Reservations, fee: Reservations accepted; $12 fee per night; American Express, MasterCard and Visa accepted. Open all year.

Who to contact: Phone (719) 873-9980 or write to P.O. Box 181, South Fork, CO 81154.

Location: From South Fork, drive one mile east on US 160 to the camp.

Trip note: This is one of three camps in the South Fork area, this being the smallest of the lot, just two acres. South Fork is a small town set along the Rio Grande River. This privately developed park covers 24 acres and has the best accommodations in the area for tent campers. A riding stable in the area provides a recreational option. See trip note for Ute Bluff Camp for other possibilities.

---

68) GREAT SAND DUNES OASIS

Reference: near Sand Dunes National Monument; map C6, grid f9.

Campsites, facilities: There are 162 tent sites and 20 sites for trailers or motor homes of any length. Picnic tables are provided. Flush toilets, bottled gas, sanitary disposal station, showers, firewood, recreation hall, store, restaurant, coffee shop, laundromat, ice, LP gas, trout pond, playground and a swimming pool are also available. Pets and motorbikes are permitted.

Reservations, fee: Reservations accepted; $9-$13.50 fee per night; MasterCard and Visa accepted. Open March to mid-November.

Who to contact: Phone (719) 378-2222 or write to 5400 Highway 150 North, Alamosa, CO 81146.

Location: From Alamosa, drive east on US 160 to Highway 150. Turn north and drive 16 miles on Highway 150 to the campground.

Trip note: This camp is set at the entrance to Great Sand Dunes National Monument. Though it offers all amenities, it is a primitive-looking camp, left purposefully that way to retain its natural atmosphere. Four-wheel-drive tours are available. If you really want to experience what it is like to live in the desert, rent one of the teepees at the park.

---

69) PINYON FLATS

Reference: at Sand Dunes National Monument; map C6, grid f9.

Campsites, facilities: There are 88 sites for tents, trailers or motor homes of any length. Picnic tables are provided. Piped water, flush toilets, and sanitary disposal station are also available. Firewood costs extra. Bottled gas is located within 2.5 miles. Some facilities are **wheelchair accessible.** Pets are permitted on leashes.

Reservations, fee: No reservations necessary; $8 fee per night. Open April to late October.

Who to contact: Phone Great Sand Dunes National Monument at (719) 378-2312 or write to Mosca, CO 81146.

Location: From Alamosa, drive 15 miles east on US 160 and 16 miles north on Country Road 150 to the park.

Trip note: This is one of two campgrounds at the Great Sand Dunes National Monument. It's a 50-square-mile sandscape that provides a strange foreground to the Rockies to the west. If you want to get lost, try walking across it. Great Sand Dunes Oasis offers a more developed (and more crowded) alternative.

---

70) WEST FORK

Reference: on the West Fork of San Juan River, San Juan National Forest; map C6, grid g2.

Campsites, facilities: There are 28 sites for tents, trailers or motor homes up to 35 feet long. Picnic tables are provided. Pit toilets, piped water and firewood are also available. Pets are permitted on leashes.

Reservations, fee: No reservations necessary; $6 fee per night. Open mid-May to mid-November.

Who to contact: Phone San Juan National Forest at (303) 264-2268 or write to Pagosa Ranger District, P.O. Box 310, Pagosa Springs, CO 81147.

Location: From the town of Pagosa Springs, drive 13.7 miles northeast on US 160, and then 1.6 miles north on Forest Service Road 684.

Trip note: Named after the West Fork of the San Juan River, this is a prime camp for fishing. Access from US 160 is a piece of cake, and there are sidetrip options if you want to stay a while. A trail follows the creek for many miles north across the divide, past hot springs and other wonders. It is advisable to obtain a Forest Service map of the area.

---

71) BIG MEADOWS

Reference: on Big Meadows Reservoir, Rio Grande National Forest; map C6, grid g2.

Campsites, facilities: There are 42 sites for tents, trailers or motor homes up to 30 feet long. Picnic tables are provided. Piped water, vault toilets and firewood are also available. A store and ice are located within five miles. Pets are permitted on leashes. Boat docks and launching facilities are nearby.

Reservations, fee: Reserve through MISTIX at (800) 283-CAMP ($6 MISTIX fee); $8 fee per night. Open mid-June to late September.

Who to contact: Phone Rio Grande National Forest at (719) 657-3321 or write to Del Norte Ranger District, P.O. Box 40, Del Norte, CO 81132.

Location: From the town of South Fork, drive 12.5 miles southwest on US 160, and then 1.8 miles southwest on Forest Service Road 410 to the campground.

Trip note: This is a premium spot located beside Big Meadows Reservoir. Take your pick: good boating and fishing at the lake, or prime backpacking trails into the Weminuche Wilderness and the Continental Divide country. This is one of the more popular National Forest camps, so reserve your spot early, and expect crowds when you get there.

---

72) HIGHWAY SPRINGS

Reference: on the South Fork of Rio Grande River, Rio Grande National Forest; map C6, grid g3.

Campsites, facilities: There are 11 sites for tents, trailers or motor homes up to 16 feet long. Picnic tables are provided. Vault toilets, piped water and firewood are also available. Showers, a store, a coffee shop, laundromat and ice are located within five miles. Pets are permitted on leashes.

Reservations, fee: No reservations necessary; no fee. Open early June to mid-September.

Who to contact: Phone Rio Grande National Forest at (719) 657-3321 or write to Del Norte Ranger District, P.O. Box 40, Del Norte, CO 81132.

Location: From the town of South Fork, drive west on US 160 for 5.2 miles to the campground.

Trip note: A nearby alternative to Beaver Creek, this campsite is set on the South Fork of the Rio Grande. With such easy access from US 160, it is a prime spot for tent campers looking for a freebie. Beware, though; others are likely to think the same thing, and you might end up wrestling for a site.

---

73) UPPER BEAVER CREEK

Reference: near Beaver Creek Reservoir, Rio Grande National Forest; map C6, grid g3.

Campsites, facilities: There are 15 sites for tents, trailers or motor homes up to 22 feet long. Picnic tables are provided. Vault toilets, piped water and firewood are also available. Sanitary disposal services, showers, a store, a coffee shop, laundromat and ice are located within five miles. Pets are permitted on leashes. Boat docks and launching facilities are nearby at Beaver Reservoir.

Reservations, fee: No reservations necessary; $8 fee per night. Open mid-June to mid-September.

Who to contact: Phone Rio Grande National Forest at (719) 657-3321 or write to Del Norte Ranger District, P.O. Box 40, Del Norte, CO 81132.

Location: From the town of South Fork, drive 2.4 miles southwest on US 160 and south on Forest Service Road 36 four miles to the campground.

Trip note: This is a good base camp for fishermen and boaters who want to hit Beaver Creek Reservoir (one mile away) by day and camp here at night. There are several other campgrounds in the area, including Highway Springs, Cross Creek and Beaver Creek, that offer alternatives.

---

74) TUCKER PONDS

Reference: near Pass Creek, Rio Grande National Forest; map C6, grid g3.

Campsites, facilities: There are 16 sites for tents, trailers or motor homes up to 22 feet long. Picnic tables are provided. Piped water, vault toilets and firewood are available. A store and ice are located within five miles. Pets are permitted on leashes.

Reservations, fee: No reservations necessary; $8 fee per night. Open late June to mid-September.

Who to contact: Phone Rio Grande National Forest at (719) 657-3321 or write to Del Norte Ranger District, P.O. Box 40, Del Norte, CO 81132.

Location: From the town of South Fork, drive 14.4 miles southwest on US 160 and 2.6 miles south on Forest Service Road 390 to the campground.

Trip note: If you want a primitive setting without driving far from the highway, you found it here. It's set on Pass Creek near two little ponds. Fishing is available at these ponds. The elevation is 9,700 feet.

---

75) PARK CREEK

Reference: on the South Fork of Rio Grande River, Rio Grande National Forest; map C6, grid g3.

Campsites, facilities: There are 16 sites for tents, trailers or motor homes up to 22 feet long. Picnic tables are provided. Vault toilets, piped water and firewood are also available. Showers, a store, a coffee shop and ice are located within five miles. Pets are permitted on leashes. Boat docks, launching facilities and rentals are available nearby.

Reservations, fee: No reservations necessary; $8 fee per night. Open mid-June to mid-September.

Who to contact: Phone Rio Grande National Forest at (719) 657-3321 or write to Del Norte Ranger District, P.O. Box 40, Del Norte, CO 81132.

Location: From the town of South Fork, drive west on US 160 for 8.9 miles to the campground.

Trip note: This is nice option for tent campers in the area. It is set where Park Creek empties into the South Fork of the Rio Grande, and there's easy access from US 160. This is a very popular spot for fishing, with many anglers utilizing the area for day-use.

76) CROSS CREEK

Reference: on Beaver Creek Reservoir, Rio Grande National Forest; map C6, grid g3.

Campsites, facilities: There are 12 sites for tents, trailers or motor homes up to 16 feet long. Picnic tables are provided. Piped water, vault toilets and firewood are available. A store, a coffee shop, laundromat and ice are located within five miles. Pets are permitted on leashes. Boat docks and launching facilities are nearby.

Reservations, fee: No reservations necessary; $8 fee per night. Open mid-June to mid-September.

Who to contact: Phone Rio Grande National Forest at (719) 657-3321 or write to Del Norte Ranger District, P.O. Box 40, Del Norte, CO 81132.

Location: From the town of South Fork, drive 2.4 miles southwest on US 160 and south on Forest Service Road 360 for 6.1 miles to the campground.

Trip note: This camp is set on the far side of Beaver Creek Reservoir. You have multiple possibilities here, including boating and fishing at the lake or hiking up the trail from camp that traces Cross Creek. It's pretty, shaded and relatively uncrowded compared to other nearby camps.

77) RIVERBEND RV PARK

Reference: near South Fork; map C6, grid g3.

Campsites, facilities: There are 60 full hookup sites for trailers or motor homes of any length. Electricity, piped water, sewer hookups and picnic tables are provided. Firewood, recreation hall and a playground are also available. Pets and motorbikes are permitted.

Reservations, fee: Reservations accepted; $14 fee per night. Open all year.

Who to contact: Phone (719) 873-5344 or write to P.O. Box 129, South Fork, CO 81154.

Location: From the town of South Fork, drive three miles west on US 160 to the campground.

Trip note: This campsite covers 60 acres but is only set up for motor homes and trailers. The sites are graveled and open. Beaver Creek Camp provides a nearby but more remote setting. Recreation includes hiking trails and a riding stable. See trip note for Ute Bluff Camp for details about the South Fork area.

78) BEAVER CREEK

Reference: near Beaver Creek Reservoir, Rio Grande National Forest; map C6, grid g3.

Campsites, facilities: There are 19 sites for tents, trailers or motor homes up to 22 feet long. Picnic tables are provided. Vault toilets, firewood and piped water are also available. Showers, sanitary disposal station, a store, a coffee shop, laundromat and ice are located within five miles. Pets are permitted on leashes. Boat docks and launching facilities are nearby at Beaver Creek Reservoir.

Reservations, fee: No reservations necessary; $8 fee per night. Open mid-June to mid-September.

Who to contact: Phone Rio Grande National Forest at (719) 657-3321 or write to Del Norte Ranger District, P.O. Box 40, Del Norte, CO 81132.

Location: From the town of South Fork, drive 2.4 miles southwest on US 160 and south on Forest Service Road 360 for three miles to the campground.

Trip note: This camp is just far enough (three miles) off the highway to get missed by a lot of out-of-town cruisers. It's a pretty spot along Beaver Creek near the confluence of the South Fork of the Rio Grande. It's a good spot for hikers and offers an assortment of trails that lead up other creeks. Boaters should consider Beaver Creek Reservoir, which has camps available.

---

79) STUNNER

Reference: on Alamosa River, Rio Grande National Forest; map C6, grid g3.

Campsites, facilities: There are 10 sites for tents, trailers or motor homes up to 16 feet long. Picnic tables are provided. Hand-pumped water and vault toilets are also available. Pets are permitted on leashes.

Reservations, fee: No reservations necessary; no fee. Open late May to mid-September.

Who to contact: Phone Rio Grande National Forest at (719) 274-5193 or write to Conejos Peak Ranger District, 21461 South Highway 285, La Jara, CO 81140.

Location: From Monte Vista, drive 12 miles south on Highway 15. Turn right and drive 33 miles west on Forest Service Road 250, then a quarter mile southwest on Forest Service Road 380 to the campground.

Trip note: This is a rustic site at 10,541 feet located on the Alamosa River about three miles northwest of Stunner Pass. Some small lakes are in the area and can be located on a Forest Service map. A trail that runs along Iron Creek to the northwest is located about two miles west of camp.

---

80) ROCK CREEK

Reference: on the South Fork of Rock Creek, Rio Grande National Forest; map C6, grid g5.

Campsites, facilities: There are 13 sites for tents, trailers or motor homes up to 16 feet long. Picnic tables are provided. Vault toilets, piped water and firewood are also available. Pets are permitted on leashes.

Reservations, fee: No reservations necessary; no fee. Open late May to late September.

Who to contact: Phone Rio Grande National Forest at (719) 657-3321 or write to Del Norte Ranger District, P.O. Box 40, Del Norte, CO 81132.

Location: From Monte Vista, drive two miles south on Highway 15, then 13.5 miles southwest on Forest Service Road 265 to the campground.

Trip note: This little-known spot set aside the South Fork of Rock Creek is a good one for hikers. It has a trail leading from camp that is routed into the adjacent wildlands along the North Fork of Rock Creek and eventually leads to the San Francisco Lakes and comes near Bennett Peak (13,190-foot elevation). The trail connects to a network of backcountry routes.

---

81) MOBILE MANOR

Reference: near Monte Vista; map C6, grid g6.

Campsites, facilities: There are 36 sites for trailers or motor homes of any length. Electricity, piped water and picnic tables are provided. Coffee shop, ice and a playground are also available. Sewer hookups are available at an additional charge. Pets are permitted on leashes.

Reservations, fee: Reservations accepted; $8-$12 fee per night; American Express, MasterCard and Visa accepted. Open late May to late September.

Who to contact: Phone (719) 852-5921 or write to 2830 West US 160, Monte Vista, CO 81144.

Location: From Monte Vista, drive two miles west on US 160.

Trip note: This motor home park covers a huge area—some 640 acres—and provides the only layover spot for motor home campers in the vicinity. The sites are open and graveled, adjacent to a motel. Not the ideal spot for wilderness-loving campers, but when you realize the nearest options are in Del Norte, 14 miles to the west, and Alamosa, 17 miles to the east, it might not look so bad.

---

82) SIERRA VISTA KOA

Reference: near Alamosa; map C6, grid g8.

Campsites, facilities: There are 30 tent sites and 52 sites for trailers or motor homes of any length. Picnic tables are provided. Flush toilets, ice, showers, a sanitary disposal station, recreation hall, store, laundromat and a playground are also available. Pets and motorbikes are permitted.

Reservations, fee: Reservations accepted; $12.50-$16.75 fee per night; MasterCard and Visa accepted. Open April through October.

Who to contact: Phone (719) 589-9757 or write to 6900 Juniper Lane, Alamosa, CO 81101.

Location: From the junction of Highway 17 and US 160 in Alamosa, drive three miles east on US 160 to the campground.

Trip note: This is the only game in town and you'd best be thankful the folks here take care of both tent campers and those with motor homes. The camp is set near Alamosa on the Rio Grande with the closest options 15 to 20 miles away. This is desert country, with sparse vegetation but spectacular mountain views. The sunsets here are unforgettable.

---

83) SAN JUAN NATIONAL FOREST HOTEL

Reference: in Pagosa; map C6, grid h1.

Campsites, facilities: There are 23 sites for trailers or motor homes of any length. Electricity, piped water and sewer hookups are provided. Flush toilets, showers, laundromat, ice and a playground are also available. Bottled gas, sanitary disposal services, a store and a coffee shop are located within one mile. Pets and motorbikes are permitted.

Reservations, fee: Reservations accepted; $15-$17 fee per night; American Express, MasterCard and Visa accepted. Open mid-May to November.

Who to contact: Phone (303) 264-2262 or write to P.O. Box 729, Pagosa Springs, CO 81147.

Location: This campground is located on the east side of the town of Pagosa Springs at 191 Pagosa Street.

Trip note: What a name, right? What they're saying is you get a mountain feeling in a privately-developed setting. The sites are open, surrounded by forest and mountains. Hotel rooms are available adjacent to the campground. Nearby recreation options include a golf course and tennis courts.

---

84) WOLF CREEK

Reference: on the West Fork of San Juan River, San Juan National Forest; map C6, grid h2.

Campsites, facilities: There are 26 sites for tents, trailers or motor homes up to 35 feet long. Picnic tables are provided. Pit toilets, firewood and piped water are also available. Pets are permitted on leashes.

Reservations, fee: No reservations necessary; $7 fee per night. Open mid-May to mid-November.

Who to contact: Phone San Juan National Forest at (303) 264-2268 or write to Pagosa Ranger District, P.O. Box 310, Pagosa Springs, CO 81147.

Location: From the town of Pagosa Springs, drive 13.7 miles northeast on US 160 and a half mile north on Forest Service Road 684.

Trip note: This site is set at an 8,000-foot elevation along Wolf Creek at the head water of the West Fork of the San Juan River. It is a good spot for hikers with the trailhead for Windy Pass and Treasure Mountain Trail at the camp.

85) EAST FORK

Reference: on the East Fork of San Juan River, San Juan National Forest; map C6, grid h2.

Campsites, facilities: There are 26 sites for tents, trailers or motor homes up to 35 feet long. Picnic tables are provided. Piped water, pit toilets and firewood are also available. Pets are permitted on leashes.

Reservations, fee: Reservations accepted; $7 fee per night. Open mid-May to mid-November.

Who to contact: Phone San Juan National Forest at (303) 264-2268 or write to Pagosa Ranger District, P.O. Box 310, Pagosa Springs, CO 81147.

Location: From the town of Pagosa Springs, drive 9.7 miles northeast on US 160 and 0.8 mile east on Forest Service Road 667 to the campground.

Trip note: This is a prime campground only a minute drive off US 160. It's a pretty spot along the East Fork of the San Juan River near its confluence with the West Fork. The camp is at the base of Turner Peak (9,248 feet), which overlooks the area. The elevation is 8,400 feet.

86) MIX LAKE

Reference: near Platoro Reservoir, Rio Grande National Forest; map C6, grid h4.

Campsites, facilities: There are 22 sites for tents, trailers or motor homes up to 22 feet long. Picnic tables are provided. Piped water and vault toilets are also available. Showers, a store, coffee shop, laundromat and ice are located within one mile. Pets are permitted on leashes. Boat docks, launching facilities and rentals are nearby.

Reservations, fee: No reservations necessary; $7 fee per night. Open late May to mid-September.

Who to contact: Phone Rio Grande National Forest at (719) 274-5193 or write to Conejos Peak Ranger District, 21461 South Highway 285, La Jara, CO 81140.

Location: From Antonito, drive 23 miles west on Highway 17. Turn right and drive 21.6 miles northwest on Forest Service Road 250, then three-quarters of a mile west on Forest Service Road 2506B to the campground.

Trip note: This is an idyllic little camp at 10,100 feet, situated beside little Mix Lake and adjacent to the larger Platoro Reservoir. It has a good fishing prospects, and for hikers, a trail crosses the road just north of camp.

87) LAKE FORK

Reference: on Conejos River, Rio Grande National Forest; map C6, grid h4.

Campsites, facilities: There are 19 sites for tents, trailers or motor homes up to 22 feet long. Picnic tables are provided. Hand-pumped water, vault toilets and firewood are also available. A store, coffee shop, laundromat and ice are located within five miles. Pets are permitted on leashes.

Reservations, fee: Reserve through MISTIX at (800) 283-CAMP ($6 MISTIX fee); $7 fee per night. Open late May to mid-September.

Who to contact: Phone Rio Grande National Forest at (719) 274-5193 or write to Route 1, P.O. Box 520G, La Jara, CO 81140.

Location: From Antonito, drive 23 miles west on Highway 17 and 16 miles northwest on Forest Service Road 250 to the campground.

Trip note: This camp is an ideal jump-off point for a backpacking trip. It is located adjacent to the South San Juan Wilderness, beside the Conejos River and below the largest mountain in the area, Conejos Peak (13,172 feet). Nearby trails provide routes to many lakes. Getting to the peak of Forest King Mountain, elevation 11,365 feet, is a worthy sidetrip for conditioned hikers.

---

88) COMSTOCK

Reference: near the North Fork of Rock Creek, Rio Grande National Forest; map C6, grid h5.

Campsites, facilities: There are eight sites for tents, trailers or motor homes up to 16 feet long. Picnic tables are provided. Piped water, vault toilets and firewood are also available. Pets are permitted on leashes.

Reservations, fee: No reservations necessary; no fee. Open late May late September.

Who to contact: Phone Rio Grande National Forest at (719) 657-3321 or write to Del Norte Ranger District, P.O. Box 40, Del Norte, CO 81132.

Location: From Monte Vista, drive two miles south on Highway 15 and 16.5 miles southwest on Forest Service Road 265 to the campground.

Trip note: This camp is an option to Rock Creek Camp (see trip note for recreation details), set just two miles from that camp.

---

89) ALAMOSA

Reference: on Alamosa River, Rio Grande National Forest; map C6, grid h5.

Campsites, facilities: There are 10 sites for tents, trailers or motor homes up to 16 feet long. Picnic tables are provided. Hand-pumped water and vault toilets are available. Pets are permitted on leashes.

Reservations, fee: No reservations necessary; no fee. Open late May to mid-November.

Who to contact: Phone Rio Grande National Forest at (719) 274-5193 or write to Conejos Peak Ranger District, 21461 South Highway 285, La Jara, CO 81140.

Location: From Monte Vista, drive 12 miles south on Highway 15 and 17.4 miles west on Forest Service Road 250.

Trip note: This is a good backcountry camp set along the Alamosa River. Several good hiking trails are in the area; see a Forest Service map for specifics.

---

90) LA JARA RESERVOIR WILDLIFE MANAGEMENT AREA

Reference: southwest of Monte Vista; map C6, grid h5.

Campsites, facilities: There are 50 primitive tent sites. Pit toilets are also available. There is **no piped water.** Pets are permitted on leashes. A boat ramp is available.

Reservations, fee: No reservations necessary; no fee. Open May to November.

Who to contact: Phone (303) 247-0855 or write to Colorado Division of Wildlife, 6060 Broadway, Denver, CO 80216.

Location: From Monte Vista, drive 20 miles south on Highway 15, west for a half mile on Forest Service Road 250, and 11 miles southwest on Ra Jadero Canyon Road to the reservoir.

Trip note: This is a popular spot for local anglers and hunters, particularly because of the waterfowl during the fall hunting season. The park covers more than 2,500 acres and gets little traffic from out-of-towners.

---

91) BLANCO RIVER

Reference: on Rio Blanco River, San Juan National Forest; map C6, grid i2.

Campsites, facilities: There are six sites for tents, trailers or motor homes up to 35 feet long. Picnic tables are provided. Pit toilets and firewood are also available. Well water is available. Pets are permitted on leashes. There is a group area for use also.

Reservations, fee: No reservations necessary; no fee on single sites; call ahead for group rates. Open mid-May to mid-November.

Who to contact: Phone San Juan National Forest at (303) 264-2268 or write to P.O. Box 310, Pagosa Springs, CO 81147.

Location: From the town of Pagosa Springs, drive 13.1 miles southeast on US 84 and 1.8 miles east on Forest Service Road 656 to the campground.

Trip note: This campground offers a primitive setting, yet it's not far from the highway. It is set along the Blanco River, a twisty river that has cut its own canyon. The stream is quite beautiful, and offers good fishing as well.

---

92) SPECTACLE

Reference: near Conejos River, Rio Grande National Forest; map C6, grid i4.

Campsites, facilities: There are 24 sites for tents, trailers or motor homes of any length. Picnic tables are provided. Hand-pumped water and vault toilets are also available. A store is located within five miles. Pets are permitted on leashes.

Reservations, fee: No reservations necessary; $7 fee per night. Open late May to mid-September.

Who to contact: Phone Rio Grande National Forest at (719) 274-5193 or write to Conejos Peak Ranger District, 21461 South Highway 285, La Jara, CO 81140.

Location: From Antonito, drive 23 miles west on Highway 17 and six miles northwest on Forest Service Road 250 to the campground.

Trip note: This camp provides an option to the adjacent Conejos Camp. It is located near the Conejos River on the border of the South San Juan Wilderness. There are several hiking trails to the north and south that lead into the backcountry.

---

93) TRUJILLO MEADOWS

Reference: near Trujillo Meadows Reservoir, Rio Grande National Forest; map C6, grid i4.

Campsites, facilities: There are 50 sites for tents, trailers or motor homes up to 30 feet. Picnic tables are provided. Piped water and vault toilets are also available. A boat ramp is available on Trujillo Reservoir. Pets are permitted on leashes. Two sites are **wheelchair accessible.**

Reservations, fee: No reservations necessary; $8 fee per night. Open mid-May to mid-September.

Who to contact: Phone Rio Grande National Forest at (719) 274-5193 or write to Conejos Peak Ranger District, 21461 South Highway 285, La Jara, CO 81140.

Location: From Antonito, drive 32 miles west on Highway 17, and three miles north on Forest Service Road 116 to the campground.

Trip note: This camp is set at 10,000 feet beside Trujillo Meadows Reservoir and just north of the Colorado-New Mexico border. A four-wheel-drive road at the north end of the lake leads north along Rio De Los Pinos, turning into a trail routed into the South San Juan Wilderness.

---

94) ELK CREEK

Reference: near Conejos River, Rio Grande National Forest; map C6, grid i5.

Campsites, facilities: There are 45 sites for tents, trailers or motor homes of any length. Picnic tables are provided. Hand-pumped water and vault toilets are also available. Showers are located within five miles. Pets are permitted on leashes.

Reservations, fee: Reserve through MISTIX at (800) 283-CAMP ($6 MISTIX fee); $8 fee per night. Open mid-May to mid-September.

Who to contact: Phone Rio Grande National Forest at (719) 274-5193 or write to Conejos Peak Ranger District, 21461 South Highway 285, La Jara, CO 81140.

Location: From Antonito, drive 23 miles west on Highway 17. Continue one mile southwest on Forest Service Road 128, then 200 yards northwest on Forest Service Road 128.1B to the campground.

Trip note: This is one of the more popular Forest Service campgrounds in the region and is set in the high country at the confluence of Elk Creek and the Conejos River. A trail that starts at camp is routed into the San Juan Wilderness and provides a chance to camp and fish at many backcountry lakes.

---

95) ASPEN GLADE

Reference: on Conejos River, Rio Grande National Forest; map C6, grid i5.

Campsites, facilities: There are 34 sites for tents, trailers or motor homes up to 25 feet. Picnic tables are provided. Piped water and vault toilets are also available. A store, coffee shop, laundromat and ice are located within five miles. Pets are permitted on leashes.

Reservations, fee: Reserve through MISTIX at (800) 283-CAMP ($6 MISTIX fee); $8 fee per night. Open mid-May to mid-September.

Who to contact: Phone Rio Grande National Forest at (719) 274-5193 or write to Conejos Peak Ranger District, 21461 South Highway 285, La Jara, CO 81140.

Location: From Antonito, drive 18 miles west on Highway 17 to the campground.

Trip note: This is one of three campgrounds set along the Conejos River on Highway 17 as you head west from Antonito. There are many trails that access the surrounding Rio Grande National Forest. A good one starts at the nearby River Springs Ranger Station and heads west along the Conejos River.

---

96) MOGOTE

Reference: on Conejos River, Rio Grande National Forest; map C6, grid i6.

Campsites, facilities: There are 41 sites for tents, trailers or motor homes up to 25 feet. Picnic tables, piped water and vault toilets are provided. A store, coffee shop, laundromat and ice are also available within one mile. Pets are permitted on leashes.

Reservations, fee: Reserve through MISTIX at (800) 283-CAMP ($6 MISTIX fee); $8 fee per night. Open mid-May to mid-November.

Who to contact: Phone Rio Grande National Forest at (719) 274-5193 or write to Conejos Peak Ranger District, 21461 South Highway 285, La Jara, CO 81140.

Location: From Antonito, drive 15 miles west on Highway 17 to the campground.

Trip note: This is one of three camps set along the Conejos River as you head west out of Antonito. See trip note for Aspen Glade Camp.

97) NARROW GAUGE RAILROAD

Reference: in Antonito; map C6, grid i7.

Campsites, facilities: There are 10 tent sites and 50 sites for trailers or motor homes of any length. Electricity, piped water, sewer hookups and picnic tables are provided. Flush toilets, sanitary disposal station, showers, recreation hall, a store, coffee shop and ice are also available. Bottled gas and a laundromat are located within one mile. Pets and motorbikes are permitted.

Reservations, fee: Reservations accepted; $10 fee per night; American Express, MasterCard and Visa accepted. Open March through mid-October.

Who to contact: Phone (719) 376-5441 or write to P.O. Box 636, Antonito, CO 81120.

Location: This campground is located in Antonito at the junction of Highways 275 and 17.

Trip note: The highlight here is taking a spectacular trip on the Cumbres Toltec Scenic Railroad which winds its way through the Rocky Mountain country from Antonito on the southwest to Chama in New Mexico. Other recreation options include hiking trails, bike paths, a riding stable and tennis courts. Or make a sidetrip to the nearby Conejos River to the north or the Rio Grande to the east.

98) CONEJOS

Reference: on Conejos River, Rio Grande National Forest; map C6, grid i4.

Campsites, facilities: There are 16 sites for tents, trailers or motor homes of any length. Picnic tables are provided. Hand-pumped water and vault toilets are also available. A store is located within five miles. Pets are permitted on leashes.

Reservations, fee: No reservations necessary; $7 fee per night. Open mid-May to mid-September.

Who to contact: Phone Rio Grande National Forest at (719) 274-5193 or write to Conejos Peak Ranger District, 21461 South Highway 285, La Jara, CO 81140.

Location: From Antonito, drive 23 miles west on Highway 17, then seven miles west on Forest Service Road 250 to the campground.

Trip note: This camp, along with Spectacle Camp, is set along the Conejos River, adjacent to South San Juan Wilderness. It's ideal for hikers because of the many trails to high mountain lakes. A Forest Service map will provide details.

Colorado Map C7
37 listings
Pages 262-279

North (C3)—see page 148
East (C8)—see page 280
South—New Mexico
West (C6)—see page 216

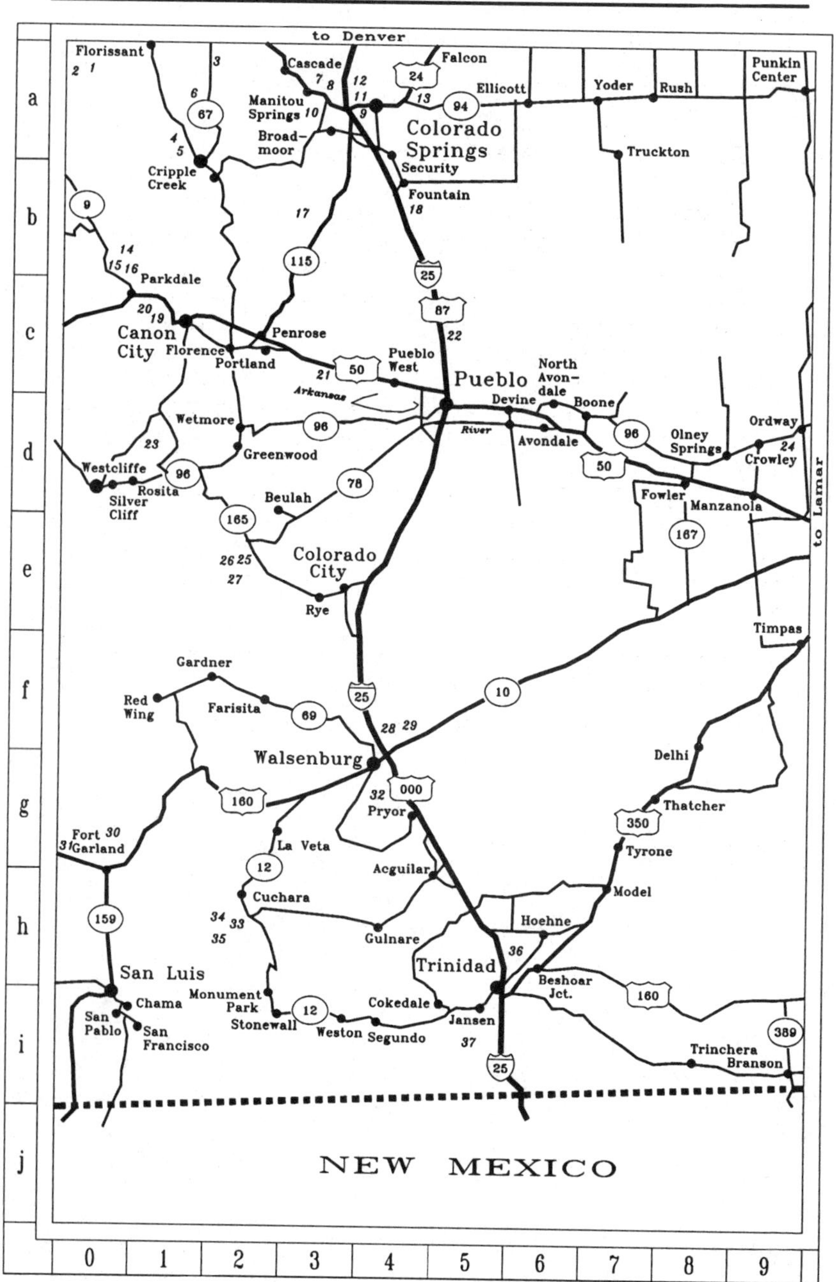

Featuring: Elevenmile Reservoir, Pike National Forest, Florissant Fossil Beds, Cripple Creek, Fountain Creek, Bear Creek, Pueblo Reservoir, San Isabel National Forest, Arkansas River, Middle Creek, Mountain Home Reservoir, Smith Reservoir, Trinchera Peak, North Fork of Purgatoire River

---

1) COVE

Reference: in Elevenmile Canyon, Pike National Forest; map C7, grid a0.

Campsites, facilities: There are five sites for tents, trailers or motor homes up to 22 feet long. Picnic tables are provided. Well water and pit toilets are also available. Pets are permitted on leashes.

Reservations, fee: No reservations necessary; $7 fee per night. Open mid-May to late September.

Who to contact: Phone Pike National Forest at (719) 836-2031 or write to South Park Ranger District, P.O. Box 219, Fairplay, CO 80440.

Location: From the town of Lake George, travel one mile southwest on County Road 61, then southwest on Forest Service Road 96 for 8.3 miles to the campground.

Trip note: This tiny, secluded spot is set near the end of Elevenmile Canyon. There are many recreation options in the surrounding area; see a Forest Service map for details. Note: there is no access to Elevenmile Reservoir from Elevenmile Canyon. You must approach from the north or the west.

---

2) SPILLWAY

Reference: in Elevenmile Canyon, Pike National Forest; map C7, grid a0.

Campsites, facilities: There are 24 sites for tents, trailers or motor homes up to 22 feet long. Picnic tables are provided. Piped water and pit toilets are also available. Pets are permitted on leashes.

Reservations, fee: No reservations necessary; $7 fee per night. Open mid-May to late September.

Who to contact: Phone Pike National Forest at (719) 836-2031 or write to South Park Ranger District, P.O. Box 219, Fairplay, CO 80440.

Location: From the town of Lake George, travel one mile southwest on County Road 61, then southwest on Forest Service Road 96 for 8.6 miles to the campground.

Trip note: Like Cove Campground, this is also set at the end of Elevenmile Canyon and provides a nearby campground option. Note: there is no access to Elevenmile Reservoir from Elevenmile Canyon. You must approach from the north or the west.

3) THE CRAGS

Reference: in Pike National Forest; map C7, grid a1.

Campsites, facilities: There are 17 sites for tents, trailers or motor homes up to 22 feet long. Picnic tables are provided. Hand-pumped water and pit toilets are also available. Pets are permitted on leashes.

Reservations, fee: No reservations necessary; no fee. Open mid-May to October.

Who to contact: Phone Pike National Forest at (719) 636-1602 or write to Pike's Peak Ranger District, 601 South Weber Street, Colorado Springs, CO 80903.

Location: From Divide, drive 4.5 miles south on Highway 67 and 3.5 miles east on Forest Service Road 1094 to the campground.

Trip note: At 10,100 feet, this is the high country. It's an ideal base camp for hikers who want to make the trip up to the crags. A trail that climbs 755 feet in 1.5 miles takes you straight up to 10,855 feet elevation. Even if you're not into hiking, it can provide a refreshing back-to-nature experience. It's remote, secluded and quiet.

4) LOST BURRO

Reference: near Florissant Fossil Beds; map C7, grid a1.

Campsites, facilities: There are 14 tent sites and 16 sites for trailers or motor homes of any length. Piped water and picnic tables are provided. Flush toilets, sanitary disposal station, showers, ice and a playground are also available. Firewood costs extra. A coffee shop is located within one mile. Pets and motorbikes are permitted.

Reservations, fee: Reservations accepted; $11-$13 fee per night. Open Memorial Day to Labor Day.

Who to contact: Phone (719) 689-2345 or write to P.O. Box 614, Cripple Creek, CO 80813.

Location: From the town of Cripple Creek, drive four miles north-west on Teller County Road 1 to the campground.

Trip note: This camp is just far enough "out there" to make a good overnighter for Colorado Springs residents. It's set on the slopes of the Rockies with hiking trails available in the adjacent National Forest. A good sidetrip is eight miles north to the Florissant Fossil Beds National Monument. In the town of Cripple Creek, you can ride the Victor Railroad or visit old gold mines. The main attraction in Cripple Creek is gambling, with several casinos to choose from.

5) CRIPPLE CREEK TRAVEL PARK

Reference: in Cripple Creek; map C7, grid a1.

Campsites, facilities: There are 28 tent sites and 50 sites for trailers or motor homes of any length. Electricity, piped water, sewer hookups and picnic tables are provided. Flush toilets, sanitary disposal station, showers, firewood, recreation hall, laundromat, ice and a playground are also available. Bottled gas, a store and coffee shop are located within one mile. Pets and motorbikes are permitted.

Reservations, fee: Reservations accepted; $15 fee per night; American Express, MasterCard and Visa accepted. Open June to mid-September.

Who to contact: Phone (719) 689-2513 or write to Cripple Creek, CO 80813.

Location: Located in Cripple Creek on Highway 67.

Trip note: This is one of four campgrounds in the Cripple Creek area. Sites are grassy and graveled, in a mountain setting. For recreation options, see trip note for Lost Burro Camp.

---

6) CRIPPLE CREEK GOLD

Reference: in Cripple Creek; map C7, grid a1.

Campsites, facilities: There are 12 tent sites and 12 sites for trailers or motor homes of any length. Piped water and picnic tables are provided. Flush toilets, sanitary disposal station, showers, firewood, a store, laundromat, ice and a playground are also available. Electricity costs extra. Pets and motorbikes are permitted.

Reservations, fee: Reservations accepted; $12-$15 fee per night. Open May to late September.

Who to contact: Phone (719) 689-2342 or write to P.O. Box 601, Cripple Creek, CO 80813.

Location: Located five miles north of Cripple Creek off of Highway 67.

Trip note: This is a private campground that covers 30 acres and is set on the slopes of the Rockies. It provides a camping option in the Cripple Creek area. For recreation possibilities, see the trip note for Lost Burro Camp.

---

7) GOLDEN EAGLE RANCH

Reference: south of Colorado Springs; map C7, grid a3.

Campsites, facilities: There are 200 tent sites and 300 sites for trailers or motor homes of any length. Picnic tables are provided. Flush toilets, sanitary disposal station, showers, a store, laundromat, ice and a playground are also available. Firewood costs extra. Pets and motorbikes are permitted.

Reservations, fee: Reservations accepted; $10-$12.50 fee per night; MasterCard and Visa accepted. Open May to late September.

Who to contact: Phone (719) 576-0450 or write to 710 Rock Creek Canyon, Colorado Springs, CO 80926.

Location: From the town of Colorado Springs, drive south on Highway 115 (Nevada Avenue) for five miles to the campground.

Trip note: This camp, along with others in the Colorado Springs area, is located at the foot of Pike's Peak. This one is set on a rustic ranch, with "natural setting" campsites. The city itself is home to almost one-quarter million people. For a city, it's a pretty good one. One highlight is the Wildlife World Museum, (303) 488-2460, which includes paintings, sculptures and taxidermist specimens of wildlife. To the west, Pike National Forest offers good camping in primitive, Rocky Mountain settings as well as hiking and fishing in high, remote areas. Nearby Cripple Creek offers gambling casinos.

---

8) PEAK VIEW

Reference: near Colorado Springs; map C7, grid a3.

Campsites, facilities: There are 25 tent sites and 100 sites for trailers or motor homes of any length. Picnic tables are provided. Flush toilets, sanitary disposal station, showers, ice, a recreation hall, store, coffee shop, laundromat, playground and a swimming pool are also available. Bottled gas is located within one mile. Pets and motorbikes are permitted.

Reservations, fee: Reservations accepted; $11.50-$18 fee per night; American Express, MasterCard and Visa accepted. Open all year.

Who to contact: Phone (719) 598-1434 or (800) 551-CAMP, or write to 4954 North Nevada Avenue, Colorado Springs, CO 80907.

Location: Take exit 146 off Interstate 25 in Colorado Springs and drive a half mile east on Garden of the Gods Road. Turn north on Nevada Avenue to the campground.

Trip note: One of many private parks in the Colorado Springs area, this one is set on the north end of the city. The park is within the city limits, heavily wooded in a semi-rural setting. Motel rooms are available adjacent to the campground. See the trip note for Golden Eagle Ranch for sidetrip options in Colorado Springs.

---

9) FOUNTAIN CREEK

Reference: in Colorado Springs; map C7, grid a3.

Campsites, facilities: There are 24 tent sites and 90 sites for trailers or motor homes up to 31 feet long. Piped water and picnic tables are provided. Flush toilets, bottled gas, sanitary disposal station, showers, recreation hall, laundromat and ice are also available. A store and coffee shop are located within one mile. Pets and motorbikes are permitted.

Reservations, fee: No reservations necessary; $10-$15 fee per night; MasterCard and Visa accepted. Open May to late October.

Who to contact: Phone (719) 633-2192 or write to 3023 1/2 West Colorado, Colorado Springs, CO 80904.

Location: Take the 31st Street exit off US 24 in Colorado Springs and drive a half block east on Colorado Avenue to the campground.

Trip note: This campground is near Old Colorado City and is one of nine camps in or near the city limits. Nearby recreation options include a golf course, a riding stable and tennis courts. See the trip note for Golden Eagle Ranch for sidetrip possibilities in area.

10) PIKE'S PEAK TRAILER PARK

Reference: near Fountain Creek; map C7, grid a3.

Campsites, facilities: There are 10 tent sites and 62 sites for trailers or motor homes of any length. Electricity, piped water, sewer hookups and picnic tables are provided. Flush toilets, sanitary disposal station, showers, recreation hall, a store, laundromat, ice, playground and a swimming pool are also available. Bottled gas and a coffee shop are located within one mile. Motorbikes are permitted.

Reservations, fee: Reservations accepted; $12-$18 fee per night; MasterCard and Visa accepted. Open May to late October.

Who to contact: Phone (719) 685-9459 or write to 320 Manitou Avenue, Manitou Springs, CO 80829.

Location: From the town of Colorado Springs, drive west on US 24 for four miles and then west on Manitou Avenue to the campground.

Trip note: This is a nice camp, a little farther from town than others in the area. It is privately developed and offers many sidetrip possibilities. One of the best is visiting Cave of the Winds, (719) 685-5444, which provides magnificent views of mountain peaks and Williams Canyon. Nearby recreation options include an 18-hole golf course, hiking trails and a riding stable.

11) GOLDFIELD

Reference: near Bear Creek; map C7, grid a3.

Campsites, facilities: There are 25 tent sites and 75 sites for trailers or motor homes of any length. Picnic tables are provided. Flush toilets, sanitary disposal station, showers, recreation hall, a store, laundromat and ice are also available. Bottled gas and a coffee shop are located within one mile. Pets and motorbikes are permitted.

Reservations, fee: Reservations accepted; $10-$13 fee per night; Open all year.

Who to contact: Phone (719) 471-0495 or write to 411 South 26th Street, Colorado Springs, CO 80904.

Location: Take exit 141 off Interstate 25 in Colorado Springs and drive west for 2.5 miles on US 24 to 26th Street. The campground is located at corner of US 24 and 26th.

Trip note: This private park is adjacent to the Bear Creek Nature Center in Colorado Springs. The park is heavily wooded. Nearby recreation options include a golf course and bike paths. A good sidetrip is Seven Falls to the west. For information about Colorado Springs, see the trip note for Golden Eagle Ranch.

12) GARDEN OF THE GODS

Reference: near Colorado Springs; map C7, grid a3.

Campsites, facilities: There are 75 tent sites and 300 sites for trailers or motor homes of any length. Piped water and picnic tables are provided. Flush toilets, bottled gas, sanitary disposal station, showers, recreation hall, a store, laundromat, ice, playground and a swimming pool are also available. A coffee shop is located within one mile. Pets are permitted on leashes.

Reservations, fee: Reservations accepted; $18-$22 fee per night; American Express, MasterCard and Visa accepted. Open April to November.

Who to contact: Phone (719) 475-9450 or write to P.O. Box RM, 3704 West Colorado, Colorado Springs, CO 80904.

Location: Take exit 141 off Interstate 25 in Colorado Springs and drive west for four miles on US 24 to Ridge Road. Travel one block north and then a quarter mile west to the campground.

Trip note: This is a massive, privately developed park that covers 22 acres adjacent to the Garden of the Gods, the ultimate tourist must-see. Guided tours are available. Nearby recreation options include a golf course, bike paths, a riding stable and tennis courts. The U.S. Air Force Academy and Seven Falls are also nearby.

---

13) WRANGLER RV RANCH

Reference: east of Colorado Springs; map C7, grid a4.

Campsites, facilities: There are 20 tent sites and 85 sites for trailers or motor homes of any length. Picnic tables are provided. Flush toilets, sanitary disposal station, showers, recreation hall, laundromat, ice and a playground are also available. A store and coffee shop are located within one mile. Pets and motorbikes are permitted.

Reservations, fee: Reservations accepted; $12.75-$16.75 fee per night; MasterCard and Visa accepted. Open all year.

Who to contact: Phone (719) 591-1402 or write to 6225 East Platte, Colorado Springs, CO 80915.

Location: East of Colorado Springs, at the junction of US 24 and Highway 94, drive east for a half mile to the campground.

Trip note: This is one of two campgrounds set just east of the city of Colorado Springs. This one covers 18 acres with nearby recreation options that include a golf course, a riding stable and tennis courts. It has sites in a desert-like setting, adjacent to a motel. See the trip note for Golden Eagle Ranch for information about Colorado Springs.

---

14) YOGI BEAR JELLYSTONE

Reference: west of Canon City; map C7, grid b0.

Campsites, facilities: There are 36 tent sites and 39 sites for trailers or motor homes of any length. Picnic tables are provided. Flush toilets, bottled gas, sanitary disposal station, showers, recreation hall, a store, laundromat, ice, playground and a swimming pool are also available.

Electricity, piped water, sewer hookups and firewood are available at an additional charge. A coffee shop is located within one mile. Pets are permitted on leashes.

Reservations, fee: Reservations accepted; $12.50-$17.50 fee per night. Open all year.

Who to contact: Phone (719) 275-2128 or write to P.O. Box 1025, Canon City, CO 81215.

Location: From Canon City, drive nine miles west on US 50.

Trip note: This is one of several campgrounds in the Canon City area. This park covers 20 acres, with simple sites among pine trees. There are hiking trails and a riding stable nearby. River rafting trips are also available. See the trip note for Mountain View Camp for possibilities in the Canon City area.

---

15) MOUNTAIN VIEW

Reference: west of Canon City; map C7, grid b0.

Campsites, facilities: There are 50 tent sites and 25 sites for trailers or motor homes. One cabin is available for rental. Picnic tables are provided. Flush toilets, sanitary disposal station, showers, recreation hall, a store, coffee shop, ice and playground are also available. Electricity, piped water, sewer hookups and firewood are available at an additional charge. Bottled gas and a laundromat are located within one mile. Pets and motorbikes are permitted.

Reservations, fee: Reservations accepted; $9-$16 fee per night; $25 per night for cabin. Visa accepted. Open all year.

Who to contact: Phone (719) 275-7232 or write to 45606 Highway 50 West, Canon City, CO 81212.

Location: From Canon City, drive eight miles west on Highway 50 to the campground.

Trip note: This camp is a nearby option to KOA Royal Gorge. This is a scenic area. The Arkansas River rumbles out of the canyon to the valley floor. A dramatic whitewater rafting trip through the Royal Gorge can be arranged with local outfitters. Sidetrips include a visit to the Canon City Municipal Museum. Local events include the Royal Gorge Rodeo in July and a Pioneer Day celebration in September. A golf course is also nearby.

---

16) GORGE KOA

Reference: west of Canon City; map C7, grid b0.

Campsites, facilities: There are 48 tent sites and 105 sites for trailers or motor homes of any length. Picnic tables are provided. Flush toilets, bottled gas, sanitary disposal station, showers, recreation hall, a store, coffee shop, laundromat, ice, playground and a swimming pool are also available. Firewood costs extra. Pets are permitted on leashes.

Reservations, fee: Reservations accepted; $14.50-$18.50 fee per night; MasterCard and Visa accepted. Open mid-April to October.

Who to contact: Phone (719) 275-6116 or write to P.O. Box 528, Canon City, CO 81212.

Location: From Canon City, drive eight miles west on Highway 50 and then one-half mile south at Royal Gorge exit.

Trip note: This is a privately developed park that covers 20 acres and has hiking trails and a riding stable nearby. RV sites are open, but the tent area is heavily wooded. For campers with kids, there is a giant slide and a miniature golf course. It is one of several campgrounds in the area. For details on the Canon City area, see the trip note for Mountain View Campground.

---

17) FORD'S MOUNTAINDALE RANCH

Reference: southwest of Colorado Springs; map C7, grid b3.

Campsites, facilities: There are 50 tent sites and 100 sites for trailers or motor homes of any length. Picnic tables are provided. Flush toilets, bottled gas, sanitary disposal station, recreation hall, a store, ice and a playground are also available. Showers and firewood are available at an additional charge. Pets are permitted on leashes.

Reservations, fee: Reservations accepted; $7-$11 fee per night. Open May to late September.

Who to contact: Phone (719) 576-0619 or write to 2000 Barrett Road, Colorado Springs, CO 80906.

Location: From the town of Colorado Springs, drive 18 miles southwest on Highway 115 (Nevada Avenue) and then two miles west on Barrett Road to the campground.

Trip note: This is a big park covering 510 acres. Privately developed, it is set just far enough out of Colorado Springs that it feels fairly remote. There are a multitude of recreation options in Colorado Springs; see trip notes for Golden Eagle Ranch and Pike's Peak Trailer Park.

---

18) COLORADO SPRINGS SOUTH KOA

Reference: south of Colorado Springs; map C7, grid b4.

Campsites, facilities: There are 230 sites for trailers or motor homes of any length. Electricity, piped water, sewer hookups and picnic tables are provided. Flush toilets, bottled gas, sanitary disposal station, showers, recreation hall, a store, laundromat, ice, miniature golf, hot tub and a swimming pool are also available. A coffee shop is located within one mile. Pets and motorbikes are permitted. There are also six camping cabins available.

Reservations, fee: Reservations accepted; $14-$20 fee per night. $28 per night for cabins. Open April to November.

Who to contact: Phone (719) 382-7575 or write to 8100 South Bonanza Trail, Fountain, CO 80817.

Location: From the town of Colorado Springs, drive nine miles south on Interstate 25 and take exit 132 to the campground.

Trip note: This park is just far enough out of Colorado Springs to give it an rural feel. The sites are large and graveled with some grass and a few trees. See trip note for Golden Eagle Camp for sidetrip details.

---

19) RV STATION

Reference: near Canon City; map C7, grid c1.

Campsites, facilities: There are 13 tent sites and 60 sites for trailers or motor homes of any length. Picnic tables are provided. Flush toilets, bottled gas, sanitary disposal station, showers and ice are also available. Electricity, piped water and sewer hookups are available at an additional charge. A coffee shop is located within one mile. Pets on leashes and motorbikes are permitted.

Reservations, fee: Reservations accepted; $9-$11 fee per night. Open all year.

Who to contact: Phone (719) 275-4576 or write to 3120 East Main, Canon City, CO 81212.

Location: In the town of Canon City, go south at the last stoplight at east end of town and drive one-half block to the campground.

Trip note: This is an option for Canon City area campers. This is an urban-style RV park, with graveled sites and little vegetation. It is set inside the city limits with all amenities nearby. For area details, see trip note for Mountain View Camp.

---

20) MAVERICK TRAILER PARK

Reference: in Canon City; map C7, grid c1.

Campsites, facilities: There are six tent sites and 12 sites for trailers or motor homes of any length. Picnic tables are provided. Flush toilets, showers and laundromat are also available. Electricity, piped water and sewer hookups are available at an additional charge. Bottled gas, a store, a coffee shop, laundromat and ice are located within one mile. Pets are permitted on leashes.

Reservations, fee: Reservations accepted; $7-$14 fee per night. Open all year.

Who to contact: Phone (719) 275-5546 or write to 295 South Reynolds Avenue, Canon City, CO 81212.

Location: Located in Canon City. Turn south off US 50 on Reynolds Avenue and drive 1.5 blocks to the campground.

Trip note: Set in the urban Canon City area, this is still a relatively wooded park. For recreation details, see the trip note for Mountain View Camp.

---

21) PUEBLO STATE PARK

Reference: west of Pueblo; map C7, grid c3.

Campsites, facilities: There are 112 tent sites and 111 drive-through sites for trailers or motor homes of any length. Note: An additional 180 new sites are scheduled. Picnic tables are provided. Flush toilets, sanitary disposal station, showers, a store, laundromat, ice and a playground are also available. Some facilities are **wheelchair accessible.** Pets are permitted on leashes. Boat docks, launching facilities and rentals are nearby.

Reservations, fee: Reserve sites by calling (800) 678-CAMP ($6.75 reservation fee); $7 fee per night plus $3 entrance fee. Open all year with limited winter facilities.

Who to contact: Phone (719) 561-9320 or write to 640 Reservoir Road, Pueblo, CO 81005.

Location: From Pueblo, drive west for six miles on US 50 to McCullough Boulevard and then south to the park.

Trip note: This is a big state park covering 15,000 acres. It sits alongside the Pueblo Reservoir at the west end of the lake. All water sports are possible including fishing, boating, sailing and waterskiing. Horseback riding, hiking trails and bicycling trails are also available. A visitor center is nearby.

---

22) PUEBLO KOA

Reference: north of Pueblo; map C7, grid c5.

Campsites, facilities: There are 25 tent sites and 75 sites for trailers or motor homes of any length. Picnic tables are provided. Flush toilets, bottled gas, sanitary disposal station, showers, recreation hall, a store, laundromat, ice, playground and a swimming pool are also available. Pets and motorbikes are permitted.

Reservations, fee: Reservations accepted; $13-$19 fee per night; MasterCard and Visa accepted. Open all year.

Who to contact: Phone (719) 542-2273 or write to 4131 Interstate 25 North, Pueblo, CO 81008.

Location: From Pueblo, drive six miles north on Interstate 25 and take exit 108 to the campground.

Trip note: This is one of several campgrounds in the Pueblo area. This one has open sites, with a few trees. See trip note for Arena RV Park for recreation possibilities.

---

23) OAK CREEK

Reference: southwest of Canon City, San Isabel National Forest; map C7, grid d1.

Campsites, facilities: There are six sites for tents, trailers or motor homes. Picnic tables are provided. Pit toilets are also available. There is **no piped water**. Pets are permitted on leashes.

Reservations, fee: No reservations necessary; no fee. Open mid-May to November.

Who to contact: Phone San Isabel National Forest at (719) 275-4119 or write to San Carlos Ranger District, 326 Dozier Street, Canon City, CO 81212.

Location: From Canon City, drive 12.3 miles southwest on County Road 143 to the campground.

Trip note: This is a primitive and rugged camp set alongside Oak Creek. It is relatively unknown. A good sidetrip is to take the two-mile trail up Lion Canyon. It's advisable to obtain a Forest Service map which details backcountry roads, trails and streams.

---

24) THE JUNCTION

Reference: in Ordway; map C7, grid d9.

Campsites, facilities: There are 15 tent sites and 36 sites for trailers or motor homes of any length. Electricity, piped water, sewer hookups and picnic tables are provided. Flush toilets, bottled gas, sanitary disposal station, showers, firewood, a store, cafe, laundromat, ice, playground and a swimming pool are also available. Pets and motorbikes are permitted.

Reservations, fee: Reservations accepted; $2-$8 fee per night; MasterCard and Visa/BankAmericard accepted. Open all year.

Who to contact: Phone (719) 267-3262, or write 18055 Road G, P.O. Box 97, Ordway, CO 81063.

Location: This campground is located in the town of Ordway at the junctions of Highway 96 and Highway 71.

Trip note: This is a 14-acre, privately developed urban park, just far enough (10 miles) off the interstate that it gets missed by a lot of folks. Some sites are shaded. Visits to nearby Lake Henry or Lake Meredith provides recreation options.

---

25) LAKE ISABEL SOUTHSIDE

Reference: northwest of Rye, San Isabel National Forest; map C7, grid e2.

Campsites, facilities: There are eight sites for tents, trailers or motor homes up to 30 feet long. Picnic tables are provided. Hand-pumped water and pit toilets are also available. A store, coffee shop, laundromat and ice are located within one mile. Pets are permitted on leashes. Boat docks and launching facilities are nearby. No motorized boats allowed on lake. There is a **wheelchair accessible** fishing pier available.

Reservations, fee: No reservations necessary; $8-$10 fee per night. Open mid-May to late October.

Who to contact: Phone San Isabel National Forest at (719) 275-4119 or write to San Carlos Ranger District, 326 Dozier Street, Canon City, CO 81212.

Location: From Rye, drive 10 miles northwest on Highway 165 and a half mile west on Forest Service Road 308 to the campground.

Trip note: This camp is set at 8,000 feet beside a small lake. It provides a good base camp for hikers. There are several good trails in the area, including the St. Charles Trail, Snowslide Trail and Cisneros Trail. The Charles River empties into the lake and continues eastward.

26) OPHIR

Reference: on Middle Creek, San Isabel National Forest; map C7, grid e2.

Campsites, facilities: There are 31 sites for tents, trailers or motor homes up to 22 feet. Picnic tables are provided. Hand-pumped water and pit toilets are also available. Pets are permitted on leashes.

Reservations, fee: No reservations necessary; $6 fee per night. Open mid-May to late October.

Who to contact: Phone San Isabel National Forest at (719) 275-4119 or write to San Carlos Ranger District, 326 Dozier Street, Canon City, CO 81212.

Location: From Beulah, drive 11.8 miles southwest on Highway 76 and 3.3 miles northwest on Highway 165 to the campground.

Trip note: This Forest Service camp provides easy access and is a pretty spot set just off the main road on Middle Creek. If you want a camp with water, Lake Isabel camps provide nearby alternatives. Several hiking trails are located to the south; see a Forest Service map for specifics.

27) LAKE ISABEL ST. CHARLES

Reference: northwest of Rye, San Isabel National Forest; map C7, grid e2.

Campsites, facilities: There are 15 sites for tents, trailers or motor homes up to 16 feet long. Picnic tables are provided. Hand-pumped water and pit toilets are also available. A store, coffee shop and ice are located within one mile. Pets are permitted on leashes. Boat docks and rentals are nearby. No motorized boats allowed on lake.

Reservations, fee: No reservations necessary; $6-$10 fee per night. Open mid-May to late October.

Who to contact: Phone San Isabel National Forest at (719) 275-4119 or write to San Carlos Ranger District, 326 Dozier Street, Canon City, CO 81212.

Location: From Rye, drive 10 miles northwest on Highway 165 and 1.1 miles west on Forest Service Road 308.

Trip note: This is one of three camps at Lake Isabel. See trip note for Lake Isabel Southside for recreation options.

28) COUNTRY BUDGET HOST RV PARK

Reference: in Walsenburg; map C7, grid f4.

Campsites, facilities: There are 17 drive-through sites for trailers or motor homes of any length. Electricity, piped water, sewer hookups and picnic tables are provided. Flush toilets, showers and laundromat are also available. Bottled gas, a store, coffee shop and ice are located within one mile. Pets are permitted on leashes.

Reservations, fee: Reservations accepted; $10.50-$15 fee per night; American Express, MasterCard and Visa accepted. Open all year.

Who to contact: Phone (719) 738-3800 or write to P.O. Box 190, Walsenburg, CO 81089.

Location: From Walsenburg, drive one mile north on Interstate 25 and take exit 52 to the west side of Interstate 25 and the campground.

Trip note: The key here is location. This motor home park is set in town near the junction of Interstate 25, US 160, and Highway 10. The sites are partially grassy and graveled with scattered trees, adjacent to a motel. One of the only restaurants in town is located directly across the street. In winter, Cuchara Ski Resort is nearby. Nearby recreation options include a golf course, bike paths and tennis courts. A good sidetrip possibility is to visit Lathrop State Park.

---

29) DAKOTA

Reference: in Walsenburg; map C7, grid f4.

Campsites, facilities: There are 50 tent sites and 72 sites for trailers or motor homes of any length. Electricity, piped water, sewer hookups and picnic tables are provided. Flush toilets, bottled gas, sanitary disposal station, firewood, recreation hall, a store, laundromat, ice and a playground are also available. Showers are available at an additional charge. A coffee shop is located within one mile. Pets on leashes and motorbikes are permitted. Boat docks and launching facilities are nearby.

Reservations, fee: Reservations accepted; $12-$15 fee per night. Open all year.

Who to contact: Phone (719) 738-9912 or write to P.O. Box 206, Walsenburg, CO 81089.

Location: From Walsenburg, drive one mile north on Business Route Interstate 25 to the campground.

Trip note: Walsenburg is not exactly a hot spot for vacations, but it can make a decent stopover for campers heading down Interstate 25 to New Mexico. See trip note for Lathrop State Park and Country Budget Host RV Park for options.

---

30) UTE CREEK

Reference: near Mountain Home Reservoir; map C7, grid g0.

Campsites, facilities: There are 30 tent sites and 26 sites for trailers or motor homes of any length. Picnic tables are provided. Flush toilets, sanitary disposal station, showers, firewood, laundromat, ice and a playground are also available. A store and coffee shop are located within one mile. Pets and motorbikes are permitted.

Reservations, fee: Reservations accepted; $3-$10 fee per night. Open April to late November.

Who to contact: Phone (719) 379-3238 or write to P.O. Box 188, Fort Garland, CO 81133.

Location: Take the Narcisso Street exit of US 160 in Fort Garland and drive one block north following the signs to the campground.

Trip note: There's not a whole lot around these parts. The campground is pleasant, with little Ute Creek running through the tent area. Rumor has it that the fishing can be decent if you hit it right, but so far, not many have. Attractions in the area include Sand Dunes National Monument, the historic Fort Garland Museum, and San Luis, the oldest town in Colorado. It is located 16 miles to the south. Also to the south, Sangre de Cristo Creek and Mountain Home Reservoir provide sidetrip possibilities.

---

31) BLANCA RV PARK

Reference: near Smith Reservoir; map C7, grid g0.

Campsites, facilities: There are 10 tent sites and 28 sites for trailers or motor homes of any length. Electricity, piped water, sewer hookups and picnic tables are provided. Flush toilets, ice, bottled gas, firewood, showers, a sanitary disposal station, recreation hall, store, coffee shop and a laundromat are also available. Pets and motorbikes are permitted.

Reservations, fee: Reservations accepted; $10-$13 fee per night; MasterCard and Visa accepted. Open all year with limited winter facilities.

Who to contact: Phone (719) 379-3201 or write to P.O. Box 64, Blanca, CO 81123.

Location: This campground is located in Blanca on US 160.

Trip note: This privately developed park covers five acres and is used primarily for a layover spot for cruisers on US 160. It is set in the tiny town of Blanca, a fairly small park surrounded by a seven-foot fence to protect campers from highway noise. It has graveled RV sites and grassy tent sites with some trees. Smith Reservoir, three miles to the south, provides a sidetrip option. It is a popular lake for fishing.

---

32) LATHROP STATE PARK

Reference: near Walsenburg; map C7, grid g4.

Campsites, facilities: There are 98 sites for tents, trailers or motor homes of any length. Piped water and picnic tables are provided. Flush toilets, sanitary disposal station, showers, laundromat and playground are also available. Electricity and firewood are available at an additional charge. Ice is located within one mile. Some facilities are **wheelchair accessible.** Pets are permitted on leashes. Boat docks and launching facilities are nearby.

Reservations, fee: Reserve sites by calling (800) 678-CAMP ($6.75 reservation fee); $6-$10 fee per night plus $3 entrance fee. Open all year with limited winter facilities.

Who to contact: Phone (719) 738-2376 or write to P.O. Box 111, Walsenburg, CO 81089.

Location: From Walsenburg, drive three miles west on US 160 to the park.

Trip note: This park is set at 6,400 feet and is a good option to Country Host RV Park and Dakota Camp, which are both located in nearby Walsenburg. Fishing, boating, waterskiing and windsurfing (when the wind is up) are all popular here. Hiking trails, bicycle trails and horseback riding are also available.

---

33) BLUE LAKE

Reference: near Trinchera Peak, San Isabel National Forest; map C7, grid h2.

Campsites, facilities: There are 15 sites for tents, trailers or motor homes up to 22 feet long. Picnic tables are provided. Hand-pumped water and pit toilets are also available. Pets are permitted on leashes.

Reservations, fee: No reservations necessary; $6-$8 fee per night. Open June to November.

Who to contact: Phone San Isabel National Forest at (719) 275-4119 or write to San Carlos Ranger District, 326 Dozier Street, Canon City, CO 81212.

Location: From La Veta, drive nine miles south on Highway 12 to Cuchara. Continue south on Highway 12 for 3.5 miles and 3.5 miles west on Forest Service Road 413 to the campground.

Trip note: This is a nearby option to Bear Lake Camp. There is good fishing in this lake, as well as Bear Lake; both are stocked with trout regularly. A hiking trail is routed south along North Purgatoire River and branching west to Trinchera Peak.

---

34) BEAR LAKE

Reference: near Trinchera Peak, San Isabel National Forest; map C7, grid h2.

Campsites, facilities: There are 14 sites for tents, trailers or motor homes up to 22 feet long. Picnic tables are provided. Piped water and pit toilets are located. Pets are permitted on leashes.

Reservations, fee: No reservations necessary; $6 fee per night. Open June to November.

Who to contact: Phone San Isabel National Forest at (719) 275-4119 or write to San Carlos Ranger District, 326 Dozier Street, Canon City, CO 81212.

Location: From La Veta, drive nine miles south on Highway 12 to Cuchara. Continue south on Highway 12 for 3.5 miles, then 4.3 miles west on Forest Service Road 413 to the campground.

Trip note: This secluded camp is set on Bear Lake, adjacent to Blue Lake Camp. It's a good spot for fishermen and hikers. Indian Trail is routed north from camp for several miles. See trip note for Blue Lake for other hiking options.

35) PURGATOIRE

Reference: on the North Fork of Purgatoire River; map C7, grid h2.

Campsites, facilities: There are 23 sites for tents, trailers or motor homes up to 22 feet long. Picnic tables are provided. Hand-pumped water and pit toilets are also available. Pets are permitted on leashes.

Reservations, fee: No reservations necessary; $6 fee per night. Open May to November.

Who to contact: Phone San Isabel National Forest at (719) 275-4119 or write to San Carlos Ranger District, 326 Dozier Street, Canon City, CO 81212.

Location: From La Veta, drive nine miles south on Highway 12 to Cuchara. Continue south on Highway 12 for 13.5 miles and drive 3.2 miles west on Forest Service Road 411.

Trip note: This is an obscure, little-known camp set along the North Fork of the Purgatoire River. A possible sidetrip is to take the six-mile hike north on the trail that leads to Bear Lake and Blue Lake—but hey, you could also drive to those lakes.

36) TRINIDAD LAKE STATE PARK

Reference: west of Trinidad; map C7, grid h6.

Campsites, facilities: There are 62 sites for tents, trailers or motor homes up to 25 feet long. Piped water and picnic tables are provided. Flush toilets, sanitary disposal station, laundromat and showers are also available. Pets are permitted on leashes. Boat launching facilities are nearby.

Reservations, fee: Reserve sites by calling (800) 678-CAMP ($6.75 reservation fee); $7-$10 fee per night plus $3 entrance fee. Open all year with limited winter facilities.

Who to contact: Phone (719) 846-6951 or write to Route 3, P.O. Box 360, Trinidad, CO 81082.

Location: From Trinidad, drive three miles west on Highway 12 to the park.

Trip note: This is a big and relatively new state park that provides a number of recreational options. Fishing is the most popular, but when the wind is up, so is windsurfing. There are several miles of excellent hiking trails as well and horseback riding is available.

37) CAWTHON

Reference: near Trinidad; map C7, grid i5.

Campsites, facilities: There are 10 tent sites and 24 sites for trailers or motor homes of any length. Electricity, piped water and picnic tables are provided. Flush toilets, sanitary disposal station, showers, laundromat, ice and a swimming pool are also available. A store and coffee shop are located within one mile. Pets and motorbikes are permitted.

Reservations, fee: Reservations accepted; $4-$14.50 fee per night; MasterCard and Visa accepted. Open all year.

Who to contact: Phone (719) 846-3303 or write to 1701 Santa Fe Trail, Trinidad, CO 81082.

Location: Take exit 13A off Interstate 25 in Trinidad and drive a half mile east to Santa Fe Trail. Turn south and follow the signs to the campground.

Trip note: This is the most developed of the three camps in the area. It offers spacious sites, both graveled and grassy, overlooking a golf course. Recreation options can be found at Trinidad Lake (two miles away) and Monument Lake (35 miles away). Both offer fishing and boating opportunities. In Trinidad, visitors can explore local museums and art galleries. Golfers take note: the course adjacent to camp is excellent, and they've got tennis courts too.

Colorado Map C8
3 listings
Pages 280-282

North (C4)—see page 180
East—Kansas
South—Oklahoma
West (C7)—see page 262

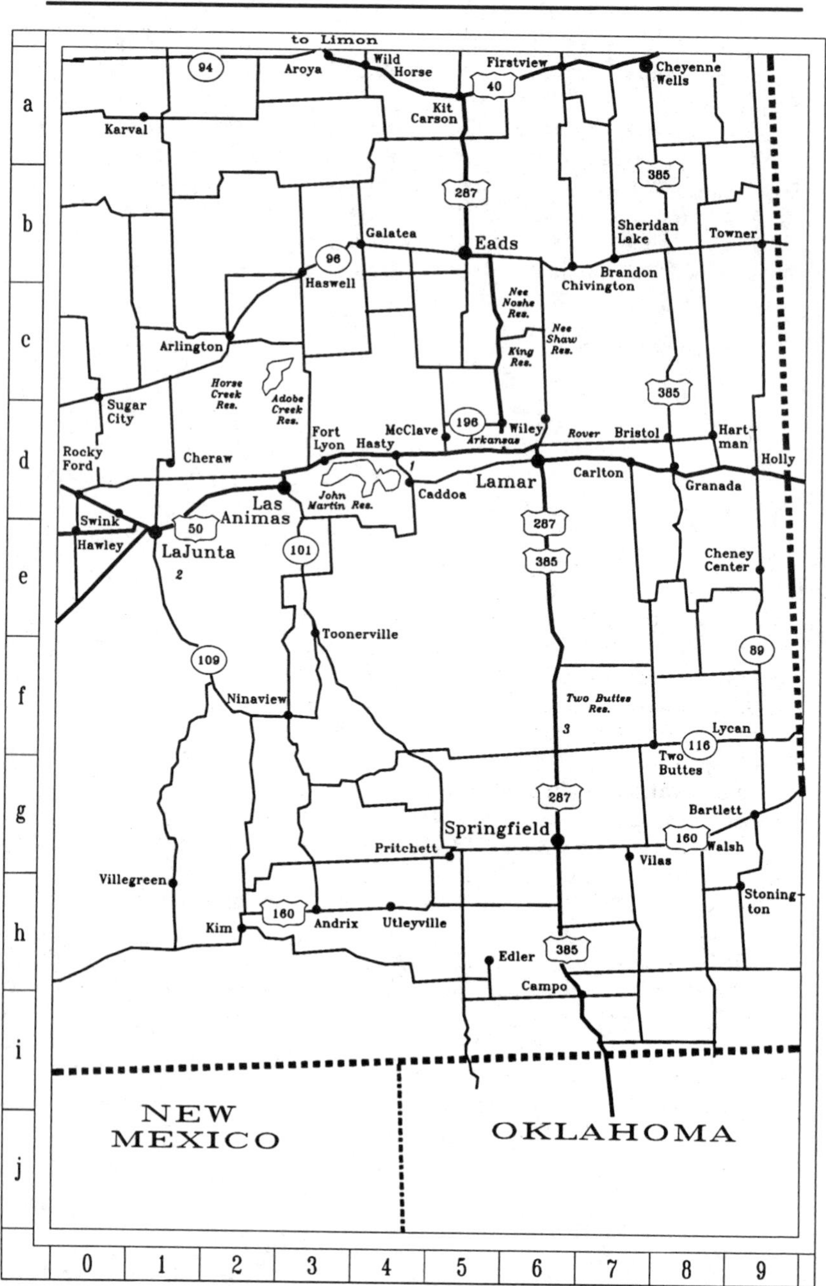

Featuring: Holbrook Lake

1) LAKE HASTY RECREATION AREA

Reference: south of Hasty; map C8, grid d4.

Campsites, facilities: There are 50 sites for tents, trailers or motor homes of any length. Picnic tables are provided. Piped water, vault toilets, sanitary disposal station, playground and a wading pool are also available. A store, a coffee shop and ice are located within one mile. Some facilities are **wheelchair accessible.** Pets are permitted on leashes. There is a boat ramp nearby at John Martin Reservoir.

Reservations, fee: No reservations; $5 fee per night. Open early April to late October.

Who to contact: Phone the Army Corps of Engineers at (719) 336-3476, or write Star Route, Hasty, CO 81044.

Location: From the town of Hasty, drive four miles south on County Road 24 road to the campground.

Trip note: The camp is set on a big lake near the John Martin Dam. Fishing, boating, swimming and waterskiing are popular during the summer months. A visitor center and tours of dam are available. It's the nicest campground in the southeast part of the state.

2) LA JUNTA KOA

Reference: near Holbrook Lake; map C8, grid e1.

Campsites, facilities: There are 10 tent sites and 44 sites for trailers or motor homes of any length. Picnic tables are provided. Flush toilets, bottled gas, sanitary disposal station, showers, firewood, a store, laundromat, ice, playground and a swimming pool are also available. A coffee shop is located within one mile. Pets and motorbikes are permitted.

Reservations, fee: Reservations accepted; $13-$18 fee per night. Open all year.

Who to contact: Phone (719) 384-9580, or write 26680 West Highway 50, La Junta, CO 80150.

Location: From the town of La Junta drive two miles west on US 50 to the campground.

Trip note: This camp is one of two choices for campers looking for a spot in La Junta. It's a simple campground, with open, grassy sites, but the surrounding area has much to offer. "La Junta" means "the junction," an historical spot where the old Santa Fe Trail and Navajo Trail intersected. Nearby Holbrook Lake provides a spot for boating, fishing and waterskiing. If you have the time, the Comanche National Grassland is located southwest of town with Highway 109 and US 350 providing access.

3) TWO BUTTES RESERVOIR

Reference: north of Springfield; map C8, grid f6.

Campsites, facilities: There are 75 tent sites and 57 sites for trailers or motor homes of any length. Picnic tables are provided. Piped water, pit toilets and a disposal station are also available. A store is located within one mile. Pets are permitted on leashes. Boat launching facilities and rentals are available.

Reservations, fee: No reservations necessary; no fee. Open May to late-October.

Who to contact: Phone (303) 297-1192, or write Colorado Division of Wildlife, 6060 Broadway, Denver, CO 80216.

Location: From the town of Springfield, drive 17 miles north on US 385/287, and then three miles east on the access road to the campground.

Trip note: This isn't much of a lake, but what the heck. The nearest campground is an hour's drive to the north, with zilch in other directions, so no complaints, please. Look on the positive side—it's free, and you're likely to have the whole place to yourself. It is a good base camp for outdoor people, particularly in the fall, when Two Buttes Reservoir attracts waterfowl making a stop on the flyway.

MONTANA

Montana Map M1
105 listings
Pages 284-331

North—Canada
East (M2)—see page 332
South (M6)—see page 364
West—Idaho

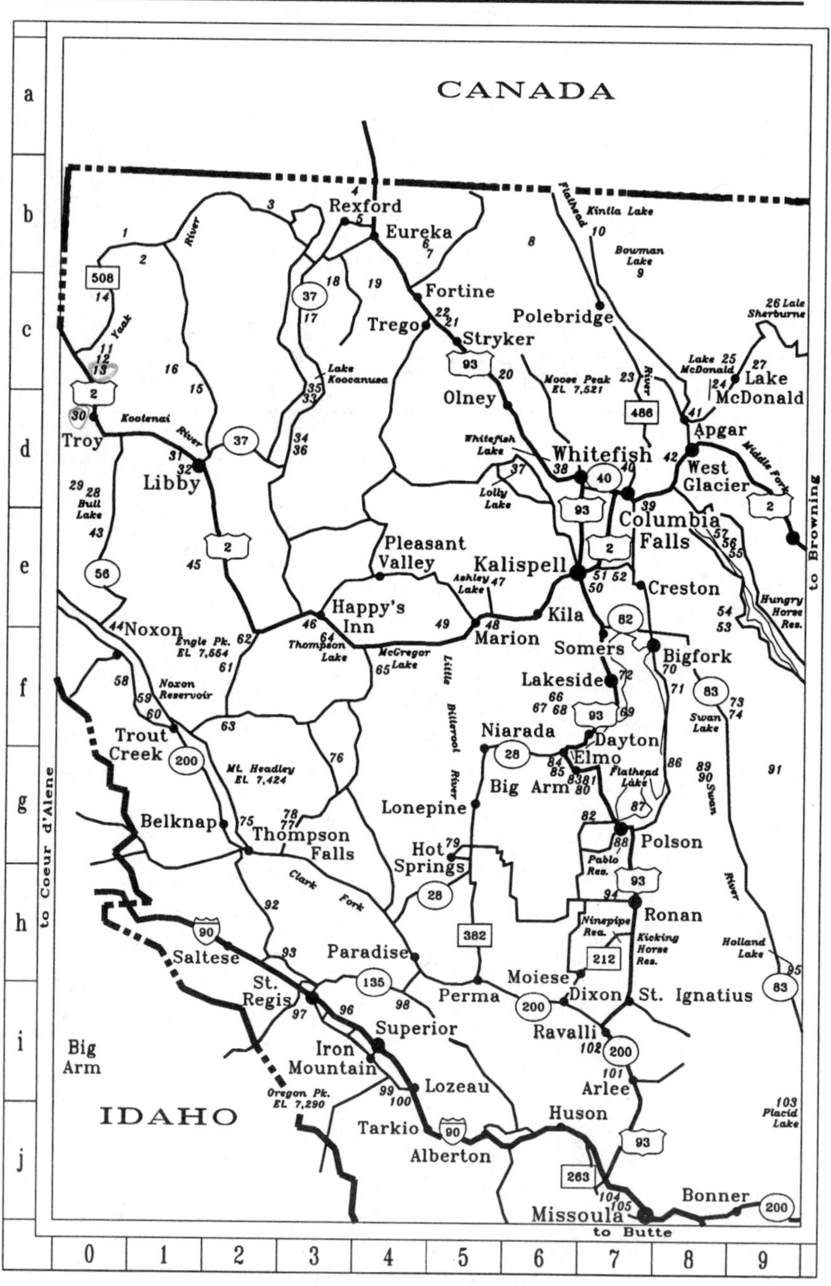

Featuring: Yaak River, Kootenai National Forest, North Fork Flathead River, Flathead National Forest, Glacier National Park, Pipe Creek, Lake Koocanusa, Pinkham Creek, Lake McDonald, Lake Sherburne, Avalanche Creek, Bull Lake, Kootenai Falls, Kootenai River, West Glacier, Columbia Falls, Cabinet Gorge Reservoir, Thompson Lake, Ashley Lake, Bitterroot Lake, Flathead Lake, Flathead River, Handkerchief Lake, Hungry Horse Reservoir, Noxon Reservoir, Cabinet Mountains Wilderness, McGregor Lake, Lake Mary Ronan, Swan Lake, Clark Fork, Fishtrap Lake, Thompson River, Lolo National Forest, Swan River State Forest, Bob Marshall Wilderness, East Fork of Dry Creek, Twelvemile Creek, Clark Fork River, Jocko River, Placid Lake

---

1) WHITETAIL

Reference: on Yaak River, Kootenai National Forest; map M1, grid b0.

Campsites, facilities: There are 12 sites for tents, trailers and motor homes up to 32 feet long. Picnic tables are provided. Hand-pumped water, vault toilets and firewood are available. A store and ice are located within five miles. Pets are permitted on leashes.

Reservations, fee: No reservations necessary; no fee. Open June to late October.

Who to contact: Phone Kootenai National Forest at (406) 295-4693, or write to Three Rivers Ranger District, 1437 North Highway 2, Troy, MT 59935.

Location: From Troy, drive 10.2 miles northwest on US 2. Turn northeast on Highway 508 and continue for 12.8 miles, then drive 11.4 miles northeast on Forest Highway 92 to the campground.

Trip note: This is a primitive, little-used camp set on the Yaak River. If the spot doesn't grab you, there are two other options, both of which are located on the Yaak River: Pete Creek Camp is upriver, and Red Top Camp (smaller and more primitive) is downriver. Small boats can be carried to the river. There are a few good hiking trails in the area, along with several Forest Service roads that are excellent for mountain biking.

---

2) PETE CREEK

Reference: near Yaak River, Kootenai National Forest; map M1, grid b1.

Campsites, facilities: There are 13 sites for tents, trailers and motor homes up to 32 feet long. Picnic tables are provided. Hand-pumped water, vault toilets and firewood are also available. A store and ice are located within three miles. Pets are permitted on leashes.

Reservations, fee: No reservations necessary; no fee. Open June to late September.

Who to contact: Phone Kootenai National Forest at (406) 295-4693, or write to Three Rivers Ranger District, 1437 North Highway 2, Troy, MT 59935.

Location: From Troy, drive 10.2 miles northwest on US 2. Turn northeast on Highway 508 and continue for 12.8 miles, then drive 14.1 miles northeast on Forest Highway 92 to the campground.

Trip note: Western Montana is loaded with these kind of camps: idyllic, little-known spots that require some driving on Forest Service roads. This one is set at the confluence of the Yaak River and Pete Creek and is just two miles from the small town of Yaak. It sits in the Purcell Mountains right below Grizzly Peak (6,500 feet). There is fishing and swimming access from the campground. Nearby Whitetail Camp offers a more primitive option.

---

3) CARIBOU

Reference: on East Fork of the Yaak River, Kootenai National Forest; map M1, grid b2.

Campsites, facilities: There are three tent sites. Picnic tables are provided. Pit toilets and firewood are also available. There is **no piped water.** Pets are permitted on leashes.

Reservations, fee: No reservations necessary; no fee. Open June to late September.

Who to contact: Phone Kootenai National Forest at (406) 295-4693, or write to Three Rivers Ranger District, 1437 North Highway 2, Troy, MT 59935.

Location: From Troy, drive 10.2 miles northwest on US 2. Turn northeast on Highway 508 and continue for 12.8 miles, then drive about 38 miles northeast on Forest Highway 92 to the campground.

Trip note: Don't expect to find a tent city way out here. It's a tiny little spot, usually devoid of humanoids, and is situated at the confluence of Caribou Creek and the East Fork of the Yaak River. There are several hiking trails in the area; see a Forest Service map. Fishing can be quite good in the Yaak River, and you get access directly from the campground.

---

4) GATEWAY BOAT-IN

Reference: on Kootenai River, Kootenai National Forest; map M1, grid b3

Campsites, facilities: There are four primitive tent sites at this boat-in campground. Picnic tables are provided. Pit toilets and firewood are also available. There is **no piped water.**

Reservations, fee: No reservations necessary; no fee. Open June to mid-October.

Who to contact: Phone Kootenai National Forest at (406) 296-2536, or write Eureka Ranger District, 1299 Highway 93 North, Eureka, MT 59917.

Location: From Eureka, drive seven miles northwest to Tobacco Plains Boat Ramp. From there, the campground is two miles by boat.

Trip note: Hey, you want the world to yourself? Then motor on out here to this boat-in camp. It gets very little use. The camp is on Lake Koocanusa and very close to the Canadian border. If you want quiet and solitude, this is your camp.

---

5) REXFORD BENCH COMPLEX

Reference: on Kootenai River, Kootenai National Forest; map M1, grid b3.

Campsites, facilities: There are about 153 sites for tents, trailers or motor homes up to 32 feet long. The sites are set in three different adjacent areas. Picnic tables are provided. Piped water, flush toilets, a sanitary disposal station, a public phone and firewood are also available. Some facilities are **wheelchair accessible.** Pets are permitted on leashes. Boat docks and launching facilities and a swimming beach are nearby.

Reservations, fee: No reservations necessary; $8 fee per night. Open early May to mid-October.

Who to contact: Phone Kootenai National Forest at (406) 296-2536, or write Eureka Ranger District, 1299 Highway 93 North, Eureka, MT 59917.

Location: From Eureka, drive a half mile north on US 93 and five miles west on Highway 37 to Rexford. The campground entrance is at the east end of town.

Trip note: A popular spot for families and groups, this campground is set on the Tobacco River arm of Lake Koocanusa. You get a beach, boat launch and relatively open camping area, but expect lots of company.

---

6) BIG THERRIAULT LAKE

Reference: near Fortine, Kootenai National Forest, map M1, grid b4.

Campsites, facilities: There are 10 sites for tents, trailers and motor homes up to 32 feet long. Picnic tables are provided. Pit toilets and firewood are also available. Hand-pumped water is available. Pets are permitted on leashes. Boat launching facilities for small boats are nearby.

Reservations, fee: No reservations necessary; no fee. Open mid-June to mid-September.

Who to contact: Phone Kootenai National Forest at (406) 882-4451, or write to Fortine Ranger District, P.O. Box 116, Fortine, MT 59918.

Location: From Fortine, drive 2.8 miles northwest on US 93. Turn northeast on County Road 1143 and drive two miles, then continue 10.6 miles northeast on Forest Service Road 114. Continue west for 13 more miles to the campground.

Trip note: You get a take-your-pick deal here, with good boating, fishing, swimming, hiking and backpacking. The camp is set at lakeside and offers numerous trails into the adjacent wildlands. The best of them are routed to the northwest, into the Ten Lakes Scenic Area (see Forest Service map). Others head south to converge at Therriault Pass. For the ambitious, one trail heads up to the top of Stahl Peak (7,430 feet).

---

7) LITTLE THERRIAULT LAKE

Reference: near Fortine, Kootenai National Forest; map M1, grid b4.

Campsites, facilities: There are seven sites for tents, trailers and motor homes up to 22 feet long. Picnic tables are provided. Hand-pumped water, pit toilets and firewood are also available. Pets are permitted on leashes.

Reservations, fee: No reservations necessary; no fee. Open mid-June to October.

Who to contact: Phone Kootenai National Forest at (406) 882-4451, or write to Fortine Ranger District, P.O. Box 116, Fortine, MT 59918.

Location: From Fortine, drive 2.8 miles northwest on US 93. Turn northeast on County Road 1143 and drive two miles, then continue 10.6 miles northeast on Forest Service Road 114. Continue west for 13.2 more miles to the campground.

Trip note: This camp is located just a quarter mile from the previous camp at Big Therriault Lake (see trip note for area details). Small boats can be carried to the lake. There is a **wheelchair accessible** fishing area also.

---

8) TUCHUCK

Reference: on the North Fork of Flathead River, Flathead National Forest; map M1, grid b6.

Campsites, facilities: There are seven sites for tents, trailers and small motor homes up to 20 feet long. Picnic tables are provided. Vault toilets are also available. There is **no piped water.** Pets are permitted on leashes.

Reservations, fee: No reservations necessary; no fee. Open mid-June to late September.

Who to contact: Phone Flathead National Forest at (406) 892-4372, or write to Tally Lake Ranger District, 1335 Highway 93 West, Whitefish, MT 59937-3153.

Location: From the town of Columbia Falls, drive 53 miles north on Forest Service Road 210. Turn west on Forest Service Road 114 and continue for 10 miles.

Trip note: This one is way out there in "booger country." If you don't want any company, this is the place to go. The camp is set at the confluence of two creeks and offers several good hiking trails: one follows Tuchuck Creek for many miles, and the other runs parallel up on the ridge to Tuchuck Mountain. In either case, a Forest Service map is advised.

9) BOWMAN LAKE

Reference: in Glacier National Park; map M1, grid b7.

Campsites, facilities: There are 48 sites for tents, trailers and motor homes up to 22 feet long. Picnic tables are provided. Piped water and pit toilets are also available. Pets are permitted on leashes. Boat launching facilities are nearby.

Reservations, fee: No reservations necessary; $8 fee per night. Open mid-May to late September, including limited and some off-season weekends.

Who to contact: Phone Waterton-Glacier International Peace Park at (406) 888-5441, or write P.O. Box 128, West Glacier, MT 59936.

Location: From the town of West Glacier, drive 32 miles northwest on North Fork Road, then six miles east on a dirt road to the campground.

Trip note: This is the most popular campground in the northwest part of Glacier National Park. Why? Because it is set along the shore of Bowman Lake, the southwest shore to be specific, and people love tenting along a pretty lake. And Bowman Lake is just that flat-out pretty. It's a long skinny lake surrounded by wild country. Many trails are in the area.

10) KINTLA LAKE

Reference: in Glacier National Park, map M1, grid b7.

Campsites, facilities: There are 13 sites for tents, trailers and motor homes up to 18 feet long. Picnic tables are provided. Piped water and pit toilets are also available. Pets are permitted on leashes. Boat launching facilities are nearby.

Reservations, fee: No reservations necessary; $8 fee per night. Open mid-May to late September, including limited and some off-season weekends.

Who to contact: Phone Waterton-Glacier International Peace Park at (406) 888-5441, or write P.O. Box 128, West Glacier, MT 59936.

Location: From the town of West Glacier, drive 47 miles northwest on North Fork Road to the campground.

Trip note: In many ways, this is an idyllic spot. It's set on the western edge of Kintla Lake in the northwestern corner of Glacier National Park and is a good spot for boating, fishing and hiking. There are numerous trails in the area including one that is routed far across the northern region of the park.

11) KILBRENNAN LAKE

Reference: in Kootenai National Forest; map M1, grid c0.

Campsites, facilities: There are five sites for tents, trailers and motor homes up to 22 feet long. Picnic tables are provided. Pit toilets and firewood are also available. There is **no piped water.** Pets are permitted on leashes. Boat docks and launching facilities are nearby.

Reservations, fee: No reservations necessary; no fee. Open late May to late September.

Who to contact: Phone Kootenai National Forest at (406) 295-4693, or write to Three Rivers Ranger District, 1437 North Highway 2, Troy, MT 59935.

Location: From Troy, drive 2.7 miles northwest on US 2. Turn northeast on Forest Service Road 2394 and continue for 10 miles to the campground.

Trip note: This is a classic lakeside spot set at the north end of Kilbrennan Lake. It's the only camp at the lake, small and primitive, but pretty and secluded as well. Fishing can be good in Kilbrennan Lake, and you probably won't find many other people here, which should help out your success rates.

---

12) YAAK RIVER

Reference: in Kootenai National Forest; map M1, c0.

Campsites, facilities: There are 43 sites for tents, trailers and motor homes of any length. Picnic tables are provided. Piped water, vault toilets and firewood are also available. Showers, a store, coffee shop and ice are located within five miles. Pets are permitted on leashes. A boat ramp is nearby.

Reservations, fee: No reservations necessary; $5 fee per night. Open mid-May to late September.

Who to contact: Phone Kootenai National Forest at (406) 295-4693, or write to Three Rivers Ranger District, 1437 North Highway 2, Troy, MT 59935.

Location: From Troy, drive 7.5 miles northwest on US 2.

Trip note: This is a popular spot compared to the other camps in the vicinity because of its easy access from Highway 2. It's also the closest campground to the Idaho border. The camp is set at the confluence of the Yaak River and Kootenai River, with access for small boats available. This area is popular with cross-country skiers in the winter, and there is some good hiking in the area. See a Forest Service map for trail information.

---

13) YAAK FALLS

Reference: on Yaak River, Kootenai National Forest; map M1, grid c0.

Campsites, facilities: There are seven sites for tents, trailers and motor homes up to 22 feet long. Picnic tables are provided. Pit toilets and firewood are also available. There is **no piped water.** Pets are permitted on leashes.

Reservations, fee: No reservations necessary; no fee. Open late May to late September.

Who to contact: Phone Kootenai National Forest at (406) 295-4693, or write to Three Rivers Ranger District, 1437 North Highway 2, Troy, MT 59935.

Location: From Troy, drive 10.2 miles northwest on US 2. Turn northeast on Highway 508 and drive 6.5 miles to the campground.

Trip note: This is a classic spot. There are several waterfalls nearby at the head of the scenic river canyon on the Yaak River, providing nearby scenic attractions. Sportsmen can fish in the Yaak River or hike a few of the trails in the area. This is one of three rustic camps in the Yaak River vicinity that are just a short drive north of Highway 2. The others are Kilbrennan Lake Camp and Yaak River Camp.

---

14) RED TOP

Reference: on Yaak River, Kootenai National Forest; map M1, grid c0.

Campsites, facilities: There are three sites for tents, trailers and motor homes up to 32 feet long. Picnic tables are provided. Pit toilets and firewood are also available. There is **no piped water.** Pets are permitted on leashes.

Reservations, fee: No reservations necessary; no fee. Open late May to late September.

Who to contact: Phone Kootenai National Forest at (406) 295-4693, or write to Three Rivers Ranger District, 1437 North Highway 2, Troy, MT 59935.

Location: From Troy, drive 10.2 miles northwest on US 2. Turn northeast on Highway 508 and drive 12.8 miles to the campground.

Trip note: Bet you didn't know about this one. It's a tiny, beautiful spot on the Yaak River. A trail is routed up to Red Top Mountain (6,226 feet). Another trail, located south of the campground at the confluence of Cyclone Creek and the Yaak River, heads west for about nine miles. If you're not into hiking, try your hand at fishing in the Yaak River.

---

15) CARRIGAN

Reference: on Pipe Creek, Kootenai National Forest; map M1, grid c1.

Campsites, facilities: There are eight sites for tents, trailers and motor homes up to 21 feet long. Picnic tables are provided. Firewood is also available. There is **no piped water.** Pets are permitted on leashes.

Reservations, fee: No reservations necessary; no fee. Open June to mid-September.

Who to contact: Phone (406) 293-4141, or write Champion International Corporation, Libby, MT 59923.

Location: From Libby, drive a half mile north on Highway 37, then 12 miles north on Pipe Creek Road to the campground.

Trip note: This is a primitive camp on Pipe Creek that doesn't get much attention, and that is primarily because almost nobody knows about it. It isn't maintained, and has no water or sewage facilities, but if you just need to get away from it all and have guaranteed solitude, this may be just the camp you're looking for.

---

16) LOON LAKE

Reference: near Libby, Kootenai National Forest; map M1, grid c1.

Campsites, facilities: There are four sites for tents, trailers and motor homes up to 32 feet long. Picnic tables are provided. Firewood and pit toilets are also available. There is **no piped water.** Pets are permitted on leashes. Small boats can be carried to the lake.

Reservations, fee: No reservations necessary; no fee. Open mid-May to early October.

Who to contact: Phone Kootenai National Forest at (406) 293-7741, or write to Libby Ranger District, 1263 Highway 37 North, Libby, MT 59923.

Location: From Libby, drive a half mile north on Highway 37. Turn north on Pipe Creek Road and drive 16 miles, then turn west on Forest Service Road 471 and continue for three miles to the campground.

Trip note: Small and quiet, this primitive spot offers lakeside access to Loon Lake, a skinny lake that sits below Turner Mountain (5,952 feet). Turner Mountain Ski Area operates in the winter. The fishing can be good here, and there is a network of Forest Service roads nearby, providing options for hikers or mountain bikers.

---

17) PECK GULCH

Reference: on Lake Koocanusa, Kootenai National Forest; map M1, grid c3.

Campsites, facilities: There are 75 sites for tents, trailers and motor homes up to 32 feet long. Picnic tables are provided. Piped water, vault toilets and firewood are also available. Some facilities are **wheelchair accessible.** Pets are permitted on leashes. Boat docks and launching facilities are nearby.

Reservations, fee: No reservations necessary; $6 fee per night. Open early May to mid-October.

Who to contact: Phone Kootenai National Forest at (406) 296-2536, or write Eureka Ranger District, 1299 Highway 93 North, Eureka, MT 59917.

Location: From Eureka, drive a half mile north on US 93. Turn west on Highway 37 and proceed five miles to Rexford, then continue 16 miles southwest on Highway 37 to the campground.

Trip note: This popular spot is set on the eastern shore of Lake Koocanusa. The campsites are open and unshaded and have picnic tables. Fishing can be good at this lake. Inch Mountain looms to the east at 6,210 feet.

18) CAMP 32

Reference: on Pinkham Creek, Kootenai National Forest; map M1, grid c3.

Campsites, facilities: There are five tent sites. Picnic tables and well water are provided. Pit toilets and firewood are also available.

Reservations, fee: No reservations necessary; no fee. Open mid-May to mid-October.

Who to contact: Phone Kootenai National Forest at (406) 296-2536, or write Eureka Ranger District, 1299 Highway 93 North, Eureka, MT 59917.

Location: From Eureka, drive a half mile north on US 93. Turn west on Highway 37 and proceed five miles to Rexford. From Rexford, drive 2.5 miles south on Highway 37, then turn southeast on Forest Service Road 856 and drive two miles. Continue for 1.5 miles southwest on Forest Service Road 7182 to the campground.

Trip note: This site is just far enough off the highway to get missed by all out-of-towners. In many ways, it is a very attractive spot. The camp is set on Pinkham Creek about a half mile west of Pinkham Falls (a definite must-go sidetrip). In addition, it is just four miles from the shore of Kootenai Lake. Overall, this site is primitive, small and quiet.

19) ROCK LAKE

Reference: in Kootenai National Forest; map M1, grid c4.

Campsites, facilities: There are five tent sites. Picnic tables are provided. Pit toilets and firewood are also available. There is **no piped water.** Pets are permitted on leashes. Boat launching facilities for small boats are nearby.

Reservations, fee: No reservations necessary; no fee. Open mid-May to mid-November.

Who to contact: Phone Kootenai National Forest at (406) 882-4451, or write to Fortine Ranger District, P.O. Box 116, Fortine, MT 59918.

Location: From Eureka, drive four miles south on the Frank Lake Road to the campground.

Trip note: This camp is set along the south shore of little Rock Lake, one of a cluster of little lakes south of Eureka. A primitive road leads to nearby Timber Lake. There is no fishing in Rock Lake. Hikers should consider exploring the myriad of trails in the forest east of US 93.

20) DOG CREEK

Reference: north of Whitefish; map M1, grid c5.

Campsites, facilities: There are 15 tent sites and 20 drive-through sites for trailers or motor homes of any length. Piped water and picnic tables are provided. Flush toilets, sanitary disposal station, showers, firewood, recreation hall, a store, laundromat, ice and a playground are also available. Electricity and sewer hookups are available at an additional charge. Pets and motorbikes are permitted. Boat rentals are nearby.

Reservations, fee: Reservations accepted; $10-$15 fee per night; MasterCard and Visa accepted. Open all year.

Who to contact: Phone (406) 881-2472, or write to P.O. Box 68, Olney, MT 59927.

Location: From Whitefish, drive 21 miles north on Highway 93 to the campground.

Trip note: This is a good layover spot for cruisers on US 93 looking to take a break. It's a pretty area with hiking trails routed into the surrounding Flathead National Forest. The camp rests on 80 acres with a stream flowing through it; streamside sites are available. Recreation options include hiking and biking on the many trails in the park.

---

21) SOUTH DICKEY LAKE

Reference: in Kootenai National Forest; map M1, grid c5.

Campsites, facilities: There are 10 sites for tents, trailers and motor homes up to 32 feet long. Picnic tables are provided. Piped water, pit toilets and firewood are also available. A store and ice are located within five miles. Pets are permitted on leashes. Boat docks and launching facilities for small boats are nearby.

Reservations, fee: No reservations necessary; $5 fee per night. Open mid-May to mid-November.

Who to contact: Phone Kootenai National Forest at (406) 882-4451, or write to Fortine Ranger District, P.O. Box 116, Fortine, MT 59918.

Location: From Stryker, drive 4.7 miles northwest on US 93. Turn southwest on County Road 3785 and drive one mile, then turn southeast on Forest Service Road 3788 and continue for two miles to the campground.

Trip note: Of the two camps on the lake, this one is more desirable, primarily because it is set on the south side of the lake and away from the highway. It is, however, set near the Burlington Northern Railroad, so you may just be exchanging the sound of cars for trains. In any case, it's a pretty campground, with full boating facilities for anglers and even a swimming beach.

---

22) NORTH DICKEY LAKE

Reference: in Kootenai National Forest; map M1, grid c5.

Campsites, facilities: There are four tent sites and 12 sites for trailers and motor homes up to 32 feet long. Picnic tables are provided. Piped water, pit toilets and firewood are also available. A store and ice are located within five miles. Pets are permitted on leashes. Boat docks and launching facilities for small boats are nearby.

Reservations, fee: No reservations necessary; $5 fee per night. Open mid-May to mid-November.

Who to contact: Phone Kootenai National Forest at (406) 882-4451, or write to Fortine Ranger District, P.O. Box 116, Fortine, MT 59918.

Location: From Stryker, drive 4.7 miles northwest on US 93, then a half mile west on County road 3785 to the campground.

Trip note: Easy access is the bonus here. The lake sits aside the highway, and the campground is located on the north shore of the lake. The Mount Marston National Recreation Trail is routed to the north of the camp, leading to the top of Mount Marston at 7,330 feet. There are miles of trails available north of there. If tent spaces at this camp are full, check out nearby South Dickey Lake.

---

23) BIG CREEK

Reference: on the North Fork of Flathead River, Flathead National Forest; map M1, grid c7.

Campsites, facilities: There are 22 sites for tents, trailers and motor homes up to 22 feet long. Picnic tables are provided. Piped water, vault toilets and firewood are also available. Pets are permitted on leashes. Boat launching facilities are nearby.

Reservations, fee: No reservations necessary; $5 fee per night. Open late May to late September.

Who to contact: Phone Flathead National Forest at (406) 892-4372, or write to Tally Lake Ranger District, 1335 Highway 93 West, Whitefish, MT 59937-3153.

Location: From the town of Columbia Falls, drive 21 miles north on Forest Service Road 210 to the campground.

Trip note: A good alternative to some of the crowded camps at nearby Glacier National Park, this lesser-used Forest Service camp is set on the North Fork of the Flathead River and is near the confluence with Big Creek. It is set just a short drive from the park entrance.

---

24) FISH CREEK

Reference: on Lake McDonald, Glacier National Park; map M1, grid c8.

Campsites, facilities: There are 180 sites for tents, trailers, or motor homes up to 26 feet long. Picnic tables are provided. Piped water, flush toilets and sanitary disposal station are also available. Some facilities are **wheelchair accessible.** Pets are permitted on leashes.

Reservations, fee: No reservations necessary; $10 fee per night. Open mid-June to late August.

Who to contact: Phone Waterton-Glacier International Peace Park at (406) 888-5441, or write P.O. Box 128, West Glacier, MT 59936.

Location: From the town of West Glacier, drive four miles north on Camas Road to the campground.

Trip note: This is another giant campground on Lake McDonald in Glacier National Park. A visitors center is located at the turnoff to the lake; rangers will be happy to provide you with maps and information. Boating and fishing are two options on Lake McDonald.

---

25) SPRAGUE CREEK

Reference: on Lake McDonald, Glacier National Park; map M1, grid c8.

Campsites, facilities: There are 25 sites for tents, trailers and motor homes up to 22 feet long. Picnic tables are provided. Piped water and flush toilets are also available. A store, coffee shop and ice are located within one mile. Some facilities are **wheelchair accessible.** Pets are permitted on leashes.

Reservations, fee: No reservations necessary; $10 fee per night. Open late June to early September.

Who to contact: Phone Waterton-Glacier International Peace Park at (406) 888-5441, or write P.O. Box 128, West Glacier, MT 59936.

Location: From the town of West Glacier, drive 10 miles northeast on Going-to-the-Sun Road.

Trip note: Located on the north end of Lake McDonald, this is a popular spot in Glacier National Park. This is by far the smallest of three camps on the lake, and with Sprague Creek running alongside, has a nice charm to it. The other camps (Apgar and Fish Creek) are more suited for boaters. This one is better for hikers and has many trails leading into the adjacent wildlands.

---

26) MANY GLACIER

Reference: on Lake Sherburne, Glacier National Park; map M1, grid c9.

Campsites, facilities: There are 117 sites for trailers or motor homes up to 35 feet long. Picnic tables are provided. Piped water, flush toilets, sanitary disposal station, a store and coffee shop are also available. Ice is located within one mile. Some facilities are **wheelchair accessible.** Pets are permitted on leashes. Boat docks and rentals are nearby.

Reservations, fee: No reservations necessary; $10 fee per night. Open mid-June to mid-September.

Who to contact: Phone Waterton-Glacier International Peace Park at (406) 888-5441, or write P.O. Box 128, West Glacier, MT 59936.

Location: From Babb, drive nine miles west on Many Glaciers Road to the campground.

Trip note: No tenters need apply. This huge site is for motor homes and trailers only. The park is set on Lake Sherburne in Glacier National Park where you can rent your own boat. Horseback riding is also an option. There are many excellent trails in the park; see a park map for details.

27) AVALANCHE

Reference: on Avalanche Creek, Glacier National Park; map M1, grid c9.

Campsites, facilities: There are 87 sites for trailers or motor homes up to 26 feet long. Picnic tables are provided. Piped water, flush toilets and a sanitary disposal station are also available. Some facilities are **wheelchair accessible.** Pets are permitted on leashes.

Reservations, fee: No reservations necessary; $8 fee per night. Open mid-June to late August.

Who to contact: Phone Waterton-Glacier International Peace Park at (406) 888-5441, or write P.O. Box 128, West Glacier, MT 59936.

Location: From the town of West Glacier, drive 12 miles northeast on Going-to-the-Sun Road.

Trip note: This is one of the few motor home/trailer-only campgrounds in Glacier National Park, but it's a good one, particularly if you want to try a hike. A trail from camp follows Avalanche Creek for several miles to Avalanche Lake. This camp gets heavy pressure in the midsummer months, so get there early.

28) DORR SKEELS

Reference: on Bull Lake, Kootenai National Forest; map M1, grid d0.

Campsites, facilities: There are six sites for tents, trailers and motor homes up to 32 feet long. Picnic tables are provided. Pit toilets and firewood are also available. There is **no piped water.** Pets are permitted on leashes.

Reservations, fee: No reservations necessary; no fee. Open mid-May to mid-September.

Who to contact: Phone Kootenai National Forest at (406) 295-4693, or write to Three Rivers Ranger District, 1437 North Highway 2, Troy, MT 59935.

Location: From Troy, drive three miles southeast on US 2. Turn south on Highway 56 and drive 12.5 miles, then one mile west on the campground entrance road.

Trip note: Like Bad Medicine Camp, this campground is also set on Bull Lake. This particular camp is ideal for picnics (eight picnic tables) and also good for swimming if you don't mind cool water. Boat launch, docks, and a swimming beach makes this a popular spot for local people and for waterskiing.

29) SPAR LAKE

Reference: in Kootenai National Forest; map M1, grid d0.

Campsites, facilities: There are eight sites for tents, trailers and motor homes up to 32 feet long. Picnic tables are provided. Pit toilets and firewood are also available. Pets are permitted on leashes. Boat launching facilities for small boats are nearby.

Reservations, fee: No reservations necessary; no fee. Open mid-May to late September.

Who to contact: Phone Kootenai National Forest at (406) 295-4693, or write to Three Rivers Ranger District, 1437 North Highway 2, Troy, MT 59935.

Location: From Troy, drive three miles east to Lake Creek Road, then head south for eight miles. The road then becomes Spar Lake Road (Forest Service Road 384). Continue on for 12 miles to the campground.

Trip note: This is an alternative to Bull Lake. It's a farther drive, yes, but far less people come with the bargain. It's a decent-sized lake that's good for fishing, but there is no swimming. A trailhead at the end of Forest Service Road 384 leads south along Cub Creek to Spar Peak (6,585 feet) or southwest along Spar Creek to Little Spar Lake.

---

30) TROY

Reference: near Kootenai Falls; map M1, grid d0.

Campsites, facilities: There are 50 tent sites and 40 sites for trailers and motor homes of any length. Piped water and picnic tables are provided. Flush toilets, bottled gas, sanitary disposal station, showers, firewood, a store, laundromat, ice and a playground are also available. Pets and motorbikes are permitted.

Reservations, fee: Reservations accepted; $10-$15 fee per night; MasterCard and Visa accepted. Open May to late October.

Who to contact: Phone (406) 295-5959, or write 2898 Highway 2N, Troy, MT 59935.

Location: From Troy, drive two miles northwest on US 2.

Trip note: This privately developed motor home park covers 10 acres and offers shaded campsites surrounded by fir and cedar trees. It is set near the Kootenai River where the fishing is good. Tenters can set up camp right next to the river. A good sidetrip is to the southeast end of town to Kootenai Falls.

---

31) MEADOWLARK GROUP PARK

Reference: near Kootenai River; map M1, grid d1.

Campsites, facilities: There are eight tent sites and 16 sites for trailers or motor homes of any length. Electricity, piped water, sewer hookups and picnic tables are provided. Flush toilets and showers are also available. A sanitary disposal station, a store, coffee shop, laundromat and ice are located within one mile. Pets are permitted on leashes.

Reservations, fee: Reservations accepted; $8-$10 fee per night. Open April to November.

Who to contact: Phone (406) 293-4825, or write 676 US Highway 2 West, Libby, MT 59923.

Location: In Libby, drive to 676 US Highway 2 West.

Trip note: Motor home cruisers might want to call this home for a while. The Kootenai River along with the surrounding mountains provide a good feel. Sidetrip possibilities include the local golf course, or visiting the Heritage Museum in town. Camp Fireman Memorial provides another option in town.

---

32) FIREMAN MEMORIAL PARK

Reference: in Libby; map M1, grid d1.

Campsites, facilities: There are 15 sites for tents, trailers and motor homes. Picnic tables are provided. Piped water, chemical toilets, sanitary disposal station and a playground are also available. A store, coffee shop, laundromat and ice are located within one mile. Pets are permitted on leashes.

Reservations, fee: No reservations necessary; no fee. Three-day stay limit. Open mid-April to October.

Who to contact: Phone (406) 293-3832/2731, or write P.O. Box 704, Libby, MT 59923.

Location: This campground is located at the west end of Libby on US 2.

Trip note: This popular city park gets fairly heavy use in the summer season. It's not the most scenic location, as it's set in town, but grassy sites are available and hey, you can't beat the price. A riding stable is nearby, and some trails are available in the park. See trip note for Meadowlark Group Camp for other details.

---

33) ROCKY GORGE

Reference: on Lake Koocanusa, Kootenai National Forest, map M1, grid d3.

Campsites, facilities: There are 120 sites for tents, trailers and motor homes of any length. Picnic tables, piped water and vault toilets are provided. A boat dock and launching facilities are available nearby. Pets are permitted on leashes.

Reservations, fee: No reservations necessary; $6 fee per night. Open early June to mid-September.

Who to contact: Phone Kootenai National Forest at (406) 296-2536 or write to Eureka Ranger District, 1299 Highway 93 North, Eureka, MT 59917.

Location: From Eureka, drive a half mile north on US 93 to Rexford. Turn south on Highway 37 and drive 23 miles to the campground.

Trip note: This is one of the most popular camps at Lake Koocanusa. It's set near the shore, with large, open sites, some partially shaded. The nearby boat ramp is a bonus for anglers, and this lake is known for good fishing.

34) YARNELL ISLAND BOAT-IN

Reference: on Lake Koocanusa, Kootenai National Forest; map M1, grid d3.

Campsites, facilities: There are eight tent sites. Picnic tables are provided. There is **no piped water.** A store, coffee shop and ice are located within five miles. Pets are permitted on leashes. Boat docks, launching facilities and rentals are nearby.

Reservations, fee: No reservations necessary; no fee. Open June to late September.

Who to contact: Phone Kootenai National Forest at (406) 293-7773, or write 12557 Highway 37 North, Libby, MT 59923.

Location: This boat-in campground is accessible from one of several launches on Lake Koocanusa. One way is to travel 25 miles northeast of Libby on Highway 37 to the Koocanusa Marina, then travel two miles southwest by boat to the island.

Trip note: This is one of the few boat-in only campgrounds in the Rocky Mountains, a primitive camp set on a pretty, secluded island in the 90-mile long Lake Koocanusa. Go by canoe, power boat or kayak, but go. Boat-in camping is a one-of-a-kind adventure.

35) McGILLIVRAY

Reference: on Lake Koocanusa, Kootenai National Forest; map M1, grid d3.

Campsites, facilities: There are 50 sites for tents, trailers and motor homes of any length. Picnic tables are provided. Piped water, flush toilets and firewood are also available. Pets and motorbikes are permitted. Some facilities are **wheelchair accessible.** Boat docks and launching facilities are nearby.

Reservations, fee: No reservations necessary; $6 fee per night. Open mid-May to late September.

Who to contact: Phone Kootenai National Forest at (406) 293-7773, or write 12557 Highway 37 North, Libby, MT 59923.

Location: From Libby, drive 14 miles northeast on Highway 37. Turn north on Forest Service Road 228 and continue for 10.5 miles to the campground.

Trip note: This is a developed Forest Service camp set on the shore of giant Lake Koocanusa, directly across from Koocanusa Marina. It is a good base camp for campers and fishermen. The full service marina and nearby riding stable provide sidetrip options. A resident campground host is in attendance from June to September. An alternative camp is Barron to the north.

36) TIMBERLANE GROUP CAMP

Reference: on Pipe Creek, Kootenai National Forest; map M1, grid d3.

Campsites, facilities: There are 14 sites for tents, trailers and motor homes up to 32 feet long. Picnic tables are provided. Hand-pumped water and vault toilets are also available. Pets are permitted on leashes.

Reservations, fee: Reservations required; $25 fee per night. Open mid-May to late September.

Who to contact: Phone Kootenai National Forest at (406) 293-7741, or write Libby Ranger District, 1263 Highway 37 North, Libby, MT 59923.

Location: From Libby, drive a half mile north on Highway 37. Turn north on Pipe Creek Road and continue for 8.1 miles to the campground.

Trip note: Here's a rare offer, and for many, it will be an offer you can't refuse—for $25, you get the whole campground. So if you have a family reunion or club trip coming up, and you want a camp all to yourselves, this is the spot. It's in a pretty, remote setting, set along Pipe Creek. There is direct fishing access from the campground.

---

37) TALLY LAKE

Reference: in Flathead National Forest; map M1, grid d5.

Campsites, facilities: There are 39 sites for tents, trailers and motor homes up to 22 feet long. Picnic tables are provided. Piped water, vault toilets and a sanitary disposal station are also available. Pets are permitted on leashes. A boat ramp and launching facilities are nearby. Some facilities are **wheelchair accessible.**

Reservations, fee: Reservations required; $6 fee per night. Open Memorial Day to Labor Day.

Who to contact: Phone Flathead National Forest at (406) 862-2508, or write to Tally Lake Ranger District, 1935 Highway 93 West, Whitefish, MT 59937.

Location: From Whitefish, drive four miles west on US 93, then 15 miles west on Forest Service Road 113 to the campground.

Trip note: The camp is set at the north shore Tally Lake, a pretty lake in Flathead National Forest. It's a good spot for boating and fishing. There is also a swimming beach. A trail that starts at the southwest end of the lake, Tally Mountain-Billy Creek Trail, is routed into the adjacent wildlands.

---

38) WHITEFISH LAKE STATE RECREATION AREA

Reference: near Whitefish; map M1, grid d6.

Campsites, facilities: There are 25 sites for tents, trailers and motor homes up to 30 feet long. Picnic tables are provided. Piped water, pit toilets and firewood are also available. Bottled gas is located within one mile. Pets are permitted on leashes. Boat launching facilities are nearby.

Reservations, fee: No reservations necessary; $5-$7 fee per night. Open mid-May to mid-September.

Who to contact:: Phone the Montana Division of Fish, Wildlife and Parks at (406) 444-2535, or write 1420 East Sixth Avenue, Helena, MT 59620.

Location: From Whitefish, drive a half mile west on US 93 to milepost 129. Turn north and continue one mile north to the campground.

Trip note: This is a popular area for both locals and out-of-towners during summer. Boating, fishing and swimming are all popular here. It's a beautiful area, surrounded by evergreens and mountains. By the way, if you don't live around these parts, you don't want to know how cold it gets in the winter here.

---

39) WEST GLACIER KOA

Reference: near West Glacier; map M1, grid d7.

Campsites, facilities: There are 16 tent sites and 100 sites for trailers and motor homes of any length. Picnic tables are provided. Flush toilets, bottled gas, sanitary disposal station, showers, recreation hall, a store, laundromat, ice and a playground are also available. Electricity, piped water, sewer hookups and firewood are available at an additional charge. Pets and motorbikes are permitted.

Reservations, fee: Reservations accepted; $13-$25 fee per night; MasterCard and Visa accepted. Open May to late September.

Who to contact: Phone (406) 387-5341, or write P.O. Box 215, West Glacier, MT 59936.

Location: From the town of West Glacier, drive 2.5 miles west on US 2. Look for the big KOA sign and travel one mile east to the campground.

Trip note: A shaded forest of lodgepole pines covers some 20 acres of private parkland here. Hiking trails in the area are just across the road from the lakes. A nearby riding stable provides a recreation possibility.

---

40) LASALLE

Reference: near Columbia Falls; map M1, grid d7.

Campsites, facilities: There are six tent sites and 35 sites for trailers and motor homes. Electricity, piped water, sewer hookups and picnic tables are provided. Flush toilets, showers, recreation hall, laundromat, ice and a playground are also available. Pets and motorbikes are permitted.

Reservations, fee: Reservations accepted; $10-$15 fee per night; MasterCard and Visa accepted. Open year-round.

Who to contact: Phone (406) 892-4668, or write 5618 Highway 2 West, Columbia Falls, MT 59912.

Location: From the town of Columbia Falls, drive 4.5 miles southwest on US 2 to the campground.

Trip note: This privately developed campground has easy access from the highway. A golf course and riding stable provide recreation possibilities. For a side trip, visit Columbia Falls, which offers many other recreational options.

---

41) APGAR

Reference: on Lake McDonald, Glacier National Park; map M1, grid d8.

Campsites, facilities: There are 196 sites for tents, trailers and motor homes up to 35 feet long. Picnic tables are provided. Piped water, flush toilets, sanitary disposal station, a store and coffee shop are also available. Bottled gas and ice are located within one mile. Some facilities are **wheelchair accessible.** Pets are permitted on leashes. Boat facilities and rentals are nearby.

Reservations, fee: No reservations necessary; $10 fee per night. Open June through September, including limited and some off-season weekends.

Who to contact: Phone Waterton-Glacier International Peace Park at (406) 888-5441, or write P.O. Box 128, West Glacier, MT 59936.

Location: From the town of West Glacier, drive two miles north on the park entrance road to the campground. It's located right near the park headquarters.

Trip note: This is one of three camps set aside Lake McDonald in world famous Glacier National Park. There is a swimming beach and boat launching facilities nearby, so it's a popular spot. Expect company from July through August.

---

42) SAN-SUZ-ED TRAILER PARK

Reference: near Glacier National Park; map M1, grid d8.

Campsites, facilities: There are 50 tent sites and 70 sites for trailers and motor homes of any length. Electricity, piped water, sewer hookups and picnic tables are provided. Flush toilets, showers, gift shop, a coffee shop, a store, laundromat, ice and a playground are also available. Pets are permitted on leashes. Boat docks, launching facilities and rentals are nearby. **Wheelchair accessible** facilities are available.

Reservations, fee: Reservations accepted; $15-$17 fee per night. Open all year.

Who to contact: Phone (406) 387-5280, or write P.O. Box 387, West Glacier, MT 59936.

Location: From the town of West Glacier, drive three miles west on US 2 to the campground entrance, located between mileposts 150 and 151. This campground is located 2.5 miles from the entrance to Glacier National Park.

Trip note: We didn't ask how this park got its name, and after deliberating, decided we didn't want to know anyway. Heh, heh. The park covers 30 acres and has several small lakes nearby, and of course, the magnificent Glacier National Park is located directly north. You get a choice of sunny or shaded sites, with hard-packed gravel sites for wheelchair campers. Tell San, Suz and Ed we sent you.

43) BAD MEDICINE

Reference: on Bull Lake, Kootenai National Forest; map M1, grid e0.

Campsites, facilities: There are 16 sites for tents, trailers and motor homes up to 32 feet long. Picnic tables are provided. Piped water, vault toilets and firewood are also available. A store and ice are located within six miles. Pets are permitted on leashes. Boat docks, launching facilities and rentals are nearby.

Reservations, fee: No reservations necessary; $5 fee per night. Open mid-May to late September.

Who to contact: Phone Kootenai National Forest at (406) 295-4693, or write to Three Rivers Ranger District, 1437 North Highway 2, Troy, MT 59935.

Location: From Troy, drive three miles southeast on US 2. Continue 18.8 miles south on Highway 56, then turn west on Forest Service Road 398 and drive one mile. Continue for one mile north on Forest Service Road 8019.

Trip note: This is one of two camps (the other is Dorr Skeels Camp) that sit along five-mile-long Bull Lake. This one is at the south end of the lake. Bull Lake is popular, getting fairly heavy use compared to other parts of the region. It offers every recreation option you could want: fishing, boating, swimming and hiking. A good sidetrip is Ross Creek Falls, located about 2.5 miles west of camp on Highway 56, and Ross Creek Cedars Scenic Area, about two miles west of the falls.

44) BULL RIVER

Reference: on Cabinet Gorge Reservoir, Kootenai National Forest; map M1, grid e0.

Campsites, facilities: There are 18 sites for tents, trailers and motor homes up to 32 feet long. Picnic tables and fire grates are provided. Piped water, flush toilets, firewood, a boat dock and launching facilities for small boats are also available. Showers, a store, coffee shop, laundromat and ice are located within one mile. Pets are permitted on leashes.

Reservations, fee: No reservations necessary; $6 fee per night. Open May to late October.

Who to contact: Phone Kootenai National Forest at (406) 827-3533 or write to Cabinet Ranger District, 2693 Highway 200, Trout Creek, MT 59874.

Location: From Noxon, drive about four miles northwest on Highway 200 to the campground.

Trip note: There are a lot of recreational options at this camp: you can hunker down here to the camp set at the confluence of Cabinet Gorge

Reservoir and Bull River, swim and fish on Bull River Bay, or maybe explore some of the many hiking trails in the area. Or, you can head south a few miles to Noxon Reservoir and go boating. The Cabinet Mountains offer a beautiful setting. The Bitterroot Mountains are to the immediate west.

45) HOWARD LAKE

Reference: in Kootenai National Forest; map M1, grid e1.

Campsites, facilities: There are nine sites for tents, trailers and motor homes up to 16 feet long. Picnic tables are provided. Hand-pumped water, vault toilets and firewood are also available. Some facilities are **wheelchair accessible.** Pets are permitted on leashes. Boat docks and launching facilities for small boats are nearby.

Reservations, fee: No reservations necessary; $5 fee per night. Open mid-May to early October.

Who to contact: Phone Kootenai National Forest at (406) 293-7741, or write to Libby Ranger District, 1263 Highway 37 North, Libby, MT 59923.

Location: From Libby, drive 12 miles south on US 2, then 11.6 miles south on Forest Service Roads 231 and 4779 to the campground.

Trip note: Howard Lake, though small and remote, has everything a camper could want—fishing, boat launching facilities, nearby hiking trails, even a swimming beach. This idyllic spot is set aside the lake, right below Midas Point, and on the edge of the Cabinet Mountains Wilderness to the west. Nearby Forest Service dirt roads provide access to wilderness trailheads. A map is essential.

46) HAPPY'S INN

Reference: near Thompson Lake; map M1, grid e3.

Campsites, facilities: There are 20 tent sites and 20 sites for trailers or motor homes of any length. Electricity, piped water and sewer hookups are provided. Flush toilets, bottled gas, sanitary disposal station, showers, recreation hall, a coffee shop, laundromat and ice are also available. No pets allowed. Boat launching facilities are nearby.

Reservations, fee: Reservations accepted; $2-$10 fee per night; MasterCard and Visa accepted. Open all year.

Who to contact: Phone (406) 293-7810 or write to 39704 US Highway 2 South, Libby, MT 59923.

Location: From Libby, drive 40 miles southeast on US 2.

Trip note: This is a privately operated camp covering 30 acres. The sites are in a large, grassy area, near Thompson Lake. The lake provides an excellent sidetrip, with fishing, boating and swimming among your options.

47) ASHLEY LAKE STATE RECREATION AREA

Reference: north of Kalispell; map M1, grid e5.

Campsites, facilities: There are 12 sites for tents. Picnic tables are provided. Pit toilets are provided, but there is **no piped water.** Pets are permitted on leashes. Boat launching facilities are nearby.

Reservations, fee: No reservations necessary; no fee. Open mid-May to mid-September.

Who to contact: Phone Montana Department of Fish, Wildlife and Parks at (406) 444-2535, or write 1420 East Sixth Avenue, Helena, MT 59620.

Location: From Kalispell, drive 16 miles west on US 2 to milepost 105, then turn north on a county road (trailers not recommended) and continue 13 miles to the campground.

Trip note: This is a good fishing spot that is popular among anglers out of Kalispell. The camp is set on the north shore of Ashley Lake. Forest wildlands border the lake to the north.

48) REST-A-DAY

Reference: near Ashley Lake; map M1, grid e5.

Campsites, facilities: There are seven tent sites and 22 sites for trailers or motor homes of any length. Electricity, piped water and picnic tables are provided. Flush toilets, bottled gas, sanitary disposal station, showers, firewood, a store, laundromat, ice and a playground are also available. Pets and motorbikes are permitted.

Reservations, fee: Reservations accepted; $7-$11 fee per night; MasterCard and Visa accepted. Open all year.

Who to contact: Phone (406) 854-2292 or write to 8405 Highway 2 West, Marion, MT 59925.

Location: From Kalispell, drive 20 miles west on US 2 to the campground.

Trip note: This is a good layover spot for folks looking to "lay-up" for the night after cruising Highway 2. It is directly off the highway. The park covers seven acres and is quite pretty, surrounded by lodgepole pines and mountains. The nearest lake is Bitterroot Lake, five miles away, with several recreation options. See trip note for Bitterroot Lake State Park.

49) BITTEROOT LAKE STATE PARK

Reference: on Bitterroot Lake; map M1, grid e5.

Campsites, facilities: There are 20 sites for tents, trailers and motor homes up to 25 feet long. Picnic tables are provided. Piped water, pit toilets and firewood are also available. Pets are permitted on leashes. Boat launching facilities are nearby.

Reservations, fee: No reservations necessary; $4-$6 fee per night. Open mid-May to mid-September.

Who to contact: Phone Montana Department of Fish, Wildlife and Parks at (406) 444-2535 or write to 1420 East Sixth Avenue, Helena, MT 59620.

Location: From Kalispell, drive 20 miles west on US 2 to milepost 101, then continue five miles north to the campground.

Trip note: This 30-acre state park is set aside Bitterroot Lake (a small lake compared to massive Flathead Lake to the southeast). Boating, fishing and swimming are popular at this lake. This site is easy to reach from US 2 and is the only campground at the lake.

---

50) GREENWOOD TRAILER VILLAGE

Reference: in Kalispell; map M1, grid e7.

Campsites, facilities: There are 25 tent sites and 45 drive-through sites for trailers or motor homes of any length. Picnic tables are provided. Flush toilets, sanitary disposal station, showers, cable TV, laundromat and ice are also available. Electricity, piped water and sewer hookups are available at an additional charge. Bottled gas, a store and coffee shop are located within one mile. Pets and motorbikes are permitted.

Reservations, fee: Reservations accepted; $10-$15.50 fee per night. Open April to late October.

Who to contact: Phone (406) 257-7719, or write 1100 East Oregon, Kalispell, MT 59901.

Location: This campground is located in Kalispell. From the town at the junction of US 2 and Highway 93, drive a quarter of a mile east on US 2 to the campground.

Trip note: This is one of two motor home parks in the Kalispell area. This one is located right on the city limits, close to shopping centers and restaurants. It is completely paved, with graveled sites and one side of the park is shaded by huge Douglas fir trees. Not exactly the wilderness, but not bad for the city.

---

51) ROCKY MOUNTAIN HI

Reference: near Flathead Lake; map M1, grid e7.

Campsites, facilities: There are 15 tent sites and 97 sites for trailers or motor homes. Picnic tables are provided. Flush toilets, sanitary disposal station, showers, recreation hall, a store, laundromat, ice and a playground are also available. Electricity, piped water, sewer hookups and firewood are available at an additional charge. Bottled gas is located within one mile. Pets and motorbikes are permitted. Boat docks are nearby.

Reservations, fee: Reservations accepted; $10-$15 fee per night. Open all year.

Who to contact: Phone (406) 755-9573, or write 825 Helena Flats, Kalispell, MT 59901.

Location: From Kalispell, drive four miles east on US 2. Turn east at the reserve entrance and follow the signs to the campground.

Trip note: This is an okay layover spot for motor home cruisers looking for a spot to park it in the Kalispell area. The park covers seven acres, and has all the amenities. It is paved, with some grassy sites.

---

52) GLACIER PINE RV

Reference: near Flathead River; map M1, grid e7.

Campsites, facilities: There are 75 tent sites and 149 drive-through sites for trailers or motor homes of any length. Electricity, piped water and picnic tables are provided. Flush toilets, sanitary disposal station, showers, firewood, a store, laundromat, ice and a playground are also available. Sewer hookups are available at an additional charge. Bottled gas is located within one mile. Pets and motorbikes are permitted.

Reservations, fee: Reservations accepted; $8-$10 fee per night; MasterCard and Visa accepted. Open April to November.

Who to contact: Phone (406) 752-2760, or write 1850 Highway 35 East, Kalispell, MT 59901.

Location: From Kalispell, drive 1.5 miles east on Highway 35 to the campground.

Trip note: This privately owned park covers 18 acres and sits near the Flathead River. It's one of three motor home parks in the immediate area. This is by far the largest, and offers every convenience a camper could want, with the exception, perhaps, of privacy.

---

53) HANDKERCHIEF LAKE

Reference: on Handkerchief Lake, Flathead National Forest; map M1, grid e8.

Campsites, facilities: There are nine sites for tents only. Picnic tables are provided. Vault toilets are also available. There is **no piped water.** Pets are permitted on leashes. Boat docks are nearby.

Reservations, fee: No reservations necessary; no fee. Open June to mid-September.

Who to contact: Phone Flathead National Forest at (406) 387-5243 or write to Hungry Horse Ranger District, P.O. Box 340, Hungry Horse, MT 59919.

Location: From Hungry Horse, drive 35 miles southeast on Forest Service Road 895, then two miles northwest on Forest Service Road 897 to the campground.

Trip note: This is a small, primitive camp set aside Handkerchief Lake at 3,920 feet elevation. It's often overlooked because of its proximity to huge Hungry Horse Reservoir. A trail starts at camp that leads into the Jewel Basin Hiking Area. There are many lakes here with hungry trout, Handkerchief Lake included. There is fishing access directly from the campground.

54) LAKEVIEW

Reference: on Hungry Horse Reservoir, Flathead National Forest; map M1, grid e8.

Campsites, facilities: There are five sites for tents, trailers and motor homes up to 21 feet long. Picnic tables are provided. Vault toilets are also available. There is **no piped water.** Pets are permitted on leashes.

Reservations, fee: No reservations necessary; no fee. Open June to mid-September.

Who to contact: Phone Flathead National Forest at (406) 387-5243 or write to Hungry Horse Ranger District, P.O. Box 340, Hungry Horse, MT 59919.

Location: From Hungry Horse, drive 24 miles southeast on Forest Service Road 895 to the campground.

Trip note: Hungry Horse Reservoir is a huge, long lake, but this spot is tiny, quiet and primitive, with direct fishing access. If there's anybody here, you can drive 10 miles farther south on Forest Service Road 895 to Graves Bay where we discovered another small campground.

55) LOST JOHNNY POINT

Reference: on Hungry Horse Reservoir, Flathead National Forest; map M1, grid e8.

Campsites, facilities: There are 26 sites for tents, trailers and motor homes up to 22 feet long. Picnic tables and pit toilets are also available. There is **no piped water**. Some facilities are **wheelchair accessible.** Pets are permitted on leashes. Boat docks and launching facilities are nearby.

Reservations, fee: No reservations necessary; $4 fee per night. Open seasonally and as weather permits.

Who to contact: Phone Custer National Forest at (406) 387-5243, or write Hungry Horse Ranger District, P.O. Box 340, Hungry Horse, MT 59919.

Location: From Hungry Horse, drive nine miles southeast on Forest Service Road 895 to the campground.

Trip note: This is one of several camps on Hungry Horse Reservoir. This one is located on the northwestern end, and is the closest to the dam. Hungry Horse is a giant reservoir, good for power boating and fishing for cutthroat trout, as well as swimming. The Jewel Basin Hiking Area is located in the high country west of the reservoir.

56) MURRAY BAY COMPLEX

Reference: on Hungry Horse Reservoir, Flathead National Forest; map M1, grid e8.

Campsites, facilities: There are 46 sites for tents, trailers or motor homes up to 22 feet long. Picnic tables are provided. Pit toilets and piped water are also available. Pets are permitted on leashes. Boat docks and launching facilities are nearby.

Reservations, fee: No reservations necessary; $4 fee per night. Open seasonally and as weather permits.

Who to contact: Phone Flathead National Forest at (406) 387-5243, or write Hungry Horse Ranger District, P.O. Box 340, Hungry Horse, MT 59919.

Location: From Martin City, drive 22 miles southeast on Forest Service Road 38. The campground is on the east shore of Hungry Horse Reservoir.

Trip note: How did Hungry Horse Reservoir get its name, you ask? Back in one of the punishing winters in the early 1900s, a couple of burly pack horses (named Tex and Jerry) meandered away from their posts. They managed to survive until they were found a month later, starved and weak. Fortunately, the story has a happy ending: Tex and Jerry were nursed back to health and were able to return to civilization strong and healthy. This camp is set on the northeast side of Hungry Horse Reservoir. Recreation options are detailed in the trip note for Lost Johnny Point Camp.

---

57) ELK ISLAND BOAT-IN

Reference: on Hungry Horse Reservoir, Flathead National Forest; map M1, grid e8.

Campsites, facilities: There are seven tent sites. Picnic tables are provided. Pit toilets and firewood are also available. There is **no piped water.** Pets are permitted on leashes. Boat docks and launching facilities are nearby.

Reservations, fee: No reservations necessary; no fee. Open seasonally and as weather permits.

Who to contact: Phone Flathead National Forest at (406) 387-5243, or write to Hungry Horse Ranger District, P.O. Box 340, Hungry Horse, MT 59919.

Location: From Martin City, drive 13 miles southeast on Forest Service Road 38, then travel two miles southeast by boat to the campground on Elk Island.

Trip note: This is one of the rare boat-in camps in the entire Rocky Mountain region. This spot is nestled on Elk Island at Hungry Horse Reservoir and is one of several camps at the lake. Lost Johnny Point and Murray Bay Complex camps provide drive-to possibilities. See trip notes for those camps for details on Hungry Horse Reservoir.

---

58) BIG EDDY

Reference: on Noxon Reservoir, Kootenai National Forest; map M1, grid f0.

Campsites, facilities: There are four sites for tents, trailers and motor homes up to 32 feet long. Picnic tables and vault toilets are provided. There is **no piped water**. A boat ramp is available. Some facilities are **wheelchair accessible**. Pets are permitted on leashes.

Reservations, fee: No reservations; no fee. Open year-round.

Who to contact: Phone Kootenai National Forest at (406) 827-3533 or write to Cabinet Ranger District, 2693 Highway 200, Trout Creek, MT 59874.

Location: From the town of Trout Creek, drive north on Highway 200 to the campground entrance on the right.

Trip note: This is a small, primitive campground with easy highway access. There is a boat ramp that will accommodate trailers up to 32 feet long, a plus for anglers with larger boats. The fishing in this area is good, and this camp is used primarily by fishermen. An alternative camp is Marten Creek, which is just as primitive but not as easily accessible.

---

59) MARTEN CREEK

Reference: on Noxon Reservoir, Kootenai National Forest; map M1, grid f1.

Campsites, facilities: There are four sites for tents, trailers and motor homes up to 32 feet long. Picnic tables and vault toilets are provided. There is **no piped water**. A boat launch is available. Pets are permitted on leashes.

Reservations, fee: No reservations; no fee. Open year-round.

Who to contact: Phone Kootenai National Forest at (406) 827-3533 or write to Cabinet Ranger District, 2693 Highway 200, Trout Creek, MT 59874.

Location: From the town of Trout Creek, drive seven miles northwest on Marten Creek Road.

Trip note: This a tiny, primitive camp in an exceptionally beautiful location. It is nestled beside Marten Creek Bay on Noxon Reservoir, with excellent fishing access and nearby facilities for boaters. There are also hiking trails close to camp. This camp is little known and little used, so you can fill up your water jug and settle in for a few days for some quiet and privacy.

---

60) NORTH SHORE

Reference: on Noxon Reservoir, Kootenai National Forest; map M1, grid f1.

Campsites, facilities: There are 12 sites for tents, trailers, and motor homes up to 32 feet long. Picnic tables are provided. Piped water, vault toilets, firewood, a boat dock and launching facilities are also available. A store, coffee shop, laundromat and ice are located within three miles. Pets are permitted on leashes.

Reservations, fee: No reservations necessary; $5 fee per night. Open May to late October.

Who to contact: Phone Kootenai National Forest at (406) 827-3533 or write to Cabinet Ranger District, 2693 Highway 200, Trout Creek, MT 59874.

Location: From the town of Trout Creek, drive 2.5 miles northwest on Highway 200, then a half mile west on Swamp Creek Road to the campground.

Trip note: This is one of the few lakeside campgrounds in this area. It's set on the north shore of Noxon Reservoir and is a good spot for boaters and fishermen. A nature trail skirts the camp. The area is surrounded by privately owned land, so don't expect to go tromping off in search of Bigfoot.

---

61) LAKE CREEK

Reference: near Cabinet Mountains Wilderness, Kootenai National Forest; map M1, grid f2.

Campsites, facilities: There are four sites for tents, trailers and motor homes up to 32 feet long. Picnic tables are provided. Hand-pumped water, pit toilets and firewood are also available. Pets are permitted on leashes.

Reservations, fee: No reservations necessary; no fee. Open mid-May to late September.

Who to contact: Phone Kootenai National Forest at (406) 293-7741 or write to Libby Ranger District, 1263 Highway 37 North, Libby, MT 59923.

Location: From Libby, drive 23 miles south on US 2; six miles west on Forest Service Road 231, then one mile west on Forest Service Road 2332 to the campground.

Trip note: This is a good jump-off spot for backpackers looking for a multi-day trip. Several trailheads are located nearby that head into the Cabinet Mountains Wilderness and south along some small streams. Anglers can try their luck at catching the elusive trout in Lake Creek.

---

62) SYLVAN LAKE

Reference: in Kootenai National Forest; map M1, grid f2.

Campsites, facilities: There are five tent sites. Picnic tables are provided. Pit toilets and firewood are also available. There is **no piped water.** Pets are permitted on leashes.

Reservations, fee: No reservations necessary; no fee. Open May to late October.

Who to contact: Phone Kootenai National Forest at (406) 293-7773 or write to 12557 Highway 37 North, Libby, MT 59923.

Location: From the town of Trout Creek, drive one mile west on Highway 200 to Vermilion River Road (Forest Service Road 154). Turn north and drive 17 miles to the campground on the left.

Trip note: Though it's fairly easy to reach, this tiny, primitive spot set along little Sylvan Lake, is little known and little used. Nearby Miller

Creek pours into the lake. Miller Lake, another tiny lake, is just to the north. There's some private land in the area, so watch for no trespassing signs.

63) WILLOW CREEK

Reference: in Kootenai National Forest; map M1, grid f2.

Campsites, facilities: There are four sites for tents, trailers or motor homes up to 16 feet long. Picnic tables are provided. Pit toilets and firewood are also available. There is **no piped water.** Pets are permitted on leashes.

Reservations, fee: No reservations necessary; no fee. Open May to late October.

Who to contact: Phone Kootenai National Forest at (406) 827-3533 or write to Cabinet Ranger District, 2693 Highway 200, Trout Creek, MT 59874.

Location: From the town of Trout Creek, drive one mile west on Highway 200 to Vermilion River Road (Forest Service Road 154). Turn north and drive 18 miles to the campground which is on the right at the junction.

Trip note: Hey, if you don't want to be bugged by anybody, this is the place. There's no one in sight. And it's a pretty spot, too, set at the confluence of Willow Creek and the Vermillion River. Good stream fishing access can be found at the campground, and hiking trails abound. In the fall, this camp is sometimes taken over by big game hunters.

64) LOGAN STATE PARK

Reference: on Thompson Lake; map M1, grid f3.

Campsites, facilities: There are 33 sites for tents, trailers and motor homes up to 30 feet long. Picnic tables are provided. Piped water, flush toilets, sanitary disposal station and firewood are also available. Pets are permitted on leashes. Boat launching facilities are nearby.

Reservations, fee: No reservations necessary; $5-$7 fee per night. Open mid-May to mid-September.

Who to contact: Phone Montana Department of Fish, Wildlife and Parks at (406) 444-2535 or write to P.O. Box 67, Kalispell, MT 59901.

Location: From Kalispell, drive 37 miles west on US 2 to milepost 77 and the campground entrance.

Trip note: This camp is set along Thompson Lake, one of three lakes in the area along US 2 that is easily accessible. The park covers 16 acres. A nature program is available in summer months. Fishing is popular here.

65) McGREGOR LAKE CAMP

Reference: on McGregor Lake, Kootenai National Forest; map M1, grid f4.

Campsites, facilities: There are 17 sites for tents, trailers and motor homes up to 32 feet long. Picnic tables are provided. Piped water and vault toilets are also available. A store, coffee shop and ice are located within two miles. Pets and motorbikes are permitted. Boat docks and launching facilities are nearby.

Reservations, fee: No reservations necessary; $4 fee per night from May to September, no fee from September through April. Open all year with limited winter facilities.

Who to contact: Phone Kootenai National Forest at (406) 293-7773 or write to Fisher River Ranger District, 12557 Highway 37 North, Libby, MT 59923.

Location: From Kalispell, drive 30 miles west on US 2 to the campground entrance.

Trip note: Easy access is the bonus here; McGregor Lake is set right off US 2. Bar Z Peak, at 6,304 feet, looms overhead to the south, with McGregor Peak, at 5,213 feet, to the northeast. If this site is full, consider Bitterroot Lake to the east or Thompson Lake to the west; or if you decide you want to vacation in style, stay at Paradise Lodge on the north side of the lake.

---

66) LAKE MARY RONAN STATE PARK

Reference: on Lake Mary Ronan; map M1, grid f6.

Campsites, facilities: There are 20 sites for tents, trailers and motor homes up to 20 feet long. Picnic tables are provided. Piped water, pit toilets and firewood are also available. Pets are permitted on leashes. Boat launching facilities are nearby.

Reservations, fee: No reservations necessary; $5-$7 fee per night. Open May to late September.

Who to contact: Phone Montana Department of Fish, Wildlife and Parks at (406) 444-2535 or write to 1420 East Sixth Avenue, Helena, MT 59620.

Location: From Polson, drive 22 miles northwest on US 93 to milepost 83 in Dayton, and then travel northwest on the park access road for seven miles to the campground.

Trip note: This 76-acre state park is one of four camps set on little Lake Mary Ronan. It's very pretty, set amidst trees, with some sunny sites. See trip note for Mountain Meadows Resort for details about the lake.

---

67) LAKE MARY RONAN LODGE

Reference: on Lake Mary Ronan; map M1, grid f6.

Campsites, facilities: There are 15 tent sites and 39 sites for trailers or motor homes of any length. Electricity, piped water and picnic tables are provided. Flush toilets, bottled gas, sanitary disposal station, showers, recreation hall, a store, coffee shop, ice and a playground are also available. Sewer hookups are available at an additional charge. Pets and motorbikes are permitted. Boat docks, launching facilities and rentals are nearby.

Reservations, fee: Reservations accepted; $7-$12 fee per night; MasterCard and Visa accepted. Open mid-May to mid-September.

Who to contact: Phone (406) 849-5454 or write to Star Route, Proctor, MT 59929.

Location: From Polson, drive 22 miles north on US 93 to Dayton. Follow the well-marked signs and drive northwest for nine miles to the campground.

Trip note: See trip note for Mountain Meadows Resort for details about Lake Mary Ronan. This park has lake frontage and covers 22 acres. The tent sites are on a pretty, sloping hill overlooking the lake. If you get tired of tent camping, rustic little cabins are also available for rental.

---

68) MOUNTAIN MEADOWS RESORT

Reference: on Lake Mary Ronan, map M1, grid f6.

Campsites, facilities: There are 15 tent sites and 50 sites for trailers or motor homes up to 60 feet long. Picnic tables are provided. Flush toilets, sanitary disposal station, showers, recreation hall, a store, coffee shop, ice and a playground are also available. Electricity, piped water, sewer hookups and firewood are available at an additional charge. Bottled gas is located within one mile. Pets and motorbikes are permitted. Boat docks, launching facilities and rentals are nearby.

Reservations, fee: Reservations accepted; $10-$13 fee per night. Open all year.

Who to contact: Phone (406) 849-5459 or write to Star Route, Proctor, MT 59929.

Location: From Polson, drive 22 miles north on US 93, then seven miles west on Highway 352 to the campground.

Trip note: This is one of four camps located on Lake Mary Ronan (a tiny lake compared to giant Flathead Lake to the west). The camp covers 15 acres in all and offers boat rentals and a dock. Fishing can be good here. Waterskiing is strictly regulated, so anglers can celebrate. A nearby riding stable provides a recreational possibility. You have a choice of sites on the lakeside, in a meadow, in the forest or in an orchard.

---

69) WEST SHORE STATE PARK

Reference: on Flathead Lake; map M1, grid f7.

Campsites, facilities: There are 30 sites for tents, trailers and motor homes up to 20 feet long. Picnic tables are provided. Piped water, pit toilets and firewood are also available. Pets are permitted on leashes. Boat launching facilities are nearby.

Reservations, fee: No reservations necessary; $5-$7 fee per night. Open mid-May to mid-September.

Who to contact: Phone Montana Department of Fish, Wildlife and Parks at (406) 444-2535 or write to 1420 East Sixth Avenue, Helena, MT 59620.

Location: From Kalispell, drive 20 miles south on US 93 to milepost 93, and turn onto the park access road.

Trip note: This is headquarters for the northwestern region of Flathead Lake. The park covers 140 acres and has lakeside access for boating, fishing and swimming. Fishing can be good, but you need a boat to get the best of it. A nature program is offered during summer months. There some pretty hiking trails nearby.

---

70) LAKESHORE TRAILER PARK

Reference: on Flathead Lake; map M1, grid f7.

Campsites, facilities: There are 20 drive-through sites for trailers or motor homes. Electricity, piped water, sewer hookups and picnic tables are provided. Flush toilets and showers are also available. A store, coffee shop and ice are located within one mile. Boat docks, launching facilities and rentals are nearby.

Reservations, fee: Reservations required; $15 fee per night. Open June to mid-September.

Who to contact: Phone (406) 844-3304 or write to P.O. Box 279, Lakeside, MT 59922.

Location: From Kalispell, drive 14 miles south on Highway 93.

Trip note: This is the most northwestern camp at Flathead Lake, and it covers five acres. It's for trailers and motor homes only, with level, grassy sites, most shaded by trees. The park is adjacent to a motel.

---

71) RONDEVUE

Reference: near Flathead Lake; map M1, grid f7.

Campsites, facilities: There are 10 tent sites and 50 sites for trailers or motor homes. Picnic tables are provided. Piped water, flush toilets, and a sanitary disposal station are also available. Showers and firewood are available. A store and laundromat are located within one mile. Pets and motorbikes are permitted. Boat docks, launching facilities and rentals are nearby.

Reservations, fee: Reservations accepted; $12 fee per night. Open May to October.

Who to contact: Phone (406) 837-6973 or write to East Lakeshore, Bigfork, MT 59911.

Location: From Bigfork, drive four miles south on Highway 35 to the campground.

Trip note: This camp is just across the highway from the northeastern shore of Flathead Lake. Fishing can be good by boat at the nearby state recreation area. This camp offers rustic sites in the trees. It's set far enough back from the highway that it's quiet and peaceful. So peaceful, in fact, that we're told the deer and wild turkey often saunter through the campground.

72) WAYFARER STATE PARK

Reference: on Flathead Lake; map M1, grid f7.

Campsites, facilities: There are 20 sites for tents, trailers and motor homes up to 20 feet long. Picnic tables are provided. Piped water, flush toilets and sanitary disposal station are also available. Pets are permitted on leashes.

Reservations, fee: No reservations necessary; $5-$7 fee per night. Open mid-May to mid-September.

Who to contact: Phone Montana Department of Fish, Wildlife and Parks at (406) 444-2535 or write to 1420 East Sixth Avenue, Helena, MT 59620.

Location: In Bigfork, turn west off Highway 35 at milepost 72, and drive a half mile to the campground.

Trip note: This is a state park that covers 49 acres. It is one of three campgrounds set on the northeastern shore of Flathead Lake. This one is the best of the three for tent campers, with pretty sites in both the shade and sun. This is one of the few camps on Flathead Lake that offers hiking trails, and you have fishing and swimming as two other options.

73) SWAN LAKE

Reference: on Swan Lake, Flathead National Forest; map M1, grid f8.

Campsites, facilities: There are 42 sites for tents, trailers and motor homes up to 30 feet long. Picnic tables are provided. Piped water and flush toilets are also available. Sanitary disposal station, showers, a store, coffee shop, laundromat and ice are located within one mile. Pets are permitted on leashes. Boat docks, launching facilities and rentals are nearby. Some facilities are **wheelchair accessible**.

Reservations, fee: No reservations necessary; $7 fee per night. Open late May to early September.

Who to contact: Phone Flathead National Forest at (406) 837-5081 or write to Swan Lake Ranger District, P.O. Box 370, Swan Lake, MT 59911.

Location: From the town of Swan Lake, drive a half mile northwest on Highway 83 to the campground.

Trip note: Set on the southern end of Swan Lake, this site is the best of the three campgrounds here for tenters. There are miles of hiking trails nearby, routed west into the backcountry, and full facilities are available just a few minutes away. Swimming, boating and fishing are some of your other options here.

74) SWAN VILLAGE MARKET

Reference: on Swan Lake; map M1, grid f8.

Campsites, facilities: There are 20 tent sites and eight sites for trailers or motor homes of any length. Electricity, piped water, sewer hookups and picnic tables are provided. Flush toilets, a store, laundromat and ice are also available. Showers are available at an additional charge. Pets are permitted on leashes. Boat docks, launching facilities and rentals are nearby.

Reservations, fee: Reservations accepted; $8-$16 fee per night; MasterCard and Visa accepted. Open May through October.

Who to contact: Phone (406) 886-2303 or write to Highway 83, Swan Lake, MT 59911.

Location: From Bigfork, drive 17 miles south on Highway 83 to the campground.

Trip note: This is one of three campgrounds near Swan Lake, a beautiful, long lake that is often overlooked by visitors because of its close proximity to giant Flathead Lake. This camp is across the highway from the lake in a park atmosphere, with graveled sites surrounded by white pine, spruce and cottonwood trees. Swan Lake is surrounded by National Forest land, which provides good hiking opportunities. See a Flathead National Forest map for trail locations.

75) THOMPSON FALLS STATE PARK

Reference: on Clark Fork; map M1, grid g2.

Campsites, facilities: There are 20 sites for tents, trailers and motor homes up to 20 feet long. Picnic tables are provided. Piped water and pit toilets are also available. Pets are permitted on leashes. Boat launching facilities are nearby.

Reservations, fee: No reservations necessary; $4-$6 fee per night. Open mid-May to mid-September.

Who to contact: Phone (406) 827-3732 or write to Thompson Falls, MT 59873.

Location: From the town of Thompson Falls, drive one mile northwest on Highway 200 to milepost 50 and into the campground.

Trip note: This 50-acre state park has a river, a nearby lake and backpacking trails. This is a popular spot compared to the other camps in the region. It's set on Clark Fork and just two miles north of the dam. Fishing can be excellent at this lake. There are numerous hiking trails in the National Forest land south of the town of Thompson Falls. See a map of Flathead National Forest for details.

76) FISHTRAP LAKE

Reference: near Fishtrap Lake, Lolo National Forest; map M1, grid g3.

Campsites, facilities: There are 11 sites for tents, trailers and motor homes up to 16 feet long. Picnic tables are provided. Hand-pumped water and pit toilets are also available. Pets are permitted on leashes. Boat docks and launching facilities are nearby.

Reservations, fee: No reservations necessary; no fee. Open June to late September.

Who to contact: Phone Lolo National Forest at (406) 826-3821 or write to Plains Ranger District, P.O. Box 429, Plains, MT 59859.

Location: From the town of Thompson Falls, drive five miles east on Highway 200, 13 miles northeast on Forest Service Road 56, 14.7 miles northwest on Forest Service Road 516, and then 1.8 miles west on Forest Service Road 7593.

Trip note: All right, you don't want any company? You get a chance for solitude here. It is set near little Fishtrap Lake. You also have the opportunity to get even farther away from the crowd if you are willing to hike a little. One of the trails in the area leads three miles north to another small lake. Also if you drive about 5.5 miles farther south via Forest Service roads, you will discover Fishtrap Creek Campground, a tiny spot with four campsites and hand-pumped water available. A Forest Service map is advised.

---

77) COPPER KING

Reference: on Thompson River, Lolo National Forest; map M1, grid g3.

Campsites, facilities: There are five sites for tents or trailers up to 12 feet long. Picnic tables are provided. Pit toilets and firewood are also available. There is **no piped water.** Pets are permitted on leashes.

Reservations, fee: No reservations necessary; no fee. Open June to late September.

Who to contact: Phone Lolo National Forest at (406) 826-3821 or write to Plains Ranger District at P.O. Box 429, Plains, MT 59859.

Location: From the town of Thompson Falls, drive five miles east on Highway 200, then four miles northeast on Forest Service Road 56 (Thompson River Road) to the campground.

Trip note: This small, primitive camp is very easy to reach, yet gets relatively little use. It's an ideal spot for a base camp for a fishing trip on the Thompson River. Clark Memorial Camp to the north provides a nearby alternative.

---

78) CLARK MEMORIAL

Reference: on Thompson River, Lolo National Forest; map M1, grid g3.

Campsites, facilities: There are five sites for tents, trailers or motor homes up to 16 feet long. Picnic tables are provided. Pit toilets are also available, but there is **no piped water.** Pets are permitted on leashes.

Reservations, fee: No reservations necessary; no fee. Open June to late September.

Who to contact: Phone Lolo National Forest at (406) 826-3821 or write to Plains Ranger District, P.O. Box 429, Plains, MT 59859.

Location: From the town of Thompson Falls, drive five miles east on Highway 200, then 5.4 miles northeast on Forest Service Road 56 to the campground.

Trip note: This is one of two small, primitive, easily accessible camps in the immediate area providing good fishing access to the Thompson River.

---

79) SHADY GROVE TRAILER PARK

Reference: in Hot Springs; map M1, grid g5.

Campsites, facilities: There are 10 tent sites and 16 sites for trailers or motor homes of any length. Picnic tables are provided. Flush toilets, sanitary disposal station, showers, firewood and laundromat are also available. Electricity, piped water and sewer hookups are available at an additional charge. Bottled gas, a store, coffee shop and ice are located within one mile. Pets are permitted on leashes.

Reservations, fee: Reservations accepted; $4-$6 fee per night. Open April to November.

Who to contact: Phone (406) 741-3845 or write to P.O. Box 548, Hot Springs, MT 59845.

Location: This campground is located in the town of Hot Springs at the west end of Central Avenue.

Trip note: You'd best stop your car and park it. That is, if it's getting late, and you are starting to hunt for a spot. This privately operated, four-acre park provides the only camping spot in town; the only spot for miles around, actually. It's set on the Flathead Indian Reservation. An excellent sidetrip is visiting the hot mineral springs one mile away.

---

80) SKIPPING ROCK TRAILER PARK

Reference: near Flathead Lake; map M1, grid g6.

Campsites, facilities: There are five tent sites and 29 drive-through sites for trailers or motor homes of any length. Electricity, piped water, sewer hookups and picnic tables are provided. Flush toilets, showers, bottled gas, firewood and a playground are also available. A store, coffee shop and ice are located within one mile. No pets allowed. Motorbikes are permitted. Boat docks and launching facilities are available at the marina.

Reservations, fee: Reservations accepted; $15-$17 fee per night. Open May to late October.

Who to contact: Phone (406) 849-5678 or write to P.O. Box 253, Big Arm, MT 59910.

Location: From Big Arm, drive a half mile north on US 93 to the campground.

Trip note: This is a nine-acre park designed primarily for trailers and motor homes. It's set near the shore of Flathead Lake. It has grassy sites shaded with evergreens and poplar trees, with a sandy, sloping swimming beach which is good for wading. This is a great place for families with small children.

---

81) BIG ARM RESORT

Reference: near Flathead Lake; map M1, grid g6.

Campsites, facilities: There are five tent sites and eight drive-through sites for trailers or motor homes. Electricity, piped water and picnic tables are provided. Flush toilets and ice are also available. A store and coffee shop are located within one mile. Pets and motorbikes are permitted. Boat docks, launching facilities and rentals are nearby.

Reservations, fee: Reservations accepted; $8-$10 fee per night; MasterCard and Visa accepted. Open June through September.

Who to contact: Phone (406) 849-5622 or write to P.O. Box 99, Big Arm, MT 59910.

Location: From Polson, drive 12 miles east on US 93 to the campground in Big Arm at the marina.

Trip note: This is a small, privately operated park that covers two acres. It's set near the western side of Flathead Lake, and is a great spot for fishing and boating access.

---

82) ROCKING G RANCH

Reference: east of Polson; map M1, grid g6.

Campsites, facilities: There are 20 tent sites and 72 drive-through sites for trailers or motor homes. Picnic tables are provided. Flush toilets, showers, firewood, recreation hall, a store, coffee shop, bar and lounge, laundromat, ice and a playground are also available. Electricity, piped water and sewer hookups are available at an additional charge. Pets and motorbikes are permitted.

Reservations, fee: Reservations accepted; $10-$17 fee per night. There is no charge for additional people. Open May to November.

Who to contact: Phone (406) 887-2537 or write to Highway 35/East Shore Route, Polson, MT 59860.

Location: From Polson, drive seven miles west on Highway 35 to the campground.

Trip note: Although it is technically a motor home station, this site boasts a park-like setting. The sites are set in a huge grassy area with no paved or graveled roads within the camping area. Poplar trees are sprinkled throughout the campground, and the park is surrounded by a vast Christmas tree plantation, providing a forest of blue spruce and Scotch pines. Across the highway are the majestic Mission Mountains. The park also has a small casino, a lounge with live music, and the only beach volleyball court from there to Missoula. The park's primary goal, says the owner, is living up to its motto: "Too much fun, Montana style."

83) SNOWBERG'S PORT AND COURT

Reference: near Flathead Lake; map M1, grid g6.

Campsites, facilities: There are 15 sites for trailers or motor homes up to 32 feet long. Electricity, piped water, sewer hookups and picnic tables are provided. Flush toilets, bottled gas, sanitary disposal station, a store, restaurant, lounge, and ice are also available. Pets and motorbikes are permitted. Boat docks, launching facilities and rentals are available at the marina.

Reservations, fee: Reservations accepted; $15-$20 fee per night; MasterCard and Visa accepted. Open mid-May to mid-October.

Who to contact: Phone (406) 849-5501 or write to P.O. Box 38, Big Arm, MT 59910.

Location: From Polson, drive 11 miles north on US 93 to the trailer campground in Big Arm.

Trip note: This is one of four camps in the immediate vicinity and one of six in the area. Take your pick. This one is set on the western shore of Flathead Lake not far from the Big Arm State Recreation Area. The lake has good fishing.

84) ELMO STATE PARK

Reference: on Flathead Lake; map M1, grid g6.

Campsites, facilities: There are 35 sites for tents, trailers and motor homes up to 25 feet long. Picnic tables are provided. Flush toilets and piped water are also available. Pets are permitted on leashes. Boat launching facilities are nearby.

Reservations, fee: No reservations necessary; $5-$7 fee per night. Open mid-May to mid-September.

Who to contact: Phone Montana Department of Fish, Wildlife and Parks at (406) 444-2535 or write to 1420 East Sixth Avenue, Helena, MT 59620.

Location: From Polson, drive 19 miles north on US 93 to milepost 78, and turn into the campground.

Trip note: An alternative to Big Arm State Recreation Area, this one is set a little farther north along the western shore of Flathead Lake. See trip note for Big Arm.

85) BIG ARM STATE PARK

Reference: on Flathead Lake; map M1, grid g6.

Campsites, facilities: There are 35 sites for tents, trailers or motor homes of any length. Picnic tables are provided. Piped water, flush toilets and firewood are also available. Pets are permitted on leashes. Boat launching facilities are nearby.

Reservations, fee: No reservations necessary; $5-$7 fee per night. Open mid-May to mid-September.

Who to contact: Phone Montana Department of Fish, Wildlife and Parks at (406) 444-2535 or write to 1420 East Sixth Avenue, Helena, MT 59620.

Location: From Polson, drive 12 miles north on US 93 to milepost 74, and then turn into the campground.

Trip note: This is recreation headquarters for the southwestern part of giant Flathead Lake. The park covers 65 acres and is nestled on a lake arm. Swimming is popular at this park. Fishing can be quite good here as well, but you need a boat to do it right. Some say a monster lurks in the depths of this lake. If you see it, get it to keep still long enough, so you can get a picture of it.

---

86) FINLEY POINT STATE PARK

Reference: on Flathead Lake; map M1, grid g7.

Campsites, facilities: There are 18 sites for tents, trailers and motor homes up to 25 feet long. Picnic tables are provided. Piped water, pit toilets and firewood are also available. Pets are permitted on leashes. Boat docks and launching facilities are nearby.

Reservations, fee: No reservations necessary; $5-$7 fee per night. Open mid-May to mid-September.

Who to contact: Phone Montana Department of Fish, Wildlife and Parks at (406) 444-2535 or write to 1420 East Sixth Avenue, Helena, MT 59620.

Location: From Polson, drive 11 miles northeast on Highway 35, and then four miles west on the park access road.

Trip note: One of the more idyllic spots on Flathead Lake, this campground is nestled on a small peninsula on the southeastern end of the lake. The park covers 24 acres and has facilities for boaters. The fishing is good, but you need a boat to get the best of it. A nature program is run by the rangers. There is also a swimming beach.

---

87) YELLOW BAY STATE PARK

Reference: on Flathead Lake; map M1, grid g7.

Campsites, facilities: There are 25 sites for tents, trailers or motor homes up to 20 feet long. Picnic tables are provided. Piped water, flush toilets and firewood are also available. Pets are permitted on leashes. Boat launching facilities are nearby.

Reservations, fee: No reservations necessary; $5-$7 fee per night. Open mid-May to mid-September.

Who to contact: Phone Montana Department of Fish, Wildlife and Parks at (406) 444-2535 or write to 1420 East Sixth Avenue, Helena, MT 59620.

Location: From Polson, drive 15 miles north on Highway 35 to milepost 17 and the entrance to the campground.

Trip note: This is one of two nice spots on the southeastern shore of Flathead Lake. Giant Flathead Lake provides good fishing by boat, and is said to be the home of a monster. See trip note for Finley Point State Park.

---

88) JIM & WANDA'S

Reference: south of Polson; map M1, grid g7.

Campsites, facilities: There are 12 tent sites and 15 sites for trailers or motor homes. Electricity, piped water and picnic tables are provided. Flush toilets, sanitary disposal station, showers, a store, coffee shop and ice are also available. Pets and motorbikes are permitted.

Reservations, fee: Reservations accepted; $10-$15 fee per night. Open May to October.

Who to contact: Phone (406) 675-8800 or write to 53140 Highway 93, Ronan, MT 59864.

Location: From Polson, drive six miles south on US 93 to the campground.

Trip note: You get a little of both the urban and country life here. A nearby golf course provides some civilized recreation. As for the untamed stuff, you can visit the nearby Pablo National Wildlife Refuge. The southern end of Flathead Lake is just a short drive to the north.

---

89) POINT PLEASANT

Reference: in Swan River State Forest; map M1, grid g8.

Campsites, facilities: There are 12 sites for tents, trailers and motor homes up to 12 feet long. Picnic tables are provided. Piped water and pit toilets are also available. Pets are permitted on leashes.

Reservations, fee: No reservations necessary; no fee. Open year-round.

Who to contact: Phone Swan River State Forest at (406) 754-2301 or write to Swan Lake, MT 59911.

Location: From the town of Swan Lake, drive seven miles south on Highway 83 to the campground.

Trip note: This is one of two camps in the immediate area. This one is set along Swan River and has easy access to the highway. There are a few riverside sites, with the rest nestled between cottonwood, cedar and lodgepole pine trees. Nearby recreation options include a riding stable. There is fishing in Swan River, but a catch-and-release regulation is strictly enforced.

---

90) CEDAR CREEK

Reference: in Swan River State Forest; map M1, grid g8.

Campsites, facilities: There are six sites for tents, trailers and motor homes up to 12 feet long. Picnic tables are provided. Piped water and pit toilets are also available. Pets are permitted on leashes.

Reservations, fee: No reservations necessary; no fee. Open year-round.

Who to contact: Phone Swan River State Forest at (406) 754-2301 or write to Swan Lake, MT 59911.

Location: From the town of Swan Lake, drive 12 miles south on Highway 83, and then at Fatty Creek Road (a gravel road at Cedar Creek) drive one mile west to the campground.

Trip note: Only a mile from the highway, this site still gets missed by virtually all out-of-town visitors. It's a little camp set along pretty Cedar Creek. Recreation options include fishing in Cedar Creek (no restrictions here), and hiking around on the many undeveloped trails.

---

91) SOUP CREEK

Reference: near Bob Marshall Wilderness, Swan River State Forest; map M1, grid g9.

Campsites, facilities: There are nine sites for tents, trailers or motor homes up to 12 feet long. Picnic tables are provided. Piped water and pit toilets are also available. Pets are permitted on leashes.

Reservations, fee: No reservations necessary; no fee. Open year-round.

Who to contact: Phone Swan River State Forest at (406) 754-2301 or write to Swan Lake, MT 59911.

Location: From the town of Swan Lake, drive six miles south on Highway 83. Turn east on Soup Creek Road (a gravel road) and drive five miles to the campground.

Trip note: The creek frontage keeps the sound of a babbling brook in your ears at night. The camp is used primarily as a jump-off point for a multi-day backpacking trip. A trail starts here that is routed into the spectacular Bob Marshall Wilderness, which is located to the east. Of the three camps in Swan River State Forest, this is the largest and nicest.

---

92) GOLD RUSH

Reference: on the East Fork of Dry Creek, Lolo National Forest; map M1, grid h2.

Campsites, facilities: There are five tent sites and only one site for either a trailer or motor home up to 16 feet long. Picnic tables are provided. Hand-pumped well water and pit toilets are also available. Pets are permitted on leashes.

Reservations, fee: No reservations necessary; no fee. Open June to late October.

Who to contact: Phone Lolo National Forest at (406) 826-3821 or write to Plains Ranger District, P.O. Box 429, Plains, MT 59859.

Location: From the town of Thompson Falls, drive nine miles south on Forest Service Road 352 (East Fork of Dry Creek Road) to the campground.

Trip note: This is an ideal base camp for a fishing trip. The camp sits aside the East Fork of Dry Creek, and so you get direct fishing access. Backpackers can use the camp as a jump-off point, because a trail from camp leads to a network of other trails up in the Coeur d'Alene Mountains, one of the most beautiful areas in the state. It is advisable to obtain a Forest Service map.

---

93) CABIN CITY

Reference: on Twelvemile Creek, Lolo National Forest; map M1, grid h3.

Campsites, facilities: There are 24 sites for tents, trailers and motor homes up to 40 feet long. Picnic tables are provided. Piped water, pit toilets and firewood are also available. A store, coffee shop and ice are located within five miles. Pets are permitted on leashes.

Reservations, fee: No reservations necessary; $4 fee per night. Open Memorial to Labor Day.

Who to contact: Phone Lolo National Forest at (406) 822-4233 or write to Superior Ranger District, P.O. Box 460, Superior, MT 59872.

Location: From Deborgia, drive 2.9 miles southeast on Highway 10. Take exit 22 and drive east for 2.5 miles on Camel's Hump Road (Number 2148). Turn left at the campground sign and drive a quarter mile.

Trip note: This is a prime spot with both easy access and good fishing. The camp is set on Twelvemile Creek where you can fish right out of camp. There are some beaver dams in the area. And if you fish right behind them, sneaking up quietly, fishing can be good. If you head north up the road a short ways, you can access a pretty hiking trail that runs along Flat Rock Creek.

---

94) MISSION MEADOWS

Reference: near Ronan; map M1, grid h7.

Campsites, facilities: There are 15 tent sites and 85 drive-through sites for trailers or motor homes. Piped water and picnic tables are provided. Flush toilets, sanitary disposal station, showers, firewood, recreation hall, store, coffee shop, laundromat, ice, playground, heated swimming pool, and hot tubs are also available. Electricity and sewer hookups are available at an additional charge. Pets and motorbikes are permitted.

Reservations, fee: Reservations accepted; $10-$12.50 fee per night. Open all year with limited facilities in the winter.

Who to contact: Phone (406) 676-5182 or write to Mission Meadows Drive, P.O. Box 98, Ronan, MT 59864.

Location: From Ronan, drive two miles north on US 93, and then a half mile west as you follow the signs to the campground.

Trip note: This is a good jump-off spot for several adventures. It is within 10 miles of three wildlife refuges, as well as close to the south end of Flathead Lake. The park covers 20 acres and has shaded sites.

---

95) HOLLAND LAKE

Reference: in Flathead National Forest; map M1, grid h9.

Campsites, facilities: There are 40 sites for tents, trailers and motor homes up to 22 feet long. Picnic tables are provided. Piped water and flush toilets are also available. A store and coffee shop are located within one mile, and showers are available. Boat docks, launching facilities and rentals are nearby.

Reservations, fee: Reservations required; $7 fee per night. Open late May to early September.

Who to contact: Phone Flathead National Forest at (406) 837-5081 or write to Swan Lake Ranger District, P.O. Box 370, Bigfork, MT 59826.

Location: From Condon, drive 8.5 miles southeast on Highway 83, then three miles east on Forest Service Road 44 to the campground.

Trip note: This is a nice camp set at the west end of Holland Lake. This is a good spot both for folks planning to hunker down for awhile, or for those ready to hike. Trails from the east end of the lake access the Holland Creek Drainage and Bob Marshall Wilderness. There is a boat ramp, a swimming beach, and plenty of fishing access.

---

96) SLOWAY

Reference: on Clark Fork River, Lolo National Forest; map M1, grid i3.

Campsites, facilities: There are 26 sites for tents, trailers, or motor homes of any length. Picnic tables are provided. Piped water, firewood, pit toilets, and a hand-launched boat ramp are also available. The facilities are **wheelchair accessible**. Pets are permitted on leashes.

Reservations, fee: No reservations necessary; $6 fee per night. Open Memorial to Labor Day.

Who to contact: Phone Lolo National Forest at (406) 822-4233 or write to Superior Ranger District, Superior, MT 59872.

Location: Between St. Regis and Superior, take the Dry Creek exit Number 43 off Interstate 90, and drive west for 3.2 miles on the north frontage road to the campground.

Trip note: This is a pretty camp set on the Clark Fork River. Fishing can be good in this area if you're the first person to hit the spots during the morning or evening bites. Horseshoe pits, a volleyball net and horse accommodations make this camp ideal for groups or families.

97) ST. REGIS

Reference: near Clark Fork; map M1, grid i3.

Campsites, facilities: There are 21 tent sites and 54 sites for trailers or motor homes of any length. Electricity, piped water and picnic tables are provided. Flush toilets, bottled gas, sanitary disposal station, showers, firewood, recreation hall, store, laundromat, ice, playground and a swimming pool are also available. Sewer hookups are available at an additional charge. A coffee shop is located within one mile. Pets and motorbikes are permitted.

Reservations, fee: Reservations accepted; $18-$19.50 fee per night. Open May to October including limited and some off-season weekends.

Who to contact: Phone (406) 649-2470 or write to P.O. Drawer A, St. Regis, MT 59866.

Location: In St. Regis, take exit 33 off Interstate 90, and drive three-quarters of a mile west on Camel's Hump Road. Follow the signs to the campground.

Trip note: This is a privately operated campground that covers 11 acres. It's an easy-to-reach spot and accesses the nearby Clark Fork River. The sites are well-shaded, on grassy meads.

98) CASCADE

Reference: near Clark Fork, Lolo National Forest; map M1, grid i4.

Campsites, facilities: There are ten sites for tents, trailers and motor homes up to 22 feet long. Picnic tables are provided. Hand-pumped well water, vault toilets and firewood are also available. Some facilities are **wheelchair accessible.** Pets are permitted on leashes. Boat docks are nearby.

Reservations, fee: No reservations necessary; $5 fee per night. Open mid-May through October.

Who to contact: Phone Lolo National Forest at (406) 826-3821 or write to Plains Ranger District, P.O. Box 429, Plains, MT 59859.

Location: From the town of Thompson Falls, drive 30 miles southeast on Highway 200 to Paradise. Continue southeast on Highway 200 for 2.5 miles, and then 6.5 miles southwest on County Road 135.

Trip note: You have plenty of options here. You can fish on the nearby Clark Fork River, take a sidetrip to Cascade Falls, or get a dunking at the Quinn Hot Springs located about four miles from camp (you'll drive right past it on your way into camp). Another choice is taking a day hike on the Cascade National Recreation Trail. The trailhead is right here at camp.

99) TROUT CREEK

Reference: near Clark Fork, Lolo National Forest; map M1, grid i4.

Campsites, facilities: There are 12 sites for tents, trailers and motor homes up to 30 feet long. Picnic tables are provided. Piped water, pit toilets and firewood are also available, but there is no garbage service. Pets are permitted on leashes.

Reservations, fee: No reservations necessary; $5 fee per night. Open Memorial Day to late September.

Who to contact: Phone Lolo National Forest at (406) 822-4233 or write to Superior, MT 59872.

Location: From Superior, drive 4.4 miles southeast on Highway 269, and then 2.5 miles southwest on Highway 257 (Trout Creek Road).

Trip note: Hey, you can fish right out of the camp. That's not too shabby. The camp is set on Trout Creek about two miles from Clark Fork. It's a good camp for a fishing trip, and offers hiking access to the Great Burn as well. This is a pretty camp with shaded sites.

---

100) QUARTZ FLAT

Reference: near Clark Fork, Lolo National Forest; map M1, grid i4.

Campsites, facilities: There are 52 sites for tents, trailers or motor homes up to 50 feet long. Piped water and picnic tables are provided. Flush toilets, sanitary disposal station ($2 fee if not staying overnight), electricity and firewood are also available. Pets are permitted on leashes.

Reservations, fee: No reservations necessary; $7 fee per night. Open May through Labor Day.

Who to contact: Phone Lolo National Forest at (406) 822-4233 or write to Superior, MT 59872.

Location: From Superior, drive 14.7 miles southeast on Interstate 90 to the rest-stop campground.

Trip note: This popular spot is set near a rest stop on Interstate 90. But that's not the main attraction. The Clark Fork River is within walking distance along with a self-guiding nature trail. If you want to drive a little ways, you can access some quality hiking trails to the west. A Forest Service map will give details.

---

101) JOCKO HOLLOW

Reference: near Jocko River; map M1, grid i7.

Campsites, facilities: There are four tent sites and 12 sites for trailers or motor homes of any length. Piped water and picnic tables are provided. Flush toilets, sanitary disposal station, laundromat, ice and a playground are also available. Electricity and showers are available at an additional charge. Bottled gas, a store and a coffee shop are located within one mile. Pets and motorbikes are permitted.

Reservations, fee: Reservations accepted; $10-$15 fee per night. Open April to October.

Who to contact: Phone (406) 726-3336 or write to Arlee, MT 59821.

Location: From Arlee, drive one mile north on US 93.

Trip note: This is one of the smaller, more intimate, privately operated campgrounds along Highway 93. The sites are grassy, with lots of trees surrounding the park. The Jocko River passes nearby.

---

102) DAY'S REST TRAILER PARK

Reference: near Jocko River; map M1, grid i7.

Campsites, facilities: There are 15 tent sites and 15 sites for trailers or motor homes of any length. Electricity, piped water and picnic tables are provided. Flush toilets, a store, laundromat and ice are also available. Sewer hookups and showers are available at an additional charge. A coffee shop is located within one mile. Pets are permitted on leashes.

Reservations, fee: Reservations accepted; $5-$8 fee per night; American Express, MasterCard and Visa accepted. Open April to late October including limited and some off-season weekends.

Who to contact: Phone (406) 745-4554 or write to Ravalli, MT 59863.

Location: This campground is located in Ravalli at the junction of US 93 and Highway 200.

Trip note: This is one of two parks in the immediate area. This one covers an acre, with grassy sites and apple and maple trees in the park. It is set just south of the National Basin Range. The Jocko River is nearby, with good fishing prospects. A nice sidetrip is to travel about five miles up to the Catholic Mission, which offers particularly scenic views of the Mission Range.

---

103) PLACID LAKE STATE PARK

Reference: on Placid Lake; map M1, grid i9.

Campsites, facilities: There are 42 sites for tents, trailers and motor homes up to 32 feet long. Picnic tables are provided. Piped water and flush toilets are also available. Some facilities are **wheelchair accessible.** Pets are permitted on leashes. Boat docks and launching facilities are nearby.

Reservations, fee: No reservations necessary; $6-$8 fee per night. Open mid-April to mid-September.

Who to contact: Phone Montana Department of Fish, Wildlife and Parks at (406) 444-2535 or write to 1420 East Sixth Avenue, Helena, MT 59620.

Location: From the town of Seeley Lake, drive three miles south on Highway 83, then three miles west on a county road. The turnoff is signed.

Trip note: This state park is on Placid Lake. Less developed than nearby Seeley Lake, this land also falls under the domain of Blackfoot Clearwater Game Range and Lolo National Forest.

104) JIM & MARY'S RV PARK

Reference: in Missoula; map M1, grid j7.

Campsites, facilities: There are 45 sites for trailers or motor homes. No tents are permitted. Picnic tables are provided. Flush toilets, showers, laundromat and a playground are also available. Bottled gas, sanitary disposal station, a store and coffee shop are located within one mile. Pets and motorbikes are permitted.

Reservations, fee: Reservations accepted; $14 fee per night; MasterCard and Visa accepted. Open April to October.

Who to contact: Phone (406) 549-4416 or write to 9800 US 93 North, Missoula, MT 59802.

Location: In Missoula, take exit 96 off Interstate 90, and drive on US 93 to the park (about three-quarters of a mile).

Trip note: One of three parks in Missoula, this offers both open and shaded sites. A good sidetrip is hiking a four-mile nature trail that begins west of Missoula at the Blue Mountain Recreation Area. It's routed to the top of Blue Mountain (6,455 feet). There's a golf course in the area. Note: This is an adult-only park, so leave the kids (or grandkids) behind.

105) MISSOULA KOA

Reference: in Missoula; map M1, grid j7.

Campsites, facilities: There are 25 tent sites and 175 sites for trailers or motor homes of any length. Piped water and picnic tables are provided. Flush toilets, sanitary disposal station, showers, firewood, recreation hall, a store, laundromat, ice, playground and a heated swimming pool are also available. Electricity and sewer hookups are available at an additional charge. Bottled gas and coffee shop are located within one mile. Pets and motorbikes are permitted.

Reservations, fee: Reservations accepted; $15-$20 fee per night; MasterCard and Visa accepted. Open all year, with limited facilities in the winter.

Who to contact: Phone (406) 549-0881 or write 3695 Tina Avenue, Missoula, MT 59802.

Location: From Interstate 90 in Missoula, take exit 101 (Reserve Street) and drive to the campground at 3695 Tina Avenue.

Trip note: This spacious and wooded 30-acre campground includes a tent area. It's a popular spot for families because it has a petting zoo. For sidetrip options, see trip note for Jim & Mary's.

Montana Map M2
33 listings
Pages 332-347

North—Canada
East (M3)—see page 348
South (M7)—see page 380
West (M1)—see page 284

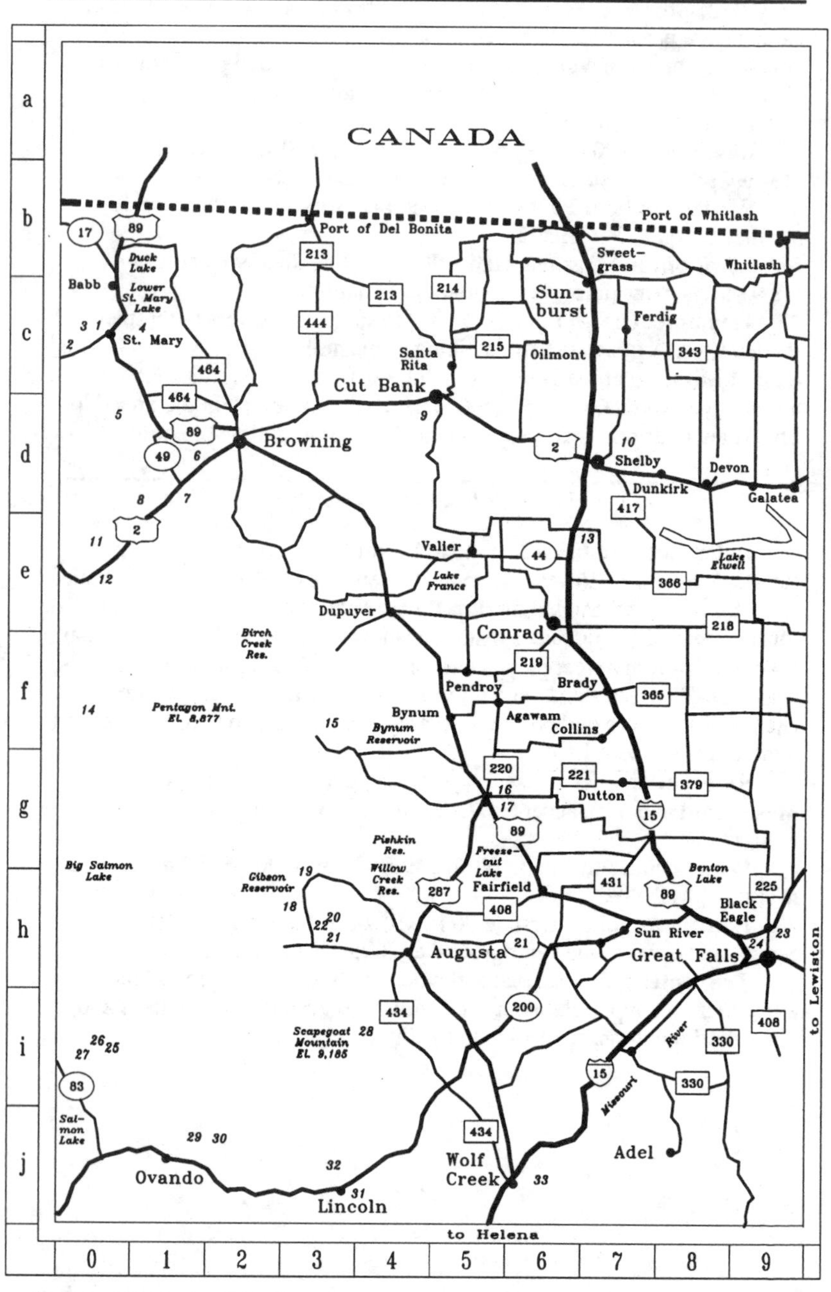

Featuring: St. Mary's Lake, Glacier National Park, Cut Bank Creek, East Glacier Park, Medicine Lake, Lewis and Clark National Forest, Marias River, Bob Marshall Wilderness, Flathead National Forest, West Fork of Teton River, Willow Creek, Sun River, Gibson Reservoir, Wood Lakes, Sun River, Missouri River, Seeley Lake, Scapegoat Mountain, Coopers Lake, Blackfoot River, Helena National Forest, Copper Creek, Holter Lake

---

1) ST. MARY'S LAKE

Reference: on St. Mary's Lake, Glacier National Park; map M2, grid c0.

Campsites, facilities: There are 156 sites for tents, trailers or motor homes up to 30 feet long. Picnic tables are provided. Piped water, flush toilets, sanitary disposal station, a store, coffee shop and ice are also available. Some facilities are **wheelchair accessible.** Pets are permitted on leashes. Boat launching facilities are nearby.

Reservations, fee: No reservations necessary; $10 fee per night. Open mid-June to late September, including limited and some off-season weekends.

Who to contact: Phone Waterton-Glacier International Peace Park at (406) 888-5441, or write P.O. Box 128, West Glacier, MT 59936.

Location: From St. Mary, drive one mile west on Going-to-the-Sun Road.

Trip note: St. Mary's Lake is the big attraction. It's a popular spot for boating and fishing and is set just outside the eastern border of Glacier National Park. A visitors center is nearby; rangers can provide maps and answer any questions you may have. Hikers should check out the many excellent trails in the park.

---

2) RISING SUN

Reference: near St. Mary Lake, Glacier National Park; map M2, grid c0.

Campsites, facilities: There are 83 sites for tents, trailers or motor homes up to 30 feet long. Picnic tables are provided. Piped water, flush toilets, sanitary disposal station, a store and a coffee shop are also available. Ice is located within one mile. Some facilities are **wheelchair accessible.** Pets are permitted on leashes. Boat launching facilities and rentals are nearby.

Reservations, fee: No reservations necessary; $10 fee per night. Open mid-June to mid-September with limited winter facilities.

Who to contact: Phone Waterton-Glacier International Peace Park at (406) 888-5441, or write P.O. Box 128, West Glacier, MT 59936.

Location: From St. Mary, drive six miles west on Going-to-the-Sun Road.

Trip note: This popular spot is great for campers who have boats and want to try fishing in St. Mary's Lake. In many ways, it's an idyllic spot in Glacier National Park.

3) JOHNSON'S

Reference: near Glacier National Park; map M2, grid c0.

Campsites, facilities: There are unlimited tent sites and 70 sites for trailers or motor homes of any length. Picnic tables are provided. Flush toilets, showers, firewood, a store, coffee shop, laundromat and ice are also available. Electricity, piped water and sewer hookups are available at an additional charge. Bottled gas and a sanitary disposal station are located within one mile. Pets and motorbikes are permitted.

Reservations, fee: Reservations accepted; $10-$15 fee per night; MasterCard and Visa accepted. Open May to mid-October.

Who to contact: Phone (406) 732-5565, or write Browning, MT 59417.

Location: This campground is located at the north end of St. Mary on US 89.

Trip note: This is one of several camps set just outside the eastern border of Glacier National Park. This one covers 35 acres, and with nearby St. Mary's Lake to the immediate east, has tremendous appeal.

4) LAKEVIEW TOURIST RESORT

Reference: near Lower St. Mary's Lake; map M2, grid c1.

Campsites, facilities: There are 25 tent sites and 15 sites for trailers or motor homes of any length. Picnic tables are provided. Flush toilets, firewood, a store, coffee shop and ice are also available. Electricity, piped water, sewer hookups and showers are available at an additional charge. Bottled gas, sanitary disposal station and laundromat are located within one mile. Pets and motorbikes are permitted. Boat docks, launching facilities and rentals are nearby.

Reservations, fee: Reservations accepted; $8-$12 fee per night; MasterCard and Visa accepted. Open mid-May to September

Who to contact: Phone (406) 732-5535, or write P.O. Box 350, Babb, MT 59411.

Location: From St. Mary, drive five miles north on US 89.

Trip note: This is a giant campground, 80 acres in all, and is set near Lower St. Mary Lake. The site is located just east of Glacier National Park. The sites are level, grassy and well treed. Many RVers make this a base camp while touring Glacier National Park.

5) CUT BANK

Reference: on Cut Bank Creek, Glacier National Park; map M2, grid d0.

Campsites, facilities: There are 19 sites for tents, trailers or motor homes up to 22 feet long. Picnic tables are provided. Piped water and pit toilets are also available. Pets are permitted on leashes.

Reservations, fee: No reservations necessary; $8 fee per night. Open June to mid-September and some off-season weekends. There are limited facilities in the winter.

Who to contact: Phone Waterton-Glacier International Peace Park at (406) 888-5441, or write P.O. Box 128, West Glacier, MT 59936.

Location: From St. Mary, drive 15 miles south on US 89 and four miles west on Cut Bank Road (it's dirt) to the campground.

Trip note: Of all the popular campgrounds at Glacier National Park, this is one of the lesser used ones. It's a pretty spot too. It's set on Cut Bank Creek just below Mount Stimson (10,142 feet) near the eastern border of the park.

---

6) FIREBRAND PASS

Reference: near East Glacier Park; map M2, grid d1.

Campsites, facilities: There are 15 tent sites and 20 sites for trailers or motor homes. Picnic tables are provided. Flush toilets, sanitary disposal station, showers, coffee shop, laundromat and ice are also available. Pets and motorbikes are permitted.

Reservations, fee: Reservations accepted; $8-$12 fee per night. Open June to mid-September.

Who to contact: Phone (406) 226-5573 or write P.O. Box 146, East Glacier Park, MT 59434.

Location: From the town of East Glacier Park, drive 3.5 miles southwest on US 2 to the campground.

Trip note: This is one of two privately run parks in the area. This camp is pretty, with wide, open sites. The folks here are real friendly, too. This camp caters more to RVs than tents; tent campers may want to investigate other nearby options. See trip note for Lazy R Trailer Park for recreation details.

---

7) LAZY R TRAILER PARK

Reference: East Glacier Park; map M2, grid d1.

Campsites, facilities: There are 20 tent sites and 15 sites for trailers or motor homes up to 30 feet long. Picnic tables are provided. Flush toilets, sanitary disposal station, showers, laundromat and a playground are also available. Bottled gas, a store, coffee shop and ice are located within one mile. Pets and motorbikes are permitted.

Reservations, fee: Reservations accepted; $8-$12 fee per night. Open June to mid-September.

Who to contact: Phone (406) 226-5573, or write P.O. Box 146, East Glacier Park, MT 59434

Location: From the junction of US 2 and Highway 49 in the town of East Glacier Park, drive one block east just past the Exxon Station.

Trip note: This is one of two choices in the town of East Glacier Park. Nearby recreation options include a golf course, hiking trails and a riding stable.

8) TWO MEDICINE

Reference: on Medicine Lake, Glacier National Park; map M2, grid d1.

Campsites, facilities: There are 99 sites for tents, trailers or motor homes up to 32 feet long. Picnic tables are provided. Piped water, flush toilets, sanitary disposal station and a store are also available. Some facilities are **wheelchair accessible.** Pets are permitted on leashes. Boat launching facilities and rentals are nearby.

Reservations, fee: No reservations necessary; $10 fee per night. Open June to early September including limited and some off-season weekends.

Who to contact: Phone Waterton-Glacier International Peace Park at (406) 888-5441, or write P.O. Box 128, West Glacier, MT 59936.

Location: From the town of East Glacier Park, drive 12 miles north on Highway 49 to the campground on Two Medicine Lake.

Trip note: Boating, fishing and swimming are the highlights at Two Medicine Lake. The site is set in Glacier National Park near its southeastern border and offers several hiking trails that traverse the area.

9) SHADY GROVE

Reference: west of Cut Bank; map M2, grid d4.

Campsites, facilities: There are 10 tent sites and 19 sites for trailers or motor homes up to 30 feet long, with an overflow area for RVs. Electricity, piped water, sewer hookups and picnic tables are provided. Flush toilets, showers, ice and a playground are also available. Pets are permitted on leashes.

Reservations, fee: Reservations accepted; $9-$12 fee per night. Open mid-May to October.

Who to contact: Phone (406) 336-2475 or write to P.O. Box 1143, Cut Bank, MT 59427.

Location: From Cut Bank, drive six miles west on US 2 to the campground.

Trip note: Stop your whimperin' and be happy you found this spot. At least they have tent sites. A lot of privately run camps don't provide even that. And they're nice, grassy sites with lots of trees around. Plus, the options are not exactly scintillating. The next nearest camp is 25 miles to the east, and there's zilch elsewhere. This camp covers four acres, and there's a nearby golf course providing a recreation possibility. Anglers should note that there are several lakes in the area that provide excellent fishing prospects.

10) LAKE SHEL-OOLE PARK

Reference: in Shelby; map M2, grid d7.

Campsites, facilities: There are 37 sites for tents, trailers or motor homes of any length. Piped water and sanitary disposal station are also available. A store, coffee shop, laundromat and ice are located within one mile.

Reservations, fee: No reservations necessary; $7-$10 fee per night. Open May to mid-October.

Who to contact: Phone (406) 434-5222 or write to Shelby, MT 59474.

Location: Take exit 364 off I-15 in Shelby, and drive a half mile south on the business bypass to the park.

Trip note: This is a 10-acre city park set near a small lake in Shelby, a town with a wild history. A lot of it is documented in the Marias Museum of History and Art which is located four blocks south of US 2 at 206 12th Avenue. This was a cowboy town, turned rich by an oil discovery in 1922. The town also has sponsored a world heavyweight fight. All kinds of high jinx occurred. A golf course provides a recreational possibility.

---

11) SUMMIT

Reference: near Glacier National Park, Lewis and Clark National Forest; map M2, grid e0.

Campsites, facilities: There are 17 sites for tents, trailers or motor homes up to 22 feet long. Picnic tables are provided. Piped water and vault toilets are also available. A store and a swimming pool are located within five miles. Pets are permitted on leashes.

Reservations, fee: No reservations necessary; $5 fee per night. Open mid-June to early September.

Who to contact: Phone Lewis and Clark National Forest at (406) 466-5341 or write Rocky Mountain Ranger District, 1102 Main Avenue NW, P.O. Box 340, Chateau, MT 59422.

Location: From the town of East Glacier Park, drive 10 miles southwest on US 2 to the campground.

Trip note: Easy access, beautiful scenery and good hiking trails are the attractions here. The camp is set along the southern border of Glacier National Park, and is adjacent to Roosevelt Monument National Historic Sites. Numerous trails are routed along various creeks. Motor home drivers may prefer Three Forks Camp, which is located just three miles away.

---

12) THREE FORKS

Reference: west of East Glacier Park; map M2, grid e0.

Campsites, facilities: There are 20 tent sites and 25 sites for trailers or motor homes of any length. A sanitary disposal station and picnic tables are provided. Flush toilets, bottled gas, sanitary disposal station, showers, laundromat, ice and a playground are also available. A coffee shop is located within one mile. Pets and motorbikes are permitted.

Reservations, fee: Reservations accepted; $10-$15 fee per night. Open mid-June to mid-September.

Who to contact: Phone (406) 226-4479, or write P.O. Box 124, East Glacier Park, MT 59434.

Location: From the town of East Glacier Park, drive 16 miles west on US 2.

Trip note: This private park covers four acres, with wide, grassy sites and lots of recreation options in the surrounding area. A riding stable is available here. See trip note for Summit Campground for area options.

---

13) WILLIAMSON MEMORIAL PARK

Reference: on Marias River; map M2, grid e6.

Campsites, facilities: There are 25 sites for tents, trailers or motor homes up to 35 feet long. Picnic tables are provided. Piped water, flush toilets, sanitary disposal station and a playground are also available. A store, coffee shop, laundromat and ice are located within five miles.

Reservations, fee: No reservations necessary; $5-$10 fee per night. Open May to mid-October

Who to contact: Phone (406) 434-5222 or write to Shelby, MT 59474.

Location: From Interstate 15 in Shelby, take exit 358 and drive seven miles south on the frontage road to the campground.

Trip note: This is one of the top spots in the region. It's a 10-acre city park set along the Marias River which is fed by big Lake Elwell to the east. And it's by far the best spot in the region for tent campers you have to drive an hour to find one as nice (Tiber Reservoir State Recreation Area).

---

14) SPOTTED BEAR

Reference: near Bob Marshall Wilderness, Flathead National Forest; map M2, grid f0.

Campsites, facilities: There are 13 sites for tents, trailers or motor homes up to 26 feet long. Picnic tables are provided. Piped water, vault toilets and sanitary disposal station are also available.

Reservations, fee: No reservations necessary; $3 fee per night. Open June to mid-October.

Who to contact: Phone Flathead National Forest at (406) 752-7345 or (406) 387-5243 or write to Spotted Bear Ranger District, P.O. Box 310, Hungry Horse, MT 59919.

Location: From Martin City, drive 55 miles southeast on Forest Service Road 38 to the campground.

Trip note: This one is way out there in "booger country"—hey, we saw two moose while driving (not hiking) out to the camp. It's a good jump-off point for entering the Bob Marshall Wilderness, the crown jewel of the nation's wilderness system. If you go, be ready to deal with possible contact with grizzly bears. There are a lot of them in the area.

15) WEST FORK

Reference: on the West Fork of Teton River, Lewis and Clark National Forest; map M2, grid f3.

Campsites, facilities: There are six sites for tents, trailers or motor homes up to 16 feet long. Picnic tables are provided. Piped water and vault toilets are also available. Pets are permitted on leashes.

Reservations, fee: No reservations necessary; no fee. Open June to November.

Who to contact: Phone Lewis and Clark National Forest at (406) 466-5341 or write to Rocky Mountain Ranger District, 1102 Main Avenue NW, P.O. Box 340, Choteau, MT 59422.

Location: From Choteau, drive 5.5 miles north on US 89. Turn northwest on County Road 144.1 and drive 33 miles, then turn north on Forest Service Road 144.2 and continue for 10 miles to the campground.

Trip note: This is one of a series of nine camps that are virtually unknown, set on the eastern border of Lewis and Clark National Forest. This one is set on the West Fork of the Teton River just below Teton Peak (8,400 feet). It's an ideal jump-off camp for backpackers. Trails start here that head west into the Bob Marshall Wilderness north along West Fork of the Teton River. Another makes a short but steep climb to Teton Peak. A Forest Service map details the trails.

16) CHOTEAU KOA

Reference: near Willow Creek; map M2, grid g5.

Campsites, facilities: There are 40 tent sites and 45 sites for trailers or motor homes of any length. Piped water and picnic tables are provided. Flush toilets, bottled gas, sanitary disposal station, showers, recreation hall, a store, miniature golf course, laundromat, ice and a playground are also available. Electricity and sewer hookups are available at an additional charge. Pets and motorbikes are permitted. A camping cabin is also available.

Reservations, fee: Reservations accepted; $11.50-$16 fee per night; MasterCard and Visa accepted. Open May to October.

Who to contact: Phone (406) 466-2615 or write to R.R. 2, P.O. Box 87, Choteau, MT 59422.

Location: From Choteau, drive three-quarters of a mile east on County Road 221 to the campground.

Trip note: This is one of two options in this town. This one covers eight acres, with graveled, sunny sites. Nearby Willow Creek is a possible sidetrip. The Old Trail Museum at the junction of US 89 and Highway 287 has historical exhibits and some baby dinosaur bones that were found in the area. For kids, the park has a miniature golf course.

17) CHOTEAU CITY PARK

Reference: near Willow Creek; map M2, grid g5.

Campsites, facilities: There are 35 sites for tents, trailers or motor homes of any length. Picnic tables are provided. Piped water, flush toilets, sanitary disposal station and playground are also available. Bottled gas, a store, coffee shop, laundromat and ice are located within one mile. Pets are permitted on leashes.

Reservations, fee: No reservations necessary; no fee. Open May to September.

Who to contact: Phone (406) 466-2510 or write to P.O. Box X, Choteau, MT 59422.

Location: This park is located in Choteau on Main Street (Highway 221).

Trip note: This is a city-managed park that covers five acres. It's not much to look at, but hey, you get what you pay for. Actually, it's not all that bad for a city campground. Willow Creek provides a sidetrip. See trip note for Choteau KOA for other recreation possibilities.

18) HOME GULCH

Reference: on Sun River, Lewis and Clark National Forest; map M2, grid h3.

Campsites, facilities: There are 15 sites for tents, trailers or motor homes up to 23 feet long. Picnic tables are provided. Piped water and vault toilets are also available. A store is located within five miles. Pets are permitted on leashes. Boat docks and launching facilities are nearby.

Reservations, fee: No reservations necessary; $5 fee per night. Open late May to mid-November.

Who to contact: Phone Lewis and Clark National Forest at (406) 466-5341 or write to Rocky Mountain Ranger District, 1102 Main Avenue NW, P.O. Box 340, Choteau, MT 59422.

Location: From Augusta, drive 22 miles northwest on County Route 108 to the campground.

Trip note: This is one of two camps in the immediate area. This one is set on Sun River about two miles east of Gibson Reservoir (Camp 23). Trails from camp follow creeks both north and south, and it's all detailed on a Forest Service map. Another trail follows the river west into the spectacular Bob Marshall Wilderness.

19) MORTIMER GULCH

Reference: near Gibson Reservoir, Lewis and Clark National Forest; map M2, grid h3.

Campsites, facilities: There are 28 sites for tents, trailers or motor homes up to 22 feet long. Picnic tables are provided. Vault toilets are also available. Pets are permitted on leashes. Boat docks and launching facilities are nearby.

Reservations, fee: No reservations necessary; $5 fee per night. Open late May to mid-November.

Who to contact: Phone Lewis and Clark National Forest at (406) 466-5341 or write to Rocky Mountain Ranger District, 1102 Main Avenue NW, P.O. Box 340, Choteau, MT 59422.

Location: From Augusta, drive 19.8 miles northwest on County Road 1081, and then seven miles west on Forest Service Road 108 to the campground.

Trip note: This camp is set on a creek that pours into Gibson Reservoir, not far from the dam. There are many hiking options here, so a Forest Service map is essential. See trip note for Home Gulch Camp.

---

20) WOOD LAKE

Reference: on Little Wood Lakes, Lewis and Clark National Forest; map M2, grid h3.

Campsites, facilities: There are nine sites for tents, trailers or motor homes up to 22 feet long. Picnic tables are provided. Piped water and vault toilets are also available. Pets are permitted on leashes.

Reservations, fee: No reservations necessary; $5 fee per night. Open June to mid-November.

Who to contact: Phone Lewis and Clark National Forest at (406) 466-5341 or write to Rocky Mountain Ranger District, 1102 Main Avenue NW, P.O. Box 340, Choteau, MT 59422.

Location: From Augusta, drive west on County Road 235 for 14 miles. Turn southwest on Forest Service Road 235 and proceed 9.6 miles to the campground.

Trip note: This is a nice little spot that few know. It's set on Wood Lake near where Ford Creek enters the lake and is a good spot to hunker down for a while. There are no trails in the immediate area.

---

21) SOUTH FORK

Reference: on Sun River, Lewis and Clark National Forest; map M2, grid h3.

Campsites, facilities: There are seven sites for tents, trailers, or motor homes up to 30 feet long. Picnic tables are provided. Piped water and vault toilets are also available. Pets are permitted on leashes.

Reservations, fee: No reservations necessary; $5 fee per night. Open June to mid-November.

Who to contact: Phone Lewis and Clark National Forest at (406) 466-5341 or write to Rocky Mountain Ranger District, 1102 Main Avenue NW, P.O. Box 340, Choteau, MT 59422.

Location: From Augusta, drive west on County Road 235 for 14 miles. Turn southwest on Forest Service Road 235 and proceed 16.5 miles to the campground.

Trip note: It's a pretty spot where the South Fork of the Sun River and other feeder streams meet to form the main Sun River. This is one of three camps in the immediate vicinity and offers good hiking possibilities. One trail is routed southwest into the Scapegoat Wilderness, another leads into the Bob Marshall Wilderness.

22) BENCHMARK

Reference: on Sun River, Lewis and Clark National Forest; map M2, grid h3.

Campsites, facilities: There are 25 sites for tents, trailers and motor homes up to 22 feet long. Picnic tables are provided. Piped water and vault toilets are also available. Pets are permitted on leashes.

Reservations, fee: No reservations necessary; $5 fee per night. Open June to November.

Who to contact: Phone Lewis and Clark National Forest at (406) 466-5341 or write to Rocky Mountain Ranger District, 1102 Main Avenue NW, P.O. Box 340, Choteau, MT 59422.

Location: From Augusta, drive west on County Road 235 for 14 miles. Turn southwest on Forest Service Road 235 and continue 15.5 miles to the campground.

Trip note: This is a trailhead camp set just south of South Fork Camp and just west of Wood Lake Camp and is located at the confluence of Wood Creek and Straight Creek (which turns into Sun River). One trail heads south into Scapegoat Wilderness and another north along Benchmark Creek past Renshaw Mountain to Renshaw Lake, and if you're up for it, far beyond to Bob Marshall Wilderness.

23) DICK'S TRAILER PARK

Reference: near Missouri River in Great Falls; map M2, grid h3.

Campsites, facilities: There are four tent sites and 40 sites for trailers or motor homes. Flush toilets, sanitary disposal station, showers and a laundromat are also available. Bottled gas, a store, coffee shop and ice are located within one mile. Pets and motorbikes are permitted.

Reservations, fee: Reservations accepted; $10.50-$15 fee per night. Open all year.

Who to contact: Phone (406) 452-0333 or write to 1403 11th Street SW, Great Falls, MT 59404.

Location: From Interstate 15 in the town of Great Falls, take the 10th Avenue exit (US 87) south. Turn east at the first light, and drive a half block to the campground.

Trip note: This is a private park that covers 16 acres, with extra-large paved and gravel sites and willow trees all around. It's set near the Missouri River and a riding stable is nearby. See trip note for Great Falls KOA for numerous sidetrip possibilities.

24) GREAT FALLS KOA

Reference: in Great Falls; map M2, grid h9.

Campsites, facilities: There are 50 tent sites and 110 sites for trailers or motor homes of any length. Picnic tables are provided. Flush toilets, bottled gas, sanitary disposal station, showers, recreation hall, store, coffee shop, laundromat, ice and a playground are also available. Electricity, piped water, sewer hookups and firewood are available at an additional charge. Pets and motorbikes are permitted.

Reservations, fee: Reservations accepted; $18-$29 fee per night; MasterCard and Visa accepted. Open all year.

Who to contact: Phone (406) 727-3191 or write to 1500 51st Street South, Great Falls, MT 59405.

Location: From Interstate 15 in the town of Great Falls, take the 10th Avenue exit (US 87). Drive five miles east to 51st Street, and then a quarter of a mile south to the campground.

Trip note: This camp has gravel sites that overlook the surrounding valleys. If you don't have an air mattress, cabins are available. Many sidetrips offer possibilities: Giant Springs Fish, Wildlife and Parks Visitor Center and Fish Hatchery, located off US 87 on River Drive; C. M. Russell Museum (cowboy artist) at 400 13th Street; Cascade County Historical Museum at 1400 First Avenue North; Malmstrom Air Force Base Museum at the base east of town off Second Avenue. A golf course in the area also provides a recreation possibility.

25) SEELEY LAKE

Reference: in Flathead National Forest; map M2, grid i0.

Campsites, facilities: There are 29 sites for tents, trailers and motor homes up to 32 feet long. Picnic tables are provided. Piped water and flush toilets are also available. Showers, a store, coffee shop, laundromat and ice are located within two miles. Some facilities are **wheelchair accessible.** Pets are permitted on leashes. Boat docks, launching facilities and rentals are nearby.

Reservations, fee: No reservations necessary; $7 fee per night. Open early June to mid-September.

Who to contact: Phone Lolo National Forest at (406) 677-2233 or write to Seeley Lake Ranger District, P.O. Box 717, Seeley Lake, MT 59868.

Location: From the town of Seeley Lake, drive one mile south on Highway 83, then three miles northwest on County Road 70 to the campground.

Trip note: This is one of two camps in the immediate area. This one is on the opposite side of the Clearwater River from River Point Camp. Swimming, fishing and boating are all options here. If you have any questions about the lake and surrounding area, visit the Seeley Lake Ranger Station at the north end of the lake. See trip note for Big Larch Camp for more details.

26) BIG LARCH

Reference: on Seeley Lake, Flathead National Forest; map M2, grid i0.

Campsites, facilities: There are 50 sites for tents, trailers and motor homes up to 32 feet long. Picnic sites are provided. Piped water and flush toilets are also available. Showers, store, laundromat and ice are located within one mile. Pets are permitted on leashes. Boat docks, launching facilities and rentals are nearby. The facilities are **wheelchair accessible.**

Reservations, fee: No reservations necessary; $7 fee per night. Open year-round.

Who to contact: Phone Lolo National Forest at (406) 677-2233 or write to Seeley Lake Ranger District, P.O. Box 717, Seeley Lake, MT 59868.

Location: From the town of Seeley Lake, drive 1.3 miles northwest on Highway 83, and then a half mile west on Forest Service Road 2199 to the campground.

Trip note: This is one of three camps nestled along Seeley Lake, a popular spot for boating, fishing, swimming and waterskiing. The entire lake is surrounded by the Seeley Lake Game Preserve. This spot is set on the east shore. There are a few hiking trails in the area.

27) RIVER POINT

Reference: on Seeley Lake, Flathead National Forest; map M2, grid i0.

Campsites, facilities: There are 27 sites for tents, trailers and motor homes up to 22 feet long. Picnic sites are provided. Piped water and pit toilets are also available. Showers, a store, laundromat and ice are located within five miles. Pets are permitted on leashes. Boat docks, launching facilities and rentals are nearby.

Reservations, fee: No reservations necessary; $7 fee per night. Open mid-June to mid-September.

Who to contact: Phone Flathead National Forest at (406) 677-2233 or write to Seeley Lake Ranger District, P.O. Box 717, Seeley Lake, MT 59868.

Location: From the town of Seeley Lake, drive one mile south on Highway 83, then two miles northwest on County Road 70 to the campground.

Trip note: This is one of two camps on the west side of Seeley Lake. This particular one is nestled adjacent to where the Clearwater River empties into the lake. The entire area is a wildlife preserve. This site offers both a swimming beach and fishing access.

28) BEAN LAKE

Reference: near Scapegoat Mountain; map M2, grid i4.

Campsites, facilities: There are 50 drive-through sites for tents, trailers or motor homes of any length. Picnic tables are provided. Pit toilets and firewood are also available. There is **no piped water.** Pets are permitted on leashes.

Reservations, fee: No reservations necessary; no fee. Open all year.

Who to contact: Phone Montana Department of Fish, Wildlife and Parks at (406) 444-2535 or write to 1420 East Sixth Avenue, Helena, MT 59620.

Location: From Augusta, drive 18 miles southwest on County Road 434 to the campground.

Trip note: This camp is set in a primitive state park that covers 17 acres. It's set below Scapegoat Mountain (9,185 feet) which is located to the immediate west. There isn't a whole lot to do here except tell ghost stories around the campfire, but you're almost guaranteed to get a site, and hey, it's free.

---

29) MONTURE

Reference: in Lolo National Forest; map M2, grid j1.

Campsites, facilities: There are five sites for tents, trailers and motor homes up to 22 feet long. Picnic tables are provided. Pit toilets are also available. There is piped water located within one mile. Pets are permitted on leashes.

Reservations, fee: No reservations necessary; no fee. Open mid-June to late September.

Who to contact: Phone Lolo National Forest at (406) 677-2233 or write to Seeley Lake Ranger District, P.O. Drawer G, Seeley Lake, MT 59868.

Location: From Ovando, drive 8.9 miles north on Forest Service Road 89 (Monture Road—good gravel road) to the campground.

Trip note: You get easy access and a small, intimate spot at this camp. For the ambitious, there are several trails in the area, though none lead directly out of camp. A Forest Service map details the possibilities.

---

30) BIG NELSON

Reference: on Coopers Lake, Lolo National Forest; map M2, grid j2.

Campsites, facilities: There are four tent sites. Picnic tables are provided. Pit toilets are also available. There is **no piped water.** Pets are permitted on leashes. A boat launch is nearby.

Reservations, fee: No reservations necessary; no fee. Open mid-June to mid-September.

Who to contact: Phone Lolo National Forest at (406) 677-2233 or write to Seeley Ranger District, P.O. Drawer G, Seeley Lake, MT 59868.

Location: From Ovando, drive 8.3 miles east on Highway 200. Turn northeast on Forest Service Road 500 and continue 11.2 miles to the campground.

Trip note: This is the most primitive of the five camps in the area and is a small site set on Coopers Lake. The lake is about a mile long and offers a boat launch. Fishing can be good here. A trail at the north end of the lake provides access to Scapegoat Wilderness which lies to the northeast. Be willing to put your time in though; it's a multi-day excursion.

---

31) ASPEN GROVE

Reference: on Blackfoot River, Helena National Forest; map M2, grid j3.

Campsites, facilities: There are 20 sites for tents, trailers and motor homes up to 20 feet long. Picnic tables are provided. Piped water and pit toilets are also available. Pets are permitted on leashes.

Reservations, fee: No reservations necessary; $5 fee per night. Open June to late September.

Who to contact: Phone Helena National Forest at (406) 362-4265 or write to Lincoln Ranger District, P.O. Box 219, Lincoln, MT 59639.

Location: From Lincoln, drive 7.1 miles east on Highway 200, then a quarter of a mile southeast on Forest Service Road 1040 to the campground.

Trip note: This is one of five Forest Service camps nestled in the Rocky Mountains. This one's just a short drive out of Lincoln and is set beside the Blackfoot River, a nice little trout stream.

---

32) COPPER CREEK

Reference: on Copper Creek, Helena National Forest; map M2, grid j3.

Campsites, facilities: There are 21 sites for tents, trailers and motor homes up to 20 feet long. Picnic tables are provided. Piped water and pit toilets are also available. Pets are permitted on leashes.

Reservations, fee: No reservations necessary; $5 fee per night. Open mid-June to late September.

Who to contact: Phone Helena National Forest at (406) 362-4265 or write to Lincoln Ranger District, P.O. Box 219, Lincoln, MT 59639.

Location: From Lincoln, drive 6.5 miles east on Highway 200. Turn northwest on Forest Service Road 330 and proceed for 8.5 miles to the campground.

Trip note: This is one of five Rocky Mountain camps in the immediate area. This one is set on Copper Creek, a short distance from Snowbank Lake, which has fishing, swimming and non-motorized boating available. This is also a prime trailhead camp. One trail leads southwest to Stonewall Mountain (8,270 feet); others are routed north through Indian Meadows and into the Scapegoat Wilderness.

33) HOLTER LAKE

Reference: on Holter Lake; map M2, grid j6.

Campsites, facilities: There are 28 sites for tents, trailers and motor homes of any length. Picnic tables are provided. Piped water and pit toilets are also available. Pets are permitted on leashes. A boat launch is nearby. Some facilities are **wheelchair accessible.**

Reservations, fee: No reservations necessary; $5-$7 fee per night. Open May to October.

Who to contact: Phone (406) 494-5059 or write to P.O. Box 3388, Butte, MT 59702.

Location: From Wolf Creek, drive two miles north on Recreation Road, across a bridge, then three miles east on a County Road to the campground.

Trip note: This is a state park campground, and it's the only camp set on upper Holter Lake, a long narrow lake which is popular for boating, fishing, swimming and waterskiing. A possible sidetrip is to visit the Beartooth Game Management Area to the southeast.

Montana Map M3
12 listings
Pages 348-355

North—Canada
East (M4)—see page 356
South (M8)—see page 408
West (M2)—see page 332

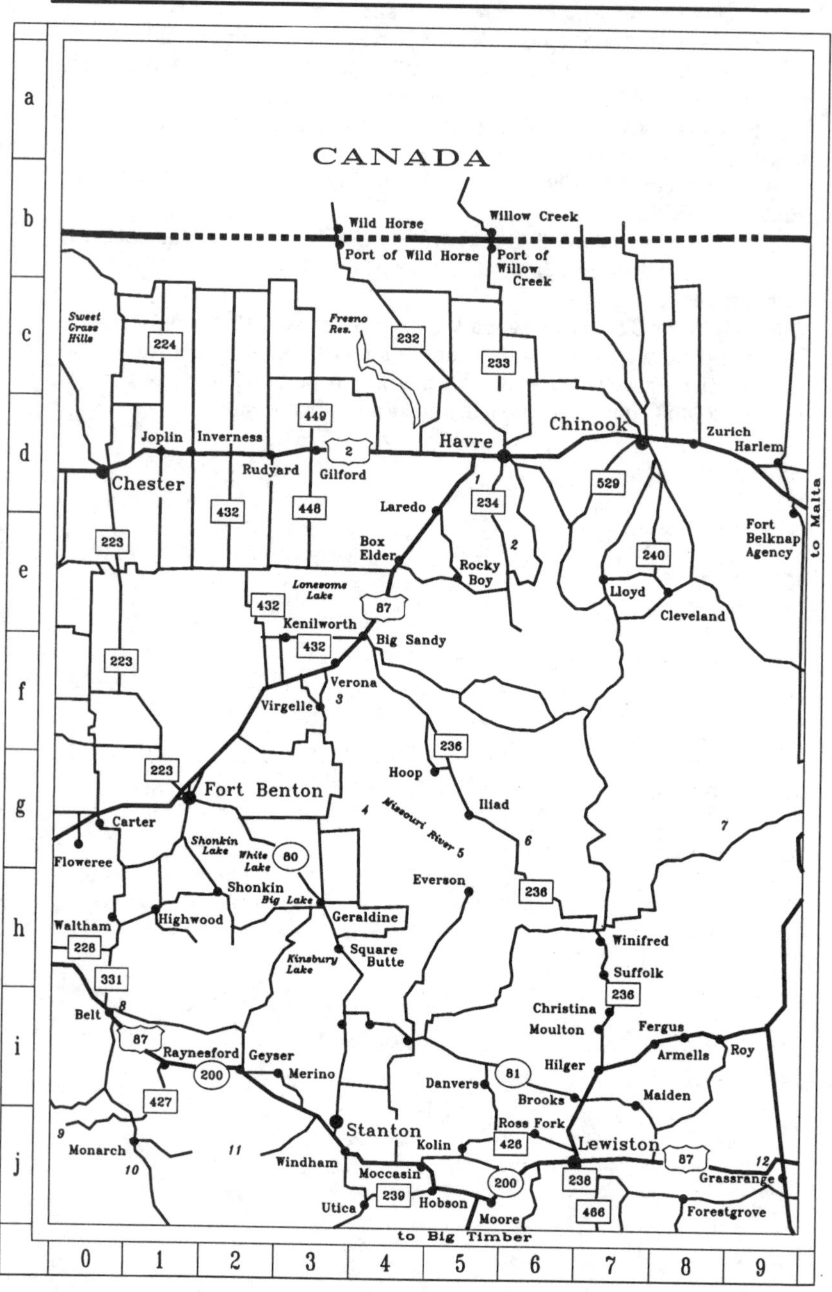

Featuring: Fresno Reservoir, Missouri River, Logging Creek, Lewis and Clark National Forest, Belt Creek, Dry Wolf Creek, Warhorse National Wildlife Refuge

---

1) EVERGREEN

Reference: near Fresno Reservoir; map M3, grid d5.

Campsites, facilities: There are 20 tent sites and 22 sites for trailers or motor homes of any length. Picnic tables are provided. Piped water, flush toilets, showers, firewood, laundromat and ice are also available. Pets and motorbikes are permitted.

Reservations, fee: Reservations accepted; $10-$15 fee per night. Open all year with limited winter facilities.

Who to contact: Phone (406) 265-8228 or write to P.O. Box 1023, Havre, MT 59501.

Location: From the junction of US 2 and US 87 in Havre, drive four miles south on US 87 to the campground.

Trip note: This is a seven-acre park that can be used as a simple layover spot, or a base camp to do some fishing. The latter can be good, especially by canoe, at the Rookery State Recreation Area on Fresno Reservoir. (From Havre, drive north on Seventh Avenue across the Milk River Bridge to River Road. Turn west and drive 4.5 miles). Canoes are ideal here, because boats must be carried in. An option for campers is to try the Bearpaw Lake State Recreation Area, 17 miles south of Havre on Highway 234, where primitive camping is available.

---

2) BEAVER CREEK PARK

Reference: south of Havre; map M3, grid e6.

Campsites, facilities: There are 250 drive-through sites Piped water is available at park office. Pit toilets and firewood are also available. Sanitary disposal station, recreation hall, a store and ice are nearby. Pets are permitted on leashes.

Reservations, fee: No reservations necessary; $5-$7 fee per night. Group camps $10 per day, available by reservation only. Open all year.

Who to contact: Phone (406) 395-4565 or write to Shamble Route, P.O. Box 368, Havre, MT 59501.

Location: From Havre, drive 15 miles south on Highway 234 to the park.

Trip note: This is a vast county park that covers more than 10,000 acres. There are lots of trails for horseback riding and hiking. This is ranch country where people bring their own horses and ride the range. Nearby Rocky Boy Indian Reservation was named after a Chippewa leader whose name was Stone Child. Why the government changed it to Rocky Boy is typical bureaucratic condescension.

3) COAL BANKS LANDING

Reference: on Missouri River; map M3, grid f3.

Campsites, facilities: There are five tent sites. Picnic tables are provided. Pit toilets are also available. There is **no piped water.** Pets are permitted on leashes.

Reservations, fee: No reservations necessary; no fee. Open May to late September.

Who to contact: Phone Montana Department of Fish, Wildlife and Parks at (406) 444-2535 or write to 1420 East Sixth Avenue, Helena, MT 59620.

Location: From the town of Fort Benton, drive 20 miles northeast on US 87 to milepost 67, eight miles south to Virgelle, and then eight miles east by boat on the Missouri River.

Trip note: Visitors might think that there are no primitive camps in this part of Montana. Wrong, providing you have a boat to get there. This is one of three boat-in camps set along the Missouri River. It is not maintained, and offers nothing more than a place to set up your tent, but you're likely to be the only one around for miles.

4) HOLE-IN-THE-WALL LANDING

Reference: on Missouri River; map M3, grid g4.

Campsites, facilities: There are five tent sites. Picnic tables are provided. Pit toilets are also available. There is **no piped water.** Pets are permitted on leashes.

Reservations, fee: No reservations necessary; no fee. Open May to late September.

Who to contact: Phone Montana Department of Fish, Wildlife and Parks at (406) 444-2535 or write to 1420 East Sixth Avenue, Helena, MT 59620.

Location: From the town of Fort Benton, drive 20 miles northeast on US 87 to milepost 67. Turn south and continue for eight miles to Virgelle, then proceed 21 miles east and south by boat on the Missouri River.

Trip note: You want to join our Five Percent Club, those few visitors who know the premium areas everybody else misses? With a boat you have a chance. That's the only way to reach this camp which covers ten acres. It's one of three on this stretch of the Wild and Scenic Missouri River. It is quite pretty, with a wilderness-like feel to it, and the fishing can be good here.

5) SLAUGHTER RIVER

Reference: on Missouri River; map M3, grid g5.

Campsites, facilities: There are five tent sites. Picnic tables are provided. Pit toilets are also available. There is **no piped water.** Pets are permitted on leashes.

Reservations, fee: No reservations necessary; no fee. Open May to late September.

Who to contact: Phone Montana Department of Fish, Wildlife and Parks at (406) 444-2535 or write to 1420 East Sixth Avenue, Helena, MT 59620.

Location: From the town of Fort Benton, drive 20 miles northeast on US 87 to milepost 67. Turn south and continue for eight miles to Virgelle, then proceed 35 miles south and east by boat along the Missouri River.

Trip note: This is one of three boat-in camps on the Missouri River around these parts. This camp covers 42 acres and is set on the north shore. You can usually expect to have the place to yourself.

---

6) JUDITH LANDING

Reference: on Missouri River; map M3, grid g6.

Campsites, facilities: There are five tent sites. Picnic tables are provided. Pit toilets are also available. There is **no piped water.** Pets are permitted on leashes.

Reservations, fee: No reservations necessary; no fee. Open late-May to late September.

Who to contact: Phone Montana Department of Fish, Wildlife and Parks at (406) 444-2535 or write to 1420 East Sixth Avenue, Helena, MT 59620.

Location: From the town of Fort Benton, drive 20 miles northeast on US 87 to milepost 67. Turn south and continue for eight miles to Virgelle, then proceed 41 miles south and east by boat along the Missouri River. By car, turn off US 87 at milepost 79 in Big Sandy, and drive 44 miles south on Highway 236 to the campground.

Trip note: This is a do-it-yourself special. It's small, unknown, primitive, and is set aside the Wild and Scenic Missouri River. It's also free, and offers the rare campground gift of solitude.

---

7) COW ISLAND LANDING

Reference: on Missouri River; map M3, grid g8.

Campsites, facilities: There are five tent sites. Picnic tables are provided. Pit toilets are also available. There is **no piped water.** Pets are permitted on leashes.

Reservations, fee: No reservations necessary; no fee. Open May to late September.

Who to contact: Phone Montana Department of Fish, Wildlife and Parks at (406) 444-2535 or write to 1420 East Sixth Avenue, Helena, MT 59620.

Location: From the town of Fort Benton, drive 20 miles northeast on US 87 to milepost 67. Turn south and continue for eight miles to Virgelle, then proceed 28 miles east and south by boat on the Wild and Scenic Missouri River.

Trip note: This is a boat-in only campsite, one of a handful on the Missouri River. Needless to say, this is a primitive camp set on an island. A good nearby, drive-to option is the James Kipp State Recreation Area, which is also set near the river.

---

8) FORT PONDEROSA

Reference: southeast of Great Falls; map M3, grid i1.

Campsites, facilities: There are 37 sites for tents, trailers and motor homes of any length. Picnic tables are provided. Flush toilets, bottled gas, sanitary disposal station, showers, firewood, laundromat, ice and a playground are also available. Electricity, piped water and sewer hookups are available at an additional charge. A store and coffee shop are located within one mile. Pets are permitted on leashes.

Reservations, fee: Reservations accepted; $10-$15 fee per night. Open all year.

Who to contact: Phone (406) 277-3232 or write to 568 Armington Road, Belt, MT 59412.

Location: From the town of Great Falls, drive 20 miles southeast on US 87. Turn north at Johnny's Bar (well signed) and drive one mile north to the campground.

Trip note: This is a good layover spot 25 miles distant from Great Falls. You get level and grassy sites sprinkled on seven acres of parkland.

---

9) LOGGING CREEK

Reference: on Logging Creek, Lewis and Clark National Forest; map M3, grid j0.

Campsites, facilities: There are 26 sites for tents, trailers and motor homes up to 22 feet long. Picnic tables are provided. Piped water and vault toilets are also available. Some facilities are **wheelchair accessible.** Pets are permitted on leashes.

Reservations, fee: No reservations necessary; no fee. Open mid-June to mid-October.

Who to contact: Phone Lewis and Clark National Forest at (406) 547-3361 or write to King's Hill Ranger District, P.O. Box A, White Sulphur Springs, MT 59645.

Location: From Monarch, drive three miles north on US 89. Turn west on County Road 427 and drive 5.7 miles, then turn southwest on Forest Service Road 253 and drive six miles to the campground.

Trip note: This is just far enough out of the way that out-of-towners miss it every time. But it's a pretty spot set beside Logging Creek. There's a short trail that runs south of camp and follows along Dry Gulch. More hiking options are available to the west; see a Forest Service map.

10) ASPEN

Reference: on Belt Creek, Lewis and Clark National Forest; map M3, grid j1.

Campsites, facilities: There are six sites for tents, trailers and motor homes up to 22 feet long. Picnic tables are provided. Piped water, firewood and vault toilets are also available. A store, coffee shop and ice are located within five miles. Some facilities are **wheelchair accessible.** Pets are permitted on leashes.

Reservations, fee: No reservations necessary; $5 fee per night. Open June to mid-October.

Who to contact: Phone Lewis and Clark National Forest at (406) 547-3361 or write to King's Hill Ranger District, P.O. Box A, White Sulphur Springs, MT 59645.

Location: From Neihart, drive four miles north on US 89 to the campground.

Trip note: This is a tiny camp set along US 89 and is along Belt Creek. A trail from camp passes the ranger station (where you can get any questions answered), and then heads west along Crawford Creek, or east along Pioneer Ridge.

11) DRY WOLF

Reference: on Dry Wolf Creek, Lewis and Clark National Forest; map M3, grid j2.

Campsites, facilities: There are 26 sites for tents, trailers, or motor homes up to 22 feet long. Picnic tables are provided. Hand-pumped water, firewood and vault toilets are also available. Dry Wolf Cabin is available for rental during the hunting season; call ranger for information. Pets are permitted on leashes.

Reservations, fee: No reservations necessary; $4 fee per night. Open June to mid-September.

Who to contact: Phone Lewis and Clark National Forest at (406) 566-2292 or write to Judith Ranger District, 109 Central Avenue, P.O. Box 484, Stanford, MT 59479.

Location: From Stanford, drive one mile west on Highway 87, then turn south on Dry Wolf Road and drive 19 miles to the campground located at the end of the road.

Trip note: This is one of two fairly remote camps in the area. This one is set on Dry Wolf Creek, a trailhead camp, and has many trails branching out in several directions to the surrounding wildlands, including Silver Gulch Trail and Placer Creek Trail. There is fishing access just upstream of the campground.

12) LITTLE MONTANA TRUCKSTOP

Reference: near Warhorse National Wildlife Refuge; map M3, grid j9.

Campsites, facilities: There are 12 drive-through sites for trailers or motor homes of any length. Piped water, sewer hookups and picnic tables are provided. Flush toilets, sanitary disposal station, showers, a store, coffee shop and ice are also available. Pets and motorbikes are permitted.

Reservations, fee: Call ahead for available space and fee; MasterCard and Visa accepted. Open all year.

Who to contact: Phone (406) 428-2270 or write to P.O. Box 831, Grass Range, MT 59032.

Location: This campground is located in Grass Range on US 87.

Trip note: This is not the most scenic area in Montana, but if you're cruising Highway 200 or US 87 looking for a camping spot, hang in there and be happy you found this one. And if you end up hanging out for awhile, a good sidetrip is to Warhorse National Wildlife Refuge set to the immediate northeast.

Montana Map M4
11 listings
Pages 356-361

North—Canada
East (M5)—see page 362
South (M9)—see page 430
West (M3)—see page 348

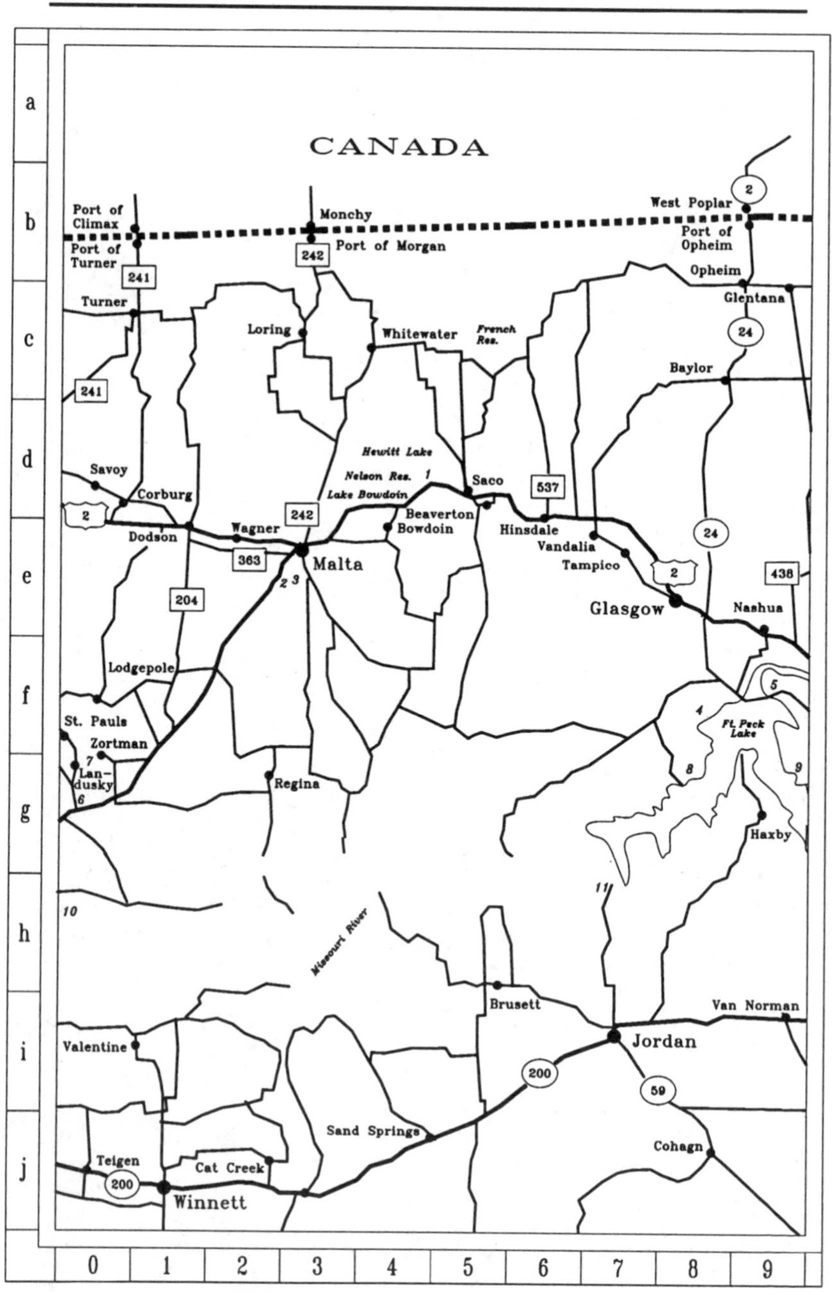

Featuring: Nelson Reservoir, Fort Peck Lake, Little Rockies, Missouri River

1) NELSON RESERVOIR

Reference: on Nelson Reservoir; map M4, grid d4.

Campsites, facilities: There are five sites for tents, trailers and motor homes of any length. Picnic tables are provided. Piped water and pit toilets are also available. A store and coffee shop are located within one mile. Pets are permitted on leashes. Boat launching facilities are nearby.

Reservations, fee: No reservations necessary; no fee. Open year-round.

Who to contact: Phone Montana Department of Fish, Wildlife and Parks at (406) 444-2535 or write to 1420 East Sixth Avenue, Helena, MT 59620.

Location: From Malta, drive 18 miles east on US 2 to milepost 488, and then two miles north on a county road to the campground

Trip note: This is a tiny spot on the eastern end of Nelson Reservoir and the only camp at the lake. It's fairly primitive, but it does offer drinking water, and hey, you can't beat the price. Boating, fishing and waterskiing are all popular here.

2) EDGEWATER INN AND CAMPGROUND

Reference: near Malta; map M4, grid e3.

Campsites, facilities: There are 30 tent sites and 40 sites for trailers or motor homes of any length. Picnic tables are provided. Flush toilets, sanitary disposal station, a store, laundromat, ice, sauna, jacuzzi, heated indoor swimming pool and exercise room are also available. Electricity, piped water, and sewer hookups are available at an additional charge. Bottled gas and coffee shop are located within one mile. Pets are permitted on leashes. Boat docks, launching facilities and rentals are nearby.

Reservations, fee: Reservations accepted; $8.50-$21 fee per night; American Express, MasterCard and Visa accepted. Open all year.

Who to contact: Phone (406) 654-1302 or write to P.O. Box 1316, Malta, MT 59538.

Location: From the junction of US 2 and Highway 242 in Malta, drive west on US 2 for a short distance to the campground.

Trip note: This is one of two parks in the area. This one is pretty, with grassy tent sites, graveled RV sites, and lots of trees and shade. It offers several nearby sidetrips. The Bowdoin National Wildlife Refuge is located west of town and is a big nesting area for the white pelican. At the east of town, there is a unique, big boulder that is shaped like a buffalo, and it has markings on it from the Assiniboine Indian tribe. You can also see pioneer and Native American relics at the Phillips County Museum at 133 South First Street.

3) TRAFTON PARK

Reference: in Malta, on Milk River; map M4, grid e3.

Campsites, facilities: There are 25 sites for tents, trailers and motor homes of any length. Picnic tables are provided. Piped water, pit toilets and a playground are also available. A store and coffee shop are located within one mile. Pets are permitted on leashes.

Reservations, fee: No reservations necessary; $3 fee per night. Open all year with limited facilities in the winter.

Who to contact: Phone (406) 654-1251 or write to P.O. Drawer L, Malta, MT 59538.

Location: At the intersection of Highways 2 and 191 in Malta, turn north at the City Center sign, and drive to the park.

Trip note: This is a good spot for tenters in the area. Set on the Milk River, it offers easy highway access in a pretty setting, with lots of trees. It's within the city limits, but far enough away from the business district that you still feel like you're in the great outdoors. It's a city-managed park that covers six acres. See the trip note for Edgewater Camp for sidetrip possibilities.

4) FORT PECK WEST RECREATION AREA

Reference: on Fort Peck Lake; map M4, grid f8.

Campsites, facilities: There are 21 sites for trailers or motor homes up to 24 feet long. Picnic tables are provided. Piped water, flush toilets, showers and a playground are also available. Sanitary disposal station are located within four miles. Some facilities are **wheelchair accessible.** Pets are permitted on leashes. Boat docks, launching facilities and rentals are nearby.

Reservations, fee: No reservations necessary; $6-$8 fee per night. Open Memorial Day to Labor Day with limited winter facilities.

Who to contact: Phone Corps of Engineers, Fort Peck Lake at (406) 526-3411 or write to P.O. Box 208, Fort Peck, MT 59223.

Location: From Glasgow, drive 19 miles southeast on Highway 24, and then two miles south on a gravel road (well signed) to the campground.

Trip note: This is a good spot for campers, boaters or fishermen. It's set near the shore of Fort Peck Lake, with wide, open sites and prairie-type vegetation. This spot is a major recreation area on Fort Peck Lake covering over 120 acres. There's a small marina and boat ramp too.

5) DOWNSTREAM CAMP

Reference: on Missouri River; map M4, grid f9.

Campsites, facilities: There are 51 sites for trailers or motor homes up to 24 feet long. Picnic tables are provided. Piped water, flush toilets, showers and a playground are also available. Sanitary disposal station, a store, coffee shop, laundromat and ice are located within one mile. Some facilities are **wheelchair accessible.** Pets are permitted on leashes. Boat launching facilities are nearby at Fort Peck Lake.

Reservations, fee: No reservations necessary; $6-$8 fee per night. Open Memorial Day to Labor Day with limited winter facilities.

Who to contact: Phone Corps of Engineers, Fort Peck Lake at (406) 526-3411 or write to P.O. Box 208, Fort Peck, MT 59223.

Location: From Glasgow, drive 23 miles southeast on Highway 24 to the campground.

Trip note: This is a 40-acre camp set one mile below the Fort Peck Dam near the Missouri River. It's a unique-looking camp, set in a river bottom in a cottonwood forest. If you prefer camping right at the lake, four camps provide that option. There is a one-mile nature trail adjacent to campground.

---

6) MONTANA GULCH

Reference: near Landusky; map M4, grid g0.

Campsites, facilities: There are five sites for tents, trailers or motor homes up to 24 feet long. Picnic tables are provided. Pit toilets and firewood are also available. There is **no piped water.** Pets are permitted on leashes.

Reservations, fee: No reservations necessary; no fee. Open May through October.

Who to contact: Phone Bureau of Land Management at (406) 255-2913 or write to P.O. Box 36800, Billings, MT 59107.

Location: From Landusky, drive a half mile northwest on a county road (well signed), and follow the signs to the campground.

Trip note: This is one of the primitive camps managed by the BLM that gets little use and is missed by most everybody, including every other camp guide published. It's set near a small creek along the slopes of the Little Rocky Mountains. There's not much out here but trees and bugs, but you're just about guaranteed solitude.

---

7) CAMP CREEK

Reference: near the Little Rockies; map M4, grid g0.

Campsites, facilities: There are nine sites for tents, trailers, or motor homes up to 24 feet long. Picnic tables are provided. Firewood and pit toilets are also available. Pets are permitted on leashes. There is **no piped water** so bring your own.

Reservations, fee: No reservations necessary; no fee. Open May to October.

Who to contact: Phone Bureau of Land Management at (406) 255-2913 or write to P.O. Box 36800, Billings, MT 59107.

Location: Drive one mile northeast of the Zortman City limits to the campground.

Trip note: This is another little, out-of-the-way place that almost nobody knows about, but the access is quite easy. The camp is set along the southern slopes of the Little Rocky Mountains. It's a good spot for hiking. There are no maintained trails in the immediate vicinity, but the ambitious can tromp around and explore anyway.

---

8) THE PINES

Reference: on Fort Peck Lake; map M4, grid g8.

Campsites, facilities: There are 35 sites for tents, trailers and motor homes up to 25 feet long. Picnic tables are provided. Pit toilets and firewood are also available. There is limited water, so bring your own. Pets are permitted on leashes. Boat launching facilities are nearby.

Reservations, fee: No reservations necessary; no fee. Open April to November.

Who to contact: Phone Corps of Engineers, Fort Peck Lake at (406) 526-3411 or write to P.O. Box 208, Fort Peck, MT 59223.

Location: From Glasgow, drive 12 miles southeast on Highway 24, and then 26 miles southwest on a gravel road (impassable when wet) to the campground.

Trip note: This is a primitive campground set on a peninsula that juts out into Fort Peck Lake along the northern shore. It covers 200 acres. An undeveloped boat ramp provides access for boaters and fishermen. The camp is sparse and doesn't offer many amenities, but it is a quieter, less expensive option to Fort Peck West Recreation Area.

---

9) ROCK CREEK STATE PARK

Reference: on Fort Peck Lake; map M4, grid g9.

Campsites, facilities: There are 25 sites for tents, trailers or motor homes of any length. Picnic tables are provided. Piped water, firewood and pit toilets are also available. Pets are permitted on leashes. Boat launching facilities are nearby.

Reservations, fee: No reservations necessary; no fee. Open May to October.

Who to contact: Phone Montana Department of Fish, Wildlife and Parks at (406) 444-2535 or write to 1420 East Sixth Avenue, Helena, MT 59620.

Location: From Glasgow, drive 43 miles south on Highway 24, and then seven miles west on a county road to the campground.

Trip note: This site is located at Fort Peck Lake. It's set on the Dry Creek arm of the lake. It's quite primitive and used primarily by fishermen. The camp covers 235 acres and has a boat launch for boating and fishing use.

---

10) JAMES KIPP STATE PARK

Reference: on Missouri River; map M4, grid h0.

Campsites, facilities: There are 30 sites for tents, trailers and motor homes up to 20 feet long. Picnic tables are provided. Firewood and pit toilets are also available. There is **no piped water** so bring your own. Pets are permitted on leashes. Boat launching facilities are nearby.

Reservations, fee: No reservations necessary; no fee. Open mid-May through November.

Who to contact: Phone Montana Bureau of Land Management at (406) 538-7461 or write P.O. Box 1160, Lewistown, MT 59457.

Location: From Lewistown, drive 65 miles northeast on Highway 191 to the campground.

Trip note: This is a big state park with the Missouri River as the centerpiece. Boating and fishing access is provided. In addition, a good adventure is awaiting you in the surrounding Charles M. Russell National Wildlife Refuge. Hiking is another option at this camp.

---

11) HELL CREEK STATE PARK

Reference: on Fort Peck Lake; map M4, grid h7.

Campsites, facilities: There are 40 sites for tents, trailers and motor homes up to 20 feet long. Picnic tables are provided. Piped water and pit toilets are also available. Pets are permitted on leashes. Boat launching facilities are nearby.

Reservations, fee: No reservations necessary; \$4-\$6 fee per night. Open mid-May to mid-September.

Who to contact: Phone Montana Department of Fish, Wildlife and Parks at (406) 444-2535 or write to 1420 East Sixth Avenue, Helena, MT 59620.

Location: At Jordan, along Highway 200, go to milepost 213 and drive 24 miles north on a county road to the campground.

Trip note: This is a pretty spot set along a cove on the southern shoreline of Fort Peck Lake. The park covers 113 acres, provides a ramp for boaters and fishermen, and is just far enough from the highway to get little use from out-of-towners. Local fishermen know about this one, though, so be sure to claim a good spot early.

Montana Map M5
2 listings
Pages 362-363

North—Canada
East—The Dakotas
South (M10)—see page 434
West (M4)—see page 356

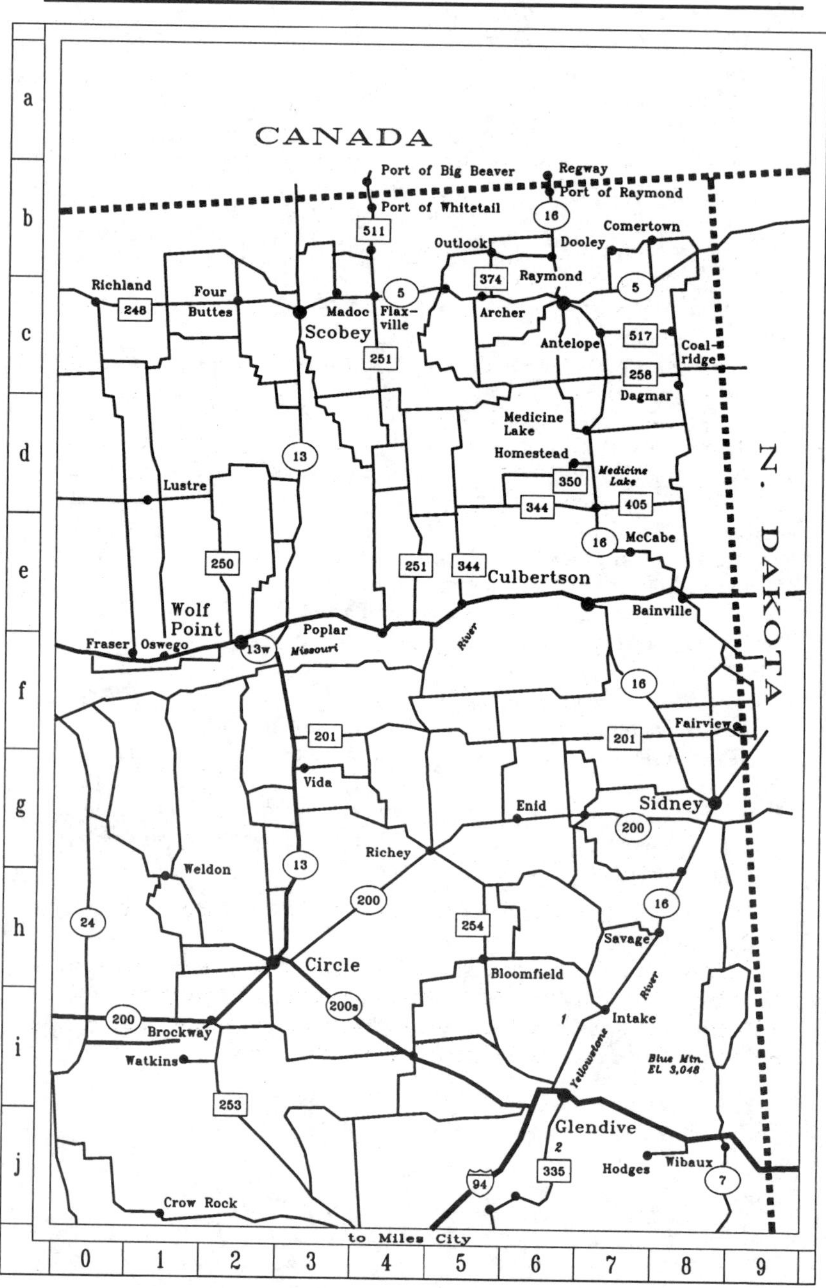

Featuring: Yellowstone River

---

1) GREEN VALLEY

Reference: on Yellowstone River; map M5, grid i6.

Campsites, facilities: There are 50 tent sites and 50 sites for trailers or motor homes of any length. Piped water and picnic tables are provided. Flush toilets, sanitary disposal station, showers, recreation hall, laundromat, ice and a playground are also available. Electricity and sewer hookups are available at an additional charge. Bottled gas, a store and coffee shop are located within one mile. Pets are permitted on leashes.

Reservations, fee: Reservations accepted; $7-$11 fee per night. Open April through October.

Who to contact: Phone (406) 359-9944 or write to P.O. Box 1396, Glendive, MT 59330.

Location: From Interstate 94 in Glendive, take exit 213. Drive a half mile north on Highway 16, and then a quarter mile east to the campground (a paved, well-signed road).

Trip note: This is one of two camps set along the northwest shore of the Yellowstone River. The park covers 15 acres and is one of the prettier spots in the region. The sites are level and grassy, with many set in the trees.

---

2) MAKOSHIKA

Reference: near Yellowstone River; map M5, grid j6.

Campsites, facilities: There are six tent sites. Picnic tables are provided. Piped water, pit toilets and firewood are also available. Pets are permitted on leashes.

Reservations, fee: No reservations necessary; no fee. Open mid-May to mid-September.

Who to contact: Phone Montana Department of Fish, Wildlife and Parks at (406) 444-2535 or write to 1420 East Sixth Avenue, Helena, MT 59620.

Location: Drive two miles southeast of Glendive on Snyder Avenue to the campground.

Trip note: This camp is set in an 800-acre state park set just south of Glendive and not far from the Yellowstone River. It's very pretty here, with nearby access to the Yellowstone River and an abundance of wildlife and vegetation. Nature trails are routed near the camp.

Montana Map M6
33 listings
Pages 364-379

North (M1)—see page 284
East (M7)—see page 380
South—Idaho
West—Idaho

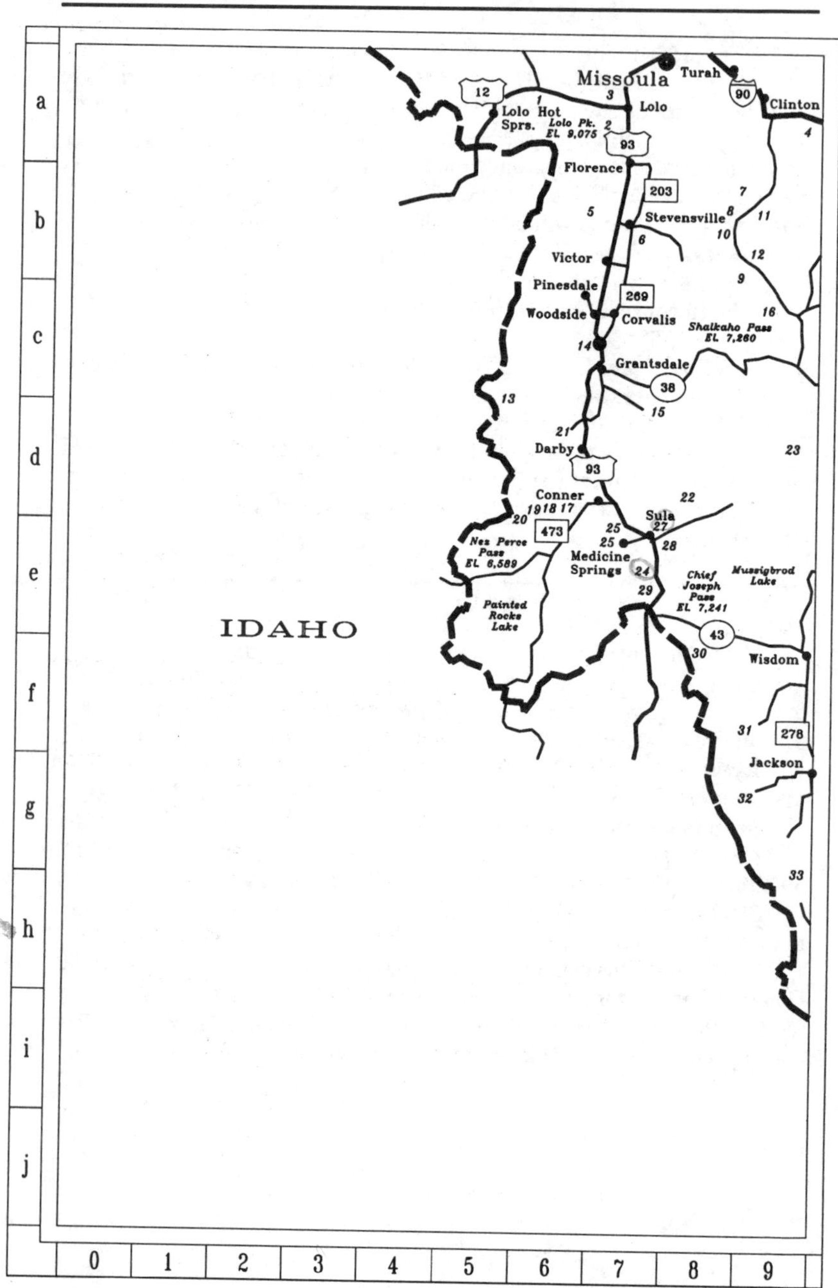

Featuring: Lolo Creek, Lolo National Forest, Clark Fork River, Bass Creek, Bitterroot National Forest, Bitterroot River, Rock Creek, Grizzly Creek, Bear Creek, Skalkaho Creek, Deerlodge National Forest, West Fork of Bitterroot River, Painted Rocks Lake, Lake Como, Moose and Martin Creeks, Moose Lake, Warm Springs Creek, Continental Divide, Beaverhead National Forest, Twin Lakes, Lower Miner Lake, Selway Mountain

---

1) LEWIS AND CLARK

Reference: near Lolo Creek, Lolo National Forest; map M6, grid a6.

Campsites, facilities: There are 17 sites for tents, trailers and motor homes up to 32 feet long. Picnic sites are provided. Piped water, firewood and vault toilets are also available. A store and ice are located within five miles. Pets are permitted on leashes.

Reservations, fee: No reservations necessary; $5 fee per night. Open Memorial to Labor Day.

Who to contact: Phone Lolo National Forest at (406) 329-3814 or write to Missoula Ranger District, Building 24-A, Fort Missoula, MT 59801.

Location: From Lolo, drive 14.8 miles west on US 12 to the campground.

Trip note: This site is set near Lolo Creek. The Lewis and Clark Trail runs nearby. Backpackers can take the trail for many miles southwest into the adjacent wildlands.

---

2) SQUARE AND ROUND DANCE RV

Reference: near Lolo Creek; map M6, grid a7.

Campsites, facilities: There are 10 tent sites and 56 sites for trailers or motor homes. Picnic tables are provided. Flush toilets, sanitary disposal station, showers and a recreation hall are also available. Electricity, piped water and sewer hookups are available at an additional charge. Bottled gas, a coffee shop and ice are located within one mile. Pets and motorbikes are permitted.

Reservations, fee: Reservations accepted; $10-$15 fee per night. Open mid-May to late September.

Who to contact: Phone (406) 273-0141 or write to 9955 US 12 West, Lolo, MT 59847.

Location: From the junction of US 93 and US 12 in Lolo, drive 2.5 miles west on US 12 to the campground.

Trip note: This is a privately operated park that covers 27 acres, with Lolo Creek flowing through the back part of the campground. It is surrounded by ponderosa pine trees, and offers a nature trail with excellent views of the surrounding mountains. There are many national forest trails available within a few minutes drive; see a Forest Service map. And for all you dosie-doers, there's a square dance center with lessons available.

3) OUTPOST

Reference: southwest of Missoula; map M6, grid a7.

Campsites, facilities: There are 30 tent sites and 20 sites for trailers or motor homes. Picnic tables are provided. Flush toilets, sanitary disposal station, showers, a store, laundromat, ice and a playground are also available. Pets and motorbikes are permitted.

Reservations, fee: No reservations necessary; $8-$10 fee per night; MasterCard and Visa accepted. Open all year.

Who to contact: Phone (406) 549-2016 or write to Highway 93 North, Missoula, MT 59802.

Location: From Missoula, drive eight miles southwest on US 93 to the campground.

Trip note: This is one of three camps in the vicinity of Lolo and is where US 12 and US 93 intersect. It has grassy, open sites surrounded by green ash and poplar trees. One sidetrip option is to visit the Fort Fizzle picnic area, which is located five miles west of Lolo on US 12. It's a wooded canyon on Lolo Creek that provides fishing access. For hikers, a trail begins from Lolo along the route of the Lewis and Clark Trail and runs westward along Lolo Creek.

4) BEAVERTAIL HILL STATE PARK

Reference: on Clark Fork River; map M6, grid a9.

Campsites, facilities: There are several tent sites and 15 drive-through sites for trailers or motor homes of any length. Picnic tables are provided. Flush toilets and piped water are also available. Pets are permitted on leashes.

Reservations, fee: No reservations necessary; $5-$7 fee per night. Open May to late September.

Who to contact: Phone Montana Department of Fish, Wildlife and Parks at (406) 444-2535 or write to 1420 East Sixth Avenue, Helena, MT 59620.

Location: From Missoula, drive 26 miles east on Interstate 90 to Beavertail exit 130, then travel three-quarters of a mile south to the park.

Trip note: This is a privately run park that covers 65 acres and is set on Clark Fork River. It's beautiful, with large sites and fishing access. It's a companion state area to Turah State Park (12 miles east of Missoula) which is also on Clark Fork.

5) CHARLES WATERS

Reference: near Bass Creek, Bitterroot National Forest; map M6, grid b6.

Campsites, facilities: There are 20 sites for tents, trailers and motor homes up to 22 feet long, five of which are pull-through, and one bicycle campsite. Picnic tables are provided. Piped water, firewood and pit toilets are also available. A store is located within five miles. Some facilities are **wheelchair accessible.** Pets are permitted on leashes.

Reservations, fee: No reservations necessary; $4 fee per night. Open June to late September.

Who to contact: Phone Bitterroot National Forest at (406) 777-5461 or write to Stevensville Ranger District, 88 Main Street, Stevensville, MT 59870.

Location: From Stevensville, drive 1.6 miles northwest on County Road 269 to US 92. Continue four miles north on US 92, then turn west on County Road 22 and drive 1.7 miles. Turn west on Forest Service Road 1316 and proceed a half mile to the campground.

Trip note: This is an ideal base camp for backpackers because a premium hiking trail starts here, leading into the Selway-Bitterroot Wilderness. The trail heads west along Bass Creek for eight miles up to Bass Lake, then circles the lake and heads south for three more miles (as you hike, three other lakes become accessible). It then heads east along Kootenai Creek, and then finally back to camp about three miles south of where the trail started. It's a great multi-day loop hike. There is a nature trail and a fitness trail in the camp. An historical point of interest is located in Stevensville: St. Mary's Mission and Fort Owen are the remainders of Montana's first white settlement.

---

6) ST. MARY'S RV PARK

Reference: near Bitterroot River; map M6, grid b7.

Campsites, facilities: There are five tent sites and 10 sites for trailers or motor homes of any length. Electricity, piped water, sewer hookups and picnic tables are provided. Flush toilets, sanitary disposal station, showers, a store, and laundromat are also available. Bottled gas and ice are located within one mile. Pets and motorbikes are permitted.

Reservations, fee: Reservations accepted; $6-$12.50 fee per night; MasterCard and Visa accepted. Open mid-April to late November.

Who to contact: Phone (406) 777-2838 or write to 3945 US 93, Stevensville, MT 59870.

Location: This campground is located in Missoula, just past the Stevensville Junction exit on Highway 93.

Trip note: This is a small, one-acre park set within walking distance of the Bitterroot River, surrounded by pine trees. There's a great multi-day loop hike nearby (see the trip note for Charles Waters Camp for details). A good sidetrip is the nearby game reserve, which has some good hiking trails.

---

7) DALLES

Reference: on Rock Creek, Lolo National Forest; map M6, grid b8.

Campsites, facilities: There are sites for tents or short trailers. Picnic tables are provided. Piped water (hand pump) and vault toilets are also available. Pets are permitted on leashes.

Reservations, fee: No reservations necessary; no fee. Open late May to late September.

Who to contact: Phone Lolo National Forest at (406) 329-3814 or write to Missoula Ranger District, Building 24-A, Fort Missoula, Missoula, MT 59801.

Location: From Clinton, drive 4.9 miles southeast on Interstate 90, and then south on Rock Creek Road (mostly a single-lane, gravel road that is narrow and rough) for 14.6 miles to the campground. The road is not suitable for long RVs.

Trip note: This is a primitive spot set on Rock Creek at the virtual edge of the Welcome Creek Wilderness. It's a good starting point for backpackers. A trail from camp ventures northwest along Welcome Creek and goes deep into the wilderness of the Sapphire Mountains.

---

8) HARRY'S FLAT

Reference: on Rock Creek, Lolo National Forest; map M6, grid b8.

Campsites, facilities: There are 18 sites for tents, trailers and motor homes up to 24 feet long. Picnic tables are provided. Hand-pumped water, firewood, and vault toilets are also available. Pets are permitted on leashes.

Reservations, fee: No reservations necessary; no fee. Open late May to late September.

Who to contact: Phone Lolo National Forest at (406) 329-3814 or write to Missoula Ranger District, Building 24-A, Fort Missoula, Missoula, MT 59801.

Location: From Clinton, drive 4.9 miles southeast on Interstate 90, and then 17.6 miles south on Rock Creek Road (mostly a single-lane, gravel road that is narrow and rough) to the campground. The road is not suitable for long RVs.

Trip note: One of a series of primitive camps, this one is set beside Rock Creek. There are no trails leading directly out of the camp, however within two miles of camp, there are several trailheads that are routed into the mountain wildlands and along creeks. A Forest Service map advised.

---

9) SIRIA

Reference: on Rock Creek, Lolo National Forest; map M6, grid b8.

Campsites, facilities: There are four primitive tent sites. Vault toilets are also available. There is **no piped water.** Pets are permitted on leashes.

Reservations, fee: No reservations necessary; no fee. Open year-round, weather permitting.

Who to contact: Phone Lolo National Forest at (406) 329-3814 or write to Missoula Ranger District, Building 24-A, Fort Missoula, Missoula, MT 59801.

Location: From Clinton, drive 4.9 miles southeast on Interstate 90, and then 29 miles south on Rock Creek Road (mostly a single-lane, gravel road that is narrow and rough) to the campground. The road is not suitable for long RVs.

Trip note: This is a tiny, primitive camp on Rock Creek and one of several camps along this stream. There are no trails leading out of this camp. Green Mountain rises to the west at 6,948 feet.

10) BITTERROOT FLAT

Reference: on Rock Creek, Lolo National Forest; map M6, grid b8.

Campsites, facilities: There are 15 sites for trailers or motor homes up to 24 feet long. Picnic tables are provided. Piped water (hand pump), firewood, and vault toilets are also available. Pets are permitted on leashes.

Reservations, fee: No reservations necessary; no fee. Open late May to late September.

Who to contact: Phone Lolo National Forest at (406) 329-3814 or write to Missoula Ranger District, Building 24-A, Fort Missoula, Missoula, MT 59801.

Location: From Clinton, drive 4.9 miles southeast on Interstate 90, and then 23.5 miles south on Rock Creek Road (mostly a single-lane, gravel road that is narrow and rough) to the campground. The road is not suitable for long RVs.

Trip note: This camp is another in a series on Rock Creek. A trail on the west side of the creek reaches Alder Creek and follows parallel to the stream for many miles.

11) GRIZZLY

Reference: on Grizzly Creek, Lolo National Forest; map M6, grid b9.

Campsites, facilities: There are nine sites for tents, trailers or motor homes up to 32 feet long. Picnic tables are provided. Piped water (hand pump), firewood, and pit toilets are also available. A store and ice are located within five miles. Pets are permitted.

Reservations, fee: No reservations necessary; no fee. Open late May to late September.

Who to contact: Phone Lolo National Forest at (406) 251-5237 or write Missoula Ranger District, Building 24-A, Fort Missoula, Missoula, MT 59801.

Location: From Clinton, drive 4.9 miles southeast on Interstate 90; south on Rock Creek Road (mostly single-lane, gravel road that is narrow and rough) for 10.6 miles, and then a half mile southeast on Forest Service Road 88 to the campground.

Trip note: It's no easy deal reaching this camp, but it's an ideal starting point for hikers—and as the rule goes, the more difficult to reach, the fewer the people. The camp is set at the confluence of Grizzly Creek and Ranch Creek (and about a mile from Rock Creek). Trails head out east and southeast from the camp along the two creeks for many miles into the surrounding wildlands.

---

12) NORTON

Reference: on Rock Creek, Lolo National Forest; map M6, grid b9.

Campsites, facilities: There are 10 sites for tent, trailers or motor homes up to 16 feet long. Picnic tables are provided. Piped water (hand pump), firewood and pit toilets are also available. A store and ice are located within five miles. Pets are permitted.

Reservations, fees: No reservations necessary; no fee. Open late May to late September.

Who to contact: Phone Lolo National Forest at (406) 251-5237 or write to Missoula Ranger District, Building 24-A, Fort Missoula, Missoula, MT 59801.

Location: From Clinton, drive 4.9 miles southeast on Interstate 90, and than south on Rock Creek Road (mostly a single-lane, gravel road that is narrow and rough) for 10 miles to the campground.

Trip note: It's a rough and tumble ride to get here, but for anglers, it's well worth the effort. The camp is set beside Rock Creek, a first class trout stream. You can practically fish from your campsite.

---

13) BEAR CREEK PASS

Reference: near Bear Creek, Bitterroot National Forest; map M6, grid c5.

Campsites, facilities: There are six sites for tents, trailers or motor homes up to 22 feet long. Picnic tables are provided. Pit toilets are also available. There is no pipes water. Pets are permitted.

Reservations, fee: No reservations necessary; no fee. Open mid-July to mid-September.

Who to contact: Phone Bitterroot National Forest at (406) 821-3913 or write Darby Ranger District, P.O. Box 388, Darby, MT 59829.

Location: From Darby, drive 7.3 miles north on US 93; 1.4 miles west on County Road 17, and then 17 miles west on Forest Service Road to the campground (very primitive road).

Trip note: This is an ideal jump-off spot for hikers looking for a small and primitive spot. This is what we call a "trailhead camp" because of all the hiking options into the Bitterroot Mountains. Some trails head west into the wilderness along Bear Creek and extend many miles. Some go east to Fish Lake and beyond into the South Fork of Lost Horse Creek.

---

14) MOUNTAIN VIEW

Reference: near Bitterroot River; map M6, grid c6.

Campsites, facilities: There are 15 sites for trailers or motor homes of any length. Flush toilets, bottled gas, showers and a laundromat are also available. A sanitary disposal station, store, coffee shop and ice are located within one mile. Pets are permitted on leashes.

Reservations, fee: Reservations accepted; $8 fee per night. Open all year.

Who to contact: Phone (406) 363-1848 or write to 1420 North First Street, Hamilton, MT 59840.

Location: From Hamilton, drive a half mile north on US 93 to the campground.

Trip note: This is a four-acre park set near the Bitterroot River. Several hiking trails are located to the west. To reach them, travel west of Hamilton on Putnam Gulch on Forest Service roads. At the end of these roads, the trails begin. They provide access to streams and small lakes in the Selway-Bitterroot Wilderness. One of the best hikes here is along Canyon Creek. It's a 4.5-mile hike that reaches Canyon Falls and Canyon Lake. A Forest Service map is advised.

---

15) BLACK BEAR

Reference: on Skalkaho Creek, Bitterroot National Forest; map M6, grid c7.

Campsites, facilities: There are six sites for tents, trailers and motor homes up to 22 feet long. Picnic tables are provided. Pit toilets are also available. There is **no piped water**. Pets are permitted on leashes.

Reservations, fee: No reservations necessary; no fee. Open June to mid-September.

Who to contact: Phone Bitterroot National Forest at (406) 821-3201 or write to 1801 North First Street, Hamilton, MT 59840.

Location: From Hamilton, drive three miles south on US 93, then 12.9 miles east on Highway 38 to the campground.

Trip note: You want everything made to order? You came to the wrong place. You want things primitive and beautiful? Okay, now we're talking. This camp is tiny and set right along Skalkaho Creek. There are several camping trails in the area for sidetrips, but none start directly at the camp. Hikers should obtain a Forest Service map.

---

16) SQUAW ROCK

Reference: on Rock Creek, Deerlodge National Forest; map M6, grid c9.

Campsites, facilities: There are 10 sites for tents, trailers or motor homes up to 32 feet long. Picnic tables are provided. Piped water and pit toilets are also available. Pets are permitted.

Reservations, fee: No reservation necessary; no fee. Open June to late September.

Who to contact: Phone Deerlodge National Forest at (406) 859-3211 or write to Philipsburg Ranger District, P.O. Box H, Philipsburg, MT 59858.

Location: From Philipsburg, drive 14 miles west on County Road 348, 4.7 miles west on County Road 102, and then 200 yards southwest on Forest Service Road 9346 to the campground.

Trip note: If you don't like this spot, well, you've got several other choices in the area. This one and seven others are set along Rock Creek.

17) SAM BILLINGS

Reference: near the West Fork of the Bitterroot River, Bitterroot National Forest; map M6, grid d6.

Campsites, facilities: There are 11 sites for tents, trailers or motor homes up to 22 feet long. Picnic tables are provided. Pit toilets are also available. There is **no piped water** here, so bring your own. Showers, coffee shop and a laundromat are located within five miles. Pets are permitted on leashes.

Reservations, fee: No reservations necessary; no fee. Open June to early September.

Who to contact: Phone Bitterroot National Forest at (406) 821-3269 or write to West Fork Ranger District, 6735 West Fork Road, Darby, MT 59829.

Location: From Darby, drive four miles south on US 93, 13 miles southwest on County Road 473, and then one mile northwest on Forest Service Road 5631 to the campground.

Trip note: This is a little-known spot set along Boulder Creek and is about a half mile from the West Fork of the Bitterroot River. It's a good jump-off point for backpackers, because there is a trail from camp that leads northwest up Boulder Creek to Boulder Lake eight miles away, a good first-day destination. The trail them continues beyond into the Selway-Bitterroot Wilderness, crossed the wilderness area, and comes to a halt at Paradise Campground on the Selway River. Using a shuttle system, this could be one fantastic trip.

18) ROMBO

Reference: on the West Fork of the Bitterroot River, Bitterroot National Forest; map M6, grid d6.

Campsites, facilities: There are 16 sites for tents, trailers or motor homes up to 22 feet long. Picnic tables are provided. Piped water and pit toilets are also available. Some facilities are **wheelchair accessible.** Pets are permitted on leashes.

Reservations, fee: No reservations necessary; $5 fee per night. Open June to mid-September.

Who to contact: Phone Bitterroot National Forest at (406) 821-3269 or write to Hamilton Ranger District, 1801 North First Street, Hamilton, MT 59840.

Location: From Darby, drive 4.1 miles south on US 93, and then 18 miles southwest on County Road 473 to the campground.

Trip note: This is a good base camp for a fishing trip, because the camp is set along the West Fork of the Bitterroot River and is close to Rombo Creek. With a county road leading directly to the campground, there is also easy access.

19) PAINTED ROCKS RESERVOIR STATE PARK

Reference: southwest of Darby; map M6, grid d6.

Campsites, facilities: There are 32 sites for tents, trailers or motor homes up to 25 feet long. Picnic tables are provided. Piped water and pit toilets are also available. Pets are permitted. Boat launching facilities are nearby.

Reservations, fee: No reservations necessary; $8 fee per night. Open May to October.

Who to contact: Phone Montana Department of Fish, Wildlife and Parks at (406) 444-2535 or write to 1420 East Sixth Avenue, Helena, MT 59620.

Location: From Darby, drive three miles south on US 93, and then 15 miles southwest on State Secondary Route 473 to the campground.

Trip note: This is the largest lake in the region, and in turn, a popular destination for locals. The lake covers 262 acres and is a good spot for boating and fishing. If the weather is good, expect some company.

20) ALTA

Reference: on the West Fork of Bitterroot River, Bitterroot National Forest; map M6, grid d6.

Campsites, facilities: There are 15 sites for tents, trailers or motor homes up to 22 feet long. Picnic tables are provided. Piped water, pit toilets and firewood are also available. Pets are permitted on leashes.

Reservations, fee: No reservations necessary; $5 fee per night. Open June to mid-September.

Who to contact: Phone Bitterroot National Forest at (406) 821-3269 or write to 1801 North First Street, Hamilton, MT 59840.

Location: From Darby, drive 4.1 miles south on US 93, 21.6 miles south on County Road 473, and then six miles south on County Road 96 to the campground.

Trip note: This one is out there in No Man's Land at the end of the West Fork Highway. The camp is set right along the West Fork of the Bitterroot River. A ranger lookout point is close by. Also, the Alta Pine National Recreation Trail passes nearby.

21) LAKE COMO

Reference: on Lake Como, Bitterroot National Forest; map M6, grid d6.

Campsites, facilities: There are 12 sites for tents, trailers or motor homes up to 22 feet long. Picnic tables are provided. Water and pit toilets are also available. Pets are permitted on leashes. Boat docks and launching facilities are nearby.

Reservations, fee: No reservations necessary; $5 fee per night. Open June to mid-September.

Who to contact: Phone Bitterroot National Forest at (406) 821-3913 or write to Darby Ranger District, P.O. Box 388, Darby, MT 59829.

Location: From Darby, drive 4.8 miles north on US 93; 3.8 miles southwest on County Road 550, and then 1.6 miles west on Forest Service Road 5621 to the campground.

Trip note: This camp is set beside Lake Como, a three-mile-long reservoir on Rock Creek. It's a good spot for boating, fishing and hiking. As for hiking, one trail from camp circles the lake, and another is routed west along Rock Creek into the wilderness.

---

22) MARTIN CREEK

Reference: on Moose and Martin Creeks, Bitterroot National Forest; map M6, grid d8.

Campsites, facilities: There are seven sites for tents, trailers or motor homes up to 22 feet long.

Reservations, fee: No reservations necessary; no fee. Open mid-June to mid-September.

Who to contact: Phone Bitterroot National Forest at (406) 821-3201 or write to Hamilton Ranger District, 1801 North First Street, Hamilton, MT 59840.

Location: From Sula, drive just north of town on US 93; four miles northeast on County Road 472, and then 12 miles northeast on Forest Service Road 80 to the campground.

Trip note: This one is set at the confluence of Moose Creek and Martin Creek and gets virtually no use from out-of-towners, who don't have a clue about it's existence. Anglers making their way along the river will discover many feeder creeks in the area. A Forest Service map is advised (many backcountry roads in the area).

---

23) COPPER CREEK

Reference: near Moose Lake, Deerlodge National Forest; map M6, grid d9.

Campsites, facilities: There are seven sites for tents, trailers or motor homes up to 30 feet long. Picnic tables are provided. Piped water and pit toilets are available. Pets are permitted. Some facilities are **wheelchair accessible.**

Reservation, fee: No reservations necessary, no fee. Open June to late October.

Who to contact: Phone Deerlodge National Forest at (406) 859-3211 or write to Philipsburg Ranger District, P.O. Box H, Philipsburg, MT 59858.

Location: From Philipsburg, drive 6.2 miles south on Montana Highway 38, 9.7 miles south on Forest Service Road 5106, and then a quarter mile on Forest Service Road 80 to the campground.

Trip note: This one's way out there in "booger country." It is a small, little-known campground set on Copper Creek. It is also only about a mile from little Moose Lake. Some hiking trails are in the area. It's advisable to obtain a Forest Service map which details the back roads and trails.

24) INDIAN TREES

Reference: on Bitterroot River, Bitterroot National Forest; map M6, grid e7.

Campsites, facilities: There are 18 sites for tents, trailers and motor homes up to 22 feet long. Picnic tables are provided. Piped water and pit toilets are also available. Pets are permitted.

Reservations, fee: No reservations are necessary; $4 fee per night. Open mid-June to mid-September.

Who to contact: Phone Bitterroot National Forest at (406) 821-3201 or write to Hamilton Ranger District, 1801 North First Street, Hamilton, MT 59840.

Location: From Sula, drive 5.8 miles south on US 93, and then one mile southwest on Forest Service Road 729 to the campground.

Trip note: This is one of the more popular Forest Service camps, and once you get here, it becomes obvious why: it is located just a mile from the highway, the campsites are set along the creek, and there are hot springs in the area.

25) SPRING GULCH

Reference: on Bitterroot River, Bitterroot National Forest; map M6, grid e7.

Campsites, facilities: There are eight sites for tents, trailers or motor homes up to 22 feet long. Picnic tables are provided. Piped water and pit toilets are also available. Showers, a laundromat and ice are located within one mile. A store and coffee shop are located within five miles. Pets are permitted on leashes.

Reservations, fee: No reservations necessary; $5 fee per night. Open June to mid-September.

Who to contact: Phone Bitterroot National Forest at (406) 821-3201 or write to Hamilton Ranger District, 1801 North First Street, Hamilton, MT 59840.

Location: From Sula, drive 4.8 miles northwest on US 93 to the campground.

Trip note: You get easy, direct access with this campground, because it is set right off the highway. You also get pretty scenery; the Bitterroot River runs right alongside.

26) SULA STORE & CAMPGROUND

Reference: south of Darby; map M6, grid e7.

Campsites, facilities: There are 10 sites and 18 drive-through sites for trailers or motor homes of any length. Electricity, piped water, sewer hookups and picnic tables are provided. Flush toilets, bottled gas, sanitary disposal station, showers, firewood, a store, coffee shop, laundromat, ice and a playground are also available. Pets and motorbikes are permitted.

Reservations, fee: Reservations accepted; $8-$12 fee per night. Open all year.

Who to contact: Phone (406) 821-3364 or write to P.O. Box 1, Sula, MT 59871.

Location: From Darby, drive eight miles south on US 93 to the campground.

Trip note: This is a privately operated park that covers four acres and is the first camp you will run into when entering Montana on US 93 from the south. It's set in the Bitterroot Mountain Range.

27) WARM SPRINGS

Reference: on Warm Springs Creek, Bitterroot National Forest; map M6, grid e7.

Campsites, facilities: There are 13 sites for tents, trailers or motor homes up to 22 feet long. Picnic tables are provided. Piped water and pit toilets are also available. Showers, a laundromat and ice are located within one mile. A coffee shop os located within five miles. Pets are permitted on leashes.

Reservations, fee: No reservations necessary; $5 fee per night. Open mid-June to mid-September.

Who to contact: Phone Bitterroot National Forest at (406) 821-3201 or write to Hamilton Ranger District, 1801 North First Street, Hamilton, MT 59840.

Location: From Sula, drive 4.8 miles northwest on US 93, and then one mile southwest on County Road 100 to the campground.

Trip note: This camp sits beside Warm Springs Creek. Trail access to the Allen Mountain Roadless Area is within a short drive.

28) CRAZY CREEK

Reference: in Bitterroot National Forest; map M6, grid e7.

Campsites, facilities: There are 14 sites for tents, trailers or motor homes up to 22 feet long. Picnic tables are provided. Water and pit toilets are also available. Showers, a laundromat and ice are located within five miles. Pets are permitted.

Reservations, fee: No reservations necessary; no fee. Open mid-June to mid-September.

Who to contact: Phone Bitterroot National Forest at (406) 821-3201 or write Hamilton Ranger District, 1801 North First Street, Hamilton, MT 59840.

Location: From Sula, drive five miles northwest on US 93; one miles southwest on County Road 100, and then three miles southwest on Forest Service Road 370 to the campground.

Trip note: This is a prime spot for both hikers and fishermen. The camp is next to Crazy Creek (for trout fishing) and also has a trail that is routed into the Allen Mountain Roadless Area.

---

29) MOOSEHEAD CAMP & STORE

Reference: south of Darby; map M6, grid e7.

Campsites, facilities: There are 20 tents sites and 16 drive-through sites for trailers or motor homes of any length. Electricity, piped water, sewer hookups and picnic tables are provided. Flush toilets, sanitary disposal station, showers, firewood, a store and ice are also available. Pets on leashes and motorbikes are permitted.

Reservations, fee: Reservations accepted; $8-$10 fee per night; MasterCard and Visa accepted. Open April to mid-November.

Who to contact: Phone (406) 821-3327 or write to HC 10, P.O. Box 49, Conner, MT 59827.

Location: From Darby, drive 15 miles south on US 93 to the campground.

Trip note: This is one in a series of campgrounds along US 93. Take your pick. This one covers 13 acres and has a riding stable nearby.

---

30) MAY CREEK

Reference: near Continental Divide, Beaverhead National Forest; map M6, grid f8.

Campsites, facilities: There are 21 sites for tents, trailers or motor homes up to 32 feet long. Picnic tables are provided. Piped water, pit toilets, sanitary disposal station and firewood are also available. Pets are permitted.

Reservations, fee: No reservations necessary; $5 fee per night. Open early July to late November.

Who to contact: Phone Beaverhead National Forest at (406) 689-3243 or write to P.O. Box 236, Wisdom, MT 59761.

Location: From Wisdom, drive 17.2 miles west on Highway 43.

Trip note: With this, you get a little-known spot with easy access, and it's right off of the two-lane highway. The camp is set along May Creek and has two good hiking options. One trail from camp heads west along May Creek to the Continental Divide; another one heads southeast and eventually ends up at the Butler Creek drainage.

31) TWIN LAKES

Reference: on Twin Lakes, Beaverhead National Forest; map M6, grid f9.

Campsites, facilities: There are 17 sites for tents, trailers or motor homes up to 32 feet long. Picnic tables are provided. Piped water, firewood and pit toilets are also available. Pets are permitted. Boat docks and launching facilities are nearby.

Reservations, fee: No reservations necessary; no fee. Open July to late November.

Who to contact: Phone Beaverhead National Forest at (406) 689-3243 or write to Wisdom Ranger District, P.O. Box 236, Wisdom, MT 59761.

Location: From Wisdom, drive 6.8 miles south on Highway 278, 7.8 miles west on Forest Service Road 945, 4.5 miles south on Forest Service Road 945.2, and then 5.8 miles southwest on Forest Service Road 183 to the campground.

Trip note: This is a prime spot virtually unknown to out-of-towners. The camp is set on the little Twin Lakes which is excellent for canoes (no motors permitted). A good sidetrip is hiking west four miles along Big Lake Creek.

32) MINER LAKE

Reference: on Lower Miner Lake, Beaverhead National Forest; map M6, grid g9.

Campsites, facilities: There are 10 sites for tents, trailers or motor homes up to 32 feet long. Picnic tables are provided. Piped water, firewood and pit toilets are also available. Pets are permitted. Boat docks and launching facilities are nearby.

Reservations, fee: No reservations necessary; no fee. Open early July to late November.

Who to contact: Phone Beaverhead National Forest at (406) 689-3243 or write to Wisdom Ranger District, P.O. Box 236, Wisdom, MT 59761.

Location: From Jackson, drive a half mile south on Highway 278, and then 10 miles west on Forest Service Road 182 to the campground.

Trip note: Bet you didn't know about this one. It's a little-known spot set along Lower Miner Lake. No motors are permitted on the lake, so it is ideal for canoes, prams and float tubes. All vehicles are prohibited on the dirt road that leads southwest out of camp, but you can hike it up to Upper Miner Lakes or farther to Rock Island Lakes. A Forest Service map is need for hikers.

33) RESERVOIR LAKE

Reference: near Selway Mountain, Beaverhead National Forest; map M6, grid h9.

Campsites, facilities: There are 16 sites for tents, trailers or motor homes up to 16 feet long. Picnic tables are provided. Piped water, firewood and pit toilets are also available. Pets are permitted. Boat docks and launching facilities are nearby.

Reservations, fee: No reservations necessary; no fee. Open mid-June to mid-September.

Who to contact: Phone Beaverhead National Forest at (406) 683-3960 or write to Dillon Ranger District, 610 North Montana, Dillon, MT 59725.

Location: From Dillon, drive 19 miles south on US 91, 16.8 miles west on County Road 324, and 10 miles northwest on Forest Service Road 1813 to the campground.

Trip note: This is one of the farthest south of the four remote, drive-to lakes in the region of the Bitterroot Mountains. Boats with motors are not permitted on the lake. A good sidetrip for the ambitious is to take the trail out of camp (starting point, 7,000 feet) and hike north to Selway Mountain (8,898 feet).

Montana Map M7
57 listings
Pages 380-407

North (M2)—see page 332
East (M8)—see page 408
South—Idaho
West (M6)—see page 364

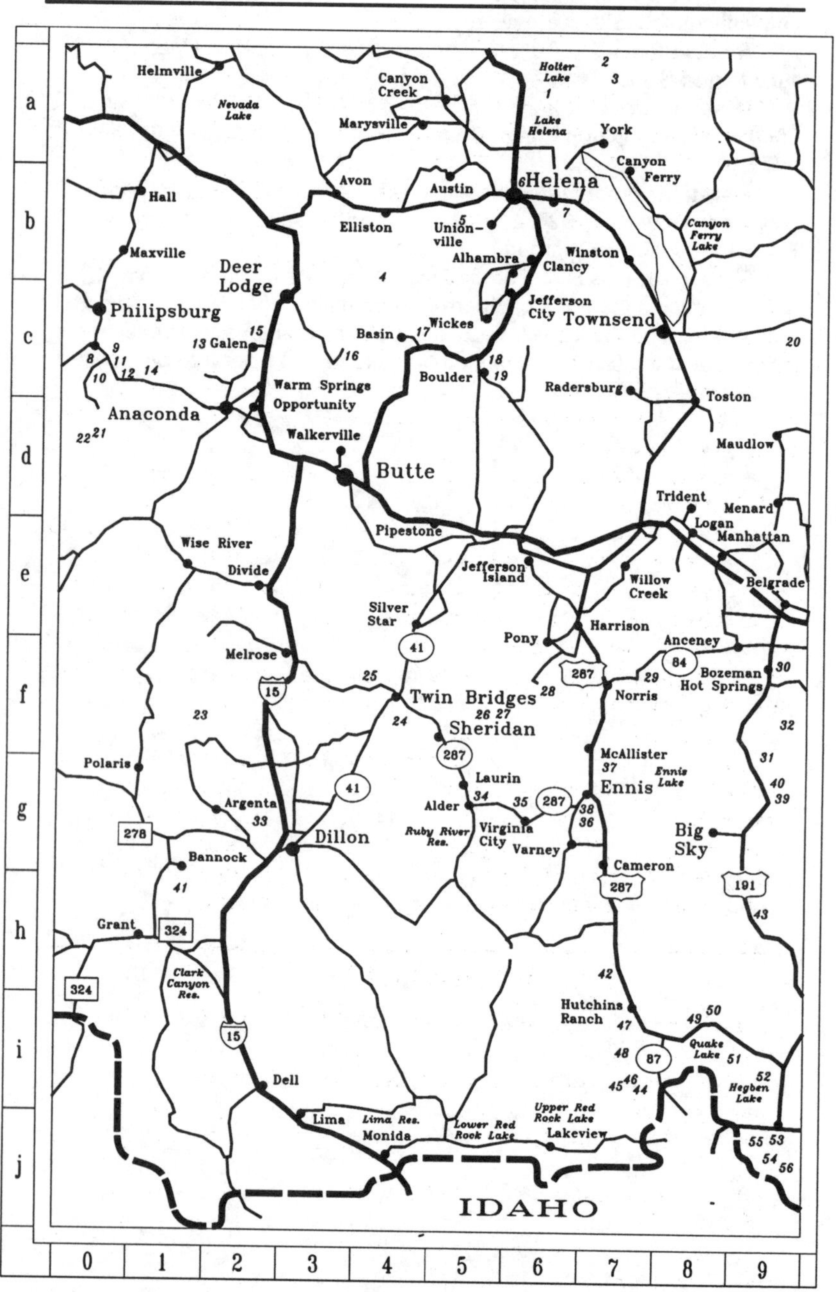

Featuring: Beaverhead National Forest, Missouri River, Gates of the Mountain Wilderness, Helena National Forest, Trout Creek, McDonald Pass, Little Blackfoot River, Ten Mile Creek, Ferry Lake, Georgetown Lake, Deerlodge National Forest, Echo Lake, Flint Creek, Warm Springs Creek, Racetrack Creek, Boulder River, Basin Creek, Ladysmith Creek, Park Lake, East Fork Reservoir, Birch Creek, Beaverhead River, Jefferson River, Mill Creek, Branham Lakes, South Willow Creek, Upper Madison River, Squaw Creek, Gallatin National Forest, Hyalite Creek, Ruby River, Madison River, Ennis Lake, Swan Creek, Grasshopper Creek, Gallatin River, Cliff Lake, Wade Lake, Earthquake Lake, Hebgen Lake, Yellowstone National Park

---

1) COULTER

Reference: boat-in, walk-in on the Missouri River, Helena National Forest; map M7, grid a6.

Campsites, facilities: There are seven 10 sites. Picnic tables are provided. Piped water and pit toilets are also available. Pets are permitted. Boat docks are nearby.

Reservations, fee: No reservations necessary, no fee. Open June to mid-September.

Who to contact: Phone Helena National Forest at (406) 449-5490 or write to Helena Ranger District, 2001 Poplar, Helena, MT 59601.

Location: This camp is accessible by boat or foot. From Interstate 15, take exit 209 to Gates of the Mountain Landing. It's 16 miles north of the city of Helena. Use your own boat or take one of the ferries that run from June through September to Meriwether Canyon picnic area, which is about a mile north of the campground. Hike the trail south along the Missouri River Canyon to the camp.

Trip note: This camp is set along the shore of the Missouri River in the Gates of the Mountain Game Preserve and is near the boundary of the Gate of the Mountain Wilderness. You get unique beauty here with limestone cliffs, 1,200 feet high, lining the canyon. A possible sidetrip is taking the trail from camp, which heads north past Meriwether Picnic Area and then east into the wilderness along Meriwether Canyon.

---

2) PIKES GULCH

Reference: near Gates of the Mountain Wilderness, Helena National Forest; map M7, grid a7.

Campsites, facilities: There are five sites for tents, trailers or motor homes up to 16 feet long. Picnic tables are provided. A pit toilet is available. There is **no piped water**, so bring your own. Pets are permitted.

Reservations, fee: No reservations necessary; no fee. Open mid-June to mid-September.

Who to contact: Phone Helena National Forest at (406) 449-5490 or write to Helena Ranger District, 2001 Poplar, Helena, MT 59601.

Location: From Helena, drive 20 miles northeast on County Road 280. Cross the bridge over Hauser Lake and continue on Forest Service Road 138 (listed as 4021 on older maps) for 29 miles northeast to the campground. The last 17 miles are winding and the road is closed to vehicle traffic from April 1st to June 15th.

Trip note: Well, you made it this far. Like Vigilante Camp, this one is way out there in No Man's Land. If you continue to drive to the end of Forest Service Road 138, you will find a trail that ventures into the Gates of the Mountain Wilderness. There is also a trailhead near Beaver Creek. The entire area has many unique rock formations. In the fall, it is a good base camp for a hunting trip.

---

3) VIGILANTE

Reference: on Trout Creek, Helena National Forest; map M7, grid a7.

Campsites, facilities: There are 10 sites for tents, trailers or motor homes up to 16 feet long. Picnic tables are provided. Piped water and pit toilets are also available. Pets are permitted.

Reservations, fee: No reservations necessary; no fee. Open June to mid-September.

Who to contact: Phone Helena National Forest at (406) 449-5490 or write to Helena Ranger District, 2001 Poplar, Helena, MT 59601.

Location: From Helena, drive 20 miles northeast on County Road 280, and then 12 miles northeast on a county road to the campground.

Trip note: This is a little-known camp set beside Trout Creek in Trout Creek Canyon. A few anglers work this spot, but it is generally free of traffic. A trail from camp heads east then south along Magpie Gulch.

---

4) KADING

Reference: on Little Blackfoot River, Helena National Forest; map M7, grid b4.

Campsites, facilities: There are 11 sites for tents, trailers or motor homes up to 22 feet long. Picnic tables are provided. Piped water and pit toilets are also available. Pets are permitted.

Reservations, fee: No reservations necessary; no fee. Open June to mid-September.

Who to contact: Phone Helena National Forest at (406) 449-5490 or write to Helena Ranger District, 2001 Poplar, Helena, MT 59601.

Location: From Elliston, drive three-quarters of a mile east on US 12, 3.6 miles south, and then 8.8 miles southwest on Forest Service Road 227 to the campground.

Trip note: This is a secluded camp nestled in a meadow along Little Blackfoot River. It's right below several peaks of the Continental Divide. Note: No vehicles are permitted beyond the camp. So you may want to venture further by hiking the trail that leads south from camp which is routed to a network of other trails in the Forest Service wildlands. See the Forest Service map.

5) MOOSE CREEK

Reference: on Ten Mile Creek, Helena National Forest; map M7, grid b5.

Campsites, facilities: There are 11 sites for tents, trailers or motor homes up to 22 feet long. Picnic tables are provided. Piped water and pit toilets are also available. Pets are permitted.

Reservations, fee: No reservations necessary; no fee. Open June to mid-September.

Who to contact: Phone Helena National Forest at (406) 449-5490 or write Helena Ranger District, 2001 Poplar, Helena, MT 59601.

Location: From Helena, drive 9.8 miles west on US 12, and then 4.3 miles south on Forest Service Road 218 to the campground.

Trip note: Here's an ideal spot for cruisers in the Helena area who want a pretty spot, yet don't want to be far from the city. The camp is set along Ten Mile Creek. A sidetrip possibility is taking the two-mile trail that starts at the nearby Ten Mile Picnic Area (north of camp) and follows Lazy Man Gulch. Cromwell Dixon Camp provides a nearby camping option.

6) HELENA KOA

Reference: in Helena; map M7, grid b6.

Campsites, facilities: There are 40 tent sites and 80 sites for trailers or motor homes of any length. Picnic tables are provided. Flush toilets, bottled gas, sanitary disposal station, showers, firewood, recreation hall, restaurant, store, laundromat, ice, playground, whirlpool and a heated swimming pool are also available. Electricity, piped water and sewer hookups cost extra. Pets and motorbikes are permitted.

Reservations, fee: Reservations accepted; $17-$21 fee per night; MasterCard and Visa accepted. Open all year.

Who to contact: Phone (406) 458-5110 or write to 5820 North Montana, Helena, MT 59601.

Location: From Helena, drive 3.5 miles north on Montana Avenue to the campground.

Trip note: This is a 12-acre, KOA park that offers a tent village and camper cabins. A golf course provides a recreation possibility. There's also a lot of sightseeing to be done in the Helena: Montana Historical Society Museum, Library and Archives at 225 North Roberts has exhibits on the history of Montana from the Ice Age until World War II, Cathedral of St. Helena on Warren Street between 9th and 10th Avenues, or the ghost town at Marysville which is 25 miles northwest of Helena via Interstate 15 and County Road 279, then follow the signs. See trip note for Branding Iron Camp for sidetrips in Helena.

7) CANYON FERRY STATE PARK

Reference: on Ferry Lake; map M7, grid b7.

Campsites, facilities: There are over 50 campsites for tents, trailers or motor homes. They are divided among nine campgrounds set around this large lake. Most, but not all have piped water. The campground names are Chinaman Gulch, Court Sheriff, Crittendon (**no piped water**), Hellgate (the largest), Indian Road, Overlook, Ponderosa (**no piped water**), Riverside and White Earth. Picnic tables are provided. Pit toilets and firewood are also available. Pets are permitted. Boat launching facilities and rentals are nearby.

Reservations, fee: No reservations necessary; $7-$9 fee per night. Open May to October.

Who to contact: Phone Montana State Parks at (406) 444-4720 or write to Regional Park Director, 1420 East Sixth Avenue, Helena, MT 59620.

Location: Access is available from different roads off of US 12/287 from 10 to 32 miles southeast of Helena. A Helena National Forest Service map provides locations of all camps and picnic areas.

Trip note: The Canyon Ferry area is a vast parkland covering both land and water. The camps are set beside Big Ferry Lake, by far the largest lake of the region. For day-use possibilities, there are a number of small picnic areas around the lake in addition to the campgrounds.

8) PINEY BAY

Reference: on Georgetown Lake, Deerlodge National Forest; map M7, grid e0.

Campsites, facilities: There are 48 sites for tents, trailers or motor homes up to 32 feet long.

Reservations, fee: No reservations necessary; $7 fee per night. Open June to October.

Who to contact: Phone Deerlodge National Forest at (406) 859-3211 or write to Philipsburg Ranger District, P.O. Box H, Philipsburg, MT 59858.

Location: From Philipsburg, drive 9.1 miles south on Montana Highway 1, 3.1 miles southwest on County Road 406, and then three-quarters of a mile southeast on Forest Service Road 505 to the campground.

Trip note: This is the smallest, most intimate camp at Georgetown Lake, and is nestled on Piney Bay. There is good boating and fishing in the summer.

9) FLINT CREEK

Reference: near Georgetown Lake, Deerlodge National Forest; map M7, grid c0.

Campsites, facilities: There are 10 sites for tents, trailers or motor homes up to 32 feet long. Picnic tables are provided. Piped water and pit toilets are also available. Some facilities are **wheelchair accessible.** Pets are permitted.

Reservations, fee: No reservations; no fee. Open May to late October.

Who to contact: Phone Deerlodge National Forest at (406) 859-3211 or write to Philipsburg Ranger District, P.O. Box H, Philipsburg, MT 59858.

Location: From Philipsburg, drive 6.4 miles south on Montana Highway 1, and then a quarter of a mile southeast to the campground.

Trip note: This one of five campgrounds located in the immediate area. Set on Flint Creek and one of the quieter spots around, there is good recreation available including a three-mile trip to Georgetown Lake and Echo Lake.

---

10) PHILIPSBURG BAY

Reference: on Georgetown Lake, Deerlodge National Forest; map M7, grid c0.

Campsites, facilities: There are 69 sites for tents, trailers or motor homes up to 32 feet long. Picnic tables are provided. Piped water and pit toilets are also available. A store, coffee shop and ice are located within five miles. Pets are permitted. Boat docks, launching facilities and rentals are nearby. Some facilities are **wheelchair accessible.**

Reservations, fee: No reservations necessary; $7 fee per night. Open mid-June to mid-October.

Who to contact: Phone Deerlodge National Forest at (406) 859-3211 or write to Philipsburg Ranger District, P.O. Box H, Philipsburg, MT 59858.

Location: From Philipsburg, drive 9.1 miles south on Montana Highway 1, 1.5 miles southwest on County Road 406, and then a half mile southeast on Forest Service Road 9460 to the campground.

Trip note: This spot is one of the options at Georgetown Lake. It provides a good base camp for anglers and boaters.

---

11) LODGEPOLE

Reference: on Georgetown Lake, Deerlodge National Forest; map M7, grid c0.

Campsites, facilities: There are 10 tent sites and 21 sites for trailers or motor homes up to 32 feet long. Picnic tables are provided. Piped water and pit toilets are also available. A store, coffee shop and ice are located within five miles. Pets are permitted. Boat docks, launching facilities and rentals are nearby.

Reservations, fee: No reservations necessary; $6 fee per night. Open June to late October.

Who to contact: Phone Deerlodge National Forest at (406) 859-3211 or write to Philipsburg, MT 59858.

Location: From Philipsburg, drive 9.8 miles south on Montana Highway 1 to the campground.

Trip note: This is one of the few Forest Service camps that is set up more for motor homes than tents. And it's a nice spot to boot because of its location next to Georgetown Lake, a popular lake for boating, fishing and waterskiing.

---

12) CABLE MOUNTAIN

Reference: near Echo Lake, Deerlodge National Forest; map M7, c0.

Campsites, facilities: There are 11 sites for tents, trailers or motor homes up to 22 feet long. Picnic tables are provided. Piped water and pit toilets are also available. A store is located within five miles. Pets are permitted. Boat docks, launching facilities and rentals are nearby at Georgetown Lake.

Reservations, fee: No reservations necessary; no fee. Open mid-June to mid-September.

Who to contact: Phone Deerlodge National Forest at (406) 859-3211 or write to Philipsburg Ranger District, P.O. Box H, Philipsburg, MT 59858.

Location: From Philipsburg, drive 12 miles south on Montana Highway 1, 3.1 miles north on Forest Service Road 65, and then a quarter mile south on Forest Service Road 242 to the campground.

Trip note: It's a take-your-pick deal with seven campgrounds in the immediate area. This one is set on North Fork of Flint Creek about a mile from Echo Lake.

---

13) SPRING HILL

Reference: near Flint Creek, Deerlodge National Forest; map M7, grid c1.

Campsites, facilities: There are 12 sites for tents, trailers and motor homes up to 22 feet long. Picnic tables are provided. Piped water and pit toilets are also available. A coffee shop is located within five miles. Pets are permitted on leashes. Boat docks and launching facilities are nearby.

Reservations, fee: No reservations necessary except for picnic area; $4 fee per night. Open mid-June to September.

Who to contact: Phone Deerlodge National Forest at (406) 846-1770 or write to Philipsburg Ranger District, P.O. Box H, Philipsburg, MT 59858.

Location: From Anaconda, drive 10.8 miles northwest on Highway 10A to the campground.

Trip note: If Warm Springs Camp seems crowded, this spot provides another option. Fishing can be good at nearby Silver Lake and Warm Springs Creek.

14) WARM SPRINGS

Reference: on Warm Springs Creek, Deerlodge National Forest; map M7, grid c1.

Campsites, facilities: There are six sites for tents, trailers and motor homes up to 22 feet long. Picnic tables are provided. Hand-pumped water and pit toilets are also available. Pets are permitted on leashes.

Reservations, fee: No reservations necessary; no fee. Open mid-June to September.

Who to contact: Phone Deerlodge National Forest at (406) 846-1770 or write to Deerlodge Ranger District, 91 North Frontage Road, Deerlodge, MT 59722.

Location: From Anaconda, drive 10.6 miles northwest on Montana Highway 1, then 2.3 miles north on Forest Service Road 170 to the campground.

Trip note: If you want to avoid the people at nearby Georgetown Lake, here's a good alternate. This tiny spot is set on Warm Springs Creek and is a five-minute drive from the highway. There is good fishing in the area.

15) RACETRACK

Reference: on Racetrack Creek, Deerlodge National Forest; map M7, grid c2.

Campsites, facilities: There are 11 sites for tents, trailers or motor homes up to 16 feet long. Picnic tables are provided. Pit toilets are also available. There is **no piped water**. Pets are permitted on leashes. Some facilities are **wheelchair accessible.**

Reservations, fee: No reservations necessary; no fee. Open mid-June to mid-November.

Who to contact: Phone Deerlodge National Forest at (406) 846-1770 or write to Deerlodge Ranger District, 91 North Frontage Road, Deerlodge, MT 59722.

Location: From Anaconda, drive 3.1 miles east on Highway 10A. Turn north and drive 6.6 miles on Highway 273, then turn right on a signed county road and proceed 6.5 miles northwest. Turn right on Forest Service Road 169 and continue five more miles northwest to the campground.

Trip note: This camp gets its name from Racetrack Creek, which the camp sits beside, as well as Racetrack Peak, which looms overhead to the west. River access is good here for drift-boat fishermen because it has a good spot for put-in or take-out. Hiking can be found up a west-bound, dirt road which accesses a trail that goes deep into the Flint Range. Many alpine lakes are tucked away here.

16) OROFINO

Reference: in Deerlodge National Forest; map M7, grid c3.

Campsites, facilities: There are 10 sites for tents, trailers and motor homes up to 22 feet long. Picnic tables are provided. Pit toilets and water are also available. Pets are permitted on leashes.

Reservations, fee: No reservations necessary; no fee. Open June to September.

Who to contact: Phone Deerlodge National Forest at (406) 846-1770 or write to Deerlodge Ranger District, 91 North Frontage Road, Deerlodge, MT 59722.

Location: From Deerlodge, drive 13 miles southeast on Forest Service Road 82 to the campground.

Trip note: Here's a primitive camp that is all by its lonesome and is set along the mountain rim in Deerlodge National Forest. There are no other camps in the area. Hiking trails are the main form of entertainment (Forest Service map required).

---

17) BASIN CANYON

Reference: on Basin Creek, Deerlodge National Forest; map M7, grid c4.

Campsites, facilities: There are three sites for tents, trailers or motor homes up to 16 feet long. Picnic tables are provided. Pit toilets are also available. There is **no piped water.** Pets are permitted on leashes.

Reservations, fee: No reservations necessary; no fee. Open mid-May to mid-September.

Who to contact: Phone Deerlodge National Forest at (406) 287-3223 or write to Whitehall Ranger District, P.O. Box F, Whitehall, MT 59759.

Location: From Boulder, drive eight miles west on Interstate 15 to Basin. Turn north on Forest Service Road 172 and continue 3.5 miles to the campground.

Trip note: This is a primitive and tiny spot set along Basin Creek. You get fishing access, a pretty stream flowing by, and not much else.

---

18) BOULDER CITY PARK

Reference: near Boulder River; map M7, grid c5.

Campsites, facilities: There are 10 sites for tents, trailers and motor homes up to 16 feet long. Picnic tables are provided. Piped water, flush toilets and sanitary disposal station are also available. Bottled gas, firewood, a store, coffee shop, laundromat and ice are located within one mile. Pets are permitted on leashes.

Reservations, fee: No reservations; no fee. Open June to mid-October.

Who to contact: Phone (406) 225-3381 or write to P.O. Box 68, Boulder, MT 59632.

Location: This park is located at the north end of Boulder on Highway 91.

Trip note: This is a five-acre park on the outskirts of Boulder. It's pretty, with open, grassy sites. The Boulder River runs nearby. A good sidetrip for hikers and anglers is to the Elder Creek Picnic Area in Deerlodge National Forest. The picnic area is about seven miles southwest of Boulder and located on Forest Service Road 86, which follows Little Boulder River and is a dirt road for the last two miles.

---

19) SUNSET TRAILER COURT

Reference: in Boulder; map M7, grid c5.

Campsites, facilities: There are eight tent sites and 18 sites for trailers or motor homes. Electricity, piped water, sewer hookups and picnic tables are provided. Flush toilets, bottled gas, sanitary disposal station, showers and a laundromat are also available. A store, coffee shop and ice are located within one mile. Pets and motorbikes are permitted.

Reservations, fee: Reservations accepted; $5-$10 fee per night. Open all year.

Who to contact: Phone (406) 225-3387 or write to P.O. Box 22, Boulder, MT 59632.

Location: From Interstate 15, take the Boulder exit onto Highway 69 in Boulder, and drive three blocks south to the campground.

Trip note: This is a private park that covers eight acres. It's one of two parks in Boulder. See trip note for Boulder City Park for sidetrip option.

---

20) SKIDWAY

Reference: near Castle Fork, Helena National Forest; map M7, grid c9.

Campsites, facilities: There are 11 sites for tents, trailers or motor homes up to 16 feet long. Picnic tables are provided. Water, firewood and pit toilets are also available. Pets are permitted on leashes.

Reservations, fee: No reservations necessary; no fee. Open June to late September.

Who to contact: Phone Helena National Forest at (406) 266-3425 or write to Townsend Ranger District, P.O. Box 29, Townsend, MT 59644.

Location: From Townsend, drive 23 miles east on US 12, and then two miles south on Forest Service Road 4042 to the campground.

Trip note: The access road here is a tricky, twisty son-of-a-gun from the Castle Fork of Battle Creek onward. Once you make it though, you can hike on a trail that is routed south along the ridge line of Grassy Mountain.

---

21) EAST FORK

Reference: near East Fork Reservoir, Deerlodge National Forest; map M7, grid d0.

Campsites, facilities: There are seven sites for tents, trailers or motor homes up to 32 feet long. Picnic tables are provided. Pit toilets are also available. There is **no piped water**. Pets are permitted on leashes. Boat docks are nearby.

Reservations, fee: Reservations accepted; no fee. Open June to late October.

Who to contact: Phone Deerlodge National Forest at (406) 859-3211 or write to Philipsburg Ranger District, P.O. Box H, Philipsburg, MT 59858.

Location: From Philipsburg, drive 6.2 miles south on Montana Highway 1, six miles southwest on Highway 38. Turn left on Forest Service Road 672 and drive 4.7 miles southeast, then a half mile on Forest Service Road 9349 to the campground.

Trip note: If you don't mind the lack of amenities, this can be an ideal spot. Just hard enough to reach to get missed by most out-of-towners, it's located in a pretty setting along East Fork Creek just a quarter mile from East Fork Reservoir. There is good fishing in East Fork Creek.

---

22) CANYON CREEK

Reference: near Melrose, Beaverhead National Forest; map M7, grid d0.

Campsites, facilities: There are three tent sites. Picnic tables are provided. Pit toilets and firewood are also available. There is **no piped water.** Pets are permitted on leashes.

Reservations, fee: No reservations necessary; no fee. Open July to mid-September.

Who to contact: Phone Beaverhead National Forest at (406) 832-3178 or write to Wise River Ranger District, P.O. Box 86, Wise River, MT 59762.

Location: From Melrose, drive a quarter mile south on Interstate 15. Turn left on County Road 1871 and drive five miles west, then turn left on Forest Service Road 1872 and proceed five miles northwest. Turn right on Forest Service Road 7401 and drive 3.5 miles southwest to the campground at the end of the road.

Trip note: Tiny, hard-to-reach, and primitive, this spot is hardly used. It is set on Canyon Creek, across from Canyon Creek Guest Ranch, and is used primarily as a staging area for hikers. A trail from camp heads southwest and then forks south along Lion Creek to some lakes, or west along Gold Creek for many miles.

---

23) DINNER STATION

Reference: on Birch Creek, Beaverhead National Forest; map M7, grid f2.

Campsites, facilities: There are 13 sites for tents, trailers or motor homes up to 16 feet long. Picnic tables are provided. Piped water, firewood and pit toilets are also available. Some facilities are **wheelchair accessible.** Pets are permitted on leashes.

Reservations, fee: No reservations necessary; no fee. Open mid-May to mid-September.

Who to contact: Phone Beaverhead National Forest at (406) 683-3960 or write to Dillon Ranger District, 610 North Montana, Dillon, MT 59725.

Location: From Dillon, drive 12 miles north on Interstate 15, then 10 miles northwest on Birch Creek Road. Turn northwest on Forest Service Road 1922 (past Aspen picnic ground) and drive two miles to the campground.

Trip note: This is the only camp in the immediate area, and it's not too shabby. It's set on a pretty tributary of Birch Creek. And because there's a trail from camp routed west for six miles to a series of alpine lakes, backpackers can use it as a base camp. There are several 10,000-foot peaks in the area as well, providing a challenge for hardy, bush-whacking types.

---

24) STARDUST TRAILER PARK

Reference: near Beaverhead River; map M7, grid f4.

Campsites, facilities: There are two tent sites and eight sites for trailers or motor homes. Picnic tables, flush toilets, sanitary disposal station and showers are also available. Bottled gas, laundromat and ice are located within one mile. Pets and motorbikes are permitted.

Reservations, fee: Reservations accepted; $6-$13 fee per night; MasterCard and Visa accepted. Open May to November.

Who to contact: Phone (406) 684-5648 or write to 409 North Main Street, Twin Bridges, MT 59754.

Location: This campground is located at the north end of Twin Bridges and is at the junction of Highway 41 and 287.

Trip note: Easy access at a major highway junction is the highlight here. It's a small urban park, set a few blocks from the Beaverhead River, amidst a mixture of willow and evergreen trees. Other than Jefferson River Park, there are no other choices in the area without a 25-minute drive.

---

25) JEFFERSON RIVER PARK

Reference: on Jefferson River; map M7, grid f4.

Campsites, facilities: There are four tent sites and seven sites for trailers or motor homes of any length. Flush toilets, sanitary disposal station and showers are also available. A store is located within one mile. Pets and motorbikes are permitted. Boat launching facilities are nearby.

Reservations, fee: Reservations accepted; $10-$15 fee per night. Open mid-May to October.

Who to contact: Phone (406) 684-5262 or write to P.O. Box 171, Highway 41 South, Silver Star, MT 59751.

Location: From Twin Bridges, drive eight miles north on Highway 287 to the campground.

Trip note: This is a small, privately operated park set on the Jefferson River. It has easy highway access and pretty, well-treed sites. There are no other camps within 10 miles.

26) MILL CREEK

Reference: on Mill Creek, Beaverhead National Forest; map M7, grid f5.

Campsites, facilities: There are nine sites for tents, trailers and motor homes up to 32 feet long. Picnic tables are provided. Pit toilets and firewood are also available. There is **no piped water.** Pets are permitted on leashes.

Reservations, fee: Reservations accepted; no fee. Open June to late October.

Who to contact: Phone Beaverhead National at (406) 842-5432 or write to Sheridan Ranger District, P.O. Box 428, Sheridan, MT 59749.

Location: From Sheridan, drive seven miles east on Mill Creek Road to the campground.

Trip note: This is one of two primitive campgrounds on the western edge of the Tobacco Root Mountains. Set beside Mill Creek, it's in a shady, wooded setting. There is a trail that heads north out of camp along Quartz Creek. The camp at Branham Lakes provides a nearby lakeside alternate.

27) BRANHAM LAKES

Reference: on Branham Lakes, Beaverhead National Forest; map M7, grid f5.

Campsites, facilities: There are six sites for tents, trailers or motor homes up to 22 feet long. Picnic tables are provided. Pit toilets are also available. There is **no piped water.** Pets are permitted on leashes. Boat docks are nearby.

Reservations, fee: No reservations necessary; no fee. Open July to mid-September.

Who to contact: Phone Beaverhead National Forest at (406) 842-5432 or write to Sheridan Ranger District, P.O. Box 428, Sheridan, MT 59749.

Location: From Sheridan, drive 13 miles east on Mill Creek Road to the campground.

Trip note: This is a spectacular setting with the little Branham Lakes sitting like jewels below the surrounding peaks (all over 10,000 feet). On a clear day, it's a real show stopper. A trail leads west out of camp and follows the South Fork of Indian Creek to the junction with the main creek. Another trail south of camp leads up to an old mining site.

28) POTOSI

Reference: on South Willow Creek, Beaverhead National Forest; map M7, grid f6.

Campsites, facilities: There are 11 tent sites and three sites for trailers or motor homes up to 32 feet long. Picnic tables are provided. Piped water, firewood and pit toilets are also available. Pets are permitted on leashes.

Reservations, fee: No reservations necessary; no fee. Open mid-June to mid-September.

Who to contact: Phone Beaverhead National Forest at (406) 682-4253 or write to Madison Ranger District, 5 Forest Service Road, Ennis, MT 59729.

Location: From Pony, drive three miles southeast on County Road 1601, and then five miles southwest on Forest Service Road 1601 to the campground.

Trip note: Set in the eastern Tobacco Root Mountains, this site is the only one in the area. The camp is set on South Willow Creek and is a good spot for backpackers. Trails head northwest and lead to several small lakes.

29) RED MOUNTAIN

Reference: on Upper Madison River; map M7, grid f7.

Campsites, facilities: There are 22 sites for tents, trailers or motor homes of any length. Picnic tables are provided. Piped water and pit toilets are located. Pets are permitted on leashes.

Reservations, fee: No reservations necessary; no fee. Open all year.

Who to contact: Phone Bureau of Land Management at (406) 255-2913 or write to P.O. Box 36800, Billings, MT 59107.

Location: From Norris, drive nine miles northeast on Highway 84.

Trip note: This camp is not well known, but the few who do know of it use it quite regularly. You can find out why, with the Upper Madison River running alongside, providing good fishing and nice scenery. It's also a good spot for hikers. You're on the threshold to the Beartrap Mountain Wilderness Area. It's a nine-mile hike by trail south to enter the wilderness.

30) BOZEMAN HOT SPRINGS KOA

Reference: southwest of Bozeman; map M7, grid f9.

Campsites, facilities: There are 50 tent sites and 95 sites for trailers or motor homes of any length. Picnic tables are provided. One and two-room camping cabins are also available. Flush toilets, bottled gas, sanitary disposal station, showers, recreation hall, a store, laundromat, ice and a playground are also available. Electricity, piped water, sewer hookups, firewood and a swimming pool are available at an additional charge. Pets and motorbikes are permitted.

Reservations, fee: Reservations accepted; $14-$19 fee per night; camping cabins are $25-$30 per night. MasterCard and Visa accepted. Open all year.

Who to contact: Phone (406) 587-3030 or write to 133 Lower Rainbow Road, Bozeman, MT 59715.

Location: From Bozeman, drive 7.7 miles southwest on US 191 to the campground.

Trip note: If you like sitting in hot springs, this place may be your calling. This campground has an indoor hot springs pool, the only one in the immediate area. Other popular hot springs are Chico Hot Springs, located 35 miles east in Livingston, and Norris Hot Springs, only 25 miles away. The park covers 20 acres, set in a valley surrounded by both evergreen and deciduous trees.

---

31) SPIRE ROCK

Reference: on Squaw Creek, Gallatin National Forest, map M7, grid f9.

Campsites, facilities: There are 10 sites for tents, trailers and motor homes up to 16 feet long. Picnic tables are provided. Pit toilets are also available. There is **no piped water.** A store, coffee shop and ice are located within five miles. Pets are permitted on leashes.

Reservations, fee: No reservations necessary; no fee. Open mid-June to mid-September.

Who to contact: Phone Gallatin National Forest at (406) 587-6920 or write to Bozeman Ranger District, 601 Nikles Avenue, P.O. Box C, Bozeman, MT 59715.

Location: From Bozeman, drive 29 miles south on US 191, and then 2 miles east on Squaw Creek Road to the campground.

Trip note: Set in Gallatin Canyon, this camp is little-known and primitive, yet easy to reach. That's a bonus. Its location along Squaw Creek is another. Garnet Peak at 8,245 feet looms overhead with unique rock formations along its rim line. If you head back west about two miles along the road you came in, you will find a trailhead that leads to the peak.

---

32) LANGOHR

Reference: on Hyalite Creek, Gallatin National Forest; map M7, grid f9.

Campsites, facilities: There are 12 sites for tents, trailers and motor homes up to 16 feet long. Picnic tables are provided. Piped water, firewood and pit toilets are also available. Pets are permitted on leashes. Boat docks and launching facilities are nearby at Hyalite Reservoir. Some sites are **wheelchair accessible.**

Reservations, fee: No reservations necessary; $7 fee per night. Open mid-June to mid-September.

Who to contact: Phone Gallatin National Forest at (406) 587-6920 or write to Bozeman Ranger District, 601 Nikles Avenue, P.O. Box C, Bozeman, MT 59715.

Location: From Bozeman, drive eight miles south on County Road 243, and then southeast on Forest Service Road 62 for five miles to the campground.

Trip note: This is one of the few secluded spots in this region. The others are along the highway and privately operated to handle the flood of vacationers heading north out of Yellowstone National Park. But not this one; it's quiet, little used and located on Hyalite Creek in Hyalite Canyon. And it has a unique bonus: a **wheelchair accessible** fishing trail runs along the creek.

---

33) DILLON KOA

Reference: on Beaverhead River; map M7, grid g3.

Campsites, facilities: There are 30 tent sites and 67 sites for trailers or motor homes of any length. Piped water and picnic tables are provided. Flush toilets, bottled gas, sanitary disposal station, showers, recreation hall, a store, coffee shop, laundromat, ice, playground and a swimming pool are also available. Electricity, sewer hookups and firewood are available at an additional charge. Pets and motorbikes are permitted.

Reservations, fee: Reservations accepted; $14-$18 fee per night; MasterCard and Visa accepted. Open March through November.

Who to contact: Phone (406) 683-2749 or write to 735 West Park Street, Dillon, MT 59725.

Location: Take I-15, exit 63 off Highway 41 in Dillon, and drive south on Montana Street to the end. Turn right on Reeder, and drive a half mile to the campground at 735 West Park Street.

Trip note: You might stop here just because you need a layover spot, but after you check out the area, you may want to stay a while. This private park covers 21 acres and is situated on the banks of the Beaverhead River, a prime trout stream. For golfers, there's a course in the area. This is one of two parks in Dillon.

---

34) ALDER/VIRGINIA KOA

Reference: near Ruby River; map M7, grid g5.

Campsites, facilities: There are 50 tent sites and 39 sites for trailers or motor homes of any length. Picnic tables are provided. Flush toilets, bottled gas, sanitary disposal station, showers, recreation hall, a store, laundromat, ice and a playground are also available. Electricity, piped water and sewer hookups are available at an additional charge. A coffee shop is located within one mile. Pets and motorbikes are permitted.

Reservations, fee: Reservations accepted; $12.50-$17 fee per night; MasterCard and Visa accepted. Open year-round.

Who to contact: Phone (406) 842-5677 or write to P.O. Box 103, Alder, MT 59710.

Location: From Alder, drive a quarter of a mile east on Highway 287 to the campground.

Trip note: This is a large KOA park on the outskirts of town, with grassy sites encircled by cottonwood, boxwood, alder and evergreen trees. The campground has an historical dredge pond where campers can fish. Sidetrip highlights are the historic towns of Virginia City and Nevada City, where gold-panning and garnet-hunting remain popular tourist activities. For outdoor purists, the nearby Ruby River and Ruby River Reservoir offer hiking, fishing and gorgeous scenic views.

---

35) VIRGINIA CITY

Reference: near Virginia City; map M7, grid g6.

Campsites, facilities: There are 26 tent sites and 22 sites for trailers or motor homes. Picnic tables are provided. Flush toilets, sanitary disposal station, volleyball, horseshoes and showers are also available. Electricity, piped water and sewer hookups are available at an additional charge. A store and coffee shop are located within one mile. Pets and motorbikes are permitted.

Reservations, fee: Reservations accepted; $14-$16 fee per night. Open late May to September.

Who to contact: Phone (406) 843-5493 or write to P.O. Box 32, Virginia City, MT 59755.

Location: From Virginia City, drive a half mile east on Highway 287 to the campground.

Trip note: This is one of four parks set up primarily for motor homes and is along little Highway 287. Virginia City KOA is nine miles to the west in Alder, and Ennis Sportsman Access and McCall's Elkhorn are some 14 miles to the east in Ennis. Virginia City has many historic points of interest, and a riding stable provides a recreational possibility in the area.

---

36) McCALL'S ELKHORN

Reference: near Madison River; map M7, grid g7.

Campsites, facilities: There are 13 sites for tent, trailers or motor homes. Flush toilets, showers, a store, bottled gas and ice are also available. A coffee shop and laundromat are located within one mile. Pets and motorbikes are permitted (pets must be on a leash).

Reservations, fee: Reservations accepted; $12-$15 fee per night. Open year-round.

Who to contact: Phone (406) 682-4273 or write to 69 Montana Highway 287, Ennis, MT 59729.

Location: This campground is located at the south end of Ennis on Highway 287.

Trip note: This pretty little camp is set in a valley. The sites are grassy and sunny, with mountain views of the Madison Range to the east and the Gravely and Tobacco Root Ranges to the rest. Fishermen might consider this a base camp for trips to the blue-ribbon Madison River to the south along US 287 or to Ennis Lake to the north. Nearby recreation options include a golf course and a riding stable.

37) LAKESHORE LODGE

Reference: on Ennis Lake; map M7, grid g7.

Campsites, facilities: There are eight tent sites and 36 sites for trailers or motor homes of any length. Electricity, piped water, sewer hookups and picnic tables are provided. Flush toilets, bottled gas, showers, firewood, recreation hall, a store, coffee shop, laundromat, ice and a playground are also available. Pets and motorbikes are permitted. Boat docks, launching facilities and rentals are available.

Reservations, fee: Reservations accepted; $10-$14 fee per night. Open mid-May to mid-October.

Who to contact: Phone (406) 682-4424 or write to P.O. Box 134, McAllister, MT 59740.

Location: From Ennis, drive eight miles north on US 287 to McAllister. Then follow the signs, turn east, and drive 2.5 miles to the campground.

Trip note: This is a 14-acre park set beside Ennis Lake, a popular lake for boating and fishing. It's quite a pretty spot, but well used, so it's advisable to reserve your site early. A golf course is also in the area.

38) ENNIS SPORTSMAN ACCESS

Reference: near Madison River; map M7, grid g7.

Campsites, facilities: There are 15 tent sites and 15 sites for trailers or motor homes up to 20 feet long. Picnic tables are provided. Piped water and pit toilets are also available. Pets are permitted on leashes. Boat launching facilities are nearby.

Reservations, fee: No reservations necessary; $3-$5 fee per night. Open May to late September.

Who to contact: Phone Montana Department of Fish, Wildlife and Parks at (406) 444-2535 or write to 1420 East Sixth Avenue, Helena, MT 59620.

Location: From Ennis, on US 287 look for milepost 48, and follow to camp.

Trip note: This is a 77-acre park that provides fishermen a base camp for the nearby Madison River. The river is a world-class trout stream and attracts anglers from throughout the hemisphere. As the name implies, it is primarily a sports camp, with not much to do besides fish. For many die-hard anglers, it's paradise.

39) SWAN CREEK

Reference: on Swan Creek, Gallatin National Forest; map M7, grid g9.

Campsites, facilities: There are 11 sites for tents, trailers and motor homes up to 16 feet long. Picnic tables are provided. Piped water, firewood and pit toilets are also available. A store, coffee shop and ice are located within five miles. Pets are permitted on leashes.

Reservations, fee: No reservations necessary; $7 fee per night. Open mid-June to mid-September.

Who to contact: Phone Gallatin National Forest at (406) 587-6920 or write to Bozeman Ranger District, 601 Nikles Avenue, P.O. Box C, Bozeman, MT 59715.

Location: From Big Sky, drive 2.2 miles east on Highway 191S. Turn north on US 191 and drive 8.4 miles, then turn east on Forest Service Road 481 and continue for one mile. Turn right on Forest Service Road 481A and proceed about 200 yards to the campground.

Trip note: Take your pick: either hunker down and watch Swan Creek babble by, maybe tossing in a line now and then, or strap on your hiking boots and go for broke. A trail out of camp follows Swan Creek for many miles east. A Forest Service map details other hiking options.

---

40) GREEK CREEK

Reference: in Gallatin Canyon, Gallatin National Forest; map M7, grid g9.

Campsites, facilities: There are 14 sites for tents, trailers and motor homes up to 16 feet long. Picnic tables are provided. Piped water, firewood and pit toilets are also available. A store, coffee shop and ice are located within five miles. Pets are permitted on leashes.

Reservations, fee: No reservations necessary; $7 fee per night. Open mid-June to mid-September.

Who to contact: Phone Gallatin National Forest at (406) 587-6920 or write to Bozeman Ranger District, 601 Nikles Avenue, P.O. Box C, Bozeman, MT 59715.

Location: From Big Sky, drive 2.2 miles east on Highway 191S. Turn north on US 191 and drive 8.4 miles, then turn east on Forest Service Road 481 and continue for one mile. Turn right on Forest Service Road 481A and proceed about 200 yards to the campground.

Trip note: It's a piece of cake to reach this spot, because it's set just off the highway. However, that doesn't detract from the area's beauty. The camp is set in the Gallatin Canyon where nearby Greek Creek empties into the Gallatin River. Fishing the Gallatin River can be a wondrous experience if you hit it at just the right time.

---

41) BANNACK STATE PARK

Reference: near Grasshopper Creek; map M7, grid h1.

Campsites, facilities: There are 10 sites for tents, trailers or motor homes up to 25 feet long. Picnic tables are provided. Piped water, firewood and pit toilets are also available. Pets are permitted on leashes.

Reservations, fee: No reservations necessary; $3-$5 fee per night. Open May to October.

Who to contact: Phone (406) 444-2750 or write to Dillon, MT 59725.

Location: This site is located in Bannack. To get there, drive five miles south of Dillon on Interstate 15. Turn west on Highway 278 and drive 21 miles, then four miles south on a county road to the park.

Trip note: This is a secluded state park that gets used primarily by locals and fisherman. Fishing can be good here at Grasshopper Creek.

---

42) WEST MADISON

Reference: on Madison River; map M7, grid h7.

Campsites, facilities: There are 28 tent sites. Picnic tables are provided. Piped water and pit toilets are also available. Pets are permitted on leashes.

Reservations, fee: No reservations necessary; $3-$5 fee per night. Open May to late November.

Who to contact: Phone Bureau of Land Management at (406) 683-2337 or write to P.O. Box 1048, Dillon, MT 59725.

Location: From Ennis, drive 18 miles south on US 287, cross the McAttee Bridge, and then drive three miles south on a BLM road to the campground.

Trip note: You can set up your fishing headquarters at this 128-acre camp. The camp is set along the Madison River which is one of America's legendary and finest trout streams. Fishing guides are available in Ennis. Two other camps are set along this stretch of the Madison; note South Madison Camp and Madison River Camp.

---

43) RED CLIFF

Reference: on Gallatin River, Gallatin National Forest; map M7, grid h9.

Campsites, facilities: There are 27 tent sites and 40 sites for trailers or motor homes up to 22 feet long. Picnic tables are provided. Piped water, firewood and pit toilets are also available. A store, coffee shop and ice are located within five miles. Pets are permitted on leashes.

Reservations, fee: No reservations necessary; $7 fee per night. Open mid-June to mid-September.

Who to contact: Phone Gallatin National Forest at (406) 587-6700 or write to Bozeman Ranger District, 601 Nikles Avenue, P.O. Box C, Bozeman, MT 59715.

Location: From Big Sky, drive 2.2 miles east on Highway 191S. Turn right on US 191 and drive 6.4 miles south, then 200 yards east on Forest Service Road 634 to the campground.

Trip note: This is a 49-acre, Forest Service site and is one of the few designed more for motor homes than tent campers. It is located along the

Gallatin River, and, boy, it's a pretty spot. For a sidetrip take the trail southeast along Elkhorn Creek, or try your hand at fishing from the campground.

---

44) CLIFF POINT

Reference: on Cliff Lake, Beaverhead National Forest; map M7, grid i7.

Campsites, facilities: There are six sites for tents, trailers and motor homes up to 15 feet long. Picnic tables are provided. Piped water, firewood and pit toilets are also available. A store is located within one mile. Pets are permitted on leashes. Boat docks, launching facilities and rentals are nearby.

Reservations, fee: No reservations necessary; $7 fee per night. Open mid-June to mid-September.

Who to contact: Phone Beaverhead National Forest at (406) 682-4253 or write to Madison Ranger District, 5 Forest Service Road, Ennis, MT 59729.

Location: From West Yellowstone, drive 12 miles north on US 191. Turn left on US 287 and drive 27 miles west, then continue seven miles west on Forest Service Road 8381. Turn at the left fork and proceed to the campground.

Trip note: Because of its near proximity to Yellowstone National Park, this spot is often overlooked. The camp is set on Cliff Lake, one of two long, narrow lakes in the immediate vicinity. This little lake offers all kinds of recreation possibilities without the crowds of Yellowstone. Boating and fishing can be good, and there is a swimming beach for those who just want to bake in the sun.

---

45) WADE LAKE

Reference: on Wade Lake, Beaverhead National Forest; map M7, grid i7.

Campsites, facilities: There are 27 sites for tents, trailers and motor homes up to 16 feet long. Picnic tables are provided. Piped water, firewood and pit toilets are also available. A store is located within one mile. Pets are permitted on leashes. Boat docks, launching facilities and rentals are nearby. Some facilities are **wheelchair accessible.**

Reservations, fee: No reservations necessary; $7 fee per night. Open mid-June to mid-September.

Who to contact: Phone Beaverhead National Forest at (406) 682-4253 or write to Madison Ranger District, 5 Forest Service Road, Ennis, MT 59729.

Location: From West Yellowstone, drive 12 miles north on US 191. Turn right and drive 27 miles west on US 287, then seven miles southwest on Forest Service Road 8381. Take the right fork and continue to the campground.

Trip note: This is one of three lakes in the immediate area. The campground is set on the shoreline of Wade Lake which is the northern most of the lakes (another is Cliff Lake). There are some trails in the area; a Forest Service map is mandatory equipment before heading out. Other recreation options include fishing, boating and swimming.

---

46) HILLTOP

Reference: between Wade and Cliff Lakes, Beaverhead National Forest; map M7, grid i7.

Campsites, facilities: There are 18 sites for trailers or motor homes up to 32 feet long. Picnic tables are provided. Piped water, firewood and pit toilets are also available. A store is located within one mile. Pets are permitted on leashes. Boat docks, launching facilities and rentals are nearby.

Reservations, fee: No reservations necessary; $7 fee per night. Open mid-June to mid-September.

Who to contact: Phone Beaverhead National Forest at (406) 682-4253 or write to Madison Ranger District, 5 Forest Service Road, Ennis, MT 59729.

Location: From West Yellowstone, drive 12 miles north on US 191. Turn right and drive 27 miles west on US 287, then seven miles southwest on Forest Service Road 8381. Take the middle fork and proceed to the campground.

Trip note: You feel like you're being tugged in two directions at this spot because this campground is set between Wade Lake and Cliff Lake. Take your pick. Or try Cliff Point Camp at Cliff Lake or Wade Lake Camp at Wade Lake. Wade Lake offers a few more recreation options; see trip note for details.

---

47) SOUTH MADISON

Reference: on Madison River; map M7, grid i7.

Campsites, facilities: There are 11 sites for tents, trailers and motor homes up to 22 feet long. Picnic tables are provided. Piped water and pit toilets are also available. Pets are permitted on leashes.

Reservations, fee: No reservations necessary; $3-$5 fee per night. Open May to late November.

Who to contact: Phone Bureau of Land Management at (406) 683-2337 or write to P.O. Box 1048, Dillon, MT 59725.

Location: From Ennis, drive 26 miles south on US 287, and then one mile west to the campground.

Trip note: This is a world-class fishing spot and the camp is absolutely free—remember where you heard it. This camp covers 41 acres and is nestled along the Madison River, famous for its trout fishing. For a sidetrip, take the dirt road east from camp and drive three miles to Wolf Creek Hot Springs.

48) MADISON RIVER

Reference: on Madison River, Beaverhead National Forest; map M7, grid i7.

Campsites, facilities: There are 10 sites for trailers or motor homes up to 32 feet long. Picnic tables are provided. Piped water, firewood and pit toilets are also available. A store and laundromat are located within one mile. Pets are permitted on leashes.

Reservations, fee: No reservations necessary; no fee. Open mid-June to mid-September.

Who to contact: Phone Beaverhead National Forest at (406) 682-4253 or write to 5 Forest Service Road, Ennis, MT 59729.

Location: From Cameron, drive 23.6 miles south on US 287. Turn southwest on County Road 8381 and drive 200 yards, then turn south on Forest Service Road 8381B and drive nine miles to the campground.

Trip note: You get two for the price of one in this trip note. Madison River camp covers 400 acres and is fantastic for fishermen. It's set right along a prime piece of the Madison River. If it is filled, here's a secret: the nearby West Fork Campground has seven sites but is often overlooked.

49) CABIN CREEK

Reference: near Earthquake Lake, Gallatin National Forest; map M7, grid i8.

Campsites, facilities: There are 15 sites for tents, trailers and motor homes up to 16 feet long. Picnic tables are provided. Piped water and pit toilets are also available. A store, coffee shop and ice are located within one mile. Pets are permitted on leashes. Boat docks, launching facilities and rentals are nearby.

Reservations, fee: Reserve through MISTIX at (800) 283-CAMP ($6 MISTIX fee); $7 fee per night. Open Memorial Day to Labor Day.

Who to contact: Phone Gallatin National Forest, Hebgen Lake Ranger District at (406) 646-7369 or write to P.O. Box 520, West Yellowstone, MT 59759.

Location: From West Yellowstone, drive eight miles north on US 191, and then 15.4 miles west on US 287 to the campground.

Trip note: This is one of the two camps near Earthquake Lake. Small and pretty, it is set where Cabin Creek empties into the Madison River. A trail from camp heads north into Cabin Creek Recreation and Wildlife Area and provides a good trek for hikers.

50) BEAVER CREEK

Reference: near Earthquake Lake, Gallatin National Forest; map M7, grid i8.

Campsites, facilities: There are 65 sites for tents, trailers and motor homes up to 32 feet long. Picnic tables are provided. Piped water and pit toilets are also available. Showers, a store, a coffee shop and ice are located within five miles. Pets are permitted on leashes. Boat docks, launching facilities and rentals are nearby.

Reservations, fee: Reserve through MISTIX at (800) 283-CAMP ($6 MISTIX fee); $7 fee per night. Open June 15 to mid-September.

Who to contact: Phone Gallatin National Forest, Hebgen Lake Ranger District at (406) 646-7369 or write to P.O. Box 520, West Yellowstone, MT 59759.

Location: From West Yellowstone, drive eight miles north on US 191, and then 17.3 miles west on US 287 to the campground.

Trip note: This is one of two camps (Cabin Creek Camp is the other) near Earthquake Lake which acts as the after bay for nearby Hebgen Lake (two camps available there). This camp sits about 500 yards above the lake, with pretty views but difficult access. The old trail to the lake was wiped out in order to protect the eagle's nest that rests nearby. A visitor center is four miles west on Highway 191.

---

51) YELLOWSTONE HOLIDAY

Reference: on Hebgen Lake; map M7, grid i9.

Campsites, facilities: There are 15 tent sites and 27 sites for trailers or motor homes of any length. Picnic tables are provided. Flush toilets, showers, firewood, a store, ice and a playground are also available. Pets on leashes and motorbikes are permitted. Boat docks, launching facilities and rentals are nearby. There are also 18 cabins available.

Reservations, fee: Reservations accepted; $10-$15 fee per night; MasterCard and Visa accepted. Cabins are approximately $30 per night. Open mid-May to October.

Who to contact: Phone (406) 646-7237 or write to Star Route, P.O. Box 120, West Yellowstone, MT 59758.

Location: From West Yellowstone, drive eight miles north on US 191, and then five miles west on US 287 to the campground.

Trip note: This is a 40-acre park set on the shore of Hebgen Lake, and, like Kirkwood Ranch, it's designed primarily for motor homes and trailers. This is an extremely popular campground; get your reservation in as early as possible. A marina with boat rentals and a riding stable provide recreational possibilities.

---

52) LONESOME HURST

Reference: on Hebgen Lake, Gallatin National Forest; map M7, grid i9.

Campsites, facilities: There are 26 sites for tents, trailers or motor homes up to 30 feet long. Picnic tables, hand-pumped water, and pit toilets are provided. A boat dock and boat launch are available. Pets are permitted on leashes.

Reservations, fee: Reserve through MISTIX at (800) 283-CAMP ($6 MISTIX fee); $8 fee per night.

Who to contact: Phone Gallatin National Forest at (406) 646-7369 or write to Hebgen Lake Ranger District, P.O. Box 520, West Yellowstone, MT 59758.

Location: From West Yellowstone, drive six miles west on Highway 20, then turn north on Hebgen Lake Road and continue 3.5 miles to the campground.

Trip note: This is one of several popular camps on pretty Hebgen Lake. This one is located on the South Fork arm, and is a popular fishing spot, with easy access to the lake. The area around this camp in particular is known for its spectacular trout fishing.

---

53) RAINBOW POINT

Reference: on Hebgen Lake, Gallatin National Forest; map M7, grid i9.

Campsites, facilities: There are 86 sites for trailers or motor homes up to 32 feet long. No tents or tent trailers are permitted. Picnic tables are provided. Piped water, firewood and pit toilets are also available. Pets are permitted on leashes. Boat docks and launching facilities are nearby.

Reservations, fee: Reserve through MISTIX at (800) 283-CAMP ($6 MISTIX fee); $8 fee per night. Open June to mid-September.

Who to contact: Phone Gallatin National Forest at (406) 646-7369 or write to Hebgen Lake Ranger District, P.O. Box 520, West Yellowstone, MT 59758.

Location: From West Yellowstone, drive 4.6 miles north on US 191, and then 5.2 miles west on Forest Service Road 610 to the campground.

Trip note: This is the major camp on Hebgen Lake. It's set on the Grayling arm on a bay of the lake. It's a pretty spot, and by far the most popular here. Boat rentals, fishing and a riding stable are some of the recreation possibilities.

---

54) BRANDIN' IRON TRAILER PARK

Reference: near Yellowstone National Park; map M7, grid j9.

Campsites, facilities: There are 17 sites for trailers or motor homes of any length. No tents are permitted. Electricity, piped water, sewer hookups and picnic tables are provided. Flush toilets, showers, and laundromat are also available. Bottled gas, a store and coffee shop are located within one mile. Pets are permitted on leashes.

Reservations, fee: Reservations accepted; $18.50 fee per night; MasterCard and Visa accepted. Open mid-May to mid-October.

Who to contact: Phone (406) 646-7664 or write P.O. Box 669, West Yellowstone, MT 59758.

Location: This trailer park is located in West Yellowstone at the junction of Boundary and Firehole Streets.

Trip note: Here is yet another possibility for motor home fun. This camp is set directly across from Yellowstone National Park, right in downtown West Yellowstone. It is adjacent to a motel, with restaurants and shopping just a short walk away. Not exactly the wilderness, but there are a few evergreens around. Why no tent camping? Too dangerous, folks—this is bear country.

---

55) BAKER'S HOLE

Reference: on Madison River, Gallatin National Forest; map M7, grid j9.

Campsites, facilities: There are 72 sites for trailers or motor homes up to 32 feet long. No tents or tent trailers are permitted. Picnic tables are provided. Piped water, firewood and pit toilets are also available. Sanitary disposal station, showers, a store, coffee shop, laundromat and ice are located within five miles. One site and one restroom are **wheelchair accessible.** Pets are permitted on leashes.

Reservations, fee: Reserve through MISTIX at (800) 283-CAMP ($6 MISTIX fee); $8 fee per night. Open June to mid-September.

Who to contact: Phone Gallatin National Forest at (406) 646-7369 or write to Hebgen Lake Ranger District, P.O. Box 520, West Yellowstone, MT 59758.

Location: From West Yellowstone, drive three miles north on US 191 to the campground.

Trip note: If you fly an airplane, this is your calling. The camp is set on the Madison River, the famed trout stream, and pilots can land their planes on the nearby air strip. Great trout fishing can be had in a matter of minutes.

---

56) LION'S HEAD RESORT

Reference: near Madison River; map M7, grid j9.

Campsites, facilities: There are 15 tent sites and 144 drive-through sites for trailers or motor homes of any length. Electricity, piped water, sewer hookups and picnic tables are provided. Flush toilets, bottled gas, sanitary disposal station, showers, firewood, recreation hall, a store, restaurant and lounge, laundromat and ice are also available. Pets and motorbikes are permitted.

Reservations, fee: Reservations accepted; $18-$20 fee per night; MasterCard and Visa accepted. Open mid-May to mid-September.

Who to contact: Phone (406) 646-7296 or (406) 646-9584 or write to 1545 Targhee Pass Road, West Yellowstone, MT 59758.

Location: From West Yellowstone, drive eight miles west on Highway 20 to 1545 Targhee Pass Road.

Trip note: This is a 37-acre, private park just a mile east of the Idaho-Montana border. It has some shady sites, but all are grassy. A riding stable nearby provides a recreation option, and of course, there's good trout fishing on the Madison River. Yellowstone National Park is just eight miles away.

57) RUSTIC RV

Reference: near Yellowstone National Park; map M7, grid j9.

Campsites, facilities: There are 10 tent sites and 40 drive-through sites for trailers or motor homes of any length. Piped water and picnic tables are provided. Flush toilets, sanitary disposal station, showers, mini-store, laundromat and ice are also available. Electricity, cable TV and sewer hookups are available at an additional charge. Bottled gas, a store and coffee shop are located within one mile. Pets are permitted on leashes.

Reservations, fee: Reservations accepted; $15-$20 fee per night. Open April through October.

Who to contact: Phone (406) 646-7387 or write P.O. Box 608, West Yellowstone, MT 59758.

Location: This campground is located less than one mile west of the park entrance in West Yellowstone.

Trip note: This park is set on the threshold of Yellowstone National Park. The park covers only two acres, so you can be kind of squeezed. This is an alternative to the sardine-like campgrounds in Yellowstone Park, but it gets heavy pressure, too, so reserve far in advance.

Montana Map M8
46 listings
Pages 408-429

North (M3)—see page 348
East (M9)—see page 430
South—Wyoming
West (M7)—see page 380

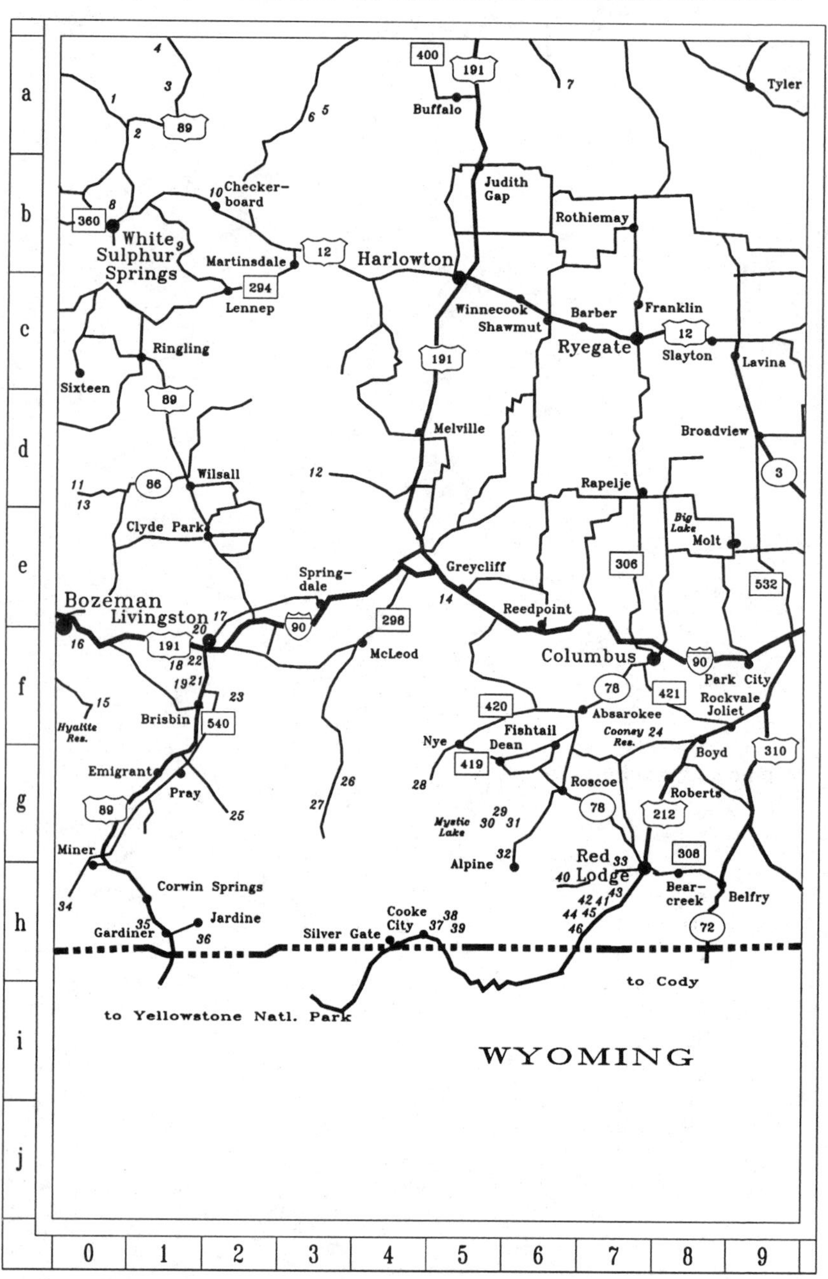

Featuring: Moose Creek, Lewis and Clark National Forest, Jumping Creek, Sheep Creek, Porphyry Peak, Judith River, Big Snowy Mountains, Grasshopper Creek, Spring Creek, Fairy Lake, Gallatin National Forest, Big Timber Creek, Battle Ridge Pass, Yellowstone River, Hyalite Reservoir, Jewel Lake, Mill Creek, Boulder River, Beartooth Wilderness, Stillwater River, Custer National Forest, Rosebud Creek, Mystic Lake, East Rosebud Lake, Trail Creek, Yellowstone National Park, Timberline Creek, Rock Creek, Steeley Creek

---

1) MOOSE CREEK

Reference: on Moose Creek, Lewis and Clark National Forest; map M8, grid a0.

Campsites, facilities: There are five sites for tents, trailers or motor homes up to 22 feet long. Picnic tables are provided. Piped water, firewood and pit toilets are also available. Pets are permitted on leashes.

Reservations, fee: No reservations necessary; no fee. Open June to late November.

Who to contact: Phone Lewis and Clark National Forest at (406) 547-3361 or write to King's Hill Ranger District, P.O. Box A, White Sulphur Springs, MT 59645.

Location: From the town of White Sulphur Springs, drive 18 miles north on US 89. Turn left on Forest Service Road 119 and drive 5.5 miles west, then turn north on Forest Service Road 204 and proceed 3.2 miles to the campground.

Trip note: Guess where this camp is set? Answer: Moose Creek. Surprised? No, but you might be at the beauty of the wildlands if you try a nearby hike. A trail starts one mile north on Forest Service Road 204 and is routed northwest up Allan Creek into Quartzite Ridge in the Little Belt Mountains. Here's today's geology lesson: quartzite is a metamorphic rock resulting from the recrystallization of quartz sandstone.

---

2) JUMPING CREEK

Reference: on Jumping Creek, Sheep Creek, Lewis and Clark National Forest; map M8, a1.

Campsites, facilities: There are 15 sites for tents, trailers and motor homes up to 22 feet long. Picnic tables are provided. Piped water, firewood and pit toilets are also available. A coffee shop is located within five miles. Pets are permitted on leashes.

Reservations, fee: No reservations necessary; $5 fee per night. Open June to late November.

Who to contact: Phone Lewis and Clark National Forest at (406) 547-3361 or write to King's Hill Ranger District, P.O. Box A, White Sulphur Springs, MT 59645.

Location: From the town of White Sulphur Springs, drive 22 miles northeast on US 89 to the campground entrance.

Trip note: You get easy access here, because the campground is set just off the highway. But don't let that distract you from enjoying the pretty setting. It's at the confluence of Sheep Creek and Jumping Creek. There are several primitive Forest Service roads in the area that are excellent for mountain biking. See a National Forest map for trail details.

---

3) KING'S HILL

Reference: near Porphyry Peak, Lewis and Clark National Forest; map M8, grid a1.

Campsites, facilities: There are 18 sites for tents, trailers and motor homes up to 22 feet long. Picnic tables are provided. Piped water, firewood and vault toilets are also available. Pets are permitted on leashes.

Reservations, fee: No reservations necessary; $5 fee per night. Open July to late September.

Who to contact: Phone Lewis and Clark National Forest at (406) 547-3361 or write to King's Hill Ranger District, P.O. Box A, White Sulphur Springs, MT 59645.

Location: From Neihart, drive nine miles south on US 89 to the campground.

Trip note: Easy to reach, this spot is perched atop King's Hill Pass, a ski area during winter. A possible sidetrip is taking the road west to Porphyry Peak; a trail there is routed south past Mizpah Peak.

---

4) MANY PINES

Reference: southeast of Neihart, Lewis and Clark National Forest; map M8, grid a1.

Campsites, facilities: There are 23 sites for tents, trailers and motor homes up to 22 feet long. Picnic tables are provided. Piped water, firewood and vault toilets are also available. A store, coffee shop and ice are located within five miles. Pets are permitted on leashes.

Reservations, fee: No reservations necessary; $5 fee per night. Open June to mid-October.

Who to contact: Phone Lewis and Clark National Forest at (406) 547-3361 or write to King's Hill Ranger District, P.O. Box A, White Sulphur Springs, MT 59645.

Location: From Neihart, drive 3.5 miles southeast on US 89 to the campground.

Trip note: This is one in a series of Forest Service camps with easy access along US 89. A unique sidetrip is the nearby hike along Memorial Creek to Memorial Falls. The trailhead is located about two miles north of this camp on the right.

---

5) INDIAN HILL

Reference: on Judith River, Lewis and Clark National Forest; map M8, grid a3.

Campsites, facilities: There are seven sites for tents, trailers and motor homes up to 22 feet long. Picnic tables are provided. Hand-pumped water, firewood and vault toilets are also available. Pets are permitted on leashes.

Reservations, fee: No reservations necessary; no fee. Open late May to October.

Who to contact: Phone Lewis and Clark National Forest at (406) 566-2292 or write to Judith Ranger District, 109 Central Avenue, P.O. Box 484, Stanford, MT 59479.

Location: From Stanford, follow Highway 87 for seven miles to Windham. At Windham, turn south on Highway 239 and travel 11 miles to Utica. Turn south on a gravel road and continue ten miles to Sapphire Village. Continue on this road (Memorial Way Road) for 5.5 miles to the campground.

Trip note: This is a little spot located beside the Judith River. There's a trail north of camp that you can hike, which reaches Indian Hill—it's routed right through Bower Canyon. Anglers should note that the South Fork of the Judith River is stocked annually just downstream from camp. This camp is used heavily by hunters during hunting season.

---

6) HAY CANYON

Reference: on Judith River, Lewis and Clark National Forest; map M8, grid a3.

Campsites, facilities: There are nine sites for tents, trailers or motor homes up to 22 feet long. Picnic tables are provided. Vault toilets and firewood are also available. There is **no piped water.** Pets are permitted on leashes.

Reservations, fee: No reservations necessary; no fee. Open year-round.

Who to contact: Phone Lewis and Clark National Forest at (406) 566-2292 or write to Judith Ranger District, 109 Central Avenue, P.O. Box 484, Stanford, MT 59479.

Location: From Hobson, drive 12 miles west on Highway 239 to Utica. Turn left on a signed county road and drive 16.5 miles southwest, then continue southwest on Forest Service Road 487 to the campground.

Trip note: Don't expect a lot of company out in this neck of the woods (with the exception of fall hunters). The camp is set in Hay Canyon along the Judith River and is frequented rarely by out-of-towners. A dirt road from camp heads west up Hay Canyon. A nearby option is Indian Hill Camp.

---

7) CRYSTAL LAKE

Reference: near Big Snowy Mountains, Lewis and Clark National Forest; map M8, grid a6.

Campsites, facilities: There are 28 sites for tents, trailers or motor homes up to 22 feet long. Picnic tables are provided. Piped water, firewood and pit toilets are also available. Pets are permitted on leashes. Boat docks and launching facilities are nearby. Crystal Lake Cabin is available for rental during the fall and winter.

Reservations, fee: No reservations necessary; $5 fee per night. Open mid-June to mid-September.

Who to contact: Phone Lewis and Clark National Forest at (406) 566-2292 or write to Judith Ranger District, 109 Central Avenue, P.O. Box 484, Stanford, MT 59479.

Location: From Stanford, travel 32 miles east on Highway 87 to Moore. Turn off at the sign for Crystal Lake onto a gravel road that leads south through Moore. Follow the signs for Crystal Lake for 20 miles to the campground.

Trip note: On a good day, Crystal Lake does look like a jewel. It's set at the foot of Mount Harlow (7,268 feet). It's quiet here too, because motor boats are not allowed, so bring your canoe. The lake is stocked each year just before Memorial Day with 1,000 seven to nine-inch rainbow trout. For hikers, there is a choice of four trails from camp: Crystal Lake Shoreline Loop Trail, Ulhorn Trail, Crystal Cascades Trail and Grandview Trail. There is a network of other trails in the Big Snowy Mountains, where you can find unique ice caves. In the winter time, there are several excellent cross-country skiing trails nearby.

---

8) SPRING CAMP

Reference: in White Sulphur Springs; map M8, grid b0.

Campsites, facilities: There are 20 sites for trailers or motor homes of any length. Electricity, piped water, sewer hookups and picnic tables are provided. Bottled gas, a store, coffee shop, laundromat and ice are located within one mile. Pets are permitted on leashes.

Reservations, fee: Reservations accepted; $10-$15 fee per night; Open April through November.

Who to contact: Phone (406) 547-3921 or write to P.O. Box 350, White Sulphur Springs, MT 59645.

Location: This campground is located in the town of White Sulphur Springs at the west end of Main Street.

Trip note: If you're looking for a break and it's late, this is the spot. It's located just on the outskirts of town (population 1400). A few sidetrips are possible. You can reach the Smith River, five miles east of town, by taking Forest Service Road 139, which starts right in town. Fishermen might consider visiting Lake Sutherlin located 10 miles northeast of town on US 12. And Castle Museum is in town and located at Second Avenue and East Baker Street.

---

9) GRASSHOPPER

Reference: on Grasshopper Creek, Lewis and Clark National Forest; map M8, grid b1.

Campsites, facilities: There are 12 sites for tents, trailers and motor homes up to 22 feet long. Picnic tables are provided. Firewood and vault toilets are also available. There is **no piped water**. Pets are permitted on leashes.

Reservations, fee: No reservations necessary; no fee. Open June through November.

Who to contact: Phone Lewis and Clark National Forest at (406) 547-3361 or write to King's Hill Ranger District, P.O. Box A, White Sulphur Springs, MT 59645.

Location: From the town of White Sulphur Springs, drive seven miles east on US 12, and then 4.2 miles south on Forest Service Road 211 to the campground.

Trip note: It's just far enough off the beaten path of US 12 that it gets missed by a lot of campers who would otherwise like to find it. The camp is set at the confluence of Grasshopper Creek and Fourmile Creek. A trail from camp is routed south along a group of peaks in the 8,200-foot range; the trail doesn't go up them but laterals around them (thank the Lord). A sidetrip for families is at the Richardson Creek Picnic Area just one mile away on Forest Service Road 211.

---

10) SPRING

Reference: on Spring Creek, Lewis and Clark National Forest; map M8, grid b2.

Campsites, facilities: There are 10 sites for tents, trailers and motor homes up to 22 feet long. Picnic tables are provided. Piped water, firewood and vault toilets are also available. Pets are permitted on leashes.

Reservations, fee: No reservations necessary; $4 fee per night. Open mid-May to late November.

Who to contact: Phone Lewis and Clark National Forest at (406) 632-4391 or write to 809 Second NW, P.O. Box F, Harlowton, MT 59036.

Location: From Harlowton, drive 33 miles west on US 12, and then four miles north on Forest Service Road 274 to the campground.

Trip note: This is a hidden spot, and the only camp in the area. It's set beside Spring Creek. At the end of the nearby road southeast of camp (you'll see it), you'll find a trail along the East Fork Spring Creek (detailed on Forest Service map). Another possibility is to go fishing at Bair Reservoir (there's no boat ramp), located seven miles northwest off Highway 11, just west of Checkerboard.

---

11) FAIRY LAKE

Reference: on Fairy Lake, Gallatin National Forest; map M8, grid d0.

Campsites, facilities: There are nine tent sites. Picnic tables are provided. Piped water, firewood and pit toilets are also available. Pets are permitted on leashes.

Reservations, fee: No reservations necessary; no fee. Open July to mid-September.

Who to contact: Phone Gallatin National Forest at (406) 587-6920 or write to Bozeman Ranger District, 601 Nikles Avenue, P.O. Box C, Bozeman, MT 59715.

Location: From Bozeman, drive 22 miles northeast on Highway 293 and 86 (Bridger Creek Road) past Bridger Bowl Ski Area. Take the middle fork at Brackett Creek, drive three miles, and then continue six miles west on Forest Service Road 74 to the campground.

Trip note: It's quite a drive to get here but a nice spot. It's one of just two camps in the whole area. This one is set along Fairy Lake with Sacagawea Peak (9,670 feet) looming overhead. A trail from camp is routed to the peak, a superb lookout point. If you wish to continue on, it connects with Bridger Mountains Trail and others (detailed on a Forest Service map). There are fish in this little lake too, so bring along your pole.

---

12) HALFMOON

Reference: on Big Timber Creek, Gallatin National Forest; map M8, grid d3.

Campsites, facilities: There are eight sites for tents, trailers or motor homes up to 16 feet long. Picnic tables are provided. Piped water and pit toilets are also available. Pets are permitted on leashes.

Reservations, fee: No reservations necessary; no fee. Open mid-June to mid-October.

Who to contact: Phone Gallatin National Forest at (406) 932-5155 or write to Big Timber Ranger District, P.O. Box 196, Big Timber, MT 59011.

Location: From Big Timber, drive 11 miles north on Highway 19. Turn west on County Road 197 (Big Timber Canyon Road) and drive eight miles, then turn on Forest Service Road 197 and continue two miles west to the campground.

Trip note: This site is at the end of the road on Big Timber Creek. Big Timber Creek Trail travels west from the camp; you can branch off to the south and hike to Blue Lake and a spectacular view of Granite Peak, or continue straight up to a 10,000-foot ridge just below Conical Peak.

---

13) BATTLE RIDGE

Reference: on Battle Ridge Pass, Gallatin National Forest; map M8, grid e0.

Campsites, facilities: There are 13 sites for tents, trailers and motor homes up to 16 feet long. Picnic tables are provided. Piped water, firewood and pit toilets are also available. Pets are permitted on leashes.

Reservations, fee: No reservations necessary; no fee. Open early June to late September.

Who to contact: Phone Gallatin National Forest at (406) 587-6920 or write to Bozeman Ranger District, 601 Nikles Avenue, P.O. Box C, Bozeman, MT 59715.

Location: From Bozeman, drive 21 miles northeast on Highway 293 and 86 (Bridger Creek Road) past Bridger Bowl Ski Area. Take the Middle Fork at Brackett Creek, and drive two miles to the campground.

Trip note: This camp is set right at Battle Ridge Pass and offers several trails. It's all detailed on a Forest Service map. The biggest attraction here is the superb scenic view.

---

14) BIG TIMBER KOA

Reference: near Yellowstone River; map M8, grid e5.

Campsites, facilities: There are 20 tent sites and 40 sites for trailers or motor homes of any length. Picnic tables are provided. Flush toilets, sanitary disposal station, showers, firewood, recreation hall, a store, laundromat, ice, playground and a swimming pool are also available. Electricity, piped water and sewer hookups are available at an additional charge. A coffee shop is located within one mile. Pets are permitted on leashes.

Reservations, fee: Reservations accepted; $15-$20 fee per night; MasterCard and Visa accepted. Open May to mid-September.

Who to contact: Phone (406) 932-6569 or write to HC88, P.O. Box 3634, Big Timber, MT 59011.

Location: From Interstate 90 in Greycliff (east of Bozeman), take exit 377 and drive a half mile west on the southern frontage road to the campground.

Trip note: This is prairie dog country, and there aren't many spots to camp. So you'd better stop here if you're getting tired. The park covers 10 acres. If you want a more primitive setting, there is a little-known spot nearby called Pelican. It is set along the Yellowstone River east of town. You get direct fishing access here.

---

15) HOOD CREEK

Reference: on Hyalite Reservoir, Gallatin National Forest; map M8, grid f0.

Campsites, facilities: There are 18 sites for tents, trailers and motor homes up to 16 feet long. Picnic tables are provided. Piped water, firewood and pit toilets are also available. Pets are permitted on leashes. Boat docks and launching facilities are nearby.

Reservations, fee: No reservations necessary; $7 fee per night. Open mid-June to mid-September.

Who to contact: Phone Gallatin National Forest at (406) 587-6920 or write to Bozeman Ranger District, 601 Nikles Avenue, P.O. Box C, Bozeman, MT 59715.

Location: From Bozeman, drive eight miles south on County Road 243, and then southeast on Forest Service Road 62 for 10 miles.

Trip note: This is a popular little spot on the eastern shore of Hyalite Reservoir. You get a myriad of recreation options: boating, swimming, hiking and fishing. Warning: Hyalite Junior Camp is at the south end of the lake. A row of mountain peaks loom overhead to the southeast. A good sidetrip is to the picnic area one mile southeast at Palisade Falls.

---

16) SUNRISE

Reference: near Bozeman; map M8, grid f0.

Campsites, facilities: There are 25 tent sites and 34 sites for trailers or motor homes of any length. Picnic tables are provided. Flush toilets, sanitary disposal station, showers, firewood, a recreation hall, laundromat, ice and a playground are also available. Electricity, piped water and sewer hookups are available at an additional charge. Bottled gas, a store and coffee shop are located within one mile. Pets and motorbikes are permitted.

Reservations, fee: Reservations accepted; $15-$20 fee per night; MasterCard and Visa accepted. Open May through October.

Who to contact: Phone (406) 587-4797 or write to 31842 Frontage, Bozeman, MT 59715.

Location: Take exit 309 off I-90 at Bozeman, and drive a quarter of a mile east on the frontage road to the campground.

Trip note: This is a six-acre, privately developed park that was once a sacred hunting ground for the Sioux Indians. It was known as Valley of the Flowers. Now, with no buffalo, it is used for farming. There's even a golf course in the area. For some, that is a shameful legacy. Two museums in town provide sidetrips: Gallatin Pioneers Museum at 301 West Main Street, and Museum of the Rockies at Montana State University (South Seventh Avenue and Kagy Boulevard).

---

17) RAINBOW HOTEL & CAMP

Reference: in Livingston; map M8, grid f1.

Campsites, facilities: There are eight tent sites and six sites for trailers or motor homes. Picnic tables are provided. Flush toilets, sanitary disposal station, ice and a playground are also available. Electricity, piped water, sewer hookups and showers are available at an additional charge. Bottled gas is located within one mile. Pets and motorbikes are permitted.

Reservations, fee: No reservations necessary; $12-$18 fee per night; MasterCard and Visa accepted. Open May to late October.

Who to contact: Phone (406) 222-3780 or write to Route 85, P.O. Box 4333, Livingston, MT 59047.

Location: This campground is located in Livingston, one mile east on Park Street.

Trip note: Of the five camps in Livingston, this spot is the friendliest to the tenters. The park covers just three acres. All the sites are grassy, with scattered trees. It's about one block from the Yellowstone River, which offers excellent fishing.

---

18) ROCK CANYON

Reference: on Yellowstone River; map M8, grid f1.

Campsites, facilities: There are 50 tent sites and 26 sites for trailers or motor homes. Piped water and picnic tables are provided. Flush toilets, showers and laundromat are also available. A small drive-in restaurant is located nearby. Pets and motorbikes are permitted.

Reservations, fee: Reservations accepted; $12 fee per night. Open mid-May to mid-October.

Who to contact: Phone (406) 222-1096 or write to Route 62, P.O. Box 3144, Livingston, MT 59047.

Location: From Interstate 90 in Livingston, take exit 333 and drive three miles south on US 89 to the campground.

Trip note: This is a good option for tent campers in the Livingston area who don't want to be in town, but just the same, find themselves in the area looking for a spot to hole up for the night. This one is just three miles out of town, with easy access from the highway. It is set along the Yellowstone River in the Paradise Valley canyon, offering riverside sites with fishing access.

---

19) BIG SPUR

Reference: near Yellowstone River; map M8, grid f1.

Campsites, facilities: There are 10 tent sites and 14 sites for trailers or motor homes of any length. Flush toilets, sanitary disposal station, showers, a store, laundromat, playground and a heated swimming pool are also available. Pets and motorbikes are permitted. Boat launching facilities are nearby.

Reservations, fee: Reservations accepted; $15-$20 fee per night; MasterCard and Visa accepted. Open May through October.

Who to contact: Phone (406) 222-7600 or write to Route 38, P.O. Box 2212, Livingston, MT 59047.

Location: From Interstate 90 in Livingston, take exit 333 and drive 10.5 miles south on US 89 to the campground.

Trip note: This is one of three camps that is a 15-minute drive south of Livingston and offers easy access off the highway. This one covers 10 acres and is not far from the Yellowstone River. This valley is known as Paradise Valley and has three nearby fishing access sites along the Yellowstone River: Mallards Rest, Loch Leven and Paradise. These all have camping areas and pit toilets, and provide direct fishing access. A riding stable provides another recreational possibility. The view is spectacular.

20) S-S MOTEL AND CAMP

Reference: in Livingston; map M8, grid f1.

Campsites, facilities: There are 10 tent sites and 14 sites for trailers or motor homes. Picnic tables are provided. Flush toilets, showers, laundromat and ice are also available. Electricity, piped water and sewer hookups are available at an additional charge. Bottled gas and sanitary disposal station are located within one mile. Pets and motorbikes are permitted.

Reservations, fee: Reservations accepted; $12-$15 fee per night; MasterCard and Visa accepted. Open June to late September.

Who to contact: Phone (406) 222-0591 or write to #1 View Vista Drive, Livingston, MT 59047.

Location: This campground is located in Livingston at the south end of Main Street.

Trip note: This is one of five camping options in town. The sites are grassy, with scattered trees throughout the camp. It is situated right in town, with a golf course, restaurants, the city park, city swimming pool, fairgrounds, shopping and the Yellowstone River all within walking distance.

21) PARADISE VALLEY KOA

Reference: near Yellowstone River; map M8, grid f1.

Campsites, facilities: There are 50 tent sites and 35 sites for trailers or motor homes of any length, with 12 full hook-ups. Picnic tables are provided. Flush toilets, sanitary disposal station, showers, recreation hall, a store, laundromat, ice, playground and a swimming pool are also available. Electricity, piped water, sewer hookups and firewood are available at an additional charge. Pets and motorbikes are permitted.

Reservations, fee: Reservations accepted; $15-$20 fee per night; MasterCard and Visa accepted. Open May through November.

Who to contact: Phone (406) 222-0992 or write to Route 38, P.O. Box 2089, Livingston, MT 59047.

Location: From Interstate 90 in Livingston, take exit 333. Drive 10 miles south on US 89, and then two miles east on a well-signed county road to the campground.

Trip note: This is a good base camp for a fishing trip to the Yellowstone River. The park covers seven acres. See trip note for Big Spur for other possible base camps for fishermen and campers.

22) OLSEN'S DRIVE-THRU TRAILER COURT

Reference: near the Yellowstone River; map M8, grid f1.

Campsites, facilities: There are 10 tent sites and 25 sites for trailers or motor homes. Electricity, piped water, sewer hookups and picnic tables are provided. Flush toilets, sanitary disposal station, cable TV, showers, laundromat, ice and a playground are also available. Bottled gas is located within one mile. Pets and motorbikes are permitted. Boat docks, launching facilities and rentals are nearby.

Reservations, fee: Reservations accepted; $10-$12 fee per night. Open all year.

Who to contact: Phone (406) 222-1028 or write to Route 62, P.O. Box 3107, Livingston, MT 59047.

Location: In Livingston, drive a half mile south on US 89, and then two blocks west on Merrit Lane to the trailer park.

Trip note: The park covers 10 acres and is not far from the Yellowstone River. A good sidetrip is to cruise US 89 south to Yellowstone National Park and enjoy the spectacular view of mountains everywhere. A riding stable and golf course in the area provide recreational options.

---

23) PINE CREEK

Reference: near Jewel Lake, Gallatin National Forest; map M8, grid f2.

Campsites, facilities: There are 26 sites for tents, trailers and motor homes up to 22 feet long. Picnic tables are provided. Piped water, firewood and pit toilets are also available. A store, coffee shop and laundromat are located within five miles. Pets are permitted on leashes.

Reservations, fee: No reservations necessary; $5 fee per night. Open June to late September.

Who to contact: Phone Gallatin National Forest at (406) 222-1892 or write to Livingston Ranger District, Route 62, P.O. Box 3197, Livingston, MT 59047.

Location: From Livingston, drive four miles south on US 89. Turn south on Highway 540 and drive 10 miles, then turn east on Forest Service Road 202 and continue 2.5 miles to the campground.

Trip note: This is a 25-acre Forest Service site with an outstanding hiking trail leading out from camp. It follows Pine Creek for four miles west, most of it up, to little Jewel Lake at the foot of Mount McKnight (10,310 feet). It's an idyllic spot, but it takes some thumping to reach it. See trip note for Big Spur Camp for other spots right along the Yellowstone River. Fishing in the creek is another recreation possibility.

---

24) COONEY RESERVOIR STATE PARK

Reference: southwest of Laurel; map M8, grid f7.

Campsites, facilities: There are 30 sites for tents, trailers and motor homes up to 20 feet long. Picnic tables are provided. Piped water, pit toilets and a playground are also available. Boat launching facilities are nearby. Pets are permitted on leashes.

Reservations, fee: No reservations necessary; $7-$9 fee per night. Open mid-May to mid-September.

Who to contact: Phone Montana Department of Fish, Wildlife and Parks at (406) 444-2535 or write to 1420 East Sixth Avenue, Helena, MT 59620.

Location: From Laurel, drive 22 miles southwest on US 212 to milepost 90, and then eight miles west on a signed county road to the park.

Trip note: This is the only camp for many miles, and it's a pretty spot. The park covers 1,000 acres and is set right along Cooney Reservoir. It's a popular spot for boating, fishing, swimming and waterskiing.

---

25) SNOW BANK

Reference: on Mill Creek, Gallatin National Forest; map M8, grid g2.

Campsites, facilities: There are 12 sites for tents, trailers and motor homes up to 22 feet long. Picnic tables are provided. Piped water, firewood and pit toilets are also available. Pets are permitted on leashes.

Reservations, fee: No reservations necessary; $5 fee per night. Open June to late September.

Who to contact: Phone Gallatin National Forest at (406) 222-1892 or write to Livingston Ranger District, Route 62, P.O. Box 3197, Livingston, MT 59047.

Location: From Livingston, drive 20 miles south on US 89, then 15 miles southeast on County Road 486 to the campground.

Trip note: This is a small camp that gets missed by most out-of-staters. The campsites are right along Mill Creek, which can offer some good fishing. It's a good camp for backpackers because of a trail leading from camp northwest into the Absaroka Wilderness. Other trails head south and connect up with a network of trails around Monitor Peak (10,400 feet). A Forest Service map is advised. A word of warning: just two miles southeast on County Road 486 is the Temple Hills Assembly Grounds—so you better not get lost, or somebody may try to convert you.

---

26) HELL'S CANYON

Reference: near Boulder River, Gallatin National Forest; map M8, grid g3.

Campsites, facilities: There are 11 sites for tents, trailers or motor homes up to 16 feet long. Picnic tables are provided. Pit toilets are also available. There is **no piped water.** Pets are permitted on leashes.

Reservations, fee: No reservations necessary; no fee. Open mid-June to October.

Who to contact: Phone Gallatin National Forest at (406) 932-5155 or write to Big Timber Ranger District, P.O. Box 196, Big Timber, MT 59011.

Location: From Big Timber, drive 25 miles south on Highway 298, and then 14 miles south on Forest Service Road 212 to the campground.

Trip note: This camp is located within walking distance of the Boulder River. One mile south of camp, a trail from the Fourmile Guard Station heads both east and west along creek drainages into the surrounding Absaroka-Beartooth Wilderness Area. This an ideal base camp for a wilderness expedition.

---

27) HICKS PARK

Reference: near Absaroka-Beartooth Wilderness, Gallatin National Forest; map M8, grid g3.

Campsites, facilities: There are 16 sites for tents, trailers or motor homes up to 22 feet long. Picnic tables are provided. Piped water and pit toilets are also available. Pets are permitted on leashes.

Reservations, fee: No reservations necessary; no fee. Open mid-June to October.

Who to contact: Phone Gallatin National Forest at (406) 932-5155 or write to Big Timber Ranger District, P.O. Box 196, Big Timber, MT 59011.

Location: From Big Timber, drive 25 miles south on Highway 298, and then 20 miles south on Forest Service Road 212 to the campground.

Trip note: This is one of the better trailhead camps in the region. One trail starts from camp and heads east along Upsidedown Creek for about four miles to Horseshoe Lake. It then continues up farther to Lake Plateau in the Absaroka-Beartooth Wilderness Area. Many small, secret lakes are tucked away below mountain peaks out in this part of the wilderness. One word of warning: If you are camping here, and not hiking away, be forewarned of a church camp nearby.

---

28) WOODBINE

Reference: on Stillwater River, Custer National Forest; map M8, grid g4.

Campsites, facilities: There are 46 sites for tents, trailers or motor homes up to 30 feet long. Picnic tables are provided. Hand-pumped water, firewood and pit toilets are also available. Pets are permitted on leashes.

Reservations, fee: No reservations necessary; $5 fee per night. Open June to October.

Who to contact: Phone Custer National Forest at (406) 446-2103 or write to Beartooth Ranger District, Route 2, P.O. Box 3420, Red Lodge, MT 59068.

Location: From Nye, drive eight miles southwest on a signed, paved County Road 419 to the campground.

Trip note: This one is way out there. It's set along the Stillwater River at the foot of the Beartooth Mountains. It's a good jump-off point for a multi-day backpack trip into the bordering the Absaroka-Beartooth Wilderness Area. A trail starting a quarter mile from camp is routed south along the river into the wilderness.

29) PINE GROVE

Reference: on Rosebud Creek, Custer National Forest; map M8, grid g5.

Campsites, facilities: There are 35 tent sites and 11 sites for trailers or motor homes up to 30 feet long. Picnic tables are provided. Hand-pumped water, firewood and pit toilets are also available. Pets are permitted on leashes. Boat docks are nearby.

Reservations, fee: No reservations necessary; $5 fee per night. Open late May through Labor Day.

Who to contact: Phone Custer National Forest at (406) 446-2103 or write to Beartooth Ranger District, Route 2, P.O. Box 3420, Red Lodge, MT 59068.

Location: From Fishtail, drive one mile west on County Road 419. Turn left on County Road 425 and drive six miles southwest, then eight miles south on Forest Service Road 72 to the campground.

Trip note: This is one of two camps in the immediate area. This one is set along Rosebud Creek about three miles east of Emerald Lake, and it's five miles west of the trailhead that provides access to Mystic Lake.

30) EMERALD LAKE

Reference: near Mystic Lake, Custer National Forest; map M8, grid g5.

Campsites, facilities: There are 21 sites for tents, trailers and motor homes up to 30 feet long. Picnic tables are provided. Hand pumped water, firewood and pit toilets are also available. Pets are permitted on leashes.

Reservations, fee: No reservations necessary; $5 fee per night. Open late May through Labor Day.

Who to contact: Phone Custer National Forest at (406) 446-2103 or write to Beartooth Ranger District, Route 2, P.O. Box 3420, Red Lodge, MT 59068.

Location: From Fishtail, drive one mile west on County Road 419. Turn left on County Road 425 and drive six miles southwest, then 11.5 miles south on Forest Service Road 72 to the campground.

Trip note: This is a pretty spot set aside little Emerald Lake. A good sidetrip is to Mystic Lake (a three-mile hike). The trip note for Pine Grove Camp details the route. Also West Rosebud Reservoir is a quarter mile upstream from camp (a 40-acre lake).

31) JIMMY JOE

Reference: on Rosebud Creek, Custer National Forest; map M8, grid g6.

Campsites, facilities: There are 10 sites for tents, trailer or motor homes up to 25 feet long. Picnic tables are provided. Pit toilets are also available. There is **no piped water.** Pets are permitted on leashes. Boat docks and launching facilities are nearby at East Rosebud Lake.

Reservations, fee: No reservations necessary; no fee. Open mid-June to mid-September.

Who to contact: Phone Custer National Forest at (406) 446-2103 or write to Beartooth Ranger District, Route 2, P.O. Box 3420, Red Lodge, MT 59068.

Location: From Roscoe, drive seven miles southwest on County Road 177, then three miles southwest on Forest Service Road 177 to the campground.

Trip note: This primitive campground is used primarily as an overflow for East Rosebud Lake to the southwest when it has too many people. The camp is set on East Rosebud Creek about five miles northeast of Alpine and East Rosebud Lake.

---

32) EAST ROSEBUD

Reference: on East Rosebud Lake, Custer National Forest; map M8, grid g6.

Campsites, facilities: There are four tent sites and eight sites for trailers or motor homes up to 16 feet long. Picnic tables are provided. Hand-pumped water, pit toilets, firewood and a store are also available. Pets are permitted on leashes. A boat launch for small craft is nearby.

Reservations, fee: No reservations necessary; $6 fee per night. Open mid-June to mid-September.

Who to contact: Phone Custer National Forest at (406) 446-2103 or write to Beartooth Ranger District, Route 2, P.O. Box 3420, Red Lodge, MT 59068.

Location: From Roscoe, drive seven miles southwest on County Road 177, and then six miles southwest on Forest Service Road 177 to the campground.

Trip note: The road ends here, and aren't you glad you came. The camp is set aside East Rosebud Lake near the tiny town of Alpine. You get many options besides just wanting to stay put. There are many hiking options. A trail from camp heads east to the Red Lodge Creek Plateau and passes several small alpine lakes on the way. Two other nearby trails provide access to the Absaroka-Beartooth Wilderness Area to both the south and west where many lakes can also be discovered. It is also possible to hike to Mystic Lake from here, a 12-mile hike on a trail that follows Phantom Creek between two peaks over 10,000 feet tall.

---

33) RED LODGE KOA

Reference: north of Red Lodge, map M8, grid g7.

Campsites, facilities: There are 18 tent sites and 58 sites for trailers or motor homes of any length. Camping cabins are also available. Picnic tables are provided. Flush toilets, sanitary disposal station, showers, a store, laundromat, ice, playground, fishing pond and a swimming pool are also available. Electricity, piped water and sewer hookups are available at an additional charge. Pets and motorbikes are permitted.

Reservations, fee: Reservations accepted; $12-$17 fee per night; $22 per night for camping cabins. MasterCard and Visa accepted. Open Mid-May through September.

Who to contact: Phone (406) 446-2364 or write to P.O. Box 936, Red Lodge, MT 59068.

Location: From Red Lodge, travel four miles north on US 212 to the campground.

Trip note: This is an easy-to-reach camp right along US 212. It's a wild, woolly and spectacular 64-mile drive from here to the northeastern entrance of Yellowstone National Park. The road is open only in the summer and reaches elevations of 11,000 feet. With the drop-offs, you feel like you are on the edge of the world. During early August at Red Lodge, there's an annual celebration called "The Festival of Nations." One last note: primitive camping is available at four nearby locations along Rock Creek that provide fishing access. Explore a little and you'll find them.

---

34) PETRIFIED FOREST

Reference: on Trail Creek, Gallatin National Forest; map M8, grid h0.

Campsites, facilities: There are 12 sites for tents, trailers or motor homes up to 22 feet long. Picnic tables are provided. Piped water, firewood and pit toilets are also available. Pets are permitted on leashes.

Reservations, fee: No reservations necessary; no fee. Open mid-May to late November.

Who to contact: Phone Gallatin National Forest at (406) 848-7375 or write to Gardiner Ranger District, P.O. Box 5, Gardiner, MT 59030.

Location: From Gardiner, drive 16 miles northwest on US 89. Turn left on County Road 63 and drive 12 miles southwest, then 3.5 miles southwest on Forest Service Road 63 to the campground.

Trip note: Like Eagle Creek Camp, this one also gets missed by many campers who would normally like to hunker down here for awhile. It is set on Trail Creek, named after the trail along the creek that heads west into the Gallatin Petrified Forest. Visiting the forest is a worthwhile sidetrip; it has an eerie, spooky quality, and trees of rock are quite a phenomenon if you've never seen them before.

---

35) EAGLE CREEK

Reference: near Yellowstone National Park, Gallatin National Forest; map M8, grid h1.

Campsites, facilities: There are 10 sites for tents, trailers or motor homes up to 16 feet long. Picnic tables are provided. Pit toilets, sanitary disposal station, a store, coffee shop, laundromat and ice are located within one mile. There is **no piped water.** Pets are permitted on leashes.

Reservations, fee: No reservations necessary; no fee. Open all year.

Who to contact: Phone Gallatin National Forest at (406) 848-7375 or write to Gardiner Ranger District, P.O. Box 5, Gardiner, MT 59030.

Location: From Gardiner, drive a half mile north on US 89. Turn north on Forest Service Road 493 and continue 3.5 miles to the campground.

Trip note: This is one of three camps in the immediate area just north of the border of Yellowstone National Park. That's why this spot also gets missed by so many, who would normally like to try it on for size. This camp is set along Eagle Creek. You get a quiet camp and pretty scenery, but that's about it.

---

36) ROCKY MOUNTAIN CAMP

Reference: near Yellowstone River; map M8, grid h1.

Campsites, facilities: There are 21 tent sites and 75 sites for trailers or motor homes of any length. Piped water and picnic tables are provided. Flush toilets, bottled gas, sanitary disposal station, showers, recreation hall, a store, coffee shop, laundromat, ice and a playground are also available. Electricity and sewer hookups are available at an additional charge. Pets and motorbikes are permitted.

Reservations, fee: Reservations accepted; $12-$16 fee per night; MasterCard and Visa accepted. Open all year with limited winter facilities.

Who to contact: Phone (406) 848-7251 or write to Jardine Route, P.O. Box 10, Gardiner, MT 59030.

Location: In Gardiner, turn east onto Jardine Road from US 89, and drive two blocks to the campground.

Trip note: Set above the town of Gardiner, this is a pretty, sunny camp. It's about one block from the Yellowstone River, with a trail leading from camp. There are a few trees and shrubs planted, but the camp is mostly open, with good views of the surrounding mountains.

---

37) SODA BUTTE

Reference: near Beartooth Wilderness, Gallatin National Forest; map M8, grid h5.

Campsites, facilities: There are 21 sites for tents, trailers or motor homes up to 22 feet long. Picnic tables are provided. Piped water, firewood and pit toilets are also available. Showers, a store, coffee shop, laundromat and ice are located within one mile. Pets are permitted on leashes.

Reservations, fee: No reservations necessary; $5 fee per night. Open July to early September.

Who to contact: Phone Gallatin National Forest at (406) 848-7375 or write to Gardiner Ranger District, P.O. Box 5, Gardiner, MT 59030.

Location: From Cooke City, drive 1.2 miles east on US 212 to the campground.

Trip note: This is a nearby alternative to Colter Camp, and it's located just across the road from it and down a bit. See the trip note for Colter Camp for hiking trip possibilities.

---

38) COLTER

Reference: near Beartooth Wilderness, Gallatin National Forest; map M8, grid h5.

Campsites, facilities: There are 15 sites for tents, trailers or motor homes up to 22 feet long. Picnic tables are provided. Piped water, firewood and pit toilets are also available. Showers, a store, coffee shop, laundromat and ice are located within five miles. Pets are permitted on leashes.

Reservations, fee: No reservations necessary; $5 fee per night. Open July to early September.

Who to contact: Phone Gallatin National Forest at (406) 848-7375 or write to Gardiner Ranger District, P.O. Box 5, Gardiner, MT 59030.

Location: From Cooke City, drive 2.3 miles east on US 212 to the campground.

Trip note: This is one of three camps in the immediate area, but this is the best base camp for hikers preparing for a backpack journey. A nearby trail provides access north along Lady of the Lake Creek to numerous small alpine lakes only four miles away at the border of the Absaroka-Beartooth Wilderness Area. A Forest Service map is advised.

---

39) CHIEF JOSEPH

Reference: near Cooke City, Gallatin National Forest; map M8, grid h5.

Campsites, facilities: There are six sites for tents, trailers or motor homes up to 22 feet long. Picnic tables are provided. Piped water, firewood and pit toilets are also available. A coffee shop and ice are located within one mile. Showers, a store and laundromat are located within five miles. Pets are permitted on leashes.

Reservations, fee: No reservations necessary; $5 fee per night. Open July to early September.

Who to contact: Phone Gallatin National Forest at (406) 848-7375 or write to Gardiner Ranger District, P.O. Box 5, Gardiner, MT 59030.

Location: From Cooke City, drive 4.8 miles east on US 212 to the campground.

Trip note: This is one of three camps in the vicinity of Cooke City, and is set along the side of the road, providing easy access for a quick layover. It's not especially pretty, but there are some good hiking trails in the area. See a Forest Service map.

40) CASCADE

Reference: on Timberline and Rock Creeks, Custer National Forest; map M8, grid h6.

Campsites, facilities: There are 10 tent sites and 20 sites for trailers or motor homes up to 32 feet long. Picnic tables are provided. Hand-pumped water and pit toilets are also available. Pets are permitted on leashes.

Reservations, fee: No reservations necessary; $5 fee per night. Open late May through Labor Day.

Who to contact: Phone Custer National Forest at (406) 446-2103 or write to Beartooth Ranger District, Route 2, P.O. Box 3420, Red Lodge, MT 59068.

Location: From Red Lodge, drive 1.5 miles south on US 212, then 9.5 miles west on Forest Service Road 71 to the campground.

Trip note: This camp is set at the confluence of Timberline Creek and Rock Creek, so it's a real nice spot. And it's ideal for hikers. A trail near camp heads south along Timberline Creek to Timberline Lakes in the Absaroka-Beartooth Wilderness Area. Two other trails begin just west of the campground. So, there are lots of options here. See a Forest Service map; you'll be glad you did.

41) LIMBER PINE

Reference: southwest of Red Lodge, Custer National Forest; map M8, grid h7.

Campsites, facilities: There are 13 sites for tents, trailers or motor homes up to 40 feet long. Picnic tables are provided. Hand pumped water and pit toilets are also available. Pets are permitted on leashes.

Reservations, fee: No reservations necessary; $6 fee per night. Open late May through Labor Day.

Who to contact: Phone Custer National Forest at (406) 446-2103 or write to Beartooth Ranger District, Route 2, P.O. Box 3420, Red Lodge, MT 59068.

Location: From Red Lodge, drive 12 miles southwest on US 212, then one mile southwest on Forest Service Road 421 to the campground.

Trip note: This is a nearby alternative to Parkside Camp. See the trip note for that camp for detailed sidetrip possibilities.

42) GREENOUGH LAKE

Reference: southwest of Red Lodge, Custer National Forest; map M8, grid h7.

Campsites, facilities: There are 17 sites for tents, trailers or motor homes up to 40 feet long. Picnic tables are provided. Hand pumped water and pit toilets are also available. Pets are permitted on leashes.

Reservations, fee: No reservations necessary; $6 fee per night. Open late May through Labor Day.

Who to contact: Phone Custer National Forest at (406) 446-2103 or write to Beartooth Ranger District, Route 2, P.O. Box 3420, Red Lodge, MT 59068.

Location: From Red Lodge, drive 12 miles southwest on US 212, then one mile southwest on Forest Service Road 421 to the campground.

Trip note: This is a nearby option to Parkside Camp. See the trip note for that camp.

---

43) PARKSIDE

Reference: on Rock Creek, Custer National Forest; map M8, grid h7.

Campsites, facilities: There are 25 sites for tents, trailers or motor homes up to 40 feet long. Picnic tables are provided. Hand-pumped water and pit toilets are also available. Pets are permitted on leashes.

Reservations, fee: No reservations necessary; $6 fee per night. Open late May through Labor Day.

Who to contact: Phone Custer National Forest at (406)446-2103 or write to Beartooth Ranger District, Route 2, P.O. Box 3420, Red Lodge, MT 59068.

Location: From Red Lodge, drive 12 miles southwest on US 212, then a half mile southwest on Forest Service Road 421 to the campground.

Trip note: This is one of four camps set in a line along Rock Creek. Several wilderness trails take off from this area. Starting at the end of Forest Service Road 346 (located two miles north off US 212), one ventures into the Absaroka-Beartooth Wilderness Area. Another trailhead is located at the end of Forest Service Road 3004 (a dirt road near camp). Both trails access numerous lakes. The Beartooth Mountains peaks (many over 12,000 feet) loom overhead.

---

44) MK CAMPGROUND

Reference: on Rock Creek, Custer National Forest; map M8, grid h7.

Campsites, facilities: There are two tent sites and eight sites for trailers or motor homes up to 22 feet long. Picnic tables are provided. Pit toilets are also available. There is **no piped water.** Pets are permitted on leashes.

Reservations, fee: No reservations necessary; no fee. Open mid-June to mid-September.

Who to contact: Phone Custer National Forest at (406) 446-2103 or write to Beartooth Ranger District, Route 2, P.O. Box 3420, Red Lodge, MT 59068.

Location: From Red Lodge, drive 12 miles southwest on US 212, then 3.5 miles southwest on Forest Service Road 421 to the campground.

Trip note: This little camp is set on Rock Creek about two miles from Parkside and two other camps. See the trip note for Parkside Camp for hiking options.

---

45) SHERIDAN

Reference: on Rock Creek and Steeley Creek; Custer National Forest; map M8, grid h7.

Campsites, facilities: There is one tent site and five sites for trailers or motor homes up to 22 feet long. Picnic tables are provided. Hand pumped water and pit toilets are also available. Pets are permitted on leashes.

Reservations, fee: No reservations necessary; $5 fee per night. Open late May through Labor Day.

Who to contact: Phone Custer National Forest at (406) 446-2103 or write to Beartooth Ranger District, Route 2, P.O. Box 3420, Red Lodge, MT 59068.

Location: From Red Lodge, drive five miles southwest on US 212, then two miles southwest on Forest Service Road 379 to the campground.

Trip note: This is an easy-to-reach yet tiny spot at the confluence of Rock Creek and Seeley Creek.

---

46) BASIN

Reference: on Rock Creek, Custer National Forest; map M8, grid h7.

Campsites, facilities: There are 30 sites for tents, trailers, or motor homes up to 40 feet long. Picnic tables are provided. Hand-pumped water and pit toilets are also available. Pets are permitted on leashes.

Reservations, fee: No reservations necessary; $6 per night. Open late May to Labor Day.

Who to contact: Phone Custer National Forest at (406) 446-2103 or write to Beartooth Ranger District, Route 2, P.O. Box 3420, Red Lodge, MT 59068.

Location: From Red Lodge, drive 1.5 miles south on US 212, then seven miles west on Forest Service Road 71 to the campground.

Trip note: This is a good base camp for hikers. The camp is set on Rock Creek where the National Recreation Trail leaves camp. The trail heads southwest for about four miles to little Basin Creek Lake which lies on the border of Absaroka-Beartooth Wilderness Area.

Montana Map M9
4 listings
Pages 430-433

North (M4)—see page 356
East (M10)—see page 434
South—Wyoming
West (M8)—see page 408

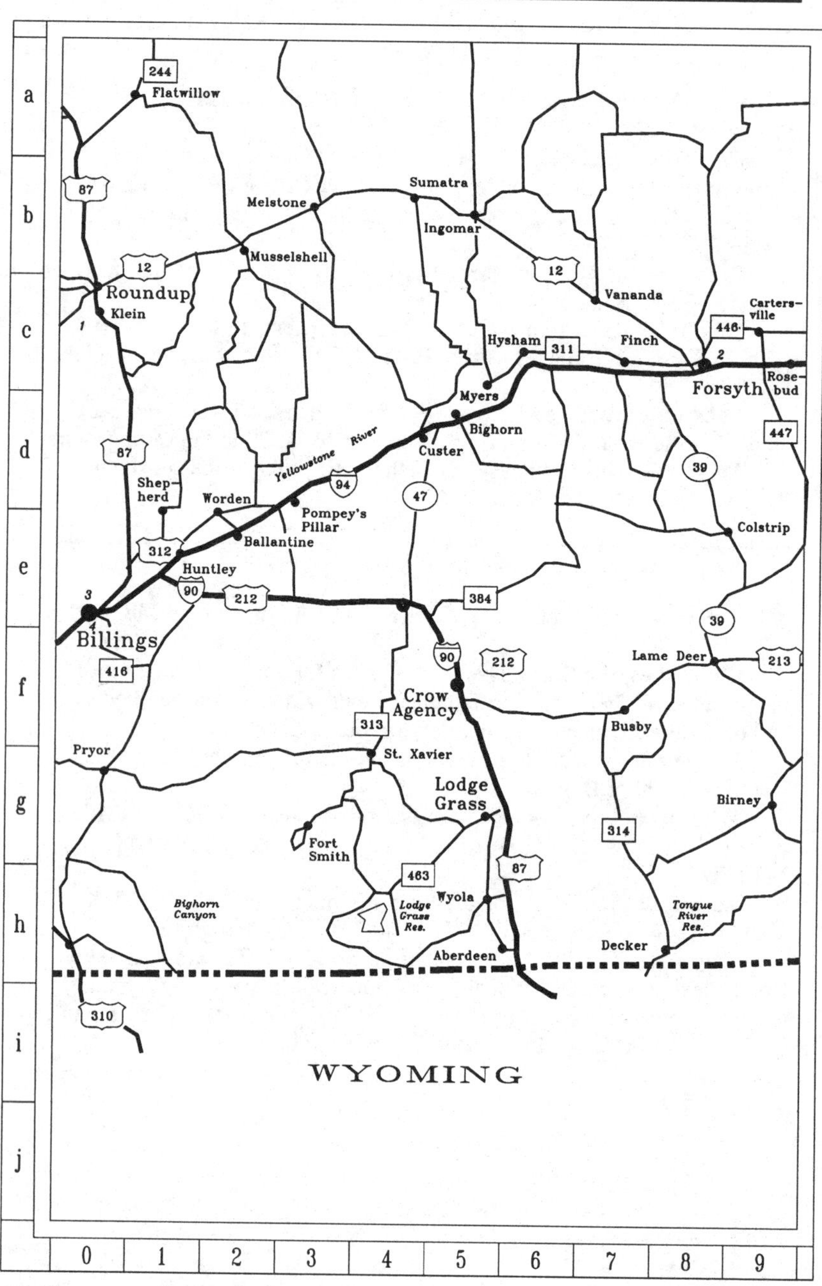

Featuring: Musselshell River, Yellowstone River, Pryor Mountains, Custer National Forest

---

1) COW BELL

Reference: near Musselshell River; map M9, grid c0.

Campsites, facilities: There are 25 sites for tents, trailers or motor homes of any length. Picnic tables are provided. Piped water, flush toilets, firewood and playground are also available. Bottled gas, sanitary disposal station, a store, coffee shop, laundromat and ice are located within one mile. Pets are permitted on leashes.

Reservations, fee: No reservations necessary; no fee. Open May through September.

Who to contact: Phone (406) 323-1104 or write to 506 Main Street, Roundup, MT 59072.

Location: This campground is located in Roundup down by the Musselshell River.

Trip note: This is the only campground around these parts, so if you're looking for a spot to grab some shut eye, you'd best take it here. A golf course in the area provides a recreational option, or checking out the Musselshell River is another possibility.

---

2) ROSEBUD STATE PARK

Reference: on Yellowstone River; map M9, grid c8.

Campsites, facilities: There are 33 sites for tents, trailers or motor homes up to 25 feet long. Picnic benches are provided. Piped water, pit toilets and a playground are also available. Ice is located within one mile. Pets are permitted on leashes. Boat launching facilities are nearby.

Reservations, fee: No reservations necessary; $7-$9 fee per night. Open mid-March through December.

Who to contact: Phone (406) 232-4365 or write to Route 1, P.O. Box 2004, Miles City, MT 59301.

Location: To get to the East Unit, take the East exit off Interstate 94 in Forsyth, and continue north along Yellowstone River. The West Unit is located west of Forsyth on Highway 12 at the south end of the Yellowstone River Bridge near milepost 270.

Trip note: This is actually two campgrounds in one with an east and west unit. It adds up to a 32-acre park and is set along the Yellowstone River. It's complete with boating access for anglers.

---

3) BIG SKY

Reference: in Billings; map M9, grid e0.

Campsites, facilities: There are 20 tent sites and 75 sites for trailers or motor homes of any length. Picnic tables are provided. Flush toilets, sanitary disposal station, showers, a store, restaurant, laundromat and ice are also available. Electricity, piped water and sewer hookups are available at an additional charge. Bottled gas is located within one mile. Pets are permitted on leashes.

Reservations, fee: Reservations accepted; $9-$14 fee per night. Open all year.

Who to contact: Phone (406) 259-4110 or write to 5516 Laurel Road, Billings, MT 59102.

Location: Take exit 446 off Interstate 90 in Billings, and drive one-half mile north to the campground.

Trip note: This is one of two campgrounds in the immediate area. This one covers 10 acres and provides more space for tent campers than the others. The area has a colorful history with the likes of Calamity Jane and the Boothill Cemetery. It's all detailed at the Yellowstone County Historical Museum located off Highway 3 at the Billings Logan International Airport. For hours and specific driving directions, call the museum at (406) 256-6811.

---

4) BILLINGS METRO KOA

Reference: near Yellowstone River; map M9, grid e0.

Campsites, facilities: There are 30 tent sites and 120 sites for trailers or motor homes of any length. Camping cabins are also available. Electricity, piped water, sewer hookups and picnic tables are provided. Flush toilets, bottled gas, sanitary disposal station, showers, recreation hall, a store, laundromat, ice, playground and a swimming pool are also available. A coffee shop is located within one mile. Pets and motorbikes are permitted.

Reservations, fee: Reservations accepted; $17-$23 fee per night; camping cabins are $27-$33 per night. MasterCard and Visa accepted. Open April through October.

Who to contact: Phone (406) 252-3104 or write to 3087 Garden Avenue, Billings, MT 59101.

Location: Take exit 450 off Interstate 90 in Billings, drive a quarter mile south on 27th Street, and then three-quarters of a mile west on Garden Avenue. Follow the signs to the campground.

Trip note: This is a popular spot with open and shaded sites. It's set near the Yellowstone River. But don't get the idea that this is out in the middle of nowhere. It ain't. In fact, they've even got a miniature golf course for your kids.

Montana Map M10
5 listings
Pages 434-436

North (M5)—see page 362
East—North Dakota
South—Wyoming
West (M9)—see page 430

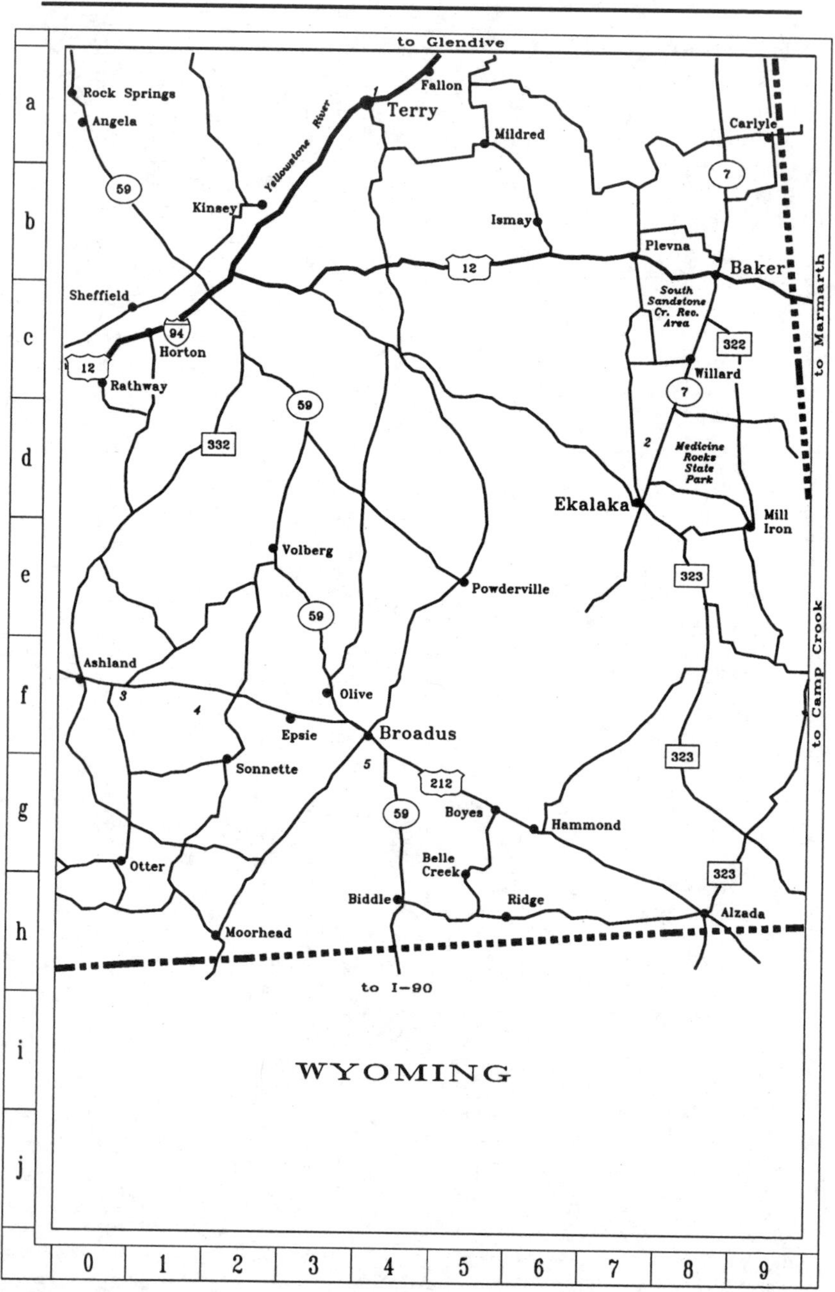

Featuring: Yellowstone River, Custer National Forest

1) ROY'S TRAILER COURT

Reference: near Yellowstone River; map M10, grid a4.

Campsites, facilities: There are 10 tent sites and 20 sites for trailers or motor homes of any length. Electricity, piped water, sewer hookups and picnic tables are provided. Flush toilets, sanitary disposal station, showers and ice are also available. Bottled gas, a store, coffee shop and laundromat are located within one mile. Pets are permitted on leashes.

Reservations, fee: Reservations accepted; $8-$10 fee per night. Open April through October.

Who to contact: Phone (406) 637-5829 or write to P.O. Box 375, Terry, MT 59349.

Location: Take exit 176 off Interstate 94 in Terry, and drive 1.2 miles west.

Trip note: This private camp covers three acres, with grassy, open sites. The Yellowstone River is a short distance away, providing excellent fishing prospects.

2) MEDICINE ROCK STATE MONUMENT

Reference: north of Ekalaka; map M10, grid d7.

Campsites, facilities: There are 10 sites for tents, trailers or motor homes up to 25 feet long. Picnic tables are provided. Piped water and pit toilets are also available. Pets are permitted on leashes.

Reservations, fee: No reservations necessary; no fee. Open May to October.

Who to contact: Phone Montana Department of Fish, Wildlife and Parks at (406) 444-2535 or write to 1420 East Sixth Avenue, Helena, MT 59620.

Location: From Baker, drive 25 miles south on Highway 7 to milepost 10, and then go one mile west on a signed county road to the campground.

Trip note: This is a big state park. It covers 320 acres and is out in the middle of nowhere. The Chalk Buttes and a chunk of the Custer National Forest, located to the south, provide a sidetrip possibilities.

3) RED SHALE

Reference: southwest of Ashland, Custer National Forest; map M10, grid f1.

Campsites, facilities: There are 14 sites for tents, trailers or motor homes up to 32 feet long. Picnic tables are provided. Piped water, firewood and pit toilets are also available. One site is **wheelchair accessible**. Pets are permitted on leashes.

Reservations, fee: No reservations necessary; $5 fee per night. Open late May through Labor Day.

Who to contact: Phone Custer National Forest at (406) 784-2344 or write to Ashland, MT 59003.

Location: From Ashland, drive 6.4 miles southeast on Highway 212 to the campground.

Trip note: You get easy access right off the highway. Back roads and trails are available in the surrounding Custer National Forest. It's all detailed on a Forest Service map. There are horseshoe pits in the camp.

---

4) LEMONADE SPRINGS CAMPGROUND

Reference: east of Ashland; map M10, grid f2.

Campsites, facilities: There are 10 tent sites and 11 sites for trailers or motor homes of any length. Picnic tables are provided. Flush toilets, sanitary disposal station, showers, ice and a playground are also available. Electricity, piped water, sewer hookups and firewood are available at an additional charge. Pets are permitted on leashes.

Reservations, fee: Reservations accepted; $8-$10 fee per night. Open June to late November.

Who to contact: Phone (406) 784-2567 or write to Ashland, MT 59003.

Location: From Ashland, drive 18 miles east on Highway 212 to the campground.

Trip note: You get plenty of room here, with shaded campsites set on 20 acres of park land. The camp is set within the Custer National Forest, with several good hiking trails nearby. Some interesting sidetrips include Custer Battlefield, the Black Hills and the Saint Labre Indian Mission.

---

5) TOWN AND COUNTRY VILLAGE

Reference: in Broadus; map M10, grid f4.

Campsites, facilities: There are 25 tent sites and 10 sites for trailers or motor homes of any length. Electricity, piped water, sewer hookups and picnic tables are provided. Flush toilets, sanitary disposal station, showers, firewood, laundromat and a playground are also available. Bottled gas, a store, coffee shop and ice are located within one mile. Pets are permitted on leashes.

Reservations, fee: Reservations accepted; $5-$12 fee per night. Open May through November.

Who to contact: Phone (406) 436-2595 or write to P.O. Box 3, Broadus, MT 59317.

Location: From Broadus, drive a half mile south on Highway 212 to the campground.

Trip note: This is a five-acre, privately run camp. It's just one in a series of four camps on Highway 212. If you're heading east, you had better pick this one, because it's zilchville for a long ways thereafter.

WYOMING

Wyoming Map W1
70 listings
Pages 438-469

North—Montana
East (W2)—see page 470
South (W5)—see page 504
West—Idaho

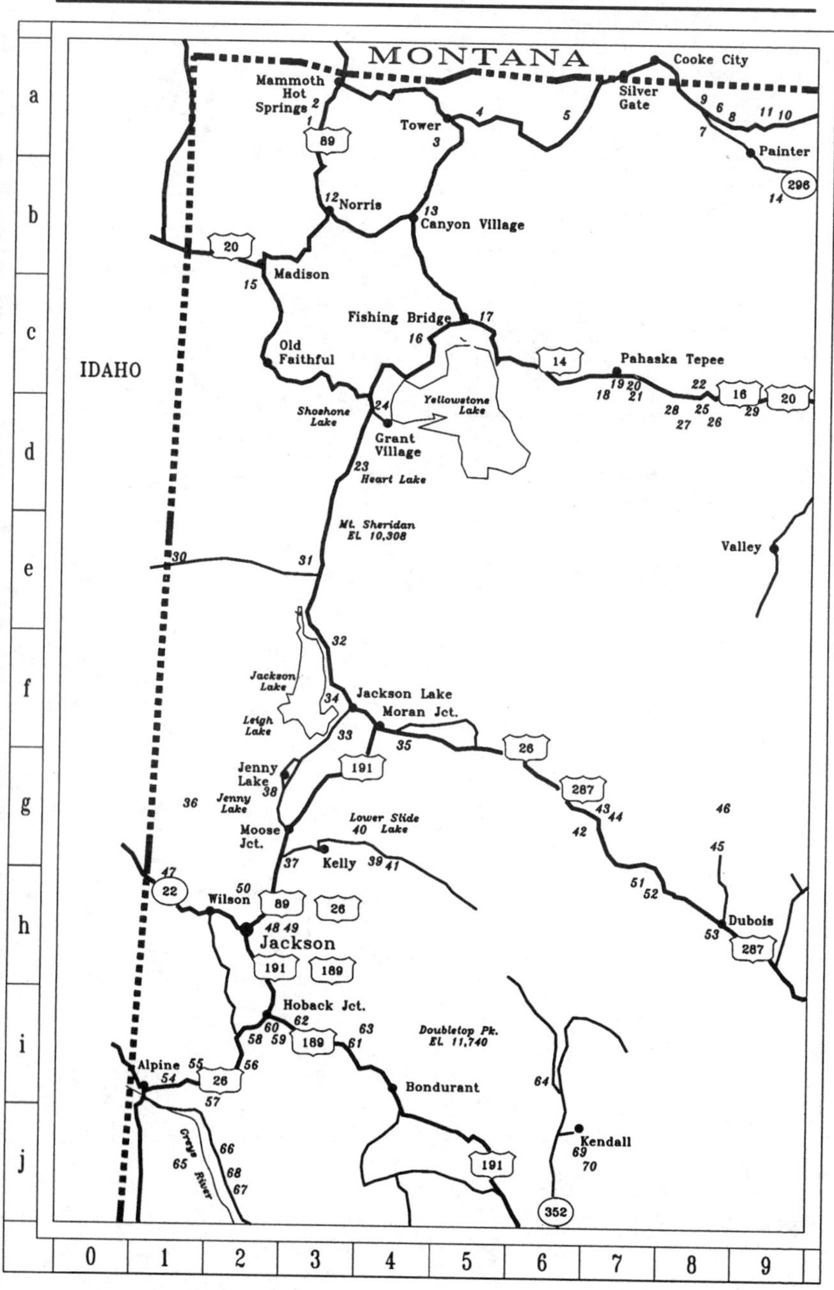

Featuring: Mammoth Hot Springs, Yellowstone National Park, Yellowstone River, Abiathar Peak, Bridger-Teton National Forest, Clarks Fork of Yellowstone River, Shoshone National Forest, Howard Eaton Trail, Grand Canyon of Yellowstone, Reef Creek, Old Faithful, Yellowstone Lake, North Absaroka Wilderness, North Fork of Shoshone River, Washakie Wilderness, Mount Sheridan, Elk Creek, Grand Targhee National Forest, Jackson Lake, Grand Teton National Park, Jedediah Smith Wilderness, Gros Ventre River, Lower Slide Lake, Brooks Lake Creek, Brooks Lake, Goodwin Lake, Snake River, Hoback River, Green River, Greys River, New Fork Lake

---

1) INDIAN CREEK

Reference: near Mammoth Hot Springs, Yellowstone National Park; map W1, grid a3.

Campsites, facilities: There are 75 sites for tents, trailers and motor homes up to 24 feet long. Picnic tables are provided. Piped water, firewood and pit toilets are also available. Pets are permitted on leashes.

Reservations, fee: No reservations necessary; $6 fee per night. Open mid-June to mid-September.

Who to contact: Phone Yellowstone National Park at (307) 344-7381 or write to P.O. Box 168, Yellowstone National Park, WY 82190.

Location: From Gardiner, Montana, drive south five miles on US 89 to the park entrance, then continue south for another 7.5 miles to the campground.

Trip note: This is a nearby alternative to Mammoth Camp and is also set in the northwest corner of Yellowstone National Park. See the trip note for Mammoth Camp.

---

2) MAMMOTH

Reference: near Mammoth Hot Springs, Yellowstone National Park; map W1, grid a3.

Campsites, facilities: There are 85 sites for tents, trailers or motor homes up to 24 feet long. Picnic tables are provided. Piped water, flush toilets and firewood are also available. A store, cafe and ice are located within one mile. Pets are permitted on leashes.

Reservations, fee: No reservations necessary; $8 fee per night. Open all year.

Who to contact: Phone Yellowstone National Park at (307) 344-7381 or write to P.O. Box 168, Yellowstone National Park, WY 82190.

Location: From the town of Gardiner, Montana, drive south five miles on US 89 to the park entrance, then continue south for five more miles to the campground.

Trip note: This camp is set in the northwest corner of Yellowstone National Park. The highlight of the area is the Mammoth Hot Springs, but the hiking trails in the area are good, too. A riding stable is also nearby, so if you want to see some of the backcountry without hoofin' it yourself, you can saddle up and take a ride.

3) TOWER FALL

Reference: near Yellowstone River, Yellowstone National Park; W1, grid a4.

Campsites, facilities: There are 32 sites for tents, trailers or motor homes up to 24 feet long. Picnic tables are provided. Piped water and pit toilets are also available. A store, cafe and ice are located within one mile. Pets are permitted on leashes.

Reservations, fee: No reservations necessary; $6 fee per night. Open June to mid-September.

Who to contact: Phone Yellowstone National Park at (307) 344-7381 or write to P.O. Box 168, Yellowstone National Park, WY 82190.

Location: From Tower Junction, drive three miles southeast.

Trip note: This is a nice spot set just below Mount Washburn (10,243 feet elevation) and is not far from the Yellowstone River to the east. Trout fishing, hiking and a nearby horse stable are the highlights.

4) SLOUGH CREEK

Reference: near Yellowstone River, Yellowstone National Park; map W1, grid a5.

Campsites, facilities: There are 29 sites for tents, trailers or motor homes up to 24 feet long. Picnic tables are provided. Piped water and pit toilets are also available. Pets are permitted on leashes.

Reservations, fee: No reservations necessary; $6 fee per night. Open late May to late October.

Who to contact: Phone Yellowstone National Park at (307) 344-7381 or write to P.O. Box 168, Yellowstone National Park, WY 82190.

Location: From Tower Junction, drive 10 miles northeast to the campground.

Trip note: This is an alternative to Tower Fall Camp. It's set a few miles east of the Yellowstone River and also has good hiking trails.

5) PEBBLE CREEK

Reference: near Abiathar Peak, Yellowstone National Park; map W1, grid a6.

Campsites, facilities: There are 36 sites for tents, trailers or motor homes up to 24 feet long. Picnic tables are provided. Piped water and pit toilets are also available. Pets are permitted on leashes.

Reservations, fee: No reservations necessary; $6 fee per night. Open mid-June to mid-September.

Who to contact: Phone Yellowstone National Park at (307) 344-7381 or write to P.O. Box 168, Yellowstone National Park, WY 82190.

Location: From Silver Gate, Montana, at the northeast entrance to the park, drive seven miles south to the campground.

Trip note: This is the first camp you run into as you drive west to Yellowstone on US 212 via Silver Gate. It is set below Abiathar Peak, elevation 10,928 feet. Some good trails are in the area.

---

6) HUNTER PEAK

Reference: on the Clarks Fork of Yellowstone River, Shoshone National Forest; map W1, grid a8.

Campsites, facilities: There are 12 sites for tents, trailers or motor homes up to 30 feet long. Picnic tables are provided. Hand-pumped water and vault toilets are also available. Pets are permitted on leashes.

Reservations, fee: No reservations necessary; $6 fee per night. Open May through November.

Who to contact: Phone Shoshone National Forest at (307) 754-7207 or write to Clarks Fork Ranger District, 1002 Road 11, Powell, WY 82435.

Location: From Cooke City, Montana, drive 14.4 miles southeast on US 212, then five miles south on Chief Joseph Scenic Highway 296 to the campground.

Trip note: This small camp is intimate and set in a beautiful spot along Clarks Fork of the Yellowstone River. It's mainly used by hunters, but it can be a good headquarters camp for hikers or anglers. The Clarks Fork Trailhead is right across the road, with facilities for horses and carcass storage racks provided. The trail follows the river along the canyon for about 15 miles.

---

7) CRAZY CREEK

Reference: on the Clarks Fork of Yellowstone River, Shoshone National Forest; map W1, grid a8.

Campsites, facilities: There are 13 tent sites and six sites for trailers or motor homes up to 30 feet long. Picnic tables are provided. Piped water and vault toilets are also available. Pets are permitted on leashes.

Reservations, fee: No reservations necessary; $6 fee per night. Open June to mid-October.

Who to contact: Phone Shoshone National Forest at (307) 754-7207 or write to Clarks Fork Ranger District, 1002 Road 11, Powell, WY 82435.

Location: From Cooke City, Montana, drive 10.4 miles southeast on US 212 to the campground.

Trip note: This is a pretty spot set beside Clarks Fork of the Yellowstone River, with big, open sites. Crazy Lakes trailhead is adjacent to the camp, leading to numerous back country lakes in the Absaroka-Beartooth Wilderness. Crazy Creek Falls is a short hike away.

---

8) LAKE CREEK

Reference: near the Clarks Fork of Yellowstone River, Shoshone National Forest; map W1, grid a8.

Campsites, facilities: There are four tent sites and two sites for trailers or motor homes up to 30 feet long. Picnic tables are provided. Hand-pumped water and vault toilets are also available. Pets are permitted on leashes.

Reservations, fee: No reservations necessary; $6 fee per night. Open June through September.

Who to contact: Phone Shoshone National Forest at (307) 754-7207 or write to Clarks Fork Ranger District, 1002 Road 11, Powell, WY 82435.

Location: From Cooke City, Montana, drive 14.4 miles southeast on US 212, then one mile south on Chief Joseph Scenic Highway 296 to the campground.

Trip note: This camp is probably the most best-used around, being the first campground travelers come across when driving south from Beartooth Highway. It is set beside Lake Creek about a mile from Clarks Fork of the Yellowstone River. Fox Creek and Crazy Creek provide nearby alternatives.

---

9) FOX CREEK

Reference: near the Clarks Fork of Yellowstone River, Shoshone National Forest; map W1, grid a8.

Campsites, facilities: There are 16 tent sites and 11 sites for trailers or motor homes up to 30 feet long. Picnic tables are provided. Piped water and vault toilets are also available. A store, cafe and ice are located within seven miles. Pets are permitted on leashes.

Reservations, fee: No reservations necessary; $6 fee per night. Open mid-June to mid-September.

Who to contact: Phone Shoshone National Forest at (307) 754-7207 or write to Clarks Fork Ranger District, 1002 Road 11, Powell, WY 82435.

Location: From Cooke City, Montana, drive 7.5 miles southeast on US 212 to the campground.

Trip note: This campground is one of several camps along the Beartooth Highway. This particular spot is very pretty, offering easy highway access and heavily wooded, private sites. You get a great view of Pilot Peak (11,708 feet), and Index Peak is visible as well. The camp is set at the confluence of Fox Creek and Clarks Fork of the Yellowstone River.

---

10) ISLAND LAKE

Reference: east of Cooke City, Shoshone National Forest; map W1, grid a9.

Campsites, facilities: There are 20 sites for tents, trailers or motor homes up to 30 feet long. Picnic tables are provided. Piped water and vault toilets are also available. A store is located within five miles. Pets are permitted on leashes. Boat docks and launching facilities are nearby.

Reservations, fee: No reservations necessary; $6 fee per night. Open July through September.

Who to contact: Phone Shoshone National Forest at (307) 754-7207 or write to Clarks Fork Ranger District, 1002 Road 11, Powell, WY 82435.

Location: From Cooke City, Montana, drive east on US 212 for 27.5 miles to the campground.

Trip note: This campsite is located on the Beartooth Plateau, adjacent to Island Lake. The Beartooth High Lakes Trail offers access to many lakes and trails in the Absaroka-Beartooth Wilderness. For anglers, the boat ramp is a plus.

---

11) BEARTOOTH LAKE

Reference: east of Cooke City, Shoshone National Forest; map W1, grid a9.

Campsites, facilities: There are 21 sites for tents, trailers or motor homes up to 30 feet long. Picnic tables are provided. Hand-pumped water and vault toilets are also available. A store is located within five miles. Pets are permitted on leashes. Boat docks and launching facilities are nearby.

Reservations, fee: No reservations necessary; $6 fee per night. Open July through September.

Who to contact: Phone Shoshone National Forest at (307) 754-7207 or write to Clarks Fork Ranger District, 1002 Road 11, Powell, WY 82435.

Location: From Cooke City, Montana, drive east on US 212 for 24.2 miles to the campground.

Trip note: This campground is adjacent to Beartooth Lake. Trails from camp provide access both to the lake and the Absaroka-Beartooth Wilderness. The surroundings at this camp are spectacular, with awesome Beartooth Butte towering above the crystalline waters of Beartooth Lake. Clay Butte Lookout is located a short distance away, with inspiring views of the Clarks Fork Valley.

---

12) NORRIS

Reference: near Howard Eaton Trail, Yellowstone National Park; map W1, grid b3.

Campsites, facilities: There are 116 sites for tents, trailers or motor homes up to 34 feet long. Picnic tables are provided. Piped water, flush toilets, firewood and ice are also available. Pets are permitted on leashes.

Reservations, fee: No reservations necessary; $8 fee per night. Open late May to mid-September.

Who to contact: Phone Yellowstone National Park at (307) 344-7381 or write to P.O. Box 168, Yellowstone National Park, WY 82190.

Location: From Norris Junction, drive one mile north.

Trip note: This Yellowstone camp is an ideal spot to start a hike from. The Howard Eaton Trail passes by camp and can provide a short sidetrip or a longer thumper; take your pick.

---

13) CANYON VILLAGE

Reference: near the Grand Canyon of Yellowstone, Yellowstone National Park; map W1, grid b4.

Campsites, facilities: There are 280 sites for trailers or motor homes up to 34 feet long. Piped water and picnic tables are provided. Flush toilets, sanitary disposal station, showers and firewood are also available. A store, cafe, laundromat and ice are located within one mile. Pets are permitted on leashes.

Reservations, fee: No reservations necessary; $8 fee per night. Open early June to mid-September.

Who to contact: Phone Yellowstone National Park at (307) 344-7381 or write to P.O. Box 168, Yellowstone National Park, WY 82190.

Location: This campground is located a quarter mile east of Canyon Village.

Trip note: The highlight at this camp is the view of the spectacular waterfalls in the Grand Canyon. Bring your camera, because you'll leave with a picture that will go on your wall for life. This spot has a way of making an Ansel Adams out of everybody. Other recreation options include hiking trails and a riding stable.

---

14) DEAD INDIAN

Reference: on Reef Creek, Shoshone National Forest; map W1, grid b9.

Campsites, facilities: There are 12 sites for tents, trailers or motor homes up to 30 feet long. Picnic tables are provided. Vault toilets are also available, and there is piped water. Pets are permitted on leashes.

Reservations, fee: No reservations necessary; no fee. Open May through November.

Who to contact: Phone Shoshone National Forest at (307) 754-7207 or write to Clarks Fork Ranger District, 1002 Road 11, Powell, WY 82435.

Location: From Cody, drive 17 miles north on Highway 120, then turn west on the Chief Joseph Scenic Highway 296. Travel 20 miles over Dead Indian Hill to the campground.

Trip note: This is a primitive, little-known spot set beside Dead Indian Creek at the base of Dead Indian Hill. It's your last chance to camp before you reach Cody if traveling on Highway 296. There is an adjacent trailhead with corrals for horses. Dead Indian Creek is known for its excellent fishing, with brook and rainbow trout along with an occasional cutthroat.

15) MADISON JUNCTION

Reference: near Old Faithful, Yellowstone National Park; map W1, grid c2.

Campsites, facilities: There are 292 sites for tents, trailers or motor homes up to 34 feet long. Picnic tables are provided. Flush toilets, piped water, sanitary disposal station, firewood and ice are also available. Some facilities are **wheelchair accessible.** Pets are permitted on leashes.

Reservations, fee: No reservations necessary; $8 fee per night. Open early May to late October.

Who to contact: Phone Yellowstone National Park at (307) 344-7381 or write to P.O. Box 168, Yellowstone National Park, WY 82190.

Location: From the town of West Yellowstone at the western entrance to the park, drive fourteen miles east to the campground.

Trip note: This is one of Yellowstone's giant campgrounds, and it's often packed. Nearby Old Faithful is why. There are several other attractions within five miles.

16) BRIDGE BAY

Reference: on Yellowstone Lake, Yellowstone National Park; map W1, grid c4.

Campsites, facilities: There are 420 sites for tents, trailers or motor homes up to 34 feet long. Picnic tables are provided. Piped water, flush toilets, sanitary disposal station, showers and firewood are also available. Bottled gas, a store, cafe, laundromat and ice are located within one mile. Pets are permitted on leashes. Boat docks, launching facilities and rentals are nearby.

Reservations, fee: Reservations necessary; $10 fee per night. Open late May to mid-September.

Who to contact: Phone Yellowstone National Park at (307) 344-7381 or write to P.O. Box 168, Yellowstone National Park, WY 82190.

Location: From the town of Lake, drive three miles south to the campground.

Trip note: This is a gigantic tent city campground set along beautiful Yellowstone Lake. There are three other camps at the lake, but this is by far the most popular. Several hiking trails are in the area, and a nearby marina provides boat access. The visitor center is located about five miles away on the north shore of the lake.

17) FISHING BRIDGE RV PARK

Reference: on Yellowstone River, Yellowstone National Park; map W1, grid c5.

Campsites, facilities: There are 345 sites for trailers or motor homes up to 40 feet long. Flush toilets, sanitary disposal station, showers, firewood and a laundromat are also available. Electricity, piped water and sewer hookups are available at an additional charge. Bottled gas, a store, cafe and ice are located within one mile. Some facilities are **wheelchair accessible.** Pets are permitted on leashes.

Reservations, fee: Reservations required; $20 fee per night. Open early June to early September.

Who to contact: Phone TW Recreational Services, Inc. at (307) 344-7311, or write to P.O. Box 168, Yellowstone National Park, WY 82190.

Location: From Pahaska at the eastern entrance to the park, drive 28 miles west to the campground entrance at Fishing Bridge Junction.

Trip note: This is one of Yellowstone's world famous camps, and the only RV camp in the entire park. It's set on the Yellowstone River just north of Yellowstone Lake. Trout fishing can be good on the river, but check park rules for special closures and catch-and-release regulations. Several good hiking trails are in the area. Note: an adjacent camp for tents has been closed in order to minimize contact between people and grizzly bears.

---

18) PAHASKA

Reference: near North Absaroka Wilderness, Shoshone National Forest; map W1, grid c7.

Campsites, facilities: There are 20 tent sites and four sites for trailers or motor homes up to 22 feet long. Picnic tables are provided. Piped water and pit toilets are also available. A store and cafe are located within one mile. Pets are permitted on leashes.

Reservations, fee: No reservations necessary; $6 fee per night. Open mid-June to late September.

Who to contact: Phone Shoshone National Forest at (307) 527-6921 or write to Wapiti Ranger District, P.O. Box 1840, Cody, WY 82414.

Location: From Cody, drive west on US 16 for 49.6 miles to the campground.

Trip note: This camp is set near the eastern boundary of Yellowstone National Park and is right on Highway 14/20. It is a good base camp for a multi-day backpack trip. Several nearby trails follow creeks into the North Absaroka Wilderness, an ideal alternative to Yellowstone. It's almost as beautiful, but there's scarcely a hint of visitor pressure. In fact the 50-mile stretch of highway that passes through the Wapiti Valley, between here and Cody, is considered by some to be the most scenic drive in the country.

---

19) THREE MILE

Reference: on the North Fork of Shoshone River, Shoshone National Forest; map W1, grid c7.

Campsites, facilities: There are 16 tent sites and 17 sites for trailers or motor homes up to 22 feet long. Piped water and picnic tables are provided. Pit toilets are available. A store and cafe are located within one mile. Pets are permitted on leashes.

Reservations, fee: No reservations necessary; $6 fee per night. Open mid-June to late September.

Who to contact: Phone Shoshone National Forest at (307) 527-6921 or write to Wapiti Ranger District, P.O. Box 1840, Cody, WY 82414.

Location: From Cody, drive west on US 14/16/20 for 48.6 miles to the campground.

Trip note: This camp is located on the North Fork of the Shoshone River, with pretty, open camps and close access to the river. It's an alternative to nearby Pahaska Camp; see the trip note for that camp. This spot is not located at a trailhead, but has several nearby. A Forest Service map details the adjacent backcountry access points.

---

20) SLEEPING GIANT

Reference: near the North Fork of Shoshone River, Shoshone National Forest; map W1, grid c7.

Campsites, facilities: There are three tent sites and three sites for trailers or motor homes up to 22 feet long. Picnic tables are provided. Piped water and pit toilets are also available. Pets are permitted on leashes.

Reservations, fee: No reservations necessary; $6 fee per night. Open mid-June to late September.

Who to contact: Phone Shoshone National Forest at (307) 527-6921 or write to Wapiti Ranger District, P.O. Box 1840, Cody, WY 82414.

Location: From Cody, drive west on US 14/16/20 for 47.6 miles to the campground.

Trip note: This is a pretty camp, tiny and secluded, with dense vegetation. Even if all the other sites are filled, you'll feel like there's no one else around. Pahaska, Three Mile and Sleeping Giant camps are just one mile apart. For sidetrip possibilities, see the trip note for Pahaska Camp.

---

21) EAGLE CREEK

Reference: near Washakie Wilderness, Shoshone National Forest; map W1, grid c7.

Campsites, facilities: There are 20 sites for tents, trailers or motor homes up to 22 feet long. Picnic tables are provided. Piped water and pit toilets are also available. A cafe is located within five miles. Pets are permitted on leashes.

Reservations, fee: No reservations necessary; $6 fee per night. Open June to late September.

Who to contact: Phone Shoshone National Forest at (307) 527-6921 or write to Wapiti Ranger District, P.O. Box 1840, Cody, WY 82414.

Location: From Cody, drive west on US 16 for 44.7 miles to the campground.

Trip note: This is one of several camps located along this incredibly scenic stretch of US 14/16/20 east of Yellowstone National Park. It's a good jump-off camp for backcountry users because there's a trail from camp that follows Eagle Creek for many miles. It will lead you south into the Washakie Wilderness. Don't be surprised if you find lots of company here. It's advisable to arrive early so you won't have to wrestle for a site.

---

22) CLEARWATER

Reference: on the North Fork of Shoshone River, Shoshone National Forest; map W1, grid c8.

Campsites, facilities: There are 32 sites for tents, trailers or motor homes up to 30 feet long. Picnic tables are provided. Piped water and pit toilets are also available. Pets are permitted on leashes.

Reservations, fee: No reservations necessary; $6 fee per night. Open June to late September.

Who to contact: Phone Shoshone National Forest at (307) 527-6921 or write to Wapiti Ranger District, P.O. Box 1840, Cody, WY 82414.

Location: From Cody, drive west on US 14/16/20 for 31.8 miles.

Trip note: This is a very pretty spot set at the confluence of Clearwater Creek and the North Fork of the Shoshone River. It's easy to reach and popular in summer months. A trail just west of camp is routed north along Clearwater Creek into the North Absaroka Wilderness.

---

23) LEWIS LAKE

Reference: near Mount Sheridan, Yellowstone National Park; map W1, grid d3.

Campsites, facilities: There are 85 sites for tents, trailers or motor homes up to 34 feet long. Picnic tables are provided. Piped water and pit toilets are also available. Pets are permitted on leashes. Boat launching facilities are nearby.

Reservations, fee: No reservations necessary; $6 fee per night. Open mid-June to late October.

Who to contact: Phone Yellowstone National Park at (307) 344-7381 or write to P.O. Box 168, Yellowstone National Park, WY 82190.

Location: From West Thumb, drive 10 miles south to the campground.

Trip note: This camp is set next to Lewis Lake, and with all the launching facilities, it's a real popular spot for boaters. Nearby Mount Sheridan (10,308 feet) is often visible in the west.

---

24) GRANT VILLAGE

Reference: on Yellowstone Lake, Yellowstone National Park; map W1, grid d4.

Campsites, facilities: There are 403 sites for tents, trailers or motor homes up to 34 feet long. Picnic tables are provided. Piped water, flush toilets, sanitary disposal station, showers and firewood are also available.

Bottled gas, cafe, laundromat and ice are located within one mile. Pets are permitted on leashes.

Reservations, fee: No reservations necessary; $8 fee per night. Open late June to mid-October.

Who to contact: Phone Yellowstone National Park at (307) 344-7381 or write to P.O. Box 168, Yellowstone National Park, WY 82190.

Location: From West Thumb, drive two miles south to the campground.

Trip note: This looks like a combination between a tent city and a wilderness town. People or not, it's an idyllic spot set along Yellowstone Lake. A Yellowstone Visitor Center is nearby.

25) ELK FORK

Reference: near Washakie Wilderness, Shoshone National Forest; map W1, grid d8.

Campsites, facilities: There are 13 sites for tents, trailers or motor homes up to 22 feet long. Picnic tables are provided. Piped water and pit toilets are also available. Pets are permitted on leashes.

Reservations, fee: No reservations necessary; $6 fee per night. Open June to late September.

Who to contact: Phone Shoshone National Forest at (307) 527-6921 or write to Wapiti Ranger District, P.O. Box 1840, Cody, WY 82414.

Location: From Cody, drive west on US 14/16/20 for 29.5 miles to the campground.

Trip note: This is a prime spot, easy to reach, beautiful, and has many sidetrip possibilities. The camp is located along Elk Creek, and a trail leading south out of camp follows the stream into the Washakie Wilderness. This makes an excellent base camp for a backpacking trip.

26) WAPITI

Reference: near Washakie Wilderness, Shoshone National Forest; map W1, grid d8.

Campsites, facilities: There are 41 sites for tents, trailers or motor homes up to 22 feet long. Picnic tables are provided. Piped water and pit toilets are also available. A store, cafe and ice are located within five miles. Pets are permitted on leashes.

Reservations, fee: No reservations necessary; $6 fee per night. Open June to late September.

Who to contact: Phone Shoshone National Forest at (307) 527-6921 or write to Wapiti Ranger District, P.O. Box 1840, Cody, WY 82414.

Location: From Cody, drive west on US 14/16/20 for 29.4 miles to the campground.

Trip note: A primitive Forest Service road runs north out of camp and is perfect for mountain bikers. This camp is set just across the road from the preceding camp. See the trip note for Elk Fork Camp for hiking possibilities.

27) REX HALE

Reference: near the North Fork of Shoshone River, Shoshone National Forest; map W1, grid d8.

Campsites, facilities: There are eight sites for trailers or motor homes up to 16 feet long. Piped water and picnic tables are provided. Pit toilets are available. Pets are permitted on leashes.

Reservations, fee: No reservations necessary; $6 fee per night. Open June to late September.

Who to contact: Phone Shoshone National Forest at (307) 527-6921 or write to Wapiti Ranger District, P.O. Box 1840, Cody, WY 82414.

Location: From Cody, drive west on US 14/16/20 for 35.9 miles to the campground.

Trip note: This camp is located just a mile east of Newton Creek Camp. At Blackwater Picnic Ground, located just west of this camp, Blackwater Fire Memorial National Recreation Trail is routed about six miles south to Clayton Mountain (11,715 feet) at the border of the Washakie Wilderness. About three miles out of camp, you can branch off to the west and hop onto the Natural Bridge Trail, which is especially pretty.

28) NEWTON CREEK

Reference: on the North Fork of Shoshone River, Shoshone National Forest; map W1, grid d8.

Campsites, facilities: There are 31 sites for tents, trailers or motor homes up to 22 feet long. Picnic tables are provided. Piped water, pit toilets and firewood are also available. Pets are permitted on leashes.

Reservations, fee: No reservations necessary; $6 fee per night. Open June to late September.

Who to contact: Phone Shoshone National Forest at (307) 527-6921 or write to Wapiti Ranger District, P.O. Box 21840, Cody, WY 82414.

Location: From Cody, drive west on US 16 for 37.3 miles to the campground.

Trip note: This is a nice camp set along the North Fork of the Shoshone River. It has easy access off US 14/16/20 too. There are several quality backcountry trails nearby including the Blackwater National Memorial Trail and Natural Bridge Trail; see trip note for Rex Hale Camp for details.

29) BIG GAME

Reference: near Elk Creek, Shoshone National Forest; map W1, grid d9.

Campsites, facilities: There are 17 sites for tents, trailers or motor homes up to 22 feet long. Picnic tables are provided. Piped water and pit toilets are also available. A store, cafe and ice are located within five miles. Pets are permitted on leashes.

Reservations, fee: No reservations necessary; $6 fee per night. Open June to late September.

Who to contact: Phone Shoshone National Forest at (307) 527-6921 or write to Wapiti Ranger District, P.O. Box 1840, Cody, WY 82414.

Location: From Cody, drive west on US 14/16/20 for 28.6 miles to the campground.

Trip note: This is one of three camps in the immediate area. It's across the road from Elk Creek about a mile from Elk Fork and Wapiti camps. See the trip note for Elk Fork.

---

30) CAVE FALLS

Reference: near Yellowstone National Park, Grand Targhee National Forest; map W1, grid e1.

Campsites, facilities: There are 23 sites for tents, trailers or motor homes up to 21 feet long. Picnic tables are provided. Piped water, pit toilets and firewood are also available. Pets are permitted on leashes.

Reservations, fee: No reservations necessary; $5 fee per night. Open mid-June to late September.

Who to contact: Phone Grand Targhee National Forest at (208) 652-7442 or write to Ashton, ID 83420.

Location: From Ashton, Idaho, drive five miles north on Highway 47. Turn right on County Road 36 and drive seven miles east, then turn east on Forest Service Road 36 and continue for 14 miles to the campground.

Trip note: This little-known camp is set just outside the southwestern boundary of Yellowstone National Park and is adjacent to the Vinegar Hole Wilderness. A trail starts at the nearby Bechler Ranger Station and follows Bechler Creek into Yellowstone for many miles. It eventually comes to Shoshone Lake. Note: you need a Wyoming fishing license for use here.

---

31) FLAGG RANCH VILLAGE

Reference: near Yellowstone National Park; map W1, grid e3.

Campsites, facilities: There are 75 tent sites and 97 sites for trailers or motor homes of any length. Electricity, piped water, sewer hookups and picnic tables are provided. Flush toilets, bottled gas, sanitary disposal station, showers, a store, cafe, laundromat and ice are also available. Firewood costs extra. Pets are permitted on leashes.

Reservations, fee: Reservations accepted; $16-$22 fee per night; MasterCard and Visa accepted. Open late May to mid-September.

Who to contact: Phone (800) 443-2311 or write to P.O. Box 187, Moran, WY 83013.

Location: From Moran Junction, drive 25 miles north on US 89 to the campground.

Trip note: This large, privately developed camp is a home for travelers stuck looking for a spot between Yellowstone to the north and the Grand Tetons to the south. Nearby recreation options include hiking trails, a marina, a riding stable and tennis courts.

---

32) COLTER BAY

Reference: on Jackson Lake, Grand Teton National Park; map W1, grid f3.

Campsites, facilities: There are 350 sites for tents, trailers or motor homes of any length. Picnic tables are provided. Piped water, flush toilets, sanitary disposal station and showers are also available. Bottled gas, a store, coffee shop, laundromat and ice are located within one mile. Some facilities are **wheelchair accessible.** Pets and motorbikes are permitted. Boat docks and rentals are nearby.

Reservations, fee: No reservations; $8 fee per night. Open late May to mid-September.

Who to contact: Phone Grand Teton National Park at (307) 733-2880 or write to P.O. Drawer 170, Moose, WY 83012.

Location: From Moran, drive north on US 89/287 for eight miles, then west for 1.5 miles to the campground.

Trip note: This giant camp is named after Jim Colter, the trailblazer who first saw the area in 1807. He wouldn't believe it if he saw it now: loaded with people in cars. And they're all here because of the lakeside beauty and the magnificent Tetons to the west. A visitor venter is nearby; so are hiking trails and bicycle rentals. A recreational program and horseback riding provide other options.

---

33) SIGNAL MOUNTAIN

Reference: near Jackson Lake, Grand Teton National Monument; map W1, grid f3.

Campsites, facilities: There are 86 sites for tents, trailers or motor homes of any length. Picnic tables are provided. Piped water, flush toilets, and sanitary disposal station are also available. Bottled gas, a store, coffee shop and ice are located within one mile. Pets and motorbikes are permitted. Boat docks, launching facilities and rentals are nearby at Jackson Lake.

Reservations, fee: No reservations; $8 fee per night. Open mid-May to late September.

Who to contact: Phone Grand Teton National Park at (307) 733-2880 or write to P.O. Drawer 170, Moose, WY 83012.

Location: From Moose, drive 18 miles north on Teton Park Road to the campground.

Trip note: This is a popular spot for boaters because of a nearby marina. There are many possible adventures here too: You could rent a boat, go for a hike, or drive up nearby Signal Mountain, which climbs 2,314 feet and has spectacular views. A recreational program is available.

34) LIZARD CREEK

Reference: on Jackson Lake, Grand Teton National Park; map W1, grid f3.

Campsites, facilities: There are 62 sites for tents, trailers or motor homes of any length. Picnic tables are provided. Piped water and flush toilets are also available. Pets and motorbikes are permitted.

Reservations, fee: No reservations; $8 fee per night. Open late June to September.

Who to contact: Phone Grand Teton National Park at (307) 733-2880 or write to P.O. Drawer 170, Moose, WY 83012.

Location: From Moran, drive north on US 89/287 for 18 miles to the campground.

Trip note: This is a popular spot, and no wonder why. It is located right at the north end of beautiful Jackson Lake with the Grand Tetons looming overhead to the west. Some hiking trails are in the area. Swimming, boating and fishing are among your options here.

35) HATCHET

Reference: in Bridger-Teton National Forest; map W1, grid f4.

Campsites, facilities: There are nine sites for tents, trailers or motor homes up to 16 feet long. Picnic tables are provided. Piped water and pit toilets are also available. Showers, a store, coffee shop and laundromat are located within one mile. Pets are permitted on leashes.

Reservations, fee: No reservations necessary; $5 fee per night. Open early June to mid-November.

Who to contact: Phone Bridger-Teton National Forest at (307) 543-2386 or write to Buffalo Ranger District, P.O. Box 278, Moran, WY 83013.

Location: From Moran, drive eight miles east on US 26 to the campground.

Trip note: This camp is set at 8,000 feet in Buffalo Valley, a good base camp for visitors heading into the interior of the Bridger Teton National Forest.

36) TETON CANYON

Reference: near Jedediah Smith Wilderness, Grand Targhee National Forest; map W1, grid g1.

Campsites, facilities: There are 11 sites for tents, trailers or motor homes up to 30 feet long. Picnic tables are provided. Piped water and pit toilets are also available. Pets are permitted on leashes.

Reservations, fee: No reservations necessary; $5 fee per night. Open July to late September.

Who to contact: Phone Grand Targhee National Forest at (208) 354-2431 or write to P.O. Box 127, Driggs, ID 83422.

Location: From Driggs, Idaho, drive 6.2 miles east on Teton Canyon Road. Turn east on Forest Service Road 2009 and drive 4.7 miles to the campground.

Trip note: This camp is known and used by just a few hikers. It's set at the foot of the Grand Tetons (elevation 13,770). The magnificent Teton Crest Trail begins here and is routed into the Jedediah Smith Wilderness.

---

37) GROS VENTRE

Reference: on Gros Ventre River, Grand Teton National Park; map W1, grid g2.

Campsites, facilities: There are 360 sites for tents, trailers or motor homes of any length. Picnic tables are provided. Piped water, flush toilets and sanitary disposal station are also available. Some facilities are **wheelchair accessible.** Pets and motorbikes are permitted.

Reservations, fee: No reservations; $8 fee per night. Open May to October.

Who to contact: Phone Grand Teton National Park at (307) 733-2880 or write to P.O. Drawer 170, Moose, WY 83012.

Location: From Jackson, drive seven miles north on US 187. Turn right on Gros Ventre Road and drive five miles northeast to the campground.

Trip note: This is a massive tent city set on the Gros Ventre River. It's a popular spot in the Jackson Hole area of the Grand Teton National Park. It also sits adjacent to the National Elk Refuge. Sleigh rides through the refuge are available from late December through March. For information stop at the information center at the north end of Jackson.

---

38) JENNY LAKE

Reference: in Grand Teton National Park; map W1, grid g2.

Campsites, facilities: There are 49 sites for tents only. Picnic tables are provided. Piped water and flush toilets are also available. Ice is located within one mile. Pets and motorbikes are permitted. Boat docks, launching facilities and rentals are nearby. Some facilities are **wheelchair accessible.**

Reservations, fee: No reservations; $8 fee per night. Open late May to mid-September.

Who to contact: Phone Grand Teton National Park at (307) 733-2880 or write to P.O. Drawer 170, Moose, WY 83012.

Location: From Moose Junction, drive eight miles north on Teton Park Road to the campground.

Trip note: This camp is set aside little Jenny Lake which often gets overshadowed by the attention paid to nearby Jackson Lake to the north and the Grand Tetons to the west. Regardless, it's a good spot, with boat rentals, fishing and horseback riding. There are hiking trails heading into the Teton Mountain Range.

39) RED HILLS

Reference: on Gros Ventre River, Bridger-Teton National Forest; map W1, grid g4.

Campsites, facilities: There are five sites for tents. Picnic tables are provided. Piped water and vault toilets are also available. Pets are permitted on leashes.

Reservations, fee: Reserve through L&L, Inc. at (800) 342-CAMP ($5 reservation fee); $5 fee per night. Open early June to late October.

Who to contact: Phone Bridger-Teton National Forest at (307) 739-5400 or write to Jackson Ranger District, P.O. Box 1689, Jackson, WY 83001.

Location: From Kelly, drive 12.8 miles east on Forest Service Road 30040 to the campground.

Trip note: This secret spot requires four miles of dirt road determination to get there. It's set aside the Gros Ventre River which feeds into Lower Slide Lake. There's good trout fishing here.

40) ATHERTON CREEK

Reference: on Lower Slide Lake, Bridger-Teton National Forest; map W1, grid g4.

Campsites, facilities: There are 20 sites for tents, trailers or motor homes up to 16 feet long. Picnic tables are provided. Piped water and vault toilets are also available. Pets are permitted on leashes. A boat ramp is nearby.

Reservations, fee: Reserve through L&L, Inc. at (800) 342-CAMP ($5 reservation fee); $5 fee per night. Open early June to late October.

Who to contact: Phone Bridger-Teton National Forest at (307) 739-5400 or write to Jackson Ranger District, P.O. Box 1689, Jackson, WY 83001.

Location: From Kelly, drive 7.3 miles east on Forest Service Road 30040 to the campground.

Trip note: This is a beautiful spot on the shore of Lower Slide Lake, but it's just enough off the beaten path of US 191 to get missed by many travelers. It has gorgeous views and good fishing at both the lake and the nearby Gros Ventre River.

41) CRYSTAL CREEK

Reference: near Gros Ventre River, Bridger-Teton National Forest; map W1, grid g4.

Campsites, facilities: There are six sites for tents. Picnic tables are provided. Piped water and vault toilets are also available. Pets are permitted on leashes.

Reservations, fee: Reserve through L&L, Inc. at (800) 342-CAMP ($5 reservation fee); $5 fee per night. Open early June to late October.

Who to contact: Phone Bridger-Teton National Forest at (307) 739-5400 or write to P.O. Box 1689, Jackson, WY 83001.

Location: From Kelly, drive 13.1 miles east on Forest Service Road 30040 to the campground.

Trip note: This is an alternative to Red Hills Camp. This one is set another mile down the road, and is located at the confluence of Crystal Creek and the Gros Ventre River. This area is very popular with fishermen, with rainbow, brook, and native cutthroat trout among the prospects.

---

42) FALLS

Reference: near Brooks Lake Creek, Shoshone National Forest; map W1, grid g7.

Campsites, facilities: There are 46 sites for tents, trailers or motor homes up to 32 feet long. Picnic tables are provided. Piped water and pit toilets are also available. Showers are located within five miles. Pets are permitted on leashes.

Reservations, fee: Reserve through MISTIX at (800) 283-CAMP ($6 MISTIX fee); $6 fee per night. Open mid-June to early September.

Who to contact: Phone Shoshone National Forest at (307) 455-2466 or write to Wind River Ranger District, P.O. Box 186, Dubois, WY 82513.

Location: From Dubois, drive 23 miles west on US 287 to the campground.

Trip note: This is one of three camps in the area. This one is set close to Togwotee Pass (9,668 feet) and Brooks Lake Creek. The others are Pinnacles Camp and Brooks Lake. It's really pretty out here. A trailhead about 2.5 miles west of camp leads southeast along River Creek.

---

43) PINNACLES

Reference: at Brooks Lake, Shoshone National Forest; map W1, grid g7.

Campsites, facilities: There are 21 sites for tents, trailers or motor homes up to 22 feet long. Picnic tables are provided. Pit toilets are available. There is hand pumped water. Pets are permitted on leashes, and boat docks are nearby.

Reservations, fee: No reservations necessary; $6 fee per night. Open late June to late September.

Who to contact: Phone Shoshone National Forest at (307) 455-2466 or write to Wind River Ranger District, P.O. Box 186, Dubois, WY 82513.

Location: From Dubois, drive 23 miles west on US 287. Turn north on Forest Service Road 14515 and drive five miles to the campground.

Trip note: This is a primitive spot set along beautiful Brooks Lake. It's a good spot for boating and fishing. The Dunoir trailhead, located on the west side of the lake near Brooks Lake Camp, follows many creeks and accesses the Washakie Wilderness.

44) BROOKS LAKE

Reference: west of Dubois, Shoshone National Forest; map W1, grid g7.

Campsites, facilities: There are 14 sites for tents, trailers or motor homes up to 22 feet long. Picnic tables are provided. Piped water, pit toilets and firewood are also available. Pets are permitted on leashes. Boat docks and launching facilities are nearby.

Reservations, fee: No reservations necessary; $6 fee per night. Open July to early September.

Who to contact: Phone Shoshone National Forest at (307) 455-2466 or write to Wind River Ranger District, P.O. Box 186, Dubois, WY 82513.

Location: From Dubois, drive 23 miles west on US 287. Turn north on Forest Service Road 14515 and drive five miles to the campground.

Trip note: This is another option for campers at Brooks Lake. See the trip note for Pinnacles Camp.

45) HORSE CREEK

Reference: north of Dubois, Shoshone National Forest; map W1, grid g8.

Campsites, facilities: There are nine sites for tents, trailers or motor homes up to 22 feet long. Picnic tables are provided. Piped water, pit toilets and firewood are also available. Pets are permitted on leashes.

Reservations, fee: No reservations necessary; $6 fee per night. Open mid-June to late October.

Who to contact: Phone Shoshone National Forest at (307) 455-2466 or write to Wind River Ranger District, P.O. Box 186, Dubois, WY 82513.

Location: From Dubois, drive 12 miles north on Forest Service Road 14507 to the campground.

Trip note: Hey, most out-of-town travelers just plain don't have a clue about this one. It's a little, secluded spot on Horse Creek. Guaranteed solitude. A trail from camp is routed to some small backcountry lakes. You need a Forest Service map to get there, but it's a go-do-it place for hikers.

46) DOUBLE CABIN

Reference: near Washakie Wilderness, Shoshone National Forest; map W1, grid g8.

Campsites, facilities: There are 15 sites for tents, trailers or motor homes up to 22 feet long. Picnic tables are provided. Piped water, pit toilets and firewood are also available. Pets are permitted on leashes.

Reservations, fee: No reservations necessary; $6 fee per night. Open late June to early September.

Who to contact: Phone Shoshone National Forest at (307) 455-2466 or write to Wind River Ranger District, P.O. Box 186, Dubois, WY 82513.

Location: From Dubois, drive 29 miles north on Forest Service Road 14508 to the campground.

Trip note: This one is out there in what we call "booger country." It's way out there, like 29 miles of dirt road, and then finally you come to the camp. It's set on the border of the Washakie Wilderness. It's a good base camp though for hikers, because there are trails heading out in three directions along various creeks.

---

47) TRAIL CREEK

Reference: near Jedediah Smith Wilderness, Grand Targhee National Forest, map W1, grid h1.

Campsites, facilities: There are 11 sites for tents, trailers or motor homes up to 30 feet long. Picnic tables are provided. Piped water and pit toilets are also available. Pets are permitted on leashes.

Reservations, fee: No reservations necessary; $6 fee per night. Open June to late September.

Who to contact: Phone Grand Targhee National Forest at (208) 354-2312 or write to P.O. Box 127, Driggs, ID 83422.

Location: From Victor, Idaho, drive 5.6 miles east on Highway 33 and look for signs to the campground.

Trip note: In many ways, this is an ideal spot: small, secluded, little known, with good side trips for hikers, and easy access. The camp is set on the border of the Jedediah Smith Wilderness.

---

48) JACKSON HOLE

Reference: in Jackson; map W1, grid h2.

Campsites, facilities: There are 60 tent sites and 120 drive-through sites for trailers or motor homes of any length. Electricity, piped water, sewer hookups and picnic tables are provided. Flush toilets, sanitary disposal station, showers, recreation hall, a store, laundromat, ice, playground and a swimming pool are also available. Bottled gas is located within one mile. Pets and motorbikes are permitted.

Reservations, fee: Reservations accepted; $15-$25 fee per night; MasterCard and Visa accepted. Open mid-May to mid-September.

Who to contact: Phone (307) 733-2927 or write to P.O. Box 2802, Jackson, WY 83001.

Location: From Jackson, drive 1.5 miles south on US 26/89/189/191 to the campground.

Trip note: This park covers eight acres. There's space for tenters and motor homes alike. It's a pretty area, grassy and shaded. Nearby recreational options include bike paths and a riding stable. The quaint town of Jackson provides many tourist attractions.

49) KOA TETON VILLAGE

Reference: near Grand Teton National Park; map W1, grid h2.

Campsites, facilities: There are 58 tent sites and 92 sites for trailers or motor homes of any length. Camping cabins are also available. Piped water and picnic tables are provided. Flush toilets, bottled gas, sanitary disposal station, showers, recreation hall, a store, laundromat, ice and a playground are also available. Firewood is available at an additional charge. A coffee shop is located within one mile. Pets and motorbikes are permitted. There are also six camping cabins available.

Reservations, fee: Reservations accepted; $19.50-$25.50 fee per night; camping cabins are $30-$35 per night. MasterCard and Visa accepted. Open May to mid-October.

Who to contact: Phone (307) 733-5354 or write to P.O. Box 38, Teton Village, WY 83025.

Location: From Jackson, drive one mile south on US 89 to Highway 22. Turn west and drive four miles to Highway 390, then turn north and continue for 1.5 miles to the campground.

Trip note: This is a popular spot for vacationers, and here are the reasons why: It is close to both Teton Village and the southern entrance to the Grand Teton National Park. And nearby are hiking trails, a golf course, a riding stable, and tennis courts. This offers a nice alternative if you want to stay away from the massive crowds at the Grand Teton camps, but it's wise to get your reservation in early.

50) CURTIS CANYON

Reference: near Goodwin Lake, Bridger-Teton National Forest; map W1, grid h2.

Campsites, facilities: There are 12 sites for tents, trailers or motor homes up to 16 feet long. Picnic tables are provided. Piped water, pit toilets and firewood are also available. Pets are permitted on leashes.

Reservations, fee: Reserve through L&L, Inc. at (800) 342-CAMP ($5 reservation fee); $7 fee per night. Open mid-June to mid-September.

Who to contact: Phone Bridger Teton National Forest at (307) 739-5400 or write to Jackson Ranger District, P.O. Box 1689, Jackson, WY 83001.

Location: From Jackson, drive east on Broadway to Elk Refuge Road. Travel north on Elk Refuge Road for five miles, then take Forest Service Road 30440 one mile to the campground.

Trip note: This is a nice hideaway near the National Elk Refuge. It takes six miles of driving on a dirt road to get here. Right there, many folks will call it quits, so if you don't mind the dust getting there, you may have the camp to yourself. There's a three-mile hike to Goodwin Lake from the camp. Goodwin Lake offers excellent fishing. This is a particularly beautiful area—bring your camera to catch the scenic views.

51) RAWHIDE RANCH

Reference: on Wind River; map W1, grid h7.

Campsites, facilities: There are 17 tent sites and 32 sites for trailers or motor homes of any length. Electricity, piped water, sewer hookups and picnic tables are provided. Flush toilets, showers, bottled gas, sanitary disposal station, showers, firewood, recreation hall, a store, coffee shop with home cooking, lounge, laundromat, ice and a playground are also available. Pets and motorbikes are permitted.

Reservations, fee: Reservations accepted; $7 fee per night; Open all year.

Who to contact: Phone (307) 455-2407 or write to P.O. Box 1307, Dubois, WY 82513.

Location: From Dubois, drive west on US 26/287 for 14 miles to the campground.

Trip note: This is one of two camps in the immediate area along the highway. It's right on the Wind River, with grassy riverside sites. This is a well-known geological area, and rockhounds come for miles around. The area also boasts the largest mountain bighorn sheep herd in the country. Other attractions include the nearby petrified forest, hiking trails, fishing and biking.

52) TRIANGLE C RANCH

Reference: west of Dubois; map W1, grid h7.

Campsites, facilities: There are 20 tent sites and 25 sites for trailers or motor homes of any length. Electricity, piped water and picnic tables are provided. Flush toilets, sanitary disposal station, showers, recreation hall, coffee shop, lounge, laundromat, ice and a playground are also available. Sewer hookups and firewood are available at an additional charge. Pets are permitted on leashes.

Reservations, fee: Reservations accepted; $10-$15 fee per night; MasterCard and Visa accepted. Open June to September.

Who to contact: Phone (307) 455-2225 or write to P.O. Box 691, Dubois, WY 82513.

Location: From Dubois, drive west on US 26/287 for 18 miles to the campground.

Trip note: This is an okay layover spot for highway cruisers. The sites are graveled and heavily wooded. Nearby riding stables provide a sidetrip.

53) CIRCLE UP CAMPER COURT

Reference: in Dubois; map W1, grid h8.

Campsites, facilities: There are 50 tent sites and 80 sites for trailers or motor homes of any length. Picnic tables are provided. Flush toilets, sanitary disposal station, firewood, recreation hall, cable TV, coffee shop, laundromat, ice, playground and an indoor swimming pool are also available. Electricity, piped water, sewer hookups and showers are available at an additional charge. Bottled gas and a store are located within one mile. Pets are permitted on leashes.

Reservations, fee: Reservations accepted; $10-$15 fee per night; MasterCard and Visa accepted. Open May to mid-October.

Who to contact: Phone (307) 455-2238 or write to P.O. Box 1520, Dubois, WY 82513.

Location: This campground is located in Dubois on US 26.

Trip note: This is the only camp in Dubois. The next closest option is Rawhide Ranch to the northeast. There are several mini-adventures at this park including a nice wildlife exhibit, a little fishing pond, and believe it or not, rental teepees.

---

54) STATION CREEK

Reference: near Snake River, Bridger-Teton National Forest; map W1, grid i1.

Campsites, facilities: There are 15 sites for tents, trailers or motor homes up to 22 feet long. Piped water and picnic tables are provided. Vault toilets and firewood are also available. Pets are permitted on leashes.

Reservations, fee: Reserve through L&L, Inc. at (800) 342-CAMP ($5 reservation fee); $7 fee per night. Open late May to early September.

Who to contact: Phone Bridger Teton National Forest at (307) 739-5400 or write to Jackson Ranger District, P.O. Box 1689, Jackson, WY 83001.

Location: From Alpine, drive 11 miles east on US 89 to the campground.

Trip note: You get easy access to this pretty spot. It's near the confluence of Station Creek and the Snake River, where you can try your hand at catching a few of the native cutthroat trout. A short trail from camp provides a sidetrip option.

---

55) EAST TABLE CREEK

Reference: near Snake River, Bridger-Teton National Forest; map W1, grid i1.

Campsites, facilities: There are 18 sites for tents, trailers or motor homes up to 22 feet long. Picnic tables are provided. Piped water, vault toilets and firewood are also available. Pets are permitted on leashes. A boat ramp is nearby.

Reservations, fee: Reserve through L&L, Inc. at (800) 342-CAMP ($5 reservation fee); $7 fee per night. Open late May to early September.

Who to contact: Phone Bridger-Teton National Forest at (307) 739-5400 or write to Jackson Ranger District, P.O. Box 1689, Jackson, WY 83001.

Location: From Alpine, drive 12.7 miles east on US 89 to the campground.

Trip note: This is another pretty spot with easy access. It is set at the confluence of East Table Creek and the Snake River near the Snake River Canyon, a stunning scenic area. A trailhead from camp provides access to a network of other trails to the north. It's all detailed on a National Forest map. This is a popular spot, so expect company.

---

56) CABIN CREEK

Reference: near Snake River, Bridger-Teton National Forest; map W1, grid i2.

Campsites, facilities: There are 10 sites for tents, trailers or motor homes up to 22 feet long. Picnic tables are provided. Piped water, vault toilets and firewood are also available. Pets are permitted on leashes.

Reservations, fee: Reserve through L&L, Inc. at (800) 342-CAMP ($5 reservation fee); $7 fee per night. Open late May to early September.

Who to contact: Phone Bridger-Teton National Forest at (307) 739-5400 or write to Jackson Ranger District, P.O. Box 1689, Jackson, WY 83001.

Location: From Alpine, drive 16.4 miles east on US 89 to the campground.

Trip note: This is one in a series of good camps in the area. This one is set close to where Cabin Creek pours into the Snake River, with both shaded and sunny sites and fishing access. A hiking trail follows Cabin Creek northeast into a network of other trails.

---

57) ELBOW

Reference: on Snake River, Bridger-Teton National Forest; map W1, grid i2.

Campsites, facilities: There are nine sites for tents, trailers or motor homes up to 22 feet long. There's an additional eight sites on the west half of the campground that are available for groups. Picnic tables are provided. Piped water, vault toilets and firewood are also available. A boat ramp is nearby. Pets are permitted on leashes.

Reservations, fee: Reserve through L&L, Inc. at (800) 342-CAMP ($5 reservation fee); $7 fee per night. Open late May to early September.

Who to contact: Phone Bridger-Teton National Forest at (307) 739-5400 or write to Jackson Ranger District, P.O. Box 1689, Jackson, WY 83001.

Location: From Alpine, drive 13.7 miles east on US 89 to the campground.

Trip note: Located near the Snake River Canyon, this spot is beautiful and quite secluded, though well-used. You'll see how the camp received its name when you arrive. It is located at the "elbow" of the Snake River, not far from where Bailey Creek empties into it. There are numerous hiking trails in the area. The fishing is good in the fall, and there's also hunting. With all these options, plan on having plenty of company.

58) LAZY J CORRAL

Reference: south of Jackson; map W1, grid i2.

Campsites, facilities: There are five tent sites and 25 sites for trailers or motor homes. Electricity, piped water, sewer hookups and picnic tables are provided. Flush toilets, sanitary disposal station, showers, a store, laundromat, ice and a playground are also available. Bottled gas and a coffee shop are located within one mile. Pets and motorbikes are permitted.

Reservations, fee: Reservations accepted; $15 fee per night. Open April to October.

Who to contact: Phone (307) 733-1554 or write to Star Route P.O. Box 24, Jackson, WY 83001.

Location: From Jackson, drive 13 miles south on Highway 189 to the campground (at the Hoback Junction).

Trip note: This camp caters primarily to motor homes, but there are spaces for tents as well. The sites are graveled, surrounded by quaking aspen and yellow pine trees. This is a great base camp for all kinds of tourist adventures; the historic town of Jackson, fishing and river rafting in the Snake and Hoback Rivers, hiking trails, bike paths and horseback riding are all close by.

59) ASTORIA HOT SPRINGS

Reference: south of Jackson; map W1, grid i2.

Campsites, facilities: There are 94 sites for tents, trailers or motor homes of any length. Picnic tables are provided. Flush toilets, sanitary disposal station, showers, a store, coffee shop, laundromat, ice and a playground are also available. Electricity, piped water, sewer hookups and a swimming pool are available at an additional charge. Pets are permitted on leashes.

Reservations, fee: Reservations accepted; $12-$15 fee per night. Open mid-May to mid-September.

Who to contact: Phone (307) 733-2659 or write to Star Route Box 18, Jackson, WY 83001.

Location: From Jackson, drive 17 miles south on US 26 to the campground.

Trip note: This area offers many choices. Set in the beautiful Snake River Canyon, this large, 160-acre camp provides open, meadow-like sites and lots of sidetrip possibilities, including hot springs and bookings for raft trips.

60) HOLIDAY TRAV-L-PARK

Reference: near Hoback River; map W1, grid i2.

Campsites, facilities: There are 79 sites for tents, trailers or motor homes of any length. Electricity, piped water, sewer hookups and picnic tables are provided. Flush toilets, sanitary disposal station, showers, firewood, recreation hall, a store, laundromat, ice, playground and a swimming pool are also available. A coffee shop is located within one mile. Pets are permitted on leashes.

Reservations, fee: Reservations accepted; $15-$21 fee per night; MasterCard and Visa accepted. Open mid-May to late September.

Who to contact: Phone (307) 733-5240 or write to Star Route P.O. Box 45, Jackson, WY 83001.

Location: From Jackson, drive 17 miles south on US 189/191 to the campground.

Trip note: This five-star rated motor home park is not your average campground. It's more like a vacation resort. Set way back in the Hoback Valley along the Hoback River, it offers pretty riverside sites and a multitude of recreation options. Campers can choose from whitewater rafting, fishing, volleyball, basketball, archery, horseback riding and hiking, just to name a few. They're well known for their huge barbecues, and every Saturday night they bring in a live band and have a barn dance. If you're looking for a place to set up and stay for awhile, check this one out.

---

61) KOZY

Reference: on Hoback River, Bridger-Teton National Forest; map W1, grid i3.

Campsites, facilities: There are eight sites for tents, trailers or motor homes up to 31 feet long. Picnic tables and piped water are provided. Vault toilets and firewood are also available. A coffee shop is located within five miles. Pets are permitted on leashes. Two campsites and one toilet are **wheelchair accessible.**

Reservations, fee: Reserve through L&L, Inc. at (800) 342-CAMP ($5 reservation fee); $6 fee per night. Open June to late September.

Who to contact: Phone Bridger Teton National Forest at (307) 739-5400 or write to Jackson Ranger District, P.O. Box 1689, Jackson, WY 83001.

Location: From Bondurant, drive northwest on US 189 for eight miles to the campground.

Trip note: This little, primitive camp is set along the Hoback River, which provides good trout fishing, especially during the evening rise throughout the summer months. It offers easy access and a pretty setting, perfect for setting up a camp chair and watching the water flow by.

---

62) HOBACK

Reference: on Hoback River, Bridger-Teton National Forest; map W1, grid i3.

Campsites, facilities: There are 14 sites for tents, trailers or motor homes up to 30 feet long. Picnic tables are provided. Piped water, vault toilets and firewood are also available. A coffee shop is located within five miles. Pets are permitted on leashes. Two campsites and one toilet are **wheelchair accessible.**

Reservations, fee: Reserve through L&L, Inc. at (800) 342-CAMP ($5 reservation fee); $7 fee per night. Open June to late September.

Who to contact: Phone Bridger-Teton National Forest at (307) 739-5400 or write to Jackson Ranger District, P.O. Box 1689, Jackson, WY 83001.

Location: From Bondurant, drive northwest on US 189 for 16 miles to the campground.

Trip note: This is a good base camp for a fishing trip in the summer or a hunting trip in the fall, and it's pretty, too. The camp is set at 6,225 feet among pine trees and is located on the Hoback River, a prime trout stream. It's a 22-mile drive out of Jackson. If you're camping in June or July, it's worth your while to seek out the spectacular wildflower displays in the Jackson area.

63) GRANITE CREEK

Reference: in Bridger-Teton National Forest, map W1, grid i4.

Campsites, facilities: There are 52 sites for tents, trailers or motor homes up to 22 feet long. Two of the units offer utility hookups for RVs. Picnic tables are provided. Piped water, vault toilets, and firewood are also available. Showers and a coffee shop are located within one mile. Pets are permitted on leashes.

Reservations, fee: Reserve through L&L, Inc. at (800) 342-CAMP ($5 reservation fee); $7 fee per night. Open mid-June to mid-September.

Who to contact: Phone Bridger-Teton National Forest at (307) 739-5400 or write to Jackson Ranger District, P.O. Box 1689, Jackson, WY 83001.

Location: From Bondurant, drive 10.1 miles northwest on Highway 189. Turn right on Forest Service Road 30500 and continue for eight miles northeast to the campground.

Trip note: Not many folks know about this one. The camp is 35 miles from Jackson. The last nine miles of the road are dirt, but the scenery is superb, and there's good fishing at Granite Creek. A special bonus is the nearby Granite Hot Springs, where you can soak or swim to your heart's content.

64) WHISKEY GROVE

Reference: near Green River, Bridger-Teton National Forest; map W1, grid i6.

Campsites, facilities: There are nine sites for tents, trailers or motor homes up to 16 feet long. Picnic tables are provided. Piped water, pit toilets and firewood are also available. Pets are permitted on leashes.

Reservations, fee: No reservations necessary; $5 fee per night. Open mid-June to early September.

Who to contact: Phone Bridger-Teton National Forest, Pinedale Ranger District at (307) 367-4326 or write to P.O. Box 220, Pinedale, WY 82941.

Location: From Pinedale, drive six miles west on US 191. Turn right on Highway 352 and drive 24 miles north, then turn on Forest Service Road 91 and continue for 2.9 miles to a signed Forest Service Road. Turn west and proceed a half mile to the campground.

Trip note: It is advisable to have a Forest Service map on this trip. The camp is a good one though and has many options: go on a fishing trip to the Green River immediately east, go on a hunting trip, or hike the surrounding Bridger-Teton National Forest (7,600 feet).

---

65) MOOSE FLAT

Reference: on Greys River, Bridger-Teton National Forest; map W1, grid j1.

Campsites, facilities: There are 10 sites for tents, trailers or motor homes up to 16 feet long. Picnic tables and piped water are provided. Pit toilets and firewood are also available. Pets are permitted on leashes.

Reservations, fee: No reservations necessary; $5 fee per night. Open mid-June to early September.

Who to contact: Phone Bridger-Teton National Forest at (307) 886-3166 or write to Greys River Ranger District, P.O. Box 339, Afton, WY 83110.

Location: From Alpine, drive three-quarters of a mile southeast on US 89. Turn on County Road 1001 and continue southeast for a half mile, then 22.5 miles southeast on Forest Service Road 10138.

Trip note: This is a secluded spot set on a dirt road along Greys River. It's adjacent to the Wyoming Range. There are hiking trails in the area, but none lead directly out of the camp. A good one starts at the confluence of Greys River and White Creek (about 4.5 miles north of this camp), heading west along White Creek, then winding south for about 10 miles.

---

66) THE BRIDGE

Reference: on Greys River, Bridger-Teton National Forest; map W1, grid j2.

Campsites, facilities: There are five sites for tents, trailers or small motor homes up to 16 feet long. Picnic tables are provided. Pit toilets and firewood are also available, but there is **no piped water.** Showers, a store, coffee shop and ice are located within five miles. Pets are permitted on leashes. Boat docks, launching facilities and rentals are nearby.

Reservations, fee: No reservations necessary; $5 fee per night. Open June to early September.

Who to contact: Phone Bridger-Teton National Forest at (307) 886-3166 or write to Greys River Ranger District, P.O. Box 339, Afton, WY 83110.

Location: From Alpine, drive three-quarters of a mile southeast on US 89. Turn on County Road 1001 and drive a half mile outheast, then 2.1 miles southeast on Forest Service Road 10138 to the campground.

Trip note: This is a tiny, primitive spot nestled along the Greys River, yet it's only a few miles out of Alpine. Fishing can be good on adjacent Mill Creek. Nearby hiking trails are detailed on the Forest Service map.

---

67) MURPHY CREEK

Reference: on Greys River, Bridger-Teton National Forest; map W1, grid j2.

Campsites, facilities: There are 10 sites for tents, trailers or motor homes up to 22 feet long. Picnic tables and piped water are provided. Pit toilets and firewood are also available. Pets are pemitted on leashes.

Reservations, fee: No reservations necessary; $5 fee per night. Open mid-June to early September.

Who to contact: Phone Bridger Teton National Forest at (307) 886-3166 or write to Greys River Ranger District, P.O. Box 339, Afton, WY 83110.

Location: From Alpine, drive three-quarters of a mile southeast on US 89. Turn on County Road 1001 and drive a half mile southeast, then 13.7 miles southeast on Forest Service Road 10138 to the campground.

Trip note: This is one of a series of primitive camps along Greys River. This one may be the best. A trail from camp heads up Hot Foot Creek to Greys Peak (8,931 feet). It then intersects with a trail that follows the middle ridge for many miles north and south. Another option is taking the trail east into the backcountry of the Little Greys River watershed. To the west is another trail (it starts off as a dirt road) that leads to little Murphy Lakes.

---

68) LYNX CREEK

Reference: on Greys River, Bridger-Teton National Forest; map W1, grid j2.

Campsites, facilities: There are 14 sites for tents, trailers or small motor homes up to 16 feet long. Picnic tables are provided. Pit toilets and firewood are also available. There is **no piped wate.** Pets are permitted on leashes.

Reservations, fee: No reservations necessary; no fee. Open mid-June to early September.

Who to contact: Phone Bridger-Teton National Forest at (307) 886-3166 or write to Greys River Ranger District, P.O. Box 339, Afton, WY 83110.

Location: From Alpine, drive three-quarters of a mile southeast on US 89. Turn on County Road 1001 and drive a half mile southeast, then 11.7 miles southeast on Forest Service Road 10138 to the campground.

Trip note: This is one of two campgrounds in the immediate vicinity, and one of five campgrounds along Greys River. This one is set at the confluence of Lynx Creek and Greys River. A huge network of hiking trails is available in the area; see a Forest Service map for details.

---

69) NEW FORK LAKE

Reference: north of Pinedale, Bridger-Teton National Forest; map W1, grid j6.

Campsites, facilities: There are 20 sites for tents, or self-enclosed trailers or motor homes up to 22 feet long. There are no picnic tables, and **no piped water.** Pit toilets and firewood are available. Pets are permitted on leashes. Boat docks and launching facilities are nearby.

Reservations, fee: No reservations and no fee for individual sites, but groups should make reservations through MISTIX at (800) 283-CAMP (reservation fee charged). Group fee ranges from $25-$75 per night, depending on number of people. Open June to early September.

Who to contact: Phone Bridger-Teton National Forest, Pinedale Ranger District at (307) 367-4326 or write to P.O. Box 220, Pinedale, WY 82941.

Location: From Pinedale, drive six miles west on US 191. Turn right on Highway 352 and drive 15 miles north, then 4.6 mile east on a signed county road. Turn right on Forest Service Road 107 and proceed 2.8 miles southeast to the campground.

Trip note: This is one of two camps at New Fork Lake. Narrows Camp is the other and is more developed. You can either stay here and boat and fish or strap on a backpack and go for broke. There are several backcountry trails that lead into the Bridger Wilderness.

---

70) NARROWS

Reference: on New Fork Lake, Bridger-Teton National Forest; map W1, grid j6.

Campsites, facilities: There are 19 sites for tents, trailers or motor homes up to 30 feet long. Picnic tables are provided. Potable water, pit toilets and firewood are also available. Pets are peritted on leashes. Boat docks and launching facilities are nearby.

Reservations, fee: Reserve through MISTIX at (800) 283-CAMP ($6 MISTIX fee); $5 fee per night. Open June to early September.

Who to contact: Phone Bridger-Teton National Forest, Pinedale Ranger District at (307) 367-4326 or write to P.O. Box 220, Pinedale, WY 82941.

Location: From Pinedale, drive six miles west on US 191. Turn right,on Highway 352 and drive 13 miles north, then turn right on Forest Service Road 107 and travel 4.6 miles east. Turn on a signed Forest Service Road and continue 2.5 miles east to the campground.

Trip note: This is an alternative to New Fork Lake Camp. It's a pretty setting, near the water and surrounded by trees and has an abundance of wildlife.

Wyoming Map W2
18 listings
Pages 470-479

North—Montana
East (W3)—see page 480
South (W6)—see page 514
West (W1)—see page 438

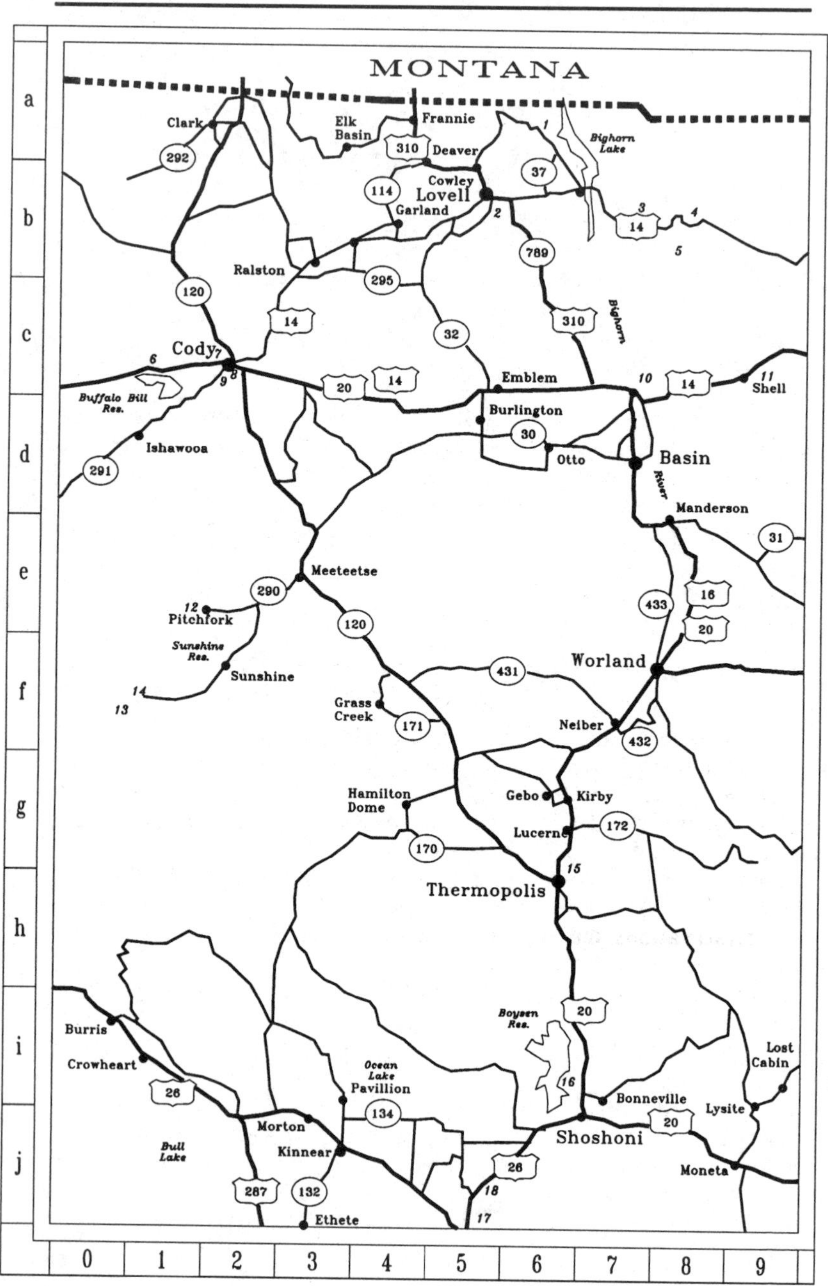

Featuring: Greys River, Bridger-Teton National Forest, Bighorn Lake, Bighorn Canyon National Recreation Area, Porcupine Falls, Bighorn National Forest, Crystal Creek, Buffalo Bill Reservoir, Shoshone River, Bighorn River, Shell Creek, Washakie Wilderness, Shoshone National Forest, Wood River, Absaroka Range

---

1) HORSESHOE BEND

Reference: on Bighorn Lake, Bighorn Canyon National Recreation Area; map W2, grid a6.

Campsites, facilities: There are 128 sites for tents, trailers or motor homes of any length. Picnic tables are provided. Piped water, pit toilets and a sanitary disposal station are also available. Pets are permitted on leashes.

Reservations, fee: No reservations necessary. Memorial Day through Labor Day, $4 fee per night; no fee remainder of the year. Open all year.

Who to contact: Phone Bighorn Canyon National Recreation Area at (307) 548-2251 or write to 20 Highway 14A East, Lovell, WY 82431.

Location: From Lovell, drive two miles east on US 14A, then 11 miles north on Highway 37 to the campground.

Trip note: This is the only campground along Bighorn Lake, so you can expect company. It's a good spot for a boating or fishing adventure though. Also bring your camera, because the area has spectacular canyons. In some places there is a half-mile vertical drop.

---

2) LOVELL CAMPER PARK

Reference: near Bighorn Lake; map W2, grid b5.

Campsites, facilities: There are 10 tent sites and five drive-through sites for trailers or motor homes of any length. Piped water and picnic tables are provided. Flush toilets, sanitary disposal station, showers and a playground are also available. Bottled gas, a store, coffee shop, laundromat and ice are located within one mile. Pets are permitted on leashes.

Reservations, fee: No reservations necessary; no fee. Open May to late September.

Who to contact: Phone (307) 548-6551 or write to P.O. Box 188, Lovell, WY 82431.

Location: In Lovell, drive to the northeast end of town on US 14A to Quebec Avenue.

Trip note: There's a two-day stay limit here, and that says it all. For many, it's an ideal spot. You get the best of both worlds. It's a small, intimate campground on the edge of a town where you can re-supply. And it's just a short drive east to Bighorn Lake and the Bighorn Canyon National Recreation Area. The visitor center for Bighorn Canyon National Recreation Area is not far from town.

3) FIVE SPRINGS FALLS

Reference: east of Lovell; map W2, grid b7.

Campsites, facilities: There are eight sites for tents, trailers or motor homes up to 22 feet long. Picnic tables are provided. Piped water and vault toilets are also available. Pets are permitted on leashes.

Reservations, fee: No reservations necessary; $5 fee per night. Open June to late October.

Who to contact: Phone the Bureau of Land Management at (307) 775-6011 or write to P.O. Box 1828, Cheyenne, WY 82001.

Location: From Lovell, drive 23 miles east on US 14A to the campground entrance road on the north side of the highway. The campground is about one mile from the highway.

Trip note: You've got to make some choices if you decide to camp here. It is set on the edge of Bighorn National Forest. The Cloud Peak Primitive Area is southeast and Bighorn Lake lies to the west. Take your pick. Access is easy here, just off the main road.

4) PORCUPINE

Reference: near Porcupine Falls, Bighorn National Forest; map W2, grid b8.

Campsites, facilities: There are 12 sites for tents, trailers or motor homes up to 22 feet long. Picnic tables are provided. Water and vault toilets are also available. Pets are permitted on leashes.

Reservations, fee: No reservations; $6 fee per night. Open June to late October.

Who to contact: Phone Bighorn National Forest at (307) 548-6541 or write to Medicine Wheel Ranger District Office, P.O. Box 367, Lovell, WY 82431.

Location: From Lovell, drive 36 miles east on US 14A, then 1.6 miles north on Forest Service Road 13 to the campground.

Trip note: This is a hiker's paradise. There are hiking trails to Porcupine Falls, Devil Canyon and Bucking Mule Falls. Bald Mountain Camp is a nearby option. Porcupine Falls are quite pretty, and there is fishing in nearby creeks.

5) BALD MOUNTAIN

Reference: on Crystal Creek, Bighorn National Forest; map W2, grid b8.

Campsites, facilities: There are two tent sites and eight sites for trailers or motor homes up to 22 feet long. Picnic tables are provided. Water and vault toilets are also available. Pets are permitted on leashes.

Reservations, fee: No reservations; $6 fee per night. Open June to late October.

Who to contact: Phone Bighorn National Forest at (307) 548-6541 or write to Medicine Wheel Ranger District Office, P.O. Box 367, Lovell, WY 82431.

Location: From Lovell, drive 36 miles east on US 14A to the campground.

Trip note: This is a pretty spot that is set on Crystal Creek in the Bighorn Mountains. For a good sidetrip, take the road on the other side of highway and head west three miles to Medicine Mountain, a place of power and mystery according to Native American legend. See trip note for Porcupine Camp for sidetrip options.

---

6) BUFFALO BILL STATE PARK

Reference: on Buffalo Bill Reservoir; map W2, grid c1.

Campsites, facilities: There are 93 sites for tents, trailers or motor homes of any length. Picnic tables are provided. Piped water, pit toilets and sanitary disposal station are also available. Pets are permitted on leashes. Boat docks and launching facilities are nearby.

Reservations, fee: No reservations; $4 fee per night plus $2 entrance fee. Open all year with limited winter facilities.

Who to contact: Phone (307) 587-9227 or write to 47 Lakeside Road, Cody, WY 82414.

Location: From Cody, drive west on US 14/16/20 for nine miles.

Trip note: This is a huge state park covering more than 10,000 acres. It borders Buffalo Bill Reservoir, where boating and fishing are popular. It's a nice park for those who want to make the short drive from Cody.

---

7) CAMP CODY

Reference: in Cody; map W2, grid c2.

Campsites, facilities: There are 53 sites for trailers or motor homes of any length. No tents are permitted. Piped water and picnic tables are provided. Flush toilets, showers, recreation hall, laundromat, ice and a swimming pool are also available. Electricity and sewer hookups are available at an additional charge. Bottled gas, a store and cafe are located within one mile. Pets are permitted on leashes.

Reservations, fee: Reservations accepted; $15 fee per night. Open all year.

Who to contact: Phone (307) 587-9730 or write to 415 Yellowstone Highway, Cody, WY 82414.

Location: From Cody, drive west on US 16 for one mile.

Trip note: This is one of a half of a dozen camps in the immediate area. It's just inside the Cody city limits, so don't expect a wilderness atmosphere, but they do offer grassy sites. Nearby recreation options include hiking trails, tennis courts and a golf course. History enthusiasts can visit the Buffalo Bill Historic Museum and the wildlife gallery across the street. And hey, they have free cable TV.

8) GATEWAY

Reference: in Cody; map W2, grid c2.

Campsites, facilities: There are 40 tent sites and 42 drive-through sites for trailers or motor homes of any length. Picnic tables are provided. Flush toilets, showers, laundromat and ice are also available. Electricity, piped water and sewer hookups are available at an additional charge. Bottled gas, a store and cafe are located within one mile. Pets and motorbikes are permitted.

Reservations, fee: Reservations accepted; $9-$12 fee per night; MasterCard and Visa accepted. Open mid-April to October.

Who to contact: Phone (307) 587-2561 or write to P.O. Box 666, Cody, WY 82414.

Location: This campground is located at the west end of Cody.

Trip note: This private park appeals to tent campers as well as motor homes cruisers. Nearby recreation options include a golf course, hiking trails and a riding stable. See trip note for Camp Cody for other sidetrip options.

9) PONDEROSA

Reference: on Shoshone River; map W2, grid c2.

Campsites, facilities: There are 80 tent sites and 102 sites for trailers or motor homes of any length. Electricity, piped water, sewer hookups and picnic tables are provided. Flush toilets, sanitary disposal station, showers, a store, laundromat, ice and a playground are also available. Bottled gas and a cafe are located within one mile. Pets and motorbikes are permitted.

Reservations, fee: Reservations accepted; $12 fee per night. Open May to mid-October.

Who to contact: Phone (307) 587-9203 or write to P.O. Box 1477, Cody, WY 82414.

Location: This campground is located in Cody on US 16.

Trip note: You get a little of both worlds here: city and country. It's set along the Shoshone River, yet it's in Cody. Nearby recreation options include a golf course, hiking trails, a riding stable and the Buffalo Bill Historic Museum.

10) GREYBULL KOA

Reference: near Bighorn River; map W2, grid c7.

Campsites, facilities: There are 23 tent sites and 37 sites for trailers or motor homes of any length. Camping cabins are also available. Piped water and picnic tables are provided. Flush toilets, bottled gas, sanitary disposal station, showers, recreation hall, a store, full-service restaurant, laundromat, ice, playground and a swimming pool are also available. Electricity, sewer hookups and cable TV are available at an additional charge. Pets and motorbikes are permitted.

Reservations, fee: Reservations accepted. $14-$18 fee per night; camping cabins are $24 per night. MasterCard and Visa accepted. Open mid-April through October.

Who to contact: Phone (307) 765-2555 or write to P.O. Box 387, Greybull, WY 82426.

Location: From US 14 in Greybull, turn east onto Fourth Avenue North, and drive four blocks. Continue north on Second Street, and drive four blocks to the campground.

Trip note: This is one of two privately developed parks in Greybull, a town located along the Bighorn River. The sites are grassy, many shaded. A golf course in the area provides a recreational possibility. Dinosaur National Monument is a short drive away, as are several mountain streams which provide good fishing.

---

11) SHELL

Reference: on Shell Creek; map W2, grid c9.

Campsites, facilities: There are 15 tent sites and 11 sites for trailers or motor homes up to 30 feet long. Electricity, piped water and picnic tables are provided. Flush toilets, sanitary disposal station, showers and a laundromat are also available. A store, coffee shop and ice are located within one mile. Pets and motorbikes are permitted.

Reservations, fee: Reservations accepted; $7-$11 fee per night. Open April through November.

Who to contact: Phone (307) 765-2342 or write to P.O. Box 16, Shell, WY 82441.

Location: From Greybull, drive 16 miles west on US 14. The campground is in Shell at the south edge of town.

Trip note: This is a privately developed camp that covers two acres. It's set near Shell Creek at the foot of the Bighorn Mountains. Many sites are grassy and shaded. Hiking and fishing are two nearby recreation options. More developed camps are located to the west in Greybull, and less developed camps to the east in Bighorn National Forest.

---

12) JACK CREEK

Reference: near Washakie Wilderness; Shoshone National Forest; map W2, grid e1.

Campsites, facilities: There are seven sites for tents, trailers or motor homes up to 21 feet long. Picnic tables are provided. Pit toilets are also available. There is **no piped water.** Pets are permitted on leashes. There are public corrals, hitching rails and feeders in the left parking area. No livestock are permitted in the campground.

Reservations, fee: No reservations necessary; no fee. Open May to late November.

Who to contact: Phone Shoshone National Forest at (307) 868-2379 or write to Greybull Ranger District, P.O. Box 158, Meeteetse, WY 82433.

Location: From Meeteetse, drive 10 miles west on Highway 290, then 20 miles west on Pitchfork Ranch Road through the oil field to the campground.

Trip note: This camp is a major jump-off for hikers heading into the Washakie Wilderness. The camp is set at the confluence of Jack Creek and the Greybull River. There are many trails and creeks in the area. It's all detailed on the Shoshone National Forest map.

13) BROWN MOUNTAIN

Reference: on Wood River, Shoshone National Forest; map W2, grid f0.

Campsites, facilities: There are six sites for tents or trailers. Picnic tables are provided. Piped water and pit toilets are also available. Pets are permitted on leashes.

Reservations, fee: No reservations necessary; $5 fee per night. Open late May through November.

Who to contact: Phone Shoshone National Forest at (307) 868-2379 or write to Greybull Ranger District, P.O. Box 158, Meeteetse, WY 82433.

Location: From Meeteetse, drive five miles southwest on Highway 290. Continue for 15.8 miles southwest on a signed county road, and then 3.2 miles west on Forest Service Road 200 to the campground.

Trip note: If Wood River Camp has too many people (like any at all), then this camp is the alternative. It's just two miles down the road. It is set along the banks of Wood River. Timber Creek Trail, accessible just west of camp, runs south along the Middle Fork of the Wood River and into the Washakie Wilderness.

14) WOOD RIVER

Reference: near Absaroka Range, Shoshone National Forest; map W2, grid f1.

Campsites, facilities: There are five sites for tents, trailers or small motor homes. Picnic tables are provided. Piped water and pit toilets are also available. Pets are permitted on leashes.

Reservations, fee: No reservations necessary; $5 fee per night. Open late May through November.

Who to contact: Phone Shoshone National Forest at (307) 868-2379 or write to Greybull Ranger District, P.O. Box 158, Meeteetse, WY 82433.

Location: From Meeteetse, drive five miles southwest on Highway 290. Continue for 15.8 miles southwest on a signed county road to the forest boundary, then three-quarters of a mile on Forest Service Road 200 to the campground.

Trip note: This is one of two camps in the immediate vicinity. Both are tiny, little-known spots. This one is located aside the Wood River.

There are several trailheads leading into the Absaroka Range. There are many streams in the area, and a Forest Service map details it all. See trip note for Brown Mountain Camp.

---

15) M-K MOBILE PARK

Reference: in Thermopolis; map W2, grid g6.

Campsites, facilities: There are 13 sites for trailers or motor homes of any length. Electricity, piped water, sewer hookups and picnic tables are provided. Flush toilets, sanitary disposal station and showers are also available. Bottled gas, a store, coffee shop, laundromat and ice are located within one mile. Pets are permitted on leashes.

Reservations, fee: Reservations accepted; $10 fee per night. Open April to October.

Who to contact: Phone (307) 864-2778 or write to 720 Shoshoni, Thermopolis, WY 82443.

Location: This campground is located at the south end of Thermopolis on US 20.

Trip note: This is a small, private park that covers just one acre. A golf course, bike paths and tennis courts are nearby. The hot mineral pool here provides a unique bonus. Fishing can be decent on the nearby Bighorn River. Another recreational option is to visit nearby Hot Springs State Park (just southeast of town), where the largest natural hot springs in the world can be found. Indoor and outdoor pools are available for use. The closest alternative is 30 miles to the south along Boysen Reservoir.

---

16) BOYSEN RESERVOIR STATE RECREATION AREA

Reference: northwest of Shoshone; map W2, grid i6.

Campsites, facilities: There are 181 sites for tents, trailers or motor homes of any length. Piped water and picnic tables are provided. Pit toilets, sanitary disposal station, a store, coffee shop, ice and a playground are also available. Some facilities are **wheelchair accessible.** Pets are permitted on leashes. Boat docks, launching facilities and rentals are located nearby.

Reservations, fee: No reservations necessary; $4 fee per night plus $2 entrance fee. Open all year with limited winter facilities.

Who to contact: Phone (307) 876-2796 or write to Shoshoni, WY 82649.

Location: From Shoshoni, drive 13 miles northwest on US 20.

Trip note: This big campground is the only camp on giant Boysen Reservoir. It's a good spot for campers, boaters and anglers. The park has boat launching facilities.

17) RUDY'S CAMPER COURT

Reference: in Riverton; map W2, grid j5.

Campsites, facilities: There are three tent sites and 21 sites for trailers or motor homes of any length. Electricity, piped water, sewer hookups and picnic tables are provided. Flush toilets, sanitary disposal station, showers and playground are also available. Bottled gas, a store, coffee shop, laundromat and ice are located within one mile. Pets are permitted on leashes.

Reservations, fee: Reservations accepted; $8.50-$13.50 fee per night. Open all year.

Who to contact: Phone (307) 856-9764 or write to 622 East Lincoln, Riverton, WY 82501.

Location: The campground is located in Riverton. Turn west on Roosevelt Avenue off US 26 at the north end of town.

Trip note: Rudy's covers just an acre and provides a layover spot for out-of-town cruisers looking for a stopping point. It's plunked right in the middle of town, surrounded by shopping centers and restaurants. The sites are graveled, with some grass and shade. A golf course provides a recreation possibility. Local attractions consist primarily of Native American celebrations, including the Riverton Rendezvous and occasional powwows.

18) OWL CREEK

Reference: near Riverton; map W2, grid j5.

Campsites, facilities: There are 20 tent sites and 19 sites for trailers or motor homes of any length. Electricity, piped water, sewer hookups and picnic tables are provided. Flush toilets, sanitary disposal station, showers, a store, laundromat, ice and a playground are also available. Pets are permitted on leashes.

Reservations, fee: Reservations accepted; $13-$16 fee per night. Open mid-May to mid-September.

Who to contact: Phone (307) 856-2869 or write to Route 1, 11124 US 26, Riverton, WY 82501.

Location: From Riverton, drive six miles east on US 26 to the campground.

Trip note: This is one of three campgrounds on the north side of Riverton and it covers four acres in a park-like setting. The sites offer grass and lots of trees. The camp is located on the Wind River Indian Reservation, which houses the Arapahoe and Shoshone tribes. A point of interest is Sacajawea's grave.

Wyoming Map W3
38 listings
Pages 480-497

North—Montana
East (W4)—see page 498
South (W7)—see page 520
West (W2)—see page 470

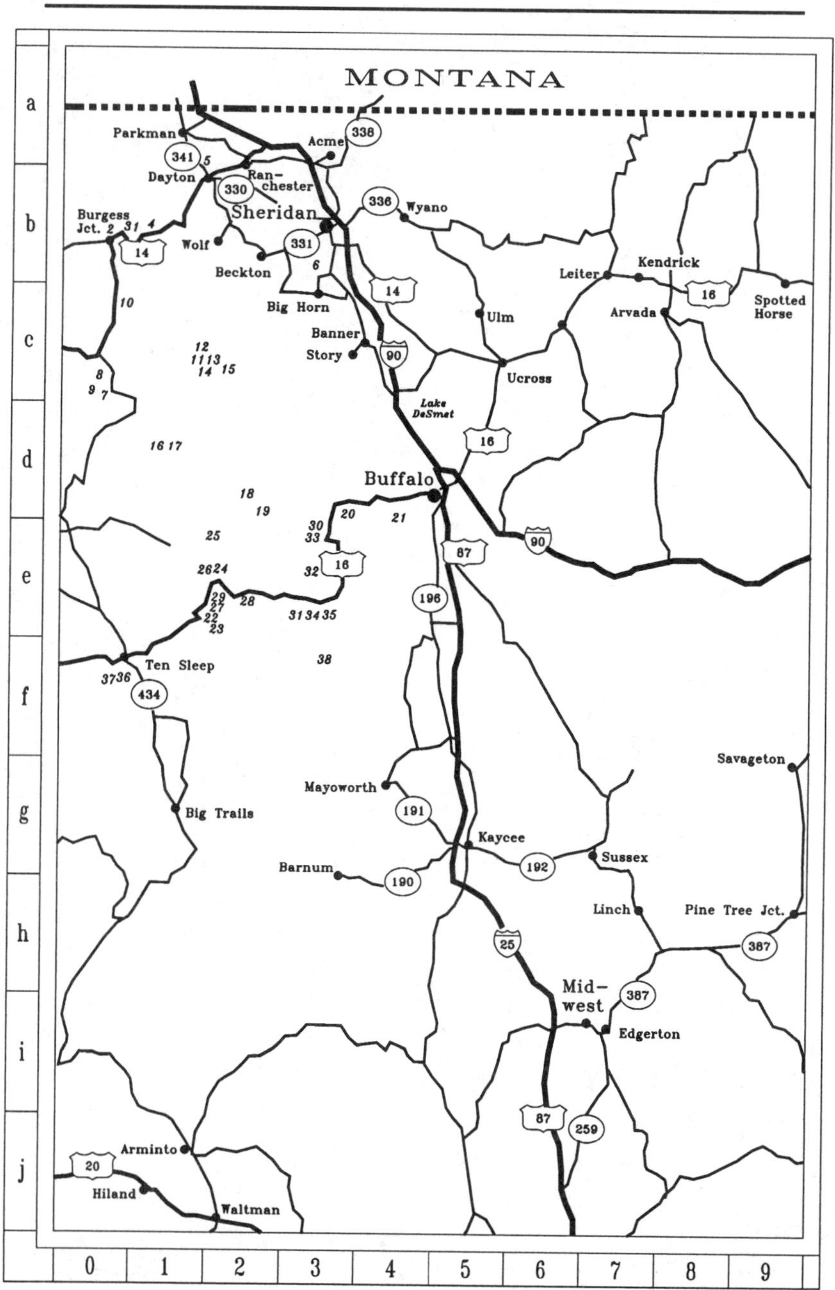

Featuring: South Tongue River, Bighorn National Forest, North Tongue River, Shell Creek, East Fork of Big Goose Creek, Cloud Peak Wilderness, Cloud Peak Primitive Area, West Fork of Little Goose Creek, Paint Rock Creek, Tensleep Lake, Middle Fork of Clear Creek, Tensleep Canyon, Meadowlark Lake, Tensleep Creek, Muddy Creek, South Fork of Clear Creek, Crazy Woman Creek, Doyle Creek

---

1) PRUNE CREEK

Reference: on South Tongue River, Bighorn National Forest; map W3, grid b0.

Campsites, facilities: There are 21 sites for tents, trailers or motor homes up to 32 feet. Picnic tables are provided. Water and vault toilets are also available. A store, coffee shop and ice are located within one mile. Pets are permitted on leashes. Boat docks and launching facilities are nearby. No motor boats are allowed however.

Reservations, fee: No reservations; $7 fee per night. Open June to late October.

Who to contact: Phone Bighorn National Forest at (307) 672-0751 or write to Supervisor's Office, 1969 South Sheridan Avenue, Sheridan, WY 82801.

Location: From Dayton, drive southwest on US 14 for 26 miles to the campground.

Trip note: This is one in a series of camps set on the South Tongue River. This one is particularly attractive since it is set near where Prune Creek pours into the river. In addition, a trail follows the river south for about five miles routing hikers to Tie Flume Camp.

---

2) TIE FLUME

Reference: on South Tongue River, Bighorn National Forest; map W3, grid b0.

Campsites, facilities: There are 25 sites for tents, trailers or motor homes up to 22 feet. Picnic tables are provided. Water and vault toilets are also available. Pets are permitted on leashes.

Reservations, fee: Reserve through MISTIX at (800) 283-CAMP ($6 MISTIX fee); $6 fee per night. Open mid-June to late October.

Who to contact: Phone Bighorn National Forest at (307) 672-0751 or write to Supervisor's Office, 1969 South Sheridan Avenue, Sheridan, WY 82801.

Location: From Dayton, drive southwest on US 14 for 34 miles, then east for two miles on Forest Service Road 26 to the campground.

Trip note: This is one in a series of camps set along the South Tongue River. There are several trails in the area including one leading to Prune Creek Camp. Fishing on the Tongue River can be quite good.

3) NORTH TONGUE

Reference: on North Tongue River, Bighorn National Forest; map W3, grid b0.

Campsites, facilities: There are four tent sites and seven sites for trailers or motor homes up to 22 feet. Picnic tables are provided. Vault toilets and water are also available. A sanitary disposal station is located nearby. A store, coffee shop and ice are located within one mile. Pets are permitted on leashes.

Reservations, fee: No reservations; $6 fee per night. Open June to late September.

Who to contact: Phone Bighorn National Forest at (307) 672-0751 or write to Supervisor's Office, 1969 South Sheridan Avenue, Sheridan, WY 82801.

Location: From Dayton, drive 29 miles southwest on US 14 and one mile north on Forest Service Road 15 to the campground.

Trip note: There are several rugged and primitive roads in the area. From the camp you get direct access to the North Tongue River. Burgess Picnic Area and Burgess Ranger Station are both located a short distance to the north.

4) SIBLEY LAKE

Reference: in Bighorn National Forest; map W3, grid b1.

Campsites, facilities: There are 10 sites for tents or trailers up to 16 feet. Picnic tables are provided. Piped water and vault toilets are also available. A store, coffee shop and ice are located within five miles. Pets are permitted on leashes. Boat docks and launching facilities are nearby, but no motors are permitted on the lake.

Reservations, fee: No reservations; $7 fee per night. Open mid-June to late September.

Who to contact: Phone Bighorn National Forest at (307) 672-0751 or write to Supervisor's Office, 1969 South Sheridan Avenue, Sheridan, WY 82801.

Location: From Dayton, drive southwest on US 14 for 25 miles to the campground.

Trip note: Whether you are ambitious are not, this is a good spot. It is set on little Sibley Lake, where you can fish or just kick back and watch the trout jump. No motorized craft are allowed on the lake, which makes for a peaceful, quiet setting. For hikers who want a challenge, take the nearby trail to the Black Mountain Lookout.

5) FOOTHILLS

Reference: on Tongue River; map W3, grid b1.

Campsites, facilities: There are 35 tent sites and 35 sites for trailers or motor homes of any length. Picnic tables are provided. Flush toilets, sanitary disposal station, laundromat and a playground are also available.

Electricity, piped water, sewer hookups and showers are available at an additional charge. A store, coffee shop and ice are located within one mile. Pets and motorbikes are permitted. A motel is adjacent to the campground.

Reservations, fee: Reservations accepted; $8.50-$13.50 fee per night. Open mid-April to late November.

Who to contact: Phone (307) 655-2547 or write to P.O. Box 174, Dayton, WY 82836.

Location: This campground is located in Dayton, at the east end of town on US 14.

Trip note: This is the only campground in the area. It covers five acres and is set on the Tongue River, right on the edge of town. Dayton is a tiny town, with a population of only 600, but it provides lots of recreation options. The Tongue River is a blue ribbon trout stream, and the surrounding area is popular with big game hunters. Hikers can explore the surrounding national forest. The camp sits at the base of the Bighorn Mountains at 4,000 feet elevation, one of the lowest locations in the state.

---

6) KOA BIGHORN

Reference: in Sheridan; map W3, grid b3.

Campsites, facilities: There are 25 tent sites and 77 sites for trailers or motor homes of any length. Camping cabins are also available. Piped water and picnic tables are provided. Flush toilets, bottled gas, sanitary disposal station, showers, recreation hall, a store, laundromat, ice, playground, and a swimming pool are also available. Electricity and sewer hookups are available at an additional charge. A coffee shop is located within one mile. Pets and motorbikes are permitted.

Reservations, fee: Reservations accepted; $14-$18 fee per night; camping cabins are $24 per night. MasterCard and Visa accepted. Open May to early October, including limited and some off-season weekends.

Who to contact: Phone (307) 674-8766 or write to 63 Decker Road, P.O. Box 35A, Sheridan, WY 82801.

Location: From Interstate 90 in Sheridan, take the Port of Entry exit 20 and drive a half mile north on Highway 338 to the campground.

Trip note: Sheridan has just one campground and this is it. So be happy with it, or be prepared to drive 20 miles to Dayton or 35 miles to Buffalo. This camp covers 15 acres and has a golf course in the area. If you plan on sticking around, a travel information center is available just off Interstate 90.

---

7) RANGER CREEK

Reference: near Shell Creek, Bighorn National Forest; map W3, grid c0.

Campsites, facilities: There are eight tent sites and two sites for trailers or motor homes up to 22 feet long. Picnic tables are provided. Water and pit toilets are also available. Pets are permitted on leashes.

Reservations, fee: No reservations; $6 fee per night. Open June to late October.

Who to contact: Phone Bighorn National Forest at (307) 765-4435 or write to Paintrock Ranger District, P.O. Box 831, Greybull, WY 82426.

Location: From Shell, drive northeast on US 14 for 15.8 miles and east on Forest Service Road 17 for two miles to the campground.

Trip note: This camp is set along Shell Creek and has a ranger station nearby where you can get all your questions answered and obtain maps of the area that can help to detail hiking and other recreation options. There is fishing in Shell Creek for determined anglers. Shell Creek Trail passes near the camp, leading up east to little Adelaide Lake. Horse rentals are available within a mile.

---

8) CABIN CREEK

Reference: northeast of Shell, Bighorn National Forest; map W3, grid c0.

Campsites, facilities: There are two tent sites and two sites for trailers or motor homes up to 22 feet long. Picnic tables are provided. Water and pit toilets are also available. Pets are permitted on leashes.

Reservations, fee: No reservations; $5 fee per night. Open June to late October.

Who to contact: Phone Bighorn National Forest at (307) 765-4435 or write to Paintrock Ranger District, P.O. Box 831, Greybull, WY 82426.

Location: From Shell, drive northeast on US 14 for 15.8 miles and east on Forest Service Road 17 for a quarter mile to the campground.

Trip note: This is a tiny spot, primitive and located very close to Cabin Creek Trailer Park and is also along Cabin Creek. The campground itself doesn't have much to offer, but there is some good hiking in the area, as well as stream fishing. Consider visiting Shell Falls, a few miles west of camp.

---

9) SHELL CREEK

Reference: northeast of Shell, Bighorn National Forest; map W3, grid c0.

Campsites, facilities: There are 11 tent sites. Picnic tables are provided. Water and pit toilets are also available. Pets are permitted on leashes.

Reservations, fee: No reservations; $6 fee per night. Open June to late October.

Who to contact: Phone Bighorn National Forest at (307) 765-4435 or write to Paintrock Ranger District, P.O. Box 831, Greybull, WY 82426.

Location: From Shell, drive northeast on US 14 for 15.8 miles and south on Forest Service Road 17 for 1.2 miles to the campground.

Trip note: This is a nearby option to Ranger Creek Camp and is also set on Shell Creek. It is fairly small, with shaded sites and lots of trees. There are hiking trails leading into the backcountry and a riding stable is nearby.

---

10) DEAD SWEDE

Reference: on South Tongue River, Bighorn National Forest; map W3, grid c0.

Campsites, facilities: There are 22 sites for tents, trailers or motor homes up to 22 feet. Picnic tables are provided. Water and vault toilets are also available. Pets are permitted on leashes.

Reservations, fee: Reserve through MISTIX at (800) 283-CAMP; $6 fee per night. Open mid-June to late October.

Who to contact: Phone Bighorn National Forest at (307) 672-0751 or write to Supervisor's Office, 1969 South Sheridan Avenue, Sheridan, WY 82801.

Location: From Dayton, drive southwest on US 14 for 34 miles and east for three miles on Forest Service Road 26 to the campground.

Trip note: Don't ask how this camp got its name. But we can tell you it is located along the South Tongue River and there are no dead Swedes strewn around. It's a real pretty spot with some good hiking trails in the adjacent wildlands. It's all detailed on a Forest Service map. Good fishing prospects can be found here.

---

11) CROSS CREEK

Reference: on the East Fork of Big Goose Creek, Bighorn National Forest; map W3, grid c1.

Campsites, facilities: There are three tent sites. Picnic tables are provided. Pit toilets are also available. There is **no piped water.** Pets are permitted on leashes.

Reservations, fee: No reservations; no fee. Open June to late October.

Who to contact: Phone Bighorn National Forest at (307) 672-0751 or write to Supervisor's Office, 1969 South Sheridan Avenue, Sheridan, WY 82801.

Location: From Bighorn, drive southwest on County Road 335 for 9.3 miles, then continue southwest on Forest Service Road 26 for eight miles. Turn on Forest Service Road 293 and proceed southwest for six miles to the campground. You need a four-wheel-drive vehicle for the last eight miles.

Trip note: Bring your four-wheel-drive vehicle, bring your own drinking water and bring some hiking boots. If that list isn't too much for you, then try this camp site on for size. It might fit pretty well. This is one of the prime base camps for a trip into the Cloud Peak Wilderness. It's set between Park and Bighorn Reservoirs on the East Fork of Big Goose Creek.

12) COFFEEN PARK

Reference: near Cloud Peak Wilderness, Bighorn National Forest; map W3, grid c1.

Campsites, facilities: There are five tent sites. Picnic tables are provided. Pit toilets and water are also available. Pets are permitted on leashes.

Reservations, fee: No reservations; no fee. Open July to late October.

Who to contact: Phone Bighorn National Forest at (307) 672-0751 or write to Supervisor's Office, 1969 South Sheridan Avenue, Sheridan, WY 82801.

Location: From Bighorn, drive southwest on County Road 335 for 9.3 miles, then continue southwest on Forest Service Road 26 for eight miles. Turn on Forest Service Road 293 and proceed southwest for eight miles to the campground (you need a four-wheel-drive vehicle for the last eight miles), park your car and hike into the campground.

Trip note: A small, primitive camp set on the edge of the Cloud Peak Wilderness. It takes a four-wheel-drive vehicle, then some hoofin' to make it here, but it's a good jump-off point for backpackers. A trail leads into the wilderness, providing access to many remote lakes. The camp itself is set along the East Fork of Big Goose Creek.

13) EAST FORK

Reference: on the East Fork of Big Goose Creek, Bighorn National Forest; map W3, grid c1.

Campsites, facilities: There are 11 sites for tents, trailers or motor homes up to 16 feet. Picnic tables are provided. Water and vault toilets are also available. Pets are permitted on leashes.

Reservations, fee: No reservations; $4 fee per night. Open mid-June to late October.

Who to contact: Phone Bighorn National Forest at (307) 672-0751 or write to Supervisor's Office, 1969 South Sheridan Avenue, Sheridan, WY 82801.

Location: From Bighorn, drive southwest on County Road 335 for 9.3 miles, southwest on Forest Service Road 26 for eight miles (trailers not advised), then south on Forest Service Road 293 for a half mile to campground.

Trip note: This is a good option to Ranger Creek Camp and is located just a mile southeast of that camp. It is located on the East Fork of Big Goose Creek. It's about three miles by dirt road to three reservoirs. Hikers can use this spot as a jump-off point. Trails start here that are routed to the Cloud Peak Wilderness.

14) RANGER CREEK

Reference: near Cloud Peak Wilderness, Bighorn National Forest; map W3, grid c1.

Campsites, facilities: There are 11 sites for tents, trailers or motor homes up to 16 feet. Picnic tables are provided. Water and vault toilets are also available. Pets are permitted on leashes.

Reservations, fee: No reservations; $4 fee per night. Open mid-June to late October.

Who to contact: Phone Bighorn National Forest at (307) 672-0751 or write to Supervisor's Office, 1969 South Sheridan Avenue, Sheridan, WY 82833.

Location: From Bighorn, drive 9.3 miles southwest on County Road 335 and 10 miles southwest on Forest Service Road 26 to the campground. (Because of the steep grades, trailers are not advised from the Bighorn side.)

Trip note: This is a good jump-off point for backpackers looking for a multi-day adventure. The camp is set on Ranger Creek and has trails that lead to Twin Lakes (an eight miler) and to the Cloud Peak Wilderness of the Bighorn Mountains. A map is essential. See the trip note for East Fork Camp for other possibilities.

---

15) LITTLE GOOSE

Reference: on the West Fork of Little Goose Creek, Bighorn National Forest; map W3, grid c2.

Campsites, facilities: There are three tent sites. Picnic tables are provided. Pit toilets and water are available. Pets are permitted on leashes.

Reservations, fee: No reservations; no fee. Open June to late October.

Who to contact: Phone Bighorn National Forest at (307) 672-0751 or write to Supervisor's Office, 1969 South Sheridan Avenue, Sheridan, WY 82801.

Location: From Bighorn, drive southwest on County Road 335 for 9.3 mile, west on Forest Service Road 314 for one mile, and south for 1.5 miles on a dirt road (four-wheel-drive vehicles needed).

Trip note: This is a tiny, little-known, little-used camp set beside the West Fork of Little Goose Creek. It takes a four-wheel-drive vehicle to get here, but once done, there are several primitive roads you can explore. You can also go for broke with a backpack and hit the trail. Either way you go, a Forest Service map is strongly advised.

---

16) PAINTROCK LAKES COMPLEX

Reference: near Cloud Peak Wilderness, Bighorn National Forest; map W3, grid d1.

Campsites, facilities: There are 17 sites for tents. No trailers are permitted. Picnic tables are provided. Water and pit toilets are also available. Pets are permitted on leashes. Boat docks are nearby.

Reservations, fee: No reservations; $5 fee per night. Open June to late October.

Who to contact: Phone Bighorn National Forest at (307) 765-4435 or write to Paintrock Ranger District, P.O. Box 831, Greybull, WY 82426.

Location: From Shell, drive northeast on US 14 for 15.8 miles and southeast on Forest Service Road 17 for 25.7 miles to the campground.

Trip note: This site consists of two small campgrounds that are a half mile apart: Upper and Lower Paintrock Lakes. The camp at Upper Paintrock Lake is concessionaire operated, and fees there are subject to change. There are two hiking trails leading out of Lower Paintrock Lake into the Cloud Peak Wilderness, making it ideal for a backpacker's base camp. An alternate camp is Medicine Lodge Lake.

---

17) MEDICINE LODGE LAKE

Reference: near Cloud Peak Wilderness, Bighorn National Forest; map W3, grid d1.

Campsites, facilities: There are two tent sites and six sites for trailers or motor homes up to 16 feet long. Picnic tables are provided. Water and vault toilets are also available. Pets are permitted on leashes. Boat docks are nearby.

Reservations, fee: No reservations; $5 fee per night. Open June to late October.

Who to contact: Phone Bighorn National Forest at (307) 765-4435 or write to P.O. Box 831, Greybull, WY 82426.

Location: From Shell, drive northeast on US 14 for 15.8 miles and southeast on Forest Service Road 17 for 25 miles to the campground. These are poor roads for trailers.

Trip note: This is a beautiful spot set amid four small lakes. You just might want to lean against a rock and watch the water. Or, you can take the trails that lead east into the Cloud Peak Wilderness in the Bighorn Mountains too. This camp generally gets less use than the nearby Paintrock Lakes Complex, and may provide a bit more privacy.

---

18) WEST TENSLEEP LAKE

Reference: in Bighorn National Forest; map W3, grid d2.

Campsites, facilities: There are 10 sites for tents, trailers or motor homes up to 16 feet long. Hand-pumped water and picnic tables are provided. Pit toilets and firewood are also available. Pets are permitted on leashes.

Reservations, fee: Reserve through MISTIX at (800) 283-CAMP ($6 MISTIX fee); $6 fee per night. Open mid-June to late October.

Who to contact: Phone Bighorn National Forest at (307) 347-8291 or write to Tensleep Ranger District, 2009 Bighorn Avenue, Worland, WY 82401.

Location: From Ten Sleep, drive 20 miles northeast on US 16, and 7.5 miles north on Forest Service Road 27 to the campground.

Trip note: In many ways, this can be an ideal spot. It's small and pretty. Set on the southern end of West Tensleep Lake, it's a long, narrow lake on Tensleep Creek. In addition, trails here lead you along Middle Creek or Tensleep Creek and into the Cloud Peak Wilderness. You could set up shop here for quite awhile (note the 14-day limit, though). Fishing can be good at Tensleep Lake.

---

19) DEER PARK

Reference: near West Tensleep Lake, Bighorn National Forest; map W3, grid d2.

Campsites, facilities: There are seven sites for tents, trailers or motor homes up to 22 feet long. Picnic tables are provided. Water and vault toilets are also available. Pets are permitted on leashes.

Reservations, fee: No reservations; $6 fee per night. Open June to late October.

Who to contact: Phone Bighorn National Forest at (307) 347-8291 or write to Tensleep Ranger District, 2009 Bighorn Avenue, Worland, WY 82401.

Location: From Ten Sleep, drive 20 miles northeast on US 16, and six miles north on Forest Service Road 27 to the campground.

Trip note: Trails from this camp are routed southeast to pretty East Tensleep Lake and north to backcountry lakes and the Cloud Peak Wilderness. This is a nearby option to West Tensleep Camp at West Tensleep Lake, located one mile to the north.

---

20) MIDDLE FORK

Reference: on the Middle Fork of Clear Creek, Bighorn National Forest; map W3, grid d3.

Campsites, facilities: There are three tent sites and six sites for trailers or motor homes up to 16 feet long. Picnic tables are provided. Water and vault toilets are also available. A store, coffee shop and ice are located within one mile. Pets are permitted on leashes.

Reservations, fee: Reserve through MISTIX at (800) 283-CAMP ($6 MISTIX fee); $7 fee per night. Open Memorial Day to mid-September.

Who to contact: Phone Bighorn National Forest at (307) 684-7981 or write to Buffalo Ranger District, 300 Spruce Street, Buffalo, WY 82834.

Location: From Buffalo, drive 13.5 miles west on US 16.

Trip note: This is one in a series of campgrounds set just off the main road. This one is located beside the Middle Fork of Clear Creek at 7,400-foot elevation. If you go across the road, you will find a trail that follows along the creek for a stretch. Fishing can be decent here.

21) BIGHORN MOUNTAIN

Reference: near Buffalo; map W3, grid d4.

Campsites, facilities: There are 30 tent sites and 40 sites for trailers or motor homes of any length. Picnic tables are provided. Flush toilets, sanitary disposal station, showers, recreation hall, a store, gift shop, laundromat, ice, playground and a swimming pool are also available. Pets are permitted on leashes.

Reservations, fee: Reservations accepted; $7-$15.50 fee per night. Open all year with limited winter facilities.

Who to contact: Phone (307) 684-2307 or write to 8935 US Highway 16 West, P.O. Box 108, Buffalo, WY 82834.

Location: From Buffalo, drive two miles west on US 16.

Trip note: This is one of three choices in the immediate Buffalo area. This privately developed park has space for tenters which is a bonus, and covers about 10 acres. A sidetrip option is to visit the Jim Gatchell Museum in Buffalo. The local golf course provides another recreational possibility.

22) LEIGH CREEK

Reference: in Tensleep Canyon, Bighorn National Forest; map W3, grid e1.

Campsites, facilities: There are four tent sites and seven sites for trailers or motor homes up to 16 feet long. Picnic tables are provided. Hand-pumped water and vault toilets are also available. A coffee shop is located within five miles. Pets are permitted on leashes.

Reservations: No reservations necessary; $6 fee per night. Open mid-May to late October.

Who to contact: Phone Bighorn National Forest at (307) 347-8291 or write to Tensleep Ranger District, 2009 Bighorn Avenue, Worland, WY 82401.

Location: From Ten Sleep, drive northeast on US 16 for eight miles, and east on Forest Service Road 18 for one mile to the campground.

Trip note: This is one of two Forest Service campgrounds in the immediate area. This one is nestled in Tensleep Canyon at the confluence of Leigh Creek and Tensleep Creek. Fishing for brook trout can be good here. Nearby Tensleep Creek Camp provides an alternative.

23) TENSLEEP CREEK

Reference: northeast of Ten Sleep, Bighorn National Forest; map W3, grid e1.

Campsites, facilities: There are five tent sites. Picnic tables are provided. Water and vault toilets are also available. A coffee shop is located within five miles. Pets are permitted on leashes.

Reservations, fee: No reservations necessary; $6 fee per night. Open mid-May to late October.

Who to contact: Phone Bighorn National Forest at (307) 347-8291 or write to Tensleep Ranger District, 2009 Bighorn Avenue, Worland, WY 82401.

Location: From Ten Sleep, drive northeast on US 16 for eight miles, and east on Forest Service Road 18 for two miles to the campground.

Trip note: If you're a tent camper who doesn't like motor homes, this is the spot. It's a tiny camp, and there just isn't room for motor homes or trailers. It is set at 5,400 feet, about a half mile north of Leigh Creek Camp on Tensleep Creek.

---

24) SITTING BULL

Reference: near Meadowlark Lake, Bighorn National Forest; map W3, grid e2.

Campsites, facilities: There are 43 sites for tents, trailers or motor homes up to 22 feet long. Picnic tables are provided. Water and vault toilets are also available. A store, coffee shop and ice are located within five miles. Pets are permitted on leashes. Boat docks, launching facilities and rentals are nearby.

Reservations, fee: Reserve through MISTIX at (800) 283-CAMP ($6 MISTIX fee); $7 fee per night. Open June to late October.

Who to contact: Phone Bighorn National Forest at (307) 347-8291 or write to Tensleep Ranger District, 2009 Bighorn Avenue, Worland, WY 82401.

Location: From Ten Sleep, drive 23 miles northeast on US 16, and one mile north on Forest Service Road 432 to the campground.

Trip note: This is one of five camps set in the vicinity of Meadowlark Lake. The camp is just one mile from the main road and about one mile from the lake. It provides good access both to the lake and also to the backcountry. A trail from camp is routed past some small lakes in the wildlands to both the north and east. A nature trail is also provided within the camp.

---

25) ISLAND PARK

Reference: on Tensleep Creek; map W3, grid e2.

Campsites, facilities: There are 10 sites for tents, trailers or motor homes up to 22 feet long. Picnic tables are provided. Water and vault toilets are also available. A store, coffee shop and ice are located within five miles. Some facilities are **wheelchair accessible.** Pets are permitted on leashes. Boat docks are nearby.

Reservations, fee: No reservations necessary; $6 fee per night. Open mid-June to late October.

Who to contact: Phone Bighorn National Forest at (307) 347-8291 or write to Tensleep Ranger District, 2009 Bighorn Avenue, Worland, WY 82401.

Location: From Ten Sleep, drive 20 miles northeast on US 16, and four miles north on Forest Service Road 27 to the campground.

Trip note: This is a good base camp for backpackers. There are several other options in the area. The camp is set along Tensleep Creek, off the main road about six miles from Meadowlark Lake. But you can expect company at the lake. Another option is to hike the trail out from camp, which heads east to East Tensleep Lake and continues north, connecting to a network of trails that lead into the Cloud Peak Wilderness.

---

26) BULL CREEK

Reference: on Meadowlark Lake, Bighorn National Forest; map W3, grid e2.

Campsites, facilities: There are 10 sites for tents, trailers or motor homes up to 16 feet long. Picnic tables are provided. Vault toilets are available. A store, coffee shop and ice are located within one mile. Water is available nearby (but not in the camp itself). Pets are permitted on leashes. Boat docks, launching facilities and rentals are nearby.

Reservations, fee: No reservations necessary; no fee. Open June to late October.

Who to contact: Phone Bighorn National Forest at (307) 347-8291 or write to Tensleep Ranger District, 2009 Bighorn Avenue, Worland, WY 82401.

Location: From Ten Sleep, drive 25 miles northeast on US 16 and a half mile north on Forest Service Road 433 to the campground.

Trip note: This is the most primitive of the two camps on Meadowlark Lake. This one is set on the southeast shore. Four-wheel-drive trails are in the area. Lakeview Campground is a nearby option.

---

27) BOULDER PARK

Reference: on Tensleep Creek; map W3, grid e2.

Campsites, facilities: There are 34 sites for tents, trailers or motor homes up to 22 feet long. Picnic tables are provided. Water and vault toilets are also available. A store, coffee shop and ice are located adjacent to the campground. Pets are permitted on leashes. Boat docks, launching facilities and rentals are nearby.

Reservations, fee: Reservations accepted for long-term camping (30-day limit); phone MISTIX at (800) 283-CAMP. $7 fee per night. Open June to September.

Who to contact: Phone Bighorn National Forest at (307) 347-8291 or write to Tensleep Ranger District, 2009 Bighorn Avenue, Worland, WY 82401.

Location: From Ten Sleep, drive northeast 20 miles on US 16, then a half mile west on Forest Service Road 27.

Trip note: This is a good spot for boaters, because the camp is located just two miles from Meadowlark Lake. The camp is set in Tensleep Canyon along Tensleep Creek. There are no hiking trails in the immediate area, but four-wheel-drive trails run nearby along the creek.

28) LAKEVIEW

Reference: on Meadowlark Lake, Bighorn National Forest; map W3, grid e2.

Campsites, facilities: There are 11 sites for tents, trailers or motor homes up to 22 feet long. Picnic tables are provided. Vault toilets are also available. There is **no piped water.** A store, coffee shop and ice are located within one mile. Some facilities are **wheelchair accessible.** Pets are permitted on leashes. Boat docks, launching facilities and rentals are nearby.

Reservations, fee: Reserve through MISTIX at (800) 283-CAMP ($6 MISTIX fee); $7 fee per night. Open June to late October.

Who to contact: Phone Bighorn National Forest at (307) 347-8291 or write to Tensleep Ranger District, 2009 Bighorn Avenue, Worland, WY 82401.

Location: From Ten Sleep, drive 24 miles northeast on US 16.

Trip note: Lakeview Camp is located on the northeast shore of Meadowlark Lake, a short way from Bull Creek Camp. It offers many amenities, including full boating facilities and a grocery store, but alas, there's no drinking water.

29) DEER HAVEN LODGE

Reference: near Meadowlark Lake; map W3, grid e2.

Campsites, facilities: There are 15 sites for trailers or motor homes. Electricity, piped water and sewer hookups are provided. A full service restaurant is also available. Flush toilets and showers are available. There are also 11 cabins available.

Reservations, fee: No reservations necessary; $5-$10 fee per night; Cabins are $20-$35 per night. Open year-round.

Who to contact: Phone (307) 366-2449.

Location: From Ten Sleep, drive 19 miles east on US 16 to the lodge and campground.

Trip note: Campers with trailers or motor homes can use this spot as a base camp for a fishing or hunting expedition. During summer, fishing can be good at nearby Meadowlark Lake in Bighorn National Forest.

30) TIE HACK

Reference: on the South Fork of Clear Creek, Bighorn National Forest; map W3, grid e3.

Campsites, facilities: There are nine sites for tents, trailers or motor homes up to 16 feet long. Picnic tables are provided. Water and vault toilets are also available. A store, coffee shop and ice are located within five miles. Pets are permitted on leashes.

Reservations, fee: No reservations; $6 fee per night. Open mid-May to late October.

Who to contact: Phone Bighorn National Forest at (307) 684-7981 or write to Buffalo Ranger District, 300 Spruce Street, Buffalo, WY 82834.

Location: From Buffalo, drive 14.5 miles west on US 16, and 1.6 miles east on Forest Service Road 21.

Trip note: If you don't like the looks of South Fork Camp, try this one on for size. It is located just 1.5 miles from South Fork Camp and is set on the South Fork of Clear Creek. It's good spot for hikers with a trail from camp leading to the Middle Fork of Clear Creek and a number of other short trails available nearby.

---

31) LOST CABIN

Reference: on Muddy Creek, Bighorn National Forest; map W3, grid e3.

Campsites, facilities: There are 20 sites for tents, trailers or motor homes up to 32 feet long. Picnic tables are provided. Water and vault toilets are also available. A store, coffee shop and ice are located within 10 miles. Pets are permitted on leashes.

Reservations, fee: Reserve through MISTIX at (800) 283-CAMP ($6 MISTIX fee); $6 fee per night. Open mid-May to late October.

Who to contact: Phone Bighorn National Forest at (307) 684-7981 or write to Buffalo Ranger District, 300 Spruce Street, Buffalo, WY 82834.

Location: From Buffalo, drive 26 miles southwest on US 16.

Trip note: Easy access is the highlight here. The camp is set just a half mile from the main road along Muddy Creek. There are long, level pull-through sites here. Crazy Woman Camp and primitive Canyon Camp provide nearby options. Despite its name, Muddy Creek can offer some pretty good fishing prospects.

---

32) SOUTH FORK

Reference: on the South Fork of Clear Creek, Bighorn National Forest; map W3, grid e3.

Campsites, facilities: There are five tent sites and 10 sites for trailers or motor homes up to 16 feet long. Picnic tables are provided. Water and vault toilets are also available. A store, coffee shop and ice are located within one mile. Pets are permitted on leashes.

Reservations, fee: Reserve through MISTIX at (800) 283-CAMP ($6 MISTIX fee); $7 fee per night. Open Memorial Day to mid-September.

Who to contact: Phone Bighorn National Forest at (307) 684-7981 or write to Buffalo Ranger District, 300 Spruce Street, Buffalo, WY 82834.

Location: From Buffalo, drive 15 miles west on US 16.

Trip note: This is an easy-to-reach Forest Service campground set along the South Fork of Clear Creek. A Forest Service road just north of the camp will lead you east to a network of hiking trails.

---

33) CIRCLE PARK

Reference: near Cloud Peak Wilderness, Bighorn National Forest; map W3, grid e3.

Campsites, facilities: There are four tent sites and six sites for trailers or motor homes up to 16 feet long. Picnic tables are provided. Water and vault toilets are also available. A store, coffee shop and ice are located within five miles. Pets are permitted on leashes.

Reservations, fee: No reservations necessary; $6 fee per night. Open mid-May to mid-September.

Who to contact: Phone Bighorn National Forest at (307) 684-7981 or write to Buffalo Ranger District, 300 Spruce Street, Buffalo, WY 82834.

Location: From Buffalo, drive 14.5 miles west on US 16, and 2.5 miles west on Forest Service Road 20 to the campground.

Trip note: This is the jump-off point for backpackers who want access to the Cloud Peak Wilderness. The camp is at the end of the Forest Service road. A trail out of camp leads to several small lakes in the wilderness. Nature trails are provided within the camp boundaries as well.

---

34) CRAZY WOMAN

Reference: on Crazy Woman Creek, Bighorn National Forest; map W3, grid e3.

Campsites, facilities: There are six tent sites. Picnic tables are provided. Water, vault toilets and firewood are also available. A store, coffee shop and ice are located within eight miles. Pets are permitted on leashes.

Reservations, fee: No reservations necessary; $6 fee per night. Open mid-May to mid-September.

Who to contact: Phone Bighorn National Forest at (307) 684-7981 or write to Buffalo Ranger District, 300 Spruce Street, Buffalo, WY 82834.

Location: From Buffalo, drive 26 miles southwest on US 16.

Trip note: We looked and looked, but couldn't find any crazy women around here. So you'll have to settle for a nice, little spot along a stream that is named Crazy Woman Creek. It's primarily a layover spot. A trail to the north leads west along Goodman Creek, with views of Sheep Mountain. It's three miles from Lost Cabin Camp.

---

35) CANYON

Reference: on the North Fork of Crazy Woman Creek, Bighorn National Forest; map W3, grid e3.

Campsites, facilities: There are four tent sites. Picnic tables are provided. Vault toilets are also available. There is **no piped water.** Pets are permitted on leashes.

Reservations, fee: No reservations necessary; no fee. Open mid-May to late September.

Who to contact: Phone Bighorn National Forest at (307) 684-7981 or write to Buffalo Ranger District, 300 Spruce Street, Buffalo, WY 82834.

Location: From Buffalo, drive 26 miles southwest on US 16, and two miles east on a Forest Service Road 33 to the campground.

Trip note: This is a quieter, smaller alternative to some of the nearby camps. This camp is far enough off the main road (two miles) to be in a more rustic setting, and is set on the North Fork of Crazy Woman Creek, where you can pull up a seat, throw in a line, and just enjoy the silence.

---

36) CIRCLE 8

Reference: near Tensleep Creek; map W3, grid f0.

Campsites, facilities: There are 10 tent sites and eight sites for trailers or motor homes of any length. Electricity, piped water, sewer hookups and picnic tables are provided. Flush toilets, bottled gas, showers, laundromat and ice are also available. Sanitary disposal station, a store and a coffee shop are located within one mile. Pets are permitted on leashes. A motel is adjacent to the campground.

Reservations, fee: Reservations accepted; $8-$10 fee per night; MasterCard and Visa accepted. Open April through October.

Who to contact: Phone (307) 366-2320 or write to P.O. Box 50, Ten Sleep, WY 82442.

Location: This campground is located in downtown Ten Sleep.

Trip note: Set near Tensleep Creek, this site covers two acres. It's one of two privately developed camps in town. This one is slightly more urban than Flagstaff, being set directly in town. Sites are paved and graveled.

---

37) FLAGSTAFF

Reference: near Tensleep Creek; map W3, grid f0.

Campsites, facilities: There are 10 tent sites and 44 sites for trailers or motor homes of any length. Electricity, piped water, sewer hookups and picnic tables are provided. Flush toilets, sanitary disposal station, showers, firewood, recreation hall, laundromat and ice are also available. Bottled gas, a store and coffee shop are located within one mile. Pets are permitted on leashes.

Reservations, fee: Reservations accepted; $10-$15 fee per night. Open June to November.

Who to contact: Phone (307) 366-2250 or write to P.O. Box 114, Ten Sleep, WY 82442.

Location: This campground is located at the west end of Ten Sleep.

Trip note: This is one of two privately developed camps in Ten Sleep. This one covers four acres and is located near the confluence of Tensleep Creek and the Norwood River.

---

38) DOYLE

Reference: on Doyle Creek, Bighorn National Forest; map W3, grid f3.

Campsites, facilities: There are 18 sites for tents, trailers or motor homes up to 22 feet long. Picnic tables are provided. Vault toilets and firewood are available. There is **no piped water.** Pets are permitted on leashes.

Reservations, fee: No reservations necessary; no fee. Open June to mid-September.

Who to contact: Phone Bighorn National Forest at (307) 684-7981 or write to Buffalo Ranger District, 300 Spruce Street, Buffalo, WY 82834.

Location: From Buffalo, drive 27 miles west on US 16. Turn left on Forest Service Road 484 and drive 5.5 miles southwest, then a quarter mile southeast on Forest Service Road 514 to the campground.

Trip note: This camp is tucked away in the southern end of Bighorn National Forest, all by its lonesome. It's a quiet, little-known and primitive camp set alongside Doyle Creek, with good fishing prospects. Some trails and dirt roads in the area are detailed on a Forest Service map.

Wyoming Map W4
8 listings
Pages 498-503

North—Montana
East—South Dakota
South (W8)—see page 542
West (W3)—see page 480

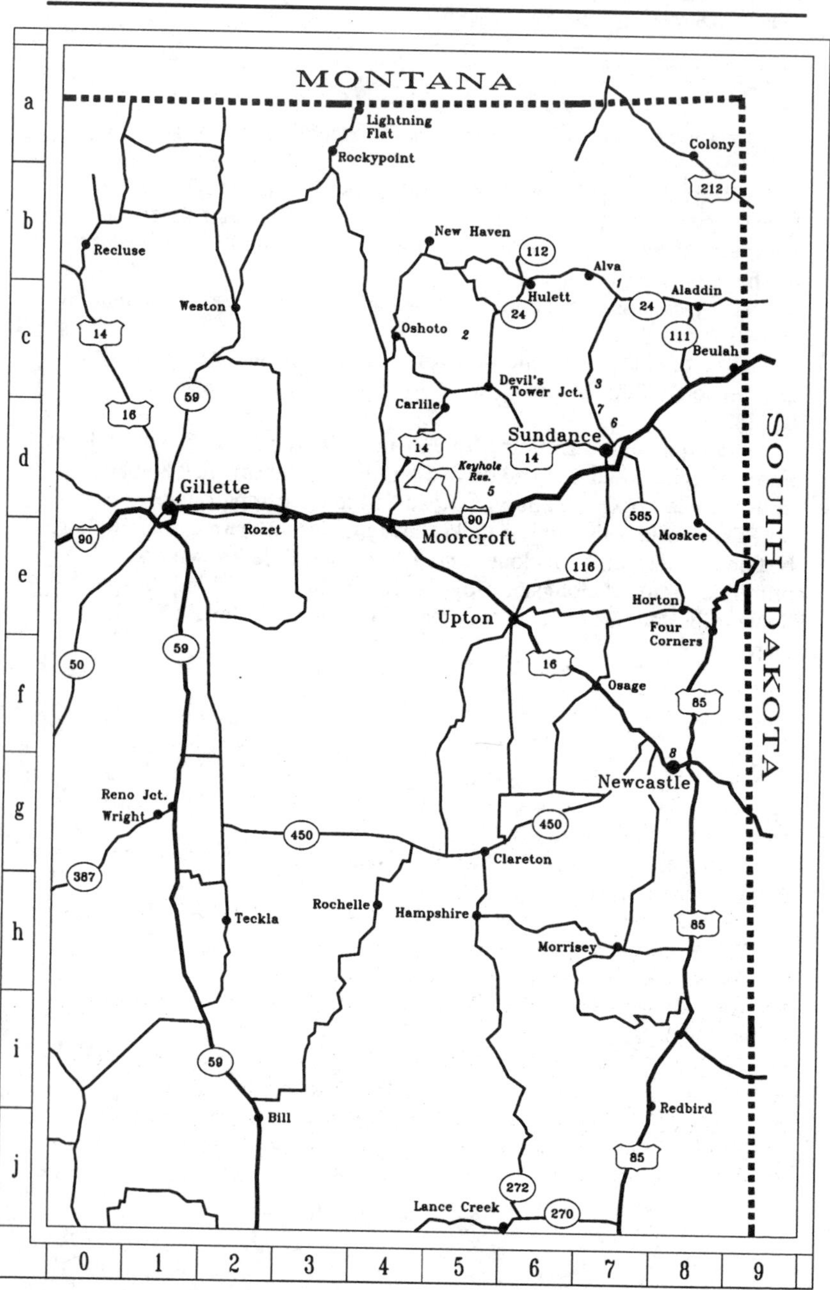

Featuring: Black Hills National Forest, Devil's Tower, Keyhole Reservoir, Jewel Cave National Monument

---

1) BEAR LODGE

Reference: southeast of Alva, Black Hills National Forest; map W4, grid b7.

Campsites, facilities: There are two tent sites and five sites for trailers or motor homes up to 22 feet long. Picnic tables are provided. Pit toilets are also available. Pets are permitted on leashes.

Reservations, fee: No reservations necessary; no fee. Open June to October.

Who to contact: Phone Black Hills National Forest at (307) 283-1361 or write to Sundance Ranger District, P.O. Box 1361, Sundance, WY 82729.

Location: From Alva, drive southeast on Highway 24 for 7.2 miles to the campground.

Trip note: This is a do-it-yourself proposition. In fact, don't expect to see anybody. Pick your own spot, take care of yourself, and then be sure to take out your own trash too. Rangers almost never come by this little spot which is set on the northeastern end of the Black Hills National Forest.

---

2) BELLE FOURCHE RIVER NATIONAL MONUMENT

Reference: in Devil's Tower; map W4, grid c5.

Campsites, facilities: There are 51 sites for tents, trailers or motor homes of any length. Picnic tables are provided. Piped water and flush toilets are also available. Firewood, a store, coffee shop and ice are located within one mile. Some facilities are **wheelchair accessible.** Pets and motorbikes are permitted.

Reservations, fee: No reservations necessary; $7 fee per night. Open all year with limited winter facilities.

Who to contact: Phone Devil's Tower National Monument at (307) 467-5370 or write to Devil's Tower, WY 82714.

Location: From Sundance, drive 23 miles northwest on US 14 and Highway 24 to Hulett. From Hulett, drive 10 miles south on Highway 24 to the campground.

Trip note: The Devil's Tower is the highlight here. It's a geological wonder: a columnar rock that juts 1,280 feet above the valley floor. About the only thing like it is the Devil's Postpile in California's Sierra Mountain Range. The park is a big one. It covers 1,347 acres and set near the Belle Fourche River.

3) COOK LAKE

Reference: north of Sundance, Black Hills National Forest; map W4, grid c7.

Campsites, facilities: There are eight tent sites and 26 sites for trailers or motor homes up to 22 feet long. Picnic tables are provided. Drinking water and pit toilets are also available. Pets are permitted on leashes. Boat docks are nearby. Some facilities are **wheelchair accessible.**

Reservations, fee: Reservations accepted; $4-$6 fee per night. Open mid-May to mid-September.

Who to contact: Phone Black Hills National Forest at (307) 283-1361 or write to Sundance Ranger District, P.O. Box 680, Sundance, WY 82729.

Location: From Sundance, drive 2.1 miles west on US 14. Turn right on Forest Service Road 838 and drive 14 miles north, then five miles east on Forest Service Road 843. Turn left on Forest Service Road 842 and continue one mile northwest to the campground.

Trip note: Cook Lake is a small lake, ideal for canoes, kayaks or rafts. No motors are allowed on boats at the lake. This keeps things calm and quiet and allows you to sneak up on your favorite fishing spot in peace. It is a newly developed campground. There is a 3.5-mile nature trail and trailhead located at the campground.

4) CRAZY WOMAN

Reference: in Gillette; map W4, grid d1.

Campsites, facilities: There are 34 tent sites and 67 sites for trailers or motor homes of any length. Picnic tables are provided. Flush toilets, sanitary disposal station, showers, recreation hall, a store, laundromat, ice and a playground are also available. Bottled gas and coffee shop are located within one mile. Pets and motorbikes are permitted.

Reservations, fee: Reservations accepted; $7-$16 fee per night; MasterCard and Visa accepted. Open year-round.

Who to contact: Phone (307) 682-3665 or write to 1001 West Second Street, Gillette, WY 82716.

Location: From Interstate 90 in Gillette, take exit 124 and drive three-quarters of a mile east on West Second Street to the campground.

Trip note: Stop your whinin' and be thankful you've got a place to sleep. In all directions, you've got zilch for an alternative. This park covers six acres and has a golf course in town as a recreation possibility. We did our best to find the crazy woman, but alas, we came up empty.

5) KEYHOLE STATE PARK

Reference: on Keyhole Reservoir; map W4, grid d5.

Campsites, facilities: There are 29 sites for tents, trailers or motor homes of any length. Picnic tables are provided. Piped water, pit toilets, sanitary disposal station, a store, coffee shop and ice are also available. Some facilities are **wheelchair accessible.** Pets are permitted on leashes. Boat docks, launching facilities and rentals are nearby.

Reservations, fee: No reservations necessary; $4 fee per night plus $2 entrance fee. Open all year with limited winter facilities.

Who to contact: Phone the park at (307) 756-3596 or write to the park at Inyan Kara Route, Moorcroft, WY 82721.

Location: From Moorcroft on Interstate 90, drive east. Take the Pine Ridge exit and drive nine miles north on a county road to the park.

Trip note: This is a good deal. It's the only camp on the only significant lake in northeastern Wyoming. It is set along the eastern shore of Keyhole Reservoir where boating, swimming and fishing are popular. On a clear day, you can see the awesome Devil's Tower to the north.

---

6) MOUNTAIN VIEW

Reference: near Sundance; map W4, grid d7.

Campsites, facilities: There are 28 tent sites and 34 sites for trailers or motor homes of any length. Piped water and picnic tables are provided. Flush toilets, sanitary disposal station, showers, playground, gift shop, store and a swimming pool are also available. Bottled gas, a store and a coffee shop are located within one mile. Pets and motorbikes are permitted.

Reservations, fee: Reservations accepted; $12-$16 fee per night. Open all year.

Who to contact: Phone (307) 283-2270 or write to P.O. Box 903, Sundance, WY 82729.

Location: This campground is located one mile east of Sundance on US 14.

Trip note: This is a private park that covers 11 acres and provides an option in the Sundance area. It has grassy sites for tents; gravel for RVs. The camp is set in a bowl surrounded by mountains on all sides, including Sugarloaf Mountain, Green Mountain and Sundance Mountain. It has easy highway access, right off the exit for Devil's Tower. This is quite an historically significant area; it's the original headquarters of—who else?—the Sundance Kid. Back in the days of the old west, it was also the prime spot for buffalo hunting, with Native Americans from as far away as Arizona coming to partake. For outdoor enthusiasts, there are 80,000 acres of national forest nearby, with access to hiking and mountain biking trails. Sand Creek, a locally acclaimed blue ribbon trout stream, is about 15 minutes away.

---

7) REUTER

Reference: near Sundance, Black Hills National Forest; map W4, grid d7.

Campsites, facilities: There are 12 tent sites and 12 sites for tents, trailers or motor homes up to 22 feet long. Picnic tables are provided.

Piped water and pit toilets are also available. A store, coffee shop, laundromat and ice are located within five miles. Pets are permitted on leashes.

Reservations, fee: Reservations accepted; $5 fee per night. Open late May through September.

Who to contact: Phone Black Hills National Forest at (307) 283-1361 or write to Sundance Ranger District, P.O. Box 680, Sundance, WY 82729.

Location: From Sundance, drive 2.1 miles west on US 14, and 2.2 miles north on paved, Forest Service Road 38 to the campground.

Trip note: This is one of two campgrounds (the other is Mountain View Camp) on the outskirts of Sundance. This one has shaded campsites and hiking trails nearby. It's advisable to obtain a Forest Service map if you plan on exploring the mountain country. A point of interest is the Warren Peak Lookout which is located nearby. From this point, you may look across the state of Wyoming and see Devil's Tower and the Bighorn Mountains. On clear days you can see three states including Montana and South Dakota. For sidetrip options, see trip note for Mountain View camp.

---

8) CRYSTAL PARK

Reference: near Jewel Cave National Monument; map W4, grid f8.

Campsites, facilities: There are 40 tent sites and 60 sites for trailers or motor homes of any length. Electricity, piped water, sewer hookups and picnic tables are provided. Flush toilets, showers, recreation hall, coffee shop, laundromat, ice, playground and a swimming pool are also available. Bottled gas, sanitary disposal station and a store are located within one mile. Pets and motorbikes are permitted.

Reservations, fee: Reservations accepted; $10-$15 fee per night; MasterCard and Visa accepted. Open May to mid-September.

Who to contact: Phone (307) 746-4426 or write to Number 3 Seminoe, Newcastle, WY 82701.

Location: This campground is located in Newcastle at the junction of US 16 and US 85.

Trip note: This is one of three privately developed parks in the Newcastle area. It is 24 miles from Jewel Cave National Monument and 60 miles from Mount Rushmore. The local golf course provides a recreational possibility.

Wyoming Map W5
18 listings
Pages 504-513

North (W1)—see page 438
East (W6)—see page 514
South—Utah
West—Idaho

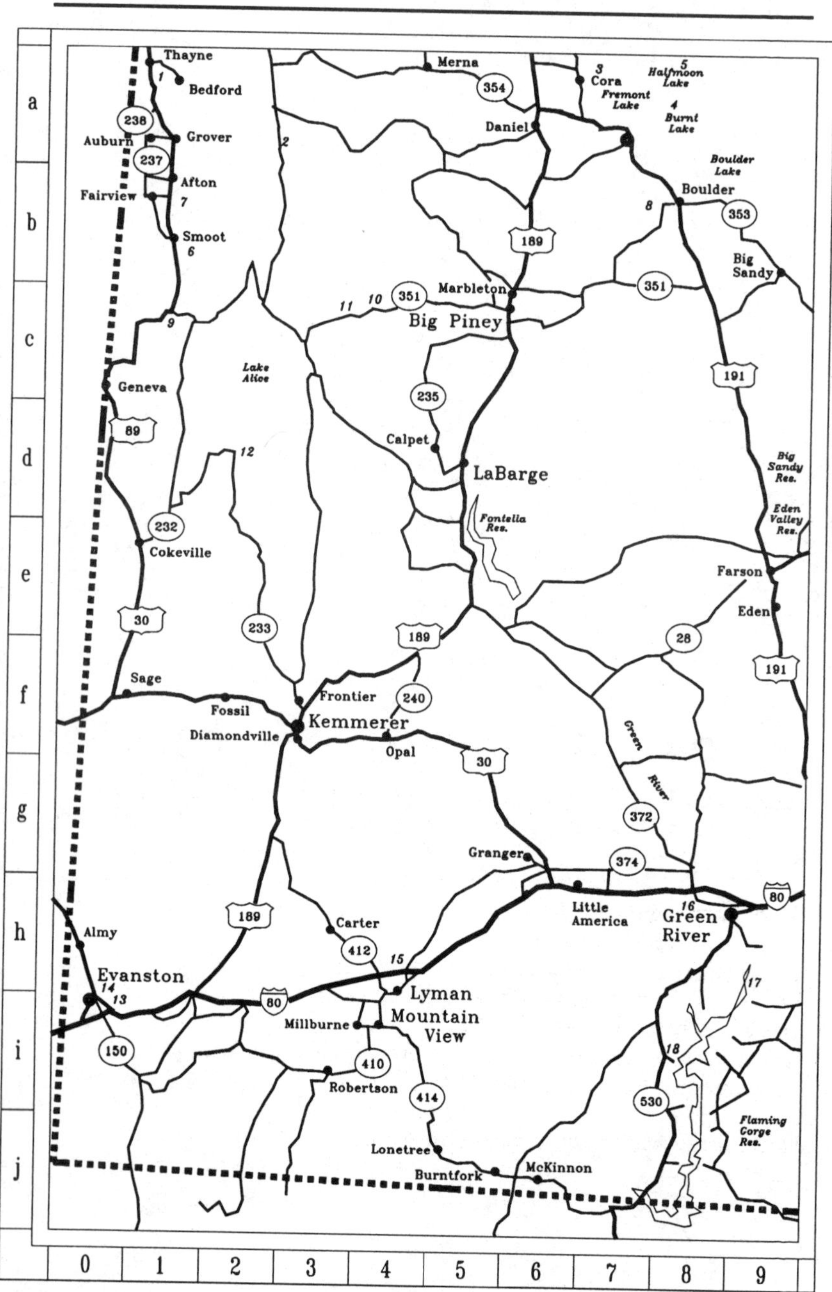

Featuring: Salt River, Greys River, Bridger-Teton National Forest, North Smith Fork of Salt River, Middle Piney Creek, Green River, Flaming Gorge Reservoir, Flaming Gorge National Recreation Area

---

1) FLAT CREEK RV PARK

Reference: near Salt River; map W5, grid a1.

Campsites, facilities: There are 12 tent sites and 26 sites for trailers or motor homes. Electricity, piped water, sewer hookups and picnic tables are provided. Flush toilets, sanitary disposal station, showers, firewood, laundromat and ice are also available. Bottled gas is located within one mile. Pets and motorbikes are permitted.

Reservations, fee: Reservations accepted; $12 fee per night. Open April through October.

Who to contact: Phone (307) 883-2231 or write to P.O. Box 239, Thayne, WY 83127.

Location: From Thayne, drive a half mile south on US 89 to the campground.

Trip note: This privately developed park covers 15 acres, and is set near the Salt River and the Caribou National Forest. The sites are mostly gravel, with little shade. There is a small creek running nearby, with limited fishing prospects. A golf course is nearby. A cheese factory in Thayne provides a possible sidetrip.

---

2) FOREST PARK

Reference: on Greys River, Bridger-Teton National Forest; map W5, grid a2.

Campsites, facilities: There are 13 sites for tents, trailers or motor homes up to 22 feet long. Picnic tables and piped water are provided. Pit toilets and firewood are also available. Pets are permitted on leashes.

Reservations, fee: No reservations necessary; $4 fee per night. Open mid-June to early September.

Who to contact: Phone Bridger-Teton National Forest at (307) 886-3166 or write to Greys River Ranger District, P.O. Box 339, Afton, WY 83110.

Location: From Alpine, drive three-quarters of a mile southeast on US 89. Turn on County Road 1001 and drive a half mile southeast, then continue for 35.3 miles southeast on Forest Service Road 10138.

Trip note: This is one of four camps along the road that runs adjacent to Greys River. It's a primitive setting. There are several trails in the area, but none lead directly out of the camp. The adjacent area to the west is designated for the protection of wintering big game and feeding grounds, closed to any public use in the winter months, and open to foot and horse travel only from May through November.

3) FREMONT LAKE

Reference: northeast of Pinedale, Bridger-Teton National Forest; map W5, grid a7.

Campsites, facilities: There are 54 sites for tents, trailers or motor homes up to 30 feet long. Picnic tables are provided. Piped water, pit toilets and firewood are also available. A coffee shop is located within five miles. Pets are permitted on leashes. Boat docks, launching facilities and rentals are nearby.

Reservations, fee: Reserve through MISTIX at (800) 283-CAMP ($6 MISTIX fee); $6 fee per night. Open late May to early September.

Who to contact: Phone Bridger-Teton National Forest, Pinedale Ranger District at (307) 367-4326 or write to P.O. Box 220, Pinedale, WY 82941.

Location: From Pinedale, drive one mile east on Highway 187. Turn north on County Road 111 and drive 2.5 miles, then continue for four miles northeast on Forest Service Road 111 to the campground.

Trip note: This is a popular big lake (by Wyoming standards—second largest in the state) that has boat rentals and good fishing. The camp is set along the southeastern shore.

4) TRAILS END

Reference: northeast of Pinedale, Bridger-Teton National Forest; map W5, grid a8.

Campsites, facilities: There are eight sites for tents, trailers or motor homes up to 22 feet long. Picnic tables are provided. Piped water, pit toilets and firewood are also available. Pets are permitted on leashes.

Reservations, fee: No reservations necessary; $5 fee per night. Open late June to early September.

Who to contact: Phone Bridger-Teton National Forest at (307) 367-4326 or write to Pinedale Ranger District, P.O. Box 220, Pinedale, WY 82941.

Location: From Pinedale, drive one mile east on Highway 187. Turn north on County Road 111 and drive 2.5 miles, then eight miles northeast on Forest Service Road 134.

Trip note: This is one of four hidden camps in the area. This one is a trailhead camp, a good jump-off point for a multi-day backpacking trip into the Bridger Wilderness. If you plan on hunkering down for awhile, check out nearby Fremont Lake, Half Moon Lake and Willow Lake, with camps at each spot.

5) HALF MOON LAKE

Reference: near Pinedale, Bridger-Teton National Forest; map W5, grid a8.

Campsites, facilities: There are 18 sites for tents, trailers or motor homes up to 16 feet long. Picnic tables are provided. Pit toilets and firewood are also available. There is **no piped water**. Pets are permitted on leashes. Boat docks, launching facilities and rentals are nearby.

Reservations, fee: No reservations necessary; $3 fee per night. Open June to early September.

Who to contact: Phone Bridger-Teton National Forest, Pinedale Ranger District at (307) 367-4326 or write to P.O. Box 220, Pinedale, WY 82941.

Location: From Pinedale, drive one mile east on Highway 187. Turn north on County Road 111 and drive 2.5 miles, then one mile east on Forest Service Road 134 to the campground.

Trip note: This is one of six lakes in the area, so if the fish aren't biting here, there's still hope. This camp is located on the north shore of the lake. Hikers have many sidetrip options. Trails in the area lead into the Bridger-Teton National Forest and Bridger Wilderness, accessing a number of lakes. Tip: Bridger Wilderness is more easily accessed from Trails End Camp.

---

6) COTTONWOOD LAKE

Reference: southeast of Afton, Bridger-Teton National Forest; map W5, grid b1.

Campsites, facilities: There are 13 sites for tents, trailers or small motor homes up to 16 feet long, and five walk-in sites. There is also one group area available. Picnic tables, piped water and pit toilets are provided. Horse holding facilities and a boat launch are also available. Pets are permitted on leashes.

Reservations, fee: No reservations necessary except for group sites; phone district ranger. $5 per night for single sites; phone ranger for group rates. Open mid-June to early September.

Who to contact: Phone Bridger-Teton National Forest at (307) 886-3166 or write to Greys River Ranger District, P.O. Box 339, Afton, WY 83110.

Location: From Afton, drive eight miles south on US 89 to Smoot. Continue south on US 89 for one mile. Turn east and drive seven miles on Forest Service Road 10208 to the campground.

Trip note: This is one of two camps in the immediate area. This one is set on the north shore of little Cottonwood Lake. It's a good spot for all—folks who just want to look at the water, enthusiastic anglers or ambitious hikers. Numerous trails are in the immediate area including one to Mount Wagner (10,709-foot elevation). Others head along Cottonwood and Trail Creeks.

---

7) SWIFT CREEK

Reference: near Afton, Bridger-Teton National Forest; map W5, grid b1.

Campsites, facilities: There are 13 sites for tents, trailers or motor homes up to 22 feet long. Picnic tables are provided. Piped water, pit toilets and firewood are also available. A store, coffee shop, laundromat and ice are located within five miles. Pets are permitted on leashes.

Reservations, fee: No reservations necessary; $5 fee per night. Open mid-May to early September.

Who to contact: Phone Bridger-Teton National Forest at (307) 886-3166 or write to Greys River Ranger District, P.O. Box 339, Afton, WY 83110.

Location: From Afton, drive 1.5 miles east on a county road and a quarter mile east on Forest Service Road 10211 to the campground.

Trip note: Campsites can be tough to come by for folks cruising US 89, but this site is an ideal choice. It's only a few minutes drive from the highway, about a mile from Afton, and right on Swift Creek. Yet it's missed by almost all. A trail along the creek provides a small sidetrip to one of the worlds only cold geysers at Periodic Springs.

---

8) OX-YOKE ACRES

Reference: near Boulder; map W5, grid b7.

Campsites, facilities: There are 21 sites for tents, trailers or motor homes of any length. Electricity, piped water and picnic tables are provided. Flush toilets, sanitary disposal station, showers, game room, firewood and ice are also available. A store is located within one mile. Pets and motorbikes are permitted.

Reservations, fee: Reservations accepted; $12-$14 fee per night. Open early May to November.

Who to contact: Phone (307) 537-5453 or write to P.O. Box 230, Boulder, WY 82923.

Location: From Pinedale, drive 11 miles south on US 191. The campground is one mile north of Boulder on the west side of the highway.

Trip note: This spot is known as the campground with the million-dollar view. It overlooks the New Fork River, with spectacular mountain vistas. The sites are grassy, some sheltered and some shaded. Fishing and hunting are popular activities here; the camp is usually busier in the early fall during hunting season than in the summer. This is also a popular camp for backpackers heading into the Big Sandy area. There are several lakes within a few minutes driving distance.

---

9) ALFRED FLAT

Reference: on the North Smith Fork of Salt River, Bridger-Teton National Forest; map W5, grid c1.

Campsites, facilities: There are 32 sites for tents, trailers or motor homes up to 22 feet long. Picnic tables are provided. Piped water, pit toilets and firewood are also available. Pets are permitted on leashes. Some facilities are **wheelchair accessible.**

Reservations, fee: No reservations necessary; $5 fee per night. Open June to early September.

Who to contact: Phone Bridger-Teton National Forest at (307) 877-4415 or write to Kemmerer Ranger District, P.O. Box 31, Kemmerer, WY 83101.

Location: From Afton, drive 23 miles south on US 89 and a quarter mile north on Forest Service Road 10131 to the campground.

Trip note: This is an ideal spot for out-of-town cruisers looking for a pretty spot. But it's also a good base camp for hikers. It is set on the North Smith Fork of the Salt River only a short hop from the highway. A trail from camp leads to the Salt River.

---

10) SACAJAWEA

Reference: on Middle Piney Creek, Bridger-Teton National Forest; map W5, grid c3.

Campsites, facilities: There are 26 sites for tents, trailers or motor homes up to 22 feet long. Picnic tables are provided. Piped water, pit toilets and firewood are also available. Pets are permitted on leashes. Boat docks are nearby.

Reservations, fee: No reservations necessary; $4 fee per night. Open mid-June to early September.

Who to contact: Phone Bridger-Teton National Forest at (307) 276-3375 or write to Big Piney Ranger District, P.O. Box 218, Big Piney, WY 83113.

Location: From Big Piney, drive 22 miles west on County Route 350 and Forest Service Road 10024 to the campground.

Trip note: This is one of two camps in the immediate area, and out here, few out-of-towners tread. This camp is set on Middle Piney Creek about two miles from Middle Piney Lake. It's a forested area. Trails in the area follow creeks into the interior of the Bridger-Teton National Forest. Camp 7 provides a nearby option but without piped water.

---

11) MIDDLE PINEY LAKE

Reference: west of Big Piney, Bridger-Teton National Forest; map W5, grid c3.

Campsites, facilities: There are six sites for tents, trailers or motor homes up to 16 feet long. Picnic tables are provided. Pit toilets and firewood are also available. There is **no piped water.** Pets are permitted on leashes. A boat launch is nearby.

Reservations, fee: No reservations necessary; no fee. Open July to late September.

Who to contact: Phone Bridger-Teton National Forest at (307) 276-3375 or write to Big Piney Ranger District, P.O. Box 218, Big Piney, WY 83113.

Location: From Big Piney, drive 20 miles west on County Road 350. Continue 4.3 miles west on Forest Service Road 10046, then 3.2 miles west on Forest Service Road 10024 to the campground.

Trip note: The road ends here, folks, and it's a good spot to stop. The camp is set on the east shore of Middle Piney Lake where the fishing can be good. Many trails and a lot of wildlife are in the area.

---

12) HAMS FORK

Reference: northeast of Cokeville, Bridger-Teton National Forest; map W5, grid d2.

Campsites, facilities: There are 10 sites for tents, trailers or motor homes up to 16 feet long. Picnic tables are provided. Piped water, pit toilets and firewood are also available. Pets are permitted on leashes.

Reservations, fee: No reservations necessary; $5 fee per night. Open mid-June to early September.

Who to contact: Phone Bridger-Teton National Forest at (307) 877-4415 or write to Kemmerer Ranger District, P.O. Box 31, Kemmerer, WY 83101.

Location: From Cokeville, drive north on Highway 232 for 12 miles, four miles northeast on a county road, and 13 miles east on Forest Service Road 10062 to the campground.

Trip note: This one is far enough "out there" to be bypassed by most folks. But it is a nice, little spot set along the Hams Fork, with excellent fishing prospects for the patient angler. There are many trails here that lead into the adjacent wildlands. This is a popular area for winter sports, including snowmobiling and cross-country skiing.

---

13) SUNSET RV

Reference: near Evanston; map W5, grid h0.

Campsites, facilities: There are four tent sites and 62 sites for trailers or motor homes of any length. Electricity, piped water, sewer hookups and picnic tables are provided. Flush toilets, sanitary disposal station, showers and a laundromat are also available. Bottled gas, a store, coffee shop and ice are located within one mile. Pets and motorbikes are permitted.

Reservations, fee: Reservations accepted; $12-$15 fee per night; MasterCard and Visa accepted. Open all year.

Who to contact: Phone (307) 789-3763 or write to 196 Bear River Drive, Evanston, WY 82930.

Location: In Evanston, take Exit 6 off Interstate 80, and drive west for a half mile on Business Interstate 80 to the campground.

Trip note: If you are going to be around Evanston for awhile, you'd better stop here and check in at the welcome center for visitors. Nearby recreation options include a golf course and tennis courts. This is one of two parks in the town. For recreation options see trip note for Philips Trailer Park.

14) PHILIPS TRAILER PARK

Reference: in Evanston; map W5, grid h0.

Campsites, facilities: There are 60 sites for trailers or motor homes of any length. Electricity, piped water, sewer hookups and picnic tables are provided. Flush toilets, showers, laundromat and a playground are also available. Bottled gas, a store, coffee shop and ice are located within one mile. Pets and motorbikes are permitted.

Reservations, fee: Reservations accepted; $13 fee per night; MasterCard and Visa accepted. Open all year with limited winter facilities.

Who to contact: Phone (307) 789-3805 or write to P.O. Box 112, Evanston, WY 82930.

Location: From Interstate 80 in Evanston, take Exit 6, and drive a half mile to the campground (camp is in the town).

Trip note: This is one of two motor home parks in Evanston. This one covers 10 acres. Nearby recreation options include a golf course and bike paths. The park is set within the city limits, with lots of shade and grass. Attractions include fishing in the Bear River, which runs right through town, and in Sulphur Creek Reservoir, located about 13 miles south. There is also hunting and hiking in the Uinta Mountains to the south.

15) LYMAN KOA

Reference: in Lyman; map W5, grid h4.

Campsites, facilities: There are 30 tent sites and 62 sites for trailers or motor homes of any length. Picnic tables are provided. Flush toilets, sanitary disposal station, showers, recreation hall, a store, laundromat, ice, playground and a swimming pool are also available. Bottled gas and a coffee shop are located within one mile. Pets and motorbikes are permitted.

Reservations, fee: Reservations accepted; $12-$16.50 fee per night; MasterCard and Visa accepted. Open mid-May to late September.

Who to contact: Phone (307) 786-2762 or write to Star Route P.O. Box 55, Lyman, WY 82937.

Location: Take Exit 41 off Interstate 80 in Lyman, and drive one mile south to the campground.

Trip note: If you're looking for a spot around these parts, you'd best stop here. There are no other camps within 30 miles in any direction. The campground is privately run and covers five acres. It's set near the historic Fort Bridger State Historical Site, established in 1843 by Jim Bridger as a trading post.

16) TEX'S TRAVEL CAMP

Reference: near Green River; map W5, grid h8.

Campsites, facilities: There are 20 tent sites and 65 sites for trailers or motor homes of any length. Picnic tables are provided. Flush toilets, sanitary disposal station, showers, a store, laundromat, ice and a playground are also available. Electricity, piped water and sewer hookups are available at an additional charge. Bottled gas is located within one mile. Pets are permitted on leashes.

Reservations, fee: Reservations accepted; $11-$18 fee per night. Open May through September including limited and some off-season weekends.

Who to contact: Phone (307) 875-2630 or write to Star Route 2, P.O. Box 101, Green River, WY 82935.

Location: From the town of Green River, drive west on Interstate 80. Take Exit 85 (Covered Wagon Road) and drive a quarter mile south, then one mile east on Highway 374 to the campground on the Green River.

Trip note: This is one of the nicer spots along Interstate 80. It covers four acres and is on the Green River. It has beautiful, private riverside sites, with lots of grass and trees and excellent fishing access. A golf course is located one mile away. Rockhounds can hunt nearby for geological treasures, and whitewater rafting is available a half mile away. Flaming Gorge Reservoir is a short drive away.

---

17) FIREHOLE

Reference: on Flaming Gorge Reservoir, Flaming Gorge National Recreation Area; map W5, grid h9.

Campsites, facilities: There are 38 sites for tents, trailers or motor homes up to 32 feet long. Piped water, flush toilets, and a sanitary disposal station are also available. Pets are permitted on leashes for an additional fee. Boat docks and launching facilities are nearby.

Reservations, fee: No reservations necessary; $6-$7 fee per night. Open late May to early September.

Who to contact: Phone Flaming Gorge National Recreation Area at (801) 784-3483 or write to Flaming Gorge Ranger District, Manila, UT 84046.

Location: From the town of Rock Springs, drive five miles southwest on Interstate 80. Take the Highway 191 exit and drive 13.7 miles south, then turn left on Forest Service Road 60106 and drive 7.2 miles southwest. Turn right on Forest Service Road 60166 and continue one mile to the campground.

Trip note: This is one of two campgrounds on the huge Flaming Gorge Reservoir, a 90-mile-long lake that is best known for huge brown trout, good waterskiing and swimming. This camp is located on the northeastern side of the lake and is the closest camp to the town of Rock Springs.

18) BUCKBOARD CROSSING

Reference: on Flaming Gorge Reservoir, Flaming Gorge National Recreation Area; map W5, grid i8.

Campsites, facilities: There are 68 sites for tents, trailers or motor homes up to 22 feet long. Picnic tables are provided. Piped water, flush toilets and a sanitary disposal station are also available. A store, coffee shop and ice are located within one mile. Pets are permitted on leashes. Boat docks and rentals are nearby.

Reservations, fee: No reservations necessary; $6-$7 fee per night. Open May to late September.

Who to contact: Phone Flaming Gorge National Recreation Area at (801) 784-3483 or write Flaming Gorge Ranger District, Manila, UT 84046.

Location: From the town of Green River, drive 25 miles south on State Route 530, then two miles east on Forest Service Road 60009 to the campground and marina.

Trip note: This is an option to Firehole Camp. This site is also set on the giant Flaming Gorge Reservoir but on the northwestern side of the lake. It's the closest camp on the lake to the town of Green River. The reservoir is 90 miles long and has giant brown trout. However they've proven to be quite elusive.

Wyoming Map W6
9 listings
Pages 514-519

North (W2)—see page 470
East (W7)—see page 520
South—Colorado
West (W5)—see page 504

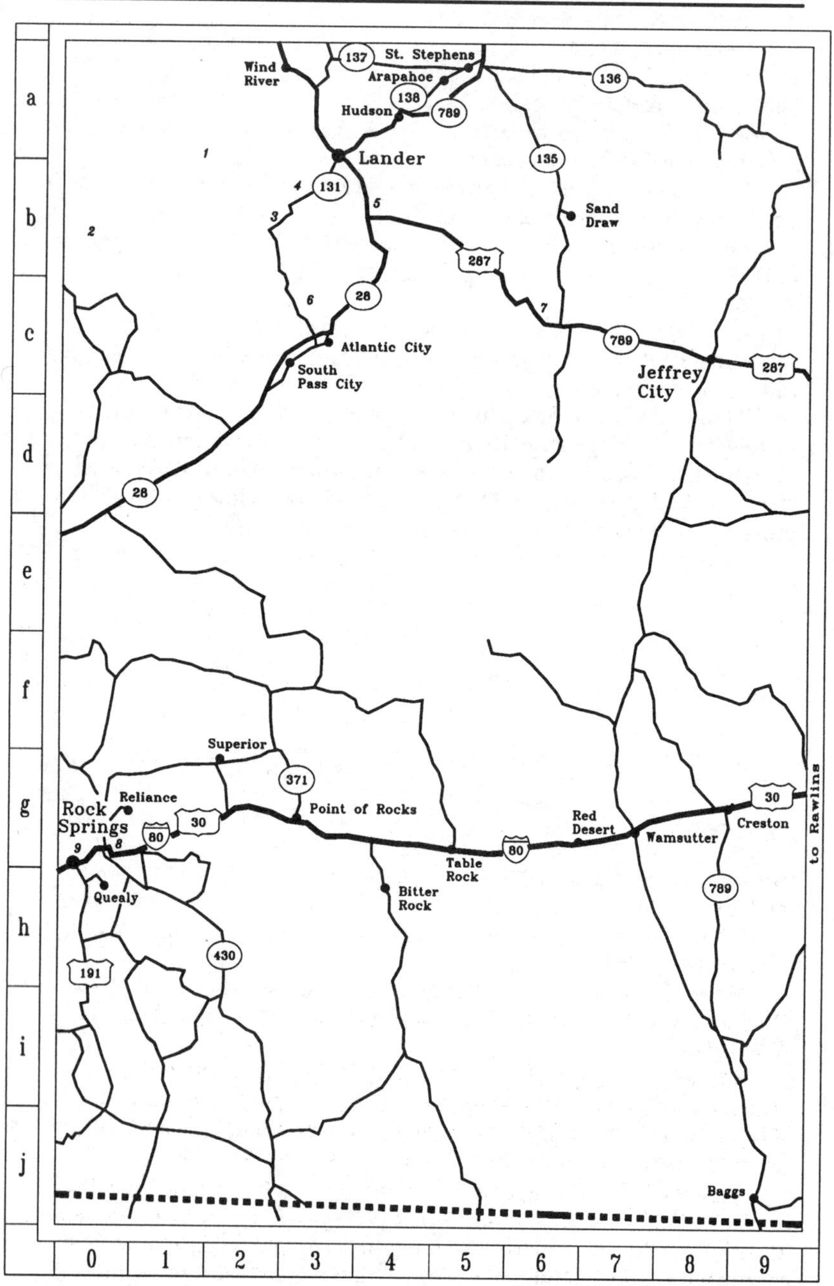

Featuring: North Fork of Popo-Agie River, Shoshone National Forest, Big Sandy River, Bridger-Teton National Forest, Little Popo-Agie Basin, Middle Fork of Popo-Agie River, Wind River Mountains, Sweetwater River, Flaming Gorge Reservoir

---

1) DICKINSON CREEK

Reference: near the North Fork of Popo-Agie River, Shoshone National Forest; map W6, grid a1.

Campsites, facilities: There are eight tent sites and seven sites for trailers or motor homes up to 16 feet long. Picnic tables are provided. Pit toilets and firewood are also available. There is **no piped water.** Pets are permitted on leashes.

Reservations, fee: No reservations necessary; no fee. Open July to late September.

Who to contact: Phone Shoshone National Forest at (307) 332-5460 or write to Washakie Ranger District, 333 Highway 789 South, Lander, WY 82520.

Location: From Lander, drive 15 miles northwest on US 287 and five miles southwest on a county road. Continue 14 miles southwest on Forest Service Road 167 and then three miles southwest on Forest Service Road 303 to the campground.

Trip note: You want solitude? You'll find it here at this little-known, primitive camp. It's set at 9,400 feet along Dickinson Creek. Many good hiking trails are in the area including along North Fork of the Popo-Agie River. Black Mountain looms to the east at 10,441 feet.

---

2) BIG SANDY

Reference: on Big Sandy River, Bridger-Teton National Forest; map W6, grid b0.

Campsites, facilities: There are 12 sites for tents, trailers or motor homes up to 22 feet long. Picnic tables are provided. Pit toilets and firewood are also available. There is **no piped water**. Pets are permitted on leashes.

Reservations, fee: No reservations necessary; no fee. Open late June to early September.

Who to contact: Phone Bridger-Teton National Forest, Pinedale Ranger District at (307) 367-4326 or write to P.O. Box 220, Pinedale, WY 82941.

Location: From Pinedale, drive 12 miles south on US 191 to Boulder. Head southeast on Highway 353 for 15 miles, then turn on County Route 23118 and drive 21 miles. Turn north on Forest Service Road 135 and continue for six miles to the campground.

Trip note: This camp gets heavy use in the summertime, probably due to the fact that it's set near the Big Sandy River (plus, you can't beat the price). There are a lot of accessible trails and small lakes in the surrounding Bridger Wilderness. It is advisable to obtain a Forest Service map.

3) SINKS CANYON

Reference: on the Middle Fork of Popo-Agie River, Shoshone National Forest; map W6, grid b2.

Campsites, facilities: There are six tent sites and four sites for trailers or motor homes up to 16 feet long. Picnic tables are provided. Water and pit toilets are also available. Pets are permitted on leashes.

Reservations, fee: No reservations necessary; $5 fee per night. Open June to late October.

Who to contact: Phone Shoshone National Forest at (307) 332-5460 or write to Washakie Ranger District, 333 Highway 789 South, Lander, WY 82520.

Location: From Lander, drive 8.7 miles southwest on Highway 701 and then a quarter mile southwest on Forest Service Road 3001B to the campground.

Trip note: This is a small, little-known camp nestled in Sinks Canyon, alongside the Middle Fork of the Popo-Agie River. It is located near a winter sports area and a geology camp. You can hop onto Cold Spring Trail about a half mile south of camp and head for the high country and several pretty alpine lakes. Bring your fishing pole.

4) SINKS CANYON STATE PARK

Reference: southwest of Lander; map W6, grid b3.

Campsites, facilities: There are four tent sites and 28 sites for trailers or motor homes of any length. Hand pumped water, pit toilets and a visitor center are also available. Some facilities are **wheelchair accessible.** Pets on leashes and motorbikes are permitted.

Reservations, fee: No reservations necessary; $4 fee per night plus $2 entrance fee. Open all year with limited winter facilities.

Who to contact: Phone (307) 332-6333 or write to Lander, WY 82520.

Location: From Lander, drive seven miles southwest on Highway 131 to the park.

Trip note: This is a 600-acre state park that comes with some nice nature trails. But the best of it is the "disappearing river," which is where the park gets its name. There's a nice trout display about one mile from the visitor center, next to park headquarters.

5) TABLE MOUNTAIN

Reference: southeast of Lander; map W6, grid b4.

Campsites, facilities: There are 17 sites for trailers or motor homes up to 30 feet long in this adult-only campground. Electricity, piped water, sewer hookups and picnic tables are provided. Flush toilets and showers are also available. A store is located within one mile. Pets are permitted on leashes.

Reservations, fee: Reservations accepted; $6 fee per night; MasterCard and Visa accepted. Open mid-May to September.

Who to contact: Phone (307) 332-3581 or write to 7335 Highway 789, Lander, WY 82520.

Location: From Lander, drive eight miles southeast on US 287 to the campground.

Trip note: This camp has an ideal location. It is set near the junction of US 287 and Highway 28. It covers seven acres. The sites are paved, with not much in the way of shade or greenery, although there is a small meadow nearby. Nearby attractions include the ghost town of South Pass City and the Wind River Indian Reservation, which houses Sacajawea's grave.

---

6) LOUIS LAKE

Reference: near Wind River Mountains, Shoshone National Forest; map W6, grid c3.

Campsites, facilities: There are four tent sites and five sites for trailers or motor homes up to 22 feet long. Picnic tables are provided. Piped water and pit toilets are also available. Pets are permitted on leashes. A primitive boat launch is nearby.

Reservations, fee: No reservations necessary; $5 fee per night. Open July to late September.

Who to contact: Phone Shoshone National Forest at (307) 332-5460 or write to Washakie Ranger District, 333 Highway 789 South, Lander, WY 82520.

Location: From Lander, drive 8.7 miles southwest on Highway 701 and then 21.4 miles southwest on Forest Service Road 308 to the campground.

Trip note: This little-known camp set along Louis Lake has several trails available that trace the nearby river and climb into the Wind River Mountains.

---

7) RIVER

Reference: on Sweetwater River; map W6, grid c6.

Campsites, facilities: There are 15 tent sites and 15 sites for trailers or motor homes of any length. Piped water and picnic tables are provided. Flush toilets, showers, a store, ice and a playground are also available. Electricity and firewood are available at an additional charge. Pets are permitted on leashes.

Reservations, fee: Reservations accepted; $7.50-$9 fee per night. Open May through September.

Who to contact: Phone (307) 544-9319 or write to Rawlins Route, P.O. Box 67, Lander, WY 82520.

Location: From Lander, drive 40 miles southeast on US 287 to the campground.

Trip note: If you are cruising US 287 and looking for a place to stop, this is your best bet. The camp is set alongside the Sweetwater River which is a good spot for fishing, picnicking, campfires and rock hunting. The closest option is Table Mountain Camp, located some 25 miles to the west. If you're heading east, you've got nothing but road for a long, long way.

---

8) ROCK SPRINGS KOA

Reference: near Flaming Gorge Reservoir; map W6, grid g0.

Campsites, facilities: There are 10 tent sites and 88 sites for trailers or motor homes of any length. Camping cabins are also available. Piped water and picnic tables are provided. Flush toilets, sanitary disposal station, showers, game room, a store, laundromat, ice, cable TV, a horse corral, swimming pool, jacuzzi, horseshoe pits and a playground are also available. Bottled gas and a coffee shop are located within one mile. Pets are permitted on leashes.

Reservations, fee: Reservations accepted; $14-$20 fee per night. Camping cabins are $25 per night. Open May through October.

Who to contact: Phone (307) 362-3063 or write to KOA #24, 86 Foothill Boulevard, Rock Springs, WY 82901.

Location: From Interstate 80 in the town of Rock Springs, take Exit 99 and drive one mile east on the N Service Road.

Trip note: This is one of two campgrounds in Rock Springs, a good layover spot for Interstate 80 cruisers. This campground covers four acres and is on the western edge of the Red Desert, below the White Mountains. Sidetrip options include Flaming Gorge Reservoir, the ghost town of South Pass City and Atlantic City historical sites, all within a short drive. There is a golf course nearby.

---

9) ALBERT'S TRAILER COURT

Reference: near Flaming Gorge Reservoir; map W6, grid g0.

Campsites, facilities: There are 20 sites for trailers or motor homes of any length. Electricity, piped water, sewer hookups and picnic tables are provided. A sanitary disposal station is also available. Bottled gas, a store, coffee shop, laundromat and ice are located within one mile. Pets are permitted on leashes.

Reservations, fee: Reservations accepted; $8-$10 fee per night. Open all year with limited winter facilities.

Who to contact: Phone (307) 382-2243 or write to 1560 Elk Street, Rock Springs, WY 82901.

Location: From Interstate 80 in the town of Rock Springs, take Exit 104. The campground is on the southeastern corner.

Trip note: This is an alternative to Rock Springs KOA. It also covers four acres in the town of Rock Springs. See trip note for Rock Springs KOA for sidetrip suggestions.

Wyoming Map W7
45 listings
Pages 520-541

North (W3)—see page 480
East (W8)—see page 542
South—Colorado
West (W6)—see page 514

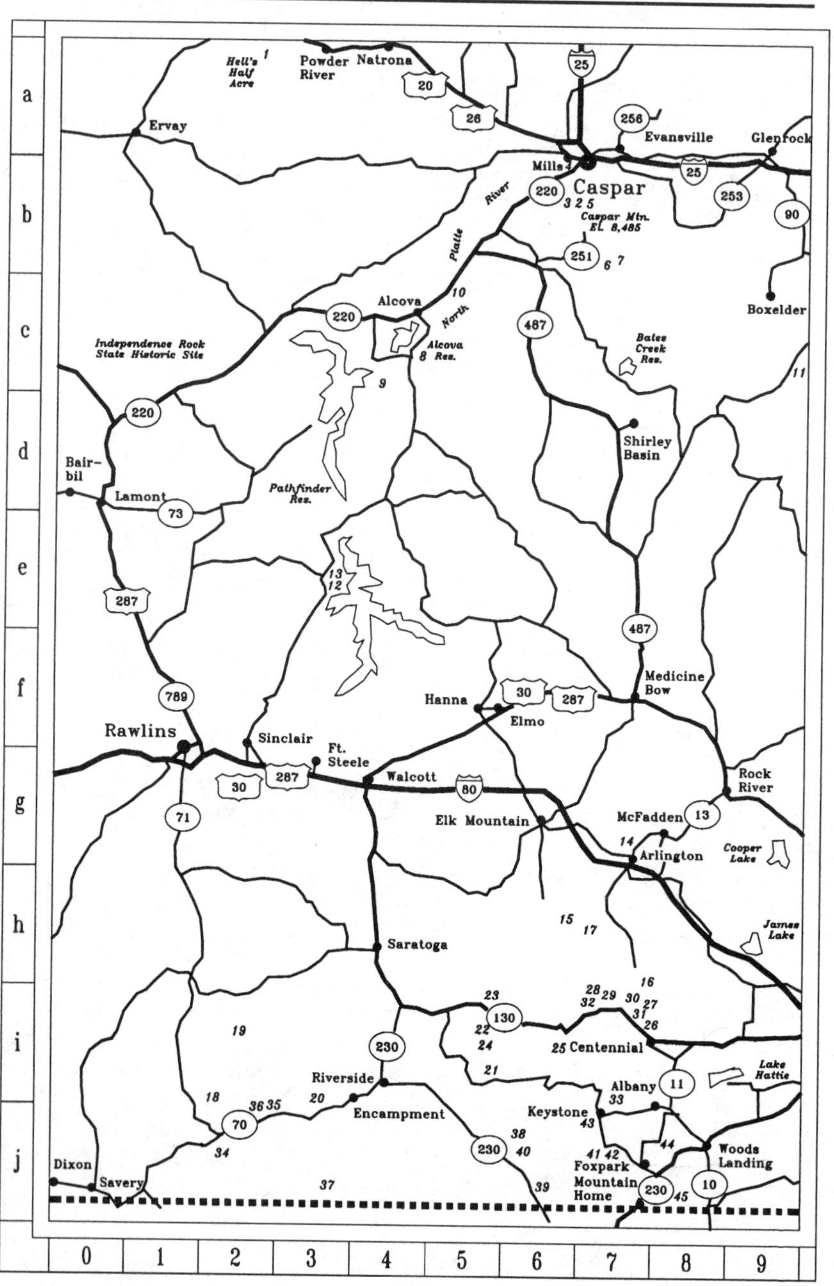

Featuring: Muddy Mountain, Fremont Canyon, Pathfinder Bird Refuge, La Prele Creek, Medicine Bow National Forest, Seminoe Reservoir, Overland Creek, Long Lake, Medicine Lake National Forest, Snowy Lakes, Little Sandstone Creek, Continental Divide, North Fork of Encampment River, North Fork of Barrett Creek, Lincoln Creek, French Creek, Libby Creek, Medicine Bow Peak, North Fork of Laramie River, Rob Roy Reservoir, North Fork of Battle Creek, Hog Park Reservoir, North Platte River, Miller Lake, Douglas Creek

---

1) HELL'S HALF ACRE

Reference: west of Casper; map W7, grid a2.

Campsites, facilities: There are 16 tent sites and 24 sites for trailers or motor homes of any length. Picnic tables are provided. Flush toilets, sanitary disposal station, showers, coffee shop, ice and a playground are also available. Electricity, piped water and sewer hookups are available at an additional charge. Pets are permitted on leashes.

Reservations, fee: Reservations accepted; $6-$13 fee per night; MasterCard and Visa accepted. Open May to November.

Who to contact: Phone (307) 472-0018 or write to Hell's Half Acre, WY 82648.

Location: From Casper, drive 45 miles west on US 26 to the campground.

Trip note: They used to find steer skeletons and the like around here. If you're short on gas or water, you're lucky this spot exists. It's set in the high Wyoming prairie and covers 320 acres. You'll find a gift shop, restaurant, lounge, motel—you get the idea. Many weird geological formations can be seen at Hell's Half Acre, located west of the park area.

---

2) CASPER MOUNTAIN

Reference: south of Casper; map W7, grid b6.

Campsites, facilities: There are several sites for tents, trailers or motor homes. Picnic tables are provided. Pit toilets are also available. Drinking water is available from early April to mid-September.

Reservations, fee: No reservations necessary; $5 fee per night. Open all year with limited winter facilities.

Who to contact: Phone Natrona County Parks Board at (307) 234-6821 or write to 4621 Cy Avenue, Casper, WY 82604.

Location: From Casper, drive eight miles south on Casper Mountain Road (Highway 251) to the campground.

Trip note: Here's a year-round county park. It's big and primitive, covering 400 acres. Water? It's a coin flip if it is running or not. In the winter, ski trails, toboggan runs and snowmobile trails are available.

---

3) BEAR TRAP MEADOW LAKE

Reference: south of Casper; map W7, grid b6.

Campsites, facilities: There are 45 tent sites and 55 sites for trailers or motor homes of any length. Picnic tables are provided. Pit toilets and firewood are available. Piped water is available from April to mid-September. Pets are permitted on leashes.

Reservations, fee: No reservations necessary; $5 fee per night. Open all year, with limited facilities in the winter.

Who to contact: Phone Natrona County Parks Board at (307) 234-6821 or write to 4621 Cy Avenue, Casper, WY 82604.

Location: From Casper, drive eight miles south on (Casper Mountain Road) Highway 251 to the campground.

Trip note: Trails for hiking and horseback riding are the highlights at this 160-acre county park. It's a fairly pretty campground, with lots of trees and grass and not too many people.

---

4) FORT CASPER

Reference: in Casper; map W7, grid b6.

Campsites, facilities: There are five tent sites and 92 sites for trailers or motor homes of any length. Electricity, piped water, sewer hookups and picnic tables are provided. Flush toilets, sanitary disposal station, showers, recreation hall, a store, laundromat, ice and a playground are also available. Bottled gas and a coffee shop are located within one mile. Pets and motorbikes are permitted.

Reservations, fee: Reservations accepted; $10-$15 fee per night. Open all year.

Who to contact: Phone (307) 234-3260 or write to 4205 Fort Casper Road, Casper, WY 82601.

Location: From Interstate 25 in Casper, take exit 188B. Drive south on Poplar to 13th Street and then west to Fort. This campground is located on Wyoming Boulevard between US 26 and Highway 220.

Trip note: What you see is what you get: A well-developed, private camp that can handle motor homes of any size. A good sidetrip is to the old Fort Casper, located just a quarter mile away.

---

5) PONDEROSA

Reference: south of Casper; map W7, grid b7.

Campsites, facilities: There are several sites for tents only. Picnic tables are provided. Pit toilets are available. There is **no piped water.** Pets are permitted on leashes.

Reservations, fee: No reservations necessary; $5 fee per night. Open all year.

Who to contact: Phone Natrona County Parks Board at (307) 234-6821 or write to 4621 Cy Avenue, Casper, WY 82604.

Location: From Casper, drive 10 miles south on Highway 1301 to the campground.

Trip note: At the three county parks south of Casper, it's a pick-your-own spot kind of deal. That's the case here along with Casper

Mountain Park and Bear Trap Meadow Park. Hiking trails provide recreation possibilities.

---

6) RIM

Reference: on Muddy Mountain; map W7, grid b7.

Campsites, facilities: There are seven sites for trailers or motor homes. Picnic tables and vault toilets are provided. Pets are permitted on leashes. There is **no piped water** at this site. Some facilities are **wheelchair accessible.**

Reservations, fee: No reservations necessary; $3-$5 fee per night. Open mid-June to late October.

Who to contact: Phone the Bureau of Land Management at (307) 775-6256 or write to P.O. Box 1828, Cheyenne, WY 82001.

Location: From Casper, drive nine miles south on Casper Mountain Road and then six miles south to Muddy Mountain and the campground.

Trip note: This is a tiny spot, remote and primitive. Hunters use this as a base camp during the fall months and the rest of the year it gets little use. Hiking trails in the area provide sidetrip options for campers.

---

7) LODGEPOLE

Reference: on Muddy Mountain; map W7, grid b7.

Campsites, facilities: There are 15 sites for trailers or motor homes. Piped water and picnic tables are provided along with vault toilets. Pets are permitted on leashes.

Reservations, fee: No reservations necessary; $3-$5 fee per night. Open mid-June to late October.

Who to contact: Phone Bureau of Land Management at (307) 775-6256 or write to P.O. Box 1828, Cheyenne, WY 82001.

Location: From Casper, drive nine miles south on Casper Mountain Road and six miles south to Muddy Mountain and the campground.

Trip note: Muddy Mountain (8,278-foot elevation) and Casper Mountain (8,485 feet) loom nearby. Set below those mountains is this camp, as well as nearby Rim Camp, where hiking and nature trails provide recreational options.

---

8) ALCOVA LAKE

Reference: in Fremont Canyon; map W7, grid c4.

Campsites, facilities: There are several tent sites and 10 full hookup sites for trailers or motor homes. Picnic tables are provided. Pit toilets and piped water are also available.

Reservations, fee: Reservations accepted; $5-$12 fee per night. Open April to mid-October.

Who to contact: Phone Natrona County Parks Board at (307) 234-6821 or write to 4621 Cy Avenue, Casper, WY 82604.

Location: From Casper, drive 28 miles west on Highway 220 and County Road 407 to the campground.

Trip note: This is one of three camping options in the immediate area. They all are set along water. The others are Grey Reef Reservoir and Pathfinder Reservoir. This spot is set in Fremont Canyon alongside Alcova Reservoir, a popular lake for boating.

---

9) PATHFINDER RESERVOIR

Reference: near Pathfinder Bird Refuge; map W7, grid c4.

Campsites, facilities: There are 50 sites for tents, trailers or motor homes. Picnic tables are provided. Pit toilets, sanitary disposal station and coffee shop are also available. Piped water is located at the dam site only. Boat docks, launching facilities and rentals are nearby.

Reservations, fee: No reservations necessary; $5 fee per night. Open April to mid-October.

Who to contact: Phone Natrona County Parks Board at (307) 234-6821 or write to 4621 Cy Avenue, Casper, WY 82604.

Location: From Casper, drive 42 miles west on Highway 220.

Trip note: Pathfinder Reservoir is one of the biggest lakes in the state and covers 26,500 acres. It is a favorite for campers and provides a spot for boating, fishing and all water sports. A marina and visitor center are nearby. The Pathfinder Bird Refuge surrounds the lake. Note: If you want piped water, go to the dam area.

---

10) GREY REEF RESERVOIR

Reference: west of Casper; map W7, grid c5.

Campsites, facilities: There are several sites for tents, trailers or motor homes. Picnic tables are provided. Pit toilets are also available. There is **no piped water.**

Reservations, fee: No reservations necessary; $5 fee per night. Open April to mid-October.

Who to contact: Phone Natrona County Parks Board at (307) 234-6821 or write to 4621 Cy Avenue, Casper, WY 82604.

Location: From Casper, drive 26 miles west on Highway 220 to the campground.

Trip note: Here's a do-it-yourself county park. You pick the site or make your own. It is set along Grey Reef Reservoir, a small lake for car-top boats and fishing.

---

11) CAMPBELL CREEK

Reference: near La Prele Creek, Medicine Bow National Forest; map W7, grid c9.

Campsites, facilities: There are nine sites for tents, trailers or motor homes up to 22 feet long. Picnic tables are provided. Hand-pumped vault toilets and firewood are also available. Pets are permitted on leashes.

Reservations, fee: No reservations necessary; no fee. Open June to mid October.

Who to contact: Phone Medicine Bow National Forest at (307) 358-4690 or write to Douglas Ranger District, 809 South Ninth, Douglas, WY 82633.

Location: From Douglas, drive one mile west on Interstate 25. Turn southwest on Highway 91 and drive 20 miles, then 13 miles southwest on County Road 24 to the campground.

Trip note: A rugged, little-used area, this is a good spot for four-wheel-drive cowboys to set up headquarters. The camp is set at the confluence of Campbell and La Prele Creeks. Get your hands on a Forest Service map which details numerous four-wheel-drive roads and hiking trails.

---

12) SEMINOE STATE PARK

Reference: on Seminoe Reservoir; map W7, grid e3.

Campsites, facilities: There are 76 sites for tents, trailers or motor homes of any length. Picnic tables are provided. Piped water, pit toilets, sanitary disposal station and a playground are also available. A coffee shop is located within 10 miles. Some facilities are **wheelchair accessible.** Pets are permitted on leashes. Boat docks and launching facilities are nearby.

Reservations, fee: No reservations necessary; $4 fee per night plus $2 entrance fee. Open all year with limited winter facilities.

Who to contact: Phone (307) 328-0115 or write to Seminoe Dam Route, Sinclair, WY 82334.

Location: Travel eight miles east of Rawlins on Interstate 80 to the Sinclair exit. From Sinclair, drive north on Seminoe Dam Road for 34 miles to the park.

Trip note: Seminoe Reservoir is one giant lake, but there are only two campgrounds here. Both this camp, and nearby Seminoe Boat Club Area, are located along the western shoreline of the lake. This is the better of the two for tent campers. Boating campers have Pathfinder Reservoir to the north.

---

13) SEMINOE BOAT CLUB AREA

Reference: on Seminoe Reservoir; map W7, grid e3.

Campsites, facilities: There are 10 tent sites and 36 drive-through sites for trailers or motor homes of any length. Electricity, piped water and sewer hookups are provided. Flush toilets, bottled gas, sanitary disposal station, a store, coffee shop and ice are also available. Showers are available at an additional charge. Pets are permitted on leashes. Boat docks and launching facilities are nearby.

Reservations, fee: Reservations accepted; $8-$10 fee per night. Open April to late October.

Who to contact: Phone (307) 328-9734 or write to P.O. Box 182, Rawlins, WY 82301.

Location: From Rawlins, travel six miles east on Interstate 80, and take the Sinclair exit. From Sinclair, drive 25 miles north on Seminoe Dam Road and 2.5 miles east on Club Drive to the camping area.

Trip note: This is a privately developed campground covering 20 acres along the western shore of Seminoe Reservoir. It is in a sparse, desert setting, but offers a multitude of recreation opportunities, including boating, fishing and swimming. Seminoe State Park provides an alternative recreational area.

---

14) OVERLAND TRAIL KOA

Reference: near Overland Creek; map W7, grid g7.

Campsites, facilities: There are 12 tent sites and 65 sites for trailers or motor homes of any length. One camping cabin is also available. Picnic tables are provided. Flush toilets, sanitary disposal station, showers, recreation hall, a store, coffee shop, laundromat, ice and a playground are also available. Electricity and sewer hookups are available at an additional charge. Pets and motorbikes are permitted.

Reservations, fee: Reservations accepted; $13-$17 fee per night; camping cabin is $26 per night. MasterCard and Visa accepted. Open mid-May to late October.

Who to contact: Phone (307) 378-2350 or write to Arlington Route, McFadden, WY 82080.

Location: From Interstate 80 in Arlington, take exit 272. The campground is on the northeastern corner.

Trip note: Vacationers can feel a lot like pioneers on Interstate 80, the original route of the Overland Trail. The park covers 30 acres and provides nearby hiking possibilities. A trail that starts at the end of the road follows Overland Creek for a short distance before looping back to the highway. Or you can follow Rock Creek for many miles into Medicine Bow National Forest.

---

15) BOW RIVER

Reference: near Long Lake, Medicine Bow National Forest; map W7, grid h6.

Campsites, facilities: There are 13 sites for tents, trailers or motor homes up to 32 feet long. Picnic tables are provided. Potable water and pit toilets are also available. Pets are permitted on leashes.

Reservations, fee: No reservations necessary; $5 fee per night. Open mid-June to mid-September.

Who to contact: Phone Medicine Bow National Forest, Saratoga Ranger District at (307) 326-5258 or write to P.O. Box 249, Saratoga, WY 82331.

Location: From the town of Elk Mountain, drive 15.3 miles south on County Road 101, then continue a quarter mile south on Forest Service Road 101 to the campground.

Trip note: This camp is set near Medicine Bow River at 8,600 feet. Good hiking trails are available nearby, and there is excellent fishing at several of the nearby lakes and streams. A Forest Service map will detail options.

---

16) BROOKLYN LAKE

Reference: northwest of Centennial, Medicine Bow National Forest; map W7, grid h7.

Campsites, facilities: There are seven sites for tents, trailers or motor homes up to 22 feet long. Picnic tables are provided. Hand-pumped water and pit toilets are also available. Pets are permitted on leashes. Boat docks are available nearby.

Reservations, fee: Reserve through MISTIX at (800) 283-CAMP ($6 MISTIX fee); $7 fee per night. Open mid-July to early September.

Who to contact: Phone Medicine Bow National Forest at (307) 745-8971 or write to Laramie Ranger District, 2468 Jackson Street, Laramie, WY 82070-6535.

Location: From Centennial, drive northwest on Highway 130 for 9.5 miles and northwest on Forest Service Road 317 for two miles to the campground.

Trip note: This is a nice spot set along the northeast shore of Brooklyn Lake. A trail leads north of camp into the backcountry, skirting several pretty alpine lakes, including North Twin Lakes, Deep Lake and get this—Mutt Lake and Jeff Lake.

---

17) DEEP CREEK

Reference: near Snowy Lakes, Medicine Bow National Forest; map W7, grid h7.

Campsites, facilities: There are 12 sites for tents, trailers or motor homes up to 22 feet long. Picnic tables are provided. Hand-pumped potable water and pit toilets are also available. Pets are permitted on leashes.

Reservations, fee: No reservations necessary; no fee. Open July to mid-September.

Who to contact: Phone Medicine Bow National Forest, Saratoga Ranger District at (307) 326-5258 or write to P.O. Box 249, Saratoga, WY 82331.

Location: From the town of Elk Mountain, drive 24.7 miles south on County Road 101.

Trip note: This is one of two camps in the immediate area. This one is set on Deep Creek at 10,200 feet elevation, about a quarter mile from Sand Lake. Hikers will do well to use this as a jump-off spot. There are many trails in this area including north along the creek and also south past several lakes and into the northern part of the Snowy Range lakes basin area.

18) LITTLE SANDSTONE

Reference: on Little Sandstone Creek, Medicine Bow National Forest; map W7, grid i2.

Campsites, facilities: There are nine sites for tents, trailers or motor homes up to 22 feet long. Picnic tables are provided. Pit toilets are available. There is **no piped water**. Pets are permitted on leashes.

Reservations, fee: No reservations necessary; no fee. Open mid-June to late October.

Who to contact: Phone Medicine Bow National Forest at (307) 327-5481 or write to Hayden Ranger District, P.O. Box 187, Encampment, WY 82325.

Location: From Savery, drive 23.6 miles northeast on Interstate 70. Continue north for 2.5 miles on Forest Service Road 801 to the campground.

Trip note: Set along Little Sandstone Creek at 8,400 feet, this campground is not far off the highway, but it's also the jump-off point for many adventurers. Numerous four-wheel-drive roads are in the area, which make great mountain biking trails.

19) JACK CREEK

Reference: near Continental Divide, Medicine Bow National Forest; map W7, grid i2.

Campsites, facilities: There are 12 sites for tents, trailers or motor homes up to 22 feet long. Picnic tables are provided. Hand-pumped water and pit toilets are also available. Pets are permitted on leashes.

Reservations, fee: No reservations necessary; $5 fee per night. Open mid-June to mid-October.

Who to contact: Phone Medicine Bow National Forest at (307) 327-5481 or write to Hayden Ranger District, P.O. Box 187, Encampment, WY 82325.

Location: From Saratoga, drive 19.1 miles west on County Road 500 and 8.1 miles south on Forest Service Road 405 to the campground.

Trip note: This is a secluded spot, ideal for hikers. It is set along Jack Creek at 8,500 feet, right along the Continental Divide. Several trails are in the area and are detailed on the map of Medicine Bow National Forest. No other camps are in the vicinity.

20) BOTTLE CREEK

Reference: near the North Fork of Encampment River, Medicine Bow National Forest; map W7, grid i3.

Campsites, facilities: There are eight sites for tents, trailers or motor homes up to 16 feet long. Picnic tables are provided. Piped water and pit toilets are also available. Pets are permitted on leashes.

Reservations, fee: No reservations necessary; $5 fee per night. Open June to late October.

Who to contact: Phone Medicine Bow National Forest at (307) 327-5481 or write to Hayden Ranger District, P.O. Box 187, Encampment, WY 82325.

Location: From Encampment, drive southwest on Highway 70 for 7.1 miles to the campground.

Trip note: This camp is easy to reach and the scenery isn't so bad either. It is set on Bottle Creek about two miles north of the North Fork of the Encampment River.

---

21) SOUTH BRUSH CREEK

Reference: southeast of Saratoga, Medicine Bow National Forest; map W7, grid i5.

Campsites, facilities: There are 21 sites for tents, trailers or motor homes up to 30 feet long. Picnic tables are provided. Hand-pumped potable water and pit toilets are also available. A store, coffee shop and ice are located within five miles. Pets are permitted on leashes.

Reservations, fee: No reservations necessary; $6 fee per night. Open mid-May to October.

Who to contact: Phone Medicine Bow National Forest, Saratoga Ranger District at (307) 326-5258 or write to P.O. Box 249, Saratoga, WY 82331.

Location: From Saratoga, drive 20.2 miles southeast on Highway 130 and 0.2 mile east on Forest Service Road 100 (North Brush Creek Road). Continue 1.1 miles southeast on Forest Service Road 200 to the campground.

Trip note: This easy-to-reach campground has just enough turns so that all out-of-towners miss it. It is set at 7,900 feet elevation on South Brush Creek about four miles from Lincoln Park (see the trip note). Several primitive roads leading from camp follow nearby creeks into the Medicine Bow Mountains.

---

22) RYAN PARK

Reference: on the North Fork of Barrett Creek, Medicine Bow National Forest; map W7, grid i5.

Campsites, facilities: There are 49 sites (including one large group area) for tents, trailers or motor homes up to 30 feet long. Water is available through a hydrant system. Picnic tables, pit toilets, a store, cafe and ice are also located within five miles. Pets are permitted on leashes.

Reservations, fee: Reserve single sites through MISTIX at (800) 263-CAMP ($6 MISTIX fee); $7 fee per night. The group site may be reserved by calling the Saratoga Ranger District; $25-$50 fee per night depending on number of people. Open mid-May to mid-October.

Who to contact: Phone Medicine Bow National Forest, Saratoga Ranger District at (307) 326-5258 or write to P.O. Box 249, Saratoga, WY 82331.

Location: From Saratoga, drive 23.3 miles southeast on Highway 130 to the campground.

Trip note: This is one of the more popular Forest Service campgrounds in the region, and that's because of the easy access. The camp is set along the North Fork of Barrett Creek, about a mile from the small mountain community of Ryan Park. This is one of the more popular camps in the area, so get your reservation in early.

---

23) LINCOLN PARK

Reference: on Lincoln Creek, Medicine Bow National Forest; map W7, grid i5.

Campsites, facilities: There are eight sites for tents, trailers or motor homes up to 22 feet long. Picnic tables are provided. Hand-pumped potable water and pit toilets are also available. A store, coffee shop and ice are located within eight miles. Pets are permitted on leashes.

Reservations, fee: No reservations necessary; $5 fee per night. Open mid-May to October.

Who to contact: Phone Medicine Bow National Forest, Saratoga Ranger District at (307) 326-5258 or write to P.O. Box 249, Saratoga, WY 82331.

Location: From Saratoga, drive 20.2 miles southeast on Highway 130 and 2.6 miles northeast on Forest Service Road 100 (North Brush Creek Road) to the campground.

Trip note: This little-known spot is set at the confluence of Lincoln and North Brush Creeks at 7,800 feet. Nearby dirt roads follow the canyons into the adjacent Medicine Bow Mountains. The name Medicine Bow comes from the days when a few Native American tribes would meet once a year here to make their bows from the mahogany that grows in the valleys. At the same time, they would exchange information on medical wisdom. Thus, early pioneers referred to the area as "the medicine bow."

---

24) FRENCH CREEK

Reference: east of Encampment, Medicine Bow National Forest; map W7, grid i5.

Campsites, facilities: There are 11 sites for tents, trailers or motor homes up to 30 feet long. Picnic tables are provided. Hand-pumped potable water and pit toilets are also available. Pets are permitted on leashes.

Reservations, fee: No reservations necessary; $5 fee per night. Open June to October.

Who to contact: Phone Medicine Bow National Forest, Saratoga Ranger District at (307) 326-5258 or write to P.O. Box 249, Saratoga, WY 82331.

Location: From Encampment, drive 4.2 miles east on Highway 230. Continue 14.3 miles east on Highway 660 and the three-quarters of a mile northeast on Forest Service Road 206 to the campground.

Trip note: Set on the western edge of the Medicine Bow National Forest, this campground is situated along French Creek at an elevation of 7,790 feet.

---

25) SILVER LAKE

Reference: near French Creek, Medicine Bow National Forest; map W7, grid i6.

Campsites, facilities: There are 19 sites for tents, trailers or motor homes up to 32 feet long. Picnic tables are provided. Piped water and pit toilets are also available. Pets are permitted on leashes. Boat docks are nearby.

Reservations, fee: No reservations necessary; $7 fee per night. Open July to mid-September.

Who to contact: Phone Medicine Bow National Forest, Saratoga Ranger District at (307) 326-5258 or write to P.O. Box 249, Saratoga, WY 82331.

Location: From Centennial, drive 16 miles northwest on Highway 130 to the campground. Or from Saratoga, drive 31.3 miles east on Highway 130.

Trip note: This beautiful spot is set alongside little Silver Lake in the high country at 10,400 feet in the Medicine Bow Mountains. A trail from camp follows a creek south to French Creek and is a good hike.

---

26) ASPEN

Reference: on Libby Creek, Medicine Bow National Forest; map W7, grid i7.

Campsites, facilities: There are eight sites for tents, trailers or motor homes up to 22 feet long. Picnic tables are provided. Piped water, pit toilets and firewood are also available. Showers, a store, coffee shop, laundromat and ice are located within five miles. Pets are permitted on leashes.

Reservations, fee: Reserve through MISTIX at (800) 283-CAMP ($6 MISTIX fee); $5 fee per night. Open June to late September.

Who to contact: Phone Medicine Bow National Forest at (307) 745-8971 or write to Laramie Ranger District, 2468 Jackson Street, Laramie, WY 82070-6535.

Location: From Centennial, drive northwest on Highway 130 for 2 miles and west on Forest Service Road 351 for several hundred yards to the campground.

Trip note: This is a take-your-pick deal. This is one of four campgrounds in the immediate area on Libby Creek. A visitor center is nearby and provides details on recreation possibilities. Corner Mountain looms to the east at 9,506 feet.

---

27) SPRUCE

Reference: on Libby Creek, Medicine Bow National Forest; map W7, grid i7.

Campsites, facilities: There are eight sites for tents, trailers or motor homes up to 16 feet long. Picnic tables are provided. Piped water and pit toilets are also available. Showers, a store, coffee shop, laundromat and ice are located within five miles. Pets are permitted on leashes.

Reservations, fee: Reserve through MISTIX at (800) 283-CAMP ($6 MISTIX fee); $5 fee per night. Open June to late September.

Who to contact: Phone Medicine Bow National Forest at (307) 745-8971 or write to Laramie Ranger District, 2468 Jackson Street, Laramie, WY 82070-6535.

Location: From Centennial, drive 2.4 miles northwest on Highway 130 to the campground.

Trip note: This is one of the camps in the Libby Creek Recreation Area complex. If this one is full, you have three others to choose from. For recreation options, the nearby visitors center can provide information.

---

28) SUGARLOAF

Reference: near Medicine Bow Peak, Medicine Bow National Forest; map W7, grid i7.

Campsites, facilities: There are 16 sites for tents, trailers or motor homes up to 22 feet long. Picnic tables are provided. Hand-pumped water and pit toilets are also available. Pets are permitted on leashes.

Reservations, fee: Reserve through MISTIX at (800) 283-CAMP ($6 MISTIX fee); $7 fee per night. Open mid-July to early September.

Who to contact: Phone Medicine Bow National Forest at (307) 745-8971 or write to Laramie Ranger District, 2468 Jackson Street, Laramie, WY 82070-6535.

Location: From Centennial, drive northwest on Highway 130 for 13 miles and north on Forest Service Road 346 for one mile to the campground.

Trip note: Here's quite a spot. The camp is set at 10,700 feet in an area with several jewel-like alpine lakes and granite peaks rising steeply above them. Those mountain tops form the Snowy Range, named because of its abundant (and often year-round) snowpack on its eastern flank. If you have the ambition, a trail from camp leads to Medicine Bow Peak, the highest peak in the range at 12,013 feet. Other trails from camp lead to numerous alpine lakes.

29) NASH FORK

Reference: on Libby Creek, Medicine Bow National Forest; map W7, grid i7.

Campsites, facilities: There are 27 sites for tents, trailers or motor homes up to 22 feet long. Picnic tables are provided. Piped water and pit toilets are also available. Pets are permitted on leashes.

Reservations, fee: No reservations necessary; $7 fee per night. Open July to early September.

Who to contact: Phone Medicine Bow National Forest at (307) 745-8971 or write to Laramie Ranger District, 2468 Jackson Street, Laramie, WY 82070-6535.

Location: From Centennial, drive northwest on Highway 130 for eight miles and north on Forest Service Road 317 for several hundred yards to the campground.

Trip note: Easy access is a highlight here. The camp is just a short hop off the highway and only two miles from Brooklyn Lake Camp. It's set alongside Libby Creek, with a scenic view to boot. By driving a short distance north, you can access several miles of hiking trails routed into the backcountry. See a Forest Service map.

30) NORTH FORK

Reference: on the North Fork of Laramie River, Medicine Bow National Forest; map W7, grid i7.

Campsites, facilities: There are 30 sites for tents, trailers or motor homes up to 22 feet long. Picnic tables are provided. Hand-pumped water and pit toilets are also available. Pets are permitted on leashes.

Reservations, fee: Reserve through MISTIX at (800) 283-CAMP ($6 MISTIX fee); $5 fee per night. Open June to early September.

Who to contact: Phone Medicine Bow National Forest at (307) 745-8971 or write to Laramie Ranger District, 2468 Jackson Street, Laramie, WY 82070-6535.

Location: From Centennial, drive northwest on Highway 130 for 3.5 miles and northwest on Forest Service Road 101 for 1.7 miles to the campground.

Trip note: You get a taste of the high country here. It's a pretty spot set along the North Fork of Laramie River. A trail out of the camp follows the river west to Brooklyn Lake, which is good for a sidetrip. Of course, you can drive to Brooklyn Lake.

31) PINE

Reference: on Libby Creek, Medicine Bow National Forest; map W7, grid i7.

Campsites, facilities: There are six sites for tents, trailers or motor homes up to 16 feet long. Picnic tables are provided. Piped water and pit toilets are also available. Showers, a store, coffee shop, laundromat and ice are located within five miles. Pets are permitted on leashes.

Reservations, fee: Reserve through MISTIX at (800) 283-CAMP ($6 MISTIX fee); $5 fee per night. Open June to late September.

Who to contact: Phone Medicine Bow National Forest at (307) 745-8971 or write to Laramie Ranger District, 2468 Jackson Street, Laramie, WY 82070-6535.

Location: From Centennial, drive northwest on Highway 130 for 2.3 miles and northwest on Forest Service Road 351 for a half mile to the campground.

Trip note: This is one of four camps set in the immediate area along Libby Creek in the Libby Creek Recreation Area complex. See the trip note for Aspen Camp or Spruce Camp.

---

32) ROB ROY

Reference: on Rob Roy Reservoir, Medicine Bow National Forest; map W7, grid i7.

Campsites, facilities: There are 43 sites for tents, trailers or motor homes up to 35 feet long. Picnic tables are provided. Piped water and pit toilets are also available. Pets are permitted on leashes. Boat launching facilities are nearby.

Reservations, fee: Reserve through MISTIX at (800) 283-CAMP ($6 MISTIX fee); $6 fee per night. Open mid-June to late September.

Who to contact: Phone Medicine Bow National Forest at (307) 745-8971 or write to Laramie Ranger District, 2468 Jackson Street, Laramie, WY 82070-6535.

Location: From Laramie, drive 22 miles west on Highway 130. Drive 11 miles southwest on Highway 11 and nine miles west on Forest Service Road 500 to the campground.

Trip note: This camp is set along Rob Roy Reservoir, a decent-sized lake on Douglas Creek. It's just hard enough to reach that it doesn't get heavy traffic, despite good boating and fishing recreational opportunities.

---

33) WILLOW

Reference: on Libby Creek, Medicine Bow National Forest; map W7, grid i7.

Campsites, facilities: There are 16 sites for tents, trailers or motor homes up to 22 feet long. Picnic tables are provided. Piped water and pit toilets are also available. A store, coffee shop, laundromat and ice are located within five miles. Pets are permitted on leashes.

Reservations, fee: Reserve through MISTIX at (800) 283-CAMP ($6 MISTIX fee); $5 fee per night. Open June to late September.

Who to contact: Phone Medicine Bow National Forest at (307) 745-8971 or write to Laramie Ranger District, 2468 Jackson Street, Laramie, WY 82070-6535.

Location: From Centennial, drive two miles northwest on Highway 130 and a half mile west on Forest Service Road 351 to the campground.

Trip note: This is one of four camps in the immediate area along Libby Creek. See the trip note for Aspen Camp.

---

34) BATTLE CREEK

Reference: on the North Fork of Battle Creek, Medicine Bow National Forest; map W7, grid j2.

Campsites, facilities: There are four tent sites. Picnic tables are provided. Hand-pumped water and pit toilets are also available. Pets are permitted on leashes.

Reservations, fee: No reservations necessary; no fee. Open June to late October.

Who to contact: Phone Medicine Bow National Forest at (307) 327-5481 or write to Hayden Ranger District, P.O. Box 187, Encampment, WY 82325.

Location: From Savery, drive 22.9 miles east on Highway 70 and south on Forest Service Road 807 for three miles to the campground. Forest Service Road 807 is a primitive dirt road.

Trip note: Campgrounds don't get much smaller or intimate than this little one. And it's pretty, too, set in the trees along the North Fork of Battle Creek. Several trails are in the area and are detailed on a Forest Service map.

---

35) HASKINS CREEK

Reference: southwest of Encampment, Medicine Bow National Forest; map W7, grid j2.

Campsites, facilities: There are 10 sites for tents, trailers or motor homes up to 22 feet long. Picnic tables are provided. Piped water and pit toilets are also available. Pets are permitted on leashes.

Reservations, fee: No reservations necessary; $5 fee per night. Open mid-June to late October.

Who to contact: Phone Medicine Bow National Forest at (307) 327-5481 or write to Hayden Ranger District, P.O. Box 187, Encampment, WY 82325.

Location: From Encampment, drive 15.3 miles southwest on Highway 401 to the campground.

Trip note: Well, you learn something every day. This camp is set on Haskins Creek. There is a monument about two miles away that marks the spot where Thomas Edison got some brilliant ideas which led to the invention of the light bulb while fishing and looking at his frayed bamboo pole. Hard as this may be to believe, it's true.

36) LOST CREEK

Reference: southwest of Encampment, Medicine Bow National Forest; map W7, grid j2.

Campsites, facilities: There are 14 sites for tents, trailers or motor homes up to 22 feet long. Picnic tables are provided. Piped water and pit toilets are also available. Pets are permitted on leashes.

Reservations, fee: No reservations necessary; $5 fee per night. Open mid-June to late October.

Who to contact: Phone Medicine Bow National Forest at (307) 327-5481 or write to Hayden Ranger District, P.O. Box 187, Encampment, WY 82325.

Location: From Encampment, drive 17.3 miles southwest on Highway 401/70 to the campground.

Trip note: Easy access is a highlight here. The camp is located right along the road, adjacent to Lost Creek. As you drive through the area, keep your eyes open for several abandoned mines. This area was once a mining center and the old mines provide a window to that period.

37) LAKEVIEW

Reference: on Hog Park Reservoir, Medicine Bow National Forest; map W7, grid j3.

Campsites, facilities: There are 50 sites for tents, trailers or motor homes up to 22 feet long. Picnic tables are provided. Piped water and pit toilets are also available. Pets are permitted on leashes. Boat docks and launching facilities are nearby.

Reservations, fee: No reservations necessary; $6 fee per night. Open mid-June to mid-September.

Who to contact: Phone Medicine Bow National Forest at (307) 327-5481 or write to Hayden Ranger District, P.O. Box 187, Encampment, WY 82325.

Location: From Encampment, drive southwest on Highway 70 for six miles and continue southwest on Forest Service Road 550 for 22 miles to the campground.

Trip note: Here's a secluded camp that can provide many different adventures. It is set on Hog Park Reservoir at 8,400 feet. This is a good lake for boating and fishing. Hikers can take one of the several trails that are routed into the adjacent wildlands and over the Continental Divide. The trails lead to several creeks with good fishing prospects.

38) PIKE POLE

Reference: near North Platte River, Medicine Bow National Forest map W7, grid j6.

Campsites, facilities: There are six sites for tents, trailers or motor homes up to 16 feet long. Picnic tables are provided. Pit toilets are also available. There is **no piped water.** Pets are permitted on leashes.

Reservations, fee: No reservations necessary; no fee. Open mid-June to mid-October.

Who to contact: Phone Medicine Bow National Forest at (307) 745-8971 or write to Laramie Ranger District, 2468 Jackson Street, Laramie, WY 82070-6535.

Location: From Foxpark, drive 23.5 miles west on Forest Service Road 512 to the campground.

Trip note: This is one of two camps in the immediate area. A trail leads out of camp, winding along Douglas Creek for about 11 miles to Pelton Creek Camp. For other hiking options, see the trip note for adjacent Pickaroon Camp.

---

39) SIX MILE GAP

Reference: near North Platte River, Medicine Bow National Forest; map W7, grid j6.

Campsites, facilities: There are seven sites for tents, trailers or motor homes up to 32 feet long. Picnic tables are provided. Hand-pumped water and pit toilets are also available. Pets are permitted on leashes. Boat docks are nearby.

Reservations, fee: No reservations necessary; no fee. Open mid-June to late October.

Who to contact: Phone Medicine Bow National Forest at (307) 327-5481 or write to Hayden Ranger District, P.O. Box 187, Encampment, WY 82325.

Location: From Encampment, drive 24.6 miles southeast on Highway 230 and two miles southeast on Forest Service Road 492.

Trip note: This is a pretty spot in North Gate Canyon. The camp is set along the North Platte River. A trail from camp follows the North Platte River north for about 10 miles to Pickaroon and Pike Pole camps. There is fishing access nearby.

---

40) PICKAROON

Reference: on North Platte River, Medicine Bow National Forest; map W7, grid j6.

Campsites, facilities: There are eight sites for tents, trailers or motor homes up to 16 feet long. Picnic tables and pit toilets are provided. There is **no piped water.** Pets are permitted on leashes.

Reservations, fee: No reservations necessary; no fee. Open mid-June to mid-October.

Who to contact: Phone Medicine Bow National Forest at (307) 745-8971 or write to Laramie Ranger District, 2468 Jackson Street, Laramie, WY 82070-6535.

Location: From Foxpark, drive 23 miles west on Forest Service Road 512 to the campground.

Trip note: This is one of two camps in the immediate vicinity (the other is Pike Pole Camp). Set at the confluence of Douglas Creek and the

North Platte River, it's a popular base camp for hikers. Trails from camp lead southeast along Douglas Creek for about 11 miles to Pelton Creek Camp and south along North Platte River to Six Mile Gap Camp. About two miles north of camp are trailheads that provide access to the Savage Run Wilderness.

---

41) BOBBIE THOMSON

Reference: near Douglas Creek, Medicine Bow National Forest; map W7, grid j7.

Campsites, facilities: There are 18 sites for tents, trailers or motor homes up to 32 feet long. Picnic tables are provided. Piped water and pit toilets are also available. Pets are permitted on leashes.

Reservations, fee: No reservations necessary; no fee. Open June to mid-October.

Who to contact: Phone Medicine Bow National Forest at (307) 745-8971 or write to Laramie Ranger District, 2468 Jackson Street, Laramie, WY 82070-6535.

Location: From Foxpark, drive 11.2 miles northwest on Forest Service Road 512 to the campground.

Trip note: This is a good base camp for anglers. There's good fishing on Douglas Creek about five miles south of Rob Roy Reservoir. Boating, fishing and swimming are options at Rob Roy Reservoir.

---

42) MILLER LAKE

Reference: near Foxpark, Medicine Bow National Forest; map W7, grid j7.

Campsites, facilities: There are seven sites for tents, trailers or motor homes up to 22 feet long. Picnic tables are provided. Piped water and pit toilets are also available. A store and a restaurant are located within one mile. Pets are permitted on leashes.

Reservations, fee: No reservations necessary; no fee. Open June to mid-October.

Who to contact: Phone Medicine Bow National Forest at (307) 745-8971 or write to Laramie Ranger District, 2468 Jackson Street, Laramie, WY 82070-6535.

Location: From Foxpark, drive one mile south on Forest Service Road 512. If you're approaching from Highway 230, drive a half mile north on Forest Service Road 512.

Trip note: This is a pretty little camp, set on the east end of tiny Miller Lake. There are no designated hiking trails near the camp, but the adventurous can strap on their boots anyway (or hop on mountain bikes) and explore the maze of old Forest Service roads to the southwest.

43) PELTON CREEK

Reference: near Douglas Creek, Medicine Bow National Forest; map W7, grid j7.

Campsites, facilities: There are 15 sites for tents, trailers or motor homes up to 16 feet long. Picnic tables are provided. Piped water and pit toilets are also available. Pets are permitted on leashes.

Reservations, fee: No reservations necessary; no fee. Open June to mid-October.

Who to contact: Phone Medicine Bow National Forest at (307) 745-8971 or write to Laramie Ranger District, 2468 Jackson Street, Laramie, WY 82070-6535.

Location: From Laramie, drive 40 miles southwest on Highway 230 and nine miles northwest on Forest Service Road 898 to the campground.

Trip note: This is a good jump-off point for hikers or folks who just want to hunker down for a while and watch the water go by. With the camp set at the confluence of Pelton and Douglas Creeks, there's a lot of water flowing by. Hikers can consider a trail that leads from camp and follows Douglas Creek for about 10 miles and leads northwest to Pickaroon Camp and Pike Pole Camp.

44) LAKE OWEN

Reference: near Foxpark, Medicine Bow National Forest; map W7, grid j8.

Campsites, facilities: There are 35 sites for tents, trailers or motor homes up to 22 feet long. Picnic tables are provided. Piped water and pit toilets are also available. Pets are permitted on leashes. A boat ramp is nearby.

Reservations, fee: No reservations necessary; no fee. Open June to mid-October.

Who to contact: Phone Medicine Bow National Forest at (307) 745-8971 or write to Laramie Ranger District, 2468 Jackson Street, Laramie, WY 82070-6535.

Location: From Foxpark, drive seven miles northeast on Forest Service Road 517 and three miles south on Forest Service Road 540 to the campground.

Trip note: Set right next to Lake Owen, this is a good spot for boating and fishing. Don't be surprised if you hear a freight train in your dreams because Union Pacific tracks run right by the lake.

45) BOSWELL CREEK

Reference: near Wyoming-Colorado border, Medicine Bow National Forest; map W7, grid j8.

Campsites, facilities: There are nine sites for tents, trailers or motor homes up to 16 feet long. Picnic tables are provided. Piped water and pit toilets are also available. A store and coffee shop are located within five miles. Pets are permitted on leashes.

Reservations, fee: No reservations necessary; no fee. Open June to mid-September.

Who to contact: Phone Medicine Bow National Forest at (307) 745-8971 or write to Laramie Ranger District, 2468 Jackson Street, Laramie, WY 82070-6535.

Location: From Laramie, drive 38 miles southwest on Highway 230 and three miles east on Forest Service Road 526 to the campground.

Trip note: Little Boswell Creek runs alongside this camp. This is a nice setting, located right off the highway near the Wyoming-Colorado border, about three miles from the little town of Mountain Home.

Wyoming Map W8
26 listings
Pages 542-554

North (W4)—see page 498
East—Nebraska
South—Colorado
West (W7)—see page 520

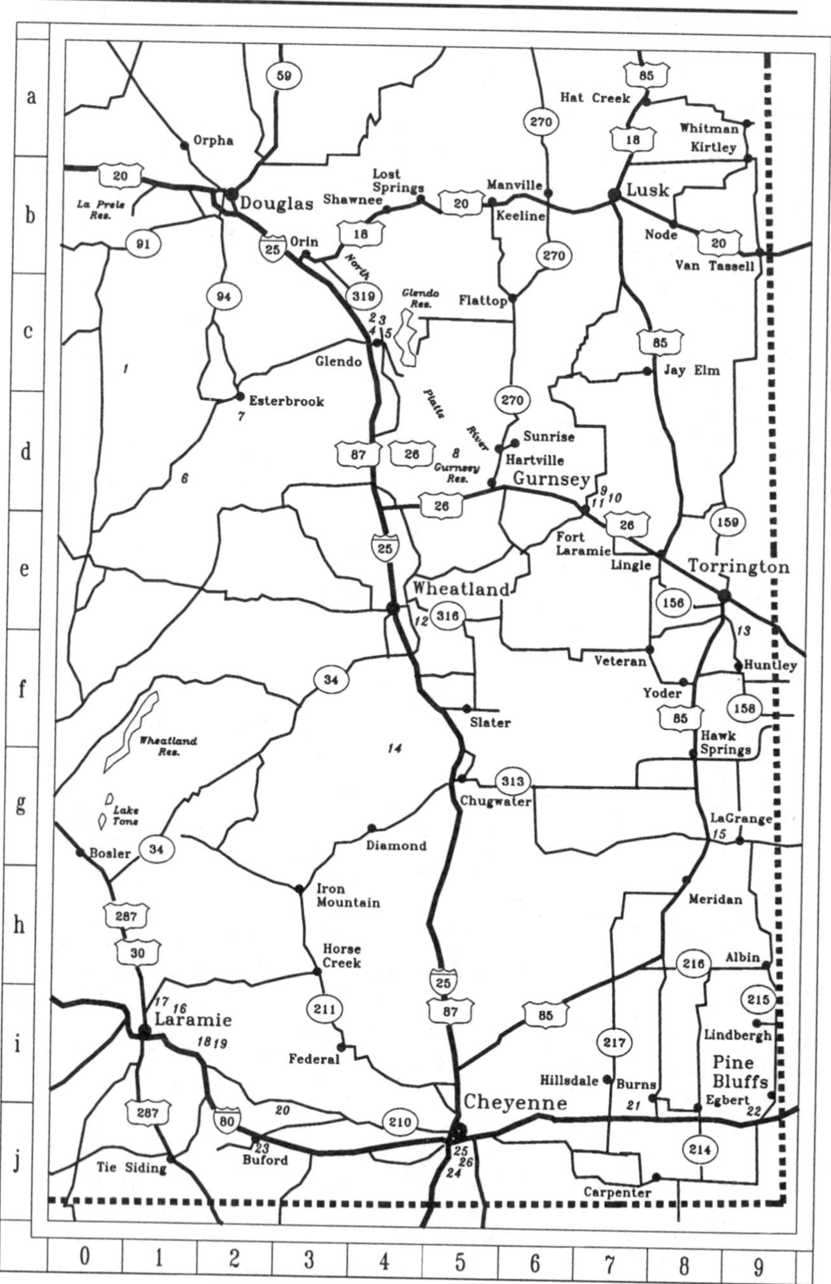

Featuring: Medicine Bow National Forest, La Bonte Creek, Glendo Reservoir, Laramie Peak, Horseshoe Creek, Guernsey Reservoir, North Platte River, Hawk Springs Reservoir, Sherman Mountains, Pole Mountain, Curt Gowdy Lake

---

1) CURTIS GULCH

Reference: on La Bonte Creek, Medicine Bow National Forest; map W8, grid c0.

Campsites, facilities: There are six sites for tents, trailers or motor homes up to 22 feet long. Picnic tables are provided. Hand-pumped water, vault toilets and firewood are also available. Pets are permitted on leashes.

Reservations, fee: No reservations necessary; no fee. Open July to mid-October.

Who to contact: Phone Medicine Bow National Forest at (307) 358-4690 or write to Douglas Ranger District, 809 South Ninth, Douglas, WY 82633.

Location: From Douglas, drive one mile west on Interstate 25 and 20 miles southwest on Highway 91. Continue 14.5 miles south on County Road 16 and four miles northeast on Forest Service Road 658 to the campground.

Trip note: Situated deep in the Laramie Mountains, the campsites are set alongside La Bonte Creek, which provides decent fishing opportunities. It's pretty here, densely-forested and shady. Trails route into the canyons to the east and south.

---

2) GLENDO MARINA

Reference: on Glendo Reservoir; map W8, grid c4.

Campsites, facilities: There are 10 sites for trailers or motor homes up to 30 feet long. Electricity, piped water and sewer hookups are provided. Bottled gas, a store, coffee shop and ice are also available. Firewood costs extra. A sanitary disposal station is located within one mile. Pets are permitted on leashes. Boat docks, launching facilities and rentals are available at the marina.

Reservations, fee: Reservations accepted; $12.50 fee per night plus state park entrance fee; MasterCard and Visa accepted. Open April to November.

Who to contact: Phone (307) 735-4216 or write to P.O. Box 187, Glendo, WY 82213.

Location: From Glendo, drive 3.5 miles southeast to the marina in Glendo State Park.

Trip note: This is an option for campers at Glendo State Park with motor homes or trailers. It's in a parking lot-type setting, with many recreation options nearby. The marina offers boating, fishing and a swimming beach. Hiking trails are available throughout the park.

3) GLENDO STATE PARK

Reference: at Glendo Reservoir; map W8, grid c4.

Campsites, facilities: There are 166 sites for tents, trailers or motor homes of any length. Picnic tables are provided. Piped water, pit toilets, sanitary disposal station, a store, coffee shop, ice and a playground are also available. Some facilities are **wheelchair accessible**. Pets are permitted on leashes. Boat docks, launching facilities and rentals are nearby.

Reservations, fee: No reservations necessary; $4 fee per night plus $2 entrance fee. Open all year with limited facilities in the winter.

Who to contact: Phone (307) 735-4433 or write to P.O. Box 57, Glendo, WY 82213.

Location: From Glendo, drive four miles east on the paved road.

Trip note: This is a popular spot for tent campers. Glendo Reservoir is the biggest lake in the area. There are many recreation options here: power boating, fishing, canoeing and hiking. Glendo Marina and Lakeview provide nearby lakeside options for campers with motor homes or trailers.

4) LAKEVIEW

Reference: on Glendo Reservoir; map W8, grid c4.

Campsites, facilities: There are 20 tent sites and 20 sites for trailers or motor homes of any length. Electricity, piped water, sewer hookups and picnic tables are provided. Flush toilets, showers and laundromat are also available. Bottled gas, a store, coffee shop and ice are located within one mile. Pets and motorbikes are permitted.

Reservations, fee: Reservations accepted; $10 fee per night. Open all year.

Who to contact: Phone (307) 735-4461 or write to P.O. Box 231, Glendo, WY 82213.

Location: This campground is located less than a mile north of Glendo on US 26.

Trip note: This is a pretty spot set alongside Glendo Reservoir, not far from Glendo State Park. See trip notes for Glendo State Park and Glendo Marina for recreation suggestions.

5) COLLINS CORRAL

Reference: on Glendo Reservoir; map W8, grid c4.

Campsites, facilities: There are 22 sites for trailers or motor homes of any length. Electricity, piped water and sewer hookups are provided. A playground is also available. A store, coffee shop, laundromat and ice are located within one mile. Pets are permitted on leashes. Boat docks, launching facilities and rentals are nearby.

Reservations, fee: Reservations accepted; $10 fee per night. Open all year.

Who to contact: Phone (307) 735-4381 or write to P.O. Box 185, Glendo, WY 82213.

Location: This trailer park is located less than a mile south of Glendo on Highway 319.

Trip note: This is one of two parks on Glendo Reservoir that post the sign "no tenters need apply." Tent campers should head to Glendo State Park.

---

6) FRIEND PARK

Reference: near Laramie Peak, Medicine Bow National Forest; map W8, grid d1.

Campsites, facilities: There are six sites for tents, trailers or motor homes up to 22 feet long. Picnic tables are provided. Hand-pumped water, vault toilets and firewood are also available. Pets are permitted on leashes.

Reservations, fee: No reservations necessary; no fee. Open mid-June to mid-October.

Who to contact: Phone Medicine Bow National Forest at (307) 358-4690 or write to Douglas Ranger District, 809 South Ninth, Douglas, WY 82633.

Location: From Douglas, drive 25 miles south on County Road 5 and 15 miles southwest on Forest Service Road 653. Continue 3.5 miles east on Forest Service Road 671 to the campground.

Trip note: If you like to hike, this is the spot for you. The camp is remote and secluded, set on Friend Creek at 7,400 feet. Laramie Peak Trail switchbacks its way up to Laramie Peak at 10,272 feet. It's not a long walk in miles, but with the elevation gain, you can plan to make a day of it.

---

7) ESTERBROOK

Reference: near Horseshoe Creek, Medicine Bow National Forest; map W8, grid d2.

Campsites, facilities: There are 12 sites for tents, trailers or motor homes up to 22 feet long. Picnic tables are provided. Hand-pumped water, vault toilets and firewood are also available. A coffee shop is located within five miles. Pets are permitted on leashes.

Reservations, fee: No reservations necessary; no fee. Open June to mid October.

Who to contact: Phone Medicine Bow National Forest at (307) 358-4690 or write to Douglas Ranger District, 809 South Ninth, Douglas, WY 82633.

Location: From Douglas, drive one mile west on Interstate 25. Take the Highway 194 exit and drive 17 miles south, then 11 miles south on County Road 5. Continue three miles east on Forest Service Road 633 to the campground.

Trip note: Of the four camps sprinkled throughout the Laramie Mountains, this one is the closest to a town. It's just three miles from Esterbrook, yet it's primitive and rugged. Four-wheel-drive roads (detailed on the Forest Service map) are in the area. Set at 6,500 feet, the site is located about 1.5 miles from Horseshoe Creek.

---

8) GUERNSEY STATE PARK

Reference: on Guernsey Reservoir; map W8, grid d5.

Campsites, facilities: There are 142 sites for tents, trailers or motor homes of any length. Picnic tables are provided. Piped water, pit toilets, sanitary disposal station and a playground are also available. Some facilities are **wheelchair accessible.** Pets are permitted on leashes. Boat docks and launching facilities are nearby.

Reservations, fee: No reservations necessary; $4 fee per night plus $2 entrance fee. Open all year with limited winter facilities.

Who to contact: Phone (307) 632-7946 or write to P.O. Box 395, Guernsey, WY 82214.

Location: From Guernsey, drive a half mile west on US 26 and then one mile north on Highway 317 to the park.

Trip note: Guernsey State Park is set along Guernsey Reservoir, which is the afterbay to its big sibling, Glendo Reservoir. This spot is smaller, but in many ways it is better because it is shielded from wind by the bluffs surrounding the reservoir. That makes it ideal for boating. A museum in the park details the historic Oregon Trail.

---

9) FORT LARAMIE MUNICIPAL PARK

Reference: on North Platte River; map W8, grid d7.

Campsites, facilities: There are 25 sites for tents, trailers or motor homes of any length. Picnic tables are provided. Piped water, flush toilets, firewood and a playground are also available. A store, coffee shop, laundromat and ice are located within one mile. Pets are permitted on leashes.

Reservations, fee: No reservations necessary; no fee. Open all year. Three-day limit.

Who to contact: Phone (307) 837-2711 or write to Fort Laramie, WY 82212.

Location: In Fort Laramie, drive west for one block on Fort Laramie Road to the park.

Trip note: The price is right, you can start with that. It's a county park set aside the North Platte River, with open sites and decent fishing in the adjacent river. Not much to look at, but it's not a bad place to set down for the night.

10) BENNETT COURT

Reference: near Fort Laramie; map W8, grid d7.

Campsites, facilities: There are 11 drive-through sites for tents, trailers or motor homes of any length. Electricity, piped water, sewer hookups and picnic tables are provided. Flush toilets, sanitary disposal station, showers and laundromat are also available. Bottled gas, a store, coffee shop and ice are located within one mile. Pets and motorbikes are permitted.

Reservations, fee: Reservations accepted; $7-$9 fee per night. Open all year.

Who to contact: Phone (307) 837-2270 or write to P.O. Box 54, Fort Laramie, WY 82212.

Location: In Fort Laramie, turn north off US 26 on Laramie Avenue and drive three blocks to the campground.

Trip note: Open, grassy sites make this attractive for campers looking to get off the highway and get some shut-eye. Historic Old Fort Laramie, three miles from this camp, is the main attraction around these parts. See trip note for Chuckwagon Drive-In for more sidetrips.

11) CHUCKWAGON DRIVE-IN

Reference: in Fort Laramie; map W8, grid d7.

Campsites, facilities: There are 10 tent sites and 15 sites for trailers or motor homes of any length. Electricity, piped water, sewer hookups and picnic tables are provided. Flush toilets, sanitary disposal station, showers and a coffee shop are also available. Bottled gas, a store, laundromat and ice are located within one mile. Pets and motorbikes are permitted.

Reservations, fee: Reservations accepted; $10 fee per night. Open mid-April to mid-October.

Who to contact: Phone (307) 837-2828 or write to P.O. Box 166, Fort Laramie, WY 82212.

Location: This campground is located less than a mile south of Fort Laramie on Highway 160.

Trip note: This is one of three choices in the area. Take your pick between Chuckwagon or Bennett Court in Fort Laramie and Pioneer Park (best for tenters) in Torrington. Chuckwagon is set in a lush plot of Kentucky bluegrass, with large, open sites. Historic Old Fort Laramie is three miles away. Another historic point of interest is 13 miles west in Gurnsey, where you can see Register Cliff, the rock where old-west pioneers carved their names. You can even see ancient wagon trail ruts there.

12) SQUAW MOUNTAIN

Reference: in Wheatland; map W8, grid e4.

Campsites, facilities: There are six tent sites and 24 drive-through sites for trailers or motor homes of any length. Electricity, piped water, sewer hookups, cable TV and picnic tables are provided. Flush toilets, bottled gas, showers, recreation hall, a store, laundromat and ice are also available. A coffee shop is located within one mile. Motorbikes are permitted. No pets allowed.

Reservations, fee: Reservations accepted; $6-$11 fee per night; MasterCard and Visa accepted. Open March through November.

Who to contact: Phone (307) 322-3253 or write to Route 1, P.O. Box 4253, Wheatland, WY 82201.

Location: From Interstate 25 in Wheatland, take the Power Plant exit and drive a half mile south on 16th Street to the campground.

Trip note: Here's a chance to stay in lovely downtown Wheatland. This the only camper park located for several miles in all directions. If you brought golf clubs along, there's a chance to use them at the local course. The only other recreation options you have here are the bowling alley and the town movie theater. You can leave your fishing pole and hiking boots at home.

---

13) PIONEER PARK

Reference: near North Platte River; map W8, grid e9.

Campsites, facilities: There are 15 tent sites and 20 sites for trailers or motor homes of any length. Piped water, sewer hookups and picnic tables are provided. Flush toilets and a playground are also available. Bottled gas, sanitary disposal station, firewood, a store, coffee shop, laundromat and ice are located within one mile. Pets are permitted on leashes.

Reservations, fee: No reservations necessary; no fee. Open early April to mid-October including limited and some off-season weekends.

Who to contact: Phone (307) 532-3879 or write to 350 West 21st Street, Torrington, WY 82240.

Location: In Torrington at the junction of US 16W and West C Street, drive south on West C Street to 15th Avenue and then two blocks west and one block south to the park.

Trip note: This is a city park set near the North Platte River. It's not the prettiest site we've ever seen, but hey, don't complain: You could be stuck in the Red Desert, out of gas and out of luck.

---

14) DIAMOND GUEST RANCH KOA

Reference: northwest of Chugwater; map W8, grid f4.

Campsites, facilities: There are 15 tent sites and 80 sites for trailers or motor homes of any length. Piped water and picnic tables are provided. Flush toilets, sanitary disposal station, showers, recreation hall, a store, restaurant, cocktail lounge, laundromat, ice, playground and a swimming pool are also available. Electricity and sewer hookups are available at an additional charge. Pets and motorbikes are permitted. There are 27 cabins available also.

Reservations, fee: Reservations recommended; $12-$15 fee per night; Cabins are $36-$50 per night. American Express, MasterCard and Visa accepted. Open May through September.

Who to contact: Phone (307) 422-3567 or write to P.O. Box 236, Chugwater, WY 82210.

Location: From Interstate 25 in Chugwater, take Exit 54 and drive west 14 miles to the park.

Trip note: This is a large, privately developed park covering 40 acres. Many recreation options are available including horseback riding, fishing or a trip to the steak house here.

---

15) BEAR MOUNTAIN STATION

Reference: near Hawk Springs Reservoir; map W8, grid g8.

Campsites, facilities: There are two tent sites and 12 sites for trailers or motor homes of any length. Picnic tables are provided. Flush toilets, sanitary disposal station, a store and ice are also available. Electricity and showers are available at an additional charge. Pets and motorbikes are permitted.

Reservations, fee: Reservations accepted; $3-$10 fee per night; MasterCard and Visa accepted. Open early April to November.

Who to contact: Phone (307) 834-2294 or write to West Route, La Grange, WY 82221.

Location: From Torrington, drive 32 miles south on US 85 to the campground.

Trip note: This is the only game in town, so if you're looking for a layover spot around these parts, you'd best head here and not complain. Other camping prospects are zilch in all directions. It's not bad really. There are some trees, and Bear Mountain Looms in the background. Hawk Springs Reservoir is located five miles to the northeast and provides a spot to blow off some steam.

---

16) N&H TRAILER RANCH

Reference: in Laramie; map W8, grid i1.

Campsites, facilities: There are 33 sites for trailers or motor homes of any length. Electricity, piped water and sewer hookups are provided. Flush toilets, showers and a laundromat are also available. Bottled gas, a store, coffee shop and ice are located within one mile. Pets and motorbikes are permitted.

Reservations, fee: No reservations necessary; $11.50 fee per night. Open all year.

Who to contact: Phone (307) 742-3158 or write to 1360 North Third Street, NBU60-9, Laramie, WY 82070.

Location: From Interstate 80 in Laramie, take the Curtis Street exit and drive east to Third Street. Turn south and drive 2.5 blocks to the campground.

Trip note: This is basically a parking lot with a little grass. It's the only camp in downtown Laramie (KOA is near the interstate). What can you say about Laramie? Well, it's the home of the University of Wyoming, and (brace yourself) has 30 native stone buildings. Nearby recreation options include a golf course, hiking trails, bike paths and tennis courts.

---

17) LARAMIE KOA

Reference: in Laramie, map W8, grid i1.

Campsites, facilities: There are 25 tent sites and 100 sites for trailers or motor homes of any length. Picnic tables are provided. Flush toilets, sanitary disposal station, showers, recreation hall, a store, RV supplies, laundromat, ice and a playground are also available. Electricity, piped water and sewer hookups are available at an additional charge. A coffee shop is located within one mile. Pets and motorbikes are permitted.

Reservations, fee: Reservations accepted; $12-$16 fee per night; MasterCard and Visa accepted. Open March to mid-November.

Who to contact: Phone (307) 742-6553 or write to 1458 McCue Street, Laramie, WY 82070.

Location: From Interstate 80 in Laramie, take the Curtis Street exit and drive to the campground.

Trip note: Easy access is a highlight here. The park which covers seven acres is located just off the highway. See the trip note for N&H Trailer Ranch.

---

18) YELLOW PINE

Reference: near Sherman Mountains, Medicine Bow National Forest; map W8, grid i2.

Campsites, facilities: There are 19 sites for tents, trailers or motor homes up to 32 feet long. Picnic tables are provided. Piped water and pit toilets are also available. Pets are permitted on leashes.

Reservations, fee: No reservations necessary; no fee. Open late May to early September.

Who to contact: Phone Medicine Bow National Forest at (307) 745-8971 or write to Laramie Ranger District, 2468 Jackson Street, Laramie, WY 82070-6535.

Location: From Laramie, drive 12.3 miles southeast on Interstate 80 and 3.1 miles east on Forest Service Road 722 to the campground.

Trip note: This camp is set adjacent to Tie City Camp. See trip note for the camp for detailed area information.

19) TIE CITY

Reference: near Pole Mountain, Medicine Bow National Forest; map W8, grid i2.

Campsites, facilities: There are 18 sites for tents, trailers or motor homes up to 32 feet long. Picnic tables are provided. Pit toilets and piped water are also available. Pets are permitted on leashes.

Reservations, fee: No reservations necessary; no fee. Open mid-May to mid-October.

Who to contact: Phone Medicine Bow National Forest at (307) 745-8971 or write to Laramie Ranger District, 2468 Jackson Street, Laramie, WY 82070.

Location: From Laramie, drive 11 miles southeast on Interstate 80 and 1.1 miles east on Forest Service Road 722 to the campground.

Trip note: This is one of two campgrounds in the immediate vicinity, located just a mile off the highway, yet provides a good jump-off point for more adventures. A trail from the nearby rest area heads up Pole Mountain (9,053 feet) and is routed into the Sherman Mountains. Many unique rock formations are in the area.

20) CURT GOWDY STATE PARK

Reference: near Curt Gowdy Lake; map W8, grid i3.

Campsites, facilities: There are 142 sites for tents, trailers or motor homes of any length. Picnic tables are provided. Piped water, pit toilets, sanitary disposal station and a recreation hall are also available. Some facilities are **wheelchair accessible.** Pets are permitted on leashes. Boat docks and launching facilities are nearby.

Reservations, fee: No reservations necessary; $4 fee per night plus $2 entrance fee. Open all year with limited winter facilities.

Who to contact: Phone (307) 632-7946 or write to Cheyenne, WY 82001.

Location: From Cheyenne, drive west for 25 miles on Happy Jack Road to Highway 210. Turn south and drive one mile to the park.

Trip note: Hey, Curt Gowdy is a pal of ours, and he's mighty proud of the park that bears his name. It covers 1,118 acres and includes two lakes. The larger of the two is good for power boating, the smaller one is ideal for shoreline fishing. There are even some hiking trails to tromp around on.

21) WYOMING

Reference: east of Cheyenne; map W8, grid i7.

Campsites, facilities: There are 100 tent sites and 50 sites for trailers or motor homes of any length. Piped water and picnic tables are provided. Flush toilets, sanitary disposal station, showers, recreation hall, laundromat, ice, playground and a swimming pool are also available. A coffee shop, cocktail lounge and a store are located within one mile. Pets and motorbikes are permitted.

Reservations, fee: Reservations accepted; $12.50-$14.50 fee per night; American Express, MasterCard and Visa accepted. Open May to September.

Who to contact: Phone (307) 547-2244 or write to 4066 I-80 Service Road, Burns, WY 82053.

Location: From Cheyenne, drive 14 miles east on Interstate 80 to the Hillsdale exit and the campground.

Trip note: This privately developed park caters to tent campers as well as motor homes. The park covers 10 acres and provides all necessary amenities. It's right off the interstate, with grassy sites and on-site recreation options including horseshoe pits, basketball court and a volleyball net. Nearby Cheyenne provides some historical points of interest; if you happen to be passing through the last week in July, check out Cheyenne Frontier Days. Terry Ranch, known as the largest buffalo ranch around, is located seven miles away, offers tours and a replica of Cheyenne as it looked in 1816.

---

22) PINE BLUFF RV VILLAGE

Reference: in Pine Bluffs; map W8, grid i9.

Campsites, facilities: There are 12 tent sites and 90 sites for trailers or motor homes of any length. Electricity, piped water, sewer hookups and picnic tables are provided. Flush toilets, sanitary disposal station, showers, laundromat and ice are also available. Bottled gas, a store and coffee shop are located within one mile. Pets and motorbikes are permitted.

Reservations, fee: Reservations accepted; $9-$14 fee per night; Open mid-April to mid-October.

Who to contact: Phone (307) 245-3665 or write to P.O. Box 1037, Pine Bluffs, WY 82082.

Location: From Interstate 80 in Pine Bluffs, take Exit 1 and drive to the campground on Old US 30 between east and west on Interstate 80.

Trip note: This is an 11-acre private park set up primarily for motor homes and trailers. A golf course is within 20 miles, and there is a free public swimming pool and tennis courts in town. The park has a deli and an old-fashioned ice cream parlor. Points of interest include nearby archeological digs, and nature trails in the surrounding bluffs.

---

23) VEDAUWOO

Reference: southeast of Laramie, Medicine Bow National Forest; map W8, grid j2.

Campsites, facilities: There are 11 sites for tents, trailers or motor homes up to 32 feet long. Picnic tables are provided. Piped water and pit toilets are also available. Pets are permitted on leashes.

Reservations, fee: No reservations necessary; $5 fee per night. Open May to late October.

Who to contact: Phone Medicine Bow National Forest at (307) 745-8971 or write to Laramie Ranger District, 2468 Jackson Street, Laramie, WY 82070-6535.

Location: From Laramie, drive 19.1 miles southeast on Interstate 80 and 1.7 miles east on Forest Service Road 700 to the campground.

Trip note: So, you ask, what the heck does "Vedauwoo" mean? Well, since you asked, it translates into "earth born" in Cheyenne. It is the name given to a big jumble of rocks found here, which the Cheyenne believed to have been piled up by playful earth spirits. Regardless of how they got here, they provide some easy rock climbing and some unique opportunities for photography. Curt Gowdy State Park is nearby.

---

24) AB

Reference: in Cheyenne; map W8, grid j5.

Campsites, facilities: There are 30 tent sites and 106 sites for trailers or motor homes of any length. Picnic tables are provided. Flush toilets, sanitary disposal station, showers, recreation hall, laundromat, ice and playgrounds are also available. Electricity, piped water and sewer hookups are available at an additional charge. Bottled gas, a store and a coffee shop are located within one mile. Pets and motorbikes are permitted.

Reservations, fee: Reservations accepted; $10-$15 fee per night. Open March through October.

Who to contact: Phone (307) 634-7035 or write to 1503 West College Drive, Cheyenne, WY 82007.

Location: From Interstate 80 in Cheyenne, take Exit 359 and drive three-quarters of a mile south on Interstate 25 to College exit 7. Drive 1.5 miles east to the campground.

Trip note: This private park has trees and grassy sites. As the capital of Wyoming, the sights in Cheyenne include the Capitol Building, Wyoming State Museum and Cheyenne Frontier Days Old West Museum. A big nine-day rodeo is held during the last full week in July each year. For other sidetrip information, see the trip note for Wyoming Camp.

---

25) GREENWAY TRAVEL PARK

Reference: in Cheyenne; map W8, grid j5.

Campsites, facilities: There are 41 drive-through sites for trailers or motor homes of any length. Electricity, piped water, sewer hookups and picnic tables are provided. Flush toilets, sanitary disposal station, showers, laundromat and ice are also available. Cable TV and phone hook-ups are available at an additional charge. Bottled gas, a store and coffee shop are located within one mile. Pets and motorbikes are permitted.

Reservations, fee: Reservations accepted; $13-$15 fee per night. Open all year.

Who to contact: Phone (307) 634-6696 or write to 3829 Greenway, Cheyenne, WY 82001.

Location: From Interstate 80 in Cheyenne, take the East Lincoln Way exit (exit 364) north and drive to the campground at 3829 Greenway Street.

Trip note: This is one of five possibilities in Cheyenne. This one has paved parking spots for motor homes. See the trip note for AB Camp for area attractions.

---

26) RESTWAY TRAVEL PARK

Reference: in Cheyenne; map W8, grid j5.

Campsites, facilities: There are 27 tent sites and 118 sites for trailers or motor homes of any length. Picnic tables are provided. Flush toilets, sanitary disposal station, showers, firewood, recreation hall, a store, coffee shop, laundromat, ice, playground, miniature golf course, horseshoes and a heated swimming pool are also available. Electricity, piped water and sewer hookups are available at an additional charge. Bottled gas is located within one mile. Pets are permitted on leashes.

Reservations, fee: Reservations accepted; $12.50-$14.50 fee per night. Open all year.

Who to contact: Phone (307) 634-3811 or (800) 443-2751, or write to P.O. Box 5088, Cheyenne, WY 82003.

Location: From Cheyenne, drive 1.5 miles east on US 30 to the campground at 4212 Whitney Road.

Trip note: This is a good spot for kids and dogs. It boasts a miniature golf course, shetland pony wagon rides, and a nightly communal fire ring for hot dog and marshmallow roasts. It also has a spectacularly beautiful view of the Rocky Mountains. See the trip note for AB Camp for sidetrip possibilities in Cheyenne.

Index

A

AB CAMP 553
AB Camp 554
Abiathar Peak 440, 441
Abrams, Mount 197
Absaroka Mountain Range 476
North 446, 448
Absaroka-Beartooth Wilderness 420, 421, 423, 426, 427, 428, 429, 441, 443
Adams, Ansel 444
Adelaide Lake 484
Afton, WY 466, 467, 468, 505, 507
ALAMOSA 256
Alamosa, CO 247, 253
Alamosa River 252, 256, 257
ALBERT'S TRAILER COURT 518
ALCOVA LAKE 523
Alcova Reservoir 524
Alder Creek 369
Alder, MT 396
ALDER/VIRGINIA KOA 395
ALFRED FLAT 508
Allan Creek 409
Allen Mountain Roadless Area 376, 377
Almont, CO 220, 224, 225, 226, 234
Alpen Rose Camp 206, 208, 209
ALPEN ROSE RV PARK 207
Alpine, WY 461, 462, 466, 467, 468, 505
ALTA 373
Alta Pine National Recreation Trail 373
Alva, WY 499
ALVARADO 242
AMPITHEATRE 197
amusement park 76
Anaconda, MT 386, 387
ANGEL OF SHAVANO GROUP CAMP 231
Animas Overlook 207
Animas Ranger District 200, 201, 202, 207
Animas River 201, 202, 206, 207, 208, 209
Animas Valley 201, 207, 208
ANSEL WATROUS 149
Antero Junction 146
Anthracite Creek 217
Anthracite Ranger Station 217
Antonito, CO 256, 258, 259, 260
APGAR 303
Apgar 296
ARAPAHO BAY 108
Arapaho National Forest
102, 106, 107, 108, 115, 116, 117, 119, 120, 121, 122
Arapahoe Indians 478
Arboles, CO 213
archeological dig 552
archery 464
Arena RV Park 272
Arkansas River
222, 229, 237, 238, 239, 240, 269
Arkansas River, South 230, 231, 236
Arlee, MT 329
Ashland, MT 435, 436
Ashley Lake 306
ASHLEY LAKE STATE RECREATION AREA 305
Ashton, ID 451
ASPEN 101, 127, 353, 531
Aspen Camp 127, 534, 535
Aspen, CO 133, 140, 141, 142, 143
ASPEN GLADE 259
Aspen Glade Camp 260
ASPEN GLEN 94
ASPEN GROVE 346
Aspen Ranger District 140, 141, 142, 143
ASPEN TRAILS 186
ASPENGLEN 105
Assiniboine Indians 357
ASTORIA HOT SPRINGS 463
ATHERTON CREEK 455
Atlantic City, WY 518
Augusta, MT 340, 341, 342, 345
Aurora, CO 160
AVALANCHE 131, 297
Avalanche Creek 131, 297
Avalanche Lake 297
Avery, Lake 61, 65
AVERY PEAK 140
Avery Peak 140

B

Babb, MT 296, 334
BABY DOE 137
BAD MEDICINE 304
Bad Medicine Camp 297
Bailey, CO 130, 131
Bailey Creek 462
Bair Reservoir 413
Baker, MT 435
BAKER'S HOLE 405
BALD MOUNTAIN 472
BALDY 163
Baldy Peak 163
BANNACK STATE PARK 398

Bar Z Peak 314
BARBOUR PONDS STATE PARK 155
Barlow Creek 199
Barnes Meadow Reservoir 95
Barrett Creek, North Fork 529
Barron 300
Basalt, CO 132, 133, 134
BASIN 429
BASIN CANYON 388
Basin Creek 388
Basin Creek Lake 429
basketball 464, 552
Bass Creek 366
Battle Creek 535
Battle Creek, Castle Fork 389
Battle Creek, North Fork 535
BATTLE RIDGE 414
Battle Ridge Pass 414, 415
Bayfield, CO 202, 208, 210, 211, 212, 213
BEAN LAKE 344
Bear Creek 128, 267, 370
Bear Creek Nature Center 267
BEAR CREEK PASS 370
BEAR LAKE 110, 277
Bear Lake 111, 277, 278
BEAR LODGE 499
Bear Mountain Looms 549
BEAR MOUNTAIN STATION 549
Bear River 111, 112, 511
Bear River Trail 110
BEAR TRAP MEADOW LAKE 521
Bear Trap Meadow Park 523
Bearpaw Lake State Recreation Area 349
Bears Ears Ranger District 61, 62
Beartooth Butte 443
Beartooth Game Management Area 347
Beartooth High Lakes Trail 443
BEARTOOTH LAKE 443
Beartooth Mountains 421, 428
Beartooth Plateau 443
Beartooth Ranger District 421, 422, 423, 427, 428, 429
Beartooth Wilderness 425, 426
Beartrap Mountain Wilderness Area 393
BEAVER CREEK 251, 402
Beaver Creek 60, 61, 97, 224, 249, 250, 382
Beaver Creek Canyon 61
BEAVER CREEK PARK 349
Beaver Creek Reservoir 249, 250, 251, 252
BEAVER LAKE 193
Beaver Ponds Picnic Ground 127
Beaver Reservoir 110
Beaverdam Creek 121
Beaverhead National Forest 377, 378, 379, 390, 392, 393, 400, 401, 402
Beaverhead River 391, 395
BEAVERTAIL HILL STATE PARK 366
Bechler Creek 451
Bechler Ranger Station 451
BEL AIRE UNIT 66
Belle Fourche River 499
BELLE FOURCHE RIVER NATIONAL MONUMENT 499
BELLE OF COLORADO 136
Bellevue, CO 96, 150
Belt Creek 353
Belt, MT 352
BENCHMARK 342
Benchmark Creek 342
BENNETT COURT 546
Bennett Court 547
Bennett Peak 253
Beulah, CO 274
bicycling (see also mountain biking) 64, 67, 72, 73, 74, 75, 94, 98, 104, 105, 125, 126, 153, 159, 160, 162, 166, 173, 191, 197, 201, 209, 222, 230, 234, 240, 241, 246, 260, 267, 268, 272, 275, 277, 294, 452, 458, 460, 463, 477, 511, 550
Big Arm, MT 320, 321, 322
BIG ARM RESORT 321
BIG ARM STATE PARK 322
Big Battlement Lake 78
BIG BEND 89
BIG BLUE 194
Big Blue Creek 194, 195
Big Blue Wilderness 195
BIG CIMARRON 194
BIG CREEK 295
BIG CREEK LAKE 87
BIG DOMINGUEZ 187
Big Dominguez Creek 187
BIG EDDY 310
Big Ferry Lake 384
Big Fish Lake 69
BIG GAME 450
Big Goose Creek, East Fork 485, 486
BIG J CAMPER COURT 75
Big Lake Creek 378
BIG LARCH 344
Big Larch Camp 343
BIG MEADOWS 248
Big Meadows Reservoir 248, 249
BIG NELSON 345
BIG PINES 173
Big Piney Ranger District 509
Big Piney, WY 509
BIG SANDY 515
Big Sandy Campground 508
Big Sandy River 515
BIG SKY 431
Big Sky, MT 398, 399
Big Snowy Mountains 411, 412
BIG SPUR 417
Big Spur Camp 418, 419
Big Timber Creek 414
Big Timber Creek Trail 414

BIG TIMBER KOA 415
Big Timber, MT 414, 415, 420, 421
Big Timber Ranger District 414, 420, 421
BIG TURKEY 172
Bigfoot 312
Bigfork, MT 316, 317, 318, 327
Bighorn Canyon National Recreation Area 471
Bighorn Lake 471, 472
BIGHORN MOUNTAIN 489
Bighorn Mountains
473, 475, 483, 487, 488, 502
Bighorn National Forest
472, 475, 481, 482, 483, 484, 485, 486, 487, 488, 489, 490, 491, 492, 493, 494, 495, 496, 497
Bighorn Ranger Station 106
Bighorn Reservoir 485
Bighorn River 474, 475, 477
Billings Logan International Airport 432
BILLINGS METRO KOA 432
Billings, MT 359, 393, 431, 432
Birch Creek 390, 391
BITTEROOT LAKE STATE PARK 306
BITTERROOT FLAT 369
Bitterroot Lake 306, 307, 314
Bitterroot Mountain Range
305, 370, 376, 379
Bitterroot National Forest
366, 370, 371, 372, 373, 374, 375, 376
Bitterroot River 367, 371, 375
Bitterroot River, West Fork 372, 373
BLACK BEAR 371
Black Canyon 188, 191
Black Hills 436
Black Hills National Forest 499, 500, 501
Black Mountain 515
Black Mountain Lookout 482
Blackfoot Clearwater Game Range 330
Blackfoot River 346, 382
Blackfoot River, MT 382
Blackhawk, CO 116, 117, 157
BLACKTAIL CREEK 112
Blackwater Fire Memorial National Recreation Trail 450
Blackwater Picnic Ground 450
Blanca, CO 276
BLANCA RV PARK 276
Blanco Ranger District
64, 65, 66, 67, 68, 69
BLANCO RIVER 257
BLODGETT 123
BLUE LAKE 277
Blue Lake 277, 278, 414
Blue Lake Camp 277
Blue Lake Trail 93
Blue Mesa Reservoir
191, 192, 232, 233, 234, 235
BLUE MOUNTAIN 168
Blue Mountain 331
Blue Mountain Recreation Area 331
Blue River 126
boating (see also canoeing, kayaking and rafting)
Colorado
62, 63, 65, 67, 68, 69, 70, 71, 73, 76, 77, 78, 79, 80, 81, 82, 83, 85, 86, 87, 88, 92, 94, 95, 100, 107, 108, 111, 113, 114, 119, 123, 124, 125, 126, 127, 132, 134, 135, 136, 137, 142, 143, 144, 145, 149, 150, 154, 155, 160, 161, 176, 177, 181, 182, 183, 185, 188, 189, 191, 192, 195, 202, 210, 211, 212, 213, 214, 218, 219, 220, 223, 226, 231, 232, 233, 234, 235, 248, 249, 250, 251, 252, 255, 257, 258, 272, 273, 274, 275, 276, 277, 278, 279, 281, 282
Montana
285, 287, 288, 289, 290, 292, 293, 294, 295, 296, 297, 299, 300, 301, 302, 303, 304, 305, 306, 307, 308, 309, 310, 311, 312, 313, 314, 315, 316, 317, 318, 320, 321, 322, 323, 327, 328, 330, 333, 334, 336, 340, 343, 344, 345, 346, 347, 349, 350, 357, 358, 359, 360, 361, 373, 374, 378, 381, 384, 385, 386, 387, 390, 391, 392, 394, 397, 400, 401, 402, 403, 404, 412, 415, 416, 417, 419, 420, 422, 423, 431
Wyoming
442, 443, 445, 448, 452, 453, 454, 455, 456, 457, 461, 466, 468, 471, 473, 477, 481, 482, 487, 488, 491, 492, 493, 500, 501, 506, 507, 509, 512, 517, 524, 525, 526, 527, 531, 534, 536, 537, 538, 539, 543, 544, 546, 551
Bob Marshall Wilderness
325, 327, 338, 339, 340, 342
BOBBIE THOMSON 538
BOGAN FLATS 139
Bolam Pass 199
Bonanza, WY 241
Bondurant, WY 464, 465
Bonny Dam Reservoir 183
BONNY LAKE STATE PARK 183
Boothill Cemetery 432
BOSWELL CREEK 539
Boswell Creek, Little 540
BOTTLE CREEK 528
Bottle Creek 529
Boulder Canyon 156
BOULDER CITY PARK 388
Boulder City Park 389
Boulder, CO
109, 110, 116, 117, 118, 156, 158
Boulder Creek 156, 372
Boulder Lake 69, 227, 372
BOULDER MOUNTAIN LODGE 156
Boulder, MT 388, 389

BOULDER PARK 492
Boulder Ranger District
109, 110, 116, 117, 118
Boulder River 388, 389, 420
Boulder, WY 508
BOW RIVER 526
Bowdoin National Wildlife Refuge 357
Bower Canyon 411
bowling 548
BOWMAN LAKE 289
Bowman Lake 289
Boyd Lake 154
BOYD LAKE STATE RECREATION AREA 154
Boysen Reservoir 477
BOYSEN RESERVOIR STATE RECREATION AREA 477
BOZEMAN HOT SPRINGS KOA 393
Bozeman, MT
393, 394, 395, 398, 399, 414, 415, 416
Bozeman Ranger District
394, 395, 398, 399, 414, 415
Brackett Creek 414
Middle Fork 415
Brainard Lake Recreation Area 116
BRANDIN' IRON TRAILER PARK 404
Branding Iron Camp 383
BRANHAM LAKES 392
Branham Lakes 392
BRB RESORT 132
Breckenridge, CO 126
BRIDGE BAY 445
BRIDGE, THE 466
Bridger Bowl Ski Area 414, 415
Bridger, Jim 511
Bridger Mountains Trail 414
Bridger-Teton National Forest
453, 455, 459, 461, 462, 464, 465, 466, 467, 468, 505, 506, 507, 508, 509, 510, 515
Briggsdale, CO 151
Broadacres Ranch 245
BROADACRES TRAVELIN' TEEPEE 245
Broadus, MT 436
BROOKLYN LAKE 527
Brooklyn Lake 527, 533
Brooklyn Lake Camp 533
BROOKS LAKE 457
Brooks Lake 456, 457
Brooks Lake Creek 456
Broomfield, CO 157, 158
BROWN MOUNTAIN 476
Browning, MT 334
BROWN'S 222
Brown's Gulch 224
BROWN'S PARK 88
Brown's Park National Wildlife Refuge
60, 61, 62
Brush, CO 182
Brush Creek, North 530
BRUSH MEMORIAL CAMPGROUND 182
Brush Memorial Campground 155
BUCKBOARD CROSSING 512
BUCKEYE 190
Buckeye Reservoir 190
Bucking Mule Falls 472
BUCKS 67
Bucks Camp 68
Buena Vista, CO 221, 222, 223
BUENA VISTA FAMILY RESORT 223
BUFFALO 163
Buffalo Camp 163, 164
Buffalo Bill Historic Museum 473, 474
Buffalo Bill Reservoir 473
BUFFALO BILL STATE PARK 473
Buffalo Creek 162, 163, 164, 165
Buffalo Creek, CO 165, 166
Buffalo Creek Ranger Station 165
BUFFALO HILLS CAMPER PARK 181
BUFFALO PASS 244
Buffalo Pass 91
Buffalo Picnic Ground 163
Buffalo Ranger District
453, 489, 493, 494, 495, 497
BUFFALO SPRINGS 146
Buffalo Valley 453
Buffalo, WY 489, 490, 493, 494, 495, 497
Bull Basin Reservoirs 61, 82
BULL CREEK 492
Bull Creek Camp 493
Bull Lake 297, 298, 304
BULL RIVER 304
Bull River 305
Bull River Bay 305
Burgess Picnic Area 482
Burgess Ranger Station 482
Burlington, CO 183
Burlington Northern Railroad 294
BURNING BEAR 128
Burns, WY 551
Burnt Timber Trail 209
BURRO BRIDGE 199
Butler Creek 377
Butte, MT 347
BYERS CREEK 115

C

C. M. Russell Museum 343
CABIN CITY 326
CABIN CREEK 402, 462, 484
Cabin Creek Camp 403
Cabin Creek 402, 462, 484
Cabin Creek Recreation and Wildlife Area
402
Cabin Creek Reservoir, Lower 121
Cabin Creek Trailer Park 484
Cabinet Gorge Reservoir 304
Cabinet Mountains 305
Cabinet Mountains Wilderness 305, 312
Cabinet Ranger District 304, 311, 313

cabins 96, 103, 132, 197, 238, 270, 315, 339, 343, 383, 403, 424, 432, 459, 474, 493, 518, 526, 548, 549
CABLE MOUNTAIN 386
Cache La Poudre River
89, 94, 96, 97, 98, 149, 150
Cache La Poudre Wilderness 97, 98
Calamity Jane 432
Calico National Recreation Trail 199
California 145
Cameron, MT 402
CAMP 32 293
Camp 7 509
CAMP CODY 473
Camp Cody 474
CAMP CREEK 359
CAMP DICK 109
CAMP HALE MEMORIAL 123
Camp Hale Recreation Area 123
CAMPBELL CREEK 524
Campbell Creek 525
canoeing (see also boating, kayaking and rafting)
110, 111, 194, 378, 412, 500, 544
Canon City, CO
239, 241, 242, 269, 271, 272, 273, 274, 277, 278
Canon City Municipal Museum 269
CANYON 495
Canyon Camp 494
CANYON CREEK 390
Canyon Creek 228, 371, 390
Canyon Creek Guest Ranch 390
Canyon Falls 371
CANYON FERRY STATE PARK 384
Canyon Lake 371
CANYON VILLAGE 444
Carbondale, CO 131, 132, 133, 134, 139
CARIBOU 286
Caribou Creek 286
Caribou National Forest 505
Carnero Creek 240
CARP LAKE 78
CARRIGAN 291
Carter Lake 153
CARTER VALLEY 153
CASCADE 230, 328
Cascade Camp 231
Cascade County Historical Museum 343
Cascade Creek 202
Cascade Falls 328
Cascade National Recreation Trail 328
CASPER MOUNTAIN 521
Casper Mountain 523
Casper Mountain Park 523
Casper, WY 521, 522, 524
Castle Museum 412
Cataract Lake 113
CATHEDRAL 246
Cathedral Creek 246
Catholic Mission 330
CAVE FALLS 451
Cave of the Winds 267
CAWTHON 278
CAYTON 199
CEBOLLA 243
Cebolla Creek 243
Cebolla Ranger District
227, 228, 229, 242, 243
CEDAR CREEK 324
Cedar Creek 325
Cedaredge, CO 78, 79, 80, 186
CEMENT CREEK 218
Centennial, WY
527, 531, 532, 533, 534, 535
CENTRAL CITY / BLACK HAWK KOA 157
Central City, CO 117, 121, 157
Chalk Buttes 435
Chalk Creek 223, 228, 230, 231
CHALK LAKE 231
Chama, NM 260
Chambers Lake 95
Champion International Corporation 291
CHAPMAN 134
Charles M. Russell National Wildlife Refuge 361
Charles River 273
CHARLES WATERS 366
Charles Waters Camp 367
Chateau, MT 337
CHATFIELD STATE RECREATION AREA 161
Cherry Creek Lake 160
CHERRY CREEK STATE RECREATION AREA 160
Cherry Creek Valley 205
Cheyenne Frontier Days Old West Museum 552, 553
Cheyenne Indians 553
Cheyenne, WY
472, 523, 551, 552, 553, 554
Chicken Creek Trail 205
Chico Hot Springs 394
CHIEF HOSA 158
CHIEF JOSEPH 426
Chinaman Gulch 384
CHINOOK 246
CHOTEAU CITY PARK 340
CHOTEAU KOA 339
Choteau KOA 340
Choteau, MT 339, 340, 341, 342
chuckwagon dinners 176
CHUCKWAGON DRIVE-IN 547
Chugwater, WY 549
Cimarron River 194
CIRCLE 8 496
CIRCLE PARK 494
CIRCLE UP CAMPER COURT 460
Cisneros Trail 273
Clark, CO 85, 86
Clark Fork River 318, 327, 328, 329, 366

CLARK MEMORIAL 319
Clarks Fork Ranger District
    441, 442, 443, 444
Clarks Fork Trailhead 441
Clarks Fork Valley 443
Clay Butte Lookout 443
Clayton Mountain 450
Clear Creek
    Middle Fork 489, 494
    South Fork 121, 493, 494
    West Fork 120
Clear Creek Ranger District
    117, 120, 121, 122
CLEAR LAKE 120
CLEARWATER 448
Clearwater Creek 448
Clearwater River 343, 344
Cliff Lake 400, 401
Cliff Lake Trail 66
CLIFF POINT 400
Cliff Point Camp 401
climbing
    ice 196
    mountain 240
    rock 156, 196, 553
Clinton, MT 368, 370
Cloud Peak Primitive Area 472
Cloud Peak Wilderness
    485, 486, 487, 488, 489, 491,
    494, 495
COACH LIGHT 172
COAL BANKS LANDING 350
COALDALE 239
Coaldale Camp 237
Coaldale, CO 237, 239, 240
Cochetopa Pass 243, 244
Cody, WY 444, 446, 447, 448, 449,
    450, 451, 473, 474
Coeur d'Alene Mountains 325
COFFEE POT SPRINGS 118
COFFEEN PARK 485
Cokeville, WY 510
COLD SPRING 226
Cold Spring Trail 516
COLD SPRINGS 61, 111, 116
Cold Springs Camp 110
Cold Springs Unit 61
Collbran, CO 74, 77, 82
Collbran Ranger District 77, 82
COLLEGIATE PEAKS 221
Collegiate Peaks Wilderness
    141, 142, 144, 220, 222
COLLINS CORRAL 544
COLORADO 175
Colorado Camp 174
Colorado Division of Wildlife
    61, 63, 65, 66, 88, 92, 100,
    158, 181, 182, 257, 282
Colorado National Monument
    61, 74, 75, 76
Colorado River 61, 71, 72, 74, 76
Colorado Springs, CO
    165, 169, 172, 174, 175, 176,
    177, 178, 264, 265, 266, 267,
    268, 270
COLORADO SPRINGS SOUTH KOA 270
COLORADO STATE FOREST 94
Colorado State Forest 93
Colorado Trail
    128, 130, 145, 163, 199, 207, 232
COLTER 426
COLTER BAY 452
Colter, Jim 452
Columbia Falls, MT 288, 295, 302
COLUMBINE 121, 190
Columbine 87
Columbine Pass 190
Comanche National Grassland 281
Comanche Peak Wilderness 95, 96, 97
COMMISSARY 189
Como, CO 138
COMO, LAKE 373
COMSTOCK 256
Condon, MT 327
CONEJOS 260
Conejos Camp 258
Conejos Peak 256
Conejos Peak Ranger District
    252, 255, 256, 258, 259, 260
Conejos River 255, 256, 258, 259, 260
Conical Peak 414
Conifer, CO 161
Conner, MT 377
Continental Divide
    87, 100, 116, 117, 164, 220,
    229, 244, 249, 377, 382, 528, 536
COOK LAKE 499
Cook Lake 500
Cooke City, MT 425, 426, 441, 442, 443
Cooney Reservoir 420
COONEY RESERVOIR STATE PARK 419
Coopers Lake 345, 346
Coors Brewery 157
COPPER CREEK 346, 374
Copper Creek 346, 375
COPPER KING 319
Corner Mountain 532
Corps of Engineers, Fort Peck Lake
    358, 359, 360
Corral Creek 96
Cortez, CO 203
COTTONWOOD CAMPER PARK 206
Cottonwood Creek 221, 222, 239, 507
COTTONWOOD LAKE 82, 221, 507
Cottonwood Lake Recreation Area 221
COULTER 381
COUNTRY BUDGET HOST RV PARK 274
Country Budget Host RV Park 275, 277
Court Sheriff 384
COVE 263
COW BELL 431
Cow Creek Swimming Beach 113

COW ISLAND LANDING 351
COWDREY LAKE 88
CRAG CREST 80
CRAGS, THE 263
Craig, CO 61, 62, 63
Crawford, CO 83, 188, 189
Crawford Creek 353
Crawford Lake 188, 189
CRAWFORD STATE RECREATION AREA 188
CRAZY CREEK 376, 441
Crazy Creek 377, 442
Crazy Creek Falls 441
CRAZY HORSE 222
Crazy Horse Camp 223
Crazy Lakes 441
CRAZY WOMAN 495, 500
Crazy Woman Camp 494
Crazy Woman Creek 495
    North Fork 495, 496
Creede, CO 245
Crested Butte, CO 140, 218
Cripple Creek, CO 264, 265
CRIPPLE CREEK GOLD 265
CRIPPLE CREEK TRAVEL PARK 264
Crittendon 384
Cromwell Dixon Camp 383
CROSS CREEK 251, 485
Cross Creek 250, 251
cross-country skiing (see also skiing) 74, 75, 83, 86, 154, 155, 160, 162, 223, 224, 233, 290, 412, 510
CROW VALLEY 150
Crystal Cascades Trail 412
CRYSTAL CREEK 455
Crystal Creek 170, 456, 472, 473
CRYSTAL LAKE 411
Crystal Lake 412
Crystal Lake Cabin 412
Crystal Lake Shoreline Loop Trail 412
CRYSTAL PARK 502
Crystal River 131, 132, 139
Cub Creek 298
Cuchara, CO 277, 278
Cuchara Ski Resort 275
Cumbres Toltec Scenic Railroad 260
Curecanti National Recreation Area 191, 192, 232, 233, 234, 235
Curt Gowdy Lake 551
CURT GOWDY STATE PARK 551
Curt Gowdy State Park 553
CURTIS CANYON 459
CURTIS GULCH 543
Cushman Lake 195
Custer Battlefield 436
Custer National Forest 309, 421, 422, 423, 427, 428, 429, 435, 436
CUT BANK 334
Cut Bank Creek 334, 335
Cut Bank, MT 336
CUTTHROAT 68
Cyclone Creek 291

D

DAKOTA 275
Dakota Camp 277
DALLES 367
Darby, MT 370, 372, 373, 374, 376, 377
Darby Ranger District 370, 374
Dark Canyon 217
DAVIS SPRINGS 114
DAY'S REST TRAILER PARK 329
Dayton, MT 314, 315
Dayton, WY 481, 482, 483, 485
DEAD INDIAN 444
Dead Indian Creek 444
Dead Indian Hill 444
DEAD SWEDE 485
DEARHAMMER 133
Deborgia, MT 326
Deception, Mount 174
DEEP CREEK 527
DEEP LAKE 71
Deep Lake 61, 71, 527
DEER CREEK 130
Deer Creek Camp 131
DEER HAVEN LODGE 493
DEER PARK 489
Deerlodge, MT 387, 388
Deerlodge National Forest 371, 374, 384, 385, 386, 387, 388, 389
Deerlodge Ranger District 387, 388
Del Norte, CO 246, 248, 249, 250, 251, 252, 253, 256
Del Norte Ranger District 246, 248, 249, 250, 252, 253, 256
DELAYNEY BUTTE LAKES 92
Delta, CO 81, 83, 185, 186, 187, 188, 189
DELTA-GRAND MESA KOA 185
DELUX RV PARK 159
Denver, CO 88, 92, 152, 155, 158, 159, 160, 162, 181, 187, 257, 282
DENVER CREEK 102
DENVER EAST STRASBURG KOA 160
Denver East Strasburg KOA 183
DENVER MEADOWS 160
DENVER NORTH KOA 157
DENVER NORTHEAST / PEPPER POD KOA 156
Denver-Rio Grande Western Railroad 230
Devil Canyon 472
Devils Gulch 103
DEVIL'S HEAD 166
Devil's Head Camp 167
Devil's Head Fire Lookout 167
Devil's Postpile 499
Devil's Tower National Monument 499
Devil's Tower, WY 499, 501

DIAMOND 175
DIAMOND GUEST RANCH KOA 548
DICKINSON CREEK 515
DICK'S TRAILER PARK 342
DIFFICULT 141
Difficult Creek 141
Dillon, CO 114, 125, 126
DILLON KOA 395
Dillon, MT 379, 391, 395, 399, 401
Dillon Ranger District 113, 114, 115, 124, 125, 126, 379, 391
Dillon Reservoir 115, 124, 125, 126
DINNER STATION 220, 390
Dinosaur, CO 62, 63
Dinosaur National Monument 61, 62, 63, 475
Dinosaur Valley 74
Divide, CO 264
DIVIDE FORK 187
DOG CREEK 293
Dollar Lake 218
Dolores, CO 198, 199
Dolores Ranger District 198, 199
Dolores River 195, 199
West 198, 199
DORCHESTER 220
Dorchester Ranger Station 220
DORR SKEELS 297
Dorr Skeels Camp 304
Dotsero, CO 119
DOUBLE CABIN 457
Douglas Creek 534, 537, 538, 539
Douglas Ranger District 525, 543, 545
Douglas, WY 525, 543, 545
DOWDY LAKE 90
DOWNSTREAM CAMP 358
DOYLE 496
Doyle Creek 496, 497
Driggs, ID 454, 458
Dry Creek 360
East Fork 325
DRY GULCH 233
Dry Gulch 352
DRY LAKE 91
DRY WOLF 353
Dry Wolf Creek 353
Dubois, WY 456, 457, 458, 460, 461
DUMONT LAKE 99
Durango, CO 200, 201, 202, 206, 207, 208, 209, 210

E

Eagle, CO 71, 118, 119, 122
EAGLE CREEK 424, 447
Eagle Creek 425, 448
Eagle Ranger District 71, 118, 119, 122
Eagle River 122, 123, 124
East Fork 123
Eagles Nest Wilderness 113, 114, 119, 125
Earthquake Lake 402, 403
East Creek 139
EAST FORK 255, 389, 486
East Fork Camp 487
East Fork Creek 390
East Fork Reservoir 389, 390
East Fork Spring Creek 413
East Fork Trail 110
East Glacier Park, MT 335, 337, 338
East Lake 93
East River 140, 234
EAST ROSEBUD 423
EAST TABLE CREEK 461
East Table Creek 462
EAST TIN CUP VILLAGE 159
ECHO LAKE 121
Echo Lake 121, 385, 386
ECHO PARK 63
Edgewater Camp 358
EDGEWATER INN AND CAMPGROUND 357
Edison, Thomas 535
Edith, Lake 122
EGGLESTON LAKE 81
Eggleston Lake 61, 79, 80
Ekalaka, MT 435
El Diente 199
ELBERT CREEK 145
Elbert Creek 145, 146
Elbert, Mount 144, 145
ELBOW 462
Elder Creek Picnic Area 389
ELEVENMILE STATE PARK 223
Elevenmile State Park 169
Elevenmile Canyon 170, 171, 263
Elevenmile Reservoir 168, 170, 223, 263
ELK CREEK 233, 258
Elk Creek 130, 131, 233, 259, 449, 450, 451
ELK FORK 449
Elk Fork Camp 449, 451
Elk Island 310
ELK ISLAND BOAT-IN 310
Elk Mountain, WY 527
Elk Mountains 131, 132
Elk River 87
ELK WALLOW 133
Elkhead Mountains 61
Elkhorn Creek 400
ELLIOT CREEK 113
Elliot Creek Camp 113, 114
Elliot State Wildlife Area 182
Elliston, MT 382
ELMO STATE PARK 322
Elwell, Lake 338
Embargo Creek 246
EMERALD LAKE 422
Emerald Lake 212, 422
Encampment River, North Fork 528
Encampment, WY 528, 529, 530, 535, 536, 537
Endlich Mesa Trail 203
Ennis Lake 397

Ennis, MT 393, 396, 397, 399, 400, 401, 402
ENNIS SPORTSMAN ACCESS 397
Ennis Sportsman Access 396
ERIKSON SPRINGS 217
ESTERBROOK 545
Esterbrook 546
Estes Park, CO
102, 103, 104, 105, 108, 152
Estes Park KOA 104
Estes-Poudre Ranger District
89, 94, 97, 98, 149
Eureka, MT 286, 287, 292, 293, 299
Eureka Ranger District
286, 287, 292, 293, 299
Eva Creek 120
Evans, Mount 121, 128
Evanston, WY 510, 511
EVERGREEN 349
Evergreen, CO 158

F

Fairplay, CO 127, 137, 138, 139, 146, 168, 170, 171, 263
FAIRY LAKE 413
Fairy Lake 413, 414
Falcon, CO 177
FALCON MEADOW 177
Fall River 103, 106
FALLS 456
FATHER DYER 135
Father Dyer 137
Ferry Lake 384
Festival of Nations, The 424
FINLEY POINT STATE PARK 323
FIREBRAND PASS 335
FIREHOLE 512
Firehole Camp 513
Fireman Memorial Camp 299
FIREMAN MEMORIAL PARK 299
FIRESIDE MOTEL 153
FISH CREEK 295
Fish Creek 296
Fish Lake 370
Fisher River Ranger District 314
fishing
Colorado
61, 62, 63, 64, 65, 66, 67, 69, 72, 73, 74, 76, 78, 79, 82, 83, 85, 86, 88, 91, 93, 94, 98, 99, 100, 105, 106, 107, 108, 109, 110, 111, 112, 114, 120, 123, 124, 125, 127, 132, 138, 140, 144, 150, 153, 154, 155, 157, 159, 160, 168, 175, 176, 177, 181, 182, 183, 186, 188, 189, 192, 193, 194, 195, 197, 199, 200, 202, 203, 205, 206, 207, 211, 212, 214, 218, 219, 220, 221, 223, 224, 226, 227, 229, 233, 234, 235, 237, 238, 239, 243, 246, 249, 250, 251, 255, 257, 259, 266, 272, 273, 276, 277, 278, 279, 281
Montana
286, 288, 289, 290, 291, 292, 294, 296, 298, 299, 300, 301, 302, 304, 305, 306, 307, 308, 309, 311, 312, 313, 315, 316, 317, 318, 319, 320, 321, 322, 323, 324, 325, 326, 327, 329, 330, 333, 336, 343, 344, 346, 347, 349, 350, 353, 357, 358, 360, 361, 366, 370, 372, 373, 374, 377, 382, 384, 385, 386, 387, 388, 389, 390, 393, 395, 396, 397, 398, 399, 400, 401, 402, 404, 405, 411, 412, 413, 414, 415, 416, 417, 418, 419, 420, 424, 431, 435
Wyoming
440, 441, 443, 444, 446, 451, 453, 455, 456, 457, 459, 460, 461, 462, 463, 464, 465, 466, 467, 468, 471, 472, 475, 477, 481, 482, 484, 485, 489, 490, 493, 494, 496, 497, 501, 505, 506, 507, 508, 509, 510, 511, 512, 513, 516, 518, 524, 526, 527, 534, 535, 536, 537, 538, 539, 543, 544, 546, 549, 551
fishing, ice 70, 73, 74, 76, 83, 86, 94, 155, 162, 224
Fishing Bridge Junction 446
FISHING BRIDGE RV PARK 445
Fishtail, MT 422
Fishtrap Creek Campground 319
FISHTRAP LAKE 318
Fishtrap Lake 318, 319
FIVE BRANCHES 210
FIVE SPRINGS FALLS 472
FLAGG RANCH VILLAGE 451
FLAGSTAFF 496
Flagstaff Mountain 156
Flaming Gorge National Recreation Area
512, 513
Flaming Gorge Ranger District 512, 513
Flaming Gorge Reservoir 512, 513, 518
FLAT CREEK RV PARK 505
Flat Rock Creek 326
FLAT ROCKS 166
Flat Tops Wilderness
66, 67, 68, 69, 70, 110, 111, 112, 119
Flathead Indian Reservation 320
Flathead Lake
307, 315, 316, 317, 318, 320, 321, 322, 323, 324, 326
Flathead National Forest
288, 294, 295, 301, 308, 309, 310, 317, 318, 327, 338, 343, 344
Flathead River 308
North Fork 288, 295
FLINT CREEK 384
Flint Creek 385
North Fork 386
Flint Range 387
FLORIDA 210
Florida Camp 211

Florissant Fossil Beds National Monument
168, 169, 170, 171, 264
FLYING A CAMPGROUND 187
FOOTHILLS 482
Ford Creek 341
FORD'S MOUNTAINDALE RANCH 270
Forest King Mountain 256
FOREST PARK 505
Forsyth, MT 431
Fort Benton, MT 350, 351
Fort Bridger State Historical Site 511
FORT CASPER 522
Fort Collins, CO
88, 89, 90, 93, 94, 95, 96,
97, 149, 154
FORT COLLINS MILE HIGH KOA 150
Fort Fizzle 366
Fort Garland, CO 275
Fort Garland Museum 276
FORT LARAMIE MUNICIPAL PARK 546
Fort Laramie, WY 546, 547
Fort Missoula 365, 368, 369, 370
Fort Morgan, CO 155
Fort Owen 367
Fort Peck Dam 359
Fort Peck Lake 358, 359, 360, 361
Fort Peck, MT 358, 359, 360
FORT PECK WEST RECREATION AREA
358
Fort Peck West Recreation Area 360
FORT PONDEROSA 352
Fortification Creek, North Fork 62
Fortine, MT 287, 288, 293, 294, 295
Fortine Ranger District
287, 288, 293, 294, 295
Fossil Ridge Area 225, 227
Fountain, CO 270
FOUNTAIN CREEK 266
Fountain Creek, CO 267
FOUR J TRAILER PARK 196
FOUR SEASONS RV PARK 237
FOURMILE 137
Fourmile Creek 137, 413
Fourmile Guard Station 420
FOX CREEK 442
Foxpark, WY 537, 538, 539
Fraser Experimental Forest 115
Fraser River 116, 120
FREEMAN 62
Freeman Reservoir 61, 62
Fremont Canyon 523, 524
FREMONT LAKE 505
Fremont Lake 506
FRENCH CREEK 530
French Creek 531
Fresno Reservoir 349
Friend Creek 545
FRIEND PARK 545
Frisco, CO 124, 126
Fruita, CO 74
FRUITA JUNCTION 74
Fruita Picnic Area 185
Fruita Reservoir 185
Frying Pan Lake 134
Frying Pan River 134
North Fork 133
FULFORD CAVE 122

G

Gallatin Canyon 394, 398
Gallatin National Forest
394, 398, 399, 402, 403, 404, 405,
413, 414, 415, 419, 420, 421, 424,
425, 426
Gallatin Petrified Forest 424
Gallatin Pioneers Museum 416
Gallatin River 398, 399, 400
GARDEN OF THE GODS 267
Garden of the Gods 268
Gardiner, MT 424, 425, 426, 439
Gardiner Ranger District 424, 425, 426
GARFIELD 230
Garfield Creek State Wildlife Area 73
Garnet Peak 394
GATES OF LODORE 62
Gates of Lodore 61
Gates of the Mountain Game Preserve 381
Gates of the Mountain Landing 381
Gates of the Mountain Wilderness 381, 382
GATEVIEW 232
GATEWAY 474
GATEWAY BOAT-IN 286
Geneva Basin 129
Geneva Creek 128
GENEVA PARK 128
Genoa Tower 168
George, Lake 168, 169, 170
Georgetown, CO 121
Georgetown Lake 384, 385, 386, 387
Giant Springs Fish, Wildlife and Parks Visitor
Center 343
Gibson Reservoir 340, 341
Gillette, WY 500
GLACIER BASIN 105
Glacier Creek 105
Glacier National Park
289, 295, 296, 297, 303,
333, 334, 335, 336, 337
GLACIER PINE RV 308
Glacier Rim 118
Glasgow, MT 358, 359, 360
GLEN ECHO RESORT 96
Glendive, MT 363
GLENDO MARINA 543
Glendo Marina 544
Glendo Reservoir 543, 544, 546
GLENDO STATE PARK 544
Glendo State Park 543, 544, 545
Glendo, WY 543, 544, 545
Glenwood Springs, CO
70, 71, 72, 73, 83, 118, 131,
132, 133, 134, 139

GOLD CREEK 226
Gold Creek 227, 390
GOLD PARK 135
GOLD RUSH 325
gold-panning 396
Golden, CO 156, 157, 158, 159
Golden Eagle Camp 270
GOLDEN EAGLE RANCH 265
Golden Eagle Ranch 266, 267, 268, 270
GOLDEN GATE CANYON STATE PARK 156
Golden Gate Canyon State Park 157
GOLDFIELD 267
golf course 72, 73, 74, 75, 76, 98, 103, 104, 105, 126, 152, 153, 158, 159, 160, 168, 174, 182, 186, 188, 191, 203, 208, 209, 222, 230, 234, 236, 254, 266, 267, 268, 269, 275, 279, 299, 303, 324, 331, 335, 336, 337, 343, 383, 395, 397, 416, 418, 419, 431, 459, 473, 474, 475, 477, 478, 483, 490, 502, 505, 510, 511, 512, 518, 548, 550, 552
golf course, miniature 98, 103, 104, 152, 181, 222, 270, 339, 432, 554
Goodman Creek 495
Goodwin Lake 459
GORE CREEK 119
Gore Mountain Range 112, 119
GORE PASS 112
Gore Pass Historic Monument 112
GORGE KOA 269
Gould, CO 93, 100
Gowdy, Curt 551
GRAHAM CREEK 211
Graham Creek Camp 211, 212
Graham Creek 213
Granby, CO 102, 107, 108, 115, 116, 120
Granby, Lake 107, 108
Granby Reservoirs 78
Grand Junction, CO 61, 73, 74, 75, 76, 78, 79, 80, 81, 185, 187
Grand Junction Ranger District 78, 79, 80, 187
Grand Lake, CO 101, 107
Grand Mesa National Forest 61, 77, 78, 79, 80, 81, 82, 185, 187
Grand Mesa Ranger District 185
Grand Targhee National Forest 451, 453, 454, 458
Grand Teton National Park 452, 453, 454, 459
GRAND VIEW 95
Grandview Trail 412
GRANITE CREEK 465
Granite Hot Springs 465
Granite Peak 414
Grant, CO 128
GRANT VILLAGE 448
Grass Range, MT 354
GRASSHOPPER 412
Grasshopper Creek 398, 413
Grassy Mountain 389
Gravely Range 397
Graves Bay 309
Great Burn 329
GREAT FALLS KOA 342
Great Falls, MT 342, 343, 352
Great Sand Dunes National Monument 247, 248
GREAT SAND DUNES OASIS 247
Great Sand Dunes Oasis 248
GREEK CREEK 398
Greeley, CO 151, 154
GREELEY RV PARK 154
Greeley RV Park 151, 155
GREEN MOUNTAIN 164
Green Mountain 369, 501
Green Mountain Falls, CO 176
Green Mountain Reservoir 113, 114, 115
Green River 61, 62, 63, 465, 466, 511, 513
Green River, WY 512, 513
GREEN VALLEY 363
GREENOUGH LAKE 427
GREENWAY TRAVEL PARK 553
GREENWOOD TRAILER VILLAGE 307
GREY REEF RESERVOIR 524
GREYBULL KOA 474
Greybull Ranger District 475, 476
Greybull River 476
Greybull, WY 475, 484, 487, 488
Greycliff, MT 415
Greys Peak 467
Greys River 466, 467, 468, 505
    Little 467
Greys River Ranger District 466, 467, 505, 507, 508
GRIZZLY 369
GRIZZLY CREEK 91
Grizzly Creek 92, 369
Grizzly Peak 286
Grizzly Reservoir 142, 143
GROS VENTRE 454
Gros Ventre River 454, 455, 456
Guanella Pass 129
Guernsey Reservoir 546
GUERNSEY STATE PARK 546
Guernsey, WY 546
Gunnison, CO 140, 189, 192, 195, 218, 219, 220, 221, 224, 225, 226, 227, 228, 232, 233, 234, 235, 242, 243
GUNNISON KOA 234
Gunnison KOA 236
Gunnison National Forest 61, 82, 140, 188, 189, 191, 217, 218, 219, 220, 221, 224, 225, 226, 227, 228, 229, 242, 243, 244

Gunnison River 186, 191, 192, 234
Lake Fork 232
Gurnsey, WY 547

H

Hahns Peak 86
HAHNS PEAK LAKE 85
Hahns Peak Ranger District 85, 87, 91, 99
Half Moon Creek 145
HALF MOON LAKE 506
HALFMOON 145
HALF MOON 414
HALL VALLEY 129
Hall Valley Camp 129, 130
Hamilton, MT
371, 372, 373, 374, 375, 376, 377
Hamilton Ranger District
372, 374, 375, 376, 377
HAMS FORK 510
HANDCART 129
Handcart Camp 129, 130
HANDKERCHIEF LAKE 308
HAPPY MEADOWS 169
HAPPY'S INN 305
Harlow, MT 412
Harlowton, MT 413
HARRY'S FLAT 368
HASKINS CREEK 535
Hasty, CO 281
HASTY RECREATION AREA, LAKE 281
HATCHET 453
HAVILAND LAKE 201
Haviland Lake 202
Havre, MT 349
Hawk Springs Reservoir 549
HAY CANYON 411
Hay Press Creek 185
hay rides 152, 176, 209, 223
HAYDEN CREEK 237
Hayden Creek Camp 239
Hayden Ranger District
528, 529, 535, 536, 537
HAYPRESS 185
Heart Lake 61, 71
HEART OF THE ROCKIES 229
HEATON BAY 125
Heaton Bay 124
Hebgen Lake 403, 404
Hebgen Lake Ranger District
402, 403, 404, 405
HELENA KOA 383
Helena, MT
302, 306, 314, 315, 317, 322, 323, 330, 345, 350, 351, 357, 360, 361, 363, 366, 373, 381, 382, 383, 384, 397, 419, 435
Helena National Forest
346, 381, 382, 383, 389
Helena Ranger District 381, 382, 383
HELL CREEK STATE PARK 361
Hellgate 384
HELL'S CANYON 420
HELL'S HALF ACRE 521
Hell's Half Acre, WY 521
Henry, Lake 273
Heritage Museum 299
Hermosa Cliffs 202
Hermosa Creek 201
East Fork 201
HERMOSA MEADOWS 209
Hesperus, CO 206
Hessie Trail 117
HI-VU 175
HICKS PARK 421
HIDDEN LAKES 92
HIDDEN VALLEY LAKE 238
HIDEOUT CABINS, THE 72
HIGHLINE STATE RECREATION AREA 73
Highline State Recreation Area 75, 76
HIGHWAY SPRINGS 249
Highway Springs 250
hiking
Colorado
62, 63, 64, 66, 67, 68, 69, 70, 71, 72, 74, 75, 77, 78, 79, 82, 83, 86, 87, 89, 90, 92, 93, 94, 95, 96, 97, 98, 99, 100, 102, 103, 104, 105, 106, 107, 108, 109, 111, 112, 113, 114, 115, 116, 117, 118, 119, 120, 121, 122, 123, 124, 125, 127, 128, 129, 130, 131, 132, 133, 134, 135, 136, 137, 139, 140, 141, 142, 143, 144, 145, 146, 150, 151, 152, 153, 154, 155, 157, 158, 159, 160, 162, 163, 164, 165, 166, 167, 169, 171, 172, 173, 174, 175, 176, 177, 178, 187, 189, 190, 193, 194, 195, 196, 197, 198, 199, 200, 201, 202, 203, 204, 205, 206, 207, 208, 209, 210, 211, 213, 214, 218, 219, 220, 221, 222, 223, 224, 225, 226, 227, 228, 230, 232, 234, 235, 236, 237, 238, 239, 240, 241, 242, 243, 244, 245, 246, 248, 249, 251, 253, 254, 255, 256, 257, 258, 259, 260, 264, 266, 267, 269, 270, 272, 273, 274, 277, 278
Montana
285, 286, 288, 289, 290, 291, 292, 293, 294, 295, 296, 297, 298, 299, 301, 302, 304, 305, 306, 308, 309, 311, 312, 313, 315, 316, 317, 318, 319, 325, 326, 327, 329, 331, 333, 335, 336, 337, 338, 339, 340, 341, 342, 344, 345, 346, 349, 352, 353, 358, 359, 360, 361, 365, 366, 367, 368, 369, 370, 371, 372, 374, 375, 377, 378, 379, 381, 382, 383, 385, 387, 388, 389, 390, 391, 392, 393, 394, 396, 398, 400, 401, 402, 403, 409, 410, 411, 412, 413, 414, 415, 416, 417, 419, 420, 421, 422, 423, 424, 425, 426, 427, 428, 429, 436

Wyoming
439, 440, 441, 443, 444, 445, 446, 447, 448, 449, 450, 451, 452, 453, 454, 455, 456, 457, 458, 459, 460, 461, 462, 463, 464, 465, 466, 467, 468, 472, 473, 474, 475, 476, 481, 482, 483, 484, 485, 486, 487, 488, 489, 490, 491, 492, 494, 495, 497, 500, 501, 502, 505, 506, 507, 508, 509, 510, 511, 515, 516, 517, 522, 523, 525, 526, 527, 528, 530, 531, 532, 533, 535, 536, 537, 538, 539, 543, 544, 545, 546, 550, 551
HILL CREEK 65
Hill Creek Trail 66
HILLTOP 401
HIMES PEAK 69
HINMAN 86
HOBACK 464
Hoback River 463, 464
Hoback Valley 464
Hobson, MT 411
Hog Park Reservoir 536
Holbrook Lake 281
HOLE-IN-THE-WALL LANDING 350
HOLIDAY TRAV-L-PARK 463
Holland Creek Drainage 327
HOLLAND LAKE 326
HOLTER LAKE 346
Holter Lake 347
Holy Cross Ranger District 119, 123, 135
Holy Cross Wilderness
122, 123, 124, 133, 135, 136
HOME GULCH 340
Home Gulch Camp 341
Homestake Creek 124
Homestake Reservoir 123, 124, 135
HOMESTEAD 170
Homestead Camp 169
HOOD CREEK 415
Hoosier Pass 164
Horn Peak 242
HORNSILVER 122
Hornsilver Camp 124
HORSE CREEK 165, 457
Horse Creek 166, 457
horseback riding
Colorado
66, 67, 68, 69, 70, 72, 73, 94, 98, 103, 105, 126, 150, 152, 153, 157, 160, 162, 173, 174, 175, 176, 191, 192, 196, 197, 201, 203, 204, 208, 209, 210, 222, 223, 234, 236, 239, 240, 246, 247, 251, 260, 266, 267, 268, 269, 270, 272, 277, 278
Montana
296, 300, 302, 303, 315, 324, 327, 336, 338, 342, 349, 396,397, 403, 404, 405, 417, 419
Wyoming
439, 440, 441, 444, 452, 455, 458, 459, 460, 463, 464, 474, 484, 505, 507, 518, 522, 549
HORSESHOE 110
HORSESHOE BEND 471
Horseshoe Creek 228, 545
Horseshoe Lake 421
horseshoes 436, 552, 554
HORSETOOTH RESERVOIR 149
Horsetooth Reservoir 149, 150
Hot Foot Creek 467
hot springs 72, 73, 198, 218, 223, 229, 237, 238, 320, 375, 394, 401, 439, 463, 465, 477
Hot Springs, MT 320
Hot Springs State Park 477
Hotchkiss, CO 188
Howard, CO 238
Howard Eaton Trail 443
HOWARD LAKE 305
Hudson, CO 156
Hulett, WY 499
Hungry Horse, MT 308, 309, 310, 338
Hungry Horse Ranger District
308, 309, 310
Hungry Horse Reservoir 308, 309, 310
HUNTER PEAK 441
Hunter-Frying Pan Wilderness 134, 143
hunting 63, 65, 70, 86, 88, 89, 93, 112, 154, 159, 175, 181, 182, 193, 214, 257, 313, 382, 411, 462, 465, 466, 483, 493, 508, 511, 523
Hyalite Canyon 395
Hyalite Creek 394, 395
Hyalite Junior Camp 416
Hyalite Reservoir 394, 415, 416

I

Ice Lake 200
ice skating 73, 76, 83, 155, 157, 162, 224
Idaho 290
Idaho Springs, CO 117, 120, 121, 122
Idalia, CO 183
IDLEWILD 116
Inch Mountain 292
Index Peak 442
INDIAN CREEK 162, 439
Indian Creek Ranger Station 162
Indian Creek, South Fork 392
INDIAN HILL 410
Indian Hill Camp 411
Indian Meadows 346
Indian Peaks Wilderness
107, 108, 110, 116, 117, 118
INDIAN RUN STATE WILDLIFE REFUGE 63
Indian Trail 277
INDIAN TREES 375
IRON CITY 228
Iron City Camp 230, 231

Iron Creek 252
IRON SPRING 192
IRWIN, LAKE 218
Isabel Camps, Lake 274
Isabel, Lake 274
ISABEL SOUTHSIDE, LAKE 273
Isabel Southside, Lake 274
ISABEL ST. CHARLES, LAKE 274
ISLAND ACRES STATE PARK 76
ISLAND LAKE 77, 442
Island Lake 61, 78, 443
ISLAND PARK 491

J

JACK CREEK 475, 528
Jack Creek 476, 528
JACKSON CREEK 167
Jackson Creek Camp 166
Jackson Gulch Reservoir 205
JACKSON HOLE 458
Jackson Hole, WY 454
Jackson Lake 155, 452, 453, 454
JACKSON LAKE STATE RECREATION AREA 155
Jackson, MT 378
Jackson Ranger District 455, 459, 461, 462, 464, 465
Jackson, WY 454, 455, 456, 458, 459, 461, 462, 463, 464, 465
JAMES KIPP STATE PARK 360
James Kipp State Recreation Area 352
JANEWAY 131
Janeway Camp 132, 139
Jedediah Smith Wilderness 453, 454, 458
Jeff Lake 527
Jefferson, CO 129, 138
JEFFERSON CREEK 126
Jefferson Creek 127, 128
Jefferson Lake 126, 127, 128
Jefferson River 391, 392
JEFFERSON RIVER PARK 391
JENNY LAKE 454
Jewel Basin Hiking Area 308, 309
Jewel Cave National Monument 502
Jewel Lake 419
JIM & MARY'S RV PARK 330
Jim & Mary's RV Park 331
JIM & WANDA'S 324
Jim Gatchell Museum 490
JIMMY JOE 422
Jinks Creek 88, 89
JOCKO HOLLOW 329
Jocko River 329, 330
Joe Wrights Creek 95
John Martin Dam 281
John Martin Reservoir 281
Johnny's Bar 352
JOHNSON'S 334
Jordan, MT 361
JUDITH LANDING 351
Judith Ranger District 353, 411, 412
Judith River 411
JUMBO 77
JUMPING CREEK 409
Jumping Creek 409, 410
JUNCTION CREEK 207
JUNCTION, THE 273
JUNCTION WEST RV PARK 75

K

KADING 382
Kalispell, MT 306, 307, 308, 313, 314, 316
Kansas 183
kayaking (see also boating, canoeing and rafting) 223, 500
KELLY DAHL 117
KELLY FLATS 97
Kelly, WY 455, 456
KELSEY 164
Kemmerer Ranger District 508, 510
Kemmerer, WY 508, 510
KENOSHA 129
Kenosha Pass 129, 130
Keyhole Reservoir 500, 501
KEYHOLE STATE PARK 500
KILBRENNAN LAKE 289
Kilbrennan Lake Camp 290, 291
Killpecker Creek 89
KING'S HILL 410
King's Hill Pass 410
King's Hill Ranger District 352, 353, 409, 410, 413
KINTLA LAKE 289
Kirkwood Ranch 403
KISER CREEK 80
KOA ASPEN BASALT 133
KOA BIGHORN 483
KOA ESTES PARK 103
KOA NORTH PARK 93
KOA OURAY 196
KOA Royal Gorge 269
KOA TETON VILLAGE 459
KOKO'S CAMPGROUND 167
Koocanusa, Lake 287, 292, 299, 300
Koocanusa Marina 300
Kootenai Creek 367
Kootenai Falls 298
Kootenai Lake 293
Kootenai National Forest 285, 286, 287, 288, 289, 290, 291, 292, 293, 294, 295, 297, 298, 299, 300, 304, 305, 310, 311, 312, 313, 314
Kootenai River 286, 287, 290, 298, 299
KOZY 464
KROEGER 205

L

L&L, Inc. 455, 456, 459, 461, 462, 465
La Bonte Creek 543
La Garita, CO 240

La Garita Mountain 246
La Garita Wilderness 243
La Grange, WY 549
La Gunita Lake 106
La Jara, CO 255, 256, 258, 259, 260
LA JARA RESERVOIR WILDLIFE MANAGEMENT AREA 257
La Junta, CO 281
LA JUNTA KOA 281
La Plata Basin 144
La Plata River 205
La Plata River Canyon 206
La Porte, CO 150
La Prele Creek 524, 525
La Veta, CO 277, 278
Lady of the Lake Creek 426
Lake City, CO 242, 243
LAKE CREEK 241, 312, 441
Lake Creek 144, 241, 312, 442
LAKE FORK 191, 255
Lake George, CO 170, 171, 223, 263
LAKE JOHN 87
LAKE SHEL-OOLE PARK 336
Lake, WY 445
LAKESHORE LODGE 397
LAKESHORE TRAILER PARK 316
Lakeside, MT 316
LAKEVIEW 144, 220, 308, 492, 536, 544
Lakeview Campground 492, 493
LAKEVIEW TOURIST RESORT 334
Lakewood, CO 128, 129, 130, 162, 163, 164, 165, 166, 167, 172
Lander, WY 515, 516, 517
Landusky, MT 359
LANGOHR 394
Laporte, CO 89, 96, 97, 149
LARAMIE KOA 550
Laramie Mountains 89, 543, 546
Laramie Peak 545
Laramie Peak Trail 545
Laramie Ranger District
527, 531, 532, 533, 534, 537, 538, 539, 540, 550, 551, 552
Laramie River 93
North Fork 533
Laramie, WY 527, 531, 532, 533, 534, 537, 538, 539, 540, 549, 550, 551, 552
Larger Leon Lake 61, 81, 82
LASALLE 302
LATHROP STATE PARK 276
Lathrop State Park 275
Laurel, MT 419
LAZY G RV PARK 203
LAZY J CORRAL 463
LAZY J RESORT AND RAFT COMPANY 239
Lazy Man Gulch 383
LAZY R TRAILER PARK 335
Lazy R Trailer Park 335
Leadville, CO 123, 135, 136, 137, 143, 144, 145, 146
Leadville Ranger District
135, 136, 137, 143, 144, 145, 146
Lee Creek 61, 82, 83
LEIGH CREEK 490
Leigh Creek 490
Leigh Creek Camp 491
Lemon Day Use Area, Upper 211
Lemon Reservoir 209, 210, 211
LEMONADE SPRINGS CAMPGROUND 436
LEWIS AND CLARK 365
Lewis and Clark National Forest
337, 339, 340, 341, 342, 352, 353, 409, 410, 411, 413
Lewis and Clark Trail 365, 366
LEWIS LAKE 448
Lewistown, MT 361
Libby Creek 531, 532, 533, 534, 535
Libby Creek Recreation Area 532, 534
Libby, MT 291, 292, 298, 299, 300, 301, 305, 312, 314
Libby Ranger District 292, 301, 305, 312
LIGHTNER CREEK 206
Lightner Creek 206, 207
Lily Lake Ranger Station 140
LIMBER PINE 427
Limon, CO 168
Lincoln Creek 141, 142, 530
LINCOLN GULCH 141
Lincoln, MT 346
LINCOLN PARK 530
Lincoln Park 529
Lincoln Ranger District 346
Lindon, CO 183
Link McIntyre Trailhead 89
Lion Canyon 273
Lion Creek 390
LION'S HEAD RESORT 405
LITTLE BEAR 78
Little Belt Mountains 409
LITTLE GOOSE 487
Little Goose Creek, West Fork 487
LITTLE MONTANA TRUCKSTOP 353
Little Rocky Mountains 359, 360
LITTLE SANDSTONE 528
Little Wood Lakes 341
Littleton, CO 162
Livingston, MT
394, 416, 417, 418, 419, 420
Livingston Ranger District 419, 420
LIZARD CREEK 453
Lizard Rock 171
Loch Leven 417
LODGEPOLE 127, 225, 385, 523
LOGAN STATE PARK 313
LOGGING CREEK 352
Lolo Creek 365, 366
Lolo, MT 365

Lolo National Forest
318, 319, 325, 326, 327, 328, 329, 343, 344, 345, 365, 367, 368, 369, 370
Loma, CO 73
LONE ROCK 166
LONESOME HURST 403
LONG DRAW 95
Long Draw Reservoir 95
Long Lake 526
Long Park 64
Longmont, CO 155
LONGS PEAK 108
Longs Peak 109
LOON LAKE 292
LORY STATE PARK 150
Los Pinos River 210
LOST BURRO 264
Lost Burro Camp 265
LOST CABIN 494
Lost Cabin Camp 495
LOST CREEK 535
Lost Creek 138, 139, 536
Lost Creek Wilderness 139, 163, 165, 171
Lost Horse Creek, South Fork 370
LOST JOHNNY POINT 309
Lost Johnny Point Camp 310
LOST LAKE 217
Lost Lake 95, 218
Lost Lake Slough 218
LOST MAN 143
Lost Man Creek 143
LOST PARK 138
Lost Park 64
LOTTIS CREEK 225
Lottis Creek 226
LOUIS LAKE 517
Loveland, CO 151, 152, 153, 154
LOVELAND RV VILLAGE 152
LOVELL CAMPER PARK 471
Lovell, WY 471, 472, 473
LOWER PIEDRA 213
LUDERS CREEK 243
Luders Creek 244
LYMAN KOA 511
Lyman, WY 511
LYNX CREEK 467
LYNX PASS 106
Lyons, CO 152

M

M-K MOBILE PARK 477
Madison Camp, South 399
MADISON JUNCTION 445
Madison Range 396
Madison Ranger District 393, 400, 401
MADISON RIVER 402
Madison River Camp 399
Madison River
396, 397, 399, 401, 402, 405
Upper 393
Magpie Gulch 382
MAKOSHIKA 363
Mallards Rest 417
Malmstrom Air Force Base Museum 343
Malta, MT 357, 358
MAMMOTH 439
Mammoth Hot Springs 439
Mancos, CO 204, 205, 206
Mancos Ranger District 205
Mancos River 204, 205
Mandall Creek 111
Mandall Trail 111
Manila, UT 512, 513
Manitou Experimental Forest 174, 175
Manitou Picnic Ground 174
Manitou Springs, CO 267
Manti Lasal National Forest 190
MANY GLACIER 296
MANY PINES 410
Margaret, Mount 90
Marias Museum of History and Art 337
Marias River 338
Marion, MT 306
Maroon Bells Snowmass Wilderness
131, 132, 139, 140, 142
Maroon Creek 140
MAROON LAKE 142
Marshall Pass 237
Marston, Mount 295
MARTEN CREEK 311
Marten Creek Bay 311
Martin City, MT 310, 338
MARTIN CREEK 374
MARVINE 67
Marvine Creek 61, 67
Marvine Lakes 67
Mary Ronan, Lake 314, 315
MARY RONAN LODGE, LAKE 314
MARY RONAN STATE PARK, LAKE 314
MARY'S LAKE 104
Marysville, MT 383
MATTERHORN 200
Matterhorn Ranger Station 200
MAVERICK TRAILER PARK 271
MAVREESO 198
MAY CREEK 377
MAY QUEEN 134
Maybell, CO 61, 62
McAllister, MT 397
McCALL'S ELKHORN 396
McCLURE 82
McClure Pass 83
McConnell, Mount 98
McDONALD FLATS 114
McDonald, Lake 295, 296, 303
McFadden, WY 526
McGILLIVRAY 300
McGregor Lake 313, 314
McGREGOR LAKE CAMP 313
McGregor Peak 314
McKnight, Mount 419

MEADOW LAKE 70
MEADOW RIDGE 177
Meadowlark Group Camp 299
MEADOWLARK GROUP PARK 298
Meadowlark Lake 491, 492, 493
MEADOWLARK MOTEL AND CAMP-GROUND 182
MEADOWS 99
MEADOWS GROUP CAMP 162
Medicine Bow Mountains 89, 94, 529, 530, 531
Medicine Bow National Forest
524, 526, 527, 528, 529, 530, 531, 532, 533, 534, 535, 536, 537, 538, 539, 543, 545, 550, 551, 552
Medicine Bow Peak 532
Medicine Bow River 527
Medicine Lake 336
MEDICINE LODGE LAKE 488
Medicine Mountain 473
MEDICINE ROCK STATE MONUMENT 435
Medicine Wheel Ranger District Office 472, 473
Meeker, CO 63, 64, 65, 66, 67, 68, 69
MEEKER PASTURE 64
Meeteetse, WY 475, 476
Melrose, MT 390
Memorial Creek 410
Memorial Falls 410
Meredith, Lake 273
MERIDIAN 130
Meriwether Canyon 381
Meriwether Picnic Area 381
MESA 235
Mesa, CO 77
Mesa Lakes 61, 77
MESA OASIS 203
Mesa Reservoir 234
Mesa Verde National Park 203, 204, 205
MESA VERDE POINT KAMPARK 204
MICHIGAN CREEK 138
Michigan Creek 94, 138
Michigan River 88, 94
South Fork 100, 101
Midas Point 305
Middle Bald Mountain 89
Middle Creek 274, 488
MIDDLE FORK 489
MIDDLE MOUNTAIN 212
MIDDLE PINEY LAKE 509
MIDDLE QUARTZ 227
Miles City, MT 431
Milk River 358
Milk River Bridge 349
MILL CREEK 392
Mill Creek 242, 392, 420, 467
MILLER CREEK 210
Miller Creek 211, 312
MILLER LAKE 538
Miller Lake 312, 538
MINER LAKE 378
Miner Lake, Lower 378
Mineral Creek, South Fork 200
Minturn, CO 119, 123, 135
MIRAMONTE RESERVOIR 195
MISSION MEADOWS 326
Mission Mountain Range 321, 330
MISSOULA KOA 331
Missoula, MT
330, 331, 366, 367, 368, 369, 370
Missoula Ranger District
365, 368, 369, 370
Missouri River 342, 350, 351, 352, 358, 359, 360, 381
Missouri River Canyon 381
MIX LAKE 255
MIZPAH 120
Mizpah Peak 410
MK CAMPGROUND 428
Moab Ranger District 190
Moab, UT 190
MOBILE MANOR 253
MOGOTE 259
MOLLY BROWN 136
Molly Brown Camp 137
Monarch, MT 352
MONARCH PARK 236
Monarch Pass 236
Monarch Ski Area 236
Monitor Peak 420
Montana Department of Fish, Wildlife and Parks
302, 306, 313, 314, 315, 317, 322, 323, 330, 345, 350, 351, 357, 360, 361, 363, 366, 373, 397, 419, 435
MONTANA GULCH 359
Montana Historical Society Museum 383
Montana Library and Archives 383
Montana State Parks 384
Montana State University 416
Monte Vista, CO 252, 253, 256, 257
Montrose, CO
188, 190, 191, 192, 193, 194, 198
MONTROSE KOA 190
MONTURE 345
Monument Lake 279
Moorcroft, WY 501
MOOSE CREEK 383, 409
Moose Creek 374, 409
MOOSE FLAT 466
Moose Lake 374, 375
Moose, WY 452, 453, 454
MOOSEHEAD CAMP & STORE 377
MORAINE PARK 105
Moran, WY 451, 453
MOREFIELD 204
Morrison, CO 161
Morrison Divide Trail 106
MORTIMER GULCH 340
MOSCA 219

Mosca, CO 248
motorbikes
Colorado
72, 74, 75, 93, 103, 132, 133, 150, 151, 152, 153, 156, 157, 158, 159, 161, 165, 170, 173, 175, 176, 186, 188, 191, 192, 196, 197, 201, 206, 207, 208, 209, 222, 223, 229, 232, 233, 234, 235, 238, 239, 241, 245, 246, 247, 251, 253, 254, 260, 264, 265, 266, 267, 268, 269, 270, 271, 272, 273, 275, 276, 278, 281
Montana
294, 302, 306, 307, 308, 314, 315, 316, 320, 321, 322, 324, 326, 327, 329, 330, 331, 334, 335, 337, 339, 342, 343, 349, 365, 366, 367, 376, 377, 383, 389, 391, 394, 395, 396, 397, 403, 405, 416, 417, 418, 419, 424, 425, 432
Wyoming
452, 453, 454, 458, 459, 460, 463, 474, 475, 483, 499, 500, 501, 502, 505, 508, 510, 511, 516, 522, 526, 544, 547, 548, 549, 550, 551, 552, 553
motorcycling 64, 223
MOUNT EVANS STATE WILDLIFE AREA 158
Mount Evans State Wildlife Area 159
Mount Evans Wilderness 120, 121, 122, 128, 130, 131
Mount Marston National Recreation Trail 295
Mount Massive Wilderness 136, 145
Mount McConnell Trail 97
Mount Princeton Hot Springs 229
Mount Zirkel Wilderness 87, 90, 91, 92
mountain biking (see also bicycling) 62, 70, 99, 100, 123, 134, 162, 228, 241, 244, 245, 285, 292, 410, 449, 501, 528, 538
Mountain Home Reservoir 275, 276
Mountain Home, WY 540
MOUNTAIN MEADOWS RESORT 315
Mountain Meadows Resort 314, 315
MOUNTAIN PARK 97
MOUNTAIN VIEW 269, 370, 501
Mountain View Camp 269, 270, 271, 502
Muddy Creek 494
Muddy Mountain 523
MURPHY CREEK 467
Murphy Lakes 467
MURRAY BAY COMPLEX 309
Murray Bay Complex 310
museum 74, 245, 265, 269, 276, 279, 299, 337, 339, 343, 357, 383, 412, 416, 432, 473, 474, 490, 546, 553
Museum of the Rockies 416
Musselshell River 431
Mutt Lake 527
Mystic Lake 422, 423

N

N&H TRAILER RANCH 549
N&H Trailer Ranch 550
NARROW GAUGE RAILROAD 260
Narrow Gauge Railroad 206, 207, 208, 209
NARROWS 468
Narrows Camp 468
NASH FORK 533
Nathrop, CO 222, 228, 230, 231
National Basin Range 330
National Elk Refuge 454, 459
NATIONAL PARK RESORT 102
Natrona County Parks Board 521, 522, 523, 524
Natural Bridge Trail 450
nature program 192, 204, 233, 235, 313, 316, 323
nature trail 76, 207, 312, 329, 331, 359, 363, 365, 367, 491, 495, 500, 516, 523, 552
Navajo Lake 213, 214
Navajo Lake Trailhead 199
NAVAJO STATE RECREATION AREA 213
Navajo Trail 281
Nederland, CO 118
Neihart, MT 353, 410
NELSON RESERVOIR 357
Neota Creek 95
Neota Wilderness 95
Nevada City, MT 396
New Castle, CO 70
NEW FORK LAKE 468
New Fork River 508
New Mexico 214, 275
Newcastle, WY 502
NEWTON CREEK 450
NORRIS 443
Norris Hot Springs 394
Norris, MT 393
NORTH BANK 224
North Bank 225
NORTH CANYON 212
NORTH CRESTONE CREEK 244
North Derby Trail 110
NORTH DICKEY LAKE 294
NORTH FORK 64, 533
North Fork Lake 231
NORTH FORK POUDRE 89
NORTH FORK RESERVOIR 230
North Fork Reservoir Camp 232
North Gate Canyon 537
North Lake 93
North Park Ranger District 87, 92, 100, 101
North Pass 244
NORTH RIM 188
North Rim Camp 191
NORTH SHORE 311
NORTH STERLING RESERVOIR CAMPGROUND 181
NORTH TONGUE 481

NORTON 370
Norwood, CO 195, 200
Norwood Ranger District 195, 200
Norwood River 496
Noxon, MT 304
Noxon Reservoir 305, 310, 311, 312

O

OAK CREEK 272
OAK RIDGE STATE WILDLIFE AREA 65
O'HAVER LAKE 236
Ohio City, CO 227
Old Colorado City, CO 266
Old Faithful 445
Old Trail Museum 339
OLIVE RIDGE 108
Olney, MT 294
OLSEN'S DRIVE-THRU TRAILER COURT 418
ONE MILE 224
One Mile Camp 224, 225
OPHIR 274
Orchard, CO 155
Ordway, CO 273
Oregon Trail 546
OROFINO 387
Ouray, CO 196, 197
Ouray Ranger District 190, 192, 193, 194
OUTPOST 366
Ovando, MT 345
Overland Creek 526
Overland Trail 526
OVERLAND TRAIL KOA 526
Overlook 384
OWEN, LAKE 539
OWL CREEK 478
OX-YOKE ACRES 508

P

Pablo National Wildlife Refuge 324
Pagoda, CO 63
Pagosa Ranger District 248, 254, 255
Pagosa Springs, CO
213, 214, 248, 254, 255, 257
PAHASKA 446
Pahaska Camp 447
Pahaska, WY 446
PAINTED ROCKS 174
Painted Rocks Camp 175
PAINTED ROCKS RESERVOIR STATE PARK 373
Paintrock Lake 488
PAINTROCK LAKES COMPLEX 487
Paintrock Lakes Complex 488
Paintrock Ranger District 484, 487
Palisade, CO 76
Palisade Falls 416
Paonia, CO 83, 217, 218
Paonia Ranger District 83, 217, 218
PAONIA RESERVOIR STATE RECREATION AREA 83
Paradise Campground 372
Paradise Lodge 314
PARADISE TRAVEL PARK 103
Paradise Valley 417
PARADISE VALLEY KOA 418
Park Cone 220
Park Mountain Range 92
PARK PLACE RESORT 151
Park Range 100
Park Reservoir 485
PARKSIDE 428
Parkside Camp 427, 428
PARRY PEAK 143
Parry Peak Camp 144
Pass Creek 250
Pathfinder Bird Refuge 524
PATHFINDER RESERVOIR 524
Pathfinder Reservoir 524, 525
PAWNEE 116
Pawnee National Grasslands 151
PEACEFUL VALLEY 109
PEAK ONE 124
PEAK VIEW 266
Pearl Lake 86
PEARL LAKE STATE PARK 86
PEBBLE CREEK 440
PECK GULCH 292
PELTON CREEK 538
Pelton Creek 539
Periodic Springs 508
PETE CREEK 285
Pete Creek 286
PETRIFIED FOREST 424
pets are permitted
Colorado
61, 62, 63, 64, 65, 66, 67, 68, 69, 70, 71, 72, 73, 74, 75, 76, 82, 83, 85, 86, 87, 88, 89, 90, 91, 92, 93, 94, 95, 96, 97, 98, 99, 100, 101, 102, 103, 104, 105, 106, 107, 108, 109, 110, 111, 112, 113, 114, 115, 116, 117, 118, 119, 120, 121, 122, 123, 124, 125, 126, 127, 128, 129, 130, 131, 132, 133, 134, 135, 136, 137, 138, 139, 140, 141, 142, 143, 144, 145, 146, 149, 150, 151, 152, 153, 154, 155, 156, 157, 158, 159, 160, 161, 162, 163, 164, 165, 166, 167, 168, 169, 170, 171, 172, 173, 174, 175, 176, 177, 181, 182, 183, 185, 186, 188, 189, 190, 191, 192, 193, 194, 195, 196, 197, 198, 199, 200, 201, 202, 203, 204, 205, 206, 207, 208, 209, 210, 211, 212, 213, 221, 222, 223, 227, 228, 229, 230, 231, 232, 233, 234, 235, 236, 237, 238, 239, 240, 241, 242, 243, 244, 245, 246, 247, 248, 249, 250, 251, 252, 253, 254, 255, 256, 257, 258, 259, 260, 263, 264, 265, 266, 267, 268, 269, 270, 271, 272, 273, 274, 275, 276, 277, 278, 281, 282

Montana
286, 287, 288, 289, 290, 291, 292, 293, 294, 295, 296, 297, 298, 299, 300, 301, 302, 303, 304, 305, 306, 307, 308, 309, 310, 311, 312, 313, 314, 315, 316, 317, 318, 319, 320, 321, 322, 323, 324, 325, 326, 327, 328, 329, 330, 331, 333, 334, 335, 336, 337, 339, 340, 341, 342, 343, 344, 345, 346, 347, 349, 350, 351, 352, 353, 354, 357, 358, 359, 360, 361, 363, 365, 366, 367, 368, 369, 370, 371, 372, 373, 374, 375, 376, 377, 378, 381, 382, 383, 384, 385, 386, 387, 388, 389, 390, 391, 392, 393, 394, 395, 396, 397, 398, 399, 400, 401, 402, 403, 404, 405, 406, 409, 410, 411, 412, 413, 414, 415, 416, 417, 418, 419, 420, 421, 422, 423, 424, 425, 426, 427, 428, 429, 431, 432, 435, 436
Wyoming
442, 443, 444, 445, 446, 447, 448, 449, 450, 451, 452, 453, 454, 455, 456, 457, 458, 459, 460, 461, 462, 463, 464, 465, 466, 467, 468, 471, 472, 473, 474, 475, 476, 477, 478, 481, 482, 483, 484, 485, 486, 487, 488, 489, 490, 491, 492, 493, 494, 495, 496, 499, 500, 501, 502, 505, 506, 507, 508, 509, 510, 511, 512, 515, 516, 517, 518, 521, 522, 523, 525, 526, 527, 528, 529, 530, 531, 532, 533, 534, 535, 536, 537, 538, 539, 543, 544, 545, 546, 547, 548, 549, 550, 551, 552, 553, 554
Phantom Creek 423
PHILIPS TRAILER PARK 510
PHILIPSBURG BAY 385
Philipsburg, MT
371, 374, 384, 385, 386, 390
Philipsburg Ranger District
371, 374, 384, 385, 386, 390
Phillips County Museum 357
Phippsburg, CO 64
PICKAROON 537
Pickaroon Camp 537, 539
PICKLE GULCH GROUP CAMP 117
Piedra River 213
Pike National Forest
126, 127, 128, 129, 130, 137, 138, 146, 162, 163, 164, 165, 166, 167, 168, 169, 170, 171, 172, 174, 175, 176, 177, 263, 264, 266
PIKE POLE 536
Pike Pole Camp 537, 539
PIKE'S GULCH 381
Pike's Peak 173, 174, 176, 265
Pike's Peak Ranger District
169, 172, 174, 177, 264
PIKE'S PEAK TRAILER PARK 266
Pike's Peak Trailer Park 270
Pilot Peak 442
PINE 533
PINE BLUFF RV VILLAGE 552
Pine Bluffs, WY 552
PINE COVE 124
Pine Cove 125
PINE CREEK 419
PINE GROVE 422
Pine Ranger District
202, 208, 210, 211, 212, 213
PINE RIVER 212
Pinedale Ranger District
466, 468, 506, 507, 515
Pinedale, WY
466, 468, 506, 507, 508, 515
PINES 100
Pines Camp 101
PINES, THE 360
PINEY BAY 384
Piney Creek, Middle 509
Pinkerton Trail 201
Pinkham Creek 293
Pinkham Falls 293
PINNACLES 456
Pinnacles Camp 456, 457
PINYON FLATS 247
PIONEER PARK 548
Pioneer Park 547
Pioneer Ridge 353
Pipe Creek 291, 300, 301
PITKIN 227
Pitkin, CO 227, 228, 229
Placer Creek Trail 353
Placid Lake 330
PLACID LAKE STATE PARK 330
Plains, MT 319, 325, 328
Plains Ranger District 319, 325, 328
Plateau, Lake 421
Platoro Reservoir 255
Platte River 158, 172
North 88, 93, 536, 537, 546, 548
South 129, 146, 154, 166, 168, 169, 170, 171
PLEASANT VALLEY 238
POINT PLEASANT 324
Pole Mountain 550, 551
POLLY'S JEEP RENTAL CAMP AND MOTEL 197
Polson, MT 314, 315, 321, 322, 323, 324
Poncha Creek 236
Poncha Springs, CO 230, 231, 236
PONDEROSA 192, 474, 522
Ponderosa Camp 189, 192, 232, 233, 384
PONDEROSA KOA 209
Pony, MT 393
Popo-Agie River
Middle Fork 516
North Fork 515
PORCUPINE 472
Porcupine Camp 473

Porcupine Falls 472
Porphyry Peak 410
PORTAL 142
POSO 240
POTOSI 393
Powderhorn Primitive Area 243
Powell, WY 441, 442, 443, 444
PRAIRIE POINT 113
Prewitt Reservoir 182
PREWITT RESERVOIR CAMPGROUND 182
Prewitt Reservoir Campground 181, 182
Princeton, Mount 221, 230
Proctor, MT 315
PROSPECTOR 125
Prospector 124
PRUNE CREEK 481
Pueblo, CO 272
PUEBLO KOA 272
Pueblo Reservoir 272
PUEBLO STATE PARK 271
Purcell Mountains 286
PURGATOIRE 277
Purgatoire River, North Fork 277, 278
PURGATORY 202
Purgatory Ski Area 202
Purgatory Trail 202
Putnam Gulch 371
Pyramid Guard Station 64

Q

QUARTZ 229
Quartz Creek 227, 228, 229, 392
QUARTZ FLAT 329
Quartzite Ridge 409
Quinn Hot Springs 328

R

RACETRACK 387
Racetrack Creek 387
Racetrack Peak 387
rafting (see also boating, canoeing and kayaking) 62, 63, 72, 111, 209, 222, 223, 224, 229, 237, 238, 240, 269, 463, 464, 500, 512
Raggeds Wilderness 83, 140, 217, 219
RAINBOW FALLS 176
RAINBOW HOTEL & CAMP 416
RAINBOW LAKES 118
RAINBOW POINT 404
Rainbow Trail 237, 239, 241, 242
Rampart Reservoir 176, 177
Rampart Reservoir Recreation Area 177
Ranch Creek 369
RANGER CREEK 483, 486
Ranger Creek Camp 484, 486, 487
Ranger Lakes 100
Ravalli, MT 330
Rawah Trail 93
Rawah Wilderness 89, 93
RAWHIDE RANCH 460
Rawhide Ranch 461
Rawlins, WY 525, 526
RED CLIFF 399
RED CREEK 232
Red Desert 518, 548
Red Feather Ranger District 88, 89, 90, 93, 95, 96
RED HILLS 455
Red Hills Camp 456
Red Lodge 423, 424
Red Lodge Creek Plateau 423
RED LODGE KOA 423
Red Lodge, MT 421, 422, 423, 424, 427, 428, 429
RED MOUNTAIN 393
RED MOUNTAIN LODGE 200
Red Rocks Ampitheater 159
RED SHALE 435
RED TOP 291
Red Top Camp 285
Red Top Mountain 291
Redcliff, CO 123, 135
Redskin Creek 162, 163
REDSTONE 139
Redstone, CO 139
Reef Creek 444
Register Cliff 547
Renshaw Lake 342
Renshaw Mountain 342
REST-A-DAY 306
RESTWAY TRAVEL PARK 554
REUTER 501
REX HALE 450
REXFORD BENCH COMPLEX 287
Rexford, MT 287, 292, 293, 299
Rich Creek-Buffalo Meadows Trail 146
Rich Creek-Tumble Creek Trail 146
Richardson Creek Picnic Area 413
Rico, CO 199, 201
Ridgway, CO 193, 195
Ridgway State Recreation Office 195
Rifle, CO 70
Rifle Creek, East 61, 70
RIFLE FALLS STATE RECREATION AREA 70
Rifle Gap Reservoir 61, 69, 70
RIFLE GAP STATE RECREATION AREA 69
RIM 523
Rio Blanco River 257
Rio De Los Pinos 258
Rio Grande National Forest 240, 243, 244, 246, 248, 249, 250, 251, 252, 253, 255, 256, 258, 259, 260
Rio Grande River 245, 246, 254
South Fork 249, 250, 252
Rio Grande Southern Railroad 201
Ripple Creek Overlook 67
RISING SUN 333
RIVER 517

RIVER BEND 151
River Creek 456
RIVER POINT 344
River Point Camp 343
River Springs Ranger Station 259
RIVERBEND RV PARK 251
RIVER'S END 219
River's End Camp 220, 221
RIVERSIDE 168
Riverside Campground 169, 384
Riverton Rendezvous 478
Riverton, WY 477, 478
RIVERVIEW 153
RIVERWOOD INN 186
Roaring Creek 89
Roaring Fork Creek 108
Roaring Fork River
61, 72, 73, 133, 141, 142, 143
ROB ROY 534
Rob Roy Reservoir 534, 538
ROBBERS ROOST 119
ROCK CANYON 417
ROCK CREEK 252
Rock Creek Camp 256
Rock Creek 112, 252, 253, 256, 367, 368, 369, 370, 371, 374, 424, 427, 428, 429, 526
Rock Creek, MT 428
ROCK CREEK STATE PARK 360
ROCK GARDENS 72
ROCK LAKE 293
ROCK SPRINGS KOA 518
Rock Springs, WY 512, 518
rockhounding 460, 512
ROCKING G RANCH 321
Rocky Boy Indian Reservation 349
ROCKY GORGE 299
ROCKY MOUNTAIN CAMP 425
ROCKY MOUNTAIN HI 307
Rocky Mountain National Park
95, 96, 97, 101, 102, 103, 104, 105, 106, 108, 109, 151, 152, 156
Rocky Mountain Ranger District
337, 339, 340, 341, 342
ROMBO 372
Rombo Creek 373
Ronan, MT 324, 326
RONDEVUE 316
Rookery State Recreation Area 349
Roosevelt Monument National Historic Sites
337
Roosevelt National Forest
88, 89, 90, 93, 94, 95, 96, 97, 98, 108, 109, 110, 116, 117, 118, 149, 151
Roosevelt National Park 97
Roscoe, MT 423
ROSE PARK MOBILE VILLAGE 76
Rosebud Creek 422, 423
Rosebud Reservoir, West 422
ROSEBUD STATE PARK 431
Ross Creek Cedars Scenic Area 304
Ross Creek Falls 304
Rosy Lane Camp 225
ROUND MOUNTAIN 170
Roundup, MT 431
Routt National Forest
61, 62, 63, 64, 85, 87, 90, 91, 92, 98, 99, 100, 101, 106, 110, 111, 112
Royal Gorge 269
Royal Gorge Rodeo 269
ROY'S TRAILER COURT 435
Ruby Mountain Range 218, 219
Ruby River 396
Ruby River Reservoir 396
RUDY'S CAMPER COURT 477
RUEDI 132
Ruedi Reservoir 132, 133, 134
Rushmore, Mount 502
RUSTIC RV 406
RV STATION 271
Ryan Gulch 174
RYAN PARK 529
Ryan Park 530
Rye, CO 273, 274

S

S-S MOTEL & CAMP 418
Sacagawea Peak 414
SACAJAWEA 509
Sacajawea's grave 478, 517
SADDLE HORN 74
Sagauche, CO 240, 244
Sagauche Ranger District 240, 244
sailboarding 86, 150
sailing (see also boating) 73, 272
Saint Labre Indian Mission 436
Salida, CO 221, 222, 227, 228, 229, 230, 231, 236, 237, 238, 239, 240
Salida Ranger District
221, 222, 228, 230, 231, 236, 237, 239
Salt River 505, 508, 509
SAM BILLINGS 372
San Carlos Ranger District
241, 242, 272, 273, 274, 277, 278
San Francisco Lakes 253
San Isabel National Forest
134, 135, 136, 137, 143, 144, 145, 146, 221, 222, 228, 230, 231, 236, 237, 239, 241, 242, 272, 273, 274, 277, 278
San Juan Mountains 245
San Juan National Forest
198, 199, 200, 201, 202, 204, 205, 206, 207, 208, 210, 211, 212, 213, 248, 254, 255, 257
SAN JUAN NATIONAL FOREST HOTEL
254
San Juan River 248, 254, 255
San Juan Wilderness 256, 258, 259, 260
San Luis, CO 276
SAN LUIS VALLEY 241

San Miguel River 200
SAN-SUZ-ED TRAILER PARK 303
Sand Creek 501
Sand Dunes National Monument 247, 276
Sand Lake 527
Sandstone Creek, Little 528
Sangre de Cristo Creek 276
Sangre de Cristo Range 242
Santa Fe Trail 279, 281
Sapphire Mountains 368
Sapphire Village 411
Saratoga Ranger District
526, 527, 529, 530, 531
Saratoga, WY
526, 527, 528, 529, 530, 531
Sargents, CO 228
Savage Run Wilderness 538
Savery, WY 528, 535
SAWMILL CREEK 61
SAWMILL GULCH 106
Sawmill Gulch Camp 102
Scapegoat Mountain 345
Scapegoat Wilderness 342, 346
Scott Gomer Creek 128
Sedalia, CO 162, 165, 166, 167
Seeley Creek 429
SEELEY LAKE 343
Seeley Lake 344
Seeley Lake Game Preserve 344
Seeley Lake, MT 330, 343, 344, 345
Seeley Lake Ranger District 343, 344, 345
SELKIRK 138
Selway Mountain 379
Selway River 372
Selway-Bitterroot Wilderness 367, 371, 372
SEMINOE BOAT CLUB AREA 525
Seminoe Reservoir 525
SEMINOE STATE PARK 525
Seminoe State Park 526
Seven Falls 267, 268
SEYMOUR LAKE 100
Shadow Mountain Reservoir 101
SHADY GROVE 336
SHADY GROVE TRAILER PARK 320
Shavano, Mount 229, 232
Sheep Creek 409, 410
Sheep Mountain 495
Shelby, MT 337, 338
SHELL 475
SHELL CREEK 484
Shell Creek 475, 483, 484
Shell Creek Trail 484
Shell Falls 484
Shell, WY 475
SHEPHERD'S RIM 68
Sherburne, Lake 296
Sheridan, Mount 448
Sheridan, MT 392
Sheridan Ranger District 392
Sheridan, WY
481, 482, 483, 485, 486, 487
Sherman, Mount 137
Sherman Mountains 550, 551
Shining, The 103
Shoshone Indians 478
Shoshone Lake 451
Shoshone National Forest
441, 442, 443, 444, 446, 447,
448, 449, 450, 456, 457, 458, 475,
476, 515, 516, 517
Shoshone River 446, 447, 448, 450, 474
Shoshoni, WY 477
SIBLEY LAKE 482
Sierra Mountain Range 499
SIERRA VISTA KOA 253
SIG CREEK 201
SIGNAL MOUNTAIN 452
Silt, CO 72
Silver Creek 117, 118
Silver Gate, MT 440
Silver Gulch Trail 353
SILVER JACK 193
Silver Jack Reservoir 193
SILVER LAKE 531
Silver Lake 386, 531
SILVER QUEEN 140
Silver Star, MT 391
Silverthorne, CO
113, 114, 115, 124, 125, 126
Silverton, CO 200, 201, 202, 208, 209
Sinclair, WY 525, 526
SINKS CANYON 516
SINKS CANYON STATE PARK 516
Sioux Indians 416
SIRIA 368
SITTING BULL 491
SIX MILE GAP 537
Six Mile Gap Camp 537
Sixmile Creek 164
Skalkaho Creek 371
SKI TOWN 98
SKIDWAY 389
skiing 120, 196, 202, 236, 275, 292, 410
skiing, cross-country
74, 75, 83, 86, 154, 155, 160,
162, 223, 224, 233, 290, 412, 510
SKIPPING ROCK TRAILER PARK 320
SLAUGHTER RIVER 350
SLEEPING ELEPHANT 94
Sleeping Elephant Mountain 94
SLEEPING GIANT 447
Slide Lake, Lower 455
SLOUGH CREEK 440
SLOWAY 327
SLUMGULLION 242
Slumgullion Pass 242
Smith Lake 112
Smith Reservoir 276
Smith River 412
Snake River 461, 462, 463
Snake River Canyon 462, 463
SNOW BANK 420

snow tubing 83, 86, 224
Snowbank Lake 346
SNOWBERG'S PORT AND COURT 321
SNOWBLIND 228
snowmobiling
74, 86, 94, 157, 223, 245, 510
Snowslide Trail 273
Snowy Lakes 527
Snowy Range 528, 532
SOAP CREEK 189
SODA BUTTE 425
Sopris, Mount 131
Sopris Ranger District
131, 132, 133, 134, 139
SOUP CREEK 325
SOUTH BRUSH CREEK 529
South Dakota 502
SOUTH DICKEY LAKE 294
South Dickey Lake 295
SOUTH FORK 66, 341, 494
South Fork Camp 342, 493
South Fork Canyon 66
South Fork, CO
245, 246, 247, 248, 249, 250,
251, 252
South Gomer 128
South Lake 93
SOUTH MADISON 401
SOUTH MEADOWS 174
SOUTH MINERAL 200
South Park Ranger District
127, 137, 138, 139, 146, 168, 169,
170, 171, 263
South Pass City, WY 517, 518
South Platte Ranger District
128, 129, 130, 162, 163, 164, 165,
166, 167, 172
SOUTH RIM 191
South Rim 188
Spar Creek 298
SPAR LAKE 297
Spar Lake, Little 298
Spar Peak 298
SPECTACLE 257
Spectacle Camp 260
spelunking 66
SPILLWAY 263
SPIRE ROCK 394
SPOTTED BEAR 338
Spotted Bear Ranger District 338
SPRAGUE CREEK 296
SPRING 413
SPRING CAMP 412
Spring Cave 66
SPRING CREEK 225
Spring Creek 225, 413
Spring Creek Reservoir 219
SPRING GULCH 375
SPRING HILL 386
SPRINGER GULCH 169
Springfield, CO 282
SPRUCE 243, 532
Spruce Camp 243, 534
SPRUCE GROVE 77, 171
SPRUCE LAKE RV PARK 104
SPRUCE LODGE 246
SQUARE & ROUND DANCE RV 365
square dance center 365
Squaw Creek 394
SQUAW MOUNTAIN 547
SQUAW ROCK 371
St. Charles Trail 273
St. Elmo, CO 228
St. Helena Cathedral 383
ST. LOUIS CREEK 115
St. Mary, MT 333, 334, 335
ST. MARY'S LAKE 333
St. Mary's Lake 333, 334
St. Mary's Mission 367
ST. MARY'S RV PARK 367
ST. REGIS 327
St. Regis, MT 327, 328
St. Vrain Creek, Middle 109, 110
STAGE STOP 161
Stahl Peak 288
Stanford, MT 353, 411, 412
Stanley Hotel 103
Stapp Lake 110
STARDUST TRAILER PARK 391
Starvation Creek 237
STATION CREEK 461
STEAMBOAT LAKE STATE PARK 86
Steamboat Lake State Park 85
Steamboat Springs, CO
64, 85, 86, 87, 91, 92, 98, 99,
100, 101, 110, 111
Steeley Creek 429
Sterling, CO 181
Sterling Reservoir, North 181
STEVENS CREEK 234
Stevensville, MT 367
Stevensville Ranger District 367
STILLWATER 107, 111
Stillwater Camp 108
Stillwater Reservoir 110, 111, 112
Stillwater River 421
Stimson, Mount 335
STONE MOUNTAIN LODGE 152
Stonewall Mountain 346
STORM KING 240
Storm King Mountain 240
Stormy Peaks 97
Straight Creek 342
Strasburg, CO 161
Stryker, MT 294, 295
STUNNER 252
Stunner Pass 252
SUGARBUSH 237
Sugarbush Camp 238
SUGARLOAF 532
Sugarloaf Mountain 501
Sula, MT 374, 375, 376, 377
SULA STORE & CAMPGROUND 376

Sulphur Creek Reservoir 511
Sulphur Ranger District
102, 107, 108, 115, 116, 120
SUMMIT 337
Summit Campground 338
SUMMIT LAKE 90
Summit Lake 91
Sun River 340, 341, 342
Sundance Kid 501
Sundance Mountain 501
Sundance Ranger District 499, 500, 502
Sundance, WY 499, 500, 501, 502
SUNNYSIDE 235
SUNRISE 416
SUNSET RV 510
SUNSET TRAILER COURT 389
SUNSHINE 195
Superior, MT 326, 327, 328, 329
Superior Ranger District 326, 327
SUPPLY BASIN 71
Sutherlin, Lake 412
SWAN CREEK 397
Swan Creek 398
SWAN LAKE 317
Swan Lake 317, 318
Swan Lake, MT 317, 318, 324, 325
Swan Lake Ranger District 317, 327
Swan River 126, 324
Swan River State Forest 324, 325
SWAN VILLAGE MARKET 317
SWEETWATER LAKE 118
Sweetwater Lake 119
Sweetwater River 517, 518
SWIFT CREEK 507
Swift Creek 508
swimming 73, 75, 76, 98, 104, 107, 113, 114, 123, 124, 126, 133, 150, 151, 152, 154, 155, 156, 157, 158, 160, 161, 176, 177, 181, 182, 185, 186, 190, 193, 195, 203, 206, 207, 208, 209, 222, 226, 229, 247, 266, 267, 268, 269, 270, 272, 273, 278, 281, 286, 287, 288, 294, 297, 298, 301, 302, 303, 304, 305, 307, 309, 316, 317, 320, 323, 326, 327, 331, 336, 337, 343, 344, 346, 347, 357, 383, 393, 395, 400, 401, 415, 416, 417, 418, 420, 424, 432, 453, 458, 461, 463, 464, 473, 474, 483, 489, 501, 502, 511, 512, 518, 526, 538, 543, 551, 552, 554
swimming pool 75, 98, 104, 126, 133, 150, 151, 152, 156, 157, 158, 160, 161, 176, 181, 182, 185, 186, 190, 203, 206, 207, 208, 209, 222, 229, 247, 266, 267, 268, 269, 270, 272, 273, 278, 281, 326, 327, 331, 337, 357, 383, 393, 395, 415, 417, 418, 424, 432, 458, 461, 463, 464, 473, 474, 483, 489, 501, 502, 511, 518, 551, 552, 554
SYLVAN LAKE 312

T

TABLE MOUNTAIN 516
Table Mountain Camp 518
TALLY LAKE 301
Tally Lake Ranger District 288, 295, 301
Tally Mountain-Billy Creek Trail 301
TARGET TREE 205
Target Tree 204
Tarryall Creek 138, 171
Taylor Canyon 224, 226, 234
Taylor Canyon Picnic Area 224
Taylor Park Reservoir
219, 220, 221, 226, 234
Taylor River 219, 221, 224, 225, 226, 234
Taylor River Ranger District
140, 189, 218, 219, 220, 221, 224, 225, 226
teepees 132, 247, 461
Telluride Blues Festival 196
Telluride, CO 195, 200
Temple Hills Assembly Grounds 420
Ten Lakes Scenic Area 288
Ten Mile Creek 383
Ten Mile Picnic Area 383
Ten Sleep, WY
488, 489, 490, 491, 492, 493, 496
tennis courts 72, 73, 98, 126, 158, 168, 174, 181, 182, 186, 188, 191, 196, 201, 208, 254, 266, 268, 275, 279, 452, 459, 473, 477, 510, 550, 552
Tensleep Camp, West 489
Tensleep Canyon 490, 492
TENSLEEP CREEK 490
Tensleep Creek 488, 490, 491, 492, 496
Tensleep Lake 488, 489, 491
TENSLEEP LAKE, WEST 488
Tensleep Ranger District
489, 490, 491, 492, 493
Tent Village 383
Terry, MT 435
Terry Ranch 552
TETON CANYON 453
Teton Crest Trail 454
Teton Mountain Range 455
Teton Peak 339
Teton River, West Fork 339
Teton Village, WY 459
Texas Creek, CO 241
TEX'S TRAVEL CAMP 511
Thayne, WY 505
Thermopolis, WY 477
THERRIAULT LAKE, BIG 287
Therriault Lake, Big 288
THERRIAULT LAKE, LITTLE 288
Therriault Pass 288
Thompson Falls 318
Thompson Falls, MT 318, 319, 325, 328
THOMPSON FALLS STATE PARK 318
Thompson Lake 305, 313, 314

Thompson River 153, 319
Big 151, 153
Little 152
THREE FORKS 337
THREE MILE 446
Three Mile 447
Three Rivers Ranger District
285, 286, 290, 291, 297, 298, 304
THREE RIVERS RESORT 233
THUNDER RIDGE 176
Thunder Ridge Camp 177
Tiber Reservoir State Recreation Area 338
TIE CITY 550
TIE FLUME 481
TIE HACK 493
TIGER RUN RESORT 126
TIMBER CREEK 101
Timber Creek Camp 105
Timber Creek 208, 209
Timber Creek Trail 476
Timber Lake 293
TIMBER RIDGE 196
TIMBERLANE GROUP CAMP 300
Timberline Creek 427
Timberline Lakes 427
Tobacco Plains Boat Ramp 287
Tobacco River 287
Tobacco Root Mountains 392, 393, 397
Togwotee Pass 456
TOM BENNETT 96
Tongue River 481, 482, 483, 485
TOP OF THE WORLD 165
Toponas, CO 106, 112
Torrington, WY 548, 549
TOWER FALL 440
Tower Junction, WY 440
TOWN & COUNTRY 173
TOWN & COUNTRY VILLAGE 436
Townsend, MT 389
Townsend Ranger District 389
TRAFTON PARK 358
TRAIL CREEK 172, 458
Trail Creek 169, 172, 424, 507
TRAILS END 506
Trails End Camp 507
TRAMWAY 164
TRANSFER 204
TRANSFER PARK 208
Transfer Park 211
Transfer Trail 205
TRAPLINE 67
Trapline Camp 69
Trappers Lake 61, 67, 68, 69
Trappers Lodge 68
Treasure Mountain Trail 254
TRIANGLE C RANCH 460
TRICKLE PEAK 79
Trinchera Peak 277
Trinidad, CO 278, 279
Trinidad Lake 279
TRINIDAD LAKE STATE PARK 278
TROUT CREEK 328
Trout Creek 175, 176, 328, 382
Trout Creek Canyon 382
Trout Creek, MT 304, 311, 312, 313
TROY 298
Troy, MT
285, 286, 290, 291, 297, 298, 304
TRUJILLO MEADOWS 258
Trujillo Meadows Reservoir 258
TUCHUCK 288
Tuchuck Creek 288
Tuchuck Mountain 289
TUCKER PONDS 250
TUNNEL 93
Turah State Park 366
Turkey Creek 172
Turkey Rock 172
Turner Mountain 292
Turner Mountain Ski Area 292
Turner Peak 255
Turquoise Lake 134, 135, 136, 137
TW Recreational Services, Inc. 446
Twelvemile Creek 326
Twin Bridges, MT 391
Twin Eagles Trail 171
TWIN LAKE 81
TWIN LAKES 377
Twin Lakes 81, 143, 144, 377, 378, 487, 527
Twin Lakes, CO 144, 145
Twin Lakes Reservoir 143, 145
TWIN PEAKS 144
TWO BUTTES RESERVOIR 282
TWO MEDICINE 336
Two Medicine Lake 336

U

U.S. Air Force Academy 268
Uinta Mountains 511
Ulhorn Trail 412
Uncompahgre National Forest
187, 190, 192, 193, 194, 195, 197, 198, 200
Uncompahgre Plateau 190
Uncompahgre Primitive Area 197
Uncompahgre River 193, 196, 197
Union Pacific 539
UNITED CAMPGROUND OF DURANGO 208
United Campground of Durango 206
UPPER BEAVER CREEK 249
Upsidedown Creek 421
UTE BLUFF 245
Ute Bluff Camp 246, 247, 251
UTE CREEK 275
Ute Creek 276
Ute Indians 205
Ute Mountain 203
Ute Mountain Casino 203

V

Vail, CO 119
VALLECITO 202
Vallecito Creek 202
Vallecito Reservoir
203, 210, 211, 212, 213
Vallecito Trailhead 203
Valley of the Flowers 416
Vasquez Mountains 115
VAUGHN LAKE 63
Vaughn Lake 64
VEDAUWOO 552
Vega Reservoir 61, 73, 74
Vega State Park 74
VEGA STATE RECREATION AREA 73
Vermillion Creek 170
Vermillion River 313
Victor, ID 458
Victor Railroad 264
VIGILANTE 382
VIKING RV PARK 71
Villa Grove, CO 241
Vinegar Hole Wilderness 451
Virgelle, MT 350, 351
VIRGINIA CITY 396
Virginia City, MT 396
VIRGINIA KOA 395
volleyball 321, 464, 552

W

WADE LAKE 400
Wade Lake Camp 400, 401
Wagner, Mount 507
WAGON TONGUE 171
Walden, CO 87, 88, 92, 94, 100
Walsenburg, CO 275, 276
WALTON CREEK 98
Walton Peak 99
WAPITI 449
Wapiti Camp 451
Wapiti Ranger District
446, 447, 448, 449, 450, 451
Wapiti Valley 446
Ward, CO 116
WARD LAKE 79
Warhorse National Wildlife Refuge 353, 354
WARM SPRINGS 376, 387
Warm Springs Camp 386
Warm Springs Creek 376, 386, 387
Warren Peak Lookout 502
Washakie Ranger District 515, 516, 517
Washakie Wilderness
447, 448, 449, 450, 457, 475, 476
Washburn, Mount 440
water slide, giant 270
Waterdog Lakes 236
waterskiing 70, 73, 74, 83, 86, 107,
132, 150, 155, 183, 189, 192, 214,
233, 272, 277, 281, 297, 344, 347,
357, 386, 420, 512
Waterton-Glacier International Peace Park
289, 295, 296, 297, 303, 333, 335, 336
WAYFARER STATE PARK 317
WEBER'S CAMP 193
WEIR & JOHNSON 81
Welcome Creek Wilderness 368
WELLER 140
Weller Camps 141
Weller Lake 141
Wellington Lake 164, 165
Wells Fargo Stage Stop 112
Weminuche Wilderness 202, 203, 209,
210, 211, 212, 213, 249
WEST 90
West Bench Trail 77
West Branch 93
WEST CHICAGO CREEK 122
West Chicago Creek 122
WEST DOLORES 198
West Elk Wilderness 189, 217, 218
WEST FORK 248, 339
West Fork Campground 402
West Fork Ranger District 372
WEST GLACIER KOA 302
West Glacier, MT 289, 295, 296, 297,
302, 303, 333, 335, 336
WEST MADISON 399
WEST SHORE STATE PARK 315
West Thumb, WY 448, 449
West Yellowstone, MT
402, 403, 404, 405, 406
West Yellowstone, WY 445
Westcliffe, CO 242
Western Narrow Gauge Railroad
201, 208, 209
WESTON PASS 146
Wheatland, WY 548
wheelchair accessible
62, 66, 73, 99, 100, 109, 110, 111,
134, 154, 160, 174, 175, 191, 193,
194, 198, 207, 220, 226, 233, 235,
247, 258, 271, 273, 276, 281, 287,
288, 292, 295, 296, 297, 300, 301,
303, 305, 309, 310, 317, 327, 328,
330, 333, 336, 343, 344, 347, 352,
353, 358, 359, 367, 372, 374, 385,
387, 390, 394, 395, 400, 405, 435,
445, 446, 452, 454, 464, 465, 477,
491, 493, 499, 500, 508, 516, 523,
525, 544, 546, 551
WHISKEY GROVE 465
White Creek 466
White Earth 384
White Mountains 518
White River 61, 64, 65, 66, 69
White River National Forest 61, 64, 65,
66, 67, 68, 69, 70, 71, 113, 114,
115, 118, 119, 122, 123, 124, 125,
126, 131, 132, 133, 134, 135, 139,
140, 141, 142, 143
WHITE STAR 144

White Sulphur Springs, MT
352, 353, 409, 410, 412, 413
WHITEFISH LAKE STATE
RECREATION AREA 301
Whitefish, MT 288, 293, 295, 301
Whitehall, MT 388
Whitehall Ranger District 388
WHITETAIL 285
Whitetail Camp 286
Whitney, Mount 145
Wiggins Unit 61
WILDHORN 169
Wildlife Management Area 182
Wildlife World Museum 265
Williams Canyon 267
Williams Fork River, South Fork 63
WILLIAMSON MEMORIAL PARK 338
WILLOW 534
WILLOW CREEK 107, 313
Willow Creek
102, 106, 107, 313, 339, 340, 393
Willow Creek Reservoir 107
Willow Lake 506
WILLOWS 113
Willows Camp 113, 114
Wilson, Mount 199
Wilson Mountains Primitive Area 200
Wilson Peak 199
Wind River 460
Wind River Indian Reservation 478
Wind River Mountains 517
Wind River Ranger District 456, 457, 458
Windham, MT 411
WINDING RIVER 101
windsurfing 73, 76, 154, 155, 160,
214, 223, 233, 277, 278
Windy Pass 254
Windy Point 124
WINDY POINT GROUP CAMP 125
Windy Point Overlook 242
Winter Park, CO 116, 120
Wisdom, MT 377, 378
Wisdom Ranger District 378
Wise River, MT 390
Wise River Ranger District 390
WOLF CREEK 254
Wolf Creek Hot Springs 401
Wolf Creek, MT 347
Wolf Creek Pass 245
Wood Creek 342
WOOD LAKE 341
Wood Lake Camp 342
WOOD RIVER 476
WOODBINE 421
Woodland Park, CO
172, 173, 174, 175, 176
Worland, WY
488, 489, 490, 491, 492, 493
WRANGLER RV RANCH 268
WYOMING 551
Wyoming Camp 553
Wyoming Range 466
Wyoming State Museum 553
Wyoming, University of 549

Y

YAAK FALLS 290
Yaak, MT 286
YAAK RIVER 290
Yaak River Camp 291
Yaak River 285, 286, 290, 291
Yamcolo Reservoir 111
Yampa, CO 64, 106, 110, 111, 112
Yampa Ranger District 64, 110, 111, 112
Yampa Reservoir 110, 111
Yampa River 61, 63, 98
YARNELL ISLAND BOAT-IN 299
YELLOW BAY STATE PARK 323
YELLOW PINE 550
Yellowstone County Historical Museum 432
YELLOWSTONE HOLIDAY 403
Yellowstone Lake 445, 446, 448, 449
Yellowstone National Park
395, 400, 404, 405, 406, 419, 424,
425, 439, 440, 443, 444, 445,
446, 447, 448, 449, 451
Yellowstone National Park, WY
439, 440, 443, 444, 445, 446,
448, 449
Yellowstone River
363, 415, 417, 418, 419, 425,
431, 432, 435, 440, 445, 446
Clarks Fork 441, 442
YOGI BEAR JELLYSTONE 268

Z

Zortman City, MT 359

About the Authors

Tom Stienstra is the outdoors writer for the *San Francisco Examiner,* which distributes his column nationally on the Scripps News Service. Among his many awards, he was named Outdoor Writer of the Year in 1990 and 1992. He continally explores the West's wild outdoors as a camper, angler and pilot.

Robyn Schlueter is the senior research editor for outdoor books published by Foghorn Press. She lives in the Rocky Mountains of Colorado, where she hikes, backpacks, snowboards, rock climbs, and travels throughout the Rocky Mountains in search of new secret spots. This is the second book she has co-authored with Tom Stienstra.

America's Secret Recreation Areas

by Award-Winning Outdoors Author Michael Hodgson

This bestselling guide details camping, hiking, rafting, mountain biking and much more in over 272 million acres of Bureau of Land Management lands in 12 western states (including the Rocky Mountains). It's the only available guide to these pristine and forgotten wilderness areas.

Regularly $15.95—now available at a special introductory price of $14.50!

ORDER TODAY—CALL (800) 842-7477

Please add $3.00 for shipping and handling and 50 cents for each additional book. (California residents add $1.20 for tax).

Foghorn Press, 555 DeHaro Street, Suite 220, San Francisco, CA 94107

• Brand New Exciting Offer •